WITHDR...
THE LIBRARY

UNIVERSITY OF
WINCHESTER

KT-150-063

Martial Rose Lil

;9

KA 0061566 8

THE TRANSFORMATION OF MEDIEVAL ENGLAND

1370–1529

THE TRANSFORMATION OF MEDIEVAL ENGLAND
1370–1529
John A. F. Thomson

THE EMERGENCE OF A NATION STATE
The commonwealth of England 1529–1660
Alan G. R. Smith

THE MAKING OF A GREAT POWER
Pre-industrial Britain 1660–1783
Geoffrey Holmes

THE FORGING OF THE MODERN STATE
Early industrial Britain 1783–1870
Eric J. Evans

THE ECLIPSE OF A GREAT POWER
Modern Britain 1870–1975
Keith Robbins

THE TRANSFORMATION
OF MEDIEVAL ENGLAND
1370–1529

John A. F. Thomson

LONGMAN
LONDON AND NEW YORK

Longman Group Limited
Longman House
Burnt Mill, Harlow, Essex, CM20 2JE, England
and Associated Companies throughout The World.

Published in the United States of America
by Longman Inc., New York

© Longman Group Limited 1983

All rights reserved. No part of this publication may be
reproduced, stored in a retrieval system, or transmitted
in any form or by any means, electronic, mechanical,
photocopying, recording, or otherwise, without the
prior permission of the Copyright owner.

First published 1983

British Library Cataloguing in Publication Data
Thomson, John A. F.
   The transformation of medieval England
   1370–1529 – (Foundations of modern Britain)
   1. Great Britain – History – 14th century
   2. Great Britain – History – Tudors, 1485–1603
   I. Title   II. Series
   942   DA225

   ISBN 0–582–48975–X
   ISBN 0–582–48976–8 Pbk

Library of Congress Cataloging in Publication Data
Thomson, John A. F.
   The transformation of medieval England, 1370–1529.

   (Foundations of modern Britain)
   Bibliography: p.
   Includes index.
   1. Great Britain – History–Medieval period,
1066–1485. 2. Great Britain – History – Tudors, 1485–1603.
I. Title.   II. Series.
DA175.T45   942.04   82–15336
ISBN 0–582–48975–X   AACR2
ISBN 0–582–48976–8 (pbk.)

KING ALFRED'S COLLEGE
WINCHESTER

942.04
THO

35516

Set in linotron 202 Times by
Printed in Singapore by
Kyodo Shing Loong Printing Industries Pte Ltd.

Contents

PART FOUR, THE STRUCTURE OF GOVERNMENT

PART FIVE, THE CHURCH AND EDUCATION

Contents

List of maps

Editor's foreword

So prodigious has been the output of specialized work on British history during the past twenty years, and so rich its diversity, that scholars and students thirst continually after fresh syntheses. Even those who read for the pure pleasure of informing themselves about the past have become quite reconciled to the fact that little can now be taken for granted. An absorbing interest in local situations, as a way to understanding more general ones; a concern with those processes of social change which accompany economic, educational and cultural development, and which often condition political activity too: these and many other strong currents of modern historiography have washed away some of our more comfortable orthodoxies. Even when we know *what* happened, there is endless scope for debate about *why* things happened and with what consequences.

In such circumstances a new series of general textbooks on British history would not seem to call for elaborate justification. However, the five volumes constituting *Foundations of Modern Britain* do have a distinct rationale and they embody some novel features. For one thing, they make a serious attempt to present a history of Britain from the point at which 'Britain' became first a recognizable entity and then a great power, and to trace the foundations of this State in the history of pre-eighteenth-century England. The fact that all five authors either have taught or are teaching in Scottish universities, while one has held a chair in the University of Wales, should at least help to remind them that one aim of the series is to avoid excessive Anglo-centricity. The first two volumes, spanning the years 1370–1660, will certainly concentrate primarily on the history of England, emphasizing those developments which first prepared the way for, and later confirmed her emergence as an independent 'commonwealth', free from Continental trammels whether territorial or ecclesiastical. But the reader should also be aware, as he reads them, of England's ultimate role as the heart of a wider island kingdom in which men of three nations came to be associated. During the period covered by volumes 3 and 4, 1660–1870, this 'United Kingdom of Great Britain' became not only a domestic reality but the centre of an Empire and the possessor of world-wide influence. Space will allow only limited treatment of Ireland and of Anglo-Irish relations until after the Union of 1801. It is appropriate, however, that in the final volume of the series reasserted nationalism should figure almost as strongly as the erosion of imperial status in the story of Britain's slide down the slippery slope from palmy greatness to anxious mediocrity. The terminal date of volume 5, 1975, is deliberately chosen: the year in which Britain, tortured once again by her Irish inheritance and facing demands for Scottish devolution, or even independence, belatedly recognized that the days of complacent self-sufficiency as regards Europe, too, were past.

As well as paying more than mere lip-service to its own title, the present series adopts an irreverent attitude to time-honoured chronological divisions. Those lines of demarcation between volumes which dominated virtually every English history series conceived before 1960 (and, with a few exceptions, have displayed a remarkable capacity for survival subsequently) are seen as a quite unnecessary obstacle to readers' understanding of the way modern historiography has reshaped whole vistas of our island's history in the past forty years. Years such as 1485, 1603, 1689, 1714, 1760 or 1815 established themselves in textbook lore at a time when they accurately reflected the heavily political and constitutional emphasis of traditional history teaching. Even on those terms they have become of limited utility. But equally seriously, the conventions which such divisions perpetuate often make it extremely difficult for authors to accommodate fundamental aspects of social and economic development within their allotted compass. The brutal slicing off of 'Tawney's century' (1540–1640) at 1603 is perhaps the worst of these atrocities; but it is not the only one.

All dates are to some extent arbitrary as lines of division, and all present their own difficulties. It is hoped, none the less, that those selected in this series to enclose periods which are in any case a good deal longer than average, may prove less inhibiting and confusing than some of their predecessors and much more adaptable to the needs of British history courses in Universities and colleges.

In one further important respect the authors have kept in mind the practical requirements of students and teachers. Their approach eschews lengthy narrative wherever possible and concentrates, within chapters short enough to be rapidly absorbed, on the development of themes and the discussion of problems. Yet at the same time they attempt to satisfy their readers' need for basic information in two ways: by providing, at appropriate stages, skeletal 'frameworks' of events, chronologically ordered, within which the subsequent analysis and interplay of argument can be set; and by placing at the end of each volume a 'compendium' of factual data, including statistics, on a scale much greater than that of normal textbook appendices.

These compendia are essential companions to the texts and are designed for ready and constant use. The frequent references to them which punctuate so many chapters in this series will be found within square brackets, for example thus [B.2]. They should be easily distinguishable from the numerous arabic numbers within round brackets inserted in each text, e.g. (117). These refer readers to the Bibliography, in which most items are thematically arranged and serially numbered. Superior numerals are for the notes which are listed at the ends of chapters.

Geoffrey Holmes

Preface

In the course of writing this book I have incurred many debts of gratitude which it is a pleasure to acknowledge. The authorship of a textbook compels one to study topics where one cannot claim real expertise and teaches one forcibly how much one must depend on the labours of others, who have done the basic research. My first debt, therefore, is to the scholars whose work I have used, some living, some dead, some known to me but many more who are strangers. The names of some are acknowledged in the bibliography, but equal thanks are due to many others who could not be mentioned because of limitations of space.

Secondly, thanks are due to those who gave more immediate assistance in the preparation of the work. Dr. Alan Smith and Dr. Michael Clanchy gave me the benefit of their specialist knowledge in particular chapters, and the general editor of the series, Professor Geoffrey Holmes scrutinized the text meticulously and made many useful suggestions for improving it. My wife suggested various improvements to the text to eliminate ambiguities in the argument and infelicities in the style, and she and my son helped in the preparation of the index. Miss Mary Brodie prepared the typescript for the publishers, dealing successfully with various drafts of it, and the staff of Longman have given support throughout the period of writing by being willing to come more than half way to meet the wishes of the author.

Finally, my greatest debt is to my colleagues and students in the History department of the University of Glasgow, in discussion with whom during the last twenty years so many of the ideas in this book were originally formulated. Their comments and questions have often forced me to rethink my views on particular problems of the period or to justify more fully views which I already held. The book is dedicated to Professor Lionel Stones, who originally appointed me to the department. His stress on the values of material as well as documentary sources for history has given me new perspectives on the subject, and his friendship and encouragement has always helped me in my work.

John A. F. Thomson

Acknowledgements

We are grateful to the following for permission to reproduce copyright material:

London School of Economics and Political Science for our table A.1 from 'Index of Prices and Wages' by H. Phelps Brown and S. Hopkins *Economica* pp 311–2, November 1956; Oxford University Press for our table A.2 (E. M. Carus-Wilson & O. Coleman 1963).

Prologue. England in 1370

On 3 June 1369 Edward III resumed the title of King of France which he had abandoned in 1360 under the terms of the Treaty of Brétigny. This action was prompted by the claim of the Valois King Charles V that he was entitled to hear appeals from the Gascon lands held by the English King. In November, the French King retaliated by declaring these lands confiscated, and the Anglo-French War was renewed. The prominence of this war in English fourteenth-century history reveals very clearly the orientation of royal policy towards western Europe. For the greater part of his reign, Edward had been largely preoccupied with defending the lands which he had inherited in south-west France, something which had been true, at any rate for part of the time, of his father and grandfather also. Indeed ever since 1066, the English crown had had territorial interests in France. During the war Edward had himself laid claim, on somewhat dubious grounds, to the French throne itself, and his military victories before 1360 had led to a large increase in the territory which was either directly under his control or ruled by men who recognized his feudal superiority. In 1360, he held the greater part of western France south of the Loire, and his eldest son, the Black Prince, had a court of his own at Bordeaux.

It is hardly surprising, therefore, that the King's mental world, and that of his closest associates, was not bounded by the English Channel. It was that of the international chivalric class, whose achievements were celebrated in the chronicle of the Hainaulter Jean Froissart, and whose prominent members were equally at home in England and on the Continent. Indeed another Hainaulter, Sir Walter Manny, was a much respected member of Edward's court, and one of the earliest knights of the King's new Order of the Garter. For such men, French was their natural tongue, as is shown by the fact that when Henry of Grosmont, duke of Lancaster and a noted war captain, wrote a religious treatise, *Le Livre de Seyntz Medecines*, this was the language which he employed. By the late fourteenth century, however, one can see signs of a decline in this employment of French and the appearance of a strong vernacular literature in writers such as Langland and Chaucer. The use of English by the latter writer, who had close connections with the court, is particularly significant as a sign of the progress of English in polite society, although one must remember that much of his writing was in a cosmopolitan European tradition in both subject and form. An equally important sign of the progress of English was the abandonment of French in some classes of official document, such as the complaints presented by Convocation to Parliament, although there were places where it was firmly rooted, notably in the conservative atmosphere of the law courts. It is likely that this widespread decline in the use of French was connected with the hostility engendered by war and its accompanying propaganda. The result was that English, for the first time in over three centuries, was becoming respectable in the upper levels of society; it was also spreading as a cultural medium below court level, and was coming to be taught in schools.

One area in which the vernacular had already become well established in the fourteenth century was in religious literature; it was almost certainly the social background of Henry of Grosmont that had led him to choose French for his book, as works which were directed to an audience lower in the social scale were already being written in English. Although the Church represented an international culture, the appearance of vernacular writings was not a peculiarly English phenomenon but may be paralleled elsewhere in Christendom, as literacy spread increasingly throughout a substantial part of lay society. The writing of vernacular sermons and the appearance of such works as *The Cloud of Unknowing* and the English writings of Richard Rolle reflect attempts to fill a gap in the spiritual life of a people who were concerned with ultimate values but who could not share the Latin culture of churchmen. Such progress in learning counted for far more in developing a national religious literature than any political factors, although it is also true that the tendency of the Church to centralization, manifest since the eleventh century, was coming under increasing strain. The suspicion that French-born popes at Avignon were politically antagonistic exacerbated resentment at papal intervention in the affairs of the English Church, and in the middle years of Edward III's reign steps were taken to curtail it. These moves were purely political and administrative, for in 1370 English religious life was strongly orthodox, and gave little indication that it was soon to be affected by a major heretical movement. The spread of devotional writings from their traditional environment in the monasteries was the only sign of how popular feeling could not be contained within its traditional limits.

There is little doubt that the country over which Edward had ruled for about forty years, and which was increasingly developing this national consciousness, was politically and economically powerful. This is clearly revealed by its successes in war against its larger neighbour France, and its limitation of the lesser threat from France's ally, Scotland. By 1370, he had abandoned attempts to dominate Scotland through a puppet ruler, but he had secured effective authority in Wales and was trying to strengthen his position in Ireland. Politically, the King made a considerable personal contribution to his country's achievements, most notably in the way in which, for most of his reign, he maintained friendly relations with the magnate class. This contrasts markedly with the unhappy experience of his father's time, when Crown and nobility had been constantly at loggerheads. One reason for this was certainly that he conformed in his life and attitudes to the ideal of kingship which was held by the magnates in a way in which his father had not, another was that he was well served in administrative matters by his principal ministers. These were still normally churchmen, although by the late fourteenth century, legally trained laymen had occasionally held important offices of State, and were encroaching on the earlier clerical monopoly of them. The King's administrators were able to mobilize effectively the nation's resources for war, and the magnate admiration for the King's military success was due as much to this as to Edward's capacity as a strategist or a tactician.

War taxation, however, also contributed to the consolidation of the nation's political identity, because the King's need for money led him to have increasingly frequent recourse to Parliament for grants, and it was during this period of war that Parliament became the effective paymaster to meet the King's needs. In 1362, it was agreed that no tax on wool should be granted by merchants or others without the consent of Parliament (53, p.161). This prevented the King from negotiating separately with any other body in the State, and by 1370 Parliament was the principal point of communication between the King and his subjects. It was still dominated by the great men who received individual writs of summons to its meetings, the future House of Lords, but the representatives of the shires and boroughs were becoming increasingly willing to voice criticisms of abuses in government and to resist taxation if they regarded it as excessive.

One of the major sources of such taxation was the levy of export duties on wool, a fact which is a reminder that the strength of the English economy rested on the country's production of raw materials rather than of manufactured goods. English wool was supplied to the looms of Flanders and Italy and was highly regarded in those countries. Politics and economics were particularly closely interrelated in Anglo-Flemish relations, because of the geographical and strategic situation of Flanders in the French War, and when in 1369 the heiress to the county married a younger brother of Charles V, Philip, duke of Burgundy, the possibility of applying economic sanctions became even more crucial. The economy of western Europe had in the earlier part of the century been affected seriously by factors beyond human control – famine between 1315 and 1317, and from the middle of the century the Black Death and subsequent epidemics. These obviously affected England also, although it is hard to judge their immediate effects. The initial effects of pestilence were not so great as to curtail the King's military activities in the 1350s, but there are signs that by 1370 the long-term effects of population decline, from an earlier peak between 4½ and 6 million, were causing some dislocation of the traditional types of manorial organization and affecting the resources of the magnate class. While it would be wrong to suggest that manorialism had remained static in character in the years before 1350, it is probably correct to say that the earlier changes were prompted by the attempts of the landowners, who held the whip-hand, to exploit their resources more fully. The balance of power between the manorial lord and his subordinates, both tenants and employed labourers, was, however, decisively upset by the labour shortage, and by 1370 the land-owning class was on the defensive. The main developments in the late-fourteenth-century economy resulted primarily from pressures from below for improved conditions in both economic and legal terms. Most notably, one can see the difficulties faced by the magnates and gentry in trying to assert their old legal rights over men who had formerly been unfree. The power of the lords had not yet been significantly reduced by 1370, and a substantial number of their men had not yet secured legal freedom, but the land-owners were having increasing problems in maintaining their old rights.

Outside manorial society, urban life had developed less fully in England than on the Continent, but London was already a great metropolis, more comparable with some of the cities of western Europe than with any other English town. With a population of probably between 30,000 and 40,000, it was more than three times the size of the next largest English towns, York and Bristol. Other major provincial centres were Norwich and Coventry, both of which had well under 10,000 inhabitants (104, p.1). London's dominance rested on a combination of factors, particularly its position near the centre of government in adjacent Westminster and its favourable geographical situation in relation to English Continental trade. The ruling mercantile group in London was perhaps the most important body of men in the country after the landed aristocracy and the higher clergy. Leading London merchants, particularly the city mayor, could play a prominent part in national politics and normally dominated England's trade with the Low Countries and northern Europe. The prominence of the Londoners was all the more marked when one sees that in general the merchant class took a very clear second place behind the landowners, nowhere more marked than in Parliament where the burgesses played only a supporting role to the more influential knights of the shire.

The renewal of the war was to lead to the revival of various tensions in English society in the 1370s. The need for war taxation gave rise to fiscal difficulties, and as the King aged he could no longer provide the kind of leadership which had carried him through the early stages of the struggle with France. The harmonious relations which had existed between the King and his subjects for over a generation were breaking down through a combination of economic problems and lack of leadership at the top.

PART ONE
Environment and economy

In the case of major epidemics, it is often impossible to specify their nature in detail, as contemporary records are often imprecise. The term 'plague' may denote an epidemic of bubonic or pneumonic plague, but it may also be used more generally to describe any pestilence. Also it is not clear what was the nature of the disease known as the 'sweating sickness'. In the table below the less precise term 'epidemic' is normally employed, rather than anything more precise, because the economic consequences of such outbreaks resulted from the fact that they occurred, not from their particular nature. It is impossible to state how widespread such epidemics were; many of those in the fifteenth century seem to have been particularly severe in London; on a number of occasions our knowledge of an outbreak depends on the fact that the meeting of Parliament was adjourned to a location in the provinces to avoid danger to those attending it.

Entries in *italics* refer to political events and have been included to provide a cross-reference to the Framework of events – Political.

1348–49	Initial attack of the Black Death.
1361–62	Epidemic.
1369	Epidemic. *Renewal of Anglo-French War.*
1373	Bristol granted legal status as a county.
1375	Epidemic.
1377	*Succession of Richard II.*
1381	Great Revolt. Main centres of disorder in Kent, Essex, East Anglia, Cambridgeshire, Hertfordshire, London. Isolated outbreaks in Bedfordshire, Buckinghamshire, Cheshire, Leicestershire, Northamptonshire, Somerset, Warwickshire, Yorkshire.
1385–88	Tension between England and the Hanse towns.
1387–88	*Revolt of the Lords Appellant against Richard II.*
1389	*Truce with France.*
1390	Epidemic.
1392–97	London lost municipal autonomy.
1396	York granted legal status as a county. *Twenty-eight-year truce with France.*
1399	*Succession of Henry IV.*
1400	Newcastle granted legal status as a county.
1404	Norwich granted legal status as a county.
1405–8	Tension between England and the Hanse towns.
1405	Epidemic.
1409	Lincoln granted legal status as a county.
1413	Epidemic. *Succession of Henry V.*
1415	*Renewal of war in France.*
1422	*Succession of Henry VI.*
1431	Rising at Abingdon, Berkshire. Supposedly Lollard, but little evidence of heresy. Trouble also in Wiltshire, Coventry and London.
1431–37	Tension between England and the Hanse towns.
1433	Epidemic.
1434	Epidemic.
1435	*Congress of Arras; Burgundian change of sides in war.*
1437	Epidemic.
1438–39	Food shortages after bad harvest.
1439	Epidemic. Peace settlement and trade agreement with Burgundy.

1440	Hull granted perpetual succession as a legal personality.
1444	Epidemic.
1446	Robert Sturmy of Bristol sent ship, the cog *Anne*, into the Mediterranean.
1448–50	Epidemics.
1449–56	Tension between England and the Hanse towns.
1450	*Loss of Normandy*. Cade's rising in Kent. Disorders in Wiltshire at the same time. Trouble persisted in Kent for two more years on a less widespread scale.
1452	Epidemic.
1453	*Final expulsion of the English from France.*
1454	Epidemic.
1457	Robert Sturmy sent ship, *Katherine*, into the Mediterranean.
1461	*Succession of Edward IV.*
1464	Epidemic. Reduction in bullion value of coinage.
1468–75	Tension between England and the Hanse towns.
1470–1	*Readeption of Henry VI.*
1471	Epidemic. During Lancastrian attack on London, Essex men with economic grievances joined Fauconberg's Kentishmen.
1475	Trade treaty with Hanse towns.
1479	Epidemic.
1480s	Search for 'island of Brasil' by ships from Bristol.
1483	*Succession of Edward V. Usurpation of Richard III.*
1485	Epidemic. *Succession of Henry VII.*
1486	Trade treaties with Brittany and France.
1489	Anti-tax revolt in Yorkshire. Murder of the earl of Northumberland.
1493	Epidemic.
1496	Trade treaty with Low Countries (*Intercursus Magnus*).
1497	John Cabot, voyaging out of Bristol, reached Newfoundland. Trade treaty with France. Cornish revolt and march on London.
1499–1500	Epidemic.
1505	Epidemic.
1509	*Succession of Henry VIII.*
1521	Epidemic.
1525	Resistance to 'Amicable Grant', particularly in East Anglia.
1526	Debasement of coinage.
1529	*Meeting of the Reformation Parliament.*
1536	The Pilgrimage of Grace. Mainly religious and political in character, but some social grievances also voiced.

CHAPTER 1

The population of England

The economic development of England between the mid fourteenth and the early sixteenth century was determined by changes in the country's population more than by any other single factor. This is undoubted, but unfortunately for historians these changes cannot be measured precisely. Three problems, in particular, confront us, the extent of the fall in England's population caused by the Black Death and by subsequent epidemics, the chronology of decline and recovery, and the possible redistribution of population throughout the country. The third question is so closely related to changes in the forms of rural settlement and to the growth and decline of towns that it is best considered in these contexts; the present chapter will concentrate on the scale of mortality and the fluctuations in the total population of England in the century and a half before 1529.

The historian's main difficulty in examining these problems is that medieval man was not statistically minded, and that consequently precise data are not available to us in our search for answers to problems. It is easier to judge the impression which the Black Death made on men's minds, for this is reflected in the chroniclers' writings, than to measure the scale of its ravages. The St Albans writer Thomas Walsingham declared that scarcely two men survived out of twenty in certain religious houses, and that many men considered that barely a tenth of the whole population remained alive (32, i, 273). Other chroniclers, such as Henry Knighton at Leicester, describe the extent of the plague locally, suggesting that there were 700 deaths in one parish and 380 in another, and some even appear to have doubted if man's life on earth was going to continue (53, p.169). Some figures of deaths in monastic houses may be accurate, but as the plague did not strike evenly throughout the country it would be foolish to deduce any estimate of national mortality from them. The same problem of interpretation arises from any use of manorial records, probably the best available documentary source; these can tell us no more than the number of holdings which fell vacant on particular estates and throw no light on mortality among landless persons.

The Black Death, which reached England in 1348, remained virulent in the following year, and recurred frequently in succeeding centuries, probably originated in central Asia and spread to the Black Sea area along the trans-Asian trade routes. From there it travelled rapidly to the Middle East, Italy and western Europe. The plague took two forms, bubonic, transmitted by a bacterium carried by the rat flea, and pneumonic, spread directly by droplet infection in a manner similar to the common cold. It is almost certain that both forms of the disease were present in late-fourteenth-century England, and it may well have been the pneumonic form, the more lethal of the two, which was responsible for the scale of the mortality in 1348–49 (53, pp.172–3). There has been some controversy in recent years over the effect which the plague had on the population, and the bacteriologist J. F. D. Shrewsbury has tried to argue that bubonic plague could not, by its nature, have destroyed as high a proportion of the population as historians have claimed (102). He does not, however, allow for the possible effects of the pneumonic form of the disease, and suggests that another epidemic, possibly of typhus, may have been responsible. As far as the effects of population change on the economy are concerned, however, the particular disease is of secondary importance.

The greatest problem for the historian of late medieval population in England is that he has no reliable figure for the number of inhabitants at the time when the plague struck the country first. Indeed, since the Domesday Survey of 1086 there had been no government measure which had produced a record of this. A generation after the first onset of the disease, the poll-tax levy of 1377 did provide such figures, but it is clearly impossible to use this to estimate the level of population before 1348 or indeed the scale of mortality in the first, or any of the intervening later, epidemics. Furthermore, although the first poll-tax was sufficiently successful as a fiscal measure for it to be repeated in 1379 and 1381, the hostility shown to it in the Great Revolt of the latter year led to its abandonment as a form of taxation; not until the sixteenth century do further governmental records become available which can be employed to estimate the size of the national population with even a modicum of confidence. These include the returns of a military survey in 1522, the subsidy rolls of 1524–25 and the chantry certificates of 1545, which report the number of communicants in each parish. In other words, in the period covered by this book, the only direct evidence on population figures comes near its start and very close to, or even after, its end. There is literally nothing of an official nature which can serve as a guide to possible fluctuations in the intervening years.

Not only is the evidence scarce, but it is often undependable. The poll-tax was payable by all over the age of fourteen, apart from genuine beggars, including the mendicant friars, who were exempted from it, and from the inhabitants of Durham and Cheshire. The historian must therefore try to estimate the population of these two shires, the proportion of the population under fourteen and, hardest of all, the extent to which the tax was successfully evaded. Certainly evasion was rife in 1381, as can be seen from the marked discrepancies between the numbers paying the tax in that year and the figures for 1377 [A.4], and there is no reason to believe that the payments in the earlier year, although more complete, provide anything close to a total record of the population. Tax evasion is a similar problem in interpreting the sixteenth-century subsidy rolls, while any deductions based on the military survey, a crude census of males over the age of sixteen, must allow not only for children but also for the balance between men and women in the population as a whole. The chantry certificates of 1545, even if one accepts their record of communicants in the parishes as accurate, do not cover the whole country, and again there is uncertainty as to the proportion of the population below communicant age.

All estimates of population size must therefore allow for a large measure of conjecture, a fact stressed by all reputable modern historians who have worked on this intractable subject. The starting-point for all later studies must be J. C. Russell's survey of British medieval population, published in 1948 (99), but more recent work has been effectively synthesized in the extended paper by J. Hatcher, dating from 1977, which also provides an excellent bibliography (75). Russell estimated the population of England at just over 2¼ million in 1377, and suggested that it rose by nearly a million between then and 1545. Hatcher, by contrast, prefers a 1377 figure in the 2¾–3 million range, and thinks it unlikely that this was exceeded until the second quarter of the sixteenth century. If there was an increase by 1545, much of it may have come in the years after 1530, and become important economically only after the period covered by this book (75, p.69). What is even harder for historians to estimate is the extent of the fall in population before 1377 from its peak in the earlier years of the century, whether or not this point was reached around 1300, the most generally accepted date, or on the eve of the cataclysm caused by the Black Death.

In any attempt to estimate the effects which population changes could have on the economy as a whole, the crucial matter is, however, not the absolute numbers of Englishmen at any particular date but the broader demographic trend. Did the population remain more or less static after the dramatic decline in the second half of the fourteenth century, or did it make a rapid recovery from the first wave of epidemics? Here the problem is less difficult than the estimation of absolute figures, because further kinds of evidence can be employed in the search for an answer. In certain social groups it is possible to examine replacement rates, namely the number of children in a family who survived to adulthood. Two such groups, which are sufficiently well documented for such a study, are tenants-in-chief and the London alderman class. Work on the former group has shown that in the century between 1341 and 1440, and more markedly in the last three-quarters of this period, the replacement rate for males was clearly below one, but rose sharply by the turn of the fifteenth and sixteenth centuries (75, p.27). In the latter group the picture was very similar, a replacement rate of one in the generation following the Black Death, below one in the sixty years before 1437, and rising above it between then and the end of the century (104, p.204). Although both these samples suggest that there was a decline until well into the fifteenth century, followed by a recovery, there are two further points which need to be taken into consideration. Firstly, figures based upon the evidence of wills, which are the main source used in the examination of the London alderman class, may exaggerate the survival rate, because in times of plague whole families might be eliminated before any will could be drawn up, or between its drafting and the death of the testator. If this were the case, the drop in population in the first half of the period could have been deeper and the subsequent recovery slower than existing replacement figures suggest. Secondly, the fortunes of tenants-in-chief or of London aldermen and their families are not necessarily the best guide to trends in the country as a whole. One may presume that the standard of living of both these groups was above the national average, and that this could have given them better resistance to disease than their poorer neighbours. In the case of the Londoners, however, they may have been more vulnerable to plague than were country dwellers, unless they themselves had, as they might, country properties to which they could flee in time of pestilence. It seems clear that epidemics of the bubonic type became increasingly limited to the towns, which provided a better habitat for the plague-carrying black rat.

Attempts to examine survival and replacement rates in rural society and in towns other than London have made it clear that conclusions can at best be tentative. There are hints that in the country there was a higher survival rate from about the 1470s, but in Bristol and Worcester it appears that there was no marked population increase until about 1510 (59; 75, pp.28–9). If this is correct, and it is impossible to be certain how far the places for which adequate data survive are typical, it may indicate that rural areas saw an earlier recovery of population than the towns and certainly suggests that there were marked variations between different regions of the country.

Indirect evidence may also help the historian to examine population variations, because it is reasonable to infer that these caused economic changes, some of which can be measured over wider and more representative areas. The main problem associated with this approach is the difficulty of judging how far a rise or fall in the number of inhabitants was the vital factor in bringing about those changes of which we can be certain, notably those in wage and price levels. An alternative explanation for price rises, for example, has been to relate them to the amount of money in circulation or the bullion value of the coinage. This may have some validity; after the devaluation of the coinage in 1465, when its silver content was cut by 20 per cent, there was a price rise of 7 per cent. The total supply of money in circulation cannot, however, be measured, because although the value of coins struck is known for individual years, there is no satisfactory way of estimating how long they remained in circulation. The increase in wages, however, seems to have persisted even in periods when there was a dearth of money, and Hatcher is prepared to accept the general line of the arguments put forward in Postan's pioneering article of 1950 that population decline was the greatest single factor in bringing about these economic changes (75, pp.47–54).

The first indirect evidence for a falling population is the movement of wage-rates. Between 1300 and 1479 payments to agricultural workers on the estates of the bishops of Winchester rose sharply, both in cash terms and in real value, measured by the price of wheat. Furthermore, the wages of artisans, although they moved at a different rate, followed the same general pattern of increasing real values at approximately the same dates. There was, moreover, a decline in wage differentials between craftsmen and unskilled workers, a development which regularly occurs when labour is scarce and higher rates have to be paid, even to the unskilled. The substantial rise in the real value of wages in the late fourteenth century and for much of the fifteenth almost certainly reflects a shortage of workers. Since Postan wrote in 1950, the figures on which historians can base their opinions have been made conveniently available with the compilation of the Phelps Brown and Hopkins indices of the cost of consumable goods, and of building wage-rates in southern England, expressed in terms of these goods [A.1]. Obviously the tables must be used with caution; one lacks information of how far the figures for southern England, for both wages and prices, can be paralleled elsewhere in the country; also some short-term price fluctuations clearly reflect an individual harvest rather than any long-term population change. It is also clear that the prices of different commodities rose at varying rates and at different times. In the early sixteenth century the prices of essential goods rose more sharply than those of inessentials, and at the same time wage differentials increased again, so it is likely that by this date population was rising again, and that as real wages declined a higher proportion of them was being spent on essential goods and less on luxuries.

A second economic indication of declining population is the fall of land values from the mid fourteenth century. Payments for leases of demesne lands, which were freely negotiated and not protected by custom, provide the clearest picture of conditions. These were already declining by 1400 and apparently continued to do so throughout the fifteenth century. Where annual rents were protected by custom, the only payment which could be varied was the entry fine payable by a new tenant, and one can see a decline in these comparable with those in payments for leases. Shortly before the plague, entry fines on the Glastonbury estates were high, at the level of £12 a virgate, but a century later they were nominal. Instead of land being in demand, lords were having to accept tenants where they could find them, on conditions which the tenants were prepared to offer. Admittedly, there were regional variations in land values, and when they began to rise again, the increase was more marked in areas round London, where the demands for food from a large urban area pushed up the value of agricultural land. At the time when rent levels were falling, some less profitable land also went out of cultivation (although the extent of this is hard to measure), so it is clear that the fall in rents must have been due to a shortage of potential tenants rather than to a greater supply of land, which might have resulted from the clearance of forest or the reclamation of fenland.

Economic evidence, then, confirms the more direct pointers to population changes such as the study of replacement rates. There was a fall during the later decades of the fourteenth century and some recovery towards the end of our period. How far can one measure the chronology of these changes or plot rises and falls within it? This is difficult, particularly as most studies of the effects of the plague have tended to concentrate on the fourteenth-century epidemics, the Black Death of 1348–49 and the further outbreaks of the next generation, rather than on the recurrent visitations of the fifteenth century (*see* Framework). Perhaps the most striking point to note at the outset is that the Black Death itself had a comparatively limited effect on wages and the supply of land. Despite the extent of mortality in the first onset of the plague (and the evidence of heriot payments on the Winchester manors shows a death-rate there of at least 50 per cent), wages did not increase startlingly, and until about 1370 there was a rise in rents which corresponded with that in prices (60). This may suggest that the Statute of Labourers, passed in 1351 to curb wage demands, had some success for a number of years. A change came in the second half of the 1370s, when there was a sharp drop in prices at a time when wages continued to rise, and from 1377 until the middle of the 1390s the Phelps Brown index shows a markedly higher level of real wages. A possible explanation for this apparently delayed effect of the Black Death is that the first onset, despite its virulence, did not harm the economy as a whole as much as might have been expected, and that it was the continuing effect of later outbreaks which did the greater damage. There seems to be little doubt that before 1348 the country was overpopulated in relation to its resources – Hatcher estimates the pre-plague population in the $4\frac{1}{2}$–6 million range, and probably nearer the higher figure (75, p.68) – and that the contribution which the extra population made to its total productivity was negligible. As a result, to quote Bridbury, the 'mid-century pestilences were more purgative than toxic' (60). If this were the case, why was there a change in the 1370s? It is possible that the earlier epidemics absorbed the existing population surplus and that the later outbreaks upset the balance between land and labour which had been re-established after 1350. It is perhaps noteworthy that two chroniclers refer to the plague of 1361 as the *pestis puerorum*, the plague of the children, and if it is true that children in particular had perished in that outbreak, it could be that by the early 1370s the supply of labour was being reduced by a shortage of new recruits, particularly as the survivors of 1361 would also have been attacked by another outbreak in 1369. The fall in population did not, however, mean a general decline in economic activity; rising wages may have served to increase consumption and give some stimulus to production, and it is worth noting that even the magnate class, which was more likely to suffer from the changed balance of power between land and labour through declining rent rolls and higher payments of wages was still able to invest considerable sums in new building during Richard II's reign.

As we move on to the fifteenth century, it is hard to judge the extent or the severity of individual outbreaks of plague or of other diseases, but it is probable that some of the epidemics which occurred in urban centres, where plague was most common, were on a sufficient scale to outweigh any natural increase in the population. In 1485 an epidemic, probably of the 'sweating sickness', carried away two mayors of London, and in the North at Ripon two mayors and six aldermen died in eight days, while York was also affected. It would be surprising if less prosperous sections of the community had not been equally attacked by disease at this time, and casualties of that extent would certainly have set back any recovery of the population. As late as the 1520s, a quarter of the property in Coventry was vacant and the population was substantially lower than in 1434, and the experience of other towns showed that this was not unique (75, p.65). The persistence of plague may have been partly responsible – the fact that the late summer remained a period of high mortality in an average year is compatible with the seasonal character of the disease (99, pp.196–8). It is probable that plague remained a constant threat, even if it is less well recorded in contemporary writings than at an earlier date; probably men were more inured to its presence than they had been in the first shock of 1348.

Population decline, of course, was not the only factor which could affect wages. Indeed, a series of bad harvests in the 1350s and 1360s, which increased food prices, may have been partly responsible for deferring the increase in real wages following the Black Death. Certainly it is noteworthy that it was 1377, a year of good harvest, which marked the start of the period when real wages remained high. Similarly, bad harvests probably explain the high prices and the sudden fall in real wages in 1482 and 1483. In this context it is worth remembering that the late Middle Ages was a period of climatic deterioration, with lower temperatures and higher rainfull than in the thirteenth century and earlier. The results of this included some abandonment of cultivation in areas such as Dartmoor, where high contour settlements seem to have been effectively deserted by 1350, and problems in farming on heavy soils which could suffer from waterlogging. However, while climatic conditions could lead to some long-term changes in the economy and to sharp annual variations in food prices, there is no reason to doubt that over a long period movements in prices and wages do indicate whether population was rising or falling.

There has been wide disagreement among historians concerning the chronology of population recovery, some suggesting that it started before the end of the fourteenth century, others favouring dates around 1430 and others again preferring the early sixteenth century (59; 75, p.15; 99, p.269). These disagreements themselves make it clear that there can have been no dramatic recovery which compensated for the losses from the fourteenth-century plagues; any such marked increase would have left no scope for argument. One must also stress that there is an insidious tendency to assume that once the population figures had reached their lowest point, their subsequent recovery was continuous; surviving evidence, however, suggests the contrary: that periods of rising population were at best intermittent and liable to sudden check from new epidemics. Whatever may have occurred earlier, it seems most likely that the sustained recovery of population did not take place until the late fifteenth or the early sixteenth century.

This conclusion would be supported by the evidence of the Phelps Brown index of real wages. The figures in this series are complete for the period covered by this book apart from a short gap between 1403 and 1411. They show considerable fluctuations in the annual level of real wages, but are markedly higher in the early fifteenth century than they had been in the late fourteenth. In some years in the 1430s wages failed to keep pace with high prices, but they rose again in the next two decades. After a slight decline in the 1460s, real wages again increased in the 1470s following a fall in prices, and the peak for the whole period of this book was reached in 1477. The 1480s show an average comparable with the 1430s, although this figure is probably depressed by the bad years of 1482 and 1483 – in the latter year prices were higher than they had been for a century, and wages did not rise proportionately. The two decades on either side of 1500 were comparatively stable, with wages being only a little lower than in the middle of the fifteenth century, but by the second decade of the sixteenth they began to decline in face of increasing prices. This decline continued, and in the 1520s wage-earners had less purchasing power than at any time since the 1370s [A.1].

Clearly, one cannot take price movements in southern England as a precise indication of population change even there, let alone over the country as a whole, but it would be extraordinary if variations in population were not an important factor affecting them, even taking into account the vagaries of individual harvests. It is possible that there may have been a recovery of population around 1430, as the previous decade was relatively free of plague, but from 1433 to 1454 epidemics again increased in frequency (*see* Framework), some being general throughout the country and others being more localized, particularly in London. This was followed by a lull of a decade before another series of major outbreaks between 1464 and 1479. This pattern of epidemics may explain the broad movement of wages in the mid fifteenth century, for the 1440s, 1450s and 1470s, when it is logical to assume that deaths were more likely to have exceeded births, were precisely those decades when wages were highest.

When prices began to rise after 1480, the sharpest increases occurred in consumable goods, such as wheat, rather than in industrial products. This divergence would be most easily explained by a rising population and a consequent labour shortage. As wages declined, less money was available for purchasing inessential goods, so the prices of these would rise less steeply. A further indication of renewed population pressure is that complaints about land enclosure became more conspicuous in the second decade of the sixteenth century, at precisely the same time as real wages began to fall.

For studying the economy it matters little whether the population of England in the 1520s had recovered to the level it had reached before the Black Death. Hatcher, the most recent writer to survey the problem, suggests that it had come nowhere near it (75, p.69). What is far more important is that the balance between land and labour, which had been favourable to labour for about a century and a half, was now tilting back decisively in favour of the landowner. Although there were various epidemics ahead, of various kinds, these no longer prevented the population from entering on a period of sustained growth between 1525 and 1550.

In conclusion, the population of England remained fairly stable for much of the fifteenth century, at a far lower level than in the first half of the fourteenth. There may have been intermittent recoveries, but the bulk of the evidence (often intractable and indirect) suggests that until around 1500 they were only temporary. This stability, not to say stagnation, underlies the whole economic condition of late medieval England. The main beneficiary of it was the agricultural worker and the principal loser the landowner. But the towns were by no means insulated from its far-reaching effects, nor, within the towns, the trading community which made a substantial contribution to the wealth of the kingdom in this period. How each of these groups was affected will be considered in the chapters which follow.

CHAPTER 2

The rural economy and standards of living

The majority of the inhabitants of late medieval England lived close to the soil and were engaged in agriculture. There were, of course, regional variations in the form of agriculture pursued, and in some parts of the country the economy was more diversified. Throughout our period, for example, tin-mining provided alternative employment in parts of Cornwall, and the demand for food by those engaged in this occupation provided a stimulus to local agriculture. The development of textile manufacturing in the fifteenth century was not only one of the most fundamental economic changes of the period, but it also took men away from farming, created a market for the sale of agricultural products and gave an incentive to the producer to grow crops and raise stock beyond the levels required for his own consumption. The development of farming beyond the subsistence level was most marked in areas of urbanization. In South-east England, for example, the demand of London for food supplies affected the neighbouring counties and gave opportunities to enterprising farmers and traders. It also tended to increase the cost of land more markedly in this region than elsewhere.

Besides the varying effects caused by such economic factors as supply and demand, the basic soil conditions of particular areas provided more fundamental reasons for a range of types of farming. Even within a single county there could be marked differences in the capacity of the soil to yield particular crops, and in ease of cultivability. Joan Thirsk's brilliant examination of these variations, region by region, illustrates this for the period from 1500 onwards (103, pp.1–112), and there is no reason to believe that a similar diversity did not exist at the earlier period also, although there were probably changes in detail in particular areas, such as those caused by climatic change to which allusion was made in Chapter 1. Also, during the fifteenth century there was a more considerable transforming influence in the movement for enclosures, which had brought an increasing area under grazing at the expense of arable (Ch.5). Most recent historical work on the rural economy has involved studies in depth of particular regions or even individual manors, and despite the patchiness of the surviving evidence it is clear that one cannot draw hard and fast lines of distinction between regions of arable farming and those of stock-rearing. Certainly, there were broad differences between areas where the plough was dominant and those where grassland was typical, but within these areas there were many deviations from the norm.

If it is hard to generalize about the pattern of farming, it is no easier to summarize the resources or standing of the men who worked on the land. The term 'peasant' is a convenient abstraction, but no more, and there was no such person as a typical peasant. Some were of servile status and others free, although with the passage of time more and more secured their freedom (Ch.4), some might occupy barely enough land to sustain themselves and their families, while others accumulated substantial farms and became themselves employers of labour. The most important common feature among them was that they did not have absolute rights over the land which they farmed, but that they were in some way dependent on a lord, who had a right to some part of their labour or their profits from the land. One must remember that in different contexts the question, 'Whose land is this?' could be answered, equally correctly, by giving the name of the lord, the peasant or possibly that of some intermediate tenant.

The availability of land played a crucial part in relations between the land-owning class and those immediately concerned with its cultivation. Before the epidemics of the mid fourteenth century a serious land shortage existed, and the landowners had the opportunity to secure high rents for lands which they leased out, and to pay low wages to men lacking other opportunities for livelihood. Because labour was cheap, there were ample advantages in cultivating the demesne, and, because land was scarce, the lord had the whip-hand also if he wished a cash rent in lieu of labour services. Surprisingly, the widespread mortality of the plague of 1349 did not completely upset the balance of power between lord and peasant. It created some problems, which prompted the issue of the Ordinance of Labourers of 1349 and the later statute of 1351, which attempted to limit mobility of labour and to peg wage-rates at the 1346 level. These measures probably had a foundation in genuine agricultural unrest – the court rolls of St Albans Abbey record an increase in the number of fugitive villeins in the 1350s – but in most places the records suggest that survivors of the epidemic took up vacant holdings, at least those on land of reasonable quality, so it appears that the population surplus from the period before the Black Death still sufficed to provide a reservoir of possible tenants. Either through this, or through their exercise of coercive powers, the great landed nobility were able to minimize damage to their incomes in the first twenty years or so after the first onset of the plague.

It was in the 1370s that the balance of the economy was seriously altered; from 1372 there was a fall in basic food prices but no drop in wages, and this continued for some years, putting pressure on the profit margins which the manorial lords could secure from their estates (60). It is not clear whether the immediate cause of this was a fortuitous series of better harvests or a further decline in population following later outbreaks of plague. The results of the changed balance are more certain; there were attempts at repressing wages by law, and this may have contributed to the outbreak of the Great Revolt of 1381 (Ch.3). The lords' position was still fundamentally weak, and the shortage of labour in relation to land was now the main characteristic of the English rural economy. This was to lead to an increase in real wages and to a decline in rents for land, and in so far as these can be used to measure the standard of living of the people, they suggest that the condition of the peasantry improved markedly in the fifteenth century. It also undermined the economic resources of the landowners, although here one must stress considerable regional variations – the land market in South-east England remained buoyant because of its proximity to the London market, which provided an outlet for agricultural produce. The complementary nature of the urban and rural economies did not, however, prevent tensions between town and country, as in 1471 when discontent in Essex at the low prices paid for food by the Londoners led men from the county to join the attack on London by the Lancastrian leader Fauconberg (40, p.218).

The shortage of labour forced the landowners to change their methods of exploiting their estates, most obviously in the abandonment of direct cultivation of the demesne by the lord's paid men in favour of leasing it out for a cash rent. Precisely when this occurred can seldom be determined on any estates, because there are few series of complete manorial records, but it is safe to say that by the early fifteenth century the change had taken place widely on both lay and ecclesiastical lands, the latter being better documented over different parts of the country. This indeed was one of the most marked steps in the transition from the traditional medieval economy to the modern.

Of the lands in lay hands, the two crown duchies of Cornwall and Lancaster possess some of the fullest records, although they are by no means unique. The Cornish lands, however, do not fit into the normal pattern of tenures, for demesne exploitation there had been abandoned before 1300, if indeed it had ever existed (76, pp.10–11). In the Norfolk manor of Forncett the policy of leasing the demesne was adopted between 1358 and 1373, but on some of the Percy lands the practice did not appear till later. Although Cockermouth was leased as early as the thirteenth century, the family's five Yorkshire manors were still in demesne in 1352, three of these being leased by 1405 and all by 1416, while their four Sussex manors were all leased between 1405 and 1416.

A similar tendency can be seen on ecclesiastical estates. On those of the archbishop of Canterbury, leasing began in the 1380s and 1390s, and despite occasional returns to direct exploitation, by 1440 all the demesne fields had been leased. The abbey of Leicester came to depend increasingly on rent income from its demesnes, and also from its tithes, and most demesnes were rented by 1477, while Owston Abbey in the same shire had abandoned direct exploitation of demesne lands in all but three villages before 1400. In the North, at Durham Priory, some leasing of demesne began in the late fourteenth century, but the main period at which it was rented out was between 1408 and 1416, perhaps some two decades later than at Christ Church, Canterbury (80, pp.79, 90, 131; 209 p.272).

How far did the abandonment of demesne lands affect the income of the landowners? Certainly when the population was declining, one would expect that tenants might be hard to find and that concessions to them might be necessary, either in the form of a rent reduction or a cut in the entry fine, or in an extension of the period of the lease. Surviving evidence suggests that this was the case, although there were many local fluctuations. On the Talbot estate of Whitchurch in North Shropshire entry fines were lower in the early fifteenth century than in the late fourteenth, and there was a decline in the rents paid for demesne lands after 1400, and little sign of recovery until well into the sixteenth century. Court profits (which included entry fines) fell before 1400 and remained depressed as late as 1507, and the revenues from mills and tolls, already declining in 1400, also showed no recovery by the early sixteenth century. On the Leicester Abbey estates, of which 75–80 per cent fell within the shire, rent income in 1408 was nearly a fifth lower than in 1341, and by 1477 had fallen by almost a third on the 1341 figure, despite the fact that the proportion of income obtained from rent as opposed to production had risen. At Forncett, the average rent per acre of lands leased was markedly lower in the fifteenth century than in the late fourteenth, although one cannot tell from the published figures how far the fluctuations may have been due to variations in the quality of the particular pieces of land being leased at the time rather than to a general decline in rent levels. On the Canterbury estates, the initial period of leasing from 1380 to 1440 was followed by a time when it was harder to secure tenants, but after about 1490 there was some recovery in revenues and evidence that there was competition for leases (80, pp.79, 86).

Further instances could be multiplied, but would add little to the general picture. More important are some of the problems implicit in it. There is little doubt that it was the labour shortage which caused the shift to leasing, but although this provided more revenue than persistence in demesne farming would have done it still left the landowner with reduced resources. Despite this, one still sees lay lords investing in land – there was no possible alternative – and the need to compensate for declining returns to maintain an existing standard of living may indeed explain some of the characteristic features of fifteenth-century society, the pursuit of heiresses, the search for the patronage of a greater man, particularly the King who could grant pensions and offices, and the desire to campaign overseas. If even attempts to improve the standard of estate management did not raise the level of the returns (and the study of the Talbot Whitchurch estates suggests that these were more affected by the underlying economic conditions than by the standard of management), the only prospect for a lord was to seek some supplementary income beyond that of his estates. The one lay lord whose scope was seriously limited in this was of course the greatest, the King, who could seek no patron, and whose fiscal resources from taxation had to be charged on men whose own landed resources were under pressure.

Ecclesiastical landowners were also at a disadvantage compared with laymen. Their own acquisitions of property were severely curtailed by the provisions of the Statute of Mortmain of 1279, and they could not seek heiresses, offices or the profits of war. But they too had expenses, notably the cost of maintaining their buildings, and if voluntary gifts were insufficient to meet requirements, they might well run into difficulties. It is more remarkable that the religious houses survived so well than that they were faced with economic problems, and if they were sometimes regarded as grasping landlords, they had little option to be anything else. Nor was it only their tenants who were resentful, but they also had to face envious glances at their lands from the laity, some of whom at any rate seem to have considered them suitable prey. A scheme of disendowment was voiced in 1395, probably by Lollard sympathizers, though it did not reach Parliament, and in 1404 and 1410 proposals were put forward in Parliament for appropriating the temporalities of the clergy. Although none of these were put into effect, they illustrate the vulnerability of clerical resources in men's minds, and the potential danger to them if the Church did not have powerful support. In practice, however, the Church lost little – the suppression of the 'alien priories' by Henry V merely saw the conversion of resources to other ecclesiastical establishments, and the disappearance of a small number of decayed religious houses in the late fifteenth and early sixteenth centuries was caused by the transfer of their endowments to other houses or to colleges at universities (218, ii, 163–5, iii, 157–8).

When lands were leased out, a wide range of people took them up. In some cases groups of villagers rented them, in others local landowners and in others again merchants, who took them on a speculative basis (209, p.282). If the tenant could not exploit the land directly himself, with his own resources and those of his family, he would have to hire labour, but it seems likely that the small farmer was able to make a better profit than the great man, because his lands were not encumbered by a costly and unproductive bureaucracy. At Durham Priory, for example, less than half of the income assigned to each office in the monastery was devoted to the activity for which the office had been created; the rest was absorbed in management costs (209, p.255).

It is in peasant society that one sees some of the main gainers from the surplus of land. It is clear that there was considerable freedom in the peasant land-market, so that individuals were able to buy parcels of land and increase their own holdings. Such peasant land purchases reflect the recognition of their rights in the land, subject to the fulfilment of obligation to their lords. Again one can see local variations: in Kent, where there was partible inheritance by the local custom called gavelkind, peasant holdings were subject to constant division and could then be reconsolidated, because the holders of land had a free right to alienate it. Even in a single shire one can see adjacent villages where there were differences. In Leicestershire, the communities at Wigston and Ulston were largely free, whereas Foston, only 2 or 3 miles from Wigston, and Galby were occupied largely by servile tenants (83, pp.53–4). It was presumably where the community was predominantly free that one finds continual buying and selling of land between peasant families and the consequent development of a group of more prosperous men in the community. Of course, differences in wealth between peasant families were not new; the evidence of the poll tax returns shows that by the last quarter of the fourteenth century peasants might employ labour on their own account and even have a servant living in their household, although it is difficult to say how common this was (81, pp.30–3; 83, p.31). Such wealthier peasants could easily become dominant figures in a village, because surprisingly few communities had a resident lord. The poll tax returns for some areas in the West Midlands suggest that little more than one village in ten had resident gentry, and in Leicestershire the situation seems to have been similar, and to have remained so into the sixteenth century. By 1525 in the latter shire a quarter of the personal estate in a sample of forty villages was owned by 4 per cent of the rural population, excluding the squires – clearly there were some members of the peasantry who must have had sufficient wealth to dominate their fellows (81, pp.26–7; 83, pp.17, 142).

The purchase of land also presupposes that the peasantry involved were able to accumulate cash, which can have been done only by the production of surplus crops and their sale in a market. In some cases the purchasers of land came from outside the village, as at Leighton Buzzard in Buckinghamshire, where recent arrivals in the manor were able to build up their holdings. Men might also leave the land, members of Wigston families migrated to Leicester into commerce, and it reflects the mobility of the population that only about 10 per cent of the families there survived in the male line from 1377 to the time of Henry VIII. Some died out or moved away, others survived only in the female line and the lands passed to another family by marriage (81, pp.43–7; 83, p.31).

It is when one recognizes the variations in peasant advancement among even individuals in a single community, as well as from one village or one region to another, that one appreciates the need for caution in calling the fifteenth century the golden age of the English labourer. Although wage-rates and rent levels provide one measure of the peasant standard of living, there are dangers in reading too much into this. Firstly, such figures give only an average, and some men would therefore do far less well. Secondly, and far more important, the main factor in most men's standard of living was not what they could earn but what they could produce, and here conditions were dominated not by economic relationships with other men but by something far more basic, the annual and unpredictable variations in the weather and the effects which this would have on the harvest. In some cases this might be literally a matter of life and death. For what this might involve, the historian must rely on literary material, and Langland's dialogue, between Piers and Hunger in the B text of *Piers Plowman* rings painfully true as a description of peasant hardship in the pre-potato age.

Piers did not have meat, but only cheese, loaves of beans and bran and various vegetables, and it was on these that he would have to live until Lammas and the new harvest. He had a cow and a calf, so he presumably would have milk, which together with the cheese could supply some protein in his diet. Indeed, milk probably became more plentiful about May, the notional time of Langland's vision, although the continuation of the passage suggests that in other respects this was a bad time of year. When harvest came, the people could put Hunger to sleep. Langland is critical of some of their actions; Waster and the beggars scorned poor food and demanded better, fine bread instead of that with beans in it and well-cooked meat. Despite the element of social criticism in the poem, Langland takes a conservative attitude to popular discontent, criticizing demands for high wages and murmurs against the Statute of Labourers. The passage concludes with a prophecy of renewed famine and deaths from hunger.

One cannot say how accurate this picture is in detail, nor if Langland is describing a famine or normal peasant conditions. However, it certainly shows the importance of seasonal variations on the normal diet of the people, and particularly of the poor. The 'poor widow' of Chaucer's *Nun's Priest's Tale* had a diet consisting mainly of milk and brown bread, with broiled bacon and the occasional egg, and this may represent a fairly normal diet. Chaucer, writing for an aristocratic audience, would be less inclined to dwell on such incidental details or to consider seasonal variations than Langland, whose central theme at this point in the work was that of hunger. A chronicle source confirms Langland's remark about bread being made from materials other than grain, namely beans, peas and vetches, but it should be noted that this year, 1439, saw a great dearth of corn, and the chronicler's comment probably reflects the unusual nature of the food, at least in his eyes; we do not know how far this view would be general and how far it was that of a man whose conditions were normally more affluent. The year 1439 was in fact one of the worst periods of famine in the fifteenth century; it had followed a harvest failure, brought about by heavy rains over the whole country throughout the summer of 1438. Wheat prices at 13s. 4d. a quarter were more than double the normal (though not as disastrously high as in the notorious famine years of 1315–17), barley at 6s.–7s. was up by over 50 per cent and peas and beans at 6s. had tripled in cost (209, pp.266–7).

These were the main items of agricultural produce, although there were many variations in the quantity of each grown, presumably resulting from local soil conditions. At four dates between 1393 and 1470, peas and beans represented from 28 to 32½ per cent of the crops on the Leicester Abbey estates, barley (presumably mainly used for brewing) from 40 to 45 per cent and wheat from 11½ to 14½ per cent. The rest of the crops consisted of oats and rye. At Wigston (also Leicestershire) in the early sixteenth century peas and beans were even more important at 49½ per cent, barley represented 43½ per cent and wheat only 6 per cent. There was a negligible quantity of rye (80, p.63; 83, p.156). The main problem of studying agricultural production is the lack of clear evidence on yields in relation to seed, although at Battle in Sussex, where this can be documented, wheat and barley yields seem to have declined and those of oats increased during the later Middle Ages. This may reflect developments elsewhere in England, as it seems to be part of a general European pattern of production.

In the mid fifteenth century Sir John Fortescue claimed that the English were richer than the French, that they normally drank ale instead of water and ate all kinds of flesh and fish in abundance (10, pp.86–7). Although his view is probably idealized and unlikely to be particularly informed about peasant conditions, there is some evidence to support his assertions. The accounts of an establishment of chantry priests at Bridport in Dorset show that their diet contained considerable quantities of flesh and fish, and that, although it normally was fairly plain, it could contain luxuries on special occasions. These priests may have been more affluent than the rest of the population, but one has evidence of flesh-eating in the artisan class too. During a heresy trial in 1429, a deposition against Margery Baxter, a wright's wife from Martham in Norfolk, stated that she had been seen boiling *unam peciam de Baken* on the Saturday after Ash Wednesday. She also said that it was better to eat left-over meat in Lent than go to market and incur debt through buying fish (241, p.128). In this remark, perhaps the earliest preserved utterance of an English housewife, she certainly seems to have assumed that such food would be a normal part of the family diet. It is likely, too, that among the peasantry occasional poaching might supplement the meat element in a family's food.

One major factor in causing seasonal variations in food supplies was the difficulty of storage. The wealthier classes might have stone-built barns, which could protect their supplies, but houses built of timber and mud, and with earth floors, would be very damp, so it would be hard to protect grains both from rotting and from the depredations of rats and mice. Building materials for peasant houses varied between different parts of the country. In the clay land areas, little stone was available for building, and timber remained the main material of houses, even as late as the fifteenth century. Excavations at two sites deserted at this period, Goltho in Lincolnshire and Barton Blount in Derbyshire, have shown this. In the West Midlands, the evidence of the Worcester court rolls suggests a prevalence of timber-framed buildings, most often consisting of three bays, although some were larger, and it is possible that the smaller houses were less well recorded. In some areas there were stone buildings, and the houses were partially paved, as at Barrow Mead in Somerset, deserted around 1400. In the last thirty years archaeological investigation of deserted village sites has added substantially to our knowledge of peasant conditions, and will probably provide more information in future, particularly by enabling fuller comparisons to be made between different parts of the country.

Such evidence, however, has its limitations. Until far more excavation has been completed, it will be hard to distinguish between what is typical of an area and what is unusual. Chronology of building forms can be established only approximately, and archaeology cannot tell us of variations in the prosperity of a community from one year to the next. As this is one of the main characteristics of the late medieval rural economy, one must not expect too much from the evidence of excavations. Documentary material, however sparse it may be, provides a firmer chronological framework for the historian.

CHAPTER 3

The Peasants' Revolt

In view of the hardships endured by many peasants, even at times when they were making some gains at the expense of their lords, it is hardly surprising that there were outbreaks of discontent, some of which took violent forms – indeed it has been said that peasant movements were as much a part of seigneurial society as strikes are of large-scale capitalism. One may pursue this parallel further, and suggest that, just as many strikes in modern industry are prompted by particular local conditions, and reflect immediate discontents rather than any general revolutionary outlook, equally many peasant movements had no wide aims, but merely indicate a grievance against a particular manorial lord.

At first sight the revolt of 1381 is different. It drew support from a wide area in South-east England, and there were associated outbreaks in other parts of the country, ranging from York and Scarborough in the North-east, to the Wirral in the North-west, and to Bridgwater and Ilchester in Somerset. It is the rising which has become known as 'the Peasants' Revolt' without any further qualification and has been seen as the most serious social revolt which occurred in medieval England. Yet despite its geographical spread, it is hard to find common features among the different risings which would justify the idea that the revolt was in any real sense a common movement. Undoubtedly the risings were connected with each other in so far as the news of the initial outbreak in Essex seems to have sparked off further unrest in adjacent counties, and later in more remote parts, and it is certain that the general circumstances of the time created an atmosphere which was ripe for revolt, but the differences of aim among the different groups of rebels suggest that each had its own grievances which it hoped to right by force. The various risings must be seen as spontaneous popular movements, and there is no reason to believe in any central leadership which attempted to control the revolt.

Indeed, the divergence in background among the different groups of rebels may reasonably raise the question whether the rising of 1381 is best described by its traditional name, whether it was in fact a peasants' revolt. The troubles at York and Scarborough, already mentioned, took place in an urban environment, and very conspicuous in the troubles was the city of London. Of the 287 participants in the rising who were excluded by name from the general amnesty, over half, 154, were Londoners (98, p.cxxiii; 109, p.55). It is clear, too, that although most of the Londoners involved were drawn from the poorer classes of society, matters were complicated by factions in the city government. An attempt was made to inculpate a group of five aldermen with participation in the troubles, but it is unlikely that in at least four cases there was any real foundation for the charge.

The revolt is well documented, both in chronicles and in the records of government.[1] Full though these are, they are not always very helpful – much of the chronicle material depends on hearsay, although the author of the *Anonimalle Chronicle* seems to have been an eye-witness of events in London or at least to have had access to some eye-witness account. A more serious problem is the bias of the sources, which reflect the views of the ruling class rather than those of the rebels and therefore tend to paint a picture of disorder rather than to record the grievances which prompted the revolt.[2] Such chronicles include letters which purport to have been written by the rebels, and note demands which were made during the rising. These, taken together with inferences drawn from what the rebels did, go some way to explaining why the revolt took place.

There is a substantial amount of evidence for peasant discontent before 1381, most of it (as far as existing evidence shows) being concentrated in the Central and East Midlands and in the Home Counties, precisely those parts of England where manorialization was most fully developed. However, there was a significant absence of such discontent in East Anglia and Kent, two of the areas most severely affected in 1381 (78, p.145). Disputes, both before and after 1381, were concerned with questions of rents to be paid and services to be performed, or with whether or not individuals were free men or villeins. Although some of the grievances voiced in 1381 concerned these same matters, there were other factors at work too, which may help to explain the special character of this rising.

The broad lines of the revolt are clear (11, pp.38–44) although there are numerous problems of detail. The first outbreak occurred in Essex in the second half of May, in the form of resistance to taxation, by early June Kent also was in revolt, and by the second week of that month East Anglia too was affected. In mid-June the Kent rebels marched on London, where they were joined by the Essex men and secured support from discontented elements in the capital. For some three days there was a virtual collapse of government, during which the rebels laid hands on and put to death the Chancellor, Archbishop Sudbury, and the Treasurer, Sir Robert Hales. The death of the rebel leader Wat Tyler on 15 June changed the situation, and by the following week the authorities were again in control in the South-east. The climax of the East Anglian revolt came slightly later; there was widespread trouble in Norfolk, Suffolk and Cambridgeshire between 12 and 21 June, in which the main victims were the Chief Justice of the King's Bench, Sir John Cavendish, and the prior of Bury St Edmunds. The man principally responsible for suppressing the trouble was Bishop Despenser of Norwich, whose force crushed various rebel groups between 18 and 25 or 26 June.

What were the causes of the rising? Were they predominantly political or social? Undoubtedly taxation provided the occasion for the revolt; this was stressed by the best informed contemporary source, the author of the *Anonimalle Chronicle*, and by the Leicester canon Henry Knighton (11, pp.124, 135). This was prompted by the costs of war – indeed, since the renewal of the conflict with France in 1369 there had been several major fiscal exactions, of which the three poll taxes were the last. In 1377 the tax had been levied at 4d. a head, in 1379 it had been graduated and in December 1380 Parliament granted a further tax at 1s. a head, and although suggestions were made that the rich should help the poor to meet this heavy burden, one suspects that these were largely unheeded. Even in 1377 there seems to have been considerable evasion; in 1381 this was certainly far worse. In those cases where the figures from counties and boroughs have survived from both 1377 and 1381, those for the latter year show an average fall of 32.54 per cent. As there is no natural reason for this, such as an epidemic, one must assume widespread evasion as the cause. In only one place, the borough of Northampton, was the 1381 figure higher than that for 1377; elsewhere it is down, sometimes by a very large amount [A.4].

The figures suggest two obvious conclusions, that the authority of the central government, as measured by its ability to secure payment, was weakest in the remote areas of the North and West, and that on the whole it was easier to enforce payments in the boroughs than in the countryside. No borough showed a drop of over 50 per cent in the numbers paying and only four over 45 per cent, whereas two counties showed one of over 60 per cent, four more of between 50 and 60 per cent and one more of over 45 per cent. At the other end of the scale, only three counties showed a fall of under 15 per cent, while nine boroughs (excluding Northampton) come into this group. Apart from these conclusions, there is little that can be safely deduced from these figures, as there is no obvious correlation between the areas of major disorder and particular levels of tax evasion. Possibly the markedly low figures for both Cambridgeshire and the town of Cambridge indicate effective enforcement of the tax, and in Kent, Norfolk and Suffolk, too, the figures are below average, although less conspicuously so, but in Essex and Hertfordshire they are higher.

The taxation in itself, however heavy, could hardly have sparked off so violent a conflagration if conditions had not been appropriate for it. One may eliminate famine as a possible underlying cause of discontent, as the harvests in the five years before 1381 were at least average and sometimes good (78, p.161). The demands made by the rebels provide the clearest guide to their grievances, and according to the *Anonimalle Chronicle* those put forward by the Essex men at Mile End on 14 June were that they should be allowed to seize and punish traitors, and that no man should be made a serf nor do homage or any type of service to a lord in return for land; instead they should hold it at a rent of 4d. an acre. This suggests that grievances were both political and social. Significantly, on the following day at Smithfield, after the deaths of Sudbury and Hales, there seem to have been no further demands concerning 'traitors', but further ones about social and legal status, that there should be no lordship apart from the King's, that the Church should be disendowed and (cryptically) that there should be no law except that of Winchester (11, pp.161–5). The other chroniclers are less explicit, but give a similar impression, complaints about servitude and oppression and demands for liberty bulking largely in their accounts. Knighton includes among the demands one for free rights of hunting and fishing, and Walsingham also reports an alleged confession by the rebel leader Jack Straw, which suggested far more revolutionary aims, the killing of all the lords and later of the King, the destruction of all possessioner clergy, leaving only the friars, and the creation of kings in all the counties (11, pp.180–6, 201–7, 365–6). This confession must be treated with scepticism, although it possibly has some factual substratum and is not merely a figment of Walsingham's imagination. The idea, however, that the rebels aimed to kill the King is unlikely – not only did the rebels show a positive loyalty to him at Mile End and Smithfield, and adopt as a watchword 'King Richard and the True Commons', but they made no attempt to take vengeance on him for the death of Wat Tyler, when he could have been at their mercy.

The actions of the rebels, as well as their demands, reflect both political and social aims. The hostility to alleged traitors took extreme form in the murders of Sudbury, Hales and Cavendish, and equally strong was the dislike of the King's uncle, John of Gaunt – his palace of the Savoy was burned down (although it is uncertain whether the Kentishmen or the Londoners played the leading part in this) and he would probably have shared the fate of Sudbury and the others if he had not had the good fortune to be in the North negotiating with the Scots. As it was, a number of the lesser victims of the rising were associates of Gaunt, and almost certainly owed their fate to his unpopularity. Other sufferers from popular hatred were foreigners, particularly Flemings, a number of whom were killed in London and East Anglia (78, pp.195–8). It is not clear if there were particular economic motives for these killings, or if they were simply a matter of xenophobia. Yet another target of the rebels' attack was lawyers and legal records. Here, particularly in the destruction of manorial court rolls, which provided a record of the obligations owed to the lords of the manors, one sees the desire to be free of the legal burdens which were laid on peasant tenants. The demand for personal freedom, a recurrent feature in late medieval peasant society, does not reflect only a wish for improved social status, but also a hope for potential economic advantages. As long as a man was unfree, he had no access to the royal courts, but could plead only in his lord's court. A free man, on the other hand, could appeal in the public courts against any increase in the burdens imposed on him. Furthermore, he could leave the manor if he so wished, and could therefore negotiate for better terms from the lord by threatening to go if the latter refused concessions (79, p.31). The most plausible explanation of the demand for the law of Winchester is probably that the rebels accepted the 1285 Statute of Winchester, which could be interpreted as giving all adult males the right to bear arms. Bearing arms and sharing in the maintenance of order, however, would give men additional powers.

Although the rebels' demands for personal freedom are conspicuous in the chronicles, this can hardly have been the main motive of the Kentishmen, one of the most prominent groups among the peasants, because in Kent there was no serfdom. Here perhaps the political factor was more significant. When Parliament met in the autumn of 1381, the Speaker expressed the view that the troubles had been caused by abuses in government, notably by purveyance for the royal household and by the levy of taxation for the defence of the realm, particularly as this did not prevent the King's enemies from raiding England. The *Anonimalle Chronicle* states that the Kentish rebels commanded those living within 12 leagues of the sea not to accompany the rebel army, but to stay at home to keep the coast free from enemies (11, pp.126–7, 330–1). As the south coast had been raided only a few years earlier, this action is understandable, and it also indicates a measure of political awareness among the peasant class. It would probably be dangerous to underestimate the amount of information which percolated down to the classes which were not themselves involved in government, and it is likely that echoes of the political crises of the 1370s, notably the events of the Good Parliament of 1376 (ch.16), were heard in the countryside. It is worth remembering that the London merchant Richard Lyons, who had been impeached in 1376, was one of the rebels' victims five years later.

It would be a mistake to assume that all participants in the revolt were involved in it for the same reasons. The rising created an atmosphere of disorder in which those with grievances felt free to take violent action against their enemies. This explains why one finds contrary demands being made by groups in different places. At Dunstable, where the rebels were townsmen, they tried to restrict freedom of trade to within the borough, whereas the rural Essex rebels had followed precisely the opposite policy, and at Yarmouth the insurgents, drawn from the neighbouring countryside attempted to overthrow the rights of the municipality (98, pp.41, 108–11).

There was little ideology in the revolt, although Christian teachings of social obligation played some part. These were voiced most clearly by the radical priest John Ball, whose record of inflammatory preaching had brought him into conflict with the authorities as early as 1366, and who had been imprisoned earlier in 1381 for his hostility to the Pope and the prelates (11, p.372). Many of his utterances were, however, sermon commonplaces, to which parallels can be found in other contemporary preaching. Even the famous couplet of Ball's sermon at Blackheath, as reported by Walsingham:

> When Adam dalf, and Eve span,
> Wo was thanne a gentilman?

was adapted from traditional preaching on the emptiness of human boasting. However, although it was not unusual for preachers to criticize social abuses and injustice, this was not necessarily given a revolutionary tone (230, pp.291, 296), and the significant point about Ball was that he adapted a traditional idea to revolutionary ends. It is also worth noting that after his death he seems to have remained as a hero in folk memory. Walsingham and Knighton also attempted to blame Wyclif and the Lollards for propagating revolt, but this must be seen only as scaremongering by the established order in the Church, attempting to tar the socially conservative academic heretic with the brush of revolution. Hilton's attempt to revive the idea of Lollard influence on the revolt by redefining Lollardy as something more than the following of Wyclif (78, p.213) disregards the general character of later Lollardy, which only rarely developed revolutionary tendencies.

Ball was the only prominent figure in the rising who had any known background of discontent; the other leaders emerged in the course of events. Even Wat Tyler, the most famous of these, does not seem to have been involved in the earliest disturbances in Kent, as he is not mentioned in indictments dealing with disorder in Canterbury on 10 and 11 June, when the leader was John Hales of Malling. Tyler is first mentioned (in conjunction with a John Rackstraw, presumably the man later known as Jack Straw) in a reference to a command issued on 13 June (11, pp.145–7). The uncertainty of even contemporary writers about who the leaders were, notably the fact that a number of them considered Straw and Tyler to be identical, illustrates how obscure they were. Attempts to trace the background even of Tyler have petered out through lack of definite evidence.

It is clear that in each area of revolt, some local figure emerged to take the lead, and this is hardly surprising when one considers the nature of fourteenth-century society. In each village and manor local men filled such offices as bailiff, and the holders of these positions were presumably the more articulate members of the community – inglorious the peasants may have been, but there is no need to regard this as synonymous with mute. Thomas Baker of Fobbing in Essex, whose resistance to the poll tax was the earliest recorded sign of revolt, had indeed been appointed to be village collector of the tax (11, p.205), but instead led the opposition to it. William Grindcob at St Albans and Geoffrey Litster in East Norfolk were local leaders as able and articulate as Tyler in Kent and London, and all seem to have had a capacity to maintain discipline. In Essex and Suffolk the rebels were sufficiently acquainted with the structure of local government to use the machinery of the hundreds for the purpose of mobilization (78, p.217). Some of the rebel leaders, notably Litster, may have appreciated their military weakness, because they attempted to involve members of the gentry in the revolt, and although they had little support of this nature, the very fact that they hoped to obtain it must argue against an interpretation of the revolt simply in class terms.

The spread of the revolt after the original outbreak reflects its improvised nature. Predictably, local risings were sporadic, but once the spark had been kindled, conditions were clearly ripe for revolt. It is hard, however, to see convincing evidence for the existence of any central revolutionary organization, and Hilton's demolition of the idea that there was something called the 'Great Society' is completely convincing (78, p.215). His translation of *magna societas* as 'large company' is far more probable, and it could refer to an individual rebel band which was threatening to dominate an area. No doubt there were communications between different groups, but the only ones preserved, those of John Ball (even if authentic), were cryptic allegorical utterances, not commands for action (11, pp.381–3; 78, p.214).

The rebels' attitude to the King is striking. Only Straw's 'confession' suggests hostility to him, and more characteristic was the attempt to identify Richard with their cause. However mistaken this attitude was, it undoubtedly was a significant factor in events (11, p.23: 78, p.225). It may explain both why the fourteen-year-old King played a prominent part in the negotiations at Mile End and Smithfield, and how he was able to avoid mob vengeance after Tyler's murder. It is not necessary to suppose that he acted on his own initiative, although this is implied in the *Anonimalle Chronicle* (11, pp.158–9): possibly his advisers felt that he might be less at risk than they themselves, and that in the circumstances a policy of temporary conciliation was the best course of action.

A problem deserving consideration is how strong the rebel forces actually were. Although all the contemporary writers depict widespread anarchy, it is hard to reconcile this with the speed of the government's reaction after Tyler's death. The mob undoubtedly was in control in London when Sudbury and Hales were executed, but on 15 June the civic leaders were able to raise a substantial force from the wards of the city and surround the rebel force at Smithfield, which immediately yielded. On this the sources are virtually unanimous (11, pp.167, 179, 186–7, 197, 204–11). If one remembers that the rebels had sympathizers in London, although these may have been partly alienated from them by the disorders, it is all the more remarkable how quickly the city authorities reasserted their control and obtained substantial support. Only one member of the feudal class, Sir Robert Knolles, is reported as playing a major part in the attack on the rebels in London, although the earl of Suffolk and Bishop Despenser of Norwich were prominent in the repression in East Anglia. Possibly the deaths of the Chancellor and the Treasurer undermined the confidence of the King's surviving ministers, and it was left to other loyalists to act on their own initiative.

The sudden collapse of the rising leaves one final question: did the revolt play any significant part in the development of English society in the following decades? The general view is that it was basic economic forces rather than the events of 1381 which brought about the end of villeinage and the enfranchisement of the peasant class (11, p.29). Alone among recent writers, Hilton suggests that the rising may have deterred the ruling class from further local attempts at repression (78, pp.231–2). One cannot judge which of these views is preferable, because one can only infer the motives of the landowners from their actions; we do not know if they were genuinely frightened by the memory of the revolt, or for how long any such fear persisted. Their treatment of those who held land from them may have been prompted as much by economic motives as by political or psychological ones. Certainly the suppression of the rising did not eliminate peasant unrest, although this reverted to being a purely local phenomenon, and in general to taking less violent forms. The most obvious casualty of the rising was the poll-tax, which was abandoned as a future source of revenue.

---

1. The main narratives and considerable documentary material are available in (11). Other documentary material is printed in the appendices to (98).
2. There is a valuable analysis of the sources in (11, pp.3–13).

CHAPTER 4

Rural society and popular movements after 1381

The rebellion of 1381 and its subsequent repression did not affect the underlying problems of the economy, notably those posed by the decline in population. The initial ruthlessness of the authorities was soon moderated, and pardons were granted to most of the participants in the rising, but sporadic disorder continued after 1381, although it was no longer a serious threat to society and government. During the fifteenth and early sixteenth centuries there were intermittent popular revolts, but apart from that of Jack Cade in 1450, they tended to be far more limited in scope than that of 1381. Also, although some of the demands which had been made in 1381 were echoed in the later risings, in none of them was there anything so clear-cut in the way of a social programme as the demands put forward at Mile End and Smithfield. Some popular attitudes did not change, and in London at any rate one sees recurrent attacks on foreigners and their property at times of civil or political commotion, as in 1456, 1457, 1463, 1470 and 1517. Such acts did not, however, amount to a programme of action; they merely represented instinctive hostility to outsiders. Although these troubles occurred in the city, foreigners were also attacked at times of peasant rioting when the rebels came to London, so it is clear that there were some sentiments which were shared by townsmen and countrymen alike.

Popular movements between the late fourteenth and the early sixteenth centuries are best understood in the broader context of developments in peasant society, even although most such risings seem to have been prompted by political or fiscal considerations rather than by social grievances. This does not, however, mean that the peasantry were contented, nor does it prove that they were particularly prosperous; rather it suggests that the peasantry found that they could secure their aims more effectively by passive resistance and the exploitation of their economic power than by violence. In Essex, a shire which had been at the heart of the 1381 troubles, the peasantry were able to improve their lot after the repression of the revolt. A statute of 1388 attempted to reinforce the Statute of Labourers, the measure enacted to control wages after the Black Death of 1348–49, but attempts in 1389 to put it into practice showed that men were trying to shake off the stigma of villein tenure, even at the cost of taking a cash wage worth less in real terms than the combination of cash and food which they had been paid previously, insisting on working by the day rather than contracting for a yearly wage, and exploiting the possibility of alternative employment (65, pp.92–5). Men who took such actions clearly felt that they had a secure prospect of work and that they did not need to be particularly submissive to their lords. The peasant's ultimate weapon was to leave the manor, and the example of Forncett in Norfolk shows that between 1400 and 1575, 126 serfs were recorded as withdrawing to 64 different places. Over half did not go beyond 10 miles, and more than half of the remainder stayed within 20. One of the most popular destinations was Norwich, 12 miles away (65, pp.123–4). By going even so short a distance, however, men could free themselves from the control of their lord and the custom of the manor, and it is clear that one can see a similar situation elsewhere in the country; families were prepared to leave the land to free themselves from their lords (79, p.35).

Custom of the manor defined peasant obligations, but it could also help to determine peasant rights. There were different kinds of customary tenure, but they had in common the fact that they gave some protection to the unfree man against arbitrary expropriation. He was not protected by the King's court as a free man was, but most lords seem to have recognized that even unfree tenants had certain rights. The fifteenth century saw the development of what was called copyhold tenure, by which a peasant possessed a copy of the entry on the manorial court roll which defined his rights and obligations, as the most common form of land-holding in early modern England. This was not universal – some tenants held land by custom alone, without possessing a copy of the court roll entry, and they were generally more vulnerable to pressure from their lords, as legal protection was gradually extended to copyhold tenants by the courts both of common law and of equitable jurisdiction during the fifteenth century. In some areas, however, customary tenants seem to have been able to obtain security comparable to that enjoyed by copyholders. In so far as tenants were able to secure the protection of copyhold, it removed the old disadvantages under which the servile tenant laboured. By the end of the Middle Ages there were various categories of copyholder, the best placed being those who held by inheritance with the entry fine to the land being fixed, while the less fortunate held for a term of life, with an uncertain entry fine to be paid by the successor, or even, although this was unusual, held only for a term of years (79, p.47; 82, pp.60–2). One demand made during the Pilgrimage of Grace in 1536 was that entry fines should not exceed the value of two years' rent, so it is likely that by this time, when a rising population was creating a shortage of land, some landlords were seeking more. More vulnerable than copyhold tenants were leaseholders, particularly when their leases were granted for limited terms such as seven or ten years, with the possibility of the rent being raised at each renewal. This could be done, and the lord would be in a position to rack-rent, if there was any demand for land, and although this latter condition was not met for much of the fifteenth century, it did apply as the sixteenth century advanced. One must not, however, classify tenants too rigidly, because the same man might hold different parts of his lands by different forms of tenure, some freehold, some copyhold and some by lease. This indeed was a factor in hastening the decay of villeinage, because a man who was free would not wish to incur servile obligations if he took possession of land which had hitherto been burdened with them.

During the fifteenth century, the laws of supply and demand worked in favour of the peasantry. Population shortage had reduced the demand for land, and it was not until the sixteenth century that demand again began to exceed supply. Significantly, it was as the population recovered that one again sees widespread movements of social unrest. An example of the practical working of the economic balance of power can be seen on the estates of the bishopric of Worcester, where the peasants were able to nullify their lord's attempts at coercion by simply refusing to pay the sums demanded. This was reflected in the increasing arrears of payments owed between the episcopate of Bishop Wakefield in 1389 and that of Bishop Carpenter in 1454. Permanent arrears were normally written off at a bishop's death, so the figures give some indication of the rate at which they accumulated. In 1389, after fourteen years of Wakefield's episcopate they were £465, in 1412, after five of Peverell's they were £252, and in 1454, after ten of Carpenter's they were £1194, representing respectively an average annual increase in arrears of £33, £50 and £119. The Worcester accounts also show that the tenants' resistance was directed particularly at payments which testified to their servile status, such as tallage and payments to commute labour service. Behind these arrears is evidence of a collective refusal to pay, which the bishop's officers could not overcome. By the early sixteenth century, however, the figure of arrears dropped; as a rising population began to press on the means of subsistence, the lord had a more powerful weapon to hand. Servile obligations did survive, albeit unevenly, throughout the country, and their persistence in this way probably reflects the unevenness of the power struggle from one manor to another. It was probably because of the greater financial power which it offered them that the lords tried, where possible, to maintain servile obligations on their tenants (79, pp.48–55).

The relative absence of major revolts during the fifteenth century probably reflects the fundamental state of the economy, and it is perhaps a reasonable assumption that the basic prosperity of the peasantry in their relations with the land-owning class contributed to this. Some of the wealthier peasants undoubtedly prospered, rising in rank to become yeomen or even gentry in the sixteenth century, but these were a minority. The basic vulnerability of the peasantry was revealed when the economic climate became chillier, and for many families this period of prosperity was to prove short-lived. In the sixteenth century, rents and entry fines began to rise again, and lords no longer felt it desirable to ensure their income by lengthening the terms of leases, when frequent renegotiation of these could give them more opportunities to raise rents.

Such popular movements as occurred between 1381 and the early sixteenth century must be seen against this background, which goes far to explain their character. The grievances which prompted them tended not to be social, but political, fiscal, or even religious. The Lollard rising of Sir John Oldcastle in 1414 had no social aims; indeed the rebels do not appear to have had any programme at all, beyond a vague idea of seizing the King (without any very clear idea of what they would then do with him). The revolt was essentially Oldcastle's attempted revenge for his arrest in the previous year, and the only economic motive which can be discerned among some of the rebels was a possible hope of seizing some ecclesiastical property. The rising at Abingdon in 1431 (with offshoots in the Midlands and London), which contemporaries associated with Lollardy, although on somewhat tenuous grounds, was undoubtedly anti-clerical, and some rebels seem to have put forward plans for ecclesiastical disestablishment.

They do not, however, seem to have possessed any programme for the betterment of lay society. Although both these revolts secured some support from fairly widespread areas, this was not strong, and they were easily suppressed.

Jack Cade's rising in 1450, which affected mainly Kent and various neighbouring counties, was a far more serious affair, and had repercussions over a much wider area. It marked the culmination of a series of political disorders, directed primarily against Henry VI's chief adviser, William de la Pole, duke of Suffolk. One of his associates, Adam Moleyns, bishop of Chichester, was murdered on 9 January, he himself was committed to the Tower on the demand of the Commons on 28 January and two sets of articles of impeachment were laid against him. Although he was pardoned by the King and sent into exile (presumably for his own protection), there were riots against him after his release from the Tower, and when he sailed from England he was intercepted and murdered on 2 May. De la Pole's unpopularity was essentially political and personal; he was associated with the failure of the war in France and was rightly suspected of exploiting royal favour in the interest of himself and his friends (Ch.22; 147, pp.44, 62). Popular unrest had begun to develop even before his death – commissions were appointed to investigate insurrections in Kent on 2 February and in Surrey on 11 April, and a London chronicle tells of the arrest and execution, at an unspecified date, of a rebel leader known as Bluebeard. (7; 22, p.158) By the end of May the Kentishmen were marching on London, in June there was a skirmish with royal forces, and they presented a formal complaint of their grievances. On 4 July they entered London, although the authorities there were able to reassert themselves more rapidly than in 1381. On the next day a pardon was offered to the rebels, who withdrew from the city, although their leader Cade remained under arms, putting himself outside the scope of the pardon, and was killed on 12 July. Another prominent man at court, the King's confessor, Bishop Ayscough of Salisbury, was murdered at Edington in Wiltshire on 29 June. The troubles in Kent dragged on sporadically for some two years; in August 1450 a certain William Parmenter virtually proclaimed himself Cade's successor by calling himself the second captain of Kent, in April 1451 there were troubles fomented by Henry Hasilden, and in May 1452 there was yet further disorder (42).

What was the cause of these disorders? The Kentishmen's statement of grievances, comprising fifteen articles and five requests to the King, throws some light on this (7; 11, pp.338–42) The first article stated that there were rumours that Kent was to be turned into a forest as a punishment for Suffolk's death. This rumour may have done what the poll tax did in 1381, set fire to a potentially explosive situation, indeed one which had already shown signs of bursting into flame. But it is clear that there were more fundamental problems. Complaints were then made about the exclusion of the lords of the King's blood from his Council, obviously an allusion to the duke of York, about purveyance of goods for the King's household, and about extortion by sheriffs and their officers. Allegations of treason were made concerning the loss of lands in France, a matter which may have particularly concerned the Kentishmen, whose vulnerability to raids was obvious, and who may well have been alarmed by the issue of a commission of array, and a command to set up warning beacons, on 14 April. Complaint was made that there was no free election of knights of the shire, and that those elected knights had taken bribes for appointing tax-collectors in it. The King was asked to take the duke of York into his counsel, to punish those responsible for the death of the duke of Gloucester and to end extortions, particularly those by four named persons.

Apart from one passing reference to the Statute of Labourers, social grievances do not appear in the petition. More important are the political demands, but most significant of all was local discontent at the action of royal officials in the shire. This was directed particularly at the sheriff, William Crowmer, and his father-in-law, Lord Say, who as Sir James Fiennes had been sheriff in 1442. Say had been Treasurer since 1449, so the attacks on him link local grievances with general hostility to the court. There is good reason to believe that these attacks were well justified, because after the defeat of the rising and Cade's death, a commission, sent into Kent to investigate extortions there, held inquests in various parts of the shire between late August and late October 1450. At these the jurors accused various officials, particularly those named in the complaint, of extortion, disseisin, forcible detention of goods and fabrication of warrants of arrest for the purpose of extorting money (42). In June too, after an attempt to repel the rebels had failed, and the leaders of the royal force, Sir Humphrey Stafford and William Stafford, had been killed at Sevenoaks, the government had tried to placate the Kentishmen by arresting Crowmer and Say and sending them to the Tower, and when Cade's men entered London in July, those two were among their earliest victims (16, p.192). The rebels also secured support in London from opponents of the court party. The courtiers' most prominent associate there was a draper, Philip Malpas, who had been chosen alderman of Lime Street ward in 1448 only through royal influence. His house was sacked during the revolt, and he himself was discharged from office; although he lived for almost twenty years more, he was not reappointed. Some of Cade's allies in the city were men of position, although the bulk of his support came from the poorer classes (128, pp.111, 115).

The evidence suggests that Cade's support was fairly widely based, and that the strength of his leadership lay in his ability to act as spokesmen for all the social groups which supported him. The revolt was not purely one of the agricultural classes, although a substantial number of those pardoned for participation in it are described as 'husbandman' or 'labourer'. A number of those involved were artisans from the Kentish towns, some of whom, particularly those connected with the cloth trade, may have had a special grievance, as a sharp decline in cloth exports after 1448 could well have caused local unemployment (66, pp.96–7). Even more striking as a pointer to the greater importance of political rather than social factors in the rebellion was the participation of men from higher up the social scale; over ninety participants are described as 'gentleman' or 'esquire', and there was even one knight in the list of those pardoned, Sir William Trussel of Aylmesthorpe, Leicestershire. It is not clear how far there were similar local grievances to those of the Kentishmen in some of the other shires which were involved in the revolt, notably Sussex and Surrey, although it is probable that the resentment of the citizens of Salisbury at the powers which the bishop exercised there may have been one factor behind the murder of Ayscough (7; 147, pp.63, 66–8).

As a leader, Cade was able to maintain discipline among his men, at least until they reached London, and his success in defeating the force sent against him argues that he possessed some military capacity. Possibly there was some break-down of control when he entered London, which may well have contributed to a reaction against him on the part of the citizens. The attack on Malpas's house certainly seems to have alarmed them and led them to co-operate with the author-ities against the rebels (22, p.161).

As in 1381 there was no specific disloyalty to the King – hatred was concen-trated on his advisers. This raises a further problem, whether or not there was, as some Tudor writers believed, Yorkist influence behind the rising. Certainly Cade's assumption of the name Mortimer, by which he was known in the earlier stages of the revolt, hints at Yorkist connections. (Indeed he was pardoned under that name, and the discovery that it was a false one provided an additional pretext for its revocation.) But Richard of York himself made no attempt to co-ordinate his movements with Cade's, and the demands for his inclusion among the King's advisers probably do no more than reflect dislike of the existing court faction.

It is worth spending considerable time in examining the causes of the 1450 rebellion, because they contrast markedly with those of the 1381 revolt. Cade and his supporters had no constructive programme for social reform, and appeared to be unconcerned about questions of servile status or land rents. Such economic grievances as existed were probably prompted by such immediate issues as the slump in the cloth industry rather than by long-term agrarian questions. The major grievances were political, although not necessarily dynastic, and reflected discontent at the abuse of power by the men who controlled the government. The rising, the most extensive popular movement between 1381 and the sixteenth cen-tury, was relatively limited in its aims and was certainly not directed at the over-throw of the social order.

During the Yorkist period there were undoubtedly some movements of pop-ular discontent; in 1471 the Essex men seem to have joined Fauconberg's attack on London because they felt that the citizens were paying insufficient prices for dairy supplies. A late and rather unreliable source also explained some of the northern discontent in 1469 as the result of the demands of the Hospital of St Leonard at York for payments of sheaves from the northern counties (13, p.121; 40, p.218). But neither of these cases really proves the existence of strong agrarian unrest; both show that local discontent could be drawn into the political struggles of contending dynasties and their magnate supporters.

In the early Tudor period, the main occasions for insurrections seem to have been fiscal. Two risings under Henry VII followed attempts to levy taxes; in 1489 the earl of Northumberland lost his life at the hands of a force of rebellious York-shiremen when he was trying to collect the subsidy granted that year, and in 1497 the levying of a tax for a war with Scotland led to a more serious revolt in Corn-wall. According to one account, the Cornishmen felt that the affairs of the North were too remote to interest them. A substantial army marched on London, and although it was defeated and the leaders were put to death, to do so the King had to divert the force which was being prepared for the campaign in Scotland (73, pp.14–16).

Resistance to taxation was not always so violent. In 1513 there was opposition to a tax imposition in Yorkshire – indeed on this occasion a remission of assessment was granted on grounds of poverty, so the government seems to have been prepared to meet genuine grievances. A decade later, there was a more serious crisis. There was opposition to a subsidy demand in 1523, and when in 1525 Henry VIII and Cardinal Wolsey attempted to levy the so-called Amicable Grant, to finance a campaign against France, they faced serious resistance. The demand was heavy, for a payment of one-sixth on the goods of the laity and of one-third on those of the clergy, and some men refused payment outright, while others put forward the plea that they could not afford to pay. The most serious trouble was in Suffolk, in the cloth-manufacturing area of Lavenham and Sudbury, where the dukes of Norfolk and Suffolk claimed that they were faced with a body of 4,000 men, who alleged that they had no work and did not know how to get their living. In fact, even in this area where the textile trade was important, such a high level of unemployment would have been surprising, for cloth exports in the mid 1520s were substantially higher than earlier in the decade, when there had been a marked recession. The authorities approached the crisis cautiously; in Suffolk the dukes arrested only the four principal offenders, and even they were pardoned when they were brought before the Star Chamber (66, pp.115–16; 73, pp.17–19). In these rebellions, the main grievances voiced were fiscal, although it is not certain how far the taxation itself was the real cause of discontent and how far merely the last straw which could not be borne in a time when land was becoming scarce and real wages were in decline [A.1].

Certainly by the second quarter of the sixteenth century there were serious social grievances which underlie such movements as the Pilgrimage of Grace of 1536 and the West Country and Norfolk revolts of 1549. Although detailed consideration of these lies beyond the scope of the present book,[1] it is worth noting that they raised more specifically social and economic grievances than the risings of the fifteenth century. Enclosure of common land, invasion of common rights and engrossing of farms were among the complaints put forward in the Norfolk rising, and there was also a demand for the ending of serfdom, although there is little evidence that there were still many men of villein status. The western rising was prompted largely by religious conservatism, although an attempt to limit the number of servants a gentleman might have had social overtones (73, p.61, 69, 136, 142–4). The most complex of the risings was the Pilgrimage of Grace, the problems of which have been covered in two important papers, both of which stress the varying motives of the participants (68; 69). In the end, the rising should probably be seen primarily as religious and political in character, although certain sectors of it, notably those in Westmorland and Craven, were concerned with such agrarian matters as enclosures and the rate of entry fines. It is possible that here, and again in Norfolk in 1549, the basic grievances lay in local rather than national conditions.

Nevertheless, it seems fair to say that by the 1530s social grievances were again being voiced to an extent that they had not been in the previous century. Behind this, almost certainly, lay the new economic pressures of an expanding population which were leaving the agricultural worker worse off than he had been in the years of land surplus. The balance of power was shifting back to favour the landlord, and it was to remain that way for a long time.

---

1. They will be considered more fully in volume II of this series, A. G. R. Smith, *The Emergence of a Nation State*.

CHAPTER 5

Enclosures and depopulation

Among the grievances of some of the rural rebels in the sixteenth century were complaints about the enclosure of lands by lords – this occurred in the north-west sector of the Pilgrimage of Grace, and the casting down of hedges marked the start of the Norfolk rising of 1549. In the 1540s, furthermore, there was a considerable quantity of writing denouncing the practice (44, pp.941–53). Criticism of it was by no means new: a generation earlier, in the second decade of the century, there had been various anti-enclosure measures, an Act in 1515 to prevent the conversion of land from tillage to pasture, and the establishment of commissions of enquiry by Wolsey in 1517 and 1518 to investigate the extent of enclosures. The returns of these commissions, together with subsequent proceedings throughout the cardinal's chancellorship against those who had broken the Act, provide much of the evidence on the whole process. At almost the same time (1516), Thomas More, in his *Utopia*, wrote the most famous of all denunciations of the evils of enclosure:

> Forsooth, my lord, quoth I, your sheep that were wont to be so meek and tame and so small eaters, now, I hear say, be become so great devourers and so wild, that they eat up and swallow down the very men themselves. They consume, destroy, and devour whole fields, houses and cities. For look in what parts of the realm doth grow the finest and dearest wool, there noblemen and gentlemen, yea and certain abbots . . . leave no ground for tillage. They enclose all pastures; they throw down houses; they pluck down towns, and leaving nothing standing but only the church to be made into a sheep-house . . . the husbandmen be thrust out of their own, or else by covin and fraud or by violent oppression they be put besides it, or by wrongs and injuries they be so wearied, that they be compelled to sell all. By one means, therefore, or by other, either by hook or crook, they must needs depart away, poor, silly, wretched souls, men, women, husbands, wives, fatherless children, widows, woeful mothers with their young babes, and their whole household small in substance and much in number, as husbandry requireth many hands. Away they trudge, I say, out of their known and accustomed houses, finding no place to rest in.

More's eloquence has set the tone for much historical writing on the subject, but while one should not deny that enclosures created a good deal of suffering, one should also remember that More was exaggerating his points for the sake of effect. Not only that, he concentrated his attack purely on enclosures as a cause of depopulation, and by so doing both failed to consider how far enclosures might have been the result rather than the cause, and omitted to mention a related question, that of the 'engrossing' or accumulation of farms by a single owner. This could be combined with enclosure, but was not necessarily identical with it. Farms could be accumulated without being enclosed, and individual yeomen could, by exchanging strips in the open fields with their neighbours, consolidate their holdings and thereby create a unit which was easier to work. Such consolidation was indeed commended by contemporary writers on agriculture. More serious was the danger to a community when enclosure by a lord took in parts of the common land, on which the villagers had relied to graze their own stock. Indeed grazing rights could be an issue in themselves, and disputes over these probably made a major contribution to bringing about the Norfolk rebellion of 1549 (73, pp.71, 142–3).

The government's motive in attacking enclosures was not simply disinterested concern for justice for the poor, although Wolsey may have been anxious about their welfare. The Crown's interest was above all the defence of the land rather than of villagers' property rights. As early as 1488–89, an Act dealing with the Isle of Wight declared that it had been made desolate by being turned into pasture, and that it could not long be defended from the King's enemies. More specifically, it attacked engrossing of holdings and provided penalties for this. In the following year a general Act condemned depopulation (although not engrossing as such), declaring that in towns where previously 200 persons were occupied, there were now only two or three herdsmen, and the rest were fallen into idleness. The same themes were reechoed in the second decade of the sixteenth century, when the government again began to take an interest in restraining enclosure, and attempted, sometimes successfully, to restore land from pasture to tillage. There were further measures in the 1530s; an Act of 1533 attempted to limit the size of the flock that one man might own and to prevent the engrossing of holdings and another in 1536 authorized the King to proceed against any encloser of land converted from tillage since 1488 (58, pp.104–6, 110–11). As the Act was largely confined to the Midlands (with the addition of Cambridgeshire and the Isle of Wight), it is unlikely that the motive of securing the defence of the realm bulked as large as in 1488–89. The aim of the measure may also have been financial, because the Crown was empowered to distrain for half of the profits resulting from the enclosure; it was not, however, an easy way to raise money, so it is unlikely to have been the only reason for the Act.

The proceedings taken under these Acts provide many of the known facts concerning enclosures and depopulation. A major defence by many of those prosecuted was that the enclosures had taken place before the practice had been made an offence, and although the practice continued after this date there is good reason to believe that this was often the case. John Hales of Coventry, a bitter opponent of enclosures, wrote in 1549 that the bulk of them had occurred before the accession of Henry VII, and the Italian historian Polydore Vergil (probably writing about 1530), said of the proceedings of 1517, that for half a century or more previously, sheep-farming nobles had tried to find devices to increase the income of their lands, and that to this end they had destroyed dwelling-houses and filled up the land with animals. Even more important is the testimony of the fifteenth-century Warwick chantry priest John Rous, who died in 1491. In his *Historia Regum Angliae* (generally a work of little value) there is an isolated and indignant digression on current depopulation in his own shire, prompted by his description of the harrying of villages by William the Conqueror. He names fifty-eight depopulated villages, almost all of which can be identified. Indeed, Rous claimed that he had petitioned Parliament in 1459 asking for legislation on enclosures, and although no such petition is preserved, there is one from as early as 1414 from the village of Chesterton in Cambridgeshire referring to depopulation there (19, pp.276–7; 58, pp.81–2, 102–3, 148).

It is clear from this that periods when enclosure was taking place do not necessarily correspond with those when articulate protests were being voiced against them. Why this was the case we shall return to later; for the moment our concern must be with the chronology, distribution and causes of the enclosures themselves. The problems connected with these are inseparable, because of the variety of local conditions, which led to them taking place at different times in various parts of the kingdom. In parts of the West Country and the South, much of the land had been enclosed long before the fifteenth century, whereas in some of the northern counties the movement did not get under way until late in the sixteenth. In Lincolnshire and the East Riding of Yorkshire, a substantial number of villages disappeared from the records in the late fourteenth and early fifteenth centuries, as well as in the second half of the fifteenth century, which seems to have been the worst period of depopulation in the area most seriously affected in the Midlands, particularly in Northamptonshire, Oxfordshire, Warwickshire, Buckinghamshire, Leicestershire and Nottinghamshire (58, pp.170–3, 220–1, 229).

Local conditions must go a long way to explaining why some villages were vulnerable to enclosure and others were not, and these variations could occur within the limits of a single shire. Although Devon is a long way from the most seriously affected areas of enclosure, it does provide well-documented evidence of such variations. In the east of the shire, there was some enclosure as early as the 1250s, it was well under way by the middle of the fourteenth century and virtually complete by the mid fifteenth. In the south of the county, it was only beginning on some manors in the late fourteenth and early fifteenth, while on others it did not occur until the sixteenth and seventeenth. The areas enclosed in the south of the county were on average larger than those in the east, so it is likely that enclosure there took place at a time when conditions were more conducive to the practice. The study of two villages, one from each part of the shire, makes it clear why this was the case. Pressure on land was fairly slack in the south (most obviously shown by the fact that when holdings were reoccupied they were often taken up by men who already held land, and not by landless men), whereas in the east there was no shortage of tenants, and the demand for land was maintained.

These distinctions in Devon are fairly clear, and should warn the historian not to simplify the picture by thinking overmuch in broad regional terms. The basic character of husbandry in a particular locality was a major factor in determining its vulnerability to the encloser. Areas of forest, where the villages already had little arable farming, were relatively immune, even in shires which were otherwise seriously affected: this can be seen in Charnwood Forest in Leicestershire and the Forest of Arden in Warwickshire. Similarly, there is little evidence of desertion in areas which had been reclaimed from marshland (58, map facing p.228, p.231).

If one works back from the sixteenth-century evidence, one is left with a strong impression that the years after 1450 saw the greatest pressure of enclosures. Detailed evidence is scarce, although recent archaelogical investigation has succeeded in identifying many deserted villages, and it is to be hoped that gradually excavation may help to clarify, at least within broad limits, when some of these desertions occurred. A more precise source for this than archaeology is the record of tax assessments, and more particularly the grants of tax relief which were made in the fifteenth-century reassessments. The basis of payment was the subsidy assessment of 1334, but although this remained in use for the following two centuries, the variations in the extent to which relief was granted in the fifteenth century to communities which had declined in size and wealth since that date suggest that a genuine effort was made to judge their capacity to pay at particular times. An important conclusion that can be drawn from the fiscal records is that the immediate effect of the Black Death in 1348–49 was slight in destroying communities, because most of the villages which eventually disappeared are still recorded as contributing to subsidies levied in the fifteenth century. There may have been a few villages abandoned in the aftermath of the plague, particularly those on poorer soil, as their inhabitants moved to better lands to take up holdings which had fallen vacant. Here it was a combination of the fall in population and local soil conditions which killed a village rather than the plague alone. If there had been land-hunger comparable to the pre-plague period, it is unlikely that the villages would have disappeared (58, pp.160–2, 209).

These factors must bulk larger in the explanation of depopulation than the sixteenth-century writers' scapegoat, the rapacious landlords. Depopulation from plague was a very real factor in the long term, and while it might not destroy a village immediately, it could weaken it as a social and economic unit. This raises another difficulty for the historian, because it is far harder to estimate the extent to which a village had shrunk or when this occurred than to note when it was finally deserted. Desertion could be marked by its disappearance from the taxation rolls, or by the union of the parish with another, whereas decay could only be hinted at by a relief of tax payments. For example, Riseholme, near Lincoln, did not finally disappear until the late sixteenth century – ecclesiastical records show that it still existed in the 1520s, but that by 1575 it had no facilities for burials. The earliest specific reference to its desertion comes from 1602. In 1428, however, it and some neighbouring villages were excused from paying the subsidy because it had less than ten households, and the excavation of one of the houses suggests that it had been deserted as early as the second half of the fourteenth century.

The case of Riseholme illustrates clearly how the casualties occurred in small settlements rather than in more substantial ones. The 1334 tax assessments and the 1377 poll-tax returns show which communities existed at those dates (the latter also showing how few had disappeared between them), and make it clear that a high proportion of those which eventually disappeared were markedly below the average size (58, pp.162–3, 207). The tax remissions of the first half of the fifteenth century show that some of the villages which later disappeared were granted substantial reliefs, although this was not universal. Unfortunately, the survival of tax records from the middle years of the century (and more especially after 1450) is more patchy than from the period immediately before, so it is not always possible to trace the disappearance of villages at precisely the time when a substantial number of the desertions seems to have occurred.

The sixteenth-century writers who condemned depopulation looked for a depopulator, and found him in the enclosing landlord, who found that stock-rearing was more profitable than corn-growing. There are some pointers to this being an accurate judgement, although the period for which wool and corn prices have been studied in detail does not go further back than 1490, and therefore does not include what are probably the most serious years of enclosure (58, p.183). However, the evidence is not entirely conclusive, and in a period when lords were having difficulty in finding tenants to take up holdings, it may well be that the conversion from arable to grazing was forced on them. The raising of sheep could bring some profit, while leaving land vacant could bring none. Furthermore, even if a surplus of wool was produced, there was perhaps more hope of selling it to the developing cloth industry than of disposing of grain which was not required, as a demand for clothing can be more flexible than one for food when men have additional purchasing power (59; 62). This is not to deny that there were unscrupulous landlords who were guilty of depopulation – the evidence that there were is clear. The danger is to exaggerate their importance, as it seems clear that their actions tended to give the final blow to communities which were already in decay rather than to destroy those which were flourishing.

The lord's power to remove the inhabitants of a village varied from place to place. Where a large number of the villagers were freeholders, they could more easily resist the lord's attempts at enclosure than where their numbers were low. Significantly, the villages which tended to disappear were those with a low proportion of peasant proprietors (83, p.28). When the tenants were copyholders, much might depend on the precise custom by which they held their land (Ch.4). Where tenure was for life only, and not by inheritance, where entry fines were not fixed by custom, it was possible for the lord, perfectly legally, to raise these to a level which a possible heir could not pay, not in the expectation of getting more money, but in the certainty that failure to pay would give him the right to evict. The process of enclosures thus illustrates the limits to the security obtained by copyholders.

In 1466 a Bohemian visitor to England commented: '. . . the peasants dig ditches round their fields and meadows and so fence them in that no one can pass on foot or on horseback except by the main roads' (25, p.53). This should remind us that not all enclosures were made by the land-owning class, but could be the work of the peasants themselves. One point, however, should be borne in mind. The Bohemian party saw only a limited part of the country, landing in Kent, and travelling via London to Reading, Salisbury and Poole, whence they sailed to France. The main areas of depopulation and enclosure in the Midlands were not on their itinerary, and in Kent, where the peasant community was free, it may well have been the peasantry who wished to consolidate their holdings. The other shires which the Bohemians visited, namely Berkshire, Hampshire and Wiltshire, were also in fact ones which were comparatively little affected by enclosures (58, pp.339–40, 351–3, 389–91).

Fifteenth-century agriculture, as we have seen (Ch.2), gave the peasantry opportunities to consolidate their holdings, and it may well be that this led to a decline in the traditional co-operative cultivation of the open-field communities, as men purchased their own draught animals and ploughs. For such men, enclosure of their lands could be the next step (62), and it is worth remembering that even John Hales, the mid-sixteenth-century opponent of enclosures, was prepared to admit that enclosure *per se* was not necessarily evil: his particular concern was with the turning of arable fields into pasture (58, p.180). Peasant enclosures, however, were not so likely to do this as those by greater men, whose lands were sufficiently extensive for them to support large flocks and who would therefore have found such a conversion of land usage economically worth while.

Despite suggestions in the preamble to a draft bill of 1514, that the men responsible for the enclosures were townsmen and speculators who were buying up land, it is clear from the evidence of the subsequent proceedings that the offenders were very largely drawn from old-established families of nobility and gentry. Indeed, the evidence goes far to bear out the criticisms made by More in *Utopia*. The evidence for Leicestershire, which had been very fully studied, shows that between 1485 and 1550, 2.1 per cent of the total enclosure was the responsibility of the Crown, 17.6 per cent that of the monasteries, 12.1 per cent that of the nobility and 67.5 per cent that of the gentry (58, pp.105, 190–1; 82, p.71).[1] There were variations in detail from shire to shire, but the predominant part played by the existing land-owning families seems to have been common.

To put these actions into perspective, however, one must remember that enclosures were by no means complete. If one again looks at Leicestershire, one sees that at most one-tenth of the open-field arable was enclosed, and this in one of the counties which was most seriously affected (82, p.69). Nor need an entire village be affected. At Cotesbach in the same county, about thirty people, from five households, were evicted about 1501, and the lands affected represented about a fifth of the manor. The rest of it remained open until the early seventeenth century, when new enclosures led to major agrarian unrest in the shire, with Cotesbach at the centre of it.

One major problem remains: if, as seems clear was the case, the main period of depopulation in the mid fifteenth century preceded public hostility to enclosures, why was there a sudden growth of the latter from the second decade of the sixteenth century onwards? The writing of *Utopia* and Wolsey's proceedings mark the start of a period in which enclosure was vigorously condemned by some, although still practised by others. There had been little sign of such popular sentiment at the time of the earlier enclosure – the attitude of John Rous cannot be matched elsewhere. Possibly the answer to this question may be found in the recovery of population, and the renewal of pressure on available land. If, as recent work has suggested (Ch.1), the sustained growth of population from the doldrums of the fifteenth century began to affect the economy in the early years of the sixteenth century rather than previously, this would come close to the period when the volume of criticism of enclosures became more vocal and more explicit. The comparative absence of protest in the fifteenth century may be explained simply by the fact that depopulation was less of a social problem, and that if a lord evicted tenants, they still had a reasonable prospect of finding land elsewhere. By the early sixteenth century, vacant holdings were again being taken up, and the level of rents and entry fines was rising; all of these changes reflect increasing demand for land (59). In consequence, enclosure of arable was now creating more social problems than it could solve. In the fifteenth century it had been a practical way of making agriculture more profitable, in the sixteenth it was more likely to create a vagrancy problem as men were dispossessed from the land, and this indeed was a social issue which came to the forefront of public attention in the Tudor period. It may well have been the realization that this was the case which led to the emergence of criticism of those responsible for enclosures.

---

1. Hoskins does not account for the remaining 0.7 per cent but states that peasantry and merchants do not feature among the enclosers.

CHAPTER 6

Urban society and economy

Throughout the Middle Ages, the bulk of the population lived in the country, but although, comparatively speaking, the number of town dwellers was small, they played a considerable part in the national economy. They were largely responsible for overseas trade, and the towns provided centres for the regional economy of their own part of the country. They were closely linked with this, and in some cases it is clear that the growth or decline of a town resulted from economic changes in the surrounding rural area. Generalizations about the state of the towns in late medieval England are, however, risky; each had its own history, which might be very different from that of its neighbour, and it is likely that even when more individual studies have been made of particular towns the general picture will be one of diversity rather than of similarity. Even when one can see a similar history of decline or recovery, this did not necessarily occur in different towns at the same time (71).

There certainly is scope for such studies: documentary material survives in town archives in such forms as deeds and rentals, and in some cases it can be supplemented by archaeological work, as twentieth-century redevelopment in town centres has given opportunities to investigate the surviving material remains below. Although such rescue excavation work cannot be more than piecemeal, as sites become available, results already obtained have provided useful information on conditions of urban life, in the types of buildings where people lived, on the desertion of houses within towns and around them, and on the distribution of trades within the towns. Unsocial crafts, such as butchering and tanning, were assigned to particular quarters, and those with a high fire risk, pottery-making or blacksmith work, were excluded from the more densely populated areas (90, pp.47–8).

Historians have taken two main approaches, the legal and the economic, to the urban history of the Middle Ages. The former is concerned with the government and status of the boroughs, and their relations with the Crown and the units of local government within which they existed, the latter with the structure of society within them and their changing economic fortunes. The earlier approach is in some ways simpler, in that one can tell precisely what was and what was not a borough, because a borough was created by charter in a formal legal act. For the same reason, it can be misleading, because not all centres of population which possessed recognizably urban characteristics, as for example the employment of the inhabitants in manufacturing or trade rather than in agriculture, were boroughs in the strict legal sense. The degree of economic specialization might vary from one centre to another, and in the last resort it is not always easy to define what was a town. Although most of the greater towns were boroughs, some major centres of manufacture, such as the cloth-making villages of Lavenham and Had-leigh, were not. Irrespective of their legal status, however, they should clearly be considered as towns in any discussion of the urban economy.

Undoubtedly the population crisis of the mid fourteenth century hit the towns severely. Insanitary conditions, and the concentration of people and rats in a lim-ited area, made them vulnerable to attacks of plague, and it is noteworthy that even when the disease had ceased to be common in the country, it persisted in urban areas. Studies of individual towns suggest that they were severely hit, that properties were deserted and that in some cases parishes had to be united, as the existing ones were too poor to maintain the services of the Church (77, pp.286–8). Many towns had to rely on immigration from the country to maintain even a reduced level of population, and the easing of pressure of population on the land in the country reduced the urge on men to move, although as we have seen in our examination of rural society men did continue to leave the land to escape the burdens of serfdom (70; 104, pp.206–10; Ch.4). The plague may not, however, have been solely responsible for urban decay, as there are few signs of the expan-sion of suburbs in English towns between 1300 and the end of the Middle Ages, and at Oxford there are references to houses falling into decay as early as 1340.

London was the greatest town in England, and during the fourteenth and fif-teenth centuries its economic resources increased more markedly than those of most other parts of the country. The 1377 poll-tax returns suggest that it was over three times the size of the largest provincial centres, Bristol and York, almost five times that of Coventry and six times that of Norwich (104, p.1). Tax returns of the 1520s do not provide an exact comparison, as they are concerned with the wealth rather than the number of the inhabitants, but they show its continued pre-eminence, almost ten times as wealthy as Norwich, and over fifteen times as wealthy as Bristol (82, pp.13–14). The fiscal evidence also points to an increase in its wealth in relation to the country as a whole: between 1334 and 1515 the assessed wealth of the city increased fifteenfold in absolute terms, and from 2 per cent to 8.9 per cent of the assessed wealth of the nation as a whole (101). Even Continental visitors were impressed by the city: a Bohemian visitor in 1466 described it as large and magnificent, with beautiful churches, in 1483 the Italian Dominic Mancini said that it was famous throughout the world, and in 1497 another Italian visitor laid stress on the wealth of its citizens. Both Italian writers commented particularly on the number of goldsmiths' shops in the city (3, pp.101–5; 25, pp.51–2; 35, pp.42–3). The anonymous writer of 1497 said that apart from London there were only two towns of importance in the country, Bris-tol and York, but in this he was misinformed, as it seems likely that Norwich, which had undoubtedly had a period of difficulties in the early fifteenth century, had begun to recover about 1465 or 1470, and was on the way to becoming the second wealthiest city in the land, as it was in the 1520s.

The dominance of London may partly reflect the decline of other centres, par-ticularly in the South and South-east, and indeed London merchants may some-times have been responsible for this. This was probably true of Southampton, towards the middle of Henry VIII's reign, although the city's decline may have been foreshadowed by earlier events. Its importance in the fifteenth century was connected with its position as the centre of Italian trade in England, but the Florentine galleys disappeared from the port after 1478 and the Venetians after 1509. The last years of Henry VII had been a prosperous period for the port – the average annual sum paid in customs dues from 1504 to 1509 was over £10,000, and in the early years of Henry VIII a group of merchants had maintained voyages to Brazil. But although trade passed through Southampton, it was not necessarily merchants of the town who were handling it. Londoners were deeply involved in the revival of the Gascon wine trade in Edward IV's reign, and also in the trade in metals, particularly Cornish tin. Improvements in shipping and the foundation of the guild of pilots of Trinity House (incorporated in 1541) made for safer navigation in the Thames, and the London merchants removed their trade nearer home. By the latter part of Henry VIII's reign the quantity of trade, as measured by customs payments, had shrunk catastrophically, to an average of just over £2,000 annually in 1535–40 and to about £663 annually in 1541–45. Although John Leland in the 1530s described a town apparently prosperous from the condition of its buildings, these may well have been erected before the decline set in.

The factors which determined the fortunes of individual towns varied. The worst case of decline, that of Boston, was brought about by the decline of the wool trade, on the export of which it had grown, and its failure to secure any substantial share of cloth exports. The Midlands cloth industry, centred on Coventry, had originally used Boston as an outlet, but by the fifteenth century was exporting mainly through London, and Coventry itself was also in decline. In the North Sea trade too, Boston had been the victim of the growing power of the German Hanse. Hull, too, suffered from the poor relations between England and the Hanse in the second half of the fifteenth century, and this may have been one factor which affected the trade of York, which had used Hull as a centre for exports. The value of York's trade at Hull probably fell from about £10,000 annually to about £2,500 between the last quarter of the fourteenth century and the middle of the sixteenth (56). In this last case there is no reason to believe that there was any direct influence of London which contributed to the decline.

Some towns, however, were able to prosper – Colchester, Salisbury and Newcastle among the larger ones, Exeter, Plymouth, Reading and Ipswich among the smaller ones – and it is likely that their prosperity depended on local factors, more particularly increasing activity in cloth manufacturing and exports, which affected the towns of the West Country and in Suffolk. Newcastle's success is less easy to explain, for as late as the early sixteenth century its main export commodity was wool, although by the reign of Henry VIII it seems to have expanded its trade in coal, iron and lead (59; 71; 75, p.45).

The dominance of London in the country has been reflected in the interests of historians, who have devoted more time to it than to provincial centres, although recent work has done something to redress the balance. It must, however, still bulk large in any examination of English urban life, not only because many of its characteristics were common to it and other towns, but also because they can be most fully studied there. Notably, one sees the dominance of a comparatively small oligarchical group of great merchants, drawn from a limited circle of the major companies. This had been consolidated in power by the end of the fourteenth century, after the one serious attempt to overthrow it. The leader of this, the draper John Northampton, although himself a member of one of the greatest companies, joined forces with the lesser guilds to try to break the control of a small group of dominant capitalists, particularly those in the victualling guilds of the fishmongers, grocers and vintners. In 1376, following the Good Parliament, in which one of the oligarchs, the alderman Richard Lyons, had been impeached, a new system was introduced by electing the city council, by crafts instead of wards. Though there may have been some hostility between the victuallers and the non-victuallers, this can hardly have been the only factor involved. For one thing, the victuallers were never able to secure a majority on the council, and for another, a substantial number of the men in the victualling guilds had other interest – grocers and fishmongers were among the most important wool exporters at this period and one does not know how far individuals actually practised the trade of their own guild – so it may have been less in their interest than has sometimes been thought to keep food prices high (84, pp.251–3; 104, pp.77–80; 109). The struggle is probably better understood as one between a dominant oligarchy and those whom they excluded from power. Until 1381 the greater merchants contrived to maintain their influence in the court of aldermen, but after the Peasants' Revolt Northampton was able to capture the mayoralty, and may have exploited the fears aroused by this disorder to try to inculpate his opponents. Certainly the five aldermen accused of collaboration with the rebels were all drawn from the victualling guilds (11, p.212). Some two years later, however, the old ruling group recovered control, election by wards was restored, and the greater men in each were again able to dominate affairs. Even the attempt to limit the number of members each guild or craft might have on the council did not curb the power of the greater companies. (104, p.79, Table 6). In the fifteenth century London remained under merchant rule: all but 6 of the 88 men who were mayor during it were drawn from the 6 greatest companies, the mercers, grocers, drapers, fishmongers, goldsmiths and skinners. The same 6 companies furnished 148 out of 173 aldermen during the same period. The first 3 of them were the most important, supplying between them 61 of the mayors and 105 of the aldermen (128, pp.107, 109).

The London merchants of this period do not, however, represent a closely connected group of families as they had done in an earlier age: the civic upper class was constantly being renewed, either as families died out, or as successful men moved out from the city to the country. It has been estimated that the majority of the great London families survived there for no more than three generations in the male line, and it was certainly rare for men to prefer city life to that of the country (104, p.205). Between 1370 and 1500 there is only one case of a father and son both being aldermen, William Reynwell (1397–1403) and his son John (1416–45) (104, pp.363–4), although there are cases when brothers or cousins both held office. Among the most prominent London citizens of the period, those who were elected mayor more than once, only a minority were of certain London origin, such as Thomas Knolles (1399–1400, 1410–11), Nicholas Wotton (1415–16, 1430–31) and Henry Barton (1416–17, 1428–29). By comparison, Richard Whittington, who was unique in holding the office thrice (1397–98,

1406–7, 1419–20), came from a minor landed family in Gloucestershire. Robert Chichele (1411–12, 1421–22) came from Higham Ferrers in Northamptonshire where his father was a burgess, although he had a family connection with London through his mother. The family was clearly influential, perhaps having been helped by his brother who was archbishop of Canterbury, and a third brother was an alderman, although he never became mayor. Stephen Broun (1438–39, 1448–49) William Estfield (1429–30, 1437–38) came respectively from Newcastle and Yorkshire, Richard Lee (1460–1, 1469–70) and John Tate (1497–98, 1504) from Worcester and Coventry (104, pp.321–77).

It is almost always difficult to discover how these men built their fortunes at the beginning, because they leave no significant mark in the records until they have already made some mark in society. There is no reason to believe that the incomers brought any large amount of capital with them, although some may have had help at the start from their families. It is hardly likely that this could have been true of the greatest of them, Whittington, because his father had died with his estate encumbered by an outlawry incurred in a plea of debt. In many cases a man made his way by individual enterprise, in others a family grew in standing from one generation to the next, with the early stages of its ascent passing unnoticed. In the case of the Reynwells, mentioned earlier, the father had begun in the lesser guild of the girdlers, and transferred to the ironmongers, while the son was a member of the great company of the fishmongers. Sometimes one sees a family moving between associated crafts: the vintners and grocers could recruit from families in the lesser victualling trades, and workers in base metals might progress to being goldsmiths (104, p.222).

It is hard to judge how far the fluidity of the London ruling class is parallelled in other towns, or whether provincial towns preserved a more closely knit society. There is scope for more work on this, but already there are tentative pointers to the picture being similar. Urban dynasties in the English towns of which studies have been made were generally short-lived, seldom surviving beyond the third generation. Many of the prominent citizens, when their origins can be traced, were drawn from the lesser landed class, who may have given them moral or financial support. At York, admissions to the freedom of the city show that in the period 1301–1550 less than one-seventh of those admitted were drawn from citizen stock, while at Romney in Kent between 1433 and 1523, a quarter of the freemen came from outside the county, and only a third from within a 5-mile radius of the town (70).

Intermarriage between members of well-connected families could at any particular time create ties between them, and have repercussions in city politics. Besides marriage, other social ties drew men together; they could serve as godparents to the others' children, or as executors of their wills. In Southampton in the 1450s, when there was considerable bitterness in civic politics over the attitude to be taken to aliens, whether they should be welcomed for bringing wealth to the town, or attacked as intruders, marriage could lead a man to switch his allegiance from one group to another. Here too, however, there is impermanence in the city ruling class: while families such as the Fetplaces and Jameses were important for more than one generation, by the early Tudor period new names appear among the ruling oligarchy, Thomas Thomas and his son Sampson, John Dawtry and Richard Palshid. While the older families derived their wealth from trade, the newer ones drew it more from investment in property, after coming to prominence initially through service to the Crown, as controllers of customs or victuallers for armies, or by serving as town clerk. Possibly the declining part played by the merchant families in town government reflects a fall in their economic power.

Oligarchy was normal in most civic government, but was often achieved only after periods of tension. In fourteenth-century Norwich, the normal assembly was not democratic, but was limited to the 'better and more discreet' of the city. In 1404 the city obtained the right to have a mayor, but this was followed by conflicts, and in 1417 a new charter was granted, which established a civic constitution. The commonalty were allowed a council of sixty, which had to assent to the decisions of the mayor and aldermen, who took over the powers of the earlier assembly of twenty-four. Later in the century there were minor changes, of which the most important was the exclusion of the general body of the commonalty from electing the mayor and sheriffs in 1447. This constitution survived with only slight modifications until the Municipal Reform Act of 1835. Similar closed bodies were established elsewhere, as at Leicester and Northampton in 1489. In some places and at different times there was some resistance, at Lincoln at the end of the fourteenth century and at Southampton, where the mayor from 1488 to 1491 made an unsuccessful attempt to preserve some semblance of democracy (77, pp.259–61). The difficulty for the historian is that evidence for how councillors were elected is often lacking, and one does not know how many freemen could participate in choosing them, nor when membership of councils came to be filled by the choice of the existing councillors. By the early sixteenth century it is clear that oligarchies were often well established: other towns where this was the case included such major centres as Bristol, Exeter and Lynn (82, pp.101–2). It was similar in the smaller towns, as can be seen from examples in Sussex and Buckinghamshire. A small group of wealthy men were responsible for the day-to-day management of community affairs, and owned a disproportionate share of the property – some 40 per cent being owned by only 5 per cent of the inhabitants.

A characteristic development in the boroughs was the practice of incorporation. This gave the borough a corporate personality at law, with the right to sue and be sued, and also empowered it to exclude the shire officials and be directly responsible to the central government. The first town to acquire this status was Bristol in 1373, and others followed, York in 1396, Newcastle in 1400, Norwich in 1404 and Lincoln in 1409. The most elaborate of the charters of incorporation was that granted to Hull in 1440. A crucial factor in the development was the growth of property-owning by towns, probably so that rent income could compensate for deficiencies of toll revenue. In the 1391 Statute of Mortmain there is mention of towns acquiring property, and the Act virtually assumes that towns already possessed a corporate and perpetual identity, although few boroughs had as yet received formal recognition of their corporate status. This mortmain legislation was followed by their being licensed to acquire lands and rents (90, pp.140–6).

Rents did not, however, necessarily solve the difficulties of town finance. The levels and movements of urban rent are hard to document, but where substantial series of records survive, it is clear that in some towns at any rate, rents fell in the fifteenth century. York provides interesting evidence, though in view of the city's declining cloth industry, it may be dangerous to regard it as typical of towns in general. In the late fourteenth century, between 1371 and 1401 when rural rents were declining, the number of tenements owned by the vicars-choral of the Minster increased from 183 to 238, and the average rent rose from 6.7 to 7.1s., an increase of just under 6 per cent. There is no particular reason to believe that this was caused merely by the newer properties being of higher value. By the second quarter of the fifteenth century, rents were in decline, and this continued after 1450. At the beginning of the sixteenth century those of the vicars-choral showed a slight increase, but this was short-lived, and after the first decade there was yet a further decline (56). A fall in urban rent values can also be seen in Oxford, although the evidence cited is less comprehensive than that for York, and the most drastic fall seems to have come in the second half of the fifteenth century after a period of relative stability. On the other hand, there is evidence in the fifteenth century of town building of both domestic and commercial property, which was clearly a speculative attempt to secure a profit, so there must have been advantages to be gained from this. One has, for example, cottage rows being erected at Winchester apparently by individuals, and shops being built by the city corporation at Exeter and by the abbey at Tewkesbury (90, pp.67–8).

It is hard to generalize safely about prosperity or decay in the late medieval English town, and different historians have interpreted the evidence in widely varying ways. The most forceful arguments for the period being one of economic growth are those put forward by Bridbury, who points rightly to the phenomenal increases paid by certain towns in taxation between 1334 and 1524. The most dramatic of these increases in percentage terms are, not surprisingly, to be found where the earlier payment was small, as at Lavenham, Totnes and Tiverton, but even major centres such as Norwich and Coventry, which had been assessed at quite a high level in 1334, showed a percentage increase above the national average. On the other hand, there were towns where the increase was small, such as York, Lincoln and Bristol, or even non-existent such as Boston (61, pp.112–13). The most recent writers on the subject have been more cautious, and have pointed out that not all towns can be fitted into the same pattern, and that local factors bulked large in each case (71; 75, p.45). While many of the towns which prospered grew on their manufacture of textiles, York, which had been a cloth town at an earlier date, had been affected by the shift of manufacturing to the West Riding, as well as by the decline of Hull as an export centre. It is also worth remembering that an increased assessment does not necessarily reflect prosperity; there is evidence of considerable urban decay, for example, at Coventry, despite the town's greater tax liability. On balance, Bridbury's more optimistic view seems hard to sustain (75, p.65).

A commonly cited piece of evidence for urban decline is the number of petitions to the Crown for relief from taxation, and equally common is the view of historians that these must be regarded with caution, as the towns were liable to paint their poverty in lurid terms, and to emulate each other in their appeals. The petitions on their own may be unreliable, but the response of the Crown to them must surely be an indication that they had some substance: a government which was regularly short of funds would be unlikely to grant remissions, and the fact that different towns were allowed varying amounts of tax allowance suggests that some attempt was made to calculate the resources available. Lincoln, which on several occasions was totally exempted from paying, seems to have been one of the worst affected (71; 77, pp.272–3).

Bridbury also suggests, from the admissions to the freedom of the boroughs, that the ranks of the citizens were being widened, and that even at a time when rural conditions provided more incentive for men to remain in the country than at an earlier date the towns were still able to attract them (61, pp.62–4 (Tables, 65–9)). The increased number of freemen need not, however, be explained by the greater attractions of town life. Dobson argues convincingly that as the admission of freemen was controlled by the borough authorities, it is more probably that the increased number of admissions was prompted by their desire to spread the load of civic obligations, and to secure money from the payments made on entry to assist shaky borough finances. Citizenship presumably had certain advantages which made it worth a man's while taking it up, but in a period of increasing civic oligarchy one may wonder how greatly these outweighed the disadvantages. Also, although there were marked fluctuations in the number of admissions from year to year, it is clear that from about 1490 the numbers of those admitted at York were consistently lower than they had been from the mid 1380s to the 1440s. There was a trough in the number admitted in the third quarter of the fifteenth century, and a rise in the 1480s was short-lived (70; 71).

One last problem remains, but is probably unanswerable. Is it possible to see private affluence co-existing with corporate poverty? Was it the towns which were poor rather than the townsmen? As far as the urban working class was concerned they may well have been better off in the fifteenth century than they had been previously or were to be later. The evidence of wage-rates, as shown expressed in real terms in the Phelps Brown and Hopkins index, [A.1] points in this direction, and if there was, as seems likely, a decline in urban rent levels, this too could have helped them. It is much harder to say if the ruling merchant employer class was affected adversely, in the same way as its rural counterpart, by the need to pay higher wages, or by a reduction in markets for the commodities which they produced at a time of population decline. Undoubtedly there were men who made substantial fortunes, but there is not sufficient evidence to say whether they were exceptional merely in the scale of their gains or because they contrived to prosper when others failed. The historian must recognize that diversity of fortune existed within towns as well as between them.

It is impossible to summarize the history of English towns in the late Middle Ages in a few convenient generalizations. The variations in their prosperity depended often on how far the developing cloth trade affected individual places; some towns undoubtedly grew, particularly in the early sixteenth century, but they often did so at the expense of others rather than through a serious movement of population from the countryside, although some such drift occurred. Nevertheless, it is likely that in the larger cities at any rate there was considerable change in the personnel of the ruling oligarchies, the members of which clearly were drawn from outside and aspired to return to the country if they could make their fortunes. As yet, there was no well-established 'city interest' to balance the power of the landed class. These oligarchies were, however, powerful and one of the most significant developments in English urban history at this time was the way in which they consolidated their control over town government. They were to continue to dominate it until the nineteenth century.

CHAPTER 7

Industry, trade and shipping

In Chapter 6, it was suggested that one factor which contributed to the variations in fortune between different towns was the extent to which they had been affected by developments in the manufacture of cloth. The growth of this industry was the most fundamental change in the country's economy in the later Middle Ages; where England had previously relied for its exports largely on the export of raw wool for the more advanced industrial economies of the Low Countries and Italy, it became in this period a manufacturing nation in its own right, and cloth replaced wool as its main resource in international trade. The rise in English textile manufacturing was accompanied by changes in its location, and this led to major alterations in the geographical distribution of wealth within the country. Behind these changes lay both developments in the European economy as a whole, and the English exploitation of new manufacturing techniques, from which particular areas benefited more than others.

Taxation of wool exports by the King to finance overseas wars was a further factor which contributed to the growth of the textile industry and of English trade. The imposition of an additional levy on alien exporters in 1303 had led to English merchants playing a major part in handling wool shipments later in the century, but it was Edward III's war taxation for his French campaigns, much of which was derived from levies on wool exports, which did most to promote the development of cloth manufacture in England, by creating a tariff barrier which raised the costs of the raw material to the foreign manufacturers. Although the wool producers seem to have borne part of the tax costs, the substantial increase in cloth production during the war is most easily explicable if a large part of the wool tax was passed on by the exporters to the foreign buyers, while the English cloth manufacturers were able to undercut their Continental rivals (88, pp.39–40). Possibly the direct effects of war on the Flemish cloth towns, which suffered from the campaigns, may have been a further benefit to English producers; indeed this may have been a more important factor in the decline of Flanders than the tariff protection enjoyed by England, because the Dutch cloth industry, which used English wool, also developed at this time at the expense of the Flemish. The extent to which English manufacturers were able to compete in Europe is shown clearly by the extent to which cloth exports increased, even after an export duty was imposed on cloth in 1347, despite the fact that there was no expansion of the market from population growth. The amount shipped abroad continued to rise till the end of the century and remained high until the mid fifteenth century. Despite a fall after the loss of Gascony, exports again increased by the 1470s. By the start of the sixteenth century, cloth had replaced wool as England's main export [A.2]. The clothiers may well have been able to obtain their raw material relatively cheap, because there is some evidence of wool prices being forced down occasionally by over-production, when growers were unable to dispose of the whole annual clip (84, p.312). As most recorded cases of this antedate the main period of enclosures in the mid fifteenth century, it is not clear if the conversion of land from arable to grazing in the period of population decline contributed to this.

Technical progress in the industry lay above all in the increased exploitation of water power. Water-powered fulling mills were not new; indeed they go back at least as far as the thirteenth century. They did, however, give England an advantage over Flanders, where windmills were more common than water-mills. Also driven by water was the 'gig-mill', used for teasing woven cloth by means of teasels secured to rollers. These raised the nap on the cloth, which could then be cropped with shears to give it a smoother finish. The main area for the manufacture of fine broadcloths was the southern Cotswolds, notably in the Stroud valley, where there was not only a supply of high-quality local wool – Cotswold wool was generally regarded as the best in England – but also quantities of fuller's earth and available water power (65, pp.153–6; 84, p.309). Other areas, such as East Anglia and Yorkshire, seem to have concentrated on rather lighter fabrics, worsteds or the narrower cloths called kerseys, and provided rivalry for the Cotswold producers. In many of the cloth-producing areas there were clear signs of prosperity, not least some of the buildings which survive from the period, notably churches such as those at Fairford in Gloucestershire or Long Melford in Suffolk.

The rise of the cloth industry considerably changed the economic geography of England, with new areas emerging to prominence as the result of industrial growth. In the late Middle Ages the West Riding of Yorkshire, particularly the Leeds–Bradford area, emerged as a major centre of the woollen textile industry, as it was to remain, overtaking York as the major centre of the cloth trade in the North (82, p.152). In the South-west, Exeter became a major centre of cloth exports from the 1490s, and by the early sixteenth century some of the smaller Devon towns were also active in the trade, this perhaps contributing to the later growth of West Country shipping activity. Wealthiest of all the centres of cloth manufacturing was East Anglia, particularly Suffolk. The richest town in the area was Lavenham, where trade developed early, and where perhaps three-quarters of the population depended directly or indirectly on cloth manufacturing. For three generations the Spring family played a dominant part in this, and when Thomas Spring III died in 1523 he was wealthier than many of the nobility and was the richest commoner in England outside London; he owned 26 manors in eastern England and held property in 130 parishes (82, pp.13, 94, 152–3). The overseas trade in cloth also contributed to the growing dominance of London, because exports were largely in the hands of the Merchant Adventurers' Company, which was increasingly dominated by the London Mercers' Company (64).

Undoubtedly the cloth industry was the most famous in late medieval England, but one should remember that its importance may have been exaggerated by its being *par excellence* an export industry, and, because its products paid dues on export, being better documented than those which met domestic requirements. Possibly the coal trade, which exported only a small proportion of its production, may have been more active than one might guess from the customs figures. There were exports, as early as the late fourteenth century, from Newcastle and Durham to places as far as Danzig, although Flanders and the Northern Netherlands were more common destinations. Much of the coal mined, however, may have been consumed domestically, or used for iron-smelting or lime-burning. It is hard to judge the extent of the industry, but later developments, particularly in the sixteenth century, seem to have been firmly based on medieval foundations. In 1508–9, 20 per cent of the value of Newcastle's trade was already in coal, and in the following decade there was a boom in coal exports which compensated for a slump in those of wool. Indeed between 1512 and 1519 some attempts were made to sink new mines, presumably to meet demand, but this expansion was followed by contraction during the general European crisis of 1521–26. The geographical spread of the mining industry is hard to ascertain, for much of it is poorly recorded, but incidental references in both ecclesiastical and secular sources show the existence of mines in Yorkshire, Staffordshire and Wales as well as in the North. Nor can one tell the normal value of a mine, although some must have given considerable yields – Wolsey, as bishop of Durham, let out one at a rent of £180 a year (82, pp.164–5).

Possibly the building industry was one of the most substantial in the country, but as it was based on small local units it is virtually impossible to study. Other forms of industry were comparatively small scale. There was some manufacture of salt, both on the east coast and at inland brine springs, but this was insufficient to meet the country's requirements, and substantial supplies had to be imported. The home product tended to be finer in quality than the imported. There is some evidence that Cornish tin-mining maintained a reasonable level of production, although with some fluctuations: a sharp drop just after the Black Death and a boom at the end of the fourteenth century were followed by a period of depression in the half-century after 1430, with a considerable recovery by the early sixteenth century. This last was perhaps due to the development of shaft-mining in addition to open-cast workings (61, pp.25–6; 76, pp.288–9; 82, pp.165–7). There are some references to other forms of metal-working in the country; most notably in the early sixteenth century the areas around Dudley and Birmingham in the Midlands, were becoming centres of ironwork, and there were further developments in such manufacturing at Sheffield where its history goes back further. Admittedly, this was still a minor part of the local economy, compared with, say, leather-working in Birmingham, but the development was to lay the foundation for later generations (82, pp.169, 173).

As noted earlier, internal trade is harder to document than external, but surviving evidence shows its variety. Southampton has some of the best records; its brokage books record tolls paid by merchants or carters entering or leaving the city. It served both as a centre of local trade for its own hinterland, and as a distribution centre for longer-distance trade. The town itself never seems to have developed much industry, but was primarily a place of exchange, from which imported goods were distributed throughout the country and export commodities sent abroad. It obtained foodstuffs from the surrounding countryside, and supplied imported fish, wine and salt in return. Much of the long-distance trade was in commodities connected with the cloth industry, notably dyestuffs such as woad and alum. It was a centre for trade going to Salisbury, the main distribution point for the Wiltshire woollen industry, and sent some goods as far as Coventry, which was famous for its woad-dyed blue cloths. In 1456 Coventry negotiated freedom from tolls in Southampton, as it had already done with another port which served it, namely Bristol. Southampton developed a considerable carting trade, possibly because neither of its rivers, the Itchen and the Test, provided scope for water-borne traffic.

The rivers indeed carried much of England's internal trade. The Severn in the West, and the Thames, the Trent, the Great Ouse and its tributaries, and the Yorkshire Ouse in the East, were undoubtedly major arteries of transport for bulk cargoes. It is noteworthy that the line of the Great North Road runs near where many of these rivers ceased to be navigable, and many towns on the road may have grown up as places where goods were transferred from water freight to carts or pack animals (82, pp.194–200). Water freight also embraced coastal shipping, particularly for heavy loads, such as the coal which was sent from the Tyne to the Thames.

Evidence for road transport is hard to come by, but it is worth remembering that the fifteenth century saw a considerable amount of bridge-building; old timber structures were replaced by stone ones, some of which still survive. It is worth noting that one source of funds for such building came from indulgences, which bishops granted for the purpose, and that another was bequests in wills, although the proportion of testators leaving money to this charity seems to have declined between 1400 and 1530 (82, pp.205–6; 242). When one recollects that bequests were made in the hope of securing the prayers of beneficiaries for the donor's soul, it may be assumed that bridges, and also roads, were in sufficient use for such gifts to be regarded as a good piece of spiritual investment.

When one turns from internal to external trade, one sees that some men at any rate recognized how important it was for England to control the sea. In the verse tract of the late 1430s, the *Libelle of Englyshe Polycye*, the anonymous author, whose sense of politics and economics was more evident than his talent for poetry, taking the design of the gold noble as his symbol, wrote:

> For iiij thynges oure noble sheueth to me,
> Kynge, shype, and swerde, and pouer of the see. (ll. 34–5)

Towards the end too, there is a long exhortation of the need to keep the sea, as the means of protecting England. The author showed shrewd perception of the powers which could be exercised by commercial blockade or by boycott, and he specifically indicates wool and tin as English products which were necessary to the Flemings, who could be brought under pressure by a withdrawal of supplies. Indeed it was the Flemings who were the main target of his attack, far more than England's older French enemies (43, pp.3–6, 15, 53–5). One suspects that this may have been due to a sense of betrayal, when Duke Philip of Burgundy's change of policy in the mid 1430s turned Flanders into a hostile country instead of an ally, and partly to the closeness of past commercial ties, when the wool trade had linked the two lands in any uneasy partnership.

External trade is better documented than internal. The material from the enrolled customs accounts provides, if not entirely reliable evidence, at least a good indication of changes in England's exports. The records of wool and cloth exported, collected by Carus-Wilson and Coleman [A.2, A.3], are an invaluable source, which should continue to yield information on a wide range of subjects. Absolute precision is impossible: there are gaps in the series of accounts from some ports, either because the records have been lost or because the customs had been farmed to the collector for a fixed sum, and there are also some irregularities in the accounting periods, although the customs year normally ran from Michaelmas to Michaelmas. Possibly goods may have been smuggled out without paying duty, although this last should not be exaggerated, because there is no reason to believe that the level of smuggling varied markedly from one period to another, and because with bulk commodities the possible gains were small and the risk of penalties was high (66, pp.21–5). The figures do afford some comparability between years, and even a brief examination of them shows the great shift from wool to cloth as England's main export commodity. This long-term change was far more striking than short-term cyclical variations brought about by political tensions or fluctuations in the general level of economic activity.

Space does not allow more than a cursory examination of the evidence, but one can illustrate its value, and the problems of using it, by looking at the question of how the balance of England's exports changed. By taking four years within our period, each half a century apart, one sees them glaringly clearly. In 1374–75, wool exports paying custom amounted to 27,637 sacks, in 1424–25 12,232 sacks, in 1474–75 8,867 sacks and in 1524–25, 3,432 sacks. Cloth exports for 1374–75 cannot be measured, as the custom on cloth for that year was farmed for all ports except London, and there are considerable gaps in the accounts for adjacent years. (In 1364–65 and 1384–85, years for which there are good sets of figures, the numbers of broadcloths exported are respectively 14,724 and 30,479.) In 1424–25 the figure was 48,368 broadcloths, in 1474–75 31,171 and in 1524–25 96,231. Clearly the cloth figures fluctuate more markedly than those for wool, although those for 1474–75 may have been artifically depressed by the absence of returns from Bristol and Newcastle. The general indication of growth is best shown by the graph compiled from the statistics of the whole period (66) [A.2]. Perhaps the most striking indication of how cloth overtook wool as the country's major export is an action of Henry VII in 1493: in order to apply economic sanctions to the Low Countries, he banned cloth exports, but not those of wool (84, p.283).

Another development clearly reflected in the customs records is the increasing dominance of London, particularly in cloth exports. In 1424–25 its share of these was just over 46 per cent of the national total, in 1474–75 (though perhaps exaggerated by the absence of the Bristol and Newcastle returns) nearly 72 per cent and in 1524–25 81.75 per cent. Its share of wool exports rose too, though less strikingly, in 1374–75 and 1424–25 the figure was between 40 and 45 per cent, by 1474–75 it exceeded 50 per cent and in 1524–25 it was 66 per cent. It is likely, particularly if one allows for the gaps in the 1474–75 returns, that the period when London secured its massive commercial lead over the rest of the country was the last quarter of the fifteenth and the first quarter of the sixteenth century. At the turn of the century, in 1499–1500, the figures (although marred by the absence of any from Southampton) show London's share of cloth exports as 68 per cent and of wool as just over 70 per cent (66, pp.77, 111).

London was also becoming dominant in other spheres of trade. By the end of the fourteenth century, the London skinners had control of the import of skins for the fur trade, and provincial merchants had been squeezed out. The records of salt imports are incomplete, and the only tables which can be compiled have to draw on several years in any period to include all the ports involved. This does not allow sufficiently for annual variations for the figures to permit strict statistical analysis, but even with these the changes are too striking to be totally ignored. In the late fourteenth century three ports, London, Exeter and Yarmouth, imported similar quantities, each taking between 13.5 per cent and 15 per cent of the national total. London's share in the mid fifteenth century was similar, but it had been overtaken by Yarmouth and Bristol, with 41.5 per cent and 19 per cent respectively. However, by the latter years of the century, both Yarmouth and Bristol had declined, and London was taking over 71 per cent of the imports.

The capital's importance in the cloth trade is seen in the part played in it by the Fellowship of the Merchant Adventurers of London. The term 'merchant adventurer' was originally applied to any merchant trading in cloth overseas; there were groups of them from various towns including Newcastle and York, and others were drawn from several of the London companies, but gradually the term was limited to a group within the Mercers. Again, originally groups of 'adventurers' were recognized in trade with various lands – one trading with Prussia secured royal recognition in 1391, another with the Netherlands in 1407 and a third with the Scandinavian lands in 1408, but eventually the Netherlands group secured for itself the specific name of the Merchant Adventurers' Company (64, pp.143–50). The company's corporate organization became tighter in the fifteenth century, particularly in the latter half of it; this culminated in 1486 with the formal recognition of the Fellowship of the Merchant Adventurers of London. From the late 1470s pressure had been put on merchants outside London to join the company there, and after some resistance they had to yield (64, pp.153–60, 172–6). The company imposed regulations on its members, but individuals still traded on their own account.

The organization of wool exports was more tightly controlled. The needs of war taxation in the fourteenth century, and the contribution which the custom on wool made to this, had led to the growth of a system whereby sales of wool had to be made through a staple town, sometimes in England and sometimes abroad. By the beginning of the fifteenth century the wool Staple was fixed at Calais, where it remained. The Staplers did not acquire a complete monopoly; merchants from the northern counties were able to export direct to the Netherlands and, more important, Italian merchants could secure licences to export wool either by land or by sea through the Straits of Gibraltar (94, pp.43–7).

The problem of keeping Calais garrisoned and of paying the troops there was closely linked with the siting of the Staple and the relations between the government and the merchants. On a number of occasions the soldiers of the garrison seized wool supplies in the town when their wages were in arrears; in 1407 they sold the wool and in 1421 the Staplers had to pay £4,000 to recover it. In the mid century too, in 1448 and 1454, the garrison again gave trouble (84, pp.258, 271, 275). In practice, money from wool taxation was the main source of funds for the garrison, and this raised problems as wool exports declined. From 1466 the company took over the financial management of the garrison, with the mayor of the Staple becoming *de facto* royal treasurer of the town. This agreement was renewed four times, the last in 1515, but eventually the company had to be released from its responsibility on grounds of poverty. It had probably been the wish to secure ready cash to pay the troops that was responsible for legislation in 1429 requiring that the entire price of the wool must be paid in gold and silver, and that one-third of the price, in bullion, be handed over to the Calais mint (84, pp.261, 275, 279–80). Political and financial considerations were probably responsible for keeping the Staple at Calais; in strictly economic terms it might have been more advantageous if it had been moved closer to the rising Dutch cloth towns.

Inside the company there were tensions, and in 1429, along with the bullion legislation, an attempt was made to change the form of trading. Instead of merchants dealing individually with clients, all wool was to be graded and pooled according to its quality, and profits were to be divided in accordance with the quantity that each had brought to the Staple. The men behind this ordinance seem to have been the greater merchants, who hoped to control the trade more strictly in their own interests, but the new system was never wholly enforced. Merchants were able to secure exemption from it, and although it is not clear who emerged more strongly from disputes in the 1440s, by the 1450s control of the Staple seems to have passed to men hostile to it (84, pp.261, 270–1, 273).

One last aspect of English trade must be considered, namely the state of the shipping industry. Our knowledge of this is patchy, and it is certain that the quantity of trade is not a precise reflection of the prosperity of English shipping, as many exports were carried in foreign vessels. The Italian wool trade, in particular, was largely carried in Venetian and Florentine galleys until the middle of the fifteenth century. Florentine shipping then declined, and the galley fleet is last recorded at Southampton in 1478. Thereafter, although the Florentines continued to import English wool, they did not carry it in their own ships, and in the 1480s proposals were made for a wool staple at Pisa, with English ships having the monopoly of the carrying. A treaty was agreed in 1490, although a concession was made to the Venetians to exempt them from the Staple. The value of the treaty, however, was short-lived, because of the disruptions of the Italian wars, and more particularly the revolt of Pisa from Florence in 1494. There is also a record of a Spanish ship carrying cloth out of Bristol in the 1460s, and it may not have been untypical, although undoubtedly English vessels were engaged in the Iberian trade. Henry VII had two Navigation Acts passed, in 1486 and 1489, but their scope was narrow, being concerned primarily with the Gascon trade, and no general attempt was made to develop English mercantile shipping (110, p.220).

The early pilot books give a fair indication of the scope of English nautical activity. They give information on the east coast of England, the English Channel and the western seaboard, including Ireland. They also contain information about the sea routes round Brittany, and south to Gascony and the Iberian peninsula, although they are markedly fuller north of Bordeaux (63, pp.24–6). They do not cover the Mediterranean, where England does not appear to have played a substantial part in trade until at least after the accession of the Tudors. There had been some earlier pioneers, notably Robert Sturmy of Bristol, who sent two ill-fated ventures there in 1446 and 1457, the first ending in the wreck of his ship off Greece and the second in a spoliation by the Genoese, which provoked retaliation against the Genoese in England and the seizure of their goods. A surviving volume of pursers's accounts shows another Bristol ship going to Oran in 1480–1 (94, pp.226–9; 100).

In the early 1480s there are some indications that English seamen were seeking to extend their activities. Portuguese protests seem to have crushed an attempt by two Englishmen, possibly with Spanish support, to secure a foothold in the Guinea trade, and around the same time, in 1480 and 1481, Bristol ships were exploring out into the Atlantic in search of the 'Isle of Brasil' (45, pp.19–23, 187–9). The available information on these voyages is sparse and the aims of the voyagers unknown, but it is possible that there was a regular series of them. It is not clear if they were being tempted to the south in search of sugar or if the Atlantic voyages were mainly concerned with fishing. Bristol had previously been heavily involved in the Iceland trade, but had been coming under pressure from increasing Hanse power there, and its merchants may well have been looking for alternative supplies of fish – it is worth stressing that the ships sent out in 1481 in search of the 'Isle of Brasil' were carrying a large quantity of salt (45, pp.188–9; 94, pp.177–82). The 'Isle of Brasil' was mythical, but fifteenth-century Atlantic charts suggest that belief in lands across the ocean was not uncommon, and there is more than just possibility that the Bristol men had heard of some landfall in them before 1480, perhaps when ships had been blown off course by abnormal wind conditions. Is it just a curious coincidence that one of the Bristol ships involved in the exploration of 1481 had on its previous voyage called at the Franciscan convent at Huelva, where Columbus was later to secure support for his proposed voyages?

The culmination of these explorations was John Cabot's discovery of Newfoundland in 1497, an event which contemporaries clearly recognized as a major achievement. Henry VII, despite his notorious parsimony, gave rewards to those who went to the new lands, and voyages continued, at least sporadically, until the end of his reign. The reaction to the discovery, that it would mean that there would be no need of the Icelandic fishing grounds in future, makes it fairly certain that even if there had been accidental sightings of the New World before that date, no systematic attempts had been made to explore it further nor to exploit the resources of the Newfoundland Banks (45, pp.214–16).

Why did England fail to exploit the discovery? No doubt Henry VIII's desire for military glory in Europe played a part; the payment of rewards recorded in the Household Books cease with his accession. It may also be that the early returns from the voyages proved small, and that it was felt that investment in them did not provide an adequate reward for those involved. Bristol, too, was in decline, losing some of its old trade to Southampton and Exeter, so its merchants could have had less to invest in this enterprise. Not until the second half of the sixteenth century, when there was a desire to combat Spanish power and to tap the resources of the Indies, did an English enterprise to North America again become attractive. Because of this delay in time, it is perhaps an exaggeration to say that the expansion of English maritime activity between 1460 and 1520 prepared the way for seizing opportunities which were opening up in many parts of the world (63, p.163).

The expansion of English shipping, however, certainly occurred. While in the fifteenth century it was rare to designate a man by the title 'shipowner', this occupation became commoner in the sixteenth (100). Some parts of the country showed more significant growth than others: on the east coast, the number of sailings not only rose in absolute terms between the 1460s and the early sixteenth century, but the proportion of those by English ships approximately doubled, although there were some exports which were largely carried in foreign vessels. In the Channel the Cinque Ports were to decline, but there was considerable growth in the West Country, between Southampton and Plymouth. In Devon and Cornwall indeed there seems to have been a long tradition of piratical and privateering activity in addition to legitimate trade, which may well have laid the foundation for the activities of seamen from this part of the country in the Elizabethan age (63, pp.159–60).

In conclusion, the main areas of growth in English trade and industry were probably in cloth and shipping, although one must always allow for the possibility that some less well-documented sectors of the economy were also making significant advances. With the growth in industry there was also a significant development of trade, particularly in the early Tudor period, and with it came the increasing dominance of London in the English economy. It was not itself a centre of manufacturing, but it outstripped all other ports as a point of transit for English exports and became thereby a major entrepôt of international trade. London merchants were able to assert their authority over their provincial rivals, and with this one can see the beginnings of centralization in the economy.

CHAPTER 8

War: profit and loss

For the first half of the period covered in this book, and again towards its end, England was involved in foreign wars. For a considerable part of the intervening period there was recurrent civil strife between magnate and dynastic factions. How far did war affect the economy or bring about social change? It had different results for various sections in the community, but all were affected by it in some way, either directly or indirectly. The military classes, the lords and the gentry, were directly involved in the wars as participants, but as landowners they also had an indirect concern, because trading changes resulting from war affected the profits of their estates. As a social group they could record both gains and losses from war, and there has been some debate among historians about how far a balance sheet can be struck for the country as a whole, whether England gained or lost from its military operations. The trading community could suffer from the hazards which war created for shipping or through the destruction of possible export markets. As we saw in Chapter 7, furthermore, the domestic cloth industry developed during the period under the tariff protection of royal taxation and as a result of war damage to existing European textile centres.

Clearly, civil war was more likely than overseas campaigns to have an immediate effect on men's lives. For members of the nobility the struggles of Lancaster and York could have drastic results, particularly for those who incurred forfeiture through ending up on the losing side; although attainders could be reversed and lands restored, this might take a long time (130, Ch.5). It is harder to measure how far the campaigns of the civil wars affected the great mass of the population or the country's internal economy, but the damage may not have been particularly great, as much of the fighting was confined to limited areas. Although the passage of an army could alarm civilians in its path, there is little evidence for mass devastations. Indeed the endemic disorder of medieval society, which was little different in the late Middle Ages from what it had been earlier, may have caused as much economic disruption in a locality such as the East Anglia of the Pastons. How far East Anglia was typical is hard to say, and the historian must guard against making generalizations from evidence which is geographically limited: certainly the Stonor correspondence suggests that Oxfordshire suffered less from the kind of violence recorded in the Paston Letters (17; 24).

England's external wars were fought principally in France, so most Englishmen had little direct experience of warfare, apart from those in the North, where relations with Scotland were always likely to break out into open hostility. However, full-scale campaigns in the northern counties were rare, and the real problem there was one of pillaging raids. This was exacerbated by the general unruliness of society, which was perhaps more deep-seated than further south, and although the emergence of the Neville and Percy families to a position of dominance in the region provided some barrier to external threats, their mutual rivalry was detrimental to local order and a potential threat to the economy of the area. Feuds lower in the social scale, such as that between the Heron and Manners families from 1428 to 1431, where both parties could count on influential support from greater men, could prove hard to solve and necessitate impartial arbitration from outside (209, pp.197–201). Despite the problems of both Scottish raids and internal disorder, the coal industry of Northumberland and Durham was able to make substantial developments, with Newcastle as the centre of exports (Ch.7; 82, pp.164–5).

England's involvement in European wars fell into two broad periods, separated by over half a century. The first ended when Gascony fell to the French in 1453, and the second began when the ambitions of Henry VIII for military glory drew the country into the conflicts of a Europe which had been greatly changed by the emergence of powerful new states in the last quarter of the fifteenth century. In the intervening years only one major English army crossed to France, in 1475, when Edward IV let himself be bought off by a treaty and substantial cash payments. Politically, relations remained tense for much of this middle period, sufficiently so to affect economic links between England and France, and England was allied with the semi-independent feudatories of the French Crown, Burgundy and Brittany, on a number of occasions until they were absorbed into the lands of the Valois dynasty in 1477 and 1492 respectively. The Burgundian alliance was closely connected with English economic interests, because the Low Countries, which were the most economically advanced section of the Burgundian duchy, were major trading partners of England, particularly as a market for exports of raw wool. This was recognized in the 1430s by the author of *The Libelle of Englyshe Polycye*, when he advocated the use of a trade embargo to force Flemish compliance with English policies (43, pp.5–6). Another overseas power with which England had uneasy relations, particularly over trading matters, was the league of Hanse towns of North Germany; there were times when these developed into open warfare, but although this affected trade, it did not have the same repercussions on society as did the wars with France.

Political ties between England and Gascony in the years before 1453 also had economic implications, because although the two had originally been linked by dynastic chance, their economies could complement each other. Gascony had developed a specialized economy dominated by viticulture, with some production of woad and iron, but its corn production was inadequate to meet its full needs. Originally England could supply the necessary quantities of corn from its own surplus, and later it was able to re-export corn from the Baltic, which was one of the major granaries for the lands of western Europe in the late Middle Ages. Gascony also provided an outlet for English cloth exports.

One effect of these trading links was that prices of wine in England were directly linked with the state of the war in South-west France. When the war was renewed in the 1370s, the price of wine in London rose to 10d. per gallon, although during the truce of 1375–77 it fell again to 6d. It was not held at this level; for most of the 1390s it was 8d. and dropped to 6d. again only in 1398. For the first half of the fifteenth century, Gascony was under less pressure, probably because Henry V's campaigns had shifted the bulk of military activity to northern France, but even so war had a serious effect on wine exports. These reached a peak during the truce of 1444–49, but were halved when war was renewed in the latter year. However, even political hostility did not entirely break these old economic links. In 1455 Charles VII of France forbade the grant of safe-conducts to the English, but this ban was relaxed and trade, albeit reduced in volume, continued until 1462. A truce in the following year did much to restore the old trade, and the Treaty of Picquigny of 1475 eased many of the restrictions which had been imposed on it (64, Ch.7; 93; 94, pp.212–13).

It is hard to judge how far and in what ways these fluctuations in the wine trade affected the population as a whole. Drinkers of wine, who would be affected by price changes, were a minority, as most Englishmen drank ale, the supply and cost of which would depend on the latest harvest. The most serious effects were probably felt by the men involved in the Gascon shipping trade, as this declined to match the reduced volume of commodities on the move. The port principally connected with this was Bristol, and it may have been the existence of surplus tonnage that led its seamen to turn their attention to new ventures in the fifteenth century, including both attempts to penetrate the Mediterranean trade and the later voyages into the Atlantic. The reduced value of trade was not confined to imports; the fall in these was parallelled, although not precisely, by a decline in cloth exports, which was particularly marked at Bristol. The customs accounts there for the decade 1450–60 show that the average annual export of broadcloths, by both denizens and aliens, was a third lower than it had been in the years 1440–50 (94, pp.334–5).[1] Wine imports over the same period were reduced by just over 40 per cent.

It is clear, therefore, that the effects of the French War on the Gascon trade were a major factor in the fortunes of Bristol; in London matters were rather different. One cannot compare exactly the customs accounts from the two ports, because those for London ending in 1460 conclude at the end of July instead of the normal date of Michaelmas, so the second period employed in the comparison is that of the eleven years 1450–61. Imports of wine suffered a similar drop to those at Bristol; indeed the average annual import fell even more drastically, by over 45 per cent, but the decline in cloth exports, by only a little over 15 per cent, was much less. The contrast is even more marked when one examines the exports in detail; those by denizens fell by only 2 per cent, those by Hansard merchants actually rose by over 6 per cent, while those by other aliens fell by over 77 per cent. Represented as a share of the market, this means that denizens increased their figure from 43.0 per cent to 49.7 per cent, the Hansards theirs from 35.6 per cent to 44.5 per cent, while other aliens, whose earlier share had been a substantial 21.4 per cent now had only 5.8 per cent (94, pp.345–6). It is not clear who these other aliens were – some were probably Italians – but it is probable that a substantial proportion of them were engaged in trade with Gascony or other French lands. On this occasion the Hansards seem to have been the main beneficiaries from the decline in the activity of other alien merchants, but they too could be affected by political rivalry, and periods of tension between England

and the Hanse towns, even if this fell short of war, were marked by substantial falls in cloth exports by the Hanse merchants. The year 1475 was to prove crucial for the recovery of cloth exports, as the Treaty of Utrecht with the Hanse and the Treaty of Picquigny with France did much to restore the level of exports in the latter years of Edward IV's reign (94, pp.26–9, 34–6). From this date onwards to the reign of Henry VIII, the trend of exports continued to rise, although there were some years when one can see a temporary decline [A.3].

The manufacture of cloth itself had of course been considerably affected by war. As we saw earlier (Ch.7), wool taxation to raise war funds had provided a protective tariff for the textile industry, and the war had damaged one of the main Continental cloth-manufacturing centres in Flanders. The effects of war, however, could also prove potentially damaging in a new way as England became more closely involved with the wider economy in western Europe; a slump in exports, even if this were due to factors outside English control, could lead to domestic unemployment, and in the 1520s complaints were made about this in the textile areas of Suffolk (Ch.4). It is probably fair to say that although some aspects of the economy were stimulated by war, for most merchants it was primarily a source of problems.

While war could create serious difficulties for the merchant class, other social groups looked at it in a different light. The values of the ruling class were essentially military, and war was not incidental to life so much as its *raison d'être*. The cult of chivalry, however artificial some aspects of it were, was one in which men really believed, and this undoubtedly contributed to a glorification of the horrors of war. The fourteenth-century French canonist Honoré Bouvet, whose *Tree of Battles* was widely circulated in various languages as well as in the original French, held that a man could engage in war on either side without imperilling his soul, and that if the combatant believed the war to be just, he might justly engage in it. Besides being a way of life, with a related set of moral values, war also had a strongly material side for the noble class, and could provide an income as well as an occupation. Some ways in which the nobility profited from war were more acceptable to the *mores* of the age than others, some more or less guaranteed reward, while others gave opportunity to gamble for high profits. Irrespective of a man's rank, it was not thought below his dignity to receive payments from the King for military service, and the wages payable varied with the rank of the individual. This remuneration was payable whether or not the war was successful. A less legitimate gain, but one which might still be made in an unsuccessful war, was to exploit the system of contracting to provide troops. A captain could economize on the equipping and provisioning of his men, or continue to draw pay for men who had died or deserted. A successful war provided other gains. Englishmen undoubtedly benefited from the fact that the great war was fought mainly on French soil, where they could loot at will, and during periods of victory successful captains were rewarded with offices in conquered territories, such as custodianships of castles, or with grants of land. Finally, and most risky, there was the possibility of ransoms. This was a gambler's reward, because the chance of war might leave a man as either the recipient or the payer of a large sum. Success could raise a man from comparative insignificance to wealth and fame, but capture could cripple an estate with the burden of payment.

The most conspicuous financial gains by English combatants were made in the earlier phase of the Anglo-French wars or in the wars with Scotland – the esquire John Coupland, who captured David II of Scotland in 1346, received lands worth £500 a year and the status of banneret, and many in the English army at Poitiers in 1356 received rich rewards (88, p.30). In the later English victories too, many men made profits. When the war went badly, however, there were corresponding losses. Robert Moleyns, Lord Hungerford, captured at Castillon in 1453, was valued for ransom at £6,000, a sum inflated to almost £10,000 by the cost of his maintenance while a prisoner till his release in 1459 and by the charges of the merchants who negotiated the exchange of the money. The family lands were mortgaged to meet the payments, and worse was to follow. Robert's loyalty to Margaret of Anjou and the Lancastrians led to attainder and forfeiture, which in turn compelled his mother to sell two manors of her own to meet the demands of creditors from whom the ransom money had been borrowed (88, pp.29–32, 126–7).

Profit and loss from war was not necessarily always a matter of individual enterprise. The relationship of brotherhood in arms among men of the military class involved support in such material matters as well as in battle and social action. It could be enforced by law, and a sworn companion could claim a right to the gains of war made by a dead partner. Similarly, if one companion were captured, his partner was under an obligation to contribute to his ransom. The best illustration of what the relationship involved is found in the careers of two esquires, Nicholas Molyneux and John Winter. In 1421 they entered a contract to be loyal to each other without dissimulation or fraud. This provided for arrangements to secure ransom money if necessary, to pool any gains of war and invest them profitably, and, if one left a widow, to make some provision for her and give some protection for surviving children. Both men were of obscure origin, but by the late 1420s they entered the service of Sir John Fastolf; by 1433 Molyneux was the latter's receiver-general, as well as serving the regent, Bedford. In the 1440s, by which time Winter had died, Molyneux entered the service of Richard, duke of York. In Winter's will, he seems to have disregarded the terms of the original partnership, for Molyneux became involved in litigation against two of the feoffees under it, and the eventual settlement suggests that his claim was justified. It should be stressed that even when the war was going badly for England, the partnership secured profits, which remained in England, even although the gains ultimately passed to other hands than those of the partners.

This point should be emphasized, because there has been debate among historians, particularly between M. M. Postan and K. B. McFarlane, about how far the war affected the total wealth of England. Postan's view was gloomy – war destroyed wealth and England grew poorer. Within the country, he argued, war transferred wealth from one group to another, and although war taxation produced a class of native financiers, as for example William de le Pole, for the first time in English history, it did not change the structure of the national economy. Wealth went on a circular tour, and royal taxation was either wasted or enriched a class of profiteers, either the war captains or the purveyors who operated between the Exchequer and the army. Wealth, originally derived from the land, returned to the purchase of land, and there was no marked constructive investment of capital. Certainly much of this is true; war led to a redistribution of wealth, but Postan does not consider whether, if there had been no war, wealth would have been more constructively employed by the land-owning class. One may doubt if it would (91; 92, pp.174–5; 93).[2]

McFarlane argued that on balance England did not lose from the war, and if one thinks in strict cash terms, the evidence supports him. French raids on the English south coast may have inflicted some damage, but in general the wealthier parts of the country were free of fighting. By contrast, war was endemic in France. English raids, even when militarily unsuccessful, provided loot for the attackers, who were sometimes paid to go away, as at St Sauveur in 1375 or Buzançais in 1412. (The buying off of Edward IV's 1475 expedition was in the same tradition.) Victorious campaigns, such as those of Henry V, led to much larger gains. The English in fifteenth-century France were like successful speculators, appropriating the assets of the conquered land, and escaping with their profits before the crash of 1453 (86; 88, pp.31–9). Even while the war was going badly for the English, they suffered fewer major military defeats, and fewer English nobles had to pay ransoms than received payments from their French equivalents. The final withdrawal without major disaster enabled them to preserve some profit. In conclusion one may say that the magnate class, and particularly the military captains, were the main beneficiaries, but that the gains of war were often fortuitous and certainly unevenly spread.

McFarlane's study of the investment of Sir John Fastolf's profits of war is the best illustration of how an individual could emerge successfully from a war which had gone badly. In 1445, his English estates had an annual value of over £1,061, and about three-quarters of this came from estates purchased out of his war gains. His inherited lands were negligible and the bulk of the balance was represented by his acquisitions through marriage. The landed purchases had cost £13,855 and some 90 per cent of them had been made after 1420. Fastolf's methods in securing gains are shown by an episode recorded in the archives of the Parlement of Paris. In 1423, the regent, Bedford, had released an important prisoner of Fastolf's, Guillaume Remon, in return for the submission of Compiègne. Fastolf sought, and obtained, compensation for this, admittedly ten years later, and also claimed a right to the ransoms of various merchants whom he had freed from Remon. His right to these was admitted – only the scale of payment was disputed. After 1445 Fastolf continued to buy property – indeed his best-known purchase, the Boar's Head Inn in Southwark, was bought for £200 in 1450. Despite some losses in the final débâcle in France, he was able to salvage something by selling lands unprofitably before the end (87).[3]

Fastolf was not unique. The Danish-born Sir Andrew Ogard, who served in France and was knighted at the Battle of Verneuil, where incidentally Fastolf was promoted banneret, received letters of denization in 1433 and held offices in France worth £1,000 annually. From these gains he bought the manors of Rye in Hertfordshire and of Emneth, near Wisbech, and indulged in substantial building and repairs there. He kept a chapel with four priests and sixteen choristers at Rye

House, at a cost of £100 a year. Nor was it only such 'new men' who devoted war gains to building. Richard Beauchamp, earl of Warwick, rebuilt the south side of Warwick Castle, enlarged the college at St Mary's Church, Warwick, and built or restored manor houses or castles in five different counties.

Although these examples suggest that the French wars did not impoverish England, clearly the inflow of bullion was not directed into economic developments which increased the country's productive capacity. This is not surprising: the military class was more concerned with conspicuous display than with the creation of national wealth, and it would be anachronistic to expect them to have any other outlook. While lords were concerned about returns from their estates, their normal practice was to exploit traditional resources rather than to seek more profitable areas for investment, even at a time when population decline made it hard for them to find tenants and had reduced rent levels and the income from them. There is, however, one other problem requiring study which could illuminate the question of how profitable the war was. The fact that lands were available for purchase presupposes that there were sellers as well as buyers, and much less is known about who these were, and why they were selling, than is known about the purchasers. A detailed examination of the causes of land sales in the fifteenth century and of the extent to which the inflow of bullion from the spoils of France affected land prices, would be a major contribution to our knowledge of how the war influenced the English economy and society.

The end of the French wars did not mean the end of warfare among Englishmen. The civil disorders and dynastic feuds between Lancaster and York presumably led to some destruction of wealth, although it is virtually impossible to judge how much. Some men certainly lost their estates, although they might recover them later as political fortunes changed, but there is no real reason to believe that the estates themselves were normally impoverished by the fighting. Also, although some families were undoubtedly hard hit by the conflicts, some men were able to avoid political entanglements and concentrate on their private interests, even men from the highest ranks of society such as John de la Pole, duke of Suffolk (148). What we do not know is how far these were typical, but it is worth remembering that the letters of both the Pastons and the Stonors are largely concerned with family concerns rather than national politics. Both families had ties with greater men, who were more concerned with affairs of State, and they were affected by political turmoil, particularly the Stonors, who suffered forfeiture in 1483 for rebelling against Richard III, but both had come through the earlier phase of the dynastic struggle with relatively minor scars.

Whereas there have been arguments over the economic consequences of overseas war in the fourteenth and fifteenth centuries, there is no disagreement that renewed English intervention in Europe in the sixteenth was massively expensive to the nation. Henry VII had been sufficiently discreet to avoid continental entanglements and their resulting expense, but his son was more concerned with illusory glory than with real power. His wars with France between 1511 and 1514 and between 1522 and 1525 brought no economic returns, the occupation of Tournai from 1513 to 1519 involved loss rather than gain and subsidy payments to continental allies involved the export of national resources (82, p.209). After the outbreak of the Reformation crisis, Henry's overseas ambitions were unabated, and it seems certain that their cost played a major part in prompting the rapacious seizure and subsequent disposal of the monastic lands, the greatest tenurial revolution in English history since the Norman Conquest.

The effects of war on the economy must be seen as uneven. It could influence individual fortunes directly as well as having more pervasive consequences for the economy as a whole. As far as the aristocracy were concerned, it did not lead to fundamental changes in the social structure; where wealth changed hands, it was generally within the existing dominant class. The financial difficulties arising out of Henry VIII's wars were, however, to clear the way for a massive redistribution of landed resources through the spoliation of the Church. The greatest changes brought about by war were probably in the development of the cloth industry and the rise of the great clothiers to prominence within the English merchant class. At the same time, one must remember that there were other aspects of the economy which were virtually unaffected by war; one sees this in the growth of the mining interest in the North-east, and most conspicuously in the continuation of trading connections with areas even after the political ties which had created them had been broken. In such cases, the effects of war lasted only as long as the duration of hostilities, and trade was resumed after the restoration of peace.

---

1. By using decades as units of comparison, one in fact underestimates the extent of the drop, which had already begun in the years 1448–50 and figures for these years lower the average for the earlier period from the peak immediately preceding the decline.
2. In Postan's latest work on the subject (92), he rather toned down some of his earlier views.
3. Fastolf's French lands, worth £85 per annum were sold for £847, approximately a rate of ten years' purchase, while the normal cost of lands was about twenty years' purchase. It is a measure of Fastolf's shrewdness that his own acquisitions, at an average of about eighteen years' purchase, cost him rather less than the current market rate for land (87).

PART TWO

The nation of England

CHAPTER 9

England: nation and localities

The study of the English economy in the late Middle Ages shows that there were wide discrepancies of fortune between different parts of the country, and that any attempt to understand its development must take into consideration not only such general factors as population change and the effects of war but also the immediate local factors which determined why one area could outstrip another in prosperity or decline. At the same time, the historian is liable to think in terms of England as a nation, and of English society as essentially one. Is this a valid belief, or should one regard society and politics also as being essentially local in character? It is fair to say, particularly when one is considering overseas relations, that there was some form of national sentiment, but at the same time one should guard against the assumption that this was a dominant force in determining men's attitudes on all occasions.

A self-conscious sense of national identity is a relatively sophisticated idea, and is unlikely to find expression outside a small educated class. It can also exist in a cruder form, whenever a man draws some distinction between himself and the member of another nation, and there is no doubt that such an attitude existed. The early-fourteenth-century chronicler, Geoffrey le Baker, tells of an episode in 1338, during a French raid on Southampton. The townsmen had secured support from the rural hinterland, and a young knight in the invading force was clubbed to the ground by an English rustic. He called for quarter, offering to pay a ransom (*Rançon*), but the peasant retorted, 'Yes, I know you're a Françon', and killed him, not knowing, as Baker says, the other's *idioma* (88, p.19). Baker tells the story partly to show the varying attitudes to war between the knightly and non-knightly classes, but it also shows how men saw in different languages a clear distinction between nations. In the late fourteenth century, one finds Wyclif using the word 'nation' (which was susceptible of a wide variety of usages), to denote men who had been bred in England (132).

Here then were two criteria, language and place of birth, which men of different kinds employed to distinguish between nations. Early in the fifteenth century, the problem of what constituted a nation arose as a practical issue at the Council of Constance, and, as might be expected in an assembly which contained many distinguished academics, the issue was debated in theoretical terms, although the original cause of the debate was essentially political. The organization of the Council, borrowed from that of the universities, was by 'nations' (principally in order to restrict the voting powers of the large number of Italians), but the French objected to the English existing as a separate nation from the Germans – significantly in the Arts Faculty at the University of Paris the English and the Germans were included in the same one. The dispute took place after the English victory at Agincourt and at a time of growing alliance between Henry V and the Emperor Sigismund against the French, and there is little doubt that the principal French spokesman on the subject, Cardinal Pierre d'Ailly, was largely concerned with cutting the enemy down to size. The argument, however, forced the English to justify their national identity, and the arguments employed give some idea of how men thought at the time. England, it was asserted, possessed all the characteristics of an authentic nation:

> whether nation be understood as a people marked off from others by blood relationship and habit of unity or by peculiarities of language, the most sure and positive sign and essence of a nation in divine and human law . . . or whether nation be understood as it should be, as a territory equal to that of the French nation (132).

The English were in fact trying to claim the authentic characteristics of a nation irrespective of how it was defined, including an attempt to cover English claims over Scotland and Ireland, despite the absence of any 'habit of unity' in the former case or of a shared language in the latter. It is however significant that blood relationship and peculiarities of speech, the criteria noted in the last paragraph, were both mentioned.

The fact that England virtually possessed a common language is also reflected in the increasing extent to which it was used both by individuals and by corporate bodies. Within the territory of England proper, the only surviving separate language was Cornish, and it is significant that this linguistic divergence was itself an issue during political troubles in the mid sixteenth century: one plea which the Cornish rebels made in 1549 in favour of the traditional liturgy was that 'we the Cornyshe men (whereof certen of us understande no Englysh) utterly refuse thys newe Englysh' (73, p.135). But Cornwall was exceptional, and one marked characteristic of the period from the late fourteenth century onwards was the increasing victory of the English tongue. Late in the reign of Edward III, it came into use as the language of the Convocation of Canterbury, instead of Latin and French, in 1399 Henry of Lancaster laid claim to the throne in English (22, p.43) and from 1395 the use of English generally became more common in wills (135, pp.209–10). In the letters of Henry V, the language was always English, a fact which was noted by his contemporaries. When the London Brewers' Company resolved in 1442 to keep its records in English, it justified its decision by the fact that Henry had preferred the 'common idiom' in his letters (135, pp.117–19). Again, when the historian considers the available sources for the late Middle Ages, it is noteworthy that one of the major collections of narratives, the London City Chronicles, was in the vernacular, although some of the earlier city chroniclers had used Latin or Anglo-Norman. In literature too, the period sees the increasing use of English, and although some bilingual (or even trilingual) writing occurs in the fifteenth century, notably in macaronic verse, the major authors, from Chaucer and Langland through Malory to Skelton and Wyatt, wrote entirely or principally in English. Admittedly, even at the end of our period, Thomas More still wrote some major works in Latin, but these were the works of a humanist scholar thinking of an international audience, and he was also prepared to produce an English version of the *History of Richard III* and to write his

Confutation of Tyndale in the vernacular. In the fifteenth century Fortescue, too, was a bilingual writer, with the English *Governance of England* and the Latin *De Laudibus Legum Anglie*. The only significant survival of French was in the specialized language of the common law and reflects the conservatism of the legal profession.

The use of English by the intellectual classes shows that it was becoming more socially acceptable, and the assertion that language was a distinguishing criterion of nationhood reveals a growing measure of national self-awareness. Furthermore, and even more important, various writers clearly show that they thought of England as a nation. Two fifteenth-century archbishops of Canterbury, Chichele and Bourchier, write of 'the Church of England' in terms which show that they regarded it as a distinctive entity within the Church Universal, and one in which they could take considerable national pride. Chief Justice Fortescue compared the prosperity of England and the quality of its law with the poverty of France and the arbitary rule of the King there (10, pp.68–9; 30, pp.113–15, 137). The Venetian author of the *Italian Relation of England* commented specifically on the English sense of national pride, and presumably was thinking of attitudes which he encountered generally and not merely the point of view of the more literate: '. . . the English are great lovers of themselves and everything belonging to them; they think that there are no other men than themselves, and no other world but England; and whenever they see a handsome foreigner, they say "he looks like an Englishman" ' (35, pp.20–1). Chronicle writings bear out the validity of this comment, for many of them are strongly patriotic, sometimes, as in the case of the *Gesta Henrici Quinti*, combining patriotism with exhortation: 'Our England (*Anglia nostra*) has reason to rejoice and reason to grieve' (at the victory of Agincourt and at the destruction and death of Christians), 'Let our England be zealous in pleasing God unceasingly.' Lest one might think that such patriotic sentiments came from a court milieu, for the anonymous author was probably a royal chaplain, one should remember that similar sentiments and the attribution of victory to God also occur in the London City Chronicles. Possibly monastic writers may have been slightly less chauvinist in outlook; the St Albans chronicler at least is less effusive about Agincourt, although he too notes the triumphant reception which the King received on his return (16, p.111; 22, p.70; 39, pp.xviii, 98–9).

The culmination of these claims to national identity and of sentiments of this nature came in the preamble to Henry VIII's Act in Restraint of Appeals of 1533: 'Where by dyvers sundrie old autentike histories and cronicles it is manifestly declared and expressed that this Realme of England is an Impire, and so hath been accepted in the world . . . .' (36, iii, 427) Here one finds an explicit statement of views on the nature of England, as well as practical conclusions drawn from them concerning the government of the Church. The idea that England was an 'Empire'[1] was not new: it was asserted in a letter from Cuthbert Tunstall to Henry VIII in 1517: 'But the Crown of England is an Empire of hitself . . .: for which cause your Grace werith a close crown.' (110, p.225 n.2) Possibly such claims were put forward even earlier, although one can only infer them from the appearance of closed crowns on the English coinage in the reign of Henry VII.

This is found on the new coin struck by Henry, the sovereign, and, more strik-ingly, on the much more widely circulated groats, where the coin type with the open crown had long remained unaltered. It is likely that the motive for the new designs may have been to enhance the dignity of the King and to stress his mag-nificence; it is impossible to say if there was any deliberate intention of claiming additional status for him, or if this was a subsequent interpretation of the imagery. In fact, closed crowns had been employed in the fifteenth century, as early as the coronation of Henry IV, but not so regularly that the historian can assume that there was any conscious policy behind the practice.

Clearly it was in the Crown's interests to stress the unity of the country as a means of enhancing its authority. Many of the writers who specifically talked of 'England' were connected with the court either through office, such as Fortescue, or even by blood, such as Bourchier. Not all writers, however, thought in national terms; the distinguished canon lawyer William Lyndwood was not prepared to identify *patria* with *regnum*, and instead thought of it as equivalent to *regio*, which for him meant the province of Canterbury (27, p.172a). Here, expressed in ecclesiastical terms, was the distinction between North and South which recurs frequently in writings of the period. A London chronicler, writing of events in early 1461, talks of the northerners almost as if they were foreign enemies: 'it was Reported that the Quene w^t the Northern men wold come downe to the Citie and Robbe and dispoile the Citie, and distroy it vtterly, and all the Sowth Cuntre' (22, p.172). The monastic continuator of the *Croyland Chronicle* wrote of the same events in hysterical terms; the northern army moved south like a swarm of locusts, ravaging all that lay in its path. Similarly, in 1469 he speaks of the rising against Edward IV as a whirlwind coming down from the North (14, pp.531, 542).

It is hard to judge how much weight should be given to such utterances; was the designation 'northerner' intended to be purely geographical and descriptive, or did it reflect a feeling that these were men almost of a different race? One suspects that the writers were not altogether clear in their own minds; the monk of Croyland, for all his extravagant remarks about the northerners, also spoke in terms of the 'sovereignty of England', when describing a prophecy among the Welsh, whom he certainly regarded as different, that they would recover it from the English, although they failed to do so in 1469 (14, p.543). Possibly one reason for the author's attitude was his ignorance of the geography of the country; a striking instance of this is his statement that in 1461 the earl of March, whom he had rightly described as being in Wales, arrived in England having enjoyed a prosperous voyage and favoured by the west wind (14, p.532). It is perhaps hard for twentieth-century man, accustomed to consult maps for any journey, to realize how limited even an intelligent man's knowledge might be, and how gaps in his information could well be filled by colourful and confused imagination. Possibly the fact that the Robin Hood ballads, which probably took their early form in this period, seem to have had a southern origin but set their events in the North (particularly in Barnsdale, north of Doncaster, rather than in Sherwood), reflects the beliefs of southerners that the North was a strange and wild world. The north-erners equally might look on the South with suspicion, or even downright hostility. During the Pilgrimage of Grace, Robert Aske talked of the northern abbeys in terms of the particular social needs of the North, and was alarmed at the prospect of their lands falling into the hands of men from the South (73, pp.34, 123). This was not new – the Dominican John Bromyard in his *Summa Predicantium* of the fourteenth century had spoken of the mutual hostility of northerners and southerners (230, p.563).

Even if one looks at the political structure of England one can see the division, and there is no doubt that political dominance was heavily weighted in favour of the South and the Midlands. The rise of the Nevilles and the Percies in the late fourteenth century was the first occasion when families of genuine northern origin came into the front rank of the nobility – one may exclude the duchy of Lancaster from any such comment, because it was closely connected with the royal family and also held substantial lands in the Midlands and the South. The Welsh Marches and the Midlands had been far more important as the power bases of major families and indeed were to remain so. The prominence of the Nevilles ended in disaster and the influence of the Percies was at best intermittent. In politics outside the magnate class one has the same picture: when one considers which boroughs were represented in fifteenth-century parliaments, one is struck by the contrasting figures from the North and the South: in Wiltshire there were sixteen boroughs and in Sussex twelve (if one includes the three Cinque Ports which fell within the shire), whereas the figures for the three northern shires of Yorkshire, Northumberland and Lancashire were three, one and none respectively. This political imbalance of North and South remained imperfectly corrected till 1832 – indeed it was to be made worse by the Tudor establishment of boroughs in the Crown duchy of Cornwall in the sixteenth century.

Yet it would be dangerous to regard such divisions as being in any way rigid. The economic crisis following the Black Death had undoubtedly given men of enterprise the opportunity to better their condition, and there was probably more mobility of population in the fifteenth century than there had been in the thirteenth. Some men may not have gone far from their original homes, but others were willing to seek their fortune at a distance: the London merchant class was recruited from every part of the country, including the far North (104, pp.210–12, 389–92). Men maintained some contact with their place of origin and might remember it in their wills. There is no surviving evidence comparable to the parish records of the seventeenth century which shows the rate of change among village inhabitants over short periods, but certainly, as we have seen (Ch.2), families died out and were replaced by others over the course of the century. There were other circumstances, too, in which men might travel about the country; knights and their retinues would go to war, merchants would pursue trade and pilgrims would travel to shrines. Margery Kempe of Lynn was perhaps exceptional in the extent of her travels, but one also remembers the *Prologue* to the *Canterbury Tales*:

> And specially, from every shires ende,
> Of Engelond, to Canterbury they wende.

In the North the shrine of St Cuthbert at Durham was second only to that of St

Thomas, although his appeal seems to have been particularly to northerners (209, pp.28–30).

A sense of nationality was not, however, incompatible with a more local loyalty, and for many members of the landed class the shire community was probably the main focus of their interests. Only occasionally did this local sentiment prove stronger than loyalty to the nation, as in 1489 when the levy of taxation for the distant Breton War led to a Yorkshire rising, in which the earl of Northumberland was murdered, and in 1497 when the Cornishmen rebelled against the payment of a subsidy for war with Scotland (73, pp.14, 15). Much work remains to be done on the structure of the shire community, and there are few shires where it has been closely analysed. A study of Cheshire in the first quarter of the fifteenth century, however, shows how the social ties of the gentry class were rooted in the locality. Families were linked by marriage alliances, and the determination of fathers to make these locally is nowhere shown more clearly than when the son of one gentleman of the shire was betrothed to the daughter of another, but the particular daughter's name was left blank in the bond of betrothal. There were also territorial ties, of lord and tenant, and of feoffees to uses and personal connections, such as those of executors. The same body of men could act as arbitrators in disputes and provide men to serve the Crown as local officials or as commissioners to levy a subsidy or array troops.

It might be argued that Cheshire was untypical: there was no great local lord, and as a palatinate jurisdiction it was specially linked to the Crown. However, the Stonor Letters suggest that the Cheshire pattern was not unique. Even a family with lands in various shires, such as the Stonors themselves, who had estates in Devon as well as their principal family holding in Oxfordshire, was closely linked by marriage to other families in its own near neighbourhood. Thomas Stonor (d.1474) was brother-in-law of Humphrey Forster of Harpeden near Henley, and father-in-law of John Barantyne of Haseley. All three of them appear quite regularly on the Oxfordshire commission of the peace. Other families who provided JPs at different times, such as the Harcourts and the Hampdens, also feature among the Stonors' correspondents (24, i, facing 7, 69–70, 113–14, 151, ii, 57–8).

The family connections of the Pastons in Norfolk do not seem to have been quite so far-reaching among the gentry families there as those of the Stonors, although Margaret Mauteby, the wife of the elder John Paston, was the daughter of another gentleman of the shire. The letters, however, show that the family was deeply involved in county affairs at a time of political turbulence, and on one occasion reveal the pride of John Paston in being a Norfolk man. In 1465 he wrote that he wished to have his doublet made of worsted 'for the worship of Norfolk' (17, iv, 188).

The community of the shire was based on a network of acquaintance and interests, and probably drew on the contacts of individuals in local government. We have seen that the Stonors and their associates served together on the Commission of the Peace, and the records of proceedings before the justices of the peace, although few in number, show how important such a group of local men was, acting along with one or two professional lawyers. Two examples will suffice to illustrate this. In Wiltshire in 1383–84, the working justices consisted of one lawyer, Sir Robert Cherleton (later Chief Justice of the Common Pleas), and four local gentry, Nicholas Bonham, Sir Philip FitzWaryn, Sir Thomas Hungerford and William de Worston. All of these men gave other service in government, as MPs, tax assessors, sheriffs, commissioners of array and so on. The Staffordshire commission of 1409–14 contained three lawyers, all active members of it, and eight gentry, who again played a part in other spheres of local government, mostly although not exclusively within the shire (31, pp.340–1, 401–2).

The extent to which a powerful magnate could dominate the shire community and act as a focus for local sentiment varied. The prominence of the duke of Norfolk in the Paston Letters reflects his local power, but the Oxfordshire of the Stonors seems to have been markedly less subject to the pre-eminence of a great man. Where there was a powerful figure, this could have important political consequences, particularly in times of civil war, as in 1471 when the Hastings connection provided important support for the newly returned Edward IV. An even more striking example of such influence was that of the Percies in Northumberland. They had been dominant there since the late fourteenth century, played an important part in Henry IV's usurpation in 1399 but were forfeited for revolt a few years later. Henry V restored them in 1416, perhaps because he hoped to use their local authority, which depended on the personal loyalty felt towards them, to safeguard his rear before further campaigns in France. Adherence to Lancaster meant a further forfeiture in 1461, but this was followed by a second restoration in 1470. Significantly, this followed the troubles in the North in the previous year, and according to one early source, the rebels then had petitioned for the earldom to be restored to the lawful heir. The most important point to note is that loyalty to such a family could survive its temporary political eclipse, and that this was rooted in the traditions of local society.

The loyalty of the North to the Percies probably reflects the more clannish nature of society in this part of the country than further south. Even when Edward IV appointed his younger brother Richard of Gloucester as his deputy in the North, the latter entered into a special indenture with Percy to define their respective powers. This system was to be the predecessor of the various experiments under the Tudors to exercise special control in the North, measures which not only reflect the problems of governing a region remote from the centre of public power but also tell us something about the tensions between a local aristocracy and the Crown. Elsewhere in the realm, in the Marches of Wales and the Principality, similar attempts were made to devolve power. Again there was a problem of lawlessness even greater than the average over the country as a whole, exacerbated by the disorders which had followed the Glyn Dŵr revolt. Men with local influence were again prominent – Edward IV relied on William Herbert, whom he made earl of Pembroke, and later on a council nominally under the prince of Wales, Richard III on his ally the duke of Buckingham, who was lord of the castle of Brecon, until the latter revolted, and Henry VII on his uncle Jasper Tudor. The first and last of these were both Welsh, (112, pp.151, 161–3) and it is likely that the element of tribal loyalty was one factor which they could employ to help in the exercise of their authority.

The establishment of such new administrative bodies in the remoter parts of the kingdom was a significant move towards building a more unified nation, but the need to create councils in the North and on the Marches is in itself an indication of how England was still divided at this date. These were only the more extreme examples of local particularism, and they were complicated by special problems, the hostile frontier in the North and the traditional privileges of the Marches in the West. Elsewhere there was no need to set up special bodies, but it is clear that much local administration had in practice to be devolved into the hands of local men.

---

1. The term 'Empire' denoted that the King owed obedience only to God and not to any temporal superior, such as the Pope or the Emperor.

CHAPTER 10

England and its neighbours

In Chapter 9, we saw that the fifteenth-century Englishman had some idea of national identity, and as being in some ways different from his neighbours. Perhaps he thought of himself more as a Kentishman or a Cornishman than as one who had something in common with men elsewhere in England, but he still distinguished Englishmen from foreigners. In the towns, one sees outbreaks of xenophobia, particularly at times of social unrest such as 1381 and 1450, when aliens were treated as scapegoats for political or economic ills. These foreigners, however, were isolated from their homelands, and more crucial for the understanding of how Britain was to develop is the consideration of how the Englishman regarded the countries closest to his own, Wales, Ireland and Scotland. Equally important was the attitude which the inhabitants of those lands had towards England.

Mental attitudes, even of individuals, are hard for the historian to ascertain, and any attempt to speak of the collective view that one nation held of another is fraught with difficulties. One may suspect that English regionalism meant that the attitude of, say, a Londoner towards the Scots was very different from that of a Northumbrian. To one, the Scot was the inhabitant of a distant land, to the other he was a potential raider who was too close for comfort. Furthermore, the relations of Wales, Ireland and Scotland to England were very different politically, and this could affect the attitudes of the ruling class to each. Since the end of the thirteenth century Wales had been subject to English rule, and remained on the whole closely bound to its larger neighbour, Ireland was divided between areas where English rule could be enforced and those where it could not, and Scotland was an independent kingdom, which had successfully resisted attempts at conquest.

If Wales possessed a sense of national identity, it owed this to its distinctive language. It had possessed no political unity at the time of the Edwardian conquest – indeed it was the very fact of its divisions which had enabled the English to carry this into effect, and unite the Principality to the kingdom by the Statute of Rhuddlan of 1284. The so-called 'Act of Union' of 1536, which will be considered later, did little more than end divisions which had persisted within Wales, and give the final blow to traditional Welsh law (110, pp.246–7). The divisions in thirteenth-century Wales had meant that political and social ties were established between English families and their Welsh neighbours, which were to persist after 1284. Edward II's Welsh officials indeed remained loyal to him against the English magnates, and later in the fourteenth and fifteenth centuries they continued to serve the Crown, even in opposition to their fellow countrymen. Even the young Owain Glyn Dŵr, later to lead a national Welsh rising, seems to have accepted the traditional friendly relationship with England, serving in the Scottish campaign of 1385, and possibly in Ireland in the 1390s. His wife was the daughter of one of the most successful Welshmen of the fourteenth century, Sir David Hanmer, who became a Justice of the King's Bench in 1383 (131, pp.22, 24, 26; 143).

Hanmer, however, was exceptional in attaining such high office, and even in Wales itself the greater administrative posts were largely filled by Englishmen, while Welshmen were limited to subordinate positions. Even more in the economic sphere there was discrimination against the native Welsh; in rural areas the settlement of Englishmen meant the transfer of the Welsh to inferior upland lands in place of their earlier more fertile valley holdings, while the towns were regarded as places for Englishmen alone. As late as 1521 ordinances were issued to prevent Welshmen becoming burgesses of Neath. Legal records also reveal the inferior status of the Welsh, most conspicuously in the term 'mere Welshmen' (*meri Wallici*), which betrays the contemptuous attitude of the English settlers. The English were privileged in court, and there were certain traditional payments which only the Welsh were liable to make, so one finds Welshmen being prepared to purchase the right to have the privileges of Englishmen (*pro libertate Anglicana habenda*) (114; 166).

The revolt of Owain Glyn Dŵr in the first decade of the fifteenth century was the greatest crisis in Anglo-Welsh relations during the later Middle Ages. It is hard to say how far this was a national rising, because Owain did not secure the support of the whole Welsh people, even at the time of his greatest military success, while there were many who deserted his cause during the English recovery (131, pp.77–80, 129–30). On the other hand, he undoubtedly attracted considerable popular support at the outbreak of the revolt, and when in 1404 he wrote to the French King as 'Owynus dei gratia princeps Wallie', he seems to have been speaking for a considerable part of his people (131, pp.35, 82–3). There is evidence for this in the support which he secured during a protracted struggle and in the difficulties which the English had in suppressing the revolt, even with some Welsh assistance, and the fact that even in defeat Owain was not betrayed to the English indicates the persistence of loyalty to him. How far he regarded himself as a national leader is hard to say – his original revolt was prompted by a private quarrel more than by national feeling, and some of his actions show little sign of being prompted by a sense of Welshness. The so-called Tripartite Indenture of 1405 between himself, Northumberland and Mortimer would have given him considerable lands in England, and the proposals to establish St Davids as a metropolitan see would have included several dioceses of western England among its suffragans (131, pp.29–31, 93–5, 120). There is, however, no doubt that during the rising he was able to exploit existing Welsh grievances.

The revolt exacerbated tension between English and Welsh. During it, the English border counties were particularly vociferous in Parliament in calling for the savage penal legislation which limited Welsh rights of office holding (112, p.148) [E], and after its suppression tests to prove Englishry were more strictly applied. As late as the 1430s, the author of the *Libelle of Englyshe Polycye* expressed a fear of further revolt in Wales (43, p.40), although there is no reason to believe that there was any serious danger of this, and this may explain why these restrictions were maintained so long. Some were relaxed by Henry VII and others removed by Henry VIII's Act of 1536. The title 'Act of Union', sometimes given to this measure is a misnomer. As its preamble makes explicit, it recognized that Wales was already incorporated with England. Its proper designation, an 'Act for Laws and Justice to be ministered in Wales in like fourme as it is in this realme', shows that its purpose was to amalgamate the legal systems of the two countries, an action which automatically removed the disabilities under which the Welsh had hitherto laboured by eliminating the legal distinctions between them and the English. It also reorganized local government in Wales, creating shires on the English pattern (36, iii, 563–9; 110, pp.253–5)

The Welsh response to Glyn Dŵr's defeat was twofold. There was certainly a tradition of resentment – fifteenth-century poetry was more bitter in tone than that of the fourteenth (143), and there was probably national sentiment behind the maintained interest in Welsh law, reflected in the survival of a considerable number of MSS of the laws of Hywel Dda, the greatest of the traditional Welsh lawgivers, from this period. Several of them contain additional notes, which show that the laws were still in practical use (166). At the same time, the fourteenth-century tradition of co-operation was restored by men who were prepared to put the past behind them and serve the English Crown. Some indeed never broke with it, such as Dafydd Gam of Brecknock, whom Henry IV ransomed from Glyn Dŵr in 1412 (112, pp.150–1; 131, p.142), and who died fighting for Henry V at Agincourt. More remarkably, the House of Tudor had been related to Glyn Dŵr and been involved in the revolt, perhaps because several of its members had served Richard II and were hostile to his supplanter; but this did not prevent Owain Tudor from entering Henry V's service and subsequently marrying his widow. Their sons, Edmund and Jasper, both became English earls, and the former's son, Henry VII (110, pp.4–6). Owain was granted the legal status of an Englishman in 1432, and after rather chequered fortunes when his secret marriage was discovered, eventually died fighting for the cause of Lancaster.

The rise of the Tudors into the aristocracy resulted from their royal connections; even more striking was that of the Herberts who had no such ties of blood. Sir William Herbert, created earl of Pembroke by Edward IV and given major responsibilities in the government of Wales, was of pure Welsh stock, and through his mother a grandson of Dafydd Gam. He served Richard, duke of York, after whose death he was closely connected with his son, both at his accession and during the early years of his reign. The favours conferred on him may well have been prompted by Edward IV's desire to secure Wales and to provide a focus for Welsh sentiment in opposition to the Tudors, who were the backbone of Lancastrian resistance in Wales, where Harlech Castle held out against Herbert for a long time. Herbert's influence enabled him to bring a substantial army to Edward's support in 1469 against the forces of the northerners who had revolted at the instigation of Warwick. One chronicle source makes it clear that the Welsh element in this army was important, and that the Welshmen suffered severe casualties in Herbert's defeat, and another speaks of the Welsh hoping at this time to recover the sovereignty of England which had been lost at the time of the

Anglo-Saxon invasions (14, p.543; 18, pp.6–7).

It is hard to say how far the accession of the Tudors contributed to a solution of Wales's problems. It seems clear that Henry VII, after his landing at Milford Haven, was helped by Welsh support, or at any rate neutrality, during the crucial weeks before Bosworth, and this was probably due to the sympathies evoked by contemporary Welsh bards. But he was only one-quarter Welsh, and his subsequent attitudes to Wales were more those of a practical politician, trying to exploit all his advantages in order to enforce his authority. Even in his relaxations of the penal legislation of the Glyn Dŵr period, there is no evidence of more than an attempt to govern more efficiently (110, pp.3–4, 256). Order, indeed, was hard to maintain, and it was probably the need to establish royal authority more securely that prompted Henry VIII's eventual solution in 1536.

Anglo-Welsh relations, then, show an alternation of hostility and co-operation on both sides, with the two lands finally being drawn more closely together. The main factor in this was the willingness of some of the Welsh gentry to come to terms and play an active part in government. The problem of Ireland was fundamentally different, although there were some aspects of Anglo-Irish relations which parallel conditions in Wales, such as the exclusion of the Gaelic Irish from the provisions of the common law, and from membership of mercantile and craft guilds in Dublin (133, pp.18, 44). But English rule, never so complete in Ireland as in Wales, had been severely shaken by the Bruce invasion of 1315–18, and had receded under Gaelic pressure during the fourteenth century. The key figures in Anglo-Irish relations were the aristocracy of English descent, a phenomenon which with rare exceptions did not occur in Wales. In particular, three great families, the Butler earls of Ormond and the Geraldine earls of Desmond and of Kildare, dominate the scene. These families, instead of representing a settler tradition and avoiding contact with the Irish, had a strong tendency to go native, intermarrying with the local aristocracy and following local customs (133, pp.57–8; 137, pp.18–21). The English authorities tried to enforce separation; the Statutes of Kilkenny of 1366, essentially a codification of earlier law, tried to forbid marriage alliances between the Anglo-Irish and the native Irish, to exclude the native Irish from benefices in cathedral or collegiate churches and to lay down that Irish living among the English should speak the English tongue (139, pp.291–2). These measures were ineffective, intermarriage continued and the Anglo-Irish magnates continued to pursue their interests with little reference to the distant Crown. Their control, even in Ireland, was patchy, for there were areas where the native Irish retained control and could cut communications between the lands which accepted a measure of English rule. Notably, the MacMurroughs of Leinster established a power in North Wexford and Carlow, which cut across the routes from Dublin to the south-west of the island, where the Desmonds and Ormonds held lands. This family was most powerful in the time of Art Mor MacMurrough, who died in 1416, after having been active from the time of Richard II (Ch.18), but it remained important and at feud with the English for most of the fifteenth and even into the sixteenth century (137, pp.170–1).

Endemic fighting went far to making Ireland ungovernable, and also made it financially unable to support the costs of administration and of frontier defence. The only English King to campaign there personally was Richard II, who had only short-lived success after his first visit, and both before and after his time successive Englishmen, sent over as Lieutenant or as Deputy, complained about inadequate financial provision. The story was the same from Sir William of Windsor in the fourteenth century, through Sir John Talbot under Henry V and Richard, duke of York, in the following reign, to the earl of Surrey under Henry VIII. The Anglo-Irish earl of Kildare, dominant in the 1470s, made similar complaints (133, p.65; 134, pp.9–10; 139, pp.297–307, 350–1, 381, 396). The English government had various expedients in its Irish policy, notably reliance on English magnates whose territorial interests in Ireland gave them some incentive to act firmly; one thinks particularly of successive members of the House of Mortimer under Richard II and again in 1423–25. All died in Ireland, although only one in battle. The duke of York, appointed Lieutenant in 1447, also inherited lands from the Mortimers. He was able to turn his power in Ireland to advantage in English domestic politics, fleeing for refuge there in 1459 after defeat at Ludford Bridge (Ch.23). Under his influence the Irish Parliament affirmed in 1460 that 'the land of Ireland is and at all times has been corporate of itself . . . freed of the burden of any special law of the realm of England' (139, pp.313–15, 334–6, 362–3, 378–87). This declaration was made by an assembly which represented the Anglo-Irish rather than the Gaelic Irish – the native population was unrepresented in Parliament until Henry VIII raised certain of the Gaelic chiefs to the peerage (133, p.33).

Native Ireland stood apart from events in England, although it might come to terms with the Anglo-Irish, who, equally with the Gaelic Irish, resented interference from across the sea. For much of the time, however, it went its own way; the native Brehon law did not begin to retreat until the sixteenth century, and the greatest of the native Irish lived in a society which was little touched by the normal customs of the rest of Christendom, even as late as the reign of Elizabeth. Native law did not distinguish between legitimate and illegitimate children, which meant that in practice marriage customs were secular and polygamous. Philip Maguire, lord of Fermanagh, who died in 1395, had twenty sons by eight different mothers, and the second earl of Clanrickard, who died in 1582, was survived by at least five of his six wives (137, pp.11, 49, 74). These native lords shared political aims with the Anglo-Irish magnates, essentially the limitation of English rule from Dublin, and as only one of the three great Anglo-Irish families, the Ormonds, had significant interests in England, it was natural that the Kildares and the Desmonds should be prepared to establish connections with Gaelic society.

Ormond support for the Lancastrians probably explains why Edward IV had assistance from Kildare and Desmond, and it was certainly this Lancastrian sympathy which led to the exile of the earl and the eclipse of the family in the third quarter of the fifteenth century. At the same time the Desmonds went increasingly native, leaving the House of Kildare politically dominant in Anglo-Irish society. Its power excited hostility and apprehension, and one sees an alternation of members of the family holding the key offices in Irish government with their opposition to anyone else who was entrusted with power. It would be fair to say that the Crown could not govern effectively without the support of the family, but dared not rely on it completely. The seventh, eighth and ninth earls effectively dominated Ireland until the 1530s. Their power was based on land (and early in the sixteenth century the grant to the eighth earl of all lands which he could recover from rebels strengthened this), but they were also connected through marriage with a number of Gaelic and Anglo-Irish families (133, pp.155–6).

Ireland did not affect English politics as much as Wales did, and it is significant that English writers say little about Irish affairs. Presumably the reason was its greater remoteness, and the lack of interest of most Englishmen in it, apart perhaps from the traders of the west coast ports such as Bristol, who bought fish, hides and timber in exchange of iron, salt and cloth (94, pp.191–201). Its main political role was its support for the House of York from 1459 onwards – as we have seen, the Irish Parliament of 1460 asserted its independence of England at a time of Lancastrian dominance, and in 1470, when Henry VI recovered the throne, Kildare held Ireland in the name of Edward IV (139, pp.394–5). After 1485, this loyalty to York took the form of supporting the pretenders, Lambert Simnel in 1487 and to a lesser extent Perkin Warbeck in 1491 (139, pp.403, 406). It was significantly just after this that one sees the strongest series of measures taken in the fifteenth century to bring Ireland under control, those taken, during a period when the Kildares were out of favour, by Sir Edward Poynings, the recently appointed Lord Deputy, in 1495. His Parliament legislated that the chief officers of Ireland should hold their posts solely at the King's will and pleasure, annulled the 1460 Act which made it treason to attack any person in Ireland under an English seal, and declared that the English seals were to be obeyed in Ireland. Its most famous enactment restricted the Irish Parliament – none was to be held until the King and the English Parliament had approved its proposed acts and a royal licence had been obtained for its summons. Another Act of the same Parliament provided that statutes made within England should apply in Ireland (133, pp.177–8).

These measures played a considerable part in establishing the governmental framework of Anglo-Irish relations for the next three centuries, although relations between Gaelic Ireland and the Anglicized areas were to be further complicated by the plantation of new immigrants at the turn of the sixteenth and seventeenth centuries. The policy pursued in the late Middle Ages, of establishing an area of English law, the so-called Pale, reflects the defensive attitude of the English to the Gaelic areas, and this seems to have become more pronounced during the fifteenth century. Although effective government had been limited to the areas near Dublin since early in the century, Poynings took steps to define the Pale more precisely, organizing a defence system, with a warning system of fires on various hills. This is a clear sign that he felt it was impossible to control the whole island and that much of it would have to be allowed to go its own way. Such a solution could satisfy no one, and left the island in a politically unstable condition, where power could rest only with those strong enough to take it by force (133, pp.132–3, 175).

If Wales was largely incorporated under English rule and Ireland precariously poised between control and independence, England's third neighbour within the

British Isles, Scotland, was politically distinct. Like Ireland, it comprised two nations, but by the late Middle Ages effective authority centred on the Lowland areas, which were linguistically, and hence culturally, closer to England than was either Ireland or Wales. In the Highland areas there were many parallels with Gaelic Ireland, with clan chiefs who paid little heed to a king in the South, or who negotiated alliances with the English King against their own ruler, but it was possible for the Scottish Crown to take some measures against them with at least limited success, and they never played so prominent a part in national affairs as did the Lowland magnates.

The accession of Robert the Steward to the Scottish throne in 1371 marked the achievement of independence against the attempts of Edward III to overthrow the settlement of 1328. Neither support for Edward Balliol, who ultimately surrendered his claims to the English King in 1356, the captivity of David II and the subsequent ransom treaty, nor a proposal in 1364 that Edward should succeed the childless David, had led to the surrender of Scottish independence (138, pp.161, 163, 193). The English did not entirely abandon their claims of overlordship, which were certainly resurrected in 1400 (possibly after a tactless letter in which Robert III addressed Henry IV as duke of Lancaster), and were probably reasserted by Henry V during the unsuccessful negotiations in 1416 for the release of James I from captivity in England. In the debates on nationality at the Council of Constance in 1417, the English claimed that the Scots were part of the English nation, along with Wales and four kingdoms in Ireland, although they do not seem to have made any specific reference to the claims of overlordship (132). Although Edward IV reasserted the claim to sovereignty in 1481, accusing James III of neglecting to do homage and affirming his intention of restoring the exiled earl of Douglas (138, p.491), this should probably be regarded as a tactical move to attract support from possible opponents of the Scottish King. Probably no English king after Edward III seriously hoped to secure rights of overlordship; it is noteworthy that no attempt was made to enforce it in the eventual ransom negotiations for James I in 1424. The effective abandonment of the claim was probably due to the fact that the English kings were more concerned with ambitions in France or were absorbed in internal faction.

Anglo-Scottish relations were not therefore affected by the tensions, found in Wales and Ireland, created by a conquest and the existence of an alien ruling class. It is not easy to obtain a clear picture of the attitudes which each nation had to the other – Scottish records and chronicles are sparse, and there are surprisingly few comments on the Scots in English writings, probably because the great bulk of the latter came from the largely indifferent south of the country. There is clearer evidence of hostility in the North; although one may discount descriptions of the Scots in the York civic records as 'enemys and rebells' and 'auncient enemys' as statements made in time of war, one cannot disregard the sentiments expressed in legal cases when a man's nationality had been questioned. In 1477, a time of peace between the two countries, there were two such: John Colyn complained that he 'was diffamyd of the chylder of iniquite be veray malesse, that he shud be a Skotte and no Ynglysman', and John Saunderson showed 'how that he of late ayanest right and gude conscience by the children of wekydness was wrongfully noysed, slaundered and defamed that he should be a Scotisheman'. Hostility to the Scots cannot, however, have been sufficient to exclude them entirely from England; not only do these cases presuppose that a man living in York might be a Scot, but also in 1480, when war was imminent, some fifty Scots resident in England sought and obtained letters of denization, so as to avoid the risk of having their property confiscated (138, p.490).

The Scots reciprocated this hostility. Aeneas Sylvius Piccolomini, later Pope Pius II, who visited Scotland in the 1430s, commented that nothing pleased the Scots more than abuse of the English (138, p.297). Walter Bower, the abbot of Inchcolm, took time in his *Scotichronicon* to reiterate the old slander against the English that they were born with tails. There was a patriotic tradition in literature, voiced in Barbour's *Bruce* in the fourteenth century and Blind Harry's *Wallace* in the fifteenth; indeed there was in the latter at least implicit criticism of the policy of *rapprochement* with England being pursued by James III. The whole corpus of ballad literature from the border areas reflects traditions of hostility, and shows how deeply they were reflected in folk memory, even although the lateness of the texts makes their value slight as a detailed source for events. Nor was it only the ballad writers who voiced such sentiments. Skelton, whose background may have been north country, was vitriolic in his attacks on the Scots, with his savage poem on Flodden and his sneering 'How the douty Duke of Albany, lyke a cowarde knyght, ran away shamfully', which probably refers to an unsuccessful Scottish raid in 1522. When, after Flodden, George Dundas reiterated the story about Englishmen with tails, Skelton retorted savagely in macaronic verse.

Yet literary evidence also shows the existence of a Scottish attraction to England. In his *Lament for the Makars* William Dunbar began his melancholy roll-call of the dead with 'the noble Chawcer, of Makaris flouir' and followed him with two other Englishmen, Gower and Lydgate. The Chaucerian tradition of writing was influential in fifteenth-century Scotland, notably in Robert Henryson but even, in some stylistic techniques, in Blind Harry. Admittedly, Dunbar was Anglophil, writing in praise of London, and, as a court poet, commemorating the marriage of James IV and Margaret Tudor. Nor were literary connections confined to the poets. In 1521 John Major, one of the leading Scots scholars of his day, wrote his *History of Greater Britain*, in which he affirmed that while there were two kingdoms in the island, the Scottish and the English, the inhabitants were all Britons, He was even eirenical on the question of tails, considering that while Englishmen had had them in the past, they no longer were so encumbered. Major's attitude to the English is all the more striking because he had spent much of his working life in France and might have been expected to stress Scotland's ancient alliance with that country.

Ultimately, however, only political moves could draw the two countries together. Although in the third quarter of the fifteenth century each country provided a refuge for rebels and exiles from the other, such as the Lancastrians in Scotland and the Douglases in England, the end of this period sees a move to peace. In the 1470s, when James III's domestic political position was fairly strong, he took steps towards two marriage alliances between the two countries. In 1474 his son, aged not quite two, was betrothed to Edward IV's five-year-old daughter, and in 1479 there were negotiations for the marriage of the King's sister to Edward's brother-in-law, Earl Rivers. One might note the preamble to the 1474 treaty: 'Forsmuche as this noble isle called Grete Britaigne canne not be kepte and mainteigned better in welthe and prosperite than such things to be practized and concluded betwene the kyngs of both reames, England and Scotland, whereby thaye and thair subgetts might be assured to lyve in peas. . . .' (138, pp.478–9, 487–9) In fact the negotiations came to nothing; when it turned out that James's sister was pregnant by William, Lord Crichton, Edward protested his outraged honour and annulled the earlier betrothal also. The initiative in these negotiations seems to have come largely from James, who may have been hoping for English neutrality while he dealt with his own troublesome subjects. Edward was less enthusiastic, although originally he was probably pleased to secure his northern frontier before invading France in 1475.

Although this proposed marriage for the Scottish prince was unsuccessful, he was eventually (nearly thirty years later as James IV) to marry another English princess. He made marriage with a daughter of Henry VII a prior condition for peace and friendship with England; this was agreed in 1502 and the marriage was celebrated in the following year (138, pp.553–4). Peace lasted until Henry VII's death, but his son was less disposed to be friendly towards the Scots. In the early years of his reign his ambitions in Europe led to a renewal of the Franco-Scottish alliance, and to the disastrous invasion of England which culminated at Flodden in 1513. Even after this, however, there were still some Scottish lords who looked for closer friendship with England rather than to the old association with France. This division in foreign policy was important for nearly half a century, down to 1560, but did not become crucial until the minority of Mary and the regency of her French mother. Many of the early moves towards the formation of a pro-English party in Scotland were little more than the old tendency for men at odds with the existing government to seek help south of the border (116, p.36), and the period when such a group became really influential lies beyond the scope of this volume. A hundred years after the marriage of 1503, the failure of the Tudor line gave the English throne to a Scottish king, and created a personal union of the two kingdoms.

So far we have considered the relations of England with its neighbours. How did the Welsh, Irish and Scots regard each other? There are some indications that they not only appreciated their common interest in resisting England but also felt themselves to be in some sense kindred. In November 1401 Owain Glyn Dŵr wrote for help to the Irish chiefs and to Robert III of Scotland, although his letters were intercepted and never reached their proposed destinations. To the former he wrote that ancient prophecies said that Irish help would be necessary for this triumph, and (more practically) that war in Wales would free Ireland from English intervention (131, pp.46–7). He also claimed kinship with the Scots, one of whom, the chronicler Bower, noted the Welsh struggle sympathetically. Scottish interest in Ireland persisted after the Bruce campaigns failed in 1318: in the mid fifteenth century the barony of the Glens of Antrim was acquired by Donald Balloch, a kinsman of the lord of the Isles, and in 1481 James III tried to rouse the native Irish against England in retaliation for Edward IV's intrigues with the restive MacDonalds (138, pp.362, 495). More striking, because there was no political pressure behind it, was the fact that when the University of Glasgow was founded in the mid fifteenth century, provision was made to include Irish students in one of its nations, Rothesay. In fact the numbers of Irish recorded were small, but there were a few, drawn from the Gaelic areas, despite the fact that much of Scotland was no longer Gaelic in character.

England's relations with its neighbours in the late Middle Ages saw some breaking down of the old barriers with Wales and Scotland. The lifting of restrictions on the Welsh was gradual, but despite them, Welshmen began to play a part in English political life. It is at least symbolically significant that Henry VII was of Welsh descent in the paternal line. Anglo-Scottish distrust, although always latent and liable to flare up into open hostility, was perhaps less profound than in the early fourteenth century, and some men at any rate saw that both countries had some interests in common. Possibly a crucial factor here was the loss by the English kings of their French lands. This made them rather more concerned with insular affairs, and as the English were less inclined to assert claims in France, the French paid less heed to maintaining an alliance, of which the main value had been to provide a diversion in the North. It is significant that the periods of Anglo-Scottish *rapprochement* in the 1470s and around 1500 coincide with times when the English kings were not particularly aggressive in Europe. Even Edward IV's campaign of 1475 must be regarded more as a demonstration than as a real attempt to recover lost lands. England's less happy relations with Ireland show that tension there was maintained, with the Irish, both Gaelic and Anglo-Irish, being forced into subordination to an alien government in Dublin. The attempt to incorporate Gaelic Ireland, through its chiefs, into one nation with the Anglo-Irish lies beyond our period, but it may well have been doomed from the start by the attitudes which had developed in the fifteenth century and earlier. Once this bitterness had been created, it was arguably impossible for later attempts to solve the Irish question to have much chance of success.

CHAPTER 11

The monarchy

Between 1370 and 1530 ten kings occupied the English throne, with the reigns of eight of them falling completely within the period. Of these eight, three (Richard II, Henry VI and Edward V) were deposed and subsequently came to violent ends, a fourth (Richard III) died in battle defending his title and a fifth (Edward IV) lost the throne for a time but subsequently recovered it. Furthermore, Richard II may have been temporarily deposed in December 1387, only to be restored for another dozen years when his enemies failed to agree on a successor, and Henry IV, Henry V and Henry VII all survived attempts to overthrow them by force. As far as the monarchy was concerned, this was a period of unequalled instability in English history, as can be seen when one looks both at earlier and at later times. Between 1066 and 1370, only Edward II had come to a violent end following a rebellion, and even John and Henry III, who had faced armed insurrections, were able to retain the throne till the ends of their lives. After 1530, only Charles I (unless one also includes Lady Jane Grey among English monarchs) was to be put to death, while James II lost the Crown by flight. The average length of each reign in this period was also markedly shorter than those before or after, a further sign of the monarchy's weakness. The most obvious problem, therefore, for the historian is why at this time the monarchy was so insecure.

The exceptional instability was partly fortuitous. The personalities of some kings contributed to their downfall, because the standing of the monarchy could not be totally separated from the individual who was king at the time, although there were certain functions of monarchy, as will be shown later, which had to be regarded as institutional rather than personal. The fact that all three kings who were ultimately deposed succeeded as minors, Henry VI as a baby and the other two before entering their teens, was probably important in only one case, that of Edward V, who was unable to defend his inheritance against his uncle Richard, duke of Gloucester, at a time when magnate rivalries were acute (Ch.25). His reign lasted for less than three months, but both Richard II and Henry VI survived minority, and it was their adult conduct which was to lead to their eventual destruction.

Richard II undoubtedly gave offence by his ambitions for the royal prerogative and the capricious arbitrariness of his conduct. This was apparent both in his political actions against his enemies (Ch.18) and in the way in which he and his advisers tried to extend the scope of the law of treason beyond that of the common law and the normal courts. Thus in 1390, the Court of Chivalry was given power to judge matters arising out of war within the realm, which could not be determined by the common law, while in Haxey's case (1397), the King persuaded the lords to declare that anyone who should excite the Commons to reform any matter touching the King's person, government or regality should be held a traitor. It is significant also that it was in Richard's reign that the term 'high treason' came into use for the first time (36, ii, 69; 161, pp.114, 137, 229). Actions such as these left Richard politically isolated in the face of the rebellion of his cousin Henry of Lancaster. In Henry VI's case, his political ineptitude was manifest long before his deposition, even indeed before his first attack of insanity posed further problems for the government of the realm (Ch.22).

Indeed, despite the instability of the monarchy at this period, it is striking how reluctant the nobility were to overthrow the King. It took a great deal of misgovernment before they would venture on so drastic a step. During the minorities of both Richard II and Henry VI, and while the latter was insane, their titles were not challenged, and the great men of the realm took steps to ensure that government would be properly conducted. No adult king was deprived of his title except as a last resort. when he had lost so much support that a rival could win the realm by force. Edward IV's temporary loss of the throne in 1470 and the overthrow of Richard III in 1485, some two years after his usurpation, both occurred when a substantial proportion of the nobility had been alienated from the Crown.

In the legal thought of the thirteenth and fourteenth centuries there was what was called a doctrine of royal capacities, whereby a distinction was drawn between the King as a person and the King as a ruler. It was to the latter that baronial loyalty was due, and it was regarded as lawful to take action against a king who failed to fulfil his obligations. Although there are still traces of this concept in fifteenth-century writings, these tended to be few, and royal authority was held to be indistinguishable from the person of the King (161, pp.98–9). A clear sign of this is to be found in the changing attitude to the offence called 'accroachment' (or usurpation) of the royal power. Numerous cases of this occurred in the early fourteenth century, but in 1388 the magnates, in revolt against Richard II and the court faction, charged the King's favourites with this crime, and the lords in Parliament declared that this was treasonable. Now there is no doubt that the accused had been acting in accordance with the King's wishes, so their actions could be regarded as treason only if the Crown were held to be distinct from the person of the King (161, pp.62–74, 96). In 1397 Richard had these sentences reversed, thereby implicitly denying that such actions could be treasonable, and it is significant that accroachment declined as a charge during the fifteenth century, not only against royal favourites but generally. The charge of compassing the King's death became more normal in prosecutions initiated by the Crown, and in the most noteworthy magnate attack on a royal favourite. that against Suffolk in 1450, the term 'accroachment' did not appear (161, pp.96–8). The civil wars of the late fifteenth century, and the alternation of tenure of the throne between Lancastrian and Yorkist kings did serve to restore the doctrine of capacities in certain circumstances: in Edward IV's reign a legal suit was brought by a man who had obtained letters of denization from Henry VI, and the question was raised whether the denization were lawful, because if it were not, the plaintiff would have no title to sue. The judges upheld the validity of the letters, and therefore that there was a possible distinction between a king *de facto* and a king *de iure* (161, pp.99–100). This must, however, be seen more as a means of solving a technical issue in the administration of the law rather than as a pronouncement on the nature of the royal title.

The possiblity of a genuine conflict of allegiance, as between 'right' and 'possession' was indeed a major problem, and one which contributed to the instability of the monarchy, because the law of succession was itself unclear. Since the accession of Henry III in 1216, the Crown had passed without dispute by male primogeniture, because there had always been a male heir of the direct line. In the twelfth century the accession of Henry II had represented the principle that a right to the Crown could be transmitted by a woman, and that of John had shown that a direct heir could be set aside. When Edward III laid claim to the French throne, this presupposed a belief in the right of a claim being transmitted through the female line, against the Valois assertion of the validity of claims through the male line only. But there is no doubt that there was in the fourteenth century a general tendency to stress the rights of male descent; not only were the French succession disputes of 1316 and 1328 settled in favour of the male heir, but in 1373 an attempt at defining the Scottish succession by the first of the Stewart kings had pronounced in favour of the male line, despite his own inheritance of it through his mother. (Ultimately, of course, this ruling was disregarded in the succession of Mary in 1542.) Even in England, there was in the fourteenth century a tendency for estates and titles to be entailed in the male line and for the claims of females to be set aside. The problem was not resolved if this procedure was to apply to the Crown as well as to lesser dignities (88, p.273; 138, p.183).

The most articulate of fifteenth-century legal writers on constitutional matters, Chief Justice Fortescue, was originally a Lancastrian partisan, and wrote in defence of the Lancastrian title, but later (after the Yorkist victory) retracted his views and admitted that the estate of the Crown was something too great for him to make any pronouncement on the matter. In this he was repeating the view expressed by himself and the other judges in 1460 when Richard, duke of York, laid claim to the throne and they were required to give their views on this subject (165, pp.22–3). At no stage did any clear legal decision on the succession secure general acquiescence, and the history of the Crown during much of this period shows that it was political power rather than any theoretical right which determined who was to obtain the throne. Successful contenders would seek to buttress their title by formulating claims of greatly varying plausibility.

The long-term problem of the succession may have lain behind some of the tensions of the 1376 Parliament, for although the death of the Black Prince while it was in session left an undoubted heir in his son Richard, the succession after Richard was uncertain. Was the next heir, Edward III's third son, John of Gaunt, the leader of the court faction, or the daughter of his late second son, Lionel of Clarence, Philippa, wife of Edmund Mortimer, earl of March, who was the leading magnate opposed to the court? [B.1] Parliament's recognition of Richard as his grandfather's heir may reflect suspicion that Gaunt already had designs on the throne, although his moderate actions on Edward III's death, when he did not even claim a formal standing as first among the young King's councillors, suggests that popular hostility to him, on this point at least, was unjustified. When Richard became king, it was presumably hoped that the succession problem would be resolved when he married and had an heir, but when his marriage remained child-less, the issue became more acute. One chronicle source suggests that the young earl of March, who succeeded his father in 1381, was formally recognized as heir; there is no official record surviving to support this, but although it is true that the writer shows considerable confusion at this point in his work (198, iii, 396 n.l), he may be reflecting popular gossip on the succession question. Seven years younger than Richard, March was too young to be politically important until the 1390s, and then it was largely in Ireland where he had lands that he was most active, being left as Lieutenant after Richard's expedition in 1395. When he was killed in 1398, his son was only six, so it may well have been his premature death which brought about a Lancastrian rather than a Mortimer succession in 1399. In the late 1390s Richard does not appear to have been particularly concerned about who was to follow him – as he was only thirty-two at the time of his dep-osition, he was perhaps hoping to live long enough to have an heir by his second wife, even although she was still only a child. His jealousy towards March, who had been popularly welcomed at the Shrewsbury Parliament in January 1398, and March's dismissal from the Irish lieutenancy later in the year before the news of his death reached England, may reflect a feeling that the man with the strongest reversionary title to the throne was a potential focus of discontent (150, pp.206–7).

In 1399 Henry of Lancaster had little option but to remove Richard from the throne, as the latter's revenge in 1397 against the Appellants, his opponents of a decade earlier, had shown that he had a long memory for grievances (Ch.18). But while many of the magnates might countenance a deposition and indeed might be relieved at it, it was less certain that they would acquiesce in a usurpation by Henry. The Percies, his most powerful allies in the North, must have been more sympathetic to a Mortimer claim, as the earl of Northumberland's son Hot-spur was married to a sister of the late earl of March. One may wonder if their support for the deposition may have been prompted by the hope that the young earl might succeed. The whole course of events in 1399 shows that the title to the throne was uncertain; undoubtedly Henry concealed his aims from friend and foe alike until he could build up his military strength and play on popular favour. Chief Justice Thirnyng opposed any claim to the throne based on conquest, and a committee of Parliament rejected as false the story that he was lawful heir by descent from Henry III through Edmund Crouchback, allegedly superseded by his brother Edward I. Henry's attempt to employ such a cock-and-bull story illus-trates the weakness of his hereditary claim, and might indeed suggest that he recognized the superiority of a Mortimer title, because he made no attempt to assert his undoubted status as the heir male of Edward III. After Richard's abdication, Henry claimed the throne 'challenging this realm of England', in vir-tue of his descent from Henry III and through God's grace, which had helped him to recover it, when it was suffering from 'default of governance and undoing of the good laws' (135, pp.52–4). The word 'challenge' is important, because it implies that Henry was putting forward a claim, which rested on the idea of the judgement of God in battle, and was not basing his title on any form of parliamentary election, which could impose conditions on him. The most marked characteristic of the claim was the vagueness of the terms in which it was expressed; it hinted at hereditary right, but was not explicit, and at divine intervention. In practice his title could not have been parliamentary, because the assembly in which he put forward his claim had no certain legal status and was not technically a parliament.

Having secured the throne by a mixture of military force and political chicanery, Henry was, however, prepared to use Parliament to consolidate his family's hold. There is record of an oath in 1404 to observe the rights of Henry's sons and the heirs of their bodies to succeed, in June 1406 a measure was agreed to exclude females from the succession, but in December of the same year, this was supplanted by a statute which entailed the Crown upon Henry's sons and the heirs of their bodies, both male and female. These measures, taken together, display continued uncertainty about the rights of women to transmit a claim to the throne (which would have justified the Mortimer claim), and doubts in theory, if not in practice, about the Lancastrian line's title. The mode of the enactment, which bore a closer resemblance to a conveyance of property than to the approval of a statute, suggests that Henry IV was unwilling to allow Parliament any claim that it could assert authority in determining the succession (165, pp.24–5). This is not surprising; any such claim would almost certainly have been regarded as extremely dubious by contemporaries.

When these measures were approved, people must have felt that most possible contingencies for the succession had been covered. The King's four living sons were aged between nineteen and sixteen, and indeed all survived to manhood. But the fecundity of the father was matched by the sterility of the sons, of whom only the eldest, Henry V, left an heir of his own. Henry V's successes in France strengthened his hold on popular support and thereby the strength of the dynasty, but his heir not only proved unsuited to the responsibilities of kingship as he grew to adulthood but also did not have an heir of his own until he had been married for eight years. When his last surviving uncle, Humphrey, duke of Gloucester, died in 1447, the problem became acute. It was a problem of succession, not of the title to the throne, as the rights of Lancaster were not yet questioned, and had not been since the failure of the plot by Richard, earl of Cambridge, in 1415 in favour of his brother-in-law the earl of March. When March died in 1425 without heirs his claim passed to his fourteen-year-old nephew, Richard, duke of York, who also represented a line of descent from Edward III's fourth son, for his uncle Edward, duke of York, had been killed at Agincourt and left no heirs, and no attempt seems to have been made to bar his claim on account of the treason of his father the earl of Cambridge.

By the middle of the fifteenth century, then, York was heir to the claim through the female line and the Mortimers, and male heir of Edward III's fourth son. But before his claim to be next heir could be admitted, two further problems needed to be solved. Firstly, the measure of 1406 had entailed the Crown on the heirs general of Henry IV's sons, but did not say whether in default of such heirs a claim might pass to descendants of John of Gaunt's daughters. Secondly, there was the problem of whether the descendants of Gaunt's third marriage were legitimate or not. By his first marriage Gaunt had two daughters who left heirs, the lines being represented respectively by the kings of Portugal and the dukes of Exeter. The daughter of his second marriage was ancestress of the fifteenth-century kings of Castile. Neither of the foreign lines seems to have been contemplated as a possible source from which a successor could be found, presumably because they were not present to assert any claim. Nor is there any sign that Henry, duke of Exeter, tried to secure recognition as heir, although he may perhaps have suggested during Henry VI's incapacity in the 1450s that he had a better claim to be Protector than had the duke of York (120).

The second problem was more complex. Gaunt's third wife, Katherine Swynford, had been his mistress before they had been able to marry, and their children, the Beauforts, had been born before the marriage. In 1396 the marriage had been confirmed by papal bull, and in 1397 Richard II had granted letters patent legitimating the issue of it (106, pp.391–2). When Henry IV confirmed the legitimation ten years later he added a clause, *excepta dignitate regali*, excluding them from the throne. At this time any prospect of a Beaufort succession was remote, so the limitation probably created little concern at the time, but there might have been doubts about its legal validity when there had been no such restriction in the original grant. Also, if one king could impose limitations, another could remove them. If a Beaufort succession were permissible, it could represent the male line of John of Gaunt, in the persons of John, duke of Somerset (d.1444) and his brother and successor, Edmund (d.1455).

Even after the death of Humphrey of Gloucester in 1447, York was slow to put forward a formal claim, and it was not perhaps quite certain, although this has been suggested (112, p.35), that he was regarded as heir presumptive. His standing certainly led him to be regarded as a possible leader of opposition to the unpopular faction at court, and when he marched on London in August 1450 he did not assert that he was heir. There are some pointers to a Beaufort claim being contemplated: Henry VI's chief adviser until 1450, the duke of Suffolk, was accused of trying to marry his son to the Beaufort heiress Margaret and claiming that she was next heiress to the throne (33, v, 277), and although there is no evidence that this charge was justified, it may reflect manoeuvres by the Beaufort faction at court. The appointment of the Beaufort Somerset as Constable to oppose York's march on London in August 1450 may have had dynastic implications, and, more significantly, when a petition was presented in Parliament in 1451 by Thomas Young, MP for Bristol, that York should be recognized as heir to the throne, the court party under Somerset's influence had him sent to the Tower. This is all the more important when one remembers that the petition did not question Henry VI's title, and merely sought recognition of York's right to succeed.

Only at the end of the following decade, one of fierce factionalism and sporadic fighting, did York go the whole way and advance a claim to the throne. This action can hardly be attributed to frustrated ambition for kingship; had this been the motive one might have expected him to act after the birth of Henry VI's son in October 1453 had removed the possibility of a peaceful inheritance of the Crown. More probably, he was acting in the hope of protecting himself after having been at grave risk in the Lancastrian triumph of the previous year, 1459. In the autumn of 1460 York was militarily in control and had the King in his custody, and he may well have thought that only drastic measures, comparable to Henry IV's in 1399, were possible (Ch.23). But the significance of the events of 1460 lay less in York's action than in the popular reaction. Even his own allies failed to support him, an indication of how the prescriptive rights of Lancaster were recognized. The resulting compromise lacked logic, but was expedient politically and militarily: Henry's title was confirmed, and York was recognized as successor, to the exclusion of the young prince. Few episodes show more clearly than this 1460 agreement that England had no precise succession law.

York had claimed the throne in virtue of descent from Edward III, and his son's title was similarly grounded. He may also, however, have believed that his title could be confirmed by military victory. Edward IV separated the ceremony of taking possession of the Crown from his coronation, which took place only after his victory at Towton, and ten years later, in his campaign to recover the throne, he affirmed in a proclamation that God's will was ascertainable in a trial by battle. In practice, the Yorkist title rested on the capacity of the kings to maintain their position, and the fact that the dynasty held the throne for only twenty-five years meant that it never really secured a measure of prescriptive justification. The deposition of Edward V was a political rather than a constitutional act, although Richard of Gloucester's methods in justifying his title suggest that he, too, was basing his claim on inheritance as the lawful heir. Richard formally claimed the throne by consanguinity, inheritance, lawful election, consecration and coronation, trying to debar his nephews on the grounds of bastardy and affirming that he himself was the lawful Yorkist claimant (165, p.32).

The less surely a title could rest on descent, the more ambiguous were the terms in which it was justified. This was true of Richard III; it was equally apparent after Henry Tudor's victory at Bosworth in 1485. No attempt was made to examine any theoretical questions of legitimacy of title or of popular election; it was merely enacted that the inheritance of the Crown rested in Henry VII 'our now sovereigne lord king' and the heirs of his body (165, pp.32–3). Henry claimed, in an address to the Commons, that he came to the throne by just hereditary title and by the judgement of God in battle. His marriage to the eldest daughter of Edward IV united Yorkist claims with his own, but he had already secured recognition of his own title, which in no way depended on the rights of his wife. The attainders of Henry's enemies after Bosworth assumed the legality of his title (110, p.63). It was once thought that an Act of 1495 distinguished between a king *de jure* and a king *de facto*, but in fact this had rather more limited scope, and was concerned with reassuring old Yorkists who had fought against Henry before 1485 that they would not be liable to charges of treason if they remained loyal to him at the time of the Act, when he was being threatened by a pretender (110, p.178).

When Henry's title was declared in 1485, one element was left uncertain, with momentous consequences. It was not stated whether the heirs of his body, to whom the succession pertained, were the heirs male or the heirs general. As he had only one surviving son, no difficulties arose in 1509 when Henry VIII became the first King for eighty-seven years to secure and hold the succession peacefully. The succession to him, however, was a fragile matter, resting for long in the sole person of the Princess Mary. As England had never had a queen regnant, this raised a genuine political problem, which should not be forgotten among the complexities of 'the King's great matter' and the consequent ecclesiastical revolution. Kinship to the reigning house and descent from Edward III played a part in bringing at least two magnates to the scaffold in the earlier part of the reign, the earl of Suffolk in 1513 and the duke of Buckingham in 1521. By 1530 a clear legal position on the subject of rightful succession to the English throne had still to be established. Henry VIII himself ultimately laid down the succession to himself by will, without establishing any binding and perpetual law on the subject.

With an unclear law of succession, there were often problems of defining the nature of treason. A statute of 1352 had limited the offence to certain precise crimes, in far less arbitrary terms than had applied earlier in the century (161, pp.87–9). Although Richard had tried to intensify the treason law, his deposition was followed by a reversion to earlier practice, with limitations being imposed on the rights of the Court of Chivalry to hear appeals of treason (161, p.145). The scope of the 1352 Act could be extended by its legal interpretation, the process called judicial construction, and there had been some debate as to whether it was held that words alone could constitute treason. Although Bellamy argues that they could, it is not clear that, in the cases cited to support his view, treasonable words were unaccompanied by actions, and the discovery of new material relating to one of these, Thomas Kerver's case in 1444, shows that the crucial article in his indictment included incitement to compass the King's death (161, pp.116–19).[1] Constructive treason did, however, give the Crown an excuse for quasi-judicial action, and one which could be abused for political ends, most notably in the actions taken by the young Henry VIII against his father's trusted, and highly unpopular, ministers Empson and Dudley in 1509–10. The Crown had a further power in the development of the procedure of attainder, which became increasingly employed in the first half of the fifteenth century, and was a fully tempered weapon by the Yorkist period (161, pp.177–205). This involved a declaration of guilt by a bill in Parliament rather than a trial. Under certain circumstances, too, when men were openly in revolt against the King, the Court of Chivalry still had jurisdiction over and above the scope of the common law, jurisdiction which enabled summary trials to be held and fierce penalties inflicted. Such were the measures taken by Edward IV's Constable, John Tiptoft, earl of Worcester, whose ferocity shocked even his contemporaries (179). These methods of supplementing the Statute of Treasons seem to have proved adequate for the Crown until the later years of Henry VIII and the breach with Rome, when there was further and savage statutory strengthening of the law.

One further problem connected with the Crown was who should have the right to exercise royal powers when the King could not do so in person, as in the periods of royal minority or insanity. In a minority, much depended on the age of the King: a boy could at least perform certain ceremonial duties, such as opening Parliament, but an infant could not. When Richard II succeeded at the age of ten, no regent was appointed, but regency powers were vested in a council, in a way similar to the actions followed after the deposition of Edward II. Richard's minority was assumed rather than formally declared, and this left some uncertainty as to when he was of age – he did not secure formal recognition of his majority until 1389, although he had been personally involved in politics at an earlier date (Ch.17). Henry VI was too young in 1422 to perform even formal royal acts, and this may have contributed to the creation of the office of Protector (195). The deathbed dispositions of Henry V, which provided for the older of his surviving brothers, the duke of Bedford, to control his son's interests in France, and the younger, Humphrey, duke of Gloucester, those in England, were fundamentally unsatisfactory, because although Humphrey's powers depended primarily on his being the child King's closest relative in England, there was always the possibility of Bedford returning there and resenting his brother's dominance. Humphrey sought powers comparable to those which had been held by William Marshal in 1216, although he was willing to waive any claim to guardianship of the King's person. (195)

The idea that the protectorship should be held by the nearest available kin, while applicable in a minority when the next of kin was an adult, could not apply during the incapacity of a king whose heir was a minor, as in 1454. It is worth noting, however, that when a protectorship was granted to the duke of York (an action which may suggest that he was regarded as next in line to the throne after the prince of Wales), a proviso was made that when the latter reached the age of discretion, he could if he wished assume power. In 1483, the powers granted to Richard of Gloucester before his usurpation included both the protectorship of the realm and the guardianship of the King's person (195). The precise formal basis for these powers is doubtful – some attention may have been paid to Edward IV's will, but as this has not survived, this can be only conjecture. In practice, however, there is no doubt that Richard secured his powers by force and used any legal claims only after the event. Although there seem to have been certain assumptions about who could be chosen Protector, in the last resort it was necessary for the individual claiming the office to have sufficient political support from the great men of the realm. In this, the protectorship resembled the monarchy itself.

---

1. This evidence was published by C. A. F. Meekings, 'Thomas Kerver's case, 1444', in *EHR*, **90** (1975), 338, 342.

CHAPTER 12

The nobility

English politics in the late Middle Ages were magnate politics, the activity of those great men whose power rested on their territorial possessions and family connections. Their influence was reflected in their summons as individuals to Parliament. Wealth and kinship to the Crown and other great magnates were not new factors in society; they had been the foundation of noble power throughout the Middle Ages, but the differentiation of a parliamentary peerage from the rest of society was new, and one of the most significant developments of the period. Indeed it was to affect the structure of English, and subsequently British, politics for half a millenium.

Who were the nobility? By the sixteenth century one can distinguish a select group, often closely related, not more than sixty in number, who were markedly more powerful than other, lesser men. This was very different from the society of around 1300, when the basic social distinction was not between noble and non-noble, but between those who were and those who were not entitled to bear arms, and the armigerous class contained about 3,000 men. There was a higher nobility, comprising a small group of earls, but it had much in common with the men who held lands by knight service. During the next two centuries, the structure of the armigerous class became more hierarchically defined, and by 1500 one can separate the nobles from a class of knights, esquires and gentlemen. The role of the latter will be considered in Chapter 13 (88, pp.6–7, 268–9).

These groups were not sharply separated. Families became extinct in the male line, and titles might die out or be re-created in collateral branches. As McFarlane said, 'the higher ranks of the nobility rarely deserve the epithet "old" ' (88, p.143). Despite the large size of some families, it was often natural failure of a line which led to extinction, though in periods of civil war political miscalculations might lead to executions which could eliminate either senior or cadet branches. If one takes the group who made up what may be called the parliamentary peerage, which emerged as a distinct group, some 135 strong, about the end of the thirteenth century, one sees that in every period of a quarter of a century between 1300 and 1500, approximately one-quarter of the families existing at the beginning of the twenty-five years failed to survive to the end. On the whole, fewer new families were raised into the group over the years, so the overall size of the peerage shrank markedly by the Tudor period. Nevertheless, it should be stressed that the percentage rate of extinction remained remarkably constant, even as the group became smaller, and the years of the most bitter struggles between Lancaster and York, in the quarter-century 1450–75, actually saw an extinction rate below the average for the two centuries as a whole (25.26 per cent as against an average of 27.17 per cent) (88, pp.172–6). When one bears these facts in mind, the famous and eloquent peroration of Chief Justice Crew, delivering the judges' opinion in the disputed claim to the earldom of Oxford in 1626, may be seen in perspective: 'For where is Bohun? where's Mowbray? where's Mortimer? nay, which is more, and most of all, where is Plantagenet? They are intombed in the urns and sepulchres of mortality.' (46, x, 256 (e))

The literal answers to Crew's rhetorical questions provide a commentary on the extinction of noble families. The last Bohun earl of Hereford died in 1373, his elder co-heiress marrying the youngest son of Edward III, Thomas, later duke of Gloucester, and the younger the future Henry IV. The last Mowbray duke of Norfolk died in 1476, and his daughter Anne in 1481, and the title passed to the collateral line of the Howards through the female line. Edward IV, in fact, tried to secure the inheritance for his second son, Richard, who married the heiress in 1478, when he was four and she was five. Her death three years later, followed by his presumed murder in 1483, meant that the Mowbray title did not pass to the royal house. The last Mortimer earl of March, Edmund, died in 1425, and the title and lands passed to his nephew, another royal cadet, Richard, duke of York. Finally, the last Plantagenet of the direct male line of Henry II, Edward, earl of Warwick, died on the scaffold in 1499 (46).

Two further examples of families where the male line died out may be noted, the Montagu earls of Salisbury and the Beauchamp earls of Warwick, in 1428 and 1446 respectively. In both cases the heiress married a member of the Neville family; indeed these two marriages were largely responsible for the dominant role of that family in English politics of the mid fifteenth century (46) [B.2]. All these families could claim respectable antiquity. The Bohuns had been earls of Hereford since 1200, and the Beauchamps had held the Warwick title since 1268. The earldoms (or dukedoms) of the Montagus, Mortimers and Mowbrays were of fourteenth-century date, although the families are recorded among the landed aristocracy earlier, the Mortimers as far back as Domesday Book, and all three of them had received individual writs of summons to Parliament before 1300 (46).

Parliament played a key part in the differentiation of a peerage. As it developed, the kings summoned individual great men as they wished on particular occasions. By about 1350, men who had once been summoned increasingly came to successive Parliaments, and were followed by their heirs, although it is clear many families which had been represented in this way in the first half of the fourteenth century later dropped out of a more limited group of peers. One may contrast McFarlane's estimate that in 1375 there were 126 families which had at some stage received an individual writ of summons with the fact that only 39 such writs were actually issued for the Parliament of 1373 (88, p.175; 188, p.371). It was even still uncertain if a man was noble or not; in 1383 Sir Thomas Camoys was elected knight of the shire for Surrey, and also received an individual writ of summons. (150, p.28).

In what came to be known as 'immemorial' baronies, it seems to have been assumed that they were created by the writ of summons, and that the dignity was tied to the lands held by the person summoned. This is shown by a case in 1497, when Sir Robert Willoughby challenged the right of Richard Neville to hold the title of Lord Latimer. Willoughby was descended in the female line from the original holders of the title, Neville from George, son of the first earl of West-morland, and his second wife. George Neville had acquired the title of Lord Latimer, and the family estates, through his first marriage, which had been child-less, but the Latimer title and lands had still remained with him and his descendants. In the discussions of 1497, however, George Neville's title was regarded not as inherited, but as having been newly created for him. The eventual compromise, which affected both lands and title, saw Willoughby renouncing his claim to the latter in return for a marriage agreement between the children of the contenders by which part of the old Latimer inheritance was restored to his family (130, p.97; 188, pp.537–8, 583–92).

The King could still promote new men into the peerage, notably his close serv-ants. In 1387, for the first time, a title was created by letters patent rather than by writ of summons, to the elderly Steward of the Household, Sir John Beau-champ. He never actually sat in Parliament, because at its next meeting, the so-called 'Merciless Parliament', he was impeached and executed. In the fifteenth century, however, creation by letters patent became the normal method of cre-ating peers (46, ii, 45–6). This had important implications: nobility was being regarded as something which flowed from a royal grant, as a result of a definite act, rather than as something which was implicit in a man's territorial power, although the summons of George Neville as Lord Latimer in 1432 shows that the territorial interpretation of nobility still survived. Although most nobles were of higher economic standing than knights, there was some overlap in their levels of wealth, but it was blood which was regarded as the factor which determined a man's status. The King had the power to enoble blood, and service to the Crown was itself sufficient to raise a man's precedence – a king's messenger had in virtue of his office the right to rank one degree above his own social level. This pre-rogative of the Crown gave it a useful means of patronage, both to reward its followers and to strengthen its influence in Parliament (15, pp.190–1; 88, p.7).

A further form of royal patronage consisted of promotion within the peerage. This idea would have been virtually incomprehensible in 1300, when only the small class of earls could be differentiated from the rest of the nobility. The title of duke first appeared in 1337, when the Black Prince was made duke of Corn-wall, but it was not granted outside the immediate royal family until Richard II's reign. Possibly it was felt that the title should be limited to close royal kin: a mid-fifteenth-century courtesy book by a servant of Humphrey, duke of Gloucester, seems to assume in its statement of precedence that a duke would be of blood royal. One early-sixteenth-century writer echoes this view, but another of 1513 does not make this assumption (15, pp.186, 284, 381). The hostility to Robert de Vere, created duke of Ireland in 1386, and to the five men on whom Richard II conferred the rank in 1397, and who were contemptuously known as 'duketti', may reflect this attitude, for although all of them could claim some royal descent, it was sometimes remote (188, pp.397–8, 418–19). Two other new titles also appeared in this period, although neither became common: that of marquess was granted to de Vere by Richard II, before he became a duke, and that of viscount was first conferred in 1440. Even as late as the mid fifteenth century, however, a writer could regard a marquess as co-equal in precedence with an earl, suggesting thereby he did not think of it as a separate grade (15, p.186).

Even within individual grades of the peerage, men strove for precedence. In 1444, Henry Beauchamp, earl of Warwick, was granted the style of premier earl of England (at the age of nineteen), with precedence after dukes and marquesses and before all other earls, and the right to wear a coronet in the King's presence. A year later he was made a duke, with precedence between two existing dukes, Norfolk and Buckingham (188, pp.473–4). No material benefits were conferred by these grants; it was the status itself which was regarded as important.

A consciousness of status and a desire for exclusiveness led to criticism of kings who were too free with grants of titles. We have seen the use of the contemptuous term 'duketti' in 1397, and it is worth noting that the first two Lancastrian kings were restrained in creations of peers. Henry VI's minority saw individual writs of summons being given particularly to men who served on the Council as knights, and there was an increasing proliferation of new titles between the end of the minority and the King's deposition in 1461 (112, pp.90–5; cf. 188, pp.452–3). Members of the court party also secured promotions, notably the earl of Suffolk, who became in turn a marquess and a duke. This may have contributed to his unpopularity and ultimate impeachment and downfall. The 'new men' in the Yorkist establishment were equally unpopular, the Herberts, Humphrey Stafford of Southwick and above all the Woodvilles, and were the main target of the revolts in the middle of Edward IV's reign. Significantly, after the Lancastrian interlude of 1470–71, Edward was markedly less lavish than before with grants of titles. Henry VII also showed restraint in creating peers: the main honour which he reserved for his closest servants was not a barony but admission to the Order of the Garter (110, pp.139–40; 112, pp.93–4). In his early years Henry VIII revived, for relatives of previous holders, various extinct titles, and later became freer with conferring new ones, but even so, by the time of the Reformation Parliament, the number of peers, not more than sixty, was fairly small (188, pp.551–65).

We have already seen that titles could be separated from the possession of particular lands, something which would have been unthinkable in the strict feudal theory of an earlier age. There were now various legal devices which restricted the rights of heirs, of which the most important were the entail and the use. The former tended to restrict succession to the male heir, when lands were granted in 'tail male', which could either exclude female descendants completely or at least until the extinction of all lineal male descendants of the original grantee (88, pp.70–3). Not all lands held by a family were necessarily held by the same tenures, so there were occasions when a fairly remote collateral heir might have reasonable claims to lands and a title. Uncertainties of succession law gave scope to the unscrupulous, particularly in attempts to convey lands to someone with a shaky title, as we saw with Edward IV's attempts to secure the duchy of Norfolk for his second son. Indeed the strong support which the collateral heir, John Howard, gave to Richard III during his usurpation was probably due to his hope, which was justified, that he could thereby secure his lawful title to the duchy.

The use was even more drastic than the entail. A man could, during his lifetime, enfeoff a group of friends, his feoffees, with all or parts of his land to hold these to his own use while he lived, and then to dispose of them in accordance with his last will. Technically the feoffees owned the lands, and the user, or *cestui que use* as he was known in law French, was a tenant. This meant that when he died the lands were not subject to feudal laws of inheritance nor liable to the payments due to the King on succession. In practice, this gave the user freedom to devise his lands at the expense of the next heir. A whole new corpus of land law developed to meet the needs of this system, notably to protect the *cestui que use* against default by his feoffees. Where the common law courts were inadequate, the equitable jurisdiction of chancery provided a remedy, and by the 1450s, some 90 per cent of the cases heard by the Chancellor were concerned with uses. (159)

The development of this system reflected royal weakness, for the King was the only landowner who could not exploit it. For the great nobility it was a two-edged weapon, for although they could employ uses to secure freedom to devise lands and to avoid payment of dues to the King, their own tenants could do the same to them. But these under-tenants were also part of the political nation, and it was community of interest between them and the magnates which enabled the propertied classes as a whole to have their way at royal expense. Whatever were the theoretical powers of kings in the fifteenth century, (and historians have long rightly abandoned the idea that they were in any sense constitutional rulers), their practical authority rested on the goodwill of landed society. If they lost that, it was the first step towards losing the Crown. In 1483, a very limited attempt to control uses, in the duchy of Lancaster alone, was modified in Parliament, and even this was repealed by Richard III in the following year. When Henry VII tried to legislate against uses, the measure applied only to cases where the *cestui que use* died intestate, a fact which itself represented a recognition that he had a right to devise lands by will (57, pp.238–48). Although the Crown could still secure the wardship and marriage of an heir, even if all the lands were enfeoffed to uses, it lacked the opportunity to exploit the lands. In practice Henry VII and Henry VIII, for more than half his reign, had tacitly to accept the system. The attack on uses was renewed only with the Reformation Parliament, and even then the first attempt at legislation, in 1532, was unsuccessful. In 1536, however, the Statute of Uses abolished the fictitious distinction between possession and ownership, and laid the rights and obligations of the latter on the *cestui que use* (57, pp.267–88). The measure was unpopular, and in the Pilgrimage of Grace demands were made for its abolition. Four years later Henry VIII, for all his power, conceded, in the Statute of Wills, substantial freedom to landowners to devise their property.

Uses enabled a man to convey lands to younger sons at the expense of the elder, to sons of a second marriage at the expense of those of the first, and they were liable to lead to the disinheritance of heiresses (88, pp.71–2). Indeed at one time, the system of inheritance by primogeniture seemed in danger. An oldest son's strongest ally, however, turned out to be his father-in-law. While the latter might not wish to endow his daughter with a large part of his lands, he would want a guarantee that her husband had sufficient resources. If the marriage was intended to cement a political alliance between two families, in fact the father of the bride might have to guarantee a substantial marriage portion if her husband-to-be was of any importance (88, p.81). In such arrangements, younger sons never were regarded as so desirable as the oldest.

Even an oldest or an only son might find his inheritance encumbered by obligations. Traditionally, a widow had the right to dower, normally a third of her late husband's landed property, so an heir might have to concede this to his mother or stepmother. Besides this, on marriage she might have been granted a jointure of all or part of her husband's lands, that is, a joint holding of lands by wife and husband and by the survivor after the death of the first party (88, p.65). This could both deplete the heir's lands and leave the dowager the prey of a fortune-hunter. One notorious case illustrates this. Katherine Neville, daughter of Ralph, first earl of Westmorland, by his second marriage, was probably born about 1400 and was widowed in 1432 by the death of her first husband, John Mowbray, second duke of Norfolk. She outlived her son, the third duke, who died in 1461 (leaving a widow, who lived till 1474), her grandson, the fourth duke, who died in 1476 and her great-granddaughter, who died in 1481. She herself survived until at least 1483, when her robes were ordered for attendance at Richard III's coronation. For most of his tenure of the duchy, then, the fourth duke's lands were charged with two dower payments, and the Duchess Katherine had also had a considerable jointure. The child heiress, Anne Mowbray, also had her estates charged with a double dower, although in fact her mother accepted a diminution of her rights in return for her daughter's marriage to the King's second son (130, pp.111 n.94).

The elder dowager, however, had not persisted in widowhood. First, she married a squire, Thomas Strangeways (posibly for love, as she later had a royal pardon for marrying without licence), and after his death Viscount Beaumont, who was killed in 1460. Finally, in the mid 1460s she married a fourth husband, John Woodville, the twenty-year-old brother of Edward IV's queen, a match which one chronicler (who ungallantly described her as about eighty), characterized as a *maritagium diabolicum* (46, ix, 607–9; 88, pp.11, 153, 180) [B.2]. It is not clear if the marriage was of the dowager's seeking, or if it was a move of the Queen's to provide for her brother, but clearly there was a danger to the Mowbray inheritance if John Woodville secured it; with powerful support at court, he might well hold it against Norfolk when the dowager died. In fact this danger was removed when he was executed in 1469, but Katherine was still able to endow a daughter of her second marriage with lands from her Mowbray jointure (130, p.111 n.96).

Her career and connections in some way caricature the position of the fifteenth-century dowager, but like a good caricature it stresses the marked characteristics. Double dowers were not unusual – the Moleyns estates were reduced by this in 1431 (95) – nor were marriages of eminent dowagers to social inferiors. Henry V's widow married Owain Tudor, their children entered the higher nobility and, after another good marriage, their grandson became King. Edward IV's father-in-law was a mere knight when he married the widow of a royal duke. Nor was it only dowagers whose marriages could raise the standing of their husbands and children. The marriage of Joan of Kent, granddaughter of Edward I, to Sir Thomas Holland gave him the rank of earl in her right, and her subsequent marriage to the Black Prince gave her Holland offspring a prominent place at the court of their half-brother, Richard II, and the family an important role in fifteenth century history, which historians have not perhaps studied as thoroughly as it deserves [B.3].

The classic example of a jointure depleting an inheritance was that of Katherine Neville's mother, Joan Beaufort. She was the second wife of Ralph, earl of Westmorland, and presumably because she was John of Gaunt's daughter, was able to secure a particularly large jointure. Her heirs, therefore, inherited a disproportionate amount of the Neville lands at the expense of the children of the earl's first family. His eldest son predeceased him, and he was succeeded in the title by his grandson, who despite having lands from his mother Elizabeth Holland, co-heiress of the earl of Kent, and from his wife Elizabeth Percy, widow of Lord Clifford, was probably less well endowed with lands as an earl than his grandfather had been as a baron (95; 130, p.98) [B.2, B.3]. Indeed the long-term effect of Joan Beaufort's jointure was to divide the Neville family into opposing factions during the civil war in the middle of the century.

One sees similar exploitation of royal connections by Edward IV's sister Anne, who had been married about 1447 to Henry Holland, duke of Exeter. Despite this marriage, Exeter adhered to Lancaster, was forfeited and went into exile on the Continent. The duchess, however, retained the estates, so her daughter was a major heiress. She was betrothed to a nephew of the earl of Warwick, so when Edward IV's queen bought the marriage for the eldest son of his first marriage, Thomas Grey, it was hardly surprising that Warwick was displeased. After his wife's death without issue, Grey was able to retain some of the Holland lands, but the duchess kept control of her jointure and other estates. She seems to have opposed the restoration of her husband, whom she divorced in 1472 to marry her lover, Thomas St Leger, an esquire of the body to Edward IV, to whom she took her estates. A postscript to this story of the Holland inheritance came in 1483, when Grey, now marquess of Dorset, contracted for a marriage between his son by his second wife and the daughter of St Leger and the duchess. She was declared heiress to the Exeter estates, apart from lands worth 500 marks a year, which were to provide for Dorset's younger brother (130, pp.112, 117, 141; 144, pp.93–4, 336–37) [B.3]. Such chicanery well illustrates how normal rights of inheritance could be set aside by those with influence in the right quarters.

Any study of fifteenth-century noble families shows a spider's web of interrelationships. Most important people were related to each other several times over, but while kinship could bring about alliances it could also cause feuds over disputed inheritances. The Woodville–Grey encroachment on the Holland inheritance, just mentioned, made Ralph, Lord Neville, later third earl of Westmorland, a loyal supporter of Richard III, because his mother was the sister and heiress of the forfeited duke of Exeter. Also, because men might have connections with both sides in a quarrel, they still had to choose which relations to support. John Holland, duke of Exeter, was executed in 1400 for rebelling against his brother-in-law Henry IV in support of his half-brother Richard II but, as we have seen, his grandson Henry, Edward IV's brother-in-law, remained firmly Lancastrian.

Were the fifteenth-century nobles particularly unruly? Can one regard the struggles of Lancaster and York as a fundamental crisis of noble society? The answer to both these questions is almost certainly no; troublesome magnates had been a problem to kings in earlier centuries, and there is no evidence of any basic weakness in the position which the magnates enjoyed in society. It is true that the nobility had to face economic difficulties, in an age when population decline had reduced their rent rolls and raised the wage-bills which they had to pay, but this did little to affect their normal style of life. It is possible that the tendency for the number of noble families to shrink may have enabled some accumulation of estates, which could compensate their owners for reduced returns on individual properties. Until the middle of the fifteenth century, individual magnates were able to exploit the economic advantages of war in France (Ch.8), or obtain offices from the Crown which could supplement landed income. Although the loss of the French lands cut off one source of additional magnate income, it is unlikely that this was the reason for later disorder – many of the feuds were already in existence before 1450. Equally, one may regard the search for patronage from the Crown as a potential cause of tension, manifested very clearly in the bitterness of the attacks launched on royal favourites such as Suffolk in the 1440s, but some magnates seem to have been able to survive without obtaining offices. On the other hand, one should not forget that by the sixteenth century the magnate class was stronger economically, so it is possible that this gave it more incentive to pursue its own interests without seeking so many favours from the King.

If there was a crisis of the nobility, it lay not in internecine struggles but in its relations with the Crown, and it was the weakness of the latter rather than the malevolence of the magnates which must bear the greater share of blame for the breakdown of order. The basic values of the nobility were those of a military class, and nothing is more apparent than the way in which military success could justify a king in the eyes of his subjects. Henry V virtually gave a moral justification to his dynasty in the esteem of the magnates, Henry VI's failures in France did more than anything else to undermine his reputation. The function of the Crown was to lead, and this was what Henry VI manifestly failed to do. Victory in civil war strengthened the respect in which Edward IV was held in the second half of his reign, and while Henry VII did not win admiration by victories, he did not lose it by defeats. Ruthlessness, such as Richard III's, did not pay because it could antagonize the great men of the realm, and the success of the early Tudors rested on the fact that they struck an acceptable balance between firm, even tyrannical rule, and conciliation of the nobility.

CHAPTER 13

Knights, esquires and gentry

In Chapter 12, we saw how the parliamentary peerage emerged in the late Middle Ages from the general range of the armigerous class. It was a social distinction rather than a purely economic one, because although the wealthiest landowners in the country were all peers, there was some overlap in income between the least prosperous of the baronage and the richest members of the non-noble class. It was also possible for a man who was not even of gentle status to be wealthier than one who was, as for example Thomas Spring of Lavenham, whose enterprise in cloth-making made him the richest man in Suffolk in the 1520s (67). A man's degree, however, was determined primarily by his descent; in Russell's *Book of Nurture* of the mid fifteenth century, it was explicitly stated that rank by blood was more important than wealth in deciding a man's status (15, p.191). Important though descent was, economic considerations were not entirely omitted, notably in certain qualifications which were required of men before they could undertake particular responsibilities, or in obligations which were laid on men with a certain income. In 1430 and 1439 men with annual incomes exceeding £40 were enjoined to assume the rank of knight (although there is ample evidence that many did not do so), and in the latter year it was laid down by statute that it was necessary for a man who was appointed a JP to have an annual income of £20. This was merely the lower limit of income at which a man could be appointed; in practice most JPs had incomes well above the minimum (74).

Nor was it only in such matters that wealth was employed as a criterion by which different classes could be distinguished. In 1363 a series of sumptuary statutes laid down the kinds of cloth which different classes were allowed to wear, and within the regulations for both knights and *esquiers & gentils gentz*, the classes were subdivided by income (36, i, 380–1) [E]. These make it clear that while a man's rank did not depend on his income only, special rights could be accorded to wealthier men of any particular degree. Equally, a man might be of gentle blood but poor, with little more than an unwillingness to undertake manual labour to distinguish him from his yeoman neighbours, who might well be richer than he (104, p.238). The sermon commonplace of John Ball's preaching in the Peasants' Revolt, (When Adam dalf . . .), makes it clear that gentility was regarded as being incompatible with such menial toil (Ch.3). It was in their social attitudes that one sees how such men were much closer to the nobility than to the peasantry. They were concerned with preserving and building up the inheritance of their families, and employed the same device of enfeoffment to uses to avoid the financial incidents of feudal tenure. Furthermore, most of them probably regarded their main function in society as fighting, the traditional role of the landed class.

It is not clear to the historian what precisely distinguished the various grades within the armigerous class, and probably contemporaries found these distinctions equally uncertain. At the same time, it is certain that the society of the late Middle Ages was acutely conscious of status, and that a man's degree in society was something which mattered greatly to him. Possibly this may have been a reaction to economic pressures; as a man found his income from land reduced by falling rents, declining prices for produce and the need to pay higher wages, he might well want to stress the one thing which remained unaffected by this, his social standing. The existence of such social gradations gave scope for ambition too, because, as we shall see in a later chapter (Ch.15) this period also saw considerable social mobility.

The grade below that of noble which was most clearly distinguishable was that of knight, because knighthood was attained through a particular ceremony, and in some cases admission to a particular order could be a mark of signal royal favour. Most select was the Garter, but there was also the Bath; knights in these orders were of higher standing than the ordinary knights bachelor. However, even the term 'knight' could be given an extended meaning, for the county representatives in Parliament, the so-called 'knights of the shire', were not necessarily men who had attained the dignity of knighthood. This term was applied to them at least as early as the 1370s. Most knights of the shire, however, would have been eligible for the dignity, and about half of those in the Parliament of 1422, the most fully studied of the period, were not only knights by rank but were also men who had followed the knightly profession of arms (194, p.92).

However, the position could also be held by men of lower rank. Readers of Chaucer will remember the description of the Franklin in the Prologue to the *Canterbury Tales*, a man who in the fifteenth century would probably have been designated by the term 'gentleman':

> At sessions ther was he lord and sire,
> Ful often time he was knight of the shire . . .
> A shereve had he ben and a countour.
> Was no where swiche a worthy vavasour.

As Chaucer was writing for a courtly audience, which would be highly aware of status, he probably took care to ensure that his picture would be credible. One sees that a man who did not even have the status of an esquire, who was a vavassor or under-tenant, was qualified to play a prominent part in local affairs. He could represent his shire in Parliament, be a JP, a sheriff and (probably) the assessor or collector of a tax. As we have seen in the sumptuary Acts of 1363, the term 'gentils gentz' could be used to describe such men, and in the fifteenth century one sees the appearance of the term 'gentleman'. This followed a statute of 1413, which laid down that in all cases concerning personal actions and in indictments which might involve outlawry, the defendant's 'estate degree or mystery' and his place of residence should be specified (36, ii, 171) [E], and some term had to be found for men between the ranks of esquire and yeoman.

A statute of 1444–45 laid down that for a man to be elected as a parliamentary knight of the shire, he had to be a knight, or an esquire or gentleman of the shire qualified to be one. Men of the rank of yeoman and below were excluded (36, ii, 342) [E]. This qualification almost certainly was an annual income of over £40, as this was the level at which men had been commanded to assume the rank. Therefore, one can see that knights of the shire, even if not actually knights, were supposed to be men of at least equivalent standing.

While knights could be clearly distinguished from esquires and gentlemen, the differences between these were less clear cut. Indeed, there does not seem to have been any uniform practice in separating them, because in a series of commissions of 1434, there were wide discrepancies in the numbers described as 'esquire' or as 'gentleman' in different shires, so it is likely that the designations appended to the names may have been somewhat arbitrary. Indeed the same man might be differently described on different occasions (74; 88, pp.6–7). However, when one considers the position of these classes in the social and political structure of the nation, such uncertainties do not greatly matter, because their more important characteristics were those which they had in common, and which indeed they shared with the knights. Positively, they were the families which were entitled to a coat of arms, and negatively, they were not sufficiently important to be summoned individually to Parliament. The first of these associated them with the nobility and distinguished them from classes lower in society, the second differentiated them from the nobility. They were not, however, a closed caste, because they might well intermarry both with the nobility and with the merchant class, and presumably also with wealthy yeoman families (Ch.15).

The possession of arms not only distinguished the classes concerned, but also throws light on their social values, because this indicates that military sentiments and interests were still their main concern. Contemporaries were uncertain whether a man was entitled to assume arms, or if they had to be granted by some authority, and two fifteenth-century writers took opposite views: Nicholas Upton declared that any man could assume arms, provided that they did not infringe on those which had been borne by anyone previously, while Richard Strangways stated that a man could not do so without permission of a herald or pursuivant. The Crown's attitude certainly seemed to favour the latter opinion because in 1417 a writ of Henry V forbade men going on the King's French expedition to bear arms unless they possessed them in the right of their ancestors (29, p.1117). This view presupposes that gentility was something which flowed from a royal grant or from long tradition, and that the structure of classes was dependent on it. Disputed claims to particular arms were heard before the Court of Chivalry, and one of the most famous proceedings there, the dispute between Sir Richard Scrope and Sir Robert Grosvenor between 1385 and 1389, over the right to bear the arms, *azure, a bend or*, shows clearly how well aware men of the noble and gentle class were of their fellows' devices. Scores of witnesses were called to testify, including men of such diverse ranks as John of Gaunt, the King's uncle, and himself claimant to the throne of Castile, and the esquire Geoffrey Chaucer, and gave evidence about the arms which they had seen the litigants bear. The evidence in these proceedings shows that men of these ranks were expected to know about other men's devices, and this reflects how coats of arms were taken to be a guarantee of an individual's social standing. The importance of a man's arms to him is also reflected in the custom, increasingly common from the fourteenth century, of appending heraldic devices to works of art, to testify to the identity of the patron. The whole development of heraldry as a formal system led to the growing importance of the College of Heralds, which was granted corporate status in 1484 (29, p.1135).

Here there was a similarity of interest between the nobility and those immediately below them, but at the same time distinctions between these groups were hardening, even apart from the distinction by writs of summons to Parliament. In 1436, the incomes of the baronial class were differently assessed from those of lesser men. The former were to be examined by the Chancellor and the Treasurer, the latter by commissioners appointed in the various counties. In fact the lists do not correspond strictly to the divisions between the parliamentary peerage and the rest of society, because a number of men with court connections are included on the baronial list. The reason for this was probably administrative convenience, rather than because service close to the King was felt to enhance a man's dignity (74).

These tax returns of 1436 give scope for analysing the social structure of England, although the evidence should be handled with care. Gray's pioneering study of 1934 should be read in conjunction with the critical reassessement by Pugh and Ross in 1953 and with Pugh's later paper of 1972 (74; 95; 112). The main criticisms in the later works are directed at Gray's views on baronial income, and there is less reason to disagree with his general description of society, although one must stress that the categories into which he divides it are arbitrary, and that there was little difference between the poorest members of one group and the wealthiest members of the next. Below a group of some 50 men, who represent the peerage, one sees between a 150 and 200 men, whom Gray calls the greater knights, with annual incomes over £100, who were either knights or eligible for knighthood. The number of men with annual incomes between £40 and £100, and therefore still potentially knights, was four or five times as great, and the class of esquires, taken to represent those with incomes between £20 and £40 per annum, was perhaps some 1,200 strong. Below this level, it is hard to differentiate gentlemen from yeomen, but there may have been between 1,000 and 2,000 in this lowest armigerous category (74). Although the total number with incomes over £20 per annum was smaller than it had been in the time of Edward I, the decline, particularly if one allows for tax evasion, was not particularly great (88, p.268), and may have been proportionately lower than the decline in population over the nation as a whole. On the other hand, the number was not large enough for every community to have a resident lord, and when one turns to the early sixteenth century, one sees that in some shires at any rate only a minority of villages had a 'squire', and control over them had passed into the hands of an absentee great landowner (67).

These men, particularly those whose annual income exceeded £40, who were eligible to sit in Parliament, were prominent in the political nation. The limitation on the right to sit in Parliament, from that of 1444–45, was more important than the earlier statute of 1429–30 which restricted the county franchise to men holding freehold land worth 40s. annually, a restriction which remained until 1832. This level, which brought the franchise into line with the qualification for jury service, could have provided a substantial electorate, extending well into the yeoman class – a generation later Fortescue described £5 as a fair living for a yeoman (194, pp.20, 27). In practice, however, many elections were uncontested, and the great men of the shire arranged the nominations, so the low income required for a man to vote was less generous than might appear. The great men were able to maintain control over the shire with little real difficulty.

Because of the size of the lesser landed class, and variations within it, generalizations about it are of little value. When one can identify members of it as individuals such as various of the Paston and Stonor families, which left sufficient surviving correspondence for the historian to see them as men and women with recognizable traits of character, one cannot assume that their outlooks and attitudes were necessarily typical of the class as a whole, though it is likely that if similar letters written by members of other families had survived – it is reasonable to assume that they were written, because the class appears to have been generally literate – many would have shown similar concerns. What one cannot tell is how far other families were concerned with public affairs in the way that this was the case with the Stonors and the Pastons; both of these families were prominent in politics and government in their respective shires, and were involved in the wars of Lancaster and York, in which the Stonors suffered forfeiture and one of the Pastons imprisonment. But one can also see that involvement in public affairs in a man's county did not necessarily involve him in political embroilments. For example, Richard Danvers, of the manor of Prescote in Oxfordshire, who was first appointed a JP in the shire in December 1453, served on forty-one consecutive Commissions of the Peace there until his death over thirty-five years later. He also served as a justice of gaol delivery, and of oyer and terminer, as an assessor of the subsidy and as a commissioner of array. Unless he was identical with a man of the same name who was Controller of the Subsidy in the port of London in 1475, we have no record of his involvement in administration outside his native shire, although he was a feoffee of two estates in neighbouring Northamptonshire (6;7). During some of the most turbulent years in English medieval history, in which other men disappeared from and reappeared on the Commission of the Peace, he never seems to have fallen foul of the faction in power. It would be unlikely that Danvers was unique, but insufficient evidence survives to say what proportion of the lesser landed class remained uninvolved in the wars, or how many members of it were active participants in them.

Danvers, as we have seen, served in local government but appears to have avoided the pitfalls of political involvement. There were other members of the landed class who did not even play a part in the affairs of their shires. Under the early Tudors, it was estimated that about a third of the gentry, most of whom were justices, were responsible for executing Crown commission. On the whole these were the wealthier men, but even a man of substance could, if he wished, play little part in such matters (67). Probably the situation in the fifteenth century was similar, so one may assume that in general the wealthier members of the shire community were the most prominent in local affairs, but that if they so desired they could avoid participation in them.

The men from the knightly and lower landed classes who appear most frequently in the records were those whose interests extended beyond their own counties, and more especially those connected with the court. The most notorious of the agents of Richard II's tyranny, Sir John Bussy, Sir William Bagot and Sir Henry Green, were all drawn from this class, and they were only three of the courtier knights. The close ties which could exist among such men are shown in McFarlane's study of the Lollard knights, all of whom were prominent in Richard II's court and Council, and who had family ties with each other through marriage. They also served as executors of other members of the group (135). Under Henry IV too, there was an inner group among the household knights, who served the King both in Council and in war, and the King seems to have followed his predecessor's example in retaining men in the counties, whose main functions were military rather than administrative. Few of them held political offices such as sheriff or JP, or were Members of Parliament, and this may reflect the reduced political importance of the household at this time (112, pp. 15–19). Less is known of relations between the court and this class under the later Lancastrians, but in Edward IV's reign one again finds such men playing an important part in enforcing royal authority in the localties. Probably a similar situation existed under Henry VI – certainly men with household connections were among the victims of the 1450 revolt (Ch.4). Under Edward IV the household group became increasingly important after the troubles of 1469, and was conspicuously larger in the second half of the reign (89).

One of Edward IV's knights of the body was Sir William Stonor, the survival of whose family papers gives the historian fuller evidence than is normally available for the careers of men of this class. His interests and social connections were wide. When he succeeded to the family estates in 1474, he was still unmarried, although in 1472 he had paid unsuccessful suit to the widowed daughter-in-law of Lord Mountjoy. In 1475 he married the daughter of a London alderman, herself the widow of a mercer's son. She died in 1479, and in the following year he married the widow of a Devonshire squire, whose grandfather had been a rich citizen of Exeter, but within a year this marriage also was broken by death. In these marriages one sees close ties between the wealthier city families and the lesser landed class, and in Stonor's case his first marriage brought him into contact with merchants involved in the wool trade. Trading interests did not prevent him from being drawn into public life; he was a JP from 1478 (7), and in the same year was created a knight of the Bath. Within two years he was made a knight of the body, and this court connection probably lay behind his third marriage in 1481, to a daughter of the higher aristocracy, Anne Neville, a niece of the great earl of Warwick and daughter of John, marquess of Montagu (24, i, xxvi–xxxiii). In material terms the marriage probably meant little, because not only did Anne have brother and sisters, but her father had fallen in revolt against the King, and his heirs had been debarred from the Neville inheritance, although he had not been attainted (130, pp.138–9). The family's comparative poverty is shown by the fact that her brother, who had been made duke of Bedford in anticipation of a marriage between him and the King's daughter, was later deprived of the title because he lacked the means to support the dignity. However, Stonor's social standing was probably enhanced by the marriage. Association with the great drew him into political intrigues, culminating in his participation in the 1483 rising against Richard III. He was forfeited, although he was able to escape to Henry Tudor and recover his estates after 1485 (24, i, xxxv). In this he was more fortunate than a fellow knight of the body, Sir Thomas St Leger, who had married the King's sister, the duchess of Exeter. He too revolted in 1483, but was taken and executed.

The fortunes of such men show that the higher a man rose, the more vulnerable he was. But only a minority of the lesser landed class acquired such prominence. Even when the household was comparatively large, as at the end of Edward IV's reign, only about thirty knights and forty esquires were closely associated with the King, and in the middle of the reign the figures were lower (89). Under Henry IV, during whose reign some 200 men were at some time described as King's knights or esquires, we do not known how many were connected with the court at any particular time (112, p.18). If one accepts, as one probably can, Gray's estimate that in 1436 there were between 2,000 and 3,000 men who were knights or esquires, it is clear that only a very small proportion of them played a significant part in national affairs. If the fifteenth century was similar to the sixteenth, probably only a minority was active, even in local government. Certainly the membership of the Commission of the Peace seems to have been drawn from only a limited proportion of it, and if one looks at the men who served in Parliament, one again has a limited field, not least because there were some regular parliamentarians, who were frequently re-elected, and thereby reduced the opportunities for others to serve there. The only fifteenth-century Parliament which has been studied in depth is that of 1422, in which there were comparatively few novices. Of the knights who were Members in this year, no fewer than sixteen sat on ten or more occasions before or after (194, p.43). The existence of such a nucleus of experienced men could have important political consequences, because it could give them assurance to stand up against the nobility and even the court. In 1376, Sir Thomas Hoo, MP for Bedfordshire, seems to have played a prominent role in stiffening the resistance of the Commons to the court, and in 1406, when the Commons attempted to control the administration of taxation, they clashed with the Lords as well as with the King (88, pp.292–3). Many knights were, of course, in baronial retinues, but this did not prevent them from playing an independent political role, either individually or collectively.

Much must remain conjectural about the general fortunes of this class. In one sense, each member of it was unique, for a man might choose whether or not to assume the rank of knight, to become involved actively in local government, or to enter service at court. Even in economic matters, where the lesser landed class was subject to the pressures of population decline and peasant prosperity, it is likely that different families had varying success in riding out the crisis; this could depend on how far individuals were able to exploit alternative sources of income such as the profits of war or the holding of offices under the Crown or members of the higher nobility. It has been said that the Dissolution of the Monasteries in the 1530s, and the release of the monastic lands on to the market, played a large part in 'the rise of the gentry' in the later sixteenth century, and there is no doubt that this contains an element of truth. But it is worth stressing that even before this date, economic forces may have already begun to work in favour of the gentry; above all, as pressure on available land increased from early in the sixteenth century, landlords were better placed to raise rents, and the result of this may have been that when the monastic lands came on the market they were better placed to take advantage of the fact. The activity of this class in the fifteenth century, however, should make it clear that their role should not be underestimated at that time, even although they had not yet acquired so influential a position as they were later to achieve.

CHAPTER 14

Indentures and retaining

In Chapters 12 and 13 we have examined the social groups within the political nation, but in order to judge their role in the events of the period we must also consider the relationships between classes and between individuals. Traditionally, the late Middle Ages have been regarded as a period of widespread political and social disorder, and the conventional villain of the piece is the 'overmighty subject', who built up a large force of retainers and was able to overshadow even the power of the King. Even some contemporary opinion was of this mind: at the end of a chapter in *The Governance of England*, in which 'he shewith the perellis that mey come to the Kyng by ouer myghtye subgettes', Sir John Fortescue wrote, 'Ther mey no grettir perell growe to a prince, than to haue a subgett equepolent to hymself.' (30, pp.127–30) Yet there is a danger in taking Fortescue's dreary tract as an accurate picture of the society of his day, and one may note that most examples which he cites of kings who suffered at the hands of their subjects were drawn from outside England or from periods other than his own. Admittedly, he may well have chosen these examples in part to avoid giving undue offence, because the political struggles of Lancaster and York created an atmosphere of uncertainty which might have made it dangerous to mention individual magnates by name. Although historians can easily identify such men, of whom the earl of Warwick was the most conspicuous, Fortescue may well have felt that it was safer to let his contemporaries apply the lessons which he had drawn rather than make his point more explicitly. At the same time, one should remember that he did not say that the threat from over-mighty subjects was more serious in his own age and country than it had been at other times and in other places. The principal problem which will be considered in this chapter is whether the bonds of social organization, what is known as bastard feudalism, were particularly conducive to disorder.

In the early Middle Ages, the tenure of land had provided the crucial tie between a lord and his followers, but by the late fourteenth century the traditional obligation of feudal society were weakening, and the power of the great lords was measured not by the number of vassals who held land from them but by the number of retainers who wore their livery and to whom they paid fees. Various factors had contributed to this change. The divisibility of estates particularly among heiresses, could reduce the average value of holdings, and the fact that feudal tenures were heritable left the lord little freedom of choice in attracting followers. The land legislation of Edward I, supplemented by various other measures down to 1327, had made it hard for new feudal tenancies to be created, while the opportunities for alienating land completely were increased (57, pp.79–103). For this reason, lords who wished to reward their followers and secure their allegiance could no longer use the traditional method of granting them land but had to find alternatives, and the most satisfactory means available was to make a payment in cash, to an individual but without any commitment to his heirs. This does not mean that the older feudal obligations disappeared overnight – lands held by feudal tenure were still subject to the old obligations, provided that these were not evaded by devices such as uses. The duchy of Lancaster records of the 1370s show that John of Gaunt took the homage of feudal vassals who inherited lands, and restored these to them when this was done. But Gaunt was also head of a retinue bound to him by indenture in the new way, and his register contains a large number of agreements between him and his retainers (1, i, 56–9, 290–350, ii, 1–7). These bound men to serve him in peace and in war for the duration of their lives, and in return receive annual fees from him. In some cases these payments were charged to the revenues of particular manors, but in others they were presumably made from the general revenues of the duchy.

The fact that the reward was in cash rather than in land is probably a less important change than the fact that the new relationship was not explicitly hereditary. Even earlier, from the twelfth century, there had been cases of lords granting a financial reward, the so-called money fief, but it had been held under similar conditions to fiefs of land, with the normal obligations of feudal land-holding. It might or might not be heritable, and can be regarded as an intermediate stage between the traditional fief and the indenture. The absence of inheritance as an essential element in the indenture system made the bonds of late medieval society far more flexible than those of the earlier period. Even although the contract in the indenture normally stipulated that it should last for life, in practice it was possible for it to be terminated earlier. A lord might withhold the payment of a fee to a retainer who did not fulfil his obligations, and it was far easier for him to do this than it would have been for his ancestor to deprive a vassal of his land. It is clear that many men did break indentures which had been made, although we do not know whether this was done by agreement between the lord and his man or by the unilateral action of one party (85). Also, when a lord died, particularly if his end was violent, his retainers were not necessarily bound to adhere to his heir. A letter of 21 June 1483, telling of political events in London, including the execution of the Lord Chamberlain, William, Lord Hastings, ended with a postscript: 'All the lord Chamberleyne mene be come my lordys of Bokynghame menne.' (24, ii, 161)

Although this terse comment on how a great lord's 'connection' could collapse provides eloquent commentary on how the bonds of society operated, one must not always see loyalty as so fleeting, nor can one totally discount the hereditary element. Hastings himself had risen to prominence through allegiance to the House of York, particularly to Edward IV, who was a personal friend as well as his lord. William's father, Sir Leonard, had been a councillor of Edward's father, Richard, duke of York, and had received an annuity from him. After Sir Leonard's death, William continued to serve the duke, fought for him in 1459 and was attainted by the Lancastrian Parliament at Coventry. He presumably entered Edward's service after the duke's death at Wakefield in 1460 (72, pp.19–20).

'Good lordship' was the principal guarantee of social order in late medieval society, and this had important implications. In times of civil disorder, a man without a lord was vulnerable, unless he could entirely avoid political entanglements. A large band of retainers would enhance a lord's prestige and strengthen him in his dealings with his fellow magnates, but this also meant that if he were aggressively inclined, he could exploit his connection to the detriment of public order. The obligations of an individual to his close associates were liable to be regarded as overriding any that he might have towards the State, if tension developed between the King and his lords. Such tension did occur in our period, although less because of any fundamental divergence in the interests of the kings and the magnates than because a number of the kings were unsuited to the tasks of ruling. It was in such circumstances that the tendency of great men to build up their own power could lead to disaster (88, pp.114, 121).

Attempts were made to limit the potential that magnate retinues had for disorder, notably by controlling the granting of liveries. The repetition of such measures suggests that they often had little effect and that the problem remained persistent, but the form of the statutes shows that distinctions were drawn between various kinds of retaining, although the precise aims of particular measures were not always clear. Effectively, one can distinguish three types of retainer, resident household dependants, men bound by indenture to their lord for life (at least in theory) and those who merely took fees and wore a lord's livery. It was above all the third group which incurred criticism, presumably because it was felt that their adherence to their lord or lords was less stable than that of the other groups. They may indeed have shown more of a tendency to take fees from several masters than other classes of retainer. It was regarded as proper that a great man should have a substantial staff of household servants, and among John of Gaunt's indentures one finds contracts with carpenters and musicians as well as with fighting men (1, i, 346, 1). The acquiescence in life indentures, which might seem as potentially dangerous as the grant of short-term liveries, was probably due to the fact that men bound to their lord in this way could provide a nucleus for the royal army. When the King, who had of course no standing army, contracted with a great man for him to furnish troops for war service, the nucleus of this force would be drawn from the magnate's indentured retinue.

In legislation against the granting of liveries, one can see, from 1390 onwards, a distinction between lawful and unlawful forms of livery, and restrictions both on those who could grant them and on those to whom they could be given. As early as 1305 and again in 1346, there had been ordinances against the retaining of men by granting of liveries and against the maintenance of quarrels (36, i, 145, 304, ii, 3) [E], but the 1390 Act laid down more precise regulations. No one below the rank of banneret was entitled to grant any 'livery of company' to knights and esquires, unless they were life retainers for peace and for war, or unless they were members of the grantor's household. In 1393 it was re-enacted that no yeoman should bear a livery unless he was a household familiar, and the earlier statutes were again renewed in 1397, and on several occasions during Henry IV's reign, although in 1411 some latitude was allowed to the men who might grant liveries: lords, knights and esquires, who were working for the King in war could do so without incurring the penalties provided by statute [E].

Although the earlier statutes were reaffirmed in 1429–30, the Act which is commonly regarded as crucial in setting severe restrictions on retaining is that of 1468, which at one time was considered to have attacked the practice as such. However, the wording of it is ambiguous, and more recent work has suggested that it was less drastic, and that it still recognized that there were circumstances in which a man could be lawfully retained. The bias in favour of the nobility appears to have been preserved, because there are no cases of lords being prosecuted for retaining after the passage of the Act, although there were actions against lesser men. It is also possible that the King exempted his own associates from the provisions of the statute, although as no written licences to retain have survived, such permission might have been only verbal (36, ii, 240–1, 426–9; 88. pp.106–7) [E].

It is, however, unrealistic to concentrate too much on the actual wording of a law, because in the Middle Ages the implementation of a statute could often be arbitrary, with the King reserving powers in it for use against his enemies rather than applying them generally. The purposes of statutes, furthermore, were often political rather than purely administrative, and the 1468 Act may well have had its origins in the particular circumstances of the time rather than in a comprehensive attempt to deal with the long-standing abuses of the indenture system. Two factors may have contributed especially to it. Shortly before it, there had been an outbreak of faction fighting between the Vernon and Grey families in Derbyshire, in which a member of the former family was murdered. This was not a feud which remained local, because various members of the nobility, including those active in the political factions at court, became involved. During the proceedings against the resulting disorder, there were prosecutions of a number of men, including members of the nobility, for retaining contrary to the law. Another possible political reason behind the measure may be suggested by a remark in a nearly contemporary chronicle. The writer described the dismissal of the earl of Warwick's brother from his post as Chancellor, in 1467 (though the chronicler misdates it to 1464), and continues: 'After that the Erle of Warwyke toke to hyme in fee as many knyghtys, squyers, and gentylmenne as he myght, to be stronge; and Kyng Edwarde dide that he myght to feble the Erles powere.' (18, pp.3–4)

The problem of liveried retainers persisted into the early Tudor period. An Act of 1487 declared that the good rule of the realm was being subverted by unlawful maintenance and the giving of liveries, and the great officers of State were authorized to summon and punish offenders (36, ii, 509–10) [E]. In 1504 a further statute was passed, the preamble of which stated that liveries and retainers were still being given and received despite the statutes against them. It laid down that all appropriate statutes were to be put into effect, and penalties of £5 per month for each man who was retained were laid down for breaches of the Act. The justices of the peace were commanded to enquire into unlawful retaining and to certify the names of offenders to the King's Bench, and proceedings could be taken against them there, in the Star Chamber or before the Council. Existing indentures contrary to the Act were declared void, although certain exemptions from it were allowed. The most important one was for men who obtained a special 'placard' from the King and indented to do war service for him, although it was made clear that men retained were not to be employed other than in accordance with the King's wishes. However, the 1504 Act still permitted the retaining of household servants and of men of law; in other words the old distinction between lawful and unlawful retaining was maintained, although the Crown was now, it seems, making a determined effort to restrict the making of contracts with fighting men (36, ii, 658–60) [E].

It was easier to pass laws than to put them into effect, and this was at the heart of the problem of retaining. From the late fourteenth century onwards there were various laws, but there is little evidence that they were implemented. The prosecution of Sir Edmund Ferrers of Chartley in 1414, for giving liveries to men who were not of his household, was an exception to the general neglect of the law of 1390, and even he was pardoned (88, p.107). In 1485–86 Chief Justice Hussey spoke cynically of lords who swore oaths not to retain and then did so (44, p.533). Even under the Tudors, when there was some increase in prosecutions, these were not frequent, although some members of the nobility were now attacked, presumably as a warning to their fellows. In 1494 the earl of Devon bound himself by recognizance not to employ retainers contrary to the law, and in 1506 he made two payments in part discharge of the recognizance, presumably because he had been guilty of a breach of his bond. In 1506 the young earl of Derby pledged himself to pay £1,000 in six instalments in part payment of a fine imposed on an uncle for unlawful retaining, and under the 1504 statute Lord Burgavenny was fined £70,650 for retaining 471 men for 30 months between June 1504 and December 1506. Most cases concerning retaining seem to have been heard in the common law courts – they are recorded in the plea rolls of the King's Bench and the Exchequer. Despite the belief that the Tudors made particular use of special courts, there is little evidence for the enforcement of laws against retaining in the Star Chamber, in the records of which references to 'retainers' occur only incidentally in pleas concerned with rioting (5, pp.cxxi–cxxv; 110, p.215).

The mention of recognizances in the earl of Devon's case reflects the successful methods employed by Henry VII to curb the nobility, and indeed these became increasingly common in the last decade of the reign. By the King's death, approximately three-quarters of the peerage families were either under attainder or liable to some form of financial penalty (130, p.292). In most cases the obligation had nothing to do with retaining, but arose from royal suspicions of disloyalty or from some infringement of the King's rights, but the same method was employed to enforce part of the penalty already mentioned on Lord Burgavenny for retaining. He had to enter into recognizances for the payment of his fine, which was reduced to £5,000, payable in ten annual instalments, presumably because the King was more concerned with obtaining the available money than with enforcing the full rigour of the law (72, pp.104–5).

But although the Tudors succeeded in controlling the practice of retaining, they were no more able than their predecessors to end it, and indeed they may not have been over-anxious to do so, because it had a useful function to fulfil in providing a means for raising an army. The strong line which was taken by Henry

VII may have been due to the absence of foreign wars in his reign, although the survival of a long and verbose licence to retain men (unfortunately undated) shows that once the Crown could control the practice, it was prepared to tolerate it. This was even more true when Henry VIII became again involved in Continental warfare and was faced the necessity of mustering troops. The later career of Lord Burgavenny, who had been fined so severely under Henry VII, shows that he received a pardon from his successor, and served as Chief Captain of the royal army in 1514, with 984 men in his company. Three years later, however, he and various other magnates were threatened with prosecution by Wolsey for granting liveries. In fact, attempts to enforce the law were sporadic, and indeed it would have been inappropriate for Wolsey, who was notorious for the magnificence of his retinue, to prosecute others for this offence (72, pp.105–6, 148–50). What the Crown had succeeded in doing was to establish that if lords were to keep retainers, royal permission was necessary for them to do so; in practice it had had to connive at some degree of retaining if it was to preserve the goodwill of the magnate class.

The legislation against retaining was based on the premise that it could cause social disorder and undermine royal authority. However, although indentured retinues could cause civil disturbance, they did not necessarily do so. Only when royal control was ineffective was the practice of retaining detrimental to good order. At other times the giving or receiving of fees, or of sinecure offices, could establish social ties which made for stability rather than instability. The indentures between Hastings and his retainers all provided that the latters' allegiance to the King had a prior claim over any obligation they had to their lord, and a man who was receiving fees from various lords had some interest in maintaining peace between them. In 1448–49 a substantial Midlands knight, Sir Humphrey Stafford of Grafton, had fees from eight lords amounting to a total of £71 annually, and his son also had a substantial number of patrons (88, pp.108–9).

In times when the King could exercise sufficient authority to prevent magnate power from getting out of hand, the influence of a courtier could be important in strengthening royal power in the local communities. This is clearly seen in the case of the Hastings retinue. He himself had risen as an adherent of the House of York, and grants which he received from various members of the nobility as well as from the King show that he was a man whose goodwill was regarded as worth having (72, p.21; 88, pp.107–8). Although most of his extant indentures date from after Edward IV's recovery of the throne in 1471, in that year he certainly had influence in the Midland shires which was of great value to his master. The official Yorkist chronicler of 1471 wrote: 'At Leycester came to the Kynge ryght-a-fayre felawshipe of folks, to the nombar of iij^M men, well habyled for the wers, such as were veryly to be trusty . . . And, in substaunce, they were suche as were towards the Lorde Hastings, the Kyngs Chambarlayne, . . .' (2, pp.8–9) This excerpt suggests that the area where Hastings exercised effective influence then was, at least in part, the same as that from which he drew many of his retainers in the 1470s – Derbyshire, Leicestershire, where his own main properties lay, Staffordshire and Nottinghamshire, especially the first three of these. His retainers were prominent in local government, serving as sheriffs and justices of the peace, and in some cases as knights of the shire in Parliament – what is less certain is whether they were already among Hastings's adherents when they held these posts, or if he recruited them because of their existing local power (72, pp.28–9, 34–9). In either case, however, he was able to put his influence at the service of his King, and even if his connection was enlarged in the 1470s with his increasing prominence at court, one cannot say whether men were seeking his 'good lordship' for this reason or if he was able to attract them to him because his service was potentially profitable. In the case of a man whose loyalty to the King was unquestioned, there was no incompatibility between his desire for a stronger band of retainers and the King's wish to maintain his authority.

The historian is therefore still left with the question: was the system of indentured retainers socially harmful or socially beneficial? There is no simple answer, because in itself it could be either, and one must remember that there was no obvious alternative to it. It is not, however, coincidental that periods of civil war saw the most vigorous recruiting of retinues, as in 1399 and after 1450 (88, p.103). Yet even at such times it is hard to say whether the indentured retainer was the cause of disorder or merely a symptom of it. Certainly at these times the system of indentures did not create the kind of stability which it provided in more peaceful times, because men who had accepted fees from more than one lord might find themselves faced with a choice of masters. A conspicuous example of this was Henry Vernon in 1471, at the time of Edward IV's return. He received letters, which still survive, from both the duke of Clarence and the earl of Warwick, commanding him to array troops on their behalf and to join their force. Despite the frantic pleas of the latter, written in his own hand, 'Henry I pray you ffayle not now as ever I may do ffor yow', Vernon followed Clarence back into Edward IV's camp (136). Men could foresee such strains on their loyalty, and when entering into indentures might except their duty to other named lords when undertaking obligations to a new one. This was done by Lord Grey of Codnor in 1464, when making an indenture with Lord Hastings; he reserved his ligeance to the King and his duty to the duke of Clarence and Sir Thomas Burgh (72, p.133).

It was normally accepted that duty to the King overrode other obligations, but even loyalty in that quarter might be overridden. In 1460 a Herefordshire esquire, Simon Milburn, bound himself by indenture to Richard, duke of York and to his son Edward, without any reservation of his allegiance (136). In such circumstances, undoubtedly, the system of retaining was a threat to law and order, but this was the case only when problems of divided loyalty arose. It is noteworthy that once royal authority was effectively restored, the retainer ceased to be a social danger.

CHAPTER 15

Social mobility

We have seen in earlier chapters that society in late medieval England was increasingly stratified. Not only did the old division persist between those who fought (essentially the land-owning class) and those who tilled the soil, but within the former, which constituted the politically significant element in society, new lines of distinction were drawn. Most important was the emergence of the peerage from the mass of armigerous families, but within both 'noble' and 'gentle' society the hierarchical principle was carried further. The new ranks of marquess and viscount were established in the peerage, and the consciousness of rank and status in the lower landed class was reflected in the classifications of knights, esquires and gentlemen. However, this social stratification was not rigid; men moved from one grade to another within the landed class, and there were even instances of recruitment into it from outside, although these were less common. It was certainly rare, though not unknown, for a man to rise directly from peasant stock, but urban society provided a common intermediate stage, by providing facilities for accumulating wealth which could then be used to acquire land. Social ambition was the main motive for acquiring land, particularly at a time when the profitability of landed wealth was at best doubtful. In this there was nothing new, and this tendency to move from city to country persisted into later centuries, so it is perhaps misleading to write, as one historian has done, of the late Middle Ages as an 'Age of Ambition'. There is no evidence to suggest that men's attitudes in this period were markedly different from those of earlier or later dates.

The movements of families within the varying ranks of landed society are better documented, and hence far easier to trace, than their origins and entry into it. When one tries to study the early history of families which rose in the world, the trail backwards tends to peter out through lack of evidence (88, pp.9–10). Indeed, in certain circumstances, men might have good reasons for concealing their family's past; a prosperous town merchant, of servile stock, might well wish to suppress his ancestry lest his former lord should try to claim him as a dependant. Again, in cases where a family's origins in the male line are traceable, no information may survive about its marriages in earlier generations, and these may well have brought non-noble blood and, more important, new wealth into it. It is quite possible that even where the name of a landed family remained unchanged, it might number among its ancestors both town dwellers and members of the yeoman class. As peerages died out, the upper division of landed society was replenished from the knights and the gentry, and may even have experienced some infiltration of blood from below this level. The movement of families into the nobility was almost entirely from below – although a few recruits were introduced into it from cadet branches of the royal family, this had little effect on the general composition of the aristocracy, as their lines died out in the male line during the civil wars of the late fifteenth century. In some cases the female line was extinguished too, in others the marriage of princesses with members of the existing aristocracy created closer ties between certain magnates and the court, sometimes rendering them more vulnerable in times of political upheaval [B.1].

Predictably, the rise of a family from obscurity was normally fairly gradual, for it took a generation or two to become fully integrated with the class into which it had risen. Indeed, on the rare occasions when the rise was rapid, a family might have to contend with conservative prejudice against the parvenu. This could apply both to movements of rank within the landed class and in circumstances when an outsider entered it. This will be illustrated later in one or two case histories. Equally, of course, a family's standing might decline, and one cannot always follow the fate of cadet lines of gentry families, nor say if their disappearance was due to the extinction of the line or merely to their failure to leave any impression in the records. In some cases, scions of such families left the country for the towns, presumably hoping to make a fortune, and later generations of such families might return to the land, although others simply disappeared into limbo.

Social mobility is an abstract idea, and to put flesh and blood on to it involves the examination of individual case histories. This method, however, raises problems for the historian, because he can no more identify an 'average family', which typifies the methods of social advancement than he can isolate that statisticians' concept, the 'average man'. Indeed the most easily identified families are those which by very virtue of their success are untypical, most notably the family of the de la Poles, which entered the nobility near the beginning of the period covered in this book and finally disappeared near its end. However, case histories do illustrate how a family's fortune could be changed, and it is hoped that those chosen will throw some light on the broader aspects of the problem.

As has been said, sudden emergence from obscurity to eminence was rare; more often a family rose gradually over a period of a generation or two, if it survived sufficiently long and did not die out from lack of heirs. The most striking rises of fortune on the whole occurred among families which were already in the landed class, rather than among those just entering it. This is understandable, because two of the most common ways of making a sudden gain were chance success in war and the making of a lucky marriage, and for a man to have the opportunity to secure either of these it was virtually essential for him to be a member of the landed class, although not necessarily prominent within it. An exceptionally fortunate beneficiary from a single military success was the Northumberland esquire John Coupland, who captured David II of Scotland at Neville's Cross in 1346. The rewards given to him, an annuity of £500 and the status of banneret, were substantial and gave him a position of eminence in the shire, but his sudden elevation in rank also raised problems. He never became properly established among the great men of the shire, and in 1363 he was murdered by a gang of fellow landowners, who were evidently jealous of his position.

Lucky marriages tended to provide more permanent gains than the windfall profits of war, and some of the most striking examples of rapid social advancement were those of families whose founder had captured the affections of a high-born widow. The rise of the Tudors began with the secret marriage of Owain Tudor to Henry V's widow, although this in itself did not guarantee automatic advancement, because it was some time before Henry VI was prepared to extend favour to his half-brothers or their father. Although he was probably aware of the marriage before his mother's death in 1437, it was not until 1452 that he created his half-brothers earls (110, pp.7, 12), significantly at a time when magnate pressure on the King was making it desirable for him to seek new allies. Even then, the Tudors might have been no more than a prominent magnate family, had it not been for two further occurrences, the failure of the main Lancastrian line and the marriage of Owain's son Edmund to Lady Margaret Beaufort, who ultimately became heiress of Lancastrian claims. The ultimate Tudor acquisition of the throne could hardly have been envisaged at the time when the family first became prominent.

The rise of the Tudors is closely parallelled by that of the Woodvilles, who emerged to prominence from the mass of lesser landed families in royal service. Richard Woodville, who was summoned to Parliament as Lord Rivers in 1449, was the son of the chamberlain to John, duke of Bedford, Henry V's brother. Richard himself was knighted in 1426 at the same time as Richard, duke of York, evidence of his early association with the court circle. In 1433, two years before his death, Bedford had married Jacquetta of Luxembourg, daughter of the great French magnate the count of St Pol, in an unsuccessful attempt to preserve the crumbling alliance between England and Burgundy. On his death, his young widow married Richard Woodville without first seeking royal assent, with the result that the couple had to pay a substantial fine. This did not, however, remove Woodville from prominence: he continued to serve in France, and in the 1440s was associated with the court party. He probably gained some advantage over his contemporaries from his marriage, which provided additional social status, and may help to explain his promotion to the peerage (130, p.105). His loyalty to the Lancastrians until their defeat at Towton was tempered by realism, and he came over to Edward IV, who pardoned both him and his eldest son (also an active Lancastrian). By 1463 he was a member of the royal Council, and this restoration to favour must have seemed in itself a considerable achievement. However, another marriage brought him to even greater prominence, when in 1464 his widowed daughter, Elizabeth, Lady Grey, married Edward IV. Rivers was raised to an earldom, and for the last five years of his life, until he fell victim in 1469 to the jealousy of the earl of Warwick, he was one of the most prominent magnates in the land (144, pp.89, 132).

The rise to prominence of the Tudors and the Woodvilles can be directly attributed to marriage, but in other cases promotion resulted from a combination of this with the unexpected disappearance of the older line of a family. For most of the fifteenth century the line of the Mowbray dukes of Norfolk survived only in a single child in each generation, and it finally expired in the daughter of the fourth duke, Anne, who died aged eight in 1481. Edward IV had attempted to secure the Mowbray lands for his second son Richard by marrying him to Anne, when the children were respectively four and five years old, and even after her death his acquisition of the Mowbray lands was confirmed in the Parliament of

January 1483. This had involved the disinheritance of the next heirs, the descendants of two daughters of the first Mowbray duke, who died in 1399, John Howard and William Berkeley. Howard, from a middling gentry family in Suffolk, had been a loyal and energetic servant of Edward IV in both war and diplomacy, being rewarded with a knighthood in 1461 and a peerage in 1470, but he was probably aggrieved at this treatment – certainly in 1483 he linked his fortunes to those of Richard, duke of Gloucester, and secured the title of duke. After his death at Bosworth, this was forfeited, and his son did not recover it until 1514. Berkeley, who had been granted a viscountcy in 1481 for renouncing his claim to any part of the Mowbray inheritance, was also promoted by Richard III, securing the title of earl of Nottingham in 1483. Unlike Howard, he himself survived the advent of the Tudors and became marquess of Berkeley in 1489 (88, p.155; 144, pp.248, 324; 188, pp.518, 523). The point that should be noted about the advancement of the Howards and the Berkeleys is that it was as fortuitous as it was fortunate, because there was no obvious likelihood of the Mowbray line becoming extinct when their ancestors had married the daughters of the first duke.

Such advancement within the landed class leaves clear traces in the records, because the inheritance of land was a vital concern for the King. Movement into this class is not always so clear, and evidence for the rise of a family is often lacking. On some occasions, indeed, it is confused by the concoction of a bogus pedigree by heralds at a later date, in an attempt to provide a successful family with respectable antiquity and origins. Historians too, who have been unwilling to assume that it was possible to rise from a low social level, have also sometimes complicated matters. The family which rose furthest in the late Middle Ages was, as already mentioned, the de la Poles. Their origin is unknown, and an attempt which has been made to argue that it may have had a Welsh aristocratic background is unconvincing. Certainly, critical comments about the family in the fourteenth century assumed that it was mercantile in its background. William de la Pole began his career as a wool merchant, became a royal financier and also served Edward III as an official. These services raised him to the status of banneret as early as 1339, although his marriage before 1330 to a sister of the Chief Baron of the Exchequer is an indication that he was already rising in social standing by that date. William's achievement in bridging the gulf from merchant to magnate in one generation was unique, and his son Michael was able to benefit from it by undertaking the traditional forms of service of the landed class. Michael served in France with the Black Prince and John of Gaunt, whose retainer he was from 1379, although this tie slackened about 1381 (46, xii (1), 434–8; 150, p.69). He remained prominent at court, and in 1383 the earl of Stafford accepted his son as a suitable husband for his daughter, although the comparative smallness of her marriage portion suggests that he may have felt that he was conferring a favour on the rising family by marrying with them. In the same year Michael became Chancellor, and in 1385 he was made earl of Suffolk, provoking the sneer from the St Albans chronicler that he was better suited to trade than to warfare (32, ii, 141; 150, p.69). The family underwent various vicissitudes in the last years of the century: Michael was attainted in 1388 and died in exile, and his son of the same name only recovered the title permanently in November 1399 – an earlier restoration by Richard II was annulled on that King's deposition. But by the time that Michael II died in 1415, it is clear that the family was accepted as impeccably aristocratic. He died at the siege of Harfleur, and his heir (Michael III) fell some six weeks later at Agincourt. The author of the *Gesta Henrici Quinti* spoke admiringly of both, the father as 'a knight of excellent and gracious name' and the son as 'as strong, as daring and as active as any member of the court' and as 'a brave young man' (39, pp.51, 97). The latter's brother and heir, William, also followed a military career. In 1415, aged nineteen, he had been invalided home from Henry V's army, and in the 1420s was one of the leading English war captains. After capture in 1429 he had to be ransomed, and he briefly resumed active service. Stories told of him suggest that he was regarded as a man who embodied the virtues of knighthood (128, pp.147–8). By the time that the family had held the earldom for a generation, therefore, no one paid any heed to its origins, and its nobility was taken for granted. Its later history saw it rising further, because William eventually became a duke, and marriage might have carried it higher still, for his son John married a sister of Edward IV, and their son, the earl of Lincoln, was Richard III's heir designate in the last months of his reign. Such family involvement in dynastic politics was not uncharacteristic of aristocratic society, and it was to lead to the fall of the de la Poles during the Tudor period. Lincoln became involved in Simnel's rising and fell at the Battle of Stoke in 1487 (Ch.25), but his younger brothers, as possible representatives of a Yorkist claim, were ruthlessly pursued by Henry VII and Henry VIII, either into exile or to the scaffold (110, pp.92–4). The final fate of the de la Poles clearly illustrates that as a family rose in rank it became increasingly vulnerable to political change.

The unique features of the de la Poles were their non-gentle origin in the male line and the rapidity of their rise in society; elsewhere among the magnates the infusion of new blood, and with it also perhaps new wealth, came through the female line and over more than one generation. In the late fourteenth century there is one case recorded of an earl who had married a merchant's daughter; at some time between 1381 and 1383 John Montagu, who became earl of Salisbury in 1397, married the daughter of Adam Francis, a former Mayor of London. It is not clear if at the time of the marriage he was already heir presumptive to the earldom, which he became following the accidental death of a cousin in 1382, although one must remember that he was heir to a peerage, as his father had received a writ of summons to Parliament in his own right. It is possible, too, that his wife's first marriage, to a man who was Constable of the Tower and a knight of the Garter, may have given her greater social standing that the average merchant's daughter (135, p.175). The passage of time clearly removed any stigma attached to mercantile origin here as with the de la Poles; few men could be haughtier about upstarts than Montagu's great-grandson, Warwick 'the Kingmaker', in his dealings with the Woodvilles, whose own origins were no humbler than his own.

Such ties between the nobility and the merchant class were rare, and intermarriages between mercantile families and the landed class were more often seen at the level of the knights and the gentry. We have already seen an example of this in the career of Sir William Stonor (Ch.13), whose three marriages marked his rise in the social scale. It is not, however, surprising that such ties existed between the great merchants and the gentry, because many of the merchants were themselves of gentle birth – the most famous English merchant of the fifteenth century, both in the eyes of contemporaries and in the memory of posterity, Whittington, was the cadet of a lesser landed family (43, p.25). As he left no heirs, he could not emulate William de la Pole in establishing a noble line – possibly indeed he rose less than one might have expected, because the early Lancastrians were more miserly in dispensing honours than some other kings. His undoubted services to the Crown did not even obtain him a knighthood, such as many mayors later in the century acquired.

The fifteenth-century mayor of London whose descendants rose highest was of similar background to Whittington. Geoffrey Boleyn, mayor in 1457–58, was one of five sons of a Norfolk landed family. He may have been helped to make his way by relatives who were established in London earlier in the century, because there are mentions of other Boleyns in company records. Geoffrey was admitted to the Mercers' Company in 1435–36 and became an alderman in 1452. He evidently prospered, for he was able to purchase the manor of Blickling in his native shire. His second wife was of noble birth, the daughter of Lord Hoo and Hastings, but it is not clear if Geoffrey was regarded as a suitable match because of his landed background or his urban wealth; possibly the former made the latter more respectable. Their elder son followed his father as a mercer and died unmarried, but their second son William entered Lincoln's Inn, was knighted in 1485 and married a daughter of Lord Ormond. His elder son Thomas rose further, marrying a daughter of the duke of Norfolk, and in the 1520s was summoned to Parliament successively as Lord Boleyn, Viscount Rochford, and earl of Wiltshire (104, p.325; 188, pp.559–65). The latter stages of his elevation were probably due to the same reasons as those which had assisted Sir Richard Woodville sixty years earlier – his daughter Anne had caught the attention of the King, and was to be the mother of a queen of England.

That same queen's greatest servant also came from a non-noble background. David Cecil of Tinwell, the grandfather of Elizabeth's minister, came from yeomen stock on the Welsh border. He joined Henry Tudor in 1485, and service to him after his accession laid the foundation of the Cecil fortunes. He received preferment as a yeoman of the guard and a steward of royal manors. Later he became an alderman at Stamford and MP for the borough, a JP in Rutland and sheriff of Northampton (67, p.469). His son Richard started higher in the social scale, serving as a royal page, and rose to be groom of the robes and Constable of Warwick Castle. The family's economic position was considerably strengthened by the plunder of the monasteries, and presumably service to the Crown helped it to secure a share of such gains. By the mid sixteenth century the Cecil family was firmly entrenched in court service, and this probably first brought young William to the notice of Protector Somerset, under whom he rose to prominence initially, although his later success undoubtedly depended on his own abilities (46, ii, 428–9).

Marriage contributed little to the rise of the Cecils; they emerged to prominence largely through service to the King at court and in administration. This kind of service, rather than that of the more traditional military kind, seems to have become increasingly common as a means of social advancement from the second half of the fifteenth century onwards, and one finds it also being followed by families which were already established. Possibly one reason for this was very simple: England was not involved in Continental wars for over half a century after 1453, and although some men secured promotion through their military activity in the civil wars, these provided less scope for major advancement than service in France had done. One route into government service, by which a man could achieve prominence and benefit his family, in an age of increasing lay literacy, itself one of the most striking new features of the age, was through the practice of the law, which may well have superseded military service as a means of self-advancement. For example, the Stonors, who at the turn of the thirteenth and fourteenth centuries were only a minor landed family, rose to greater importance through the actions of Sir John Stonor, Chief Justice of the Common Pleas under Edward II and Edward III. He was able to consolidate existing family lands in Oxfordshire and to acquire property elsewhere (24, i, vii–x). Higher in the social scale, the two families of Scrope both derived their origin from chief justices of the same period, and it was the law, too, which played a large part in the emergence of the Bourchiers, one of whom, Sir Robert, was the first layman to be Chancellor (1340–41). This family's later gains, however, came from more traditional methods – marriage and service in war. Indeed, the Chancellor Sir Robert was himself prepared to abandon legal service to go and fight in France, an action indicative of the values of fourteenth-century society. In the fifteenth century marriages in successive generations to a granddaughter of Edward III and to a sister of Richard, duke of York, herself twice descended from the same king, brought the family close to the politics of the court (55, p.210; 88, pp.12–13; 144, p.6).

All these families had already begun within the landed class; the history of the Pastons has particular interest because it illustrates how a man of non-gentle origin could rise into the gentry. Again it was the law which provided the means of advancement for William Paston, who became a justice of the Common Pleas in 1429. His father Clement was a husbandman and, according to the allegations of an enemy, his mother was of servile stock. The same account suggested that Clement borrowed money to educate his son, who then studied law (17, i, 28–30, 225). Whether or not the allegation of servile origin is true, it is certain that before the judge's time the family were very obscure, whereas afterwards they held a prominent place among the Norfolk gentry. The later Pastons, the survival of whose letters has made them familiar individuals to students of the period, shared all the interests and values of the land-owning class. Under Henry VII, two of the King's important servants, Richard Empson and Edmund Dudley, had made their career through the law, and rose to influence without the assistance of powerful relatives and friends (110, p.317 n.2), and lawyers were to continue to play an important part in government and administration, and to find in their profession a means of social advancement, in the centuries which followed.

It was possibly in the Church that talent had the greatest opportunity to overcome disadvantages of birth. This can be seen even at the highest levels of ecclesiastical preferment; between William of Wykeham at the beginning of our period and Thomas Wolsey at the end, one can see examples of men who rose through ability from humble backgrounds, and in some cases incurred unpopularity as upstarts. The rule of celibacy, however, meant that their role in advancing their families was limited by the extent to which they could exercise patronage. The extent of this is hard to measure, but seems to have been comparatively rare on a large scale, although Wykeham did endow a great-nephew with the manors of Broughton and North Newington in Oxfordshire, worth £400 annually, and this gave the latter's descendants sufficient standing to marry into various prominent families (88, p.12). Not all prelates' relations who rose to prominence owed their success to such patronage; certainly the two brothers of Archbishop Chichele of Canterbury who became London aldermen had already begun to make their way in the city before the latter rose to eminence in the Church (21, i, xxv). Some economic gains may have accrued to the kindred of prominent churchmen, through grants of leases of ecclesiastical demesne lands, although only a very few of those granted by Archbishop Warham of Canterbury appear to have been leased at below the market rate. Where prelates extended their patronage, it was more often in favour of ecclesiastical relatives, and there were bishops whose early careers were aided by family ties; Archbishop Whittlesey of Canterbury was a nephew of Simon Islip, his predecessor but one, Archbishop Bainbridge of York was a nephew of Bishop Langton of Salisbury and Bishop Thomas Kemp of London was a nephew of John Kemp, who held the sees of York and Canterbury successively. It seems that it was rare for clerical patronage to lay the foundations of a family's fortune – Wykeham's relatives were probably exceptional – but that it could sometimes confer considerable benefits.

One can see, therefore, that the extent of social mobility was fairly closely circumscribed. There was certainly no opportunity for a different class to take over the reins of power, and it was hard, though not impossible, for men from outside the landed class to break into it. Families such as the Pastons who rose from the agricultural class through acquiring a professional skill were a pointer to the future, and it is possible that by the early Tudor period there were more opportunities for yeomen to rise into the gentry. It is clear, however, that the relative prosperity of the peasantry in the years of land surplus and labour shortage did not provide a marked increase in social fluidity. Possibly some families may have moved from the land into the towns, and acquired sufficient wealth there to return to the country higher in the social scale, but one should also note that a substantial number of merchants were themselves cadets of landed families (104, pp.211–13). On the other hand, it is undoubtedly the case that a merchant who prospered would tend to buy land and that his heirs would be more likely to be brought up as gentlemen than to follow their father's trade.

It is easier to see the considerable fluidity which existed at the higher levels of society, because it is better documented. This was prompted in part by the propensity of noble families to die out, leaving gaps in the upper reaches of society which might be filled by lesser men. The means of rising into the aristocracy were varied in detail, but generally service to the Crown was the most important factor in social mobility at this level. It might take the form of traditional military service, this being marked in the periods of the French wars, and to a lesser extent during the civil wars of Lancaster and York, but it could also involve service in government and administration. At this level, the fortunes of individual families were closely bound up with political factors, and the capacity of a magnate to support the winning cause, and it is to the politics of the period that we must now turn.

PART THREE

The course of politics

1369	Renewal of Anglo-French War. French raid on Portsmouth.
1370–71	Fighting in Gascony.
1371	Return of Black Prince to England as an invalid. Marriage of John of Gaunt to Constance of Castile. Political crisis – replacement of clerical ministers by laymen. Parish tax approved by Parliament.
1372	English naval defeat off La Rochelle.
1373	Unsuccessful *chevauchée* from Calais to Bordeaux by John of Gaunt. French occupation of much of Brittany.
1375	Negotiations with France. Truce till 1377.
1376	'Good' Parliament. Attack on courtiers. Death of Black Prince.
1377	(Jan) Parliament more favourable to court. First poll tax. (June) Death of Edward III, succeeded by Richard II, aged 10. Rye and Portsmouth attacked by French.
1377–80	Period of 'continual councils'.
1378	Great Schism of Papacy.
1379	Second poll tax. Campaign in Brittany.
1380	Gravesend and Winchelsea burned by French. Third poll tax.
1381	(June) Great Revolt (see Framework – Economic and social). (Nov) Two governors appointed to control person of King.
1382	French victory over Flemings at Roosebek.
1383	Bishop Despenser's campaign in Flanders.
1385	Campaign in Scotland. (Oct) Parliament tried to curb royal extravagance.
1386	(July) Departure of John of Gaunt for Spain. (Oct) 'Wonderful' Parliament impeached Chancellor, Michael de la Pole.
1387	King's questions to the judges concerning actions of 1386 Parliament. (Nov) Appeal of treason against the King's advisers. (Dec) Battle of Radcot Bridge; defeat of royalist army under Robert de Vere.
1388	'Merciless' Parliament. Execution of those supporters of King who had not fled abroad.
1389	(May) Reassertion of personal authority by Richard II. (June) Three-year truce with France signed at Leulingham. (Nov) Return of Gaunt from Spain.
1390	Gaunt created duke of Aquitaine.
1393	Revolt in Cheshire, apparently against peace policy.
1394–95	Richard's first Irish campaign.
1396	Twenty-eight-year truce with France. Richard's second marriage, to Isabella of France.
1397	(Jan) Haxey's bill complaining about costs of royal household. (July) Arrest of duke of Gloucester, earls of Arundel and Warwick. (Sept) Gloucester murdered, Arundel executed, Warwick exiled to Isle of Man.
1398	Shrewsbury Parliament strongly subservient to King. Earl of March killed in Ireland. Exile of dukes of Norfolk and Hereford.
1399	(Feb) Death of John of Gaunt. (May) Richard's second Irish campaign. (July) Return of Henry of Lancaster. (Aug) Surrender of Richard. (Sept) Deposition of Richard.
1399–1400	Magnate revolt to restore Richard unsuccessful.
1400	(? Jan) Death of Richard, probably murdered. (Aug) Campaign in Scotland. (Sep) Glyn Dŵr's revolt.

1402	'Hotspur' defeated Scots at Homildon Hill.
1403	Defeat of Percy revolt at Shrewsbury. French attack on Gascony.
1404	Commons insist on appointing war treasurers.
1405	Northern revolt. Execution of Archbishop Scrope.
1406	Parliament demand right to audit taxes granted in 1404. Prince James of Scotland captured at sea.
1408	Defeat of earl of Northumberland at Bramham Moor.
1409	Dismissal of Chancellor and Treasurer. Replaced by supporters of the prince of Wales.
1410	Outbreak of civil war in France.
1411	(Oct) English support sent to Burgundians. (Nov) Supporters of the King recovered control of government.
1412	(Aug) English support sent to the Armagnacs.
1413	(Mar) Death of Henry IV and succession of Henry V.
1414	Revolt of Sir John Oldcastle. Opening of Council of Constance.
1415	(Aug) Plot of earl of Cambridge detected on the eve of Henry V's voyage to France. (Oct) Battle of Agincourt.
1416	Emperor Sigismund visits England.
1417	Renewal of campaign in France. Beginning of systematic conquest of Normandy.
1419	(Jan) Fall of Rouen. (Sept) Murder of duke of Burgundy by Armagnacs at Montereau. (Dec) Anglo-Burgundian alliance.
1420	Treaty of Troyes. Henry V recognized as heir of France.
1421	Battle of Baugé. Death of duke of Clarence.
1422	Death of Henry V and succession of Henry VI. Duke of Bedford in control of English interests in France, and duke of Gloucester Protector in England.
1423	French defeat at Battle of Cravant. Marriages of Bedford to Anne of Burgundy and Gloucester to Jacqueline of Hainault. Triple alliance of England, Burgundy and Brittany.
1424	Franco-Scottish Army destroyed at Verneuil. Burgundian truce with Dauphin Charles.
1425	Gloucester deserts Jacqueline of Hainault. Tension in England between Gloucester and Cardinal Beaufort. Settlement imposed by Bedford.
1428	English besiege Orleans.
1429	(Apr) Appearance of Joan of Arc. (May) Raising of Siege of Orleans. (June) French victories at Jargeau and Patay. (July) Coronation of Charles VII at Rheims. (Nov) Coronation of Henry VI as King of England.
1430	Capture of Joan of Arc (executed 1431).
1431	Coronation of Henry VI as King of France at Paris.
1433	Return of Bedford to England. Lord Cromwell's 'budget' statement.
1434	Deterioration of English position in France. Return of Bedford to Continent.
1435	Congress of Arras; Burgundian settlement with France. Death of Bedford.
1436	Unsuccessful Burgundian attack on Calais. Recapture of Paris by French.
1437	Threat to Paris by English. Appointment of new 'prive counseill' in England.
1439	Peace settlement with Burgundy, but abortive negotiations with France.
1440–41	Temporary English successes in France.
1441	Condemnation of duchess of Gloucester for sorcery.
1442	Successful French campaign in south of France.
1443	Unsuccessful Norman campaign by the duke of Somerset.

1444	Truce of Tours. Marriage of Henry VI to Margaret of Anjou.
1447	(Feb) Arrest and death of duke of Gloucester. (Apr) Death of Cardinal Beaufort.
1448	Surrender of Maine to the French.
1449	(Mar) Seizure of Fougères. Renewal of war by French. (Oct) Fall of Rouen to French.
1450	(Jan) Impeachment of duke of Suffolk (Apr) Battle of Formigny, followed by loss of Normandy. (May) Suffolk exiled and later killed. (June) Cade's rebellion.
1451	Fall of Bordeaux; loss of Gascony.
1451–52	Military activities of duke of York against court faction.
1452	Pro-English revolt in Bordeaux. Reinforcements sent to Gascony.
1453	(July) Battle of Castillon. (Aug) Henry VI's first attack of insanity. Disorder in north of England between the Percies and the Nevilles. (Oct) Birth of Edward, prince of Wales. Fall of Bordeaux to French.
1454	(Mar) Duke of York appointed Protector. (Dec) Recovery of Henry VI from insanity, and lapse of protectorship.
1455	(May) First Battle of St Albans. York reappointed Protector. (Oct) Conflict in Devon between Courtenays and Bonvilles.
1456	York relieved of protectorship.
1458	Attempt by Henry VI to reconcile rival factions.
1459	(June) Exclusion of York and Nevilles from Council meeting at Coventry. (Sept) Battle of Blore Heath. (Oct) Battle of Ludford Bridge; flight of Yorkists. (Nov) Coventry Parliament, at which Yorkists were attainted.
1460	(July) Yorkist victory at Northampton; capture of Henry VI. (Oct) Claim to throne put forward by York in Parliament. Not accepted, but compromise on succession. (Dec) York killed at Wakefield.
1461	(Feb) Battles of Mortimer's Cross and second St Albans (Mar) Edward of York proclaimed King. Consolidated position by victory at Towton.
1462	Earl of Oxford's plot.
1464	(May) Marriage of Edward IV and Elizabeth Woodville. Defeat of last major Lancastrian force at Hexham.
1465	Capture and imprisonment of Henry VI.
1467	Diplomatic negotiations with Burgundy. Dismissal of Archbishop George Neville as Chancellor.
1468	Burgundian marriage of Margaret of York.
1469	(Apr) Risings in North of England. (July) Marriage of duke of Clarence to daughter of earl of Warwick. Manifesto of Warwick and Clarence against courtiers. Battle of Edgecote, followed by Edward IV being taken into custody. Released later in year.
1470	(Mar) Lincolnshire rebellion, followed by flight of Warwick and Clarence to France. (July) Agreement between Warwick and Margaret of Anjou. (Sept) Lancastrian invasion. (Oct) Edward IV's flight to the Low Countries.
1471	(Mar) Return of Edward IV. (Apr) Edward victorious at Barnet and (May) Tewkesbury. Death of prince of Wales. Rising in Kent. Henry VI put to death.
1473	Seizure of St Michael's Mount by earl of Oxford.
1475	Edward IV's expedition to France. Treaty of Picquigny.
1477	Death of duke of Burgundy, followed by international struggles over succession to his lands. Arrest of duke of Clarence.

1478	Attainder and execution of Clarence.
1482	War with Scotland. England ignored in Treaty of Arras between Louis XI and Maximilian of Habsburg.
1483	(Apr) Death of Edward IV. (June) Usurpation of Richard III. (Oct) Revolt of duke of Buckingham, followed by his execution.
1485	Henry Tudor's invasion of England and victory at Bosworth.
1486	Marriage of Henry VII to Elizabeth of York.
1487	Revolt of Lambert Simnel defeated at Stoke.
1489	Treaty of Medina del Campo with Spanish kingdoms. Tax revolt in Yorkshire; murder of earl of Northumberland.
1491	Marriage of Duchess Anne of Brittany to Charles VIII of France. Perkin Warbeck in Ireland.
1492	English siege of Boulogne. Treaty of Étaples with France.
1493	Support for Warbeck from Habsburgs and in Burgundy.
1494	French invasion of Italy and start of Italian wars.
1495	Suppression of Yorkist conspiracy in England.
1496	Scottish attack on northern England, nominally in support of Warbeck.
1497	Cornish rising against taxation. In aftermath of its suppression, attempt by Warbeck to secure support there. Capture of Warbeck.
1499	Executions of Warbeck and of Edward, earl of Warwick (last Yorkist of the male line).
1501	Earl of Suffolk's conspiracy.
1502	Death of Arthur, prince of Wales.
1503	Death of Elizabeth of York. Marriage of Margaret Tudor and James IV of Scotland.
1509	Death of Henry VII. Succession of Henry VIII.
1510	Renewal of truce with France.
1511	'Holy League' against France, joined by England.
1513	(Apr) Naval defeat at Brest. (Aug) English victory at 'Battle of the Spurs'. (Sept) Battle of Flodden.
1514	Anglo-French treaty.
1517	Anti-foreign riots in London.
1518	Treaty of London to establish peace settlement in Europe.
1519	Disputed imperial election.
1520	Henry VIII's meetings with Charles V (May, July) and Francis I (June) (Field of Cloth of Gold).
1521	Execution of duke of Buckingham for treason.
1522	War with France.
1523	Criticism of Continental war by Commons.
1525	(Feb) Defeat of Francis I at Pavia. (Apr–May) Resistance to levy of the 'Amicable Grant'.
1526	League of Cognac against the Emperor. England stands aloof.
1527	(Apr) Anglo-French treaty. (May) Sack of Rome by imperial troops. Opening of proceedings by Henry VIII for the annulment of his marriage to Catherine of Aragon.
1529	(May) Legatine court opened proceedings on Henry's marriage. (July) Court adjourned. (Aug) Peace of Cambrai left England diplomatically isolated. (Oct) Dismissal of Wolsey from chancellorship. (Nov) Meeting of Reformation Parliament.

CHAPTER 16

The last years of Edward III

The renewal of the Anglo-French War in 1369 is generally taken, and with some justification, to be a turning-point in the history of Edward III's reign. Had the King died then, there is little doubt that he would have been regarded with few qualifications as a successful ruler, whose victories overseas contributed to his success in keeping on good terms with the great men of the realm. The Treaty of Brétigny of 1360 could be taken to mark the peak of his achievement, providing a solution for the difficult problem of relations between England and France over the lands in Gascony, which the English King was to hold in full sovereignty in return for abandoning any claim to the French throne. Final ratification of the treaty was deferred, however, with the result that Charles V of France was able to exploit discontent among the Gascon nobles over taxation to reassert his own claims, and this in turn led to renewed war. In this the English no longer enjoyed success such as they had had earlier, and defeat abroad bred discontent at home, which flared up in a number of political crises.

Almost certainly, military failure was the fundamental cause of these crises. The politically dominant landed class was essentially military in outlook, and saw the King's main function as one of providing leadership in war. In his earlier years Edward III had taken advantage of this attitude, both in actual campaigning and in the development of the cult of chivalry, centring on his newly established Order of the Garter, which included among its members most of the leading captains in his army. When the war was renewed, the English nobility and knights probably expected that it would be marked by victories similar to those of Crécy and Poitiers, but this was not to be the case.

This expectation was probably unjustified. The English now lacked the leadership which had carried them to their earlier victories; the King's health was failing and he was more inclined to seek the attractions of his mistress Alice Perrers than to take the lead in war, and when in 1372 he planned to lead a naval expedition he was kept in port by unfavourable winds. The leadership of the English armies would naturally have devolved to his heir, the Black Prince, who was also a noted soldier, but he too was sick. He gave up his lieutenancy in Aquitaine in 1371 to return to England, but during the last five years of his life was unable to play any major political role. As Edward's second son, Lionel of Clarence, had died in 1368, it was his third son, John of Gaunt, duke of Lancaster in the right of his wife and territorially the most important magnate in England, who was the leading figure in the royal family. For the next three decades, Gaunt was a man to be reckoned with in English politics, a man who inspired hate and mistrust at some times and confidence at others, who was the vigorous defender of the court of a senile father and the stabilizing force behind an unpredictable nephew. His character and aims are hard to ascertain; in his early days he was undoubtedly ambitious, but there is no reason to suspect that he was ever inclined to be disloyal, and indeed his respect for the position of monarch is perhaps the most consistent element in his political conduct. As he himself laid claim to a throne, that of Castile, in the right of his second marriage, this is hardly surprising. However, in his last years personal ambition seems to have declined, and he was to be the elder statesman who helped to smooth over political tensions in the 1390s.

It is not, however, clear how prominent Gaunt was in the early 1370s, nor how far he can be blamed for the failures in war and the corruption at court during this decade. He may have had some responsibility for the former, for he played an active part in the fighting, in Gascony from the late summer of 1370 to the autumn of 1371, and in a futile *chevauchée* through France from Calais to Bordeaux between August and December 1373 (106, pp.79, 86–93, 105–16). He also played a significant part in diplomatic negotiations with the French in 1375, culminating in a truce in June of that year. At the same time, and again under his auspices, an agreement was made with the Papacy concerning various matters concerning provisions to benefices and taxation (124, pp.34–48). England stood to gain certain practical advantages from both these agreements, but at the price of concessions which were likely to be unpopular and regarded as humiliating. It has been suggested that Gaunt's ambitions in Castile, and English xenophobia against the Castilian exiles in London, may have also contributed to his unpopularity, but at most this seems to have been a minor factor in English politics. Although Gaunt married the Castilian heiress Constance in 1371, it was not until the 1380s that he made a serious attempt to assert his claims there.

The importance of Castile in the politics of the 1370s lay less in Gaunt's claim than in its diplomatic and military alignment with France, and particularly in the naval support which it gave the latter. During the peace between 1360 and 1369, Anglo-French rivalry had taken the form of support for opposing claimants to the Castilian throne, and in 1367 the Black Prince had won a major victory at Nájera in support of Peter the Cruel against his half-brother Henry of Trastamara. The Black Prince was unable to exploit the advantages of this victory, and Peter failed to meet the debts to the English which he had incurred during the campaign, although he may have tried to do so. Before the year was out, Henry was able to return to Castile with French help, and although Peter made further attempts to secure English support, his envoys to London were unsuccessful. In 1369 he was murdered, and Henry secured control of the country. The result of this was the establishment of a Franco-Castilian alliance, which led to Castilian naval activity against the English lines of communication to Gascony and even in the Channel. Gaunt's marriage to Peter's daughter Constance in 1371 exacerbated the hostility of the Trastamaran line to England, but it did not cause it (145, pp.109–113, 144–8, 165–9).

If English intervention in Spain in the 1360s was to be to their disadvantage when the French War was renewed, the situation in another theatre, Brittany, appearing more promising. A pro-English claimant to the duchy had been victorious in 1364, and although the treaty which followed this victory saw him doing homage to the French King (141, p.152), his sympathies were still pro-English, and English garrisons remained in the duchy. The surrender of these garrisons in 1374 and 1375 contributed markedly to the growing criticism of the court, because attempts to maintain the position in Brittany had played a major part in English strategy until this time.

The early stages of the war were inconclusive; in fighting on the Gascon borders the French generally had the advantage, both before and after the withdrawal of the Black Prince to England, although his last campaign ended successfully in the brutal sacking of Limoges (106, pp.80–4). Nearer home, the French raided Portsmouth in 1369 (forcing the establishment of a garrison in the Isle of Wight to defend the south coast against further raids), and there were some ineffective campaigns in northern France, a raid by Gaunt through Picardy and Artois in 1369 and a *chevauchée* from Calais to Brittany in 1370 led by Sir Robert Knolles (141, p.164; 150, p.14). Although the latter ended with the English rearguard being defeated by a force under the French Constable, Du Guesclin, the war as a whole had shown lack of success rather than any serious disaster when for the first time open hostility to the King's ministers emerged.

The political crisis of 1371 has never attracted as much attention as that of 1376, partly because it is less well documented and partly because it lacks both the dramatic qualities or the constitutional novelties of the later one. Nevertheless it is important, because it illustrates the growth of discontent with the King's clerical ministers who were made the scapegoats – the Chancellor and the Treasurer, William of Wykeham and Thomas Brantingham, had to resign and were replaced by laymen. The basic trouble may well have been financial, because there were fierce debates over taxation (53, pp.260–1), and the unwillingness of the clergy to contribute to royal demands for money without the agreement of Convocation may have been one reason for the growth of anticlericalism, including demands from the friars for measures against the prelates and the possessioner clergy. There was also a legacy of financial problems from the 1360s, particularly in 1364, although royal expenditure had been high throughout the decade. Some 40 per cent of Exchequer expenditure was in the private interests of the King, notably on building and on the refurnishing of royal residences and castles (173, pp.483–7, 496). As the King himself was still popular, he could be criticized only through an attack on his ministers. It is hardly surprising that the landed class, which might benefit from a military victory, sought to blame someone for the lack of return on their taxes, because their resources were being strained by the economic pressures of population decline, which were intensifying at this date. The King's financial difficulties, and the consequent demands on his subjects, persisted throughout the 1370s, being indeed exacerbated by demands for money from the Papacy, though these were firmly resisted (124, p.14). Anti-papalism, however, cannot have been the cause of the attack on Edward's clerical ministers in 1371, because it was not until the following year that the first papal demand for a subsidy was made. It is not certain who took the initiative in the attack on these ministers, but it may have been the young earl of Pembroke, who received military command, with disastrous results, the next year (53, p.261).

Indeed, England's first really conspicuous setback in the war was in 1372, when

Pembroke, newly appointed as Lieutenant in Aquitaine, was defeated and captured by a Castilian fleet off La Rochelle. The main strategic effect of this was in Aquitaine, where the failure of the English reinforcements to arrive aided the French advance, and these gains in 1372 were followed in the next year by French occupation of the greater part of Brittany. This period saw a marked indecisiveness in English war plans. As already mentioned, a proposed naval expedition in 1372 under the King's personal command never sailed because of contrary winds, and later attempts to strengthen the country's resources at sea soon slackened. Although in 1373 and 1374 the English seem to have retained control of the Channel, and to have built new ships, by 1375 the Castilians were again able to intervene effectively, capturing or destroying thirty-seven vessels in the fleet bringing salt from the Bay of Biscay (124, p.22).

The main effort at war on land, Gaunt's great *chevauchée* through France in 1373, was monumentally futile, never bringing the French to a major battle and losing men, horses and supplies in the barren lands of the Auvergne (106, pp.105–16). The sole gain was a temporary consolidation of the English hold on some of the contested lands on the borders of Gascony, but the price was very high. There followed a period of military inactivity, and although plans were made for an expedition to Brittany in the late summer of 1374, it was not until after the surrender of the major castle of Bécherel in November that one sees any sense of urgency, and no troops were actually sent until April 1375. By the time that the 1375 campaign was properly under way, Gaunt had decided to negotiate with the French, and although the English forces besieging Quimperlé were near success, they had to abandon this when a truce was agreed at Bruges. The truce also provided for the handing over of the other major fortress in English hands, St Sauveur in the Cotentin, although in the end this seems to have been surrendered in accordance with an agreement made locally. It was probably about this time that Gaunt became the really dominant figure in determining English policy, and the war leaders in Brittany almost certainly resented his truce negotiations, which had deprived them of a victory. Certainly some of them were prominent in the parliamentary attack on the court party in 1376 (124, pp.37–45).

When Parliament, the so-called 'Good Parliament', met in April 1376 and the Chancellor put forward a demand for money, the government had to face discontent. The war had been unsuccessful and the truce was unpopular. Grievances were voiced at the high level of taxation and allegations were made of funds being misappropriated. When, after some days of desultory discussion, the Commons faced a royal demand for a reply to this request for money, they declared through their spokesman Sir Peter de la Mare that they wished to be joined by certain bishops, earls and barons to consider matters in the realm which required amendment. A few days later these matters were clarified, and allegations of financial corruption were made against three named persons, the King's Chamberlain, Lord Latimer, a London merchant, Richard Lyons, and the King's mistress, Alice Perrers. Pressure was maintained by the Commons and accusations were also brought against the Steward of the Household, John Neville of Raby, two further London merchants, John Pecche and Adam Bury and a Yarmouth merchant William Elys. It is worth stressing that the attack was directed primarily at a group with close court connections and not at the administration as a whole; by contrast with 1371, both the Chancellor and the Treasurer emerged unscathed from the crisis (124, pp.100–6, 157). This suggests that, whichever persons were responsible for the attack – and who these were will be considered later – they selected their targets carefully, and were not merely manifesting a general sense of grievance.

Initially, criticisms were directed at financial abuses, the loss of revenue through the issue of licences to evade the Staple at Calais in the export of wool and the arrangement of loans to benefit certain individual creditors of the Crown. All the merchants who were attacked seem to have exploited court favour for personal gain, thereby provoking the hostility of commercial rivals, as there was another group of Stapler merchants apparently prepared to grant a loan to the King on terms favourable to him if the Staple was enforced (124, p.110–12). While Parliament was sitting, a further set of charges was launched against Latimer, relating to misconduct in Brittany. These were allegations of financial malpractice in the form of extortion there, but more important were charges that he was responsible for the loss of the fortresses of Bécherel and St Sauveur. He had been Captain of Bécherel since 1368, but although at one time he had also been Captain of St Sauveur, he had ceased to hold this post in 1371, when it had been granted to another courtier, Sir Alan Buxhill. It is true that the latter's deputy Thomas Catterton, who was commander on the spot at the time of the surrender, may possibly have been a retainer of Latimer's, and Catterton undoubtedly received money at the time of the surrender. This does not, however, necessarily mean that his action was treasonable, because even before the fortress was handed over, financial terms for the surrender were being negotiated at Bruges. Neither of the military charges against Latimer seems to have been well founded (124, pp.43–4, 127, 131–2).

The attack on the courtiers was launched by the Commons, but there has been debate among historians as to whether it was they who took the initiative or if their actions were inspired by a magnate group hostile to the court. How politically mature were the knights of the shire? The best informed source for the events of the Good Parliament, the *Anonimalle Chronicle*, certainly gives the impression that the knights were by no means overawed by the lords, and it is worth remembering that in the 1360s the Commons had shown increasing assurance in voicing the interests of the middling propertied classes on such matters as the enforcement of the Statute of Labourers (173, p.507). In this, of course, their interests corresponded closely with those of the magnates, and in 1376 also there was undoubtedly magnate sympathy for the attacks on the courtiers. The key figure in the Commons was the man chosen as its Speaker, Sir Peter de la Mare, one of the knights of the shire for Hereford. All the contemporary writers stress his role, which appears to have been more pronounced than that of any previous spokesman of the Commons (193, p.16). The fact that he was victimized by Gaunt after the recovery of the court party further indicates his importance, as is the way in which he was regarded as a popular hero on his release from custody after the accession of Richard II (150, p.35). De la Mare's popularity also reflects the existence of some kind of public opinion which supported the actions of the Commons. A further indication of the Commons' initiative may be seen in the procedure known as 'intercommuning', when discussions were held between the Commons and the Lords; by the 1370s and afterwards, the form was that the Commons requested that certain lords, named by them, should be assigned to represent the Upper House.

On the other hand, it must be remembered that Sir Peter was the steward of the earl of March, one of the most prominent magnates outside the group close to Gaunt. Indeed, as son-in-law to Lionel of Clarence, March's territorial interests were probably second only to Gaunt's among the English nobility, and he had various reasons for hostility to him. In 1373 he had been debarred from going to Ireland, where he had substantial interests, to replace the incompetent William of Windsor, and in 1375 he had been one of the leaders of the attack on Quimperlé, which had been called off, following Gaunt's negotiation of a truce, when it appeared to be on the verge of success (124, p.45; 150, p.22). Furthermore, with the death of the Black Prince and the succession to the senile King being certain only in the young Richard of Bordeaux, the question of whether March's son, as a descendant of Lionel of Clarence, had a prior claim over Gaunt, cannot have failed to cross his mind. Whether or not he played a large part in initiating the attack on the courtiers, there is no doubt that he lent his support to the Commons, and their choice of him for the intercommuning committee was probably prompted by their knowledge that he was opposed to the court. The other lay lords chosen for it were also men with a military background, who were presumably dissatisfied at the conduct of the war. Possibly, too, Gaunt's younger brothers, Edmund of Langley and Thomas of Woodstock, may not have been averse to the attack on courtiers who had been treated far more generously than they, because they certainly took part in a banquet at the close of the Parliament (124, pp.107, 149, 156). It would undoubtedly be fallacious to think of the royal family as a single political bloc.

Another factor which may have contributed to magnate criticism of the court was the death of some of Edward III's old comrades in arms, such as the earls of Warwick and Hereford, in the 1360s and early 1370s (150, p.19). Men who had shared in earlier triumphs of war with a successful King might well have felt a residual loyalty to him, whereas their heirs were more likely to feel aggrieved at the lack of opportunity they had to emulate their fathers' successes and inclined to criticize the failings of the court. Such failings would be more of a grievance to those who were not in the inner circle of those in favour – those in office are more likely to regard as legitimate perquisites what others would call corruption – and this feeling of exclusion could bind together nobility and gentry in a common interest. In these circumstances it is unrealistic to debate which of them took the initiative in the attack.

The issues raised in the Good Parliament were not necessarily the ones which bulked most largely in men's minds. The motives for the attack were more probably connected with military failure rather than with financial corruption and fiscal grievances, however genuine the latter were (124, p.155). Lack of success in war, however, did not provide charges which could stick, whereas the other matters could serve as a basis for criminal charges on which the court faction could be prosecuted. The procedure of impeachment, which was developed for the first time as a political weapon in 1376, was a flexible method of bringing an action by a community against an individual, which had been utilized earlier in different circumstances. In an age when the concept of political responsibility had not been developed, criminal proceedings were the only possible way in which to get rid of unpopular royal servants. This weapon of impeachment was to have a long future, despite periods when it fell into disuse, and played a major part in tipping the constitutional balance in England from the Crown to Parliament.

Although the events of the Good Parliament showed the development of a political consciousness and the influence which the 'political nation' could exercise against the court, the aftermath of the crisis revealed their limitations. The fundamental role of the King in government was still unshaken. In the recovery of the court faction Gaunt played a dominant part, and in the autumn of 1376 the acts of the Good Parliament were annulled, de la Mare was arrested and Latimer and Alice Perrers were pardoned. Slightly later, proceedings were taken against another active critic of the court, William of Wykeham, who was deprived of his temporalities. When a new Parliament met early in 1377, it was prepared to acquiesce in Lancaster's demands, the intercommuning committee, with its membership largely changed from that of 1376, was favourable to him, and his steward, Thomas Hungerford, was chosen as Speaker (124, pp.160–4, 179, 186). One factor which may have contributed to the court's recovery was that the threat from France was increasing and that there were fears that England might be attacked. This seems to have concentrated the minds of those present wonderfully, and led them to seek greater solidarity with the government than in the Good Parliament – it is perhaps paradoxical that it was the unpopular truce and the temporary respite from the threat of attack that gave the Commons in 1376 extra freedom for uninhibited criticism, which could not have been made so easily when the country was under threat.

One further question arises out of this change of parliamentary attitudes: was it due to the rigging of the elections or merely to better management of the Commons by Lancaster and his supporters? It has been pointed out that comparatively few knights who had sat in the Good Parliament were re-elected in January 1377, but these did include at least one prominent opponent of the court, and the small number was comparable with figures of re-elections in earlier Parliaments (124, p.184). On the whole this suggests that the gains made by the court do not reflect any exceptional influence on the elections, and that better management was therefore a more important factor. It is also noteworthy that when another Parliament met in October 1377, to which a substantial number of Good Parliament knights were re-elected and in which Sir Peter de la Mare was again chosen as Speaker, good relations were maintained with the court. Admittedly, by then the political situation had changed, with the accession and coronation of Richard II apparently creating an atmosphere of goodwill, which was to be rare for the rest of the reign. Gaunt on this occasion seems to have acted with considerable discretion, and may well indeed have already discovered the advantages of a more conciliatory approach before his father's death. Certainly it was three days before Edward died that the King and Council ordered the restoration to William of Wykeham of the temporalities of his see (124, pp.178–9; 150, p.32).

CHAPTER 17

Richard II: the young king

Richard II's character has been a matter of debate among historians, and disagreements over it have been the basis of arguments about the motives behind his political actions. Many events of the reign, moreover, were highly dramatic, Richard's personal appearance on the scene at the height of the Peasants' Revolt in 1381, the execution or exile of his friends and associates in 1388, his revenge in 1397 and his own downfall two years later. This series of crises has attracted historians' attention, not least in recent years, in which a substantial number of articles and several important books have been published. There is a notable work by Tuck on domestic political struggles (150), and a valuable study of foreign relations by Palmer (140); these may be supplemented by an examination of the aims and interests of the King's opponents (118), a consideration of how deliberately the King pursued a despotic policy (125) and a volume of essays covering a wide range of topics on the reign (117).

The reign (1377–99) may be conveniently divided in May 1389, when Richard ended the supervision imposed on him a year earlier by the Lords Appellant at the time of the appropriately called Merciless Parliament. Although this assertion of authority was perhaps less sudden than some historians have suggested, it was undoubtedly a drastic political move when the King dismissed two of his principal opponents from the Council and changed the major officers of State. After this date too, there was no doubt that the King's personal wishes played a major part in determining policies. This period will be discussed in Chapter 18.

The earlier part of the reign lacks any such factor which gives coherence to political manoeuvres; indeed one of the main problems for the historian is to estimate where authority in the country lay and when Richard's own influence began to be significant in politics. Clearly, when he succeeded as a boy of ten, his role could be only formal, but despite this fact no regent was appointed to rule in his name. This apparently surprising fact can be explained, however, by the political situation at the time of his accession. The events of the last year of Edward III's life had left the obvious candidate for a regency, Richard's uncle John of Gaunt, too unpopular to be acceptable either to the magnates or to the Commons in Parliament. At the same time, he was too important to be bypassed if a regent were to be appointed. Under the circumstances, the system of councils which evolved provided a workable solution; they could carry on the routine business of the realm and deal with the many problems which persisted from the previous reign. The continual councils of the first three years of the reign, in effect, provided a collective regency. Within them, the most substantial group of councillors consisted of men who had been associated with the Black Prince, whose widow, Princess Joan, almost certainly played a significant part behind the scenes. Gaunt, too, probably still exercised considerable influence informally, and councils seem to have sought advice widely when they required it (150, pp.37–40).

The continual councils were ended in 1380, following a request by the Commons, who pointed out that Richard was almost the same age as his grandfather had been at the time of his coronation. (This, of course, disregarded the fact that Edward had not assumed personal control of the government until he was eighteen.) It is hard to say who exercised most power in the next few years, but clearly neither the magnates nor the officers of State showed much effective leadership. The most important official was probably the Chancellor, Archbishop Sudbury of Canterbury, but also influential was the Chamberlain, Aubrey de Vere, acting on behalf of his under-age nephew Robert, to whom the office pertained by hereditary right (150, pp.44–9). Aubrey was probably responsible for introducing Robert to court, where the personal favour he received from the King aroused hostility among other members of the nobility.

As at the end of Edward III's reign, the two main problems of government were defence and finance. Richard's accession was heralded by Franco-Castilian raids on the south coast, while attempts to counter these by attacks on France were unsuccessful (53, pp.257–9). At first the Commons were prepared to grant taxes; the grant of two-fifteenths and two-tenths in Richard's first Parliament was a generous one, although it was accompanied by a condition that two treasurers should be appointed to supervise the collection and expenditure of the money (55, p.402). This was a development beyond the demands made in Edward III's reign for taxation to be employed for specific ends, and was to be employed again in Henry IV's time (Ch.19). While it may foreshadow the eventual development of parliamentary control of the executive, however, it would be anachronistic to see it as the foundation of any such change – the demand was essentially an *ad hoc* measure, prompted by the particular circumstances of the time. In the next Parliament, however, there was criticism of how the last tax had been spent, the Commons claimed that they could be taxed for defence only, and it was suggested that the resources of the Crown should be sufficient to meet the King's needs. The tax offered was small (140, p.9; 150, p.42). In the spring of 1379 there was further discontent, and although a grant was made in the form of a graduated poll-tax, the Commons asked for a committee of lords to investigate the King's finances. The final attempt to raise money in Richard's early years, the third poll-tax, contributed to the outbreak of the Peasants' Revolt. It is likely that the initiative in this criticism of the government came from the Commons, and reflected their willingness to act independently, because a substantial section of the magnates were represented on the councils.

Although, as we have seen (Ch.3), the 1381 rising did not bring about noteworthy changes in peasant conditions, such as were sought by the rebels, it had important incidental effects on the government of the realm. The young King may well have been impressed by the popular loyalty to him, and this may have contributed to his later overweening self-assurance. However, this should not be over-stressed, because his accession at a young age and the absence of formal tutelage thereafter would have been enough in themselves to give him inflated notions of his own importance as he grew to adolescence. Perhaps more important were the murders during the revolt of the Chancellor and the Treasurer, which led to administrative disruption and the increasing intervention in government of members of the court group, notably Aubrey de Vere and the Under-Chamberlain, Sir Simon Burley. Tuck has shown that there was a sharp increase in the number of grants under the great seal which were authorized (or, to use the technical term, warranted) by immediate royal authority. The phrase used on the warranty notes was *per ipsum regem*, whereas at an earlier date the grant might have been warranted by the Council. Furthermore, a substantial number of the grants of this period were to members of the royal household, who seem to have exploited the confusion in government for their own advantage (117, p.6). The main uncertainty about this warranting of grants is whether the initiative lay with the King or with his associates.

It may have been such attempts to exploit governmental difficulties which prompted the Parliament of November 1381 to appoint two governors, who were to be placed in the household to control the person of the King. This appointment, of two men who were later to be bitter enemies, the earl of Arundel and Michael de la Pole, seems to have reduced courtier activity, as measured by the notes of warranty (150, p.57), at least until the summer of 1382. In a crisis at that time, the Chancellor, Sir Richard Lescrope, was dismissed for refusing to seal certain grants, which, according to the St Albans chronicler, the King wished to make. His successor, Robert Braybrook, bishop of London, was probably more congenial to the King, both as a kinsman and as a former secretary.

One does not know if the chronicler, writing retrospectively, was correct to blame Richard personally for Lescrope's dismissal, and the King's personal role in government can be inferred only from the criticisms which were made of it. Some evidence is ambiguous; when in October 1383 Richard was urged to assume personal control of the government and complaints were made that he was listening to foolish advice, he can hardly have been thought to be his own master, but his reported reply, that he would be guided by whomsoever he wished, suggests that he believed that he did possess real power. Three years later the situation was certainly different. A threat to depose him would hardly have been made if he were still thought to be in tutelage, and his alleged retort to the Commons' demand for the dismissal of the Chancellor and the Treasurer, that he would not dismiss a scullion from his kitchen at their demand, shows his autocratic temperament. Possibly 1385 may have been the year when Richard's real influence came to the fore. During the Scottish campaign of that year, he was involved in a dispute over strategy with Gaunt, and had his way, probably wisely, in limiting the scope of the army's activity (150; pp.91, 97–8, 105). At the start of this campaign too, the King's two younger uncles were made dukes and an earldom was granted to Michael de la Pole who had now adhered to the court group and had been appointed Chancellor in 1383. Possibly attempts were also made to confer earldoms on Lord Neville and Sir Simon Burley. In these actions, the King may have been asserting his position as the source of honours. There may also have been a political motive for the promotion of his uncles. In view of his strong distrust of Gaunt in the 1380s, he may have been seeking an alternative ally within his own family, although in the case of Gloucester, his youngest uncle, such a hope would have been sadly mistaken.

By this time, when Richard's personal role in government was increasing, a number of incidents were showing that his character had a tendency to violence. In 1384, when the earl of Arundel attacked the way in which the realm was being governed, Richard told him to go to the devil, and in 1385 he threatened the life of Archbishop Courtenay of Canterbury when he voiced complaints about the actions of some of the King's associates (150, pp.92, 96). It is debatable how far these actions reflect merely adolescent petulance and how far Richard was deliberately asserting royal authority. While it has been argued persuasively that Richard's tutor, Sir Simon Burley, may have trained his pupil in the absolutist ideas of Giles of Rome (125, pp.143, 155, 161), the evidence for this is purely circumstantial and the case cannot be proved beyond reasonable doubt. One should also guard against the assumption that Richard's policy was consistent throughout the reign, and that the events of the late 1390s, when his aims were clearly despotic, reflect an attitude which he had held from the outset of his personal involvement in politics. It may well have been in response to pressure on him from the magnates that Richard developed autocratic policies; his first clear assertion of his rights was a protest at the end of the 1386 Parliament that his prerogative was being infringed, and in the following year, when he submitted a series of questions to the judges on the legality of that Parliament's actions, one can see a conscious political move to absolutism (111; 113). From 1389 his actions became more cautious and more deliberate. However much Richard's personality contributed to the troubles of his reign, one must stress that it was not the sole cause of them.

If the importance of Richard's personal share in the politics of the 1380s is uncertain, it is equally hard to judge who else were influential. Despite royal distrust, Gaunt still had a major role to play, and he seems to have been a moderating influence until his departure for Spain in 1386. Princess Joan, Richard's mother, also may have played a part behind the scenes as a mediator – she certainly worked to reconcile her son with Gaunt in 1385 (150, p.95). The earlier part of the decade also saw a growth in the size of the royal household, with marked increases in the numbers of chamber knights, esquires and yeomen, men who were bound by special obligations to the King. Several of the knights, indeed, were granted custody of royal castles (150, pp.59–60). While this could have political consequences, particularly by creating factional ill-feeling when household men took over positions held by members of the Arundel family, these men were probably not concerned with the making of policy. Probably the most influential man in this sphere was the Chancellor, Michael de la Pole – certainly he was the prime target for aristocratic criticism as it developed. Of the other members of the court group, Burley seems to have kept rather more in the background, and Robert de Vere, five years older than Richard, seems to have had few concerns beyond his own advancement. The balance of the evidence suggests that the main characteristic of governmental action at this period was its indecisiveness, and this may reflect the absence of any person who was both able and willing to lay down a line of policy.

As criticism developed in the period after the Peasants' Revolt, the old issues persisting from the beginning of the reign, finance and war, were combined with a new element, hostility towards the court circle by men who felt excluded from government, in both policy and patronage. Different kinds of criticism emanated from different sources. Among the nobility there was a strong element of simple jealousy, while the Commons in Parliament probably showed the most marked hostility to alleged royal extravagance. Only one of the four Parliaments which met between November 1381 and February 1382 made a grant of supply, although the Council had support from the magnates in trying to raise money (140, p.10). This situation was similar to that which had existed between 1377 and 1381, so there is no reason to believe that the criticisms were yet directed at Richard personally. The issues of finance and war were, of course, closely connected, because the main need for money was to meet the costs of the struggle with France, which had continued, although generally at a fairly low level of activity, with raids rather than major campaigns, from the ending of the truce in 1377. This curtailment of military activity by both sides reflects the fact that both kingdoms were facing the problems of minority rule and perhaps also financial difficulties. In England, the magnates seem to have wished to increase the scale of campaigning, but the Commons were less enthusiastic about this.

In 1378, furthermore, the war had been further complicated by the outbreak of the Great Schism of the Papacy, because England and France had aligned themselves behind rival claimants, who were then trying to harness political rivalries in attempts to reduce the other's area of obedience. Two possible theatres of war, where the Church might bless an English campaign, were the Low Countries and the Iberian peninsula. In England there was a clear preference among the Commons for the former, while the principal advocate of the latter was John of Gaunt, who still had designs on the Castilian throne. For most Englishmen, however, Flanders was important as a market for wool, and in 1382, England's allies in Ghent had been severely defeated by the French. It was not until the Portuguese defeated the Castilians at Aljubarrota in 1385 that Gaunt was able to secure support for his expedition, which left in the following year (150, pp.98–9).

The expedition to Flanders in 1383 under the leadership of Bishop Despenser of Norwich had, however, been a fiasco. It had some support from the Commons, who had granted a small subsidy, which had been supplemented by the sale of indulgences granted by Urban VI for a campaign against the schismatics, a method of war finance which showed the desire of Parliament for military success on the cheap. At first the expedition appeared to be successful, but it soon petered out, perhaps because the bishop had in his force no magnates who might have provided greater military experience, and as the English began to retreat, negotiations were launched for a truce which might extricate Despenser's army (140, p.50). Palmer has argued that de la Pole had been working for a peace policy from the start, but this is, to say the least, doubtful, because when he appeared in Parliament in October 1383, he presented the government's demand for money in a distinctly aggressive tone, affirming that the honourable course of action was to fight (33, iii, 150). The lack of any real enthusiasm for peace is also suggested by the fact that the negotiations led only to a truce, which was allowed to expire, rather than to any peace settlement. De la Pole, however, certainly did consider that peace was a possible alternative to continued fighting, whereas some magnates, notably Arundel, were far more bellicose in their sentiments, and did regard the court's sympathy for a less aggressive policy as one of its major failings.

The resistance of the Commons to taxation should probably be explained simply by economic factors rather than by any dislike of war. Since 1370 landed revenues had not been keeping pace with the sharp rise of real wages (Chs 2, 3) and the gentry class was probably hit severely by this. Criticism of the high level of court expenditure and refusal of grants would be natural responses from men who were suffering from the general economic crisis, and the men in the Commons were probably more aware of this than the greater magnates who, though similarly affected, had greater basic resources on which to fall back. Possibly a military victory and its concomitant spoils might have reconciled them to paying taxes for war, because this would have given them some feeling that this was a profitable return. As it was, the ineffectiveness of the campaigns fought, as before 1381, made the situation worse.

Opposition to taxation was one thing; quite another matter was the fierce attacks which were launched against the court from 1385 onwards, which are best understood as a clash of opposed factions over a range of grievances. One should remember that the antagonists did not represent the whole of the nobility, because there seems to have been a substantial middle group which remained more or less neutral, at times tried to mediate and in the end could tip the balance in favour of either the King or his opponents. Such moderates could be found among the higher nobility, such as the King's uncle the duke of York, and the earl of Northumberland. They may well have been more common among the gentry in Parliament, many of whom had little hope of gains from either side.

The nucleus of the opposition to the King in the worst crisis of the reign, that of 1387–88, comprised the five magnates known as the Lords Appellant from the appeal of treason which they made against the courtiers. Most of these had particular grievances against the court. The most intransigent was the earl of Arundel, whose bellicosity not only reflects a desire to emulate his father, who had been a successful military commander under Edward III, but also may have been prompted by the vulnerability of his estates in South-east England to French raids. Furthermore, he was a major exporter of wool, so he was in favour of intervention in Flanders, where no agreement had been secured either by war or by diplomacy by 1385. Even more highly placed was Richard's youngest uncle, the duke of Gloucester, who had long been poorly endowed with land for one of his rank and was dependent for much of his income on Exchequer annuities. This left him vulnerable to the King's ill-will, which might lead to these payments being terminated, and he also appears to have been jealous at his exclusion from court. The only one of the five with no known particular grievance against the court was the earl of Warwick. These three were joined by two younger earls, Henry of Derby, Gaunt's son, and Thomas Mowbray, earl of Nottingham. The latter was married to Arundel's daughter, and he also may have resented the way in which Robert de Vere had supplanted him in Richard's favour. There seems to have been personal dislike between Derby and the King, and he possibly had a grievance against de Vere's uncle Aubrey, who may have used court favour to protect him in a legal suit (118, pp.109, 121, 152; 135, pp.19, 29–30; 150, pp.45, 84, 101–2).

It was a community of hostility rather than of interest which bound together Richard's opponents, and it was at best fragile. During the Merciless Parliament, the two younger Appellants were prepared to oppose the execution of Sir Simon Burley, although their seniors succeeded in securing this. Derby may also have saved Richard from deposition at the end of 1387 when there is some reason to suspect that Gloucester may have tried to secure the throne for himself. Even more striking is the position of Arundel's brother Thomas, bishop of Ely, who had been appointed Chancellor in 1386. Although in many ways he was closely allied with his brother, and was exiled in Richard's revenge in 1397, he may have tried to mediate between the King and the lords in December 1387. The bishop's friendships, too, show that one cannot always draw a clear distinction between the court and its opponents; two of his close friends, Sir John Lovell and Sir Richard Adderbury, were among the men removed from court after the Merciless Parliament (204, pp.182–3, 193, 343). The bishop was probably more concerned with dealing with particular favourites than with a general attempt to restrict the King.

Why were the favourites so unpopular? It is worth stressing that it was not until the appeal of treason in late 1387 that they were all attacked, and that the crisis had developed over a much longer period, from the Parliament of October 1385 onwards. At this meeting, some of the King's recent grants were attacked, and an attempt was made to obtain their revocation. Furthermore, the Commons tried to secure safeguards against future royal extravagance, restricting the King's power to make grants, and appointing a committee of lords to view Exchequer income and expenditure. On matters of supply, the Commons compelled the King to abandon an attempt to levy scutage, and withheld the wool tax for over five weeks. When supply was granted, it was subjected to fairly rigorous conditions. In none of these measures was there an explicit attack on any individual favourite, although the restriction of grants probably implied hostility to them as a group. In the next Parliament, a demand for a massive grant of supply, four-tenths and four-fifteenths within a year, sparked off a new crisis. The Commons, supported by the Lords, demanded that the Chancellor and the Treasurer be dismissed, and although the King tried to resist, he was threatened with deposition and gave way. De la Pole, the Chancellor, was then impeached, the most serious charge against him being that he had disregarded the Commission appointed in the previous year, although he was also accused of exploiting his position for personal advantage. He was sentenced to imprisonment, and another Commission was established to oversee the government, including the royal household. The new officers of State, headed by Bishop Arundel as Chancellor, and the members of the Commission, were men unlikely to be sympathetic to the King (150, pp.99–107).

During the next year, the King made persistent attempts to undermine the Commission, and the savagery of the attack on the favourites when Parliament met next in 1388 probably reflects in part their activity in the intervening months. De la Pole was already unpopular, and may also have been trying to recruit forces at Calais, but when the lords made their appeal of treason in November 1387, they added four names to the list, Robert de Vere, Chief Justice Tresilian, Archbishop Neville of York and a former mayor of London, Nicholas Brembre. Apart from the archbishop, all of these are known to have acted at this time in a way which angered the lords. De Vere, who had already incurred jealousy as the beneficiary of Richard's generosity, which had raised him to the title of duke of Ireland, and who had given offence by divorcing his wife, although she was the King's cousin, to marry a Bohemian attendant of the Queen, had tried to mobilize an army for Richard in Cheshire (140, p.111; 150, pp.78, 114–18). The Chief Justice was anathema to the lords because during the summer of 1387 he and his fellow judges had declared, in response to questions from the King, that the Commission established by the 1386 Parliament was derogatory to the royal prerogative, and that those who had procured it deserved to be punished by death. Brembre may have tried to rally support for the King in London, and also perhaps had been lending money to him, so that he could bypass the control on the income of the chamber, which had been imposed by the Commission. The archbishop's inclusion among the alleged traitors is more surprising, as he does not seem to have been heavily involved in politics, but his undoubted support for the court may have gone further than the surviving evidence shows (150, pp.110–16). Among the other victims of the lords in the Merciless Parliament were the other judges, who had declared in favour of the prerogative, who were banished to Ireland, and four chamber knights who were executed. As already noted, these included Richard's tutor, Sir Simon Burley, who may have been trying to raise troops in the Cinque Ports and was perhaps also regarded as a baneful influence on the King, and Sir John Beauchamp of Holt, who had been a major beneficiary of royal grants when he was receiver of the chamber, and whom Richard had appointed as Steward of the Household in 1387 in defiance of the Commission of 1386 (140, p.110; 150, pp.73, 106, 108).

Richard's recourse to attempted military action was probably the main factor in provoking the Appellants to such savage revenge. Even in their moment of triumph, however, they did not always have easy success. Three of the five main accused escaped abroad, and only Brembre stood trial in person before Parliament. There a committee of twelve peers reported that it could find nothing in his actions worthy of death, and he was finally executed on the basis of a declaration by the mayor, aldermen and recorder of London, where he had many enemies, that he was more likely to be guilty than not. The others were found guilty in their absence, and Tresilian, who was discovered in sanctuary, was taken out of it and also put to death. The Appellants themselves were not always unanimous, as can be seen from differences in their attitude to Burley.

The absence of solidarity among the Appellants meant that once they had begun to lose popular favour (and they may well have had more support from the Commons than among their fellow lords) Richard might hope to find allies to help him in reasserting his position. Nor was it long before their support dwindled. When the next Parliament met at Cambridge in the autumn of 1388, the

Commons were in a critical mood, despite the fact that a substantial number of members of the Merciless Parliament had been re-elected. They were reluctant to grant supply, criticized Arundel's conduct of a naval campaign and were concerned with the problem of lawlessness and with abuses in the retaining system. Above all, there were in the Parliament measures of labour legislation, attempting to lay down wage-scales and control mobility of labour. Such matters, more than constitutional issues of royal authority, preoccupied the gentry class at a time when they were facing economic pressures. Richard seems to have intervened in the debates over retaining in the unaccustomed role of mediator, and may thereby have obtained some goodwill which assisted in his reassertion of royal authority in May 1389.

This was not a sudden act, although the dismissal of the chief officers of State and their replacement by veteran administrators was a dramatic gesture. From the winter of 1388–89 one can trace the reappearance in government of some of the old courtiers, and one must assume that the coup of 3 May was carefully prepared (150, pp.136–7). The ease with which Richard recovered power suggests that his two strongest opponents, Gloucester and Arundel, who were removed from the Council, had drifted into a position of isolation, and that the Appellant coalition, always uneasy, had fallen apart. It also reflects the fundamental strength of the monarchy; except as a last resort, curbs on a King were not regarded as acceptable. This was Richard's greatest asset in the last decade of his reign.

CHAPTER 18

Richard II: triumph and disaster

The most striking thing about Richard II's reassertion of his personal share in government, on 3 May 1389, was the ease with which he accomplished it. He certainly showed skill in his actions, and perhaps even more in his omissions. He did not recall de Vere, de la Pole and Neville from exile, although they may perhaps have hoped for this, and this willingness of the King to lay down his friends for his life shows that he was politically more ruthless, and more astute, than his great-grandfather Edward II. What, if anything, this cost Richard personally cannot be known, though one may infer from the way in which he brought back de Vere's body for reburial in 1395 that in that case, at least, he felt a sense of loss. Richard may have benefited too from the chance that all three died early, de la Pole in late 1389 and de Vere and Neville in 1392, because this saved him from any temptation to bring them back. The appointment of two veteran administrators, Bishop Wykeham of Winchester and Bishop Brantingham of Exeter, as Chancellor and Treasurer respectively, clearly gave no cause for alarm – both had been members of the committee set up in 1385 to investigate the King's revenues and of the Commission of 1386 to supervise the administration (150, pp.100, 106, 138). The removal of Gloucester and Arundel from the Council was certainly a serious move, but the senior Appellants had been losing popularity, and the natural propensity of the magnate class to accept royal rule, except in extreme circumstances, must have simplified matters for Richard in choosing his own councillors.

Royal authority was further buttressed six months later when John of Gaunt returned from Spain. Abandonment of his claim to Castile in the right of his wife may have been a blow to his pride, but he was compensated for it by the betrothal of his daughter to the heir of the rival line and by substantial monetary compensation (145, pp.509–10). Richard was to treat him with a new friendliness, perhaps appreciating, after his experience of Gloucester, the advantages of having an uncle of undoubted loyalty and less ambition. De Vere's removal by the Appellants also helped, as he was probably responsible for sowing distrust between Gaunt and Richard in the early 1380s. For almost a decade Gaunt's support was to be one of Richard's main political assets, and the country benefited from it. His mediation secured the restoration of Gloucester and Arundel to the Council at the end of 1389, and in 1390 it was agreed that any grant which had financial implications should have the assent of at least two of a group which comprised the Chancellor and the King's three uncles, Lancaster, York and Gloucester. York and the earl of Northumberland, who had been moderates in 1387–88, also remained active in the Council (150, pp.140–2).

Besides the magnate element on the Council, the household was represented there by a group of chamber knights. Their backgrounds varied; Sir Edward Dallingridge was an old retainer of Arundel, whom he had served as Deputy Captain of Brest. When Arundel was replaced as Captain by the King's half-brother, the earl of Huntingdon, Dallingridge remained as Deputy, and it may have been Huntingdom who brought him into the King's service. In 1392–93, he was one of the most regular attenders at the Council, and when Richard suspended the liberties of London in 1392, it was Dallingridge whom he appointed as warden and escheator of the city. Another prominent group consisted of men who had served the Black Prince and Edward III, Sir Richard Sturry, Sir Lewis Clifford, Sir William Neville and Sir John Clanvow. Their importance as a group of sympathizers with heresy will be examined later (Ch.40); for the moment we are concerned with their service in government. Although they were in royal service before 1388, they must have kept in the background, for they were not attacked in the Merciless Parliament, and it was after 1389 that they became particularly prominent. Even so, their rewards were less lavish than their predecessors', as the King seems to have taken the lesson of 1388 to heart (117, pp.184–5; 118, p.116; 150, pp.141–3). Clanvowe and Neville soon died, apparently having gone to fight the infidel, but Clifford and Sturry, along with other chamber knights, appear prominently in Council sederunt lists, which survive from 1392 onwards. Membership of the Council suggests that a balance was held between a court group and the magnates, and this probably explains the relative political tranquillity of the early 1390s.

The King's recruitment of Dallingridge from Arundel's retinue foreshadows his later building up of support from the lesser landed class. The chronology of Richard's retaining could repay further study, but one thing is clear; he cast a wide net in picking his men. His notorious trio of advisers in his last years, Sir John Bussy, Sir William Bagot and Sir Henry Green, all received pardons in 1398 for having supported the Appellants. Some of their early appointments, for example as justices of the peace, reflect social standing rather than a close connection with the court, but Bussy, while remaining a retainer of Gaunt, was granted a fee of 40 marks per annum in 1391 by the King, when he was retained for life. The other two were retained in 1397, Green for a fee of 40 marks and Bagot for one of £60. In 1397 too, Bussy and Green were charged to attend the Council during the King's pleasure, receiving grants of £100, and Bagot was granted the same sum on being retained as a Council member in 1399 (7). These fees were not large, and this economy might well have been designed to forestall public criticism. The only one of Richard's advisers in this period who was ennobled, although not himself from the magnate class, was Sir William Lescrope, created earl of Wiltshire in 1397. He was appointed Under-Chamberlain in 1393 and held numerous posts towards the end of the decade. His promotion was more comparable with those of the victims of 1388, and may explain his especial unpopularity (118, pp.36, 148; 150, pp.143, 181, 193; 193, pp.350–1).

While one can follow the King's actions from the records, it is harder to judge his aims. He may have been genuinely willing to compromise, and renewed hostility may have arisen out of disputes over foreign policy. On the other hand, he may always have planned revenge for his humiliation in 1388, and the compromise could have been merely a smoke-screen – certainly his actions in 1397 show that he had not forgotten the Merciless Parliament. Gaunt probably restrained him, and also by his very presence overshadowed his son Derby, who went to fight for the Teutonic Order against the Lithuanians, and his brother Gloucester, who made an unsuccessful attempt to do the same. Warwick's retirement from the scene and Nottingham's willingness to rejoin the court faction after de Vere's exile left Arundel as the sole intransigent of the five Appellants (150, pp.153–7). Even Arundel's brother, who had secured the archbishopric of York in place of Neville, was restored to the chancellorship in September 1391, holding it until he succeeded Courtenay at Canterbury in 1396 (204, pp.353, 363). If Richard wished revenge, he certainly disguised his aims.

The main political development of the early 1390s lay in the peace negotiations with France. For all their bellicosity, the Appellants, partly for financial reasons, had been compelled to resume earlier peace moves which had been broken off in the spring of 1388. By the time of Richard's coup in 1389 discussions were already well advanced, and the King immediately renewed the safe-conducts to the French ambassadors. On 18 June 1389 a three-year truce was sealed at Leulingham, between Calais and Boulogne, and it was to be twice extended thereafter for two further years. Throughout this period, 1389–96, there were constant attempts to reach a definitive peace settlement. Both sides were willing to compromise, and at first sight there seemed to be only minor set-backs. Gaunt probably desired peace as much as his nephew, for he had failed in his negotiations with the Castilians to persuade them to give up the French alliance, despite pressure from England to insist on this (140, p.142; 145, pp.505–6). The key issue between England and France was the status of Aquitaine, and the relationship of the English King, as duke there, to his overlord the King of France. In 1390 Gaunt was created duke of Aquitaine, probably in the hope that this would cut the Gordian knot by establishing him and his heirs as an independent house, holding the lands from the French Crown. Although Aquitaine was regarded as a possession of the English Crown (even by Edward III after he assumed the French royal title), the grant to Gaunt said that he was to hold Aquitaine from Richard as from the King of France (*ut de Rege Francie*). The French offered generous boundaries; although the lands proposed in the 1393 negotiations were less than those held by England by the Treaty of Brétigny of 1360, when English military successes were near their zenith, they were substantially more than England had had at the outbreak of the war. In return, the English were willing to acknowledge French sovereignty over the duchy, and to include Scotland in the treaty (140, pp.147–8; 150, p.164). This last they had originally not wanted to do, presumably in the hope that they could bring pressure to bear on the Scots if they were isolated.

The Gascons, however, disliked these proposals, fearing lest the grant to Gaunt might be prejudicial to their liberties, which were best secured by the absence of an immediate lord. While they do not seem to have resisted him personally, they refused the possibility of a permanent separation from the English Crown. (140, pp.154–6). When in 1394 the duchy was formally granted to Gaunt *and his heirs*, there was open revolt; even Gaunt's personal presence in Aquitaine a year later failed to bring about submission. Significantly, it was then that the negotiators agreed on a long truce instead of a permanent settlement. They clearly felt that the latter could not be attained.

The Gascons were not the only opponents of peace; not all of the political nation was behind Richard and Gaunt in this policy. The Commons' attitude was ambiguous – although they disliked war taxation, the old xenophobic bellicosity died hard, and some knights probably hoped to exploit the war in their own interest through wages and spoils. The only open revolt against the peace policy was in 1393, rather surprisingly in Cheshire where Richard was strong; this was easily suppressed and Gaunt recruited many of the rebels into the army which he took to Aquitaine. Although Gloucester may have hoped that if Gaunt were diverted to Aquitaine, as envisaged in the peace proposals, he himself might attain greater importance at home, he too, somewhat contradictorily, favoured a more aggressive policy to France. This brought him closer to his old ally Arundel, who was hostile to the proposed settlement and clashed with Gaunt over it in the Parliament of January 1394. Richard supported Gaunt, and Arundel's ill-will led him later in the year to offend the King at Queen Anne's funeral, thereby earning a brief spell of incarceration in the Tower. Another section of the nobility which may have had reservations about the peace was the northerners, especially the Percy family, whose power rested partly on the powers of patronage which they could exercise through their tenure of military office in the northern counties, office which might become superfluous by the inclusion of the Scots in the treaty (150, pp.158–69).

In the latter stages of the negotiations Richard had a further bargaining counter in his own person. His queen, Anne of Bohemia, had died in 1394, leaving no heir, so, despite his undoubted affection for her, it seemed inevitable that he should soon marry again. Initially, for diplomatic reasons, he seems to have looked to Aragon for a wife, but the French opposed this, and instead offered him a choice of three French brides. Before he even replied to this, a new offer was made of the six-year-old Isabella of France. When a twenty-eight-year truce was finally agreed in 1396, it was sealed by a marriage treaty. In the dowry negotiations, Richard's ambassadors were instructed to ask (as one possibility) for French aid against his subjects and those who ought to obey him (140, pp.168, 173). This was not included in the final agreement, and historians have probably overrated its importance, in suggesting that it shows the King's despotic tendencies and foreshadows his later tyranny. It may indeed have been an allusion to the situation in Gascony or to Richard's claims in Scotland rather than an attempt to secure allies against domestic foes. At the same time, if news of this instruction leaked out, its very vagueness might have given rise to alarm.

While the French negotiations were in progress, Richard was involved elsewhere, in an expedition to Ireland. One need not doubt that his main aim was what he claimed, an attempt to restore order, for, as we have seen (Ch.10), English control was patchy and a financial drain on royal resources. He may also have been trying to create a new outlet for military activity as fighting ceased on the Continent. The winter campaign of 1394–95 secured some success, particularly in Leinster, where Art Mor MacMurrough submitted to the King. In Ulster the expedition left a less happy legacy in a dispute over its lordship between the great-est of the Anglo-Irish magnates, the earl of March, and the native chieftain, Niall Óg O'Neill. However, the settlement soon broke down, even in Leinster, and Richard was already planning a further expedition in 1398, even before the Irish situation deteriorated further with the death in battle of the earl of March. In 1399 the King did make this expedition, and it was to contribute to his downfall (150, pp.170–7, 206–11).

On the whole the magnates were less concerned with Ireland than was the King, so Richard's success there won him little prestige. It was soon after his second marriage that political tensions re-emerged. In the Parliament of January 1397, a certain Thomas Haxey presented a bill to the Commons, complaining about the failure to guard the Scottish border, the disregard of the statute against liveried retainers and the excessive costs of the royal household. This last criticism stung the King, who insisted that the author of the bill be produced. Despite this attack, the King generally seems to have controlled this Parliament, probably through the Speaker, his retainer Sir John Bussy, who had had experience in the post in 1394 (193, pp.133, 350). The Lords, too, were pliant, and were persuaded to declare criticism of the household treasonable, although Haxey himself was pardoned as a cleric. Richard's influence is also shown in an Act of the Parliament recalling from exile the judges who had been banished to Ireland by the Merciless Parliament. Haxey's case raises problems for the historian. He himself is unlikely to have initiated the complaints, being a king's clerk, who was proctor of the abbot of Selby. Little is known of how Commons' bills were drafted, and the issues of the Scottish border and of retaining were certainly matters in which the Commons were concerned, so it is possible that the attack arose spontaneously and that Haxey was made the scapegoat for others. It has also been suggested that he was a cat's-paw of a disaffected noble, although as the nobility were not backward in criticizing the King, one may wonder why anyone should prefer this indirect form of attack. Yet another possibility is that he was a stool-pigeon, act-ing on the King's behalf, so that Richard could secure a parliamentary declaration against such criticism. Improbable as this may seem at first sight, for it would hardly have been in Richard's interest to have attention drawn to possible house-hold extravagance, still less to suggest it if it did not exist, it is none the less lent a certain plausibility by Haxey's official position and his early pardon (125, pp.71–3; 150, pp.181–3). The atmosphere of this Parliament suggests increasing political tension, and the refusal of Gloucester and Arundel to attend a council a month later cannot have reassured the King as to the prospect of continuing peace with his old enemies.

Another of Richard's problems was finance. His better relations with the Com-mons in the middle of the decade may have been partly due to his reduced demands for taxation from them as the war petered out, although he did com-pensate for this by finding other ways of levying money. He was able to raise it in North Wales and Cheshire, lands which were in the patrimony of the prince of Wales, but which were in the King's hands on account of Richard having no heir, because these were outside the scope of Parliament's authority, he secured money by distraint of knighthood, and also attempted to raise loans (150, pp.144–5). These were not always successful, notably when he tried to borrow from the city of London or from individual citizens there. Throughout the decade the city suffered from royal extortion; an outbreak of disorder in 1392 gave him a pretext for forfeiting the city's liberties, imposing a royal nominee as warden in place of the mayor and nominating the sheriffs and aldermen. A corporate fine of £100,000 was imposed on the city, although this was later pardoned, but the payment that the citizens had to make for the restoration of their liberties, and then only during the King's pleasure, was still £10,000. In 1394 the city lent the King 10,000 marks, although this was soon repaid. Here there was a change from the civic reluctance to lend to the King a few years earlier, and there is little doubt that Richard was exploiting the citizens' fear to his own advantage. In the summer of 1397 Richard again raised a loan of 10,000 marks, through the agency of his new ally in the city, Mayor Whittington. He had been appointed by royal authority, contrary to the city's liberties, when the existing mayor had died in office. Two days after his appointment, however, the King granted a charter, restoring these liberties in perpetuity, and as the 'loan' was not repaid, it was clearly a gift to recover these (117, pp.178–99). The King raised other loans during this summer, an action which has been taken to mark the beginning of Richard's tyranny. The actual levy of the loans does not seem to have been considered illegal, for no reference was made to it in the deposition articles of 1399, more than half of which refer to royal actions which affected the people's possessions. An accusation which does appear well substantiated was that Richard was dilatory in repaying the loans (108).

By the time that the King was taking these moves to strengthen his finances, he had also, in July, arrested the three senior Appellants, alleging that they were guilty of new treasons. His actions from then till the end of his reign appear deliberately planned, and the cool skill with which they were implemented argues against any belief that Richard was mentally unstable. When Parliament met in September 1397 (for only twelve days), the King had his way by a mixture of threats and skilful manipulation. His bodyguard of Cheshire archers was available to overawe those present, and his councillor Sir John Bussy was again chosen as Speaker. The proclamation that fifty (unnamed) persons would be excluded from a general pardon to those involved in the events of 1386–88 would leave anyone who had supported the Appellants sufficiently uncertain of their position to make them toe the King's line. The appointment of a lay proctor to act on behalf of the clergy could have been made either to enable them to participate in judgments of blood or to save them from having to take part in the trial of their archbishop. Another procedural move to strengthen the King's position was to revoke earlier pardons before bringing charges against Gloucester, Warwick and the Arundel brothers (150, p.188). There is no doubt that Richard was guilty of deception; despite the allegations made when he arrested the Appellants, the charges against them referred to the events of 1386–88. The trial of Archbishop Arundel, who was arrested at the beginning of the Parliament, was perhaps shaky in law, as he was prevented from making a defence and was tried *in absentia* (204, pp.370–2). His brother had a public trial, but his defence was useless, and he was condemned and executed, after a defiant resistance which gave his death a dignity which he had not always shown in his life. By contrast Warwick grovelled at his trial, confessing all the charges against him, thereby saving his life, but neither his estates nor his reputation. Gloucester was probably murdered at Calais, a fact which, if true, suggests that Richard did not dare to bring him to trial. He was condemned posthumously on the basis of a confession which was conveniently produced from him admitting his guilt. When the archbishop was exiled, the King took rapid action to have him replaced, and wrote to the Pope about him in hostile terms. Indeed it is possible that one of the actions most commonly adduced as evidence for Richard's tendency to megalomania, his negotiations with the German Electors for the imperial Crown, may have been a calculated move to align himself with Boniface IX, who opposed the existing Emperor Wenceslas, in order to secure papal support in removing the archbishop (140, p.218).

The confiscated lands of the victims provided rewards for Richard's supporters, and there was a mass grant of titles. Various earls became dukes, including the two younger Appellants, Derby and Nottingham, who were now closely connected with the court. They secured the titles of Hereford and Norfolk respectively, and others received lesser titles. Some lands were annexed to the Crown, notably certain Arundel lordships in Shropshire and North Wales, which were joined to the county palatine of Cheshire, which was raised to the status of a principality. Rewards were for past services as well as recent ones; 4,000 marks were provided for distribution among the Cheshire men who had suffered for supporting the King in de Vere's Radcot Bridge campaign of 1387 (117, pp.256–61).

When Parliament reassembled in January 1398 at Shrewsbury, significantly close to Richard's power base in Cheshire, the King again used threats to keep the Commons subservient. Those who had ridden with the Appellants were already being granted pardons from October 1397, and between then and September 1398, 596 were issued. This was probably done in return for money; various shires also made payments to the King for pardon (108). This Parliament also made a notable and unprecedented grant to the King, that of the customs for life, a measure which met some of the problems which he had had to face earlier in the reign, not only because of financial difficulties as such, but also because these had led to the calling of parliaments which had criticized him (150, pp.194–5). In the course of the fifteenth century, this grant was gradually to be established as the norm, but this does not detract from the significance of Parliament's action on this occasion (Ch.29).

The support of Gaunt and of his son Hereford had been of great assistance to Richard in the autumn of 1397, and the latter's fall, following a quarrel with his former friend Norfolk, may well have been unexpected. There are difficult problems of evidence in trying to judge which of them originally expressed doubts as to their safety and the King's good faith in pardoning them. McFarlane suggests that it may have been Hereford, who then attempted to cast the blame on Norfolk, but this is based purely on an interpretation of the characters of the two men and can be no more than speculation. Tuck prefers to accept at face value Hereford's accusation that it was Norfolk (135, pp.44–7; 150, pp.208–9). It took over half a year before Hereford's charge culminated in the abortive trial by battle at Coventry in September 1398, which Richard stopped, exiling Norfolk for life and Hereford for ten years. later reduced to six. By this act, Richard's policy of divide and rule appeared to have destroyed the Appellants completely.

One cloud remained on Richard's horizon; what action was he to take on the death of John of Gaunt? The duke was now approaching sixty, and as he died within six months of his son being exiled may well already have been failing. It was presumably as a sop to him that Richard allowed Hereford an annuity of £2,000 while he was in exile and promised that he would succeed to his father's duchy. Indeed this may have been a calculated deception, so as to retain Gaunt's support, for on the latter's death, Richard confiscated the lands and increased the sentence of exile to life (135, p.47). This act is often regarded as Richard's crowning folly, and in retrospect this is no doubt a fair judgement. However, it may well have appeared less foolish at the time. For one thing, it is hard to see what other option Richard had, as the restoration of a man who had been an enemy in 1387–88 and whose exile provided him with a new reason for hostility to the King, to the position of the wealthiest magnate in the land would have been to provide a focus for all who had a grievance against him. For another, Richard had had a remarkable run of success in the previous two years and had no reason to think that his good fortune would not last. His marriage in 1396 to a child who could not be expected to produce an heir for a decade shows that he was then confident of his secure hold on the throne, and the ease of his victory over the Appellants could only have bolstered this self-assurance, perhaps blinding him to the antagonism aroused by his actions. Barron's important article on Richard's tyranny shows beyond doubt that he was pursuing a deliberate policy of keeping his subjects insecure by demands for money and for oaths of loyalty, but her conclusion that he was a man who was afraid is not altogether convincing (108). It is more likely that his policy was aimed at revenge rather than at self-protection.

Richard's final miscalculation, in leaving England for his second Irish campaign, is also best understood if one believes that he was over-confident of his position. This error of judgement may have been partly prompted by the belief that his friends at the French court could prevent Henry, who was in exile there, from moving against him, but during the summer of 1399 the duke of Orleans, who was less well disposed to Richard than the King or the duke of Burgundy, became more dominant there, and gave Henry support which may have encouraged him to invade (150, pp.212–13).

If anyone was afraid in England, it was not the King but the nobility. The confiscation of the Lancaster lands must have alarmed the propertied classes, already subjected to Richard's financial demands. When Henry arrived in northern England with a small force in the summer of 1399, he could rally support not only from the duchy of Lancaster estates but also from various northern magnates, including the earls of Northumberland and Westmorland, traditionally rivals for influence, but drawn together by Richard's tendency to bring outsiders into positions of authority in the area. Although the duke of York, whom Richard had left in control of England, succeeded in raising an army, he did not use it against the invader, and when Richard returned from Ireland, before he had had time to secure any success there, his own army deserted him (150, pp.216, 218).

Men who were loyal to Richard through fear now felt free to desert him, and as Henry's force increased in strength it was clear that desertion was more likely than loyalty to serve the cause of self-preservation. When the nobility deserted Richard's cause, they took their men with them.

The same motive was the ultimate reason for Henry's usurpation. When he had Richard as his prisoner, he was well aware that he would neither forgive nor forget; that was the lesson of 1397. Richard was still only thirty-two, and if spared might well live for another twenty years or more. He had shown a willingness to wait for revenge on the Appellants, and if he were to recover power, Henry and his supporters could not feel safe. Deposition was a drastic act, and there is evidence that there was some opposition to it, despite the official record which suggests that all went smoothly. The very doctoring of the Parliament roll in the Lancastrian interest indicates the weakness of Henry's position and his need to compensate for this with effective propaganda. Richard's actions, however, had left his opponents with no alternative.

CHAPTER 19

The establishment of Lancaster

Henry IV's accession marked the arrival of a new dynasty, but in no other way was it a dividing line in English history. Many of the problems which had faced Richard II persisted into his successor's reign, and the circumstances of the usurpation made it even harder for the new King to deal with them decisively. In 1399 he had shown that a king was vulnerable to a revolt by a determined magnate, and in order to secure his hold on the throne, he had to pay a price to his supporters and conciliate his enemies. He was extravagant with pensions and gifts in the first year of his reign, almost certainly in an attempt to buy support from the political nation (112, pp.19–20). When one remembers that in the Parliaments of Richard II royal extravagance had provoked hostility, it is hardly surprising that criticism continued under his successor. Henry IV's reign sees some of the most determined attempts by the Commons to control the King's expenditure at any time in the Middle Ages, and as Henry needed money he had to make concessions at least intermittently, although he strove to his fullest ability to ensure that the rights of the Crown were preserved intact.

But what were 'the rights of the Crown'? When deposition articles were brought against Richard, it was implied that he had overstepped the lawful limits of royal power, but no attempt was made to define these limits precisely. Parliament as a collective body did not claim an executive role in government, although individual lords and members of the Commons might hope for a place in royal service, with its responsibilities and emoluments; it did, however, claim a right to criticize and to seek redress of grievances from the King, and it was discovering that it could compel the King to provide such redress by refusing to grant supply until its demands were met. It was still recognized, as it always had been, that the King had the right to choose his councillors and officials, but the feeling was growing that in some ways Parliament had a right to examine their actions. One cannot talk to explicit constitutional principles, but one can see an implicit idea that Parliament could restrict the royal prerogative (135, pp.79–80).

Richard II's refusal to dismiss de la Pole in 1386 and his response to Haxey's bill in 1397 both show that his concept of monarchy did not allow for such criticisms of the prerogative. Henry had not been born in the purple, and after his seizure of the throne had to tread delicately. However much he might try to veil the fact in the ambiguities by which he laid claim to the throne, he and his supporters knew that his title rested on a combination of deception and force. It is noteworthy that he did not dismiss his army until after the dissolution of his first Parliament (129, p.79), a fact which suggests that he may have needed to overawe potential opposition quite as much as Richard had in 1397. The uncertainties of English succession law had enabled him to supplant a possible rival heir in the person of the young earl of March (Ch.11) [B.1], but this same uncertainty could be turned against him, so he could not afford to alienate the magnates on whose support he had depended.

Henry's greatest asset in the early months of his reign was Richard's unpopularity, but although Richard had been deserted by virtually all his supporters in 1399, not all of them may have done so from conviction as much as from a desire to end up on the winning side. Henry did not stain his accession with a blood-bath; apart from the earl of Wiltshire, Bussy and Green, who had been executed in the course of the invasion, and a valet called John Hall, who had been involved in the duke of Gloucester's death, there were no deaths among Richard's henchmen in 1399. Richard himself was still held in custody, and the lords who had been given new titles in 1397 were deprived of them, although one of them, Henry's half-brother John Beaufort, who reverted to his old title of earl of Somerset, was appointed Chamberlain and remained loyal to the new King. In other cases this initial clemency was unrewarded, and some of the lords revolted on Richard's behalf in the winter of 1399–1400. The rising was betrayed by the shifty earl of Rutland, who thereby saved his own skin and his succession to his father's duchy of York in 1402 (112, p.3; 129, pp.57, 78, 87). Several leaders of this plot fell victims to lynching by the mob in various places, a fact which suggests that the new King still had considerable popular support. In the long run the revolt probably benefited Henry, as it eliminated a substantial number of magnates whose loyalty was doubtful. Also it almost certainly sealed Richard's fate, although rumours of his survival in Scotland continued after his death (probably early in 1400), and futile conspiracies in his name persisted for well over a decade. The rumour was sufficiently credible for the Percies to spread it during their revolt in 1403, although this was almost certainly a tactical move to try to secure support from old Riccardians, as their real candidate for the throne was probably the earl of March. After 1400 it was the March claim which posed the most serious dynastic threat to Henry, and an attempt to abduct the heirs of this line to South Wales in February 1405 had the support of a number of magnates, including the duke of York (129, pp.141, 155, 171, 183; 241, pp.10, 13, 16).

Where Henry probably had his own way most successfully was in some of his appointments to office. The main positions in the household went to men with old Lancastrian connections, and the post of Treasurer of the realm to Henry's esquire John Norbury, who was appointed to this even before the usurpation was legalized, and was continued in office afterwards. At the same time the post of Chancellor went to a professional chancery clerk, John Scarle, who had earlier served in the administration of the duchy of Lancaster (129, pp.65–6, 71–2). Scarle's experience helped to preserve institutional continuity, as did the retention in office of Richard II's Keeper of the Privy Seal, Richard Clifford.

These appointments, although strengthening Henry's power in government, did not affect his position in relation to the magnates. The families which had been victims of Richard II rallied to Henry, although as the heir of Arundel was under age in 1399 and the heir of Warwick, who succeeded his discredited father in 1401, was also, their roles were unimportant in the early years. More important were the two great northern families which had avoided involvement in the struggles of Richard II's middle years but had supported Henry in 1399, the Nevilles and the Percies. Ralph Neville had been created earl of Westmorland in 1397, but he had a family connection with Henry; his second wife was the King's youngest half-sister. He was to be one of the King's most loyal supporters throughout the reign (135, pp.64–6, 71).

The three Percies were completely different. They had played a major part in Richard's deposition, but may have been hoping for the succession of the young earl of March, who was nephew to the youngest of them, the thirty-five-year-old 'Hotspur'. He, his father the earl of Northumberland and his uncle the earl of Worcester all received substantial offices from Henry, Hotspur and Northumberland mainly in the North and Worcester more at the centre of affairs, where he had already held office under Richard II, before deserting him on his return from Ireland (112, pp.8–10; 135, pp.72–3). Henry probably had no option but to gamble on their loyalty, and they seem to have tried to exploit his weakness to the full; when they failed to secure what they wanted, they rose in revolt. Although the King was probably dilatory in repaying his debts to them, they do not seem to have been worse treated than any other royal creditors. Henry's refusals to ransom Hotspur's brother-in-law Sir Edmund Mortimer from the Welsh in 1402, and to allow the Scots prisoners taken at Homildon Hill in the same year to be ransomed without his consent, created further tension, although in the following year he was still prepared to make grants to secure their loyalty. The Percies' aims are not certain, but they were probably seeking further power, and thought that they might obtain this from another change of king.

They remained persistent rebels. Even after the defeat and death of Hotspur at the Battle of Shrewsbury in 1403, and the subsequent execution of Worcester, Northumberland, who had not been openly involved, survived. Henry obviously suspected him, but in the first Parliament of the following year he was pardoned at the request of the Commons. He rebelled in 1405, joining with Archbishop Scrope of York, the young earl of Nottingham and Lord Bardolf. Prompt action by Westmorland secured the persons of the archbishop and Nottingham, who were executed as traitors. Northumberland and Bardolf escaped to Scotland and continued to plot against Henry, invading England in January 1408, only to be defeated by the sheriff of Yorkshire at Bramham Moor in the following month (129, pp.165, 186–7, 219). This marked the end of serious attempts to overthrow Henry – indeed it is probably fair to say that his victory at Shrewsbury had secured his position, for neither of the later revolts had much support. By the middle of the reign, Henry had secured his dynastic position against rival claimants, and he himself must deserve much of the credit for this. Although Shrewsbury was his only full-scale military victory, it was the only time when he needed to fight such a battle. On this occasion he caught Hotspur by surprise by his rapid march west and defeated him before he could be reinforced either by his father or by Glyn Dŵr's Welshmen. The same personal vigour can be seen in 1405, when he was prepared to set off in pursuit after the abduction of the Mortimer heirs and in his rapid northwards move to deal with Scrope's rebellion, although then he did not need to fight, as Westmorland already had two of the rebel leaders in custody and the other two in flight (129, pp.156, 183, 185).

The measure of Henry's early achievement can be seen in his later years. Although he himself became increasingly ineffective politically because of recurring illnesses, there was no challenge to the House of Lancaster. Indeed it could even afford the luxury of internal disagreements, as opposition to the King centred not on a rival line but on his own heir the prince of Wales. When this heir succeeded peacefully in 1413, there is little doubt that the country was generally reconciled to the new dynasty. Henry IV did not attain the same popular acclaim as did his son; indeed he may have disappointed some of the magnates who remembered him as a crusader and chivalric hero in the early 1390s, and who may have hoped that he would renew the war in France, but he was too much of a realist to be tempted into such ambitions, and he had to devote his efforts to dealing with more immediate problems. However Henry V's successes, both in the French War and in peace at home, must be attributed, at least partly, to the foundations which his father had laid.

Henry IV's main problem in government was finance. Parliament was reluctant to grant him taxes, and behind this lay an uncertainty about when a king was entitled to levy taxation. It was recognized that in a national emergency the King could demand money from his subjects, and this was usually taken to mean the costs of a foreign war. Under Richard II, demands for taxation had often been accompanied by royal pledges to campaign in person. At the same time it was felt that the ordinary revenues of the Crown, essentially those from its demesne lands, the financial incidents of feudalism and judicial rights, should suffice to meet routine costs of government and the court; the corollary to this was that objections were raised to the employment of parliamentary taxes for ends other than those for which they had been approved (192). These objections became increasingly vociferous when England was technically at peace with France between 1389 and 1415. If there was no war, the Commons were reluctant to vote money to the King and they were unsympathetic to requests for assistance in meeting other government expenditure. Even with the duchy of Lancaster revenues added to those of the Crown, Henry's resources were probably inadequate to meet all the expenses of government. Henry probably had the worst of both worlds; because he was theoretically at peace with France, it was hard to persuade the Commons to agree to taxation, but in practice he had to meet considerable military expenditure. Despite the truce there was fighting in Gascony, and there were even raids on the English coast (129, pp.124, 171; Ch.20). The problems of suppressing magnate unrest in the first half of the reign, hostility from the Scots and above all the protracted revolt of Owain Glyn Dŵr and Welsh raids into England, all put demands on the King's resources (192). When Henry tried to campaign in Scotland in 1400, he had to rely to a considerable extent on borrowing, because although Parliament had renewed the customs to him in 1399, it had not made any further grant. Henry had a further problem in that customs revenues dropped in the first three years of his reign by some £4,000 annually, compared with the last three of Richard II, a fall of 9.3 per cent, and this was followed by a further disastrous fall of over £13,000 in the King's fourth year. Even the subsequent recovery left revenues 16.3 per cent lower than at the end of the fourteenth century (129, p.127). He also had to face reductions in other sections of his revenues; the royal estates, like those of the magnates, were probably giving reduced returns because of the general state of the economy, and revenues from feudal incidents were being curtailed by the development of uses.

Although the King had these problems and the parsimony of the Commons suggests that they were being unrealistic, one must remember that they too had difficulties. The decline in customs revenues marks a cut-back in the wool trade, and this would have affected the incomes of the sheep-rearers and wool merchants who paid taxes and whose interests were represented by both county and borough members. Henry clearly understood the principle that extraordinary taxation was justified by war; when his ministers sought grants from Parliament, they emphasized military necessity. The Commons were not entirely blind to the King's needs, although in 1407 they tried to argue that responsibility for suppressing the Welsh revolt should be borne by the magnates in the disturbed area (192). At the same time, they tried to take advantage of the King's needs for their own ends, notably by asking for an answer to their petitions before they granted supply. The King refused to accept this as a principle, but in practice had often to concede it (129, p.112; 135, pp.96–7).

More important were the financial restrictions which the Commons tried to impose. On several occasions stipulations were made that the money granted should be employed for defence and in 1404, the Commons appointed four war treasurers to collect and spend the tax. This was to be levied in a new way, partly as a flat rate payment of 20s. on each knight's fee, and partly as a payment of a shilling in the pound on lands, goods and other sources of income. Two war treasurers were appointed in the second Parliament of the year, although on that occasion the Commons were more generous with grants (129, pp.168, 175; 192). A natural sequel to the appointment of treasurers was an insistence on auditing the accounts. Here the Commons had to face royal opposition, but in 1406, by making their grant conditional on auditing the 1404 taxes, they had their way after a protracted struggle, the details of which are not clear (129, pp.202, 206; 135, p.99). As in the similar case in Richard II's reign (Ch.17), one should guard against seeing these actions as the assertion of a constitutional principle, however far they may appear to foreshadow later ideas of the appropriation of supply. One certainly must not regard them as representing 'Lancastrian constitutionalism' because it is clear that the pressures came from the Commons, the members of which were defending their own financial interests, and that the King resisted any encroachments on his prerogatives. The Commons also tried to restrain the King's expenditure, particularly in the granting of annuities, and there were some attempts to recover royal estates which had been alienated. More immediately, there were proposals to reduce expenditure in the royal household, an approach which may put Haxey's case of 1397 into perspective, suggesting that this was a long-standing grievance of Parliament and not one particularly directed at Richard II. The most important step in this direction occurred in 1406, when the Speaker, Sir John Tiptoft, was appointed Treasurer of the Household. He may have been a compromise figure; as a chamber knight he was probably acceptable to the King, although as he replaced an old and trusted servant of Henry's, the appointment may well have been forced on him by Parliament. In this post Tiptoft seems to have succeeded both in curbing household expenditure in the next two years and in winning royal confidence, because in 1408 he was appointed Treasurer of the realm, apparently on the King's initiative. It was probably the renewal of open conflict with France (though without the formal abandonment of the truce) that increased Henry's receipts of taxes in his last years, as in these circumstances Parliament recognized its obligation to give subventions to the King beyond his normal revenue (192). Relations with France will be considered in Chapter 20; for the moment attention will be devoted to domestic affairs.

The King's problems from about 1409 were less financial than political; new factions emerged among the nobility and the prince of Wales began to be prominent in opposition to his father. The politics of these years, however, tend to be obscure, and events are much less well documented than earlier in the reign. Those chronicles which cover the period, such as Walsingham's, tend to concentrate more on ecclesiastical affairs than on politics and their references to the latter cannot always be clearly set in context. Probably personal rivalries counted for more in the struggles of 1409–13 than disputes over policy, as there seems to have been only one major issue which divided the factions, namely relations with the feuding parties in France. The group around the prince of Wales, consisting largely of magnates of the younger generation, with some support from his Beaufort relations, favoured a pro-Burgundian policy, while the King, supported by Archbishop Arundel, who had returned with him in 1399 and on whom he relied increasingly, and his second son Prince Thomas, seems to have been more prepared to come to terms with the Armagnacs, at least from 1412 onwards. Prince Henry's motives can only be conjectured, but he may well have had some personal dislike for his father; he certainly had an affection for the memory of Richard II, whom he was to have honourably reburied soon after his accession (135, pp.106–9, 121–2). Basically he seems to have been ambitious for power and for an opportunity to exercise his talents, particularly after the end of the Welsh revolt had removed him from a sphere of active usefulness to attendance at the Council, where he may well have felt circumscribed.

The circumstances in which the prince's supporters gained control of the major offices of State are obscure. The first obvious sign of trouble was the dismissal of Tiptoft as Treasurer, followed by that of Archbishop Arundel as Chancellor, in December 1409. The delay in appointing successors to both of them probably reflects the King's resistance, but nothing is known of the pressures behind this. Certainly the appointment of Sir Thomas Beaufort as Chancellor and of Lord Scrope as Treasurer was a victory for the prince's faction, which succeeded in retaining power for almost two years. It, too, had financial problems and had to face a reluctant Commons in 1410. By the following year, the situation seems to have become acute, and a further Parliament met in November. Shortly afterwards Arundel returned to the chancery and a new Treasurer was appointed (129, pp.231–2, 238–42). The removal of the prince's men is almost as puzzling as their earlier appointment, but a possible explanation may be that Bishop Henry Beaufort suggested that Henry might resign the Crown to his eldest son, and that this stirred the ailing King to action, so that he reasserted his own influence. During 1412, the prince of Wales was certainly out of favour, but the King cannot have been pursuing his supporters vindictively, because although the creation of Prince Thomas as duke of Clarence may have been intended to counterbalance Prince Henry's influence, Sir Thomas Beaufort, the Chancellor during the period of the prince's power, was created earl of Dorset at the same time (129, p.243). Possibly the King was hoping to detach him from his son's connection. There seems to have been a lot of court intrigue during this summer, perhaps prompted by the King's ill-health and a jockeying for position among the princes and their friends. Prince Henry certainly claimed that rumours were being spread about him by various sons of iniquity and sowers of division, and he produced documents to defend himself against charges that he had retained money paid to him as Captain of Calais. A reconciliation was patched up in October, which lasted until the King's death five months later (135, pp.110–12).

The succession was peaceful, and Henry V's title was never seriously challenged during his nine years' reign. There was only one rising which needed to be suppressed by force, that of the Lollards under Sir John Oldcastle, and this was hardly a serious threat to the King, who defeated it with no difficulty. Although there were some subsequent plots in which the Lollards were involved, none of them came to anything (241, pp.10–17). The only really dangerous plot was that of the earl of Cambridge in 1415, but it was revealed to the King by its intended beneficiary, the earl of March (39, pp.188–90). Herein perhaps lay the Lancastrians' greatest advantage, in that their most likely potential rival was not prepared to act against them. Henry's magnanimity to March, whom he had restored to his estates in 1413, may have been one reason for this. It was characteristic of the King to let bygones be bygones; he also restored the heirs of the earls of Huntingdon and Northumberland, whose fathers had been forfeited in 1400 and 1405 respectively, and despite the political tensions of 1412 he never showed any hostility to his brother Clarence after his accession.

The new King had one important characteristic which his father lacked, a personal charisma, although its precise character does not emerge clearly from the surviving records. His capacity as a military leader, which will be considered in Chapter 20, contributed to it, but even before he could display this in France, he had already secured support from Parliament. The first one of the reign renewed the customs and granted a subsidy, and that of November 1414 voted a double subsidy, which was valuable in itself and also gave Henry security for borrowing (197, pp.149, 151). His victory at Agincourt in 1415 seems to have created a mood of national euphoria, which benefited him both by strengthening the standing of the dynasty – victory clearly was proof of God's blessing – and by making his subjects more willing to unloose their purse-strings, both in grants and in loans. In 1415 the Commons granted the custom on wool for life and a new subsidy, as well as agreeing to earlier payment of the second half of the double one voted previously, and in 1416 they approved another double payment. In 1417 the King was able to raise over £34,000 in loans (53, pp.360, 366; 186). A further subsidy was granted in 1419, but after the Treaty of Troyes of 1420, Parliament made only one further grant, in 1421. Not only that, the King had to have recourse to forced loans, which provoked popular antagonism (53, p.377; 197, pp.162–3). The nature of these loans is not clear, and it is likely that they were of the kind on which no interest was payable to the lender, because they were regarded as an obligation due to the King at a time of national emergency. Certainly the evidence of some of the loans made to the Crown by Richard Whittington suggests that no interest was paid to him when repayment was made of the principal. The surviving records are, however, insufficient to provide absolutely certain evidence of whether or not some financial inducement was held out to lenders, and the historian must rely on parallels with rather better documented loans later in the century (Ch.29). Henry's reliance on loans may have been prompted at the end of the reign by the attitude of the Commons to the treaty of 1420, that once Henry had been recognized as heir to the French throne, the wars were no longer for the defence of England, and that the obligation to pay taxes no longer existed. Henry, however, cannot have shared this view, if he put forward demands for free loans as a right. He did, however, try to increase his resources by exploiting the conquered lands in Normandy from 1417 onwards, and this was not without success, although the revenues which he derived from them did not meet all the costs of the war, even with the Norman Exchequer under the control of as experienced an official as Tiptoft (186). The King's finances in England were probably affected by a decline in wool exports, and hence in both customs revenues and the resources of the wool producers, from 1419–20 onwards. Average exports in the last three years of the reign were over 14 per cent lower than the average for the first six (66, pp.56–7) [A.2]. Nevertheless, it is a tribute to the effectiveness of Henry's government that it was still able to finance the vigorous prosecution of a major war.

As a monarch, Henry was willing to pay attention to detail in every branch of government and to act decisively. Documents in his own hand reflect the man of action; they are blunt and to the point. The same tone appears in other royal mandates, and it is likely that they were dictated by him. Possibly the fact that they were always in English may have been one reason why he made so vivid an impression on his subjects. He was a king about whom legends gathered (often to survive in the portrait drawn by Shakespeare), and whether they were true or false, this tells the historian something about the reputation of the man among his contemporaries. Their letters to him display both admiration and affection, and go some way to explaining his success as a king (135, pp.117–19, 125, 132). It was essentially his personal qualities which contributed most to this, and which marked him out from his father, whose own achievements should not be underrated. Henry V was able to build on the foundations which his father had laid securely, adding popular acclaim to political and military control. Less than a quarter of a century after the usurpation of 1399, the third King of the House of Lancaster succeeded unchallenged as an infant, when his father died unexpectedly and prematurely aged about thirty-five. The long duration of the succeeding reign was not an achievement of Henry VI, but a tribute to his father and grandfather.

CHAPTER 20

England and Europe, 1399–1422

When Henry IV seized the English throne, he not only had to obtain acceptance at home, but also had to secure recognition abroad. More especially, he succeeded to the perennial problem of relations with France. Richard II's last years had seen some *rapprochement* between the two realms, and although it had not been possible to settle all the matters at issue between them, a long-term truce had been agreed, and had been reinforced by Richard's marriage to a daughter of Charles VI. Had the French court been united behind this policy of peace and friendship with England, Henry might never have been able to launch his invasion, but matters were not as simple as this. For the whole period from the 1390s to the 1430s, there was extreme factiousness at the French court, which was to be crucial not only in France's internal affairs but also in its external relations. The main reason for this was that from 1392 till his death in 1422 Charles VI was subject to periodic fits of insanity, which tended to increase in length as the years went by. His inability to govern personally left the country prey to the rivalries of the royal kindred, of whom the two most important in the early period were Charles's brother, Louis of Orleans, and his uncle, Philip of Burgundy. The latter had been the better disposed to Richard, possibly because of the economic ties between his lands in Flanders and England, but in 1399 Orleans was dominant at the French court and was prepared to support Henry.

There was no real goodwill behind this assistance – one suspects that Orleans's main aim was to embarrass Burgundy – and after Henry's victory Orleans was no longer so friendly. However, the existing truce was extended in November 1399, the main reason being that neither side was in a fit state to renew the conflict. Although Henry may have obtained some popularity from those who disliked Richard's policy of peace with France, his main concern was to consolidate his hold at home. He also had the problem of Richard's queen, Isabella, since the deposition, and later the death, of her husband left him with the obligation to return both her and her dowry. Negotiations over this were protracted, partly because Henry could use Isabella as a hostage to prevent French attack, and partly because he had used the last of the dowry to keep his Exchequer solvent (129, p.120). Proposals were mooted that she might marry the prince of Wales, but these were abandoned, and Isabella returned to France in 1401. Henry delayed action on the question of the dowry, and demanded in return that the French should meet the unpaid balance of the ransom of John of France, captured at Poitiers almost half a century before and dead since 1364. In the meantime, the truce was again renewed (129, p.122).

The English lands in South-west France posed the most insoluble problem in Anglo-French relations. There had been disputes over these since the loss of

Normandy in 1204, and rivalry over ultimate sovereignty there had been a major factor in the outbreak of the Hundred Years War. Throughout various attempts at settlement, no compromise could be reached which satisfied the demands of the rival monarchs, not least because the local inhabitants preferred a remote ruler in London to a closer, and perhaps more interferring, one in Paris. Furthermore, the economy of the Bordeaux region was closely linked to that of England. The landed aristocracy cared little for either king, and paid slight heed to the bonds of loyalty. Sometimes, indeed, branches of great families might preserve close ties with each other, but still owe allegiance to rival rulers. The frontiers of the English lands were ill-defined, and this gave scope for diplomatic intrigue, which could alter the balance of power between the two kings. In 1401 Henry appointed his cousin, the earl of Rutland, as his Lieutenant in Gascony (151, pp.42, 154–5), though his aim in this may have been as much to remove a potential trouble-maker from the English political scene as to strengthen his position in France. However Rutland, in a stay of about a year, did succeed in restoring English authority, by no means an easy task, and one made worse by the distrust which the Gascons had shown for the House of Lancaster in the 1390s. Until 1403 there was no open war, but rather an uneasy condition between war and peace, with active diplomatic manoeuvring. In this the English lost some frontier castles, and the count of Foix defected to Charles VI. In October 1403 the French invaded Guienne and blockaded Bordeaux, although they never formally repudiated the truce between England and France (151, p.48). During the next few years armed hostility persisted in Gascony, although there were no full-scale campaigns; in these the French made gains despite the intermittent dispatch of military assistance from England. It was not until the winter of 1407–8 that a further local truce was agreed (129, pp.180, 188, 210–11).

Politically and strategically, the French had the initiative, and they were able to carry it further into the enemy's camp by sending support to Glyn Dŵr in Wales. One thing, however, prevented them from turning their initiative into victory, the mutual hostility and continuing vendetta of the houses of Orleans and Burgundy. This struggle, and the associated search for allies by both parties, was a constant factor in English foreign policy for the next thirty years, because English rulers could play them off against each other. The death of Duke Philip and the succession of his son John in 1404 made matters even worse, as he was even more hostile to Louis of Orleans and lacked the authority of age which his father had possessed and which had served as a check on his rival. The main aim of the Burgundian dukes was to obtain influence in France, although the economic ties between their lands in the Low Countries and England may have disposed them rather more than the Orleanists to seek an accommodation with England. Philip's interests outside France may also have encouraged him to further Henry's diplomacy in Germany and the marriage alliance between the latter's daughter Blanche and the son of Rupert of the Palatinate, the German Emperor-elect (129, pp.138–9; 141, p.225). Henry's motive for this alliance was probably to avoid the isolation of England in European politics, as the Empire might serve as a counterbalance to France. (The other marriage alliance which he made, between his daughter Philippa and Eric of Denmark, was similar in character, in that he was seeking allies in the Baltic area against the hostility of the Hanse towns.)

The murder of the duke of Orleans by Burgundian agents in November 1407 was a turning-point in Anglo-French relations. Bitter though the earlier feuds had been, they were slight compared with what followed. After two years of uneasy temporizing, civil war broke out in 1410, and after a brief peace was renewed in the following year. As the Burgundians became increasingly powerful, the Orleanist faction rallied round the new duke's father-in-law Bernard of Armagnac, and John of Burgundy was driven out of Paris. He then took the fateful step of turning to England for help, offering to surrender certain Flemish towns and to marry his daughter to the prince of Wales, then dominant in Henry's Council. Troops were sent and contributed to his victory. While the marriage negotiations were still continuing, the Armagnacs also looked to England for help. They offered substantial concessions in Guienne, and the King, who had regained control of the Council during the winter, came to terms with them in 1412. In fact the Armagnacs renounced the alliance after some two months, and when an English expeditionary force under the duke of Clarence arrived, it found that the French factions had patched up another short-lived reconciliation. However, Clarence demonstrated the military weakness of France by marching from Normandy to Bordeaux without opposition, and by receiving substantial payments to buy him off (53, p.321; 129, pp.236–7; 151, pp.58–62)..

The next decade saw conspicuous duplicity on all sides, with opportunism being the most marked characteristic of all parties. Possibly the prince of Wales might have pursued a more consistent pro-Burgundian policy if he had remained in power after 1411, but this is not certain; as king he was undoubtedly prepared to deal with whichever party in France offered him the best terms. The political turmoil there enabled him to drive a hard bargain, and during 1414, the year after his accession, he negotiated simultaneously with both Burgundy and Armagnac for a possible marriage alliance. At the same time, the two French factions were trying to patch up an agreement. Of the three parties, Henry was probably the most determined on war and the Armagnacs the most inclined for peace. They offered substantial concessions, the marriage of Henry to Charles VI's daughter Catherine with a dowry increased from 600,000 to 800,000 crowns during the bargaining, and substantial territory in South-west France. John of Burgundy promised in the summer of 1414 not to ally himself with the English, but still remained in touch with Henry, whose policy was almost certainly to delay the start of a war until he could complete his preparations for it. These preparations were diplomatic as well as military. He negotiated for political support in Europe, sending embassies to the Emperor-elect Sigismund and to the King of Aragon, and blaming the French for the failure of negotiations in which his own demands were exorbitant (39, pp.12–17; 53, pp.356–8).

It is not easy to be certain of Henry's war aims. Possibly the principal one was war in itself; his military experience in Wales had given him a taste for fighting and revealed his gifts as a leader; he may well have wished to seek renown in a wider sphere, and calculated rightly that a campaign abroad would appeal to the magnate and knightly classes and thereby strengthen their loyalty to him and his family. He seems to have convinced himself that he had a rightful title to the

French throne, in defiance of logic – if the French succession passed through the female line (which would be necessary to justify the claims of Edward III and his heirs), the earl of March's title would be stronger than Henry's. As early as the summer of 1414, however, Henry was talking in terms of recovering his just inheritance, the realm of France, and he voiced this claim also during the negotiations in the summer of 1415, thereby provoking a sharp retort from the French envoys (23, pp.24–6). This claim, however, may never have been seriously meant, and certainly Henry cannot have hoped that it would be conceded. He may indeed have put it forward to ensure the breakdown of talks. The well-informed author of the *Gesta Henrici Quinti* lays particular stress on his claims in Normandy and Aquitaine (39, pp.16–17), which may well have been his primary objective.

The 1415 campaign had only limited aims, and Henry does not appear to have settled his strategy until the middle of the summer. Early in the year he may have considered the possibility of a campaign in South-west France, but in the end he launched his attack in Normandy. He landed in mid-August, and as it took over five weeks to reduce Harfleur, which he presumably wished to secure as a base, it was obvious that he would have to restrict further military activity. As late as the beginning of September Henry's plans still seem to have been for a march through France to Bordeaux, in which he hoped to capture Rouen and Paris *en route* (151, pp.72–5). This argues a totally unrealistic optimism on Henry's part, but he may at least have hoped to emulate Clarence's expedition of 1412 and give a demonstration of strength. Harfleur's stubborn resistance compelled him to reconsider his strategy, because the siege was costly in both time and casualties, not only in the fighting but also, and apparently more seriously, from an outbreak of dysentery, which killed many men and necessitated the invaliding home of others (39, pp.26–59).

At this stage the campaign looked close to disaster. The need to garrison Harfleur depleted the English army, and its numbers were further reduced by desertions. It was in these circumstances that Henry, against the advice of the majority of his Council, decided to march to Calais, believing that the 150-mile march could be accomplished in eight days (39, pp.58–61). The risk was clearly immense, and the historian is probably justified in considering it foolhardy. Henry's dilemma was that the capture of Harfleur was a small gain to show to his country, and that if he were to pursue the safe course and return home, Parliament might be reluctant to make him further grants, whereas a march through hostile country was a gamble. Even a successful march to Calais would mean little; his only real hope was to bring the French to battle and secure a victory. Not even the first of these was a certainty, still less the second. It has been reasonably argued that the march was a deliberate attempt to lure the French to battle (135, pp.126–7), but the odds against which Henry would have to fight meant that this was an enormously risky undertaking at which even his associates quailed. Crucial to any judgement of Henry's action is his assessment of the capacity of the French leadership. The older men in it, notably the King's last surviving uncle, the duke of Berry, who could remember how effectively Charles V's strategy of avoiding battle had worked in the 1370s, advised against taking up the challenge, and they may well have prevailed in the early stages of the march. Later, less cautious counsels prevailed, possibly because the French had information about Henry's problems, notably the sickness in the army (23, pp.46–7), and regarded victory as likely. This probably was what tempted them into battle at Agincourt, where they blundered to defeat, with immense casualties in both dead and prisoners, while Henry displayed his consummate skill as a solider in his tactical handling of his troops.

Strategically, this campaign should not be overrated. Essentially it was a raid, similar to many others, and the chance success in battle had no long-term military consequences. Henry's only tangible gain in 1415 was Harfleur, and as it needed to be reinforced against French attacks it was perhaps a potential liability rather than an asset. Henry's brother, the duke of Bedford, was able to raise a siege in 1416 by a naval victory in the Seine, but it was attacked again in the following year, and another fleet under the earl of Huntingdon had to be sent to relieve it (23, pp.69–71, 77–8). Henry's greatest benefit from Agincourt was less material than moral. It enhanced his reputation and, as we saw in Chapter 19, totally consolidated his position in England. It also increased his standing in western Europe, where the main political concern at the time was the attempt to end the Schism in the Church at the Council of Constance. The most influential prince there, the Emperor-elect Sigismund, wished for assistance in this from England and France, and was desirous of mediating between them. In March 1416 he went to Paris, where the French, clearly shaken by their defeat, agreed to him acting as an intermediary. At the beginning of May he arrived in England, but it soon became clear that there was no prospect of anything more than a truce, as the gap between Henry's demands and any possible French concessions was too great to be bridged (53, pp.361–2).

At this point, divisions in France again played into Henry's hands. Whereas in March the more influential of Charles VI's councillors had favoured a truce, by July Armagnac, who favoured a tougher policy, was dominant. He tried to delay agreement on a truce in the hope of first recovering Harfleur, in order to negotiate from a position of greater strength. However, Sigismund regarded this as a snub to his mediation, and in consequence accepted Henry's moves for an Anglo-imperial alliance (53, pp.362–3). They then tried to persuade John of Burgundy to join them in a set of secret negotiations, and Henry even produced a draft treaty by which the duke would renounce his allegiance to Charles. There is, however, no evidence that any firm agreement was reached (152, pp.214–15).

These manoeuvres had little long-term consequence, because in the autumn of 1417 war was renewed, and in a very different form from the raid of 1415. Henceforward, Henry's strategy suggests greater deliberation than his gambler's adventure two years before. Diplomatically he had the advantage of a renewed Burgundian attack on the Armagnacs, for although Duke John still proclaimed his loyalty to Charles VI, he seized control of most of the important towns in the neighbourhood of Paris. Although he did not capture the capital itself until May 1418, he had already in the previous November secured possession of the Queen and won her support (152, pp.216–17, 220–7). These struggles left Henry a free hand, and he was able to consolidate his position stage by stage before making any further advance. He landed at Touques, on the opposite side of the Seine estuary from Harfleur, and embarked on a campaign in western Normandy, reducing it town by town. After a slow but steady progress he laid siege to Rouen in the summer of 1418. It fell in the following January as a result of famine, because neither of the contending French factions was able to relieve it. The defenders attempted to prolong the siege by driving out the poor who could not contribute to the defence, but Henry was ruthless; although he did grant them some food supplies at Christmas, they had to remain in the town ditch between the two forces, and later the King refused them further food, saying that it was the defenders who were responsible for their fate (16, pp.21–2, 30).

During the siege, negotiations had been resumed between the contending parties, the English, the Burgundians and the old Armagnacs, now under the leadership of the Dauphin Charles. Each was trying to find an ally to isolate the third, but while the talking went on, Henry's military position, and consequently his political bargaining power, steadily improved. An attempt to reach an accommodation between the dauphin and Burgundy, in which the latter at any rate seems to have been willing to come to terms, was instead to make such agreement impossible. During a meeting between Charles and Duke John at Montereau in September 1419 the latter was murdered by members of the Dauphin's entourage, almost certainly as the result of a premeditated plan, although it is not clear if they were all involved in the plot (152, pp.274–86).

In the negotiations before Montereau, Henry's demands had been for marriage to Catherine, a suitable dowry, and full sovereign rights over Normandy and the English lands in South-west France. In Normandy he was already consolidating his position, by granting lands to his followers there, both as a reward for past services and in order to create a substantial group of men with an interest in maintaining the conquest. At the same time, by restraining his armies from what they might regard as their rights of pillage, he tried to avoid antagonizing the local population (53, pp.370–1; 135, p.127). It may well be that these demands represented Henry's real aims at this time, and that the increase in what he sought subsequently was essentially an opportunist move prompted by the incredible crassness of his opponents. Philip of Burgundy would probably have preferred to dominate France in his own right rather than co-operate with Henry, but desire for revenge on his father's murderers drove him into the English camp. Henry now laid claim to the French Crown seriously, and his only concession was that Charles VI should retain it as long as he lived. A formal Anglo-Burgundian alliance was agreed on Christmas Day 1419, and in the following spring a treaty was agreed at Troyes between Henry and the party headed by Burgundy and the Queen. This provided for Henry's marriage to Catherine and his succession to Charles VI, although the union of the realms was to be purely personal and they were to remain distinct in government and law. Henry also agreed to conquer on behalf of his father-in-law the lands which still adhered to the Dauphin. Gascony was to remain in English possession as part of the Lancastrian inheritance, but Normandy, while it was to remain under English rule until Charles's death, was then to revert to French control within the dual monarchy. (28, p.226; 151, pp.80, 85). This suggests at least a partial reversal of Henry's policy before Montereau, although there was still to be no displacement of the English lords who had obtained Norman lands.

Although the Treaty of Troyes was in form a peace settlement between England and France, in practice it was no more than a pact between Henry and one of the contending French factions. The stipulation concerning the reconquest of lands under the Dauphin's control emphasizes this point, and Henry's efforts in his two remaining years were largely devoted to this end. Apart from some four months in early 1421 when he returned to England to have his queen crowned and to raise more money for the war, these years were spent in campaigning. During Henry's absence there was a clear indication that the Dauphin's forces were by no means negligible; an army of French and Scots defeated and killed Henry's brother Clarence at Baugé in Maine. Two earls, Somerset and Huntingdon, were captured, and although the earl of Salisbury successfully extricated the main English force, and indeed launched an effective counter-attack, the result raised morale in the Dauphin's camp, and diplomatically encouraged the duke of Brittany to negotiate a truce with the Dauphin. A further sign of stiffening resistance to Henry after his return to France can be seen in the protracted character of some of the sieges – that of Meaux in the winter of 1421–22 took longer than that of Rouen and took a heavy toll of the English. The dysentery which depleted the troops also broke Henry's constitution. Although Meaux fell in May 1422, Henry could no longer play an active part in the war; he had to be carried on a litter to his last siege in July, and died at the end of August (53, pp.375–7; 135, p.132).

Henry's greatest achievements were as a soldier and as a diplomatist, and with his preference for fighting he may have regarded diplomacy as war continued by other means. He undoubtedly had a talent for exploiting a political situation to his best advantage, and his capacity for skilful planning was joined with an inspired opportunism, which enabled him to outmanoeuvre his more heavy-footed contemporaries. In an age when political conditions gave rise to duplicity on all sides, he was more than a match in unscrupulousness for his rivals.

A recent judgement on Henry described him as 'the greatest man that ever ruled England'. Certainly contemporaries regarded him highly; to his fellow-countrymen he was the hero-king *par excellence*, and his enemies looked on him as a just man and an honourable opponent (135, pp.130–3). By comparison with his successor, his memory shone bright, and a century after his accession the author of the *First English Life* regarded him as outstanding among English kings (23, p.4). The very fact that he chose to write about Henry, and to collect the views of men nearer to him in the time reflects the memory which he left. His sources include both the official tradition, embodied in the *Vita Henrici Quinti* by Tito Livio of Forli, who was commissioned to write it by Henry's brother, Humphrey, duke of Gloucester, and a series of memories preserved in the Ormonde family. The survival of these is further testimony to the esteem in which Henry was held.

If reputation alone were the criterion by which a king can be judged, undoubtedly Henry was great, but there is a danger that panegyrics may be carried too far. Untimely though his death was for the English campaigns in France, it may have been timely for his memory. The hardening of French resistance after 1420, despite the country's political divisions, suggests that a final English victory was not as near as it appeared at the time of the Treaty of Troyes, and that Henry might have had the same problems as were faced by his successors. McFarlane's view (135, p.125) that, had he lived, he might have dominated Europe and fulfilled his ambition to defeat the Turks, can be no more than speculation. It is possible, but the odds seem weighted against it. His greatest successes were achieved against ineffective opposition, and one cannot say how he would have coped with the situation which existed after his death. Good fortune as well as ability contributed to his victories. His very success left a *damnosa hereditas* to his heir and the regents who acted on his behalf, because they felt obliged to try and retain what he had won, and had to do so with resources which could not sustain the war to which Henry had committed them. The short-term gains in France were obvious, and the benefits which accrued to the King in the form of magnate goodwill equally so, but it is not necessarily a retrospective judgement to accuse Henry of short-sightedness for renewing and persisting in the war, as the experience of the previous century had shown the capacity of the French to recover from a desperate situation.

CHAPTER 21

Henry VI: minority and dual monarchy[1]

Henry V's death left England with its second minority in fifty years and with all the problems of government which this entailed. There are some parallels between the years after 1377 and those following 1422, notably in domestic political tensions and in the activity of the minority Council, but there are even more marked differences, which can be largely explained by relations with France. In 1377 French power had been in the ascendant, and threats to the English coast had helped to draw together earlier contending factions around the young King. In 1422, Henry V left his son as heir to France as well as to England, and when Charles VI died some seven weeks later, the infant Henry VI was left with an impossible inheritance. The Treaty of Troyes in 1420 had provided that the two kingdoms of England and France were to remain distinct, and this necessitated separate arrangements for ruling each of them on behalf of the new King. A determined adult ruler might have been able to control both, but no regent possessed the moral authority to do so, and the problem of who would exercise the regency in each kingdom was subject to its own particular political pressures. The division of authority between Henry V's surviving brothers, John, duke of Bedford, and Humphrey, duke of Gloucester, involved a danger that their own interests might be in opposition. More seriously, the division of the kingdoms meant that Bedford, as regent in France, could not appeal to England for financial assistance as confidently as Henry V had done.

It reflects the importance of the French lands that it was Bedford, the older and abler brother, who took control there. Although Henry V had stipulated that the duke of Burgundy, if he wished, should have the right to the regency, Philip turned it down, and the post passed to Bedford. The older view is that the duke acted in this way because he foresaw the risks which would follow from his accepting office under English protection, and that by handing back the poisoned cup to Bedford he preserved his freedom of action, so that in the long run he would secure real rather than illusory power in France (141, pp.268–70). More recently it has been convincingly argued that Philip, unlike his father, was not particularly concerned with obtaining power in France, and that his major concern was with his lands in the Low Countries. His refusal of the regency, therefore, was prompted by a desire to concentrate his activity elsewhere rather than by a calculation that it would do him little good (153, pp.16–17). While desire for revenge on the murderers of his father affected his policy, this was only one influence on him, and when he became involved in the Anglo-French fighting, it was only to protect his own lands.

Bedford's actions as regent can all be explained by his objective of pursuing to its culmination the campaign against the Dauphin in which his brother had been engaged at the time of his death. The military problem did not appear particularly difficult; an attempt by the Dauphinists to seize the strategic initiative after Henry V's death ended when their force, commanded by the Scottish earl of Buchan, was defeated at Cravant in 1423. In the following year, the Franco-Scottish army was virtually destroyed at Verneuil; French casualties were heavy, and the two leading Scots, the earls of Buchan and Douglas, were among the dead (53, p.383). But although Bedford was successful in battle, his policy of a steady reduction of the lands north of the Loire, similar to Henry V's conquest of Normandy after 1417, was perhaps a less appropriate strategy than it had been for his brother. Henry's real aims, at least until the time of Montereau, may have been limited primarily to conquests in northern France, so he could afford to move gradually. For Bedford, whose main objective was to eliminate the Dauphin and his claim to the throne, so as to secure Henry VI's title, more rapid and decisive action might have been preferable. The longer the Dauphin survived at Bourges, the more doubts might arise in the minds of trimmers as to whether an English victory was possible.

However, Bedford's ability should not be underestimated, and it is a tribute to it that the English position in France survived so long in face of many difficulties, most serious of which was the financial problem. As regent in France alone, he had to rely largely on the French lands to provide him with money to maintain his armies. This probably explains why he could not follow up the victories at Cravant and Verneuil, for although he had power to raise taxes in Normandy, he still was short of funds even for defending the duchy properly, let alone launching an effective attack on the 'kingdom of Bourges'. At this stage, he was able to obtain little support from England; by the end of Henry V's reign there had already been resistance to the King's financial demands, and the Exchequer was under severe pressure (53, p.375; 181; 186).

The mid 1420s therefore saw a consolidation of the English position rather than a further advance, and it was only in 1428 that a new strategic move was made. The earl of Salisbury, one of the ablest English field commanders, besieged Orleans, presumably hoping that its capture would give him control of the Loire valley and a springboard for a campaign towards Bourges. In November, however, he was killed by a cannon-ball, and his successor in command, the earl of Suffolk, could not push home the attack. In the late spring of 1429, the appearance of Joan of Arc marked a turning-point in the campaign, the siege was raised, and soon afterwards the English suffered two severe defeats, at Jargeau and Patay, within a week of each other. The most striking point about the subsequent campaign, in the course of which the Dauphin was crowned at Rheims, was the willingness of the towns to open their gates to Joan's army. When one compares this with their earlier reluctance to submit to the English, it shows clearly that Bedford's power had rested less on French acquiescence than on his military force. It is, however, only in retrospect that one can see this campaign as the turning-point in the war, and contemporaries might have been pardoned for viewing Joan's career as a meteor which was soon burnt out. The fortunes of war had changed so often in the past that the war party in England might well have hoped for a revival; this indeed occurred in 1430 when Joan was captured, to be put to death in the following year, and after a lull in 1432–33, the English made further gains in 1434 (53, pp.386–8). Henry VI's coronation as King of France in 1431 was presumably intended as a counter-measure to that of the Dauphin, now Charles VII, in 1429 but its propaganda effect may well have misfired through its being held at Paris instead of at Rheims, the traditional place for coronations of the French kings.

English diplomacy also had varying success. Bedford's principal objective here was to maintain alliances with the enemies of the Valois King, particularly the dukes of Burgundy and Brittany. The former's desire to avenge his father's death, at Montereau had driven him into alliance with Henry V and had contributed to the English paper victory in the Treaty of Troyes, but the Anglo-Burgundian friendship had no strong foundation. Bedford had difficulties in keeping the partnership intact and may have himself contributed to its prolongation by his marriage to Duke Philip's sister in 1423. It certainly helped to tide over a crisis prompted by the clumsy manoeuvrings of his brother, Humphrey of Gloucester.

In 1421, Jacqueline, countess of Hainault and Holland in her own right, had fled to England from her husband, John of Brabant. The marriage had been childless, and Philip of Burgundy, who was heir to the Brabant lands, hoped to absorb Jacqueline's also. Why Henry V received her in England is not known, as this action was out of character with his usual acute sense of what was diplomatically wise. After Henry's death, Gloucester took up Jacqueline's cause, obtained a dissolution of her marriage from the old, and discredited, Avignon Pope of the Schism, Benedict XIII, and married her in 1423. He then tried to raise an army to recover her lands. In view of Philip's concern with consolidating his lands in the Low Countries, his interests could hardly have been crossed more explicitly than by Humphrey's actions, so that it is scarcely surprising that he was prepared to consider coming to terms with France, provided that some reparation be made for his father's death (53, p.382; 115, p.165). From Bedford's point of view, his brother's action was all the more damaging in so far as his attachment to Jacqueline, and her lands, proved transient. After a truce in March 1425, and proposals to resolve the issue by a duel between Philip and Humphrey, the latter deserted his wife, returning to England with one of her ladies-in-waiting, Eleanor Cobham, whom he was to marry in 1428 when Martin V nullified his marriage to Jacqueline. Bedford gave no support to his brother in these irresponsible antics; indeed in the winter of 1425–26 he even warned Philip that Humphrey was trying to raise another force (153, pp.38–49). This shows clearly that Bedford saw that a quarrel with Burgundy could be highly detrimental to the English position in France.

Bedford had another potential ally in France in Duke John V of Brittany, whose relations with the Valois King were uneasy. As the duke lacked military power, it was essential for him to trim his sails to changes in the political wind. Although in 1421 he signed an alliance with the Dauphin and sent one of his brothers to help him, he simultaneously encouraged another brother, Arthur of Richemont, to fight for the English. In 1423 he joined a triple alliance with Burgundy and Bedford; at the time when one of Philip's sisters married Bedford another married Richemont (153, p.7). Even before Verneuil in 1424, however, Duke

John switched his allegiance to the Dauphinists, and after the battle Richemont followed suit, being appointed Constable of France. Gloucester's incursions in the Low Countries at this time led Philip of Burgundy to regard this change of sides benevolently; he was not so closely bound to the English alliance as to regret seeing his brothers-in-law, Richemont and Bedford, in opposition to each other. The former, indeed, played an important part in the Franco-Burgundian *rapprochement*. After his appointment as Constable, Philip made a truce with the Dauphin in 1424, and when Richemont was supplanted in the Dauphin's favour by Georges de la Trémoille, Philip temporarily broke off negotiations with the court of Bourges. Contacts between Burgundy and France in 1429 came to nothing, as can be seen from Philip's willingness to hand over Joan of Arc to the English after her capture at Compiègne in 1430. Only after la Trémoille's fall in 1433 and Richemont's return to power were serious negotiations resumed (53, pp.385–9; 115, pp.165–6).

The fluctuations in Philip's policy reflect immediate circumstances. There was, however, among the Burgundian lords a substantial number, including Philip's Chancellor, Rolin, and other councillors, who were inclined to come to terms with the French King (115, p.58; 153, p.66). These Francophils were probably most numerous in the lands of Burgundy itself, although some came from the duke's lands in the Low Countries. There, however, pro-English sentiments were stronger, and some lords there were to remain Anglophil even after 1435. In some ways these sentiments were surprising, because it was precisely in these lands that one finds economic tensions, both over English demands for bullion payments for wool bought at the Calais Staple, and over cloth imports which were resented by the manufacturing towns of Holland and Brabant. These even obtained from the duke in 1428 an ordinance banning such imports, though it soon had to be withdrawn. However, although one cannot entirely disregard the ill-will generated by such matters, they were probably subordinate to political issues in the minds of those most concerned in deciding what policy to pursue.

By the beginning of 1435, Philip seems to have decided to come to terms with the French King. At Nevers in January, agreement was reached between French emissaries and the duke that a further meeting should be held at Arras, to which the English should be invited. There the French were to put forward peace proposals, and if the English did not respond to these, the duke was to work for an agreement with Charles VII. By the time the Congress of Arras met, Anglo-Burgundian relations were cool, and while it was in progress Burgundian social contacts were markedly more cordial with the French than with the English (115, pp.121, 125, 163–4). A contributory factor to the deterioration in Anglo-Burgundian relations was the death of Philip's sister, the duchess of Bedford, in 1433. Not only did this break the personal tie between the two brothers-in-law, but Bedford's remarriage, to Jacquetta of Luxembourg, further antagonized Philip, because she was the daughter of one of his vassals, and his permission had not been sought for the marriage. By 1435, Bedford's own health was failing, and he could not go to Arras, but one doubts if even his diplomatic skill could have preserved the alliance which he had striven to uphold in the previous dozen years. His death at Rouen, between the departure of the English embassy from Arras and the final conclusion of the Franco-Burgundian agreement, removed the man who had done most to maintain English dominance in northern France.

Again it is only in retrospect that the Treaty of Arras can be seen as a decisive turning-point. The English military position should not be underrated, and the Burgundian change of sides merely stiffened a determination to fight on England's part. During a brief conflict with Burgundy, England had the advantage, holding Calais against an attempted siege and making a successful raid into West Flanders. Commercial ties were restored by 1439 – evidently the need for English wool supplies counted for more than the bullion and cloth issues (153, pp.77–85, 108). Meanwhile, in France, although Paris fell to Charles in 1436, English troops had some success in the following year, and contemporaries might have thought that the fortunes of war could turn again in England's favour. Certainly the situation in France at the beginning of Henry VI's personal rule was not one of unrelieved gloom.

The minority years had been difficult in England as well. Bedford's absence in France left Gloucester as the most prominent adult member of the royal house, but his claim to be Protector of the realm provoked opposition from his fellow magnates (156, p.30). They succeeded in imposing strict limits to the power which he held, stipulating that when Bedford was in England, he was to have the power of protector and that the Council rather than the Protector was to exercise the greater part of Crown patronage. Probably the man most vigorous in resisting Humphrey's claims was Bishop Henry Beaufort, but one must also stress the willingness of the Council to act collectively and responsibly in difficult political circumstances. Although they opposed the grant of extensive powers to Gloucester, they were still prepared to collaborate with him in the government of the realm, provided that he did not try to exploit his office too far for personal gain. The weakness of the Council lay less in the political sphere than in its inability to impose order on its own members, for personal hostilities between them could lead to public disorder (53, pp.410–11, 421–3).

The situation was complicated by the feud between Gloucester and Beaufort, which underlies many of the tensions in English politics between the 1420s and the 1440s. Both sought to turn their position during the minority to the furtherance of their own ambitions, but Beaufort, who became Chancellor for the third time in 1424, was the more skilful at making his own interests coincide with those of the country. As his widespread estates exported considerable quantities of wool to the Low Countries, he was sympathetic to Bedford's policy of maintaining good relations with Burgundy, and hostile to Gloucester's pursuit of the claims of Jacqueline of Hainault. The main weapon in Beaufort's armoury was his wealth, which he was prepared to lend to the Crown (as he had been since the time of Henry V), in return for various benefits, such as licences to export wool bypassing the Staple, opportunities to purchase Crown lands and the right to appoint collectors of customs, so as to ensure that he would be repaid. The older belief that he charged usury on these loans has recently been effectively criticized, but there is no doubt that his incidental economic gains and his political influence were for him a fair return for his outlay (53, p.413; 172, pp.141–6). It may also explain why, when Pope Martin V renewed the offer of a cardinal's hat, which

Beaufort had had to refuse under pressure from Henry V in 1418, no obstacle was put in the way of him accepting it.

Tension between Beaufort and Gloucester was liable to erupt into open hostility and even into violence, as in 1425 after the duke's return from his abortive expedition to Hainault. At this time the Council seems to have supported Beaufort, when he reinforced the Tower and ordered the arrest of a number of London citizens, who supported the duke. When Parliament met, however, it showed sympathy to Gloucester and hostility to the bishop, a fact which suggests that Humphrey had greater support in the country at large than among the councillors. This crisis was sufficiently serious for Bedford to be called in to resolve the dispute, and it is a tribute to his authority that he was able to impose a settlement which at least papered over the cracks, and which cannot have been entirely pleasing to either of the rivals. Beaufort gave up the chancellorship to John Kemp, then in the process of translation from the see of London to that of York, and went abroad with Bedford when he returned to the Continent. There he eventually received the red hat which had been bestowed on him ten years before, but which he had never been allowed to receive. He was appointed papal legate for Bohemia, and for a time was to be more active in the wider affairs of the Church than in those of England. Before leaving for France, Bedford succeeded in imposing a settlement on Gloucester, in which the lords of Council secured a confirmation from the older duke that he accepted their view of the relations between themselves and his brother.

These limits on Humphrey's power were soon to lead to a further clash between him and the Council, and when Parliament met in 1427–28 he made a further effort to reassert his authority. This was unsuccessful; the lords of Council, fifteen clerical and twelve lay, put forward a formal document requiring him to be content with the declaration of his authority to which he and Bedford had set their seals. Gloucester's position was further weakened by the emergence of hostility to him among the Commons, where he had previously had a greater measure of support than in the Council. The grant of taxation made by this Parliament was accompanied by a demand that measures should be taken for the safety of his deserted wife, Jacqueline of Hainault (53, pp.415–16; 156, pp.42–5). Opposition to Gloucester, however, did not mean support for Beaufort; when the latter returned to England and published his commission as papal legate to raise a force against the Hussites, the Council approved the duke's protest, and before the matter of raising troops could be discussed, the cardinal had to affirm that he had no intention of contravening royal rights of jurisdiction. The army was raised, but it was never to go to Bohemia, being instead diverted to reinforce the English in France after the French relief of Orleans and the Battle of Patay. This may have proved Beaufort's patriotism to his friends in England, but it signified his abandonment of any claim to be a powerful figure in the ecclesiastical politics of Christendom (156, pp.56–7).

The young King's coronation in England in November 1429 ended the formal protectorate, but made little difference in practice, as Gloucester was still recognized as chief councillor, and the Council itself still provided an overriding collective authority. The balance of support in both the Council and the country seems to have swung back to Beaufort, whom the Commons specially commended for his services when they made a grant of taxation in December of the same year (193, p.200). When Henry was taken to France in 1431 for his coronation there, however, Gloucester remained as regent in England, and was able to exploit this to his own advantage, both securing an increase in his salary and taking proceedings against Beaufort for retaining the see of Winchester, alleging that it could not be held along with a cardinalate. Gloucester also secured changes in a number of important offices, probably in the hope of removing Beaufort's supporters from positions of influence. In fact, that cardinal rode out the storm, although he had to make further loans to the government as the price of obtaining formal authorization to retain his see (156, pp.67–8).

By the early 1430s, the government was faced with a lack of popular confidence in its ability to maintain order, and, even more serious, with financial problems. The war was expensive, and the cost of taking the King to France for his coronation may have added to the burden. When Bedford returned to England in 1433, it is clear that the Commons regarded him as the man best suited to meeting the nation's difficulties, for the Speaker petitioned him not to return to France. Bedford accepted this request, but made the condition that he should have greater powers of patronage than anyone since 1422 (53, pp.417–23; 156, pp.71–2; 193, pp.210–11). The first action taken to meet the financial crisis was to replace Gloucester's ally Lord Scrope as Treasurer by a former Chamberlain, Lord Cromwell, who took steps to draw up a statement of royal revenue, expenditure and debts. This revealed accumulated debts amounting to some £165,000, although it is possible that some elements in the account may have been exaggerated (181).[2] As far as the annual balance was concerned, net receipts from ordinary revenue appear to have amounted to some three-fifths of estimated expenditure, but calculations based on the issues made by the Exchequer in the previous dozen years suggest that Cromwell may have overestimated expenses and underestimated revenues, perhaps as a tactical move to encourage Parliament to be generous. The deficit, therefore, was one which might reasonably have been covered by a grant of taxation, but in general the Commons were not obliging. Despite the fact that prices were high in 1429 and 1430 [A.1] the immediate shock of the reverses in France did prompt them to make substantial grants in those years, but they were much more niggardly in 1432 and 1433. Indeed in the latter year they reduced the assessment of the subsidy to provide relief for towns which were impoverished, or where they regarded the old level as too high (Ch.29; 53, pp.419–20; 197, pp.203–5). It was not until after the Burgundian *volte-face* at Arras that Parliament was shocked into making any further sizeable grant.

A strong man was really necessary to cope with this increase in domestic problems, but Bedford, who might have possessed the necessary authority, even despite being attacked by Gloucester for his conduct in France (156, p.76), was compelled to return to the Continent in 1434 by the deterioration in the fortunes of war. A year later he died. With his death, there was no one who had the standing to overrule the contesting factions among the magnates, and when the young King came of age, it soon became clear that he lacked the capacity to translate the power which he derived from his royal dignity into effective practical authority. During the minority a precarious balance had been preserved between the ambitions of rival nobles, largely perhaps because men were prepared to look to Bedford as a *deus ex machina* when the situation threatened to get out of hand. In the years which followed, this balance could not be maintained.

---

1. Since the completion of this book, a major new work has appeared on the period 1422 –61, R. A. Griffiths, *The Reign of King Henry VI* (1981). This furnishes much detail on the topics considered in Chapters 21–3.
2. Kirby suggests that the largest single item in this, payments due on uncashed tallies, may be inaccurate and that there may have been substantial sums paid but not accounted for.

189

CHAPTER 22

Henry VI: the loss of France

Henry VI's tragedy was that even after he came of age he never attained maturity. After reaching his majority, he did not take over control of policy, as a king might be expected to do, and when he tried to intervene personally in public affairs his participation was at best ill-judged and at worst disastrous. Above all, he lacked the detachment which was required for a successful king; he did not stand above the feuds among the nobility, notably that between Gloucester and Beaufort, which continued unappeased after Bedford's death in 1435 had removed the one man capable of holding them both in check, but persistently displayed favouritism towards the cardinal and hostility to the duke. In his patronage too, Henry lacked the strength of purpose to resist the pressures from his entourage, who were the men who made the most conspicuous gains in lands and offices from the mid 1430s to about 1450. More seriously, the King's favouritism of his immediate followers could lead to the perversion of justice, and offenders going unpunished (156, pp.106–26).

The King was probably deemed to have come of age in 1436, when petitions were granted to an increasing degree only on the authority of the royal sign manual, and when the phrase 'with the assent of our council' began to disappear from the warrants to chancery letters. It is perhaps hardly surprising that at this stage Henry's personal role was still slight – he was only about fifteen – although it is worth remembering that at the same age his father had successfully exercised real responsibility in military affairs. What was more serious was that from the early 1440s, one finds men being accused of saying that the King was mentally feeble, and these allegations continued to be made throughout the decade (147, pp.31, 34–5). As these views had popular currency, it is probable that those close to the court had even fuller knowledge of the King's weakness, although they may also have been aware that there were times when Henry could display an obstinacy when he had set his mind on a particular course. If he suspected an individual's loyalty, he was capable of pursuing him with resentment and lending his ear to any charges brought by his enemies.

In general, the men who played the most influential part in domestic politics in the years between 1435 and 1450 were connected with the Beauforts. When a new 'prive counseill' was appointed in November 1437, the great majority were men who had been associated with the cardinal. As he aged, he became less active, though he was still influential, and the man who fell heir to his prominence and who, through assiduity in Council attendance, came to dominate the court party, was the earl of Suffolk, William de la Pole. In his early years he had been an active soldier, but seems to have been persuaded of the desirability of peace as early as 1433. His wife was related to the Beauforts, with whom he was politically associated, although he had also been favoured by Bedford, during whose period of dominance in England in 1433 Suffolk was appointed Steward of the Household, a post which he retained till 1446. This office brought him into touch with the young King, and when Henry came of age Suffolk soon benefited from his favour; he became High Steward of the duchy of Lancaster in 1437 and Chief Justice of South Wales in 1438 (53, p.427; 128, pp.147–51; 199). When the cardinal began to fade from the scene, the other Beauforts seem to have accepted Suffolk's dominance, perhaps because they appreciated that he was the man who could best advance their interests with Henry.

Suffolk's position was further enhanced by the decline in Gloucester's influence. From about 1440, Humphrey's appearances at the Council were infrequent, evidence perhaps that he was being edged out of political power. He suffered a further blow in 1441 when his wife Eleanor was accused and found guilty of involvement in sorcery, though she denied a charge of plotting to destroy the King by magic. Initially it was members of her household who were charged with sorcery, but they inculpated her in their confessions. An attempted flight to sanctuary did not protect her from being cited to answer charges of heresy and treason, and although she admitted only a few of the accusations, this was enough to secure her condemnation. Before final sentence, she was divorced from her husband, and was put to public penance in London before being committed to perpetual custody. There is no reason to believe that Eleanor's trial was deliberately planned to discredit Gloucester; the evidence suggests that she may have dabbled in necromancy; but it is clear that members of the Council hostile to the duke, including the two cardinals, Beaufort and Kemp, and Adam Moleyns, the clerk of the council, who was to be closely associated with Suffolk later, took part in the proceedings. The aged Archbishop Chichele of Canterbury, politically more friendly to Humphrey, also took in the condemnation, but his role may have been rather more formal. Although no suggestion was ever made that Gloucester himself was guilty of similar practices, the duchess's condemnation clearly redounded to his disadvantage, and although he never disappeared from the scene entirely, he was not in future to play any major part in the nation's affairs. In the 1440s there was no obvious magnate leader who could serve as a focus of opposition to the court; even the duke of York, who was later to take this role, and who was generally friendly to Gloucester, was prepared to use Suffolk as an intermediary in seeking, albeit unsuccessfully, a French marriage for his oldest son (112, p.38).

As Suffolk's dominance increased, the circle of prominent men at court contracted, and even some men previously associated with Cardinal Beaufort, such as Lord Cromwell, ceased to play an active part in government. The cardinal's two nephews, John Beaufort, earl (and later duke) of Somerset, and his brother Edmund, who succeeded to this title in 1444, remained attached to Suffolk [B.2]. Indeed, after de la Pole's death, Edmund was to inherit his role as the leading magnate in the court faction. Suffolk's activity in foreign policy will be considered later, for it was his failure abroad that led to his fall. In domestic affairs he also incurred criticism, and there is no doubt that much of this was justified, because of the way in which he exploited his favoured position at court to his own advantage. Materially he benefited from receiving exemption from the payment of customs duties, and he gained also in status, being promoted marquess in 1444 and duke in 1448. He also was undoubtedly guilty of maintaining the interests of his retainers and associates, and of interfering with the processes of justice. The most serious case of this occurred in 1449, when he blocked an attempt by Lord Cromwell to secure redress for an assault on him by William Tailboys, a client of Suffolk's and a man already accused of numerous acts of violence in Lincolnshire (156, p.116).

The rivalries among the magnates at home, which often broke out into violence, which the King's actions did nothing to appease, came eventually to be linked with the problems of the King's lands in France and the related issue of peace and war. Indeed, relations with France remained the central issue of English politics until the 1450s, when the French finally were victorious and ended almost four centuries of territorial bonds across the Channel. Some historians have talked about a 'peace party' and a 'war party' in England, the first represented by the Beaufort–Suffolk connection and the second by the supporters of the dukes of Gloucester and of York. Such a view, however, is too simple; we have already noted that York was prepared to contemplate a French marriage for his son, and sought Suffolk's assistance in this, and we shall see later that John Beaufort was willing to serve as an English commander in France. It is clear that even among those most disposed to reach a peaceful settlement, there was no desire for peace at any price, but rather a hope that something might be gained by cutting English losses. Historians have tended to sympathize with this point of view, but it should be stressed that this attitude is at least partly based on hindsight, in the knowledge that the French succeeded in driving out the English. For contemporaries, however, it was by no means so clear that a peace policy was more realistic than one of vigorous prosecution of the war. The inhabitants of the shires bordering on the Channel could see obvious advantages in a war policy which aimed at keeping the French coast under English control; this denied French ships the opportunity of making raids. Men who had shared in the conquest of Normandy and been granted lands or offices there had a vested interest in retaining them. In Gascony, too, there were families for whom the English King was their traditional lord.

Furthermore, such men could hope that a policy of active war might be successful. Even after the Burgundian *volte-face* and the fall of Paris to the French in 1436, the English position was not hopeless. They still held extensive lands in Normandy and showed themselves capable of fighting back. In 1437 they threatened Paris, in 1440 the French Constable, Richemont, was defeated, and in 1441 a small army under the duke of York and Lord Talbot raised the siege of Pontoise against a much larger French force. This last, admittedly, was a short-lived triumph, because lack of money for reinforcements compelled them to withdraw to Rouen and abandon the town. Also, Charles VII's position was by no means firmly entrenched, despite the steps which he was taking to strengthen royal authority. He still had to face the kind of dissensions which Henry V had been able to exploit so successfully in the years before 1420. Although Charles was able to overcome various plots and revolts in 1437, 1440 and 1442, the troubles which he faced showed that there was scope for diplomatic manoeuvres to under-mine his position (53, p.395; 141, pp.307–8).

The major reason why Charles was victorious despite his difficulties was almost certainly the indecisiveness of the English. Henry VI's policies vacillated between peace and war; indeed he sometimes tried to pursue negotiations simultaneously with war preparations. Militarily, no clear decision was ever taken on whether to concentrate on the defence of Normandy or to give priority to Gascony, but resources were dissipated between them until it was too late. The King himself must bear much of the responsibility for this, at first perhaps because he was liable to pay too much attention to the last advice which he had received, and later because of his willingness to see good faith in Charles VII, who consistently outmanoeuvred him.

The first major attempt at negotiations took place at Gravelines in 1439, and involved the Burgundians as well as the French. Despite the Franco-Burgundian agreement at Arras in 1435, the mercantile ties between the duchy and England made it desirable for the duke to reach some settlement with Henry. Indeed in 1439 it was the Anglo-Burgundian discussions which achieved a measure of suc-cess, while those between England and France proved abortive. The conference, however, showed the extent of the gulf between England and France. The original instructions to the English ambassadors were completely uncompromising, reas-serting Henry VI's claim to the French throne, but these were essentially a formal gesture and more flexible powers of treating were granted to Cardinal Beaufort, the head of the English delegation. These were not clearly defined, but were certainly intended to leave room for manoeuvre. It was clearly recognized that if peace were to be secured a new approach was required, and that the full claims put forward were unrealistic. Beaufort accepted that although a peace settlement might be unattainable, it might be possible to reach a truce, by which it would be possible to salvage some of the lands which were still in English possession. There were still stumbling-blocks to an agreement and the negotiations were obscured by the fact that there were discrepancies between the verbal and written demands put forward by the French. The English were unwilling to concede that the claim to the throne be renounced, that they do homage for lands still to be held in France, and that French lords and clergy who had fled before the English advance be restored (105).

Even the terms for a truce, by which Henry would cease to use the French title, Charles would make no demand for homage, and the territorial status quo would be maintained, could not be agreed. Beaufort was not prepared to accept responsibility for them, and referred the terms back to England, where the more militant section of the Council headed by Gloucester opposed them firmly. It was claimed that the truce represented surrender, and that the King's subjects were being allowed to defy him. The opponents of the truce also argued that men who had been granted Norman lands should have a right to compensation. With Beau-fort in France, the case for the truce may not have been put particularly forcefully by Cardinal Kemp, and the suspicions of the more bellicose were probably inten-sified by doubts as to the sincerity of the French, when, during the recess in the negotiations, the Constable Richemont attacked and captured Meaux. In general,

Henry bowed to the wishes of the militants, apart from agreeing to the temporary release of the duke of Orleans, a prisoner in England since Agincourt, so that he might work for peace. In fact the French did not even send ambassadors back to the conference, and when Orleans was released in the following year it was the result of unilateral action by the English. Beaufort was violently attacked by Gloucester for the release of Orleans, but the King himself took the responsibility for it, claiming that it would lead to the attainment of peace. In fact Orleans failed to achieve anything, because on his return to France he was rebuffed by Charles. Instead of acting as an honest broker between the rival kings, as he may well have hoped to do, he became involved in a rebellious league of the French princes, which, among other things, accused Charles VII of evasiveness over the proposals put forward at Gravelines (156, pp.148–50, 157–9).

It was in the context of this rebellion that in 1442 negotiations were undertaken for the marriage of Henry VI to a daughter of the count of Armagnac, whose support for the English could have reinforced the military position in Gascony. The scheme failed when the French King's appearance with an army in South-west France deterred the count from the match. This campaign indeed was a considerable success for the French; various castles fell to them and there were subsequent defections from the English among the local nobility, including those of the Landes, who had hitherto been loyal to Henry (151, pp.123–7, 221–2). Small reinforcements were sent to Gascony under Sir William Bonville in March 1443, but shortly afterwards the bulk of the force raised was diverted to Normandy.

Generally, the English concentrated their military activity more in the North. Even at the time of Orleans's release, an attempt was made to strengthen the position in Normandy by reappointing the duke of York as the King's Lieutenant there, a post which he had held, with some success despite his youth, in 1436–37. It has been suggested that the purpose of the appointment was to strengthen the English negotiating position compared with the situation in 1439 (105), but as York was generally more friendly with Gloucester than with Beaufort, it may have been the war faction in the Council which was responsible for sending him to France, where he replaced the cardinal's nephew, John, earl of Somerset. The absence of further negotiations in the next two years also suggests that there was a more deliberate effort to pursue the war, and indeed in 1441 York and Talbot fought a successful campaign, though without securing any long-term gains.

War, however, was pursued as half-heartedly as peace, largely because of the shortage of money. The Treasurer, Lord Cromwell, made it clear that the country could not afford to mount simultaneous campaigns in both North and South in 1443, and it was decided to concentrate attention on Normandy. As we have seen, men originally assigned to Bonville's force in Gascony were diverted north. Somerset was appointed commander, disregarding the position of York as the King's established Lieutenant in France. Indeed the promotion of Somerset from earl to duke in advance of the campaign seems to have been a deliberate action to give the two men equal status. Although the original intention seems to have been that they should co-operate, Somerset in fact never joined York. There is little doubt that he was less concerned with advancing English interests than with acquiring land for himself in Anjou and Maine. He failed to bring any major enemy force to battle, and his one major success, the siege and capture of the stronghold of La Guerche, then in French hands, had awkward repercussions, because the town was claimed by the duke of Brittany, still regarded by the English as an ally. The campaign also led to antagonism between Somerset and York, because the former was given preferential treatment at the Exchequer for meeting the expenses of his expedition, although York was owed substantial sums for the arrears of his men's pay (156, pp.162–8). The resultant enmity between them was a vital factor in the later development of civil war in England.

Even before this campaign was over, new moves had begun for a truce, largely, it seems, under the auspices of Charles of Orleans. After the failure of the Armagnac marriage proposals in 1442, Charles put forward the name of Margaret of Anjou, the French Queen's niece. It was on this occasion that Suffolk became involved in English foreign affairs, at the request of the French – he had had custody of Orleans when the latter had been a prisoner in England. Initially, Suffolk resisted involvement in the negotiations, for fear that he might incur unpopularity, but later he was pressed to act by the Council, at which Gloucester was present, though it is not clear if the latter was genuinely supporting peace moves or merely trying to force his enemy into an unpopular position, so that he himself might recover some of the favour which he had lost with the people in recent years (128, p.155).

The two-year truce agreed at Tours settled nothing beyond the marriage of Henry to Margaret, and no agreement was reached on the more fundamental issues, such as the relationship between the two realms and the extent of the lands which were to be held by the English. It is hardly surprising that the French were reluctant to compromise, as they had had the military advantage in the two previous years a fact emphasized by the futility of Somerset's expedition of 1443. Charles VII, however, made real gains; he acquired in Margaret of Anjou a useful agent at the English court, who did much to influence her husband to pursue policies which seriously weakened his country, and, when the English offered as a concession that in return for Gascony and Normandy in full sovereignty Henry would abandon his claim to the French throne, he learned that Henry regarded his claims as negotiable (156, pp.175–6, 182–3). Initially the English reaction to the truce was favourable, and Suffolk, the chief negotiator, received a triumphant welcome on his return home, but it proved impossible to turn it into a permanent settlement. The basic problems remained intractable, and all that could be done was to extend the truce. Charles VII turned this time to good account, displaying a consistency of purpose lacking in Henry; he consolidated his power and strengthened his government, while the threat to him from the territorial princes receded, leaving the English less scope for diplomatic manoeuvres. Henry was persuaded to make concessions, largely under the influence of his queen; the most serious of these was the promise in December 1445 to surrender Maine, 'in good faith and on our kingly word', as a means of arriving at a final peace. It is not clear how far the King's advisers were aware of his actions, but there is good reason to believe that Henry acted without their approval (53, p.400; 156, pp.185, 189). In the end, however, Suffolk was to become the scapegoat for his master's actions.

In the 1920s, Kingsford attempted to rescue Suffolk's reputation from traditional obloquy, but more recent historical work has not supported his rehabilitation. As far as domestic matters were concerned, as we have seen, little can be said in his favour, but it is primarily on his foreign policy that any defence of Suffolk's reputation as a statesman must rest, notably on the claim that he was the man who sought to detach England from impossible commitments on the continent. One need not doubt that he wished for peace, provided that it could be honourably achieved, and his willingness to keep the Norman garrisons reinforced in the late 1440s shows that he had no intention of betraying English interests, as his enemies alleged against him in 1450 (128, pp.158, 162). One of the crucial questions is how far he was aware of the King's promise to surrender Maine, and Kingsford may well have been correct in suggesting that Suffolk's dilatoriness in fulfilling the King's pledge showed his disagreement with it. It is hard to imagine that he was totally unaware of his master's action, in view of the reliance which Henry placed upon him, but he may well have felt obliged to acquiesce eventually in the King's wishes, both because of his undoubted sense of loyalty and because he recognized that if he were to maintain his influence at court, it would be necessary to prove accommodating to the Queen's wishes; although she was still only in her teens, it may well have been clear already that she was likely to be a more dominant political force than her husband.

Maine was not surrendered immediately after Henry's pledge to the French King, and it was not until 1448, when Charles VII brought up an army to Le Mans, that the English garrison was eventually compelled to leave. It is hard to judge how far the government at home connived at the procrastination by the commissioners appointed to hand over the castles, but they may well have done so to mollify opinion at home, which seems to have been outraged by the surrender (156, pp.193–9). Popular sentiment, however, is hard to judge precisely, as most chroniclers pass over the actual abandonment of Maine, but there are sufficient pointers to the existence of widespread discontent. In May 1447 Suffolk was allowed to make a public declaration that he had never been party to proposals for the surrender, and actions were subsequently taken against Humphrey of Gloucester, potentially their most dangerous critic, once these proposals became public. Parliament was summoned to Bury, away from the duke's London sympathizers, and in the shire where Suffolk's influence was strong. This suggests a premeditated attempt to avoid pressure for a tougher policy in France, and there is no doubt that Humphrey's arrest on his arrival there was intended to forestall criticism from him. Shortly after his arrest the duke died, probably of a heart attack, although later allegations were made that he was murdered. His death perhaps saved Suffolk from deciding whether to bring charges against him, and it is just possible that some coup may have been planned against the court faction; certainly some members of Gloucester's household, including a bastard son, were later accused of treason, found guilty and sentenced to death, although they were reprieved at the last minute (16, p.188; 22, pp.157–8; 53, p.401).

It is hard to assess how serious a threat Gloucester was to Suffolk's position, because he had been in political eclipse since the early 1440s. He still, however, had sufficient popular support to be a possible focus of opposition to the court, and it is undeniable that Suffolk had a motive for having him out of the way; it was probably for this reason that responsibility for Humphrey's death was laid at Suffolk's door, albeit unjustifiably. Indeed, Humphrey may have constituted a more serious threat to Suffolk dead than he had ever been living, being seen as a martyr rather than as a political blunderer. When Gloucester was followed to the grave shortly afterwards by his old rival, Cardinal Beaufort, under whose auspices Suffolk had risen to power, the latter appeared to have been left as the dominant man in England, unmatched in his experience of politics and government. The swiftness of his fall, however, shows that his position was far more fragile than it might have appeared.

Because of his dominance in English politics, he must bear responsibility for a disastrous misjudgement which was to lead to the final collapse of the English position in France. Having been hitherto identified with a peace policy, which many men regarded as one of surrender, he now, unexpectedly, adopted a more aggressive attitude. In March 1449 the town of Fougères in Brittany was seized by François de Surienne, an Aragonese mercenary in English pay. The English never admitted that his action was authorized, but he probably had secret support from them; certainly they failed to persuade him to withdraw from the town or to compensate the duke of Brittany. The evidence of various witnesses to a French enquiry into the incident, in October 1449, while not absolutely conclusive, makes it highly probable that the scheme had been planned for a long time (as far back as 1446) and that Suffolk was privy to it (126). This makes Keen's view, that Suffolk's aim was to placate opinion at home, preferable to Perroy's, that he had reacted violently against Charles VII for the way in which the surrender of Maine had been enforced. The initial English reaction when Surienne wrote to Suffolk about the seizure of the town, was to approve it, a jingoistic response which illustrates both the absence of genuine sentiments in favour of peace and the short-sightedness of the English Council as a whole (53, p.401; 141, p.317; 185).

The background to this affair must be sought in Brittany. As we have seen (Ch.21), duke John V had steered a precarious course between England and France. After his death in 1442, Francis I, still formally an ally of England, had to tread delicately in his dealings with the French court, with which he also had connections; his wife was the Dauphine's sister and his uncle Richemont Constable. The existence of another family, the Penthièvres, with a rival claim to the duchy gave the French King a useful form of moral pressure to make the Breton duke toe the line. His youngest brother Gilles, however, had been brought up at the English court and was ambitious to increase his power in the duchy, and the English saw Gilles as a possible ally who could redress the decline of their influence in northern France. In fact, their support for him was probably counterproductive, and contributed to the increasingly Francophil attitude shown by the duke, who, as we have seen, may also have been antagonized by Somerset's attack on La Guerche in 1443. In 1446 Francis did homage to the French King and soon afterwards placed his brother under arrest. However in 1448, at the time of the surrender of Le Mans, the English surreptitiously listed the duke of Brittany among their allies and Henry VI's lieges (despite the duke's homage of

1446), and subsequently used this as justification for putting pressure on him to release Gilles and, when he refused to comply, for attacking Fougères (126).

The repercussions were disastrous. The act gave the French an ideal pretext for renewing the war, on the justifiable ground that the English had broken the truce. Militarily they were stronger, for although the English had been considering reinforcements for their lands in France, fear that the levying of troops could lead to greater disorder at a time of popular discontent may have prevented these from being raised in time. When the attack came, the French advance was rapid on all sectors of the front. At Rouen, the inhabitants opened the gates to the French in October 1449, and reinforcements sent from England in the following spring, too little and too late, were destroyed at Formigny before they could even join up with the main English force. Caen fell in July, Cherbourg in August and with that Normandy was lost (53, pp.403–4; 185).

Domestic troubles in England contributed to the failure to reinforce the garrisons in France. The first Parliament of 1449 had made only a meagre grant of taxation, and when another met in November, its main concern was the impeachment of Suffolk, who was committed to the Tower. Over the course of the next six weeks he had two sets of articles of indictment laid against him, covering both mismanagement of foreign affairs and misgovernment and corruption at home. The details of many of the charges were undoubtedly exaggerated, or even false, and they were essentially pretexts to remove an unpopular minister. Against a background of disorder – the Keeper of the Privy Seal, Bishop Adam Moleyns, who had been closely associated with Suffolk, was murdered by mutinous soldiers at Portsmouth on 9 January – Henry decided to banish the duke for five years, less as a scapegoat for failure than to save him from a worse fate. However, the ship on which he was going into exile was intercepted, and he was taken by two shipmen and summarily beheaded (156, pp.221–9; 197, pp.232–3). Suffolk's death did not mean the end of disorder, but proved to be the prelude to a more substantial period of trouble in Jack Cade's rising. Political grievances undoubtedly played a part in this, and during it more of Suffolk's former associates were put to death (Ch.4).

In home affairs, 1450 marks a clear dividing line, and later developments will be covered Chapter 23, but the end of the war is best treated here. The concentration of political activity on bringing down Suffolk may have contributed to the failure to reinforce Normandy; the troubles of 1450 possibly played a part in the loss of Gascony. There had been little trouble there after the truce of 1444, although the English may have felt aggrieved when Charles VII came to terms with the count of Armagnac in the following year. When the war was renewed, there were delays in levying troops for dispatch to Gascony under Lord Rivers, and Bordeaux fell to the French at the end of June 1451, before the relief force even sailed (151, pp.131, 136–7). This was not quite the end of the war, for in the autumn of 1452 a force under one of the greatest of the English war captains, John Talbot, now earl of Shrewsbury, arrived off Bordeaux. This caught the French off guard, for although an English counter-attack was not unexpected its location was; Normandy seems to have been regarded as a more likely target. Within Bordeaux there were some sympathizers who opened the gates, though the extent of Gascon support for the English return has probably been exaggerated in the past. The recovery, however, was short-lived. Although Talbot was reinforced early in 1453, his army was too small to defeat the French, and he was crushed at Castillon in July. The French followed this by a naval blockade of the Gironde and a siege of Bordeaux, which fell, this time finally, in October. Apart from Calais, there was now no English-held land in France.

CHAPTER 23

From Lancaster to York

The 1450s were one of the most turbulent decades in English history, with civil strife culminating in Henry VI's deposition. In many ways, however, the crucial problem is less why he was deposed than how he survived as king for so long. Two reasons for this survival are the fundamental respect which was paid to the royal dignity, despite Henry's manifest lack of authority as a ruler, and the existence of a group of magnates who had a vested interest either in his remaining king or in excluding any possible rival. Indeed for much of the time the ambitions of individual nobles were devoted more to gaining control of the King's person, so that the powers of kingship might be employed in their interest, than to trying to diminish such powers.

Before one examines the reasons for the civil war and the ultimate dynastic change, it is necessary to establish how the participants' aims were moulded by events and developed over a number of years. The struggle of Lancaster and York had no single cause, but resulted from various factors coming together at the same time. Fortunately for historians the events leading up to the usurpation of 1461 have been studied in considerable detail in several important books and papers. The fullest studies are Storey's (147) and Wolffe's (156), and there are crucial articles by McFarlane (136), Griffiths (119, 120) and Armstrong (107). Although there are divergencies of interpretation among some of these writers, which will be discussed later, there are also various points on which there is a substantial measure of agreement. Both Storey and Griffiths show that the years 1450–61 saw an increasing breakdown of government in the localities and the impotence of the central authority to enforce order on rival great men. The threat to the King came less from an individual overmighty subject than from the magnates' disregard for the King and their willingness to settle scores with each other by force. The existence of feuds, Neville and Percy in the North, Bonville and Courtenay in the West, did not in itself cause the civil war, but it did create an atmosphere of faction and a situation in which local rivalries could become aligned with political hostilities at the centre, as those concerned in both sought assiduously for allies in their own quarrels.

Magnate rivalries were not all, and popular sentiment in some ways knew nothing of them. The bill of the commons of Kent in 1450, directed against Suffolk and his affinity, besought the King to take into his council not only the duke of York, but also the dukes of Exeter, Buckingham and Norfolk (136). Of these, Exeter and Buckingham were to end up on the Lancastrian side, Norfolk on the Yorkist. Clearly, the polarization of the magnate class into rigid factions was by no means established at the start of the decade, and even later one should not think of factions as exclusive. Men trimmed their sails to changes in the political wind, and some managed to avoid embroilment in the struggle, though this was perhaps more marked after 1461 than before it.

Suffolk's removal from political dominance in 1450, first by his impeachment and then by his murder, was certainly a turning-point in internal English politics. Although he had undoubtedly maintained supporters in disorderly conduct if it suited him, he had been a strong force in national politics, particularly after Humphrey of Gloucester's death in 1447. His disappearance, followed by the disorder of Cade's rebellion, left the government of the country shaken, and the immediate outcome was the emergence of rivalry for influence at court between the dukes of York and Somerset. This was the central issue of politics until the latter's death in 1455. Somerset, who had been closely associated with Suffolk, secured support from the Queen, who became an increasingly important political force. The court connection was vital to him, because his landed resources were small, and over three-quarters of his income derived from crown pensions and offices (147, p.135 n). This was in marked contrast to York, the greatest landowner in the country after the King. There was old hostility between the two men; York felt he had been left in the lurch both militarily and financially during Somerset's brother's Norman campaign in 1443 (Ch.22). There was also a potential dynastic issue between them; Somerset was the male heir of John of Gaunt's line after the King, though as a Beaufort the extent of his family's legitimation might be questioned, while York was Henry's male heir from the line of Edward III, as well as possessing a potentially stronger claim than the King himself in the female line from Lionel of Clarence. Recent historical work has tended to play down this issue, and it is true that York did not claim the throne till 1460, when he appalled even his own allies by so doing – however, one should remember that for contemporaries the succession problem was sufficiently important for men to be accused in 1450 of plotting to put York on the throne and for a petition to be presented in the 1451 Parliament, of which York's chamberlain, Sir William Oldhall, was Speaker, that York be recognized as heir (147, p.81; 156, p.240). The birth of the King's son in 1453 made the succession question less immediately important, but it cannot have been forgotten, not least because when the King had gone insane earlier in the same year, this had raised in acute form the problem of choosing a Protector for the realm.

The deaths of Suffolk and various of his associates in 1450 left little clear leadership in government; neither Somerset nor York was present in the immediate aftermath of Cade's rising, the former returning from defeat in France in August and the latter from Ireland in September. On his return York was apprehensive, alleging that attempts might be made to accuse him of treason, and protesting his loyalty to Henry. He seems to have made public letters which he sent to the King defending himself against such accusations, presumably in order to obtain some popular support (119). Indeed he seemed to secure this in the Parliament which met in November, when he even had to rescue his rival Somerset from attack by a rabble of ex-soldiers. York set himself up as the champion of order, circulating bills affirming the need to reform judicial administration, and declining to act against Somerset except by lawful procedures. Before long, however, the court recovered its confidence. An attempt to attaint Suffolk posthumously was refused by the King, and Thomas Young, the lawyer MP for Bristol who had petitioned to have York recognized as heir to the throne, was sent to the Tower. An attempt to prosecute Somerset for his failure in France came to nothing, and his appointment as Captain of Calais gave him a powerful military base, as well as indicating that the King repudiated the charges against him (119; 147, pp.80, 93).

York's response in the winter of 1451–52 was to assert his position by force; his agents stirred up trouble in both the West Country and the East Midlands and he sent appeals to various towns for help in removing Somerset from the King's presence. When he marched into Kent, however, the shire did not rise, and when he was confronted by the royal army at Dartford, all he could do was to demand Somerset's arrest. During the negotiations he seems to have been tricked, for when he dismissed his army on the basis of assurances as to his safety, he was detained as a prisoner, although there were enough members of the Council, notably the Neville earls of Salisbury and Warwick, who were able to resist his being brought to trial and to secure the grant of a general pardon. In the ensuing months the King played an active personal part in two judicial perambulations in the West Country and the Midlands, in both of which he was accompanied by Somerset. The subsequent Parliament of March 1453 was strongly pro-court, being perhaps encouraged by the apparently improved situation in France following Shrewsbury's recapture of Bordeaux. It granted the King a whole subsidy, and asked for the attainder of York's chamberlain, Sir William Oldhall (147, pp.94–103; 156, pp.253–64).

York appeared isolated; indeed, he even lost his lieutenancy of Ireland. Then, in August 1453, the King went out of his mind, and the political situation was transformed. That this was the case probably reflects the personal influence which Henry exercised, and suggests that Somerset's power in 1453, as much as Suffolk's a few years earlier, was largely due to royal favour. Once the King's own authority ceased to operate, it was striking that the magnates showed a capacity for collective action not dissimilar to that which they had displayed during the minority. The lords resisted Somerset's attempt to exclude York from the Council, an action which suggests that there may have been resentment at how the King's favour had given him such overriding influence. The Council seems to have tried to pursue a policy of stability, and when York was received back into the ruling group of magnates, he behaved with considerable restraint. Possibly the birth of the King's son in October, and the easing of the succession question, may have lifted possible suspicions as to York's aims and motives. His main hostility was directed against Somerset alone, who was confined to the Tower shortly before Christmas. A newsletter of 19 January 1454 shows that the political outlook was uncertain. There were reports of magnates raising troops; these included men such as the veteran Chancellor, Cardinal Kemp, who was not tied to any political faction, as well as friends of York and Somerset. A more serious report was that the Queen was seeking powers to rule the land, appoint the great officers of State and exercise ecclesiastical patronage (17, ii, 295–9). The Council moved very tentatively: in February York was appointed as King's Lieutenant to open Parliament, and it was another month before he was appointed Protector, with powers similar to those which Humphrey of Gloucester had exercised during the minority. The death of the Chancellor may have forced the Council to take more decisive action, rather than to hope for the King's recovery, and the appointment of Richard Neville, earl of Salisbury, to the vacant post seems to have been supported by political neutrals in the Council as well as by York. York's appointment as Captain of Calais should probably be seen as an attempt to ensure that the town and fortress should be under a capable soldier, who could defend them against a possible French attack, rather than as the duke's attempt to secure a military base for himself. Also, those present at the Council on 18 July, when York's refusal to release Somerset on bail was upheld, were by no means all his partisans. The Council seems to have tried genuinely to exercise its collective authority for the good of the realm rather than in the interests of any individual (156, pp.278–84).

One major problem which York had to face during his protectorate was the rebellion of Henry Holland, duke of Exeter, who joined forces with Lord Egremont, a younger son of the Percy earl of Northumberland, the head of a family which had long been bitterly hostile to the Nevilles, who were themselves close to the Protector through marriage. Exeter and Egremont may have been drawn together by hostility to the veteran administrator Lord Cromwell, whose territorial gains included lands to which each of them might hope to lay claim. The outbreak of hostility in Yorkshire in 1453, in a battle which one contemporary writer saw as the beginning of the troubles in England, was probably prompted by the marriage of one of Salisbury's younger sons, Sir Thomas Neville, to Cromwell's heiress. Exeter may also have been jealous of York's position as Protector, claiming a right to it in virtue of being the King's closest relative [B.1]. In May 1454 Exeter and Egremont took up arms, but York was soon able to march north and act firmly against their supporters. When Exeter fled south into sanctuary, he was removed from it and taken into custody for several months. Later in the year further trouble between the Nevilles and the Percies saw Egremont also being committed to prison (120).

As Protector, York seems to have maintained order and political stability at least as effectively as the King's government had done before Henry's insanity. The struggles of the magnates were renewed when the King recovered his senses and resumed an active part in public affairs. Somerset, and later Exeter, were freed from custody. There were changes in the great offices of State, although Salisbury's replacement as Chancellor by the new archbishop of Canterbury, Thomas Bourchier, can hardly be construed as violently hostile to York, whose sister Isabel was married to the archbishop's brother, Henry. At this date the Bourchiers are best regarded as non-partisan, a fact well illustrated by the archbishop's retention of the Great Seal after Somerset's death at St Albans in 1455. As his brother became Treasurer after this battle, the family may have already been showing the pro-York attitude which was to secure greater promotion for them in the following reign.

Nevertheless, York and the Nevilles may have feared some reprisals from the court party. Somerset's summons of a reinforced Council to Leicester, away from London where he was unpopular, was probably intended as a prelude to action against York. There were some parallels between this Council and a Parliament, although no burgesses were summoned and the knights were chosen arbitrarily. There may have been a plan to isolate York, and leave him open to attack, in a similar way to the arrest of Humphrey of Gloucester at Bury St Edmunds in 1447. York and the Nevilles raised an armed force, but news of this probably reached Somerset late, because his own troops, assembled somewhat hastily, were fewer than those of his enemies when they met at St Albans. The King seems to have tried to act on his own initiative, replacing Somerset as commander of his army by the duke of Buckingham, Humphrey Stafford, who then tried to negotiate with York. The rebels' later claim that they were loyal to the King personally may be borne out by the fact that York's demand on this occasion was for the surrender of Somerset to him and his allies (107).

After the negotiations failed, the royal banner was displayed, and armed conflict broke out. The ensuing struggle was more of a skirmish than a battle, and the number of casualties was comparatively slight. It was the ranks of some of the victims which gave the clash its real importance, for they included Somerset himself, Northumberland and Lord Clifford. Politically too, St Albans was a watershed, for after it York and the Nevilles secured control. Some office-holders were changed, though others survived, and some magnates ill-disposed to the victors, including Exeter, were kept in custody, but generally York seems to have sought support from as wide a group as possible of his fellow peers. An oath of personal loyalty to the King was taken by the lords, including some who were still under age and would not have received a summons to Parliament (107), so it is clear that whatever York may have wished for himself, the dynastic issue was not given any prominence.

There has been disagreement among historians as to whether or not the King relapsed into insanity again after the battle, and the evidence on the matter is not entirely conclusive.[1] Certainly he seems to have been able to take some formal part in public affairs, unlike in 1453–54, but it is worth stressing that the patent by which York was again appointed Protector made specific reference to Henry's sickness. York's appointment followed a petition of the Commons, but it is not known whether this was spontaneous or inspired by a Yorkist partisan. Before the duke undertook the task, he sought and secured the fulfilment of certain conditions, most notably that the appointment should no longer be held at the King's pleasure, but that his tenure of it could be ended only by the King in Parliament. Clearly he was guarding himself against the possibility of another sudden dismissal following a reassertion of royal power, such as he had suffered after the King's recovery at the beginning of the year.

Behind York's appointment lay the fact that there was public anxiety over the increasing degree of anarchy in the country; when the Commons sought the appointment, the formal reason which they gave for it was the need to restore order. The problem was particularly pressing in the South-west, where the rivalry between the Courtenay earl of Devon and Lord Bonville, which had already led to violence earlier in the decade, had again broken out into open conflict. Bonville, originally a protégé of Suffolk, had later adhered to Somerset, but in late 1455 came to terms with York and the Nevilles, perhaps in the hope of curbing Devon's actions against him. If this was his aim, he did not succeed, for Devon continued on his violent way, and although York had the earl imprisoned in the Tower, he was not brought to trial (147, pp.84–92, 166–73; 156, pp.294–300).

This may have accompanied a decline in York's influence. He was relieved of the protectorate in February 1456, probably through the actions of the Queen, who was increasingly becoming the leading figure among his opponents. A letter to John Paston on 9 February, about a fortnight before the termination of the protectorate, refers to her activity in trying to secure power for herself (17, iii, 75). The King himself showed no sign of hostility to York, who still remained active in public affairs, serving on the Scottish border to defend it against raids. Troubles in Wales gave the Queen an opportunity to turn on York's followers, Sir William Herbert and Sir Walter Devereux, and suspicions were cast on York's own actions. The more moderate magnates, Buckingham and his half-brothers the Bourchiers, may have tried to restrain the Queen, but the outcome was the dismissal of the Bourchiers from their offices early in October 1456. The new Treasurer, Shrewsbury, was a powerful figure in his own right, and was married to a sister of the strongly pro-court magnate Wiltshire. Margaret also obtained support from the new earls of Somerset and Northumberland, whose fathers had been killed at St Albans, and exploited York's new friendship with Bonville to attract Devon to her side. The one moderate who retained some influence was Buckingham, whose undoubted loyalty to Henry did not yet lead him to support the Queen. An external threat from France may have helped to preserve an uneasy peace for a year between the rival factions, and in January 1458 the King attempted to reconcile them, through the mediation of Archbishop Bourchier and his successor as Chancellor, Bishop Waynflete of Winchester. A temporary settlement was agreed, with financial and territorial compensation (147, pp.177–85).

This proved superficial, although it is not quite clear why it broke down into a further civil war, which saw violent fluctuations of fortune. The Queen seems to have strengthened her hold on the administration in various appointments to offices, and in the autumn Warwick fled to Calais after he had been attacked in London. By the summer of 1459 it was clear that the Queen was determined to crush her enemies, and that those magnates who had hitherto acted as a moderating force were being compelled to choose sides. When a Great Council met at Coventry in late June, not only were York and the Nevilles excluded, but so also were the Bourchiers and the earl of Arundel. Buckingham, on the other hand, had joined the Queen. In September the two factions came to blows at Blore Heath in Staffordshire, where Salisbury fought off an attempt to prevent him from bringing northern troops to join York at Ludlow, but in the following month, when the royal army (with Henry present) confronted them at Ludford Bridge, the Yorkist leaders had to flee, prompted perhaps by their followers' unwillingness to fight against the King. York and his second son Edmund fled to Ireland and his oldest son Edward joined Salisbury and Warwick, going first to Devon and then to Calais. These two places were to be the springboards for the Yorkist recovery in 1460 (97, pp.25–6; 144, pp.20–1; 147, p.86).

The violence of the court's revenge in the Parliament which met at Coventry, a month after Ludford (the first for three and three-quarter years) [D] may have been critical in hardening York's attitude to the King. He and his two eldest sons were attainted, as were the two Nevilles, Salisbury and Warwick, and a number of their followers. The Queen was clearly determined to consolidate her control by giving her allies a vested interest in her success, so the proscription of the Yorkists was accompanied by a distribution of forteited lands. For example, Buckingham received property forfeited by York's chamberlain, Sir William Old-hall (97, p.26). But although this may have bound some men closer to the court party, such interference with property rights probably created apprehension elsewhere. This was exploited in a manifesto issued by the Yorkist lords in the summer of 1460, shortly before their return to England, when they alleged that the court lords, notably Shrewsbury and Wiltshire, had planned the Coventry attainders to enrich themselves. Certainly there was sufficient dislike for the court for the invasion of the Yorkist earls to attract substantial support from its landing in Kent, through its progress to London and thence into the Midlands. By the time they confronted Henry at Northampton, they probably had a larger force than the King. Despite this, the court refused to parley, and in the ensuing battle the leading royal captains, Buckingham and Shrewsbury, were killed and the King was captured.

Possession of the King gave the Yorkists power to exercise government in his name and change the great officers of state. Viscount Bourchier returned to the treasurership, and Warwick's brother, the bishop of Exeter, became Chancellor. All this occurred before York himself returned from Ireland, when he promptly put the cat among the pigeons by asserting a claim to the throne, taking his friends by surprise as much as his enemies. Even with a number of Lancastrian sympathizers excluded from the Parliament, there is no doubt that the claim provoked considerable dissent, and it took some time before a compromise was reached, that Henry would be allowed to remain King during his life, but that York would be recognized as his heir. As York's claim rested on his descent from Lionel of Clarence, this was essentially illogical, but it reflected political attitudes – men were reluctant to abandon Henry, to whom they had sworn oaths of loyalty, but they were much less prepared to defend the claims of the prince and his mother, whose actions had done much to precipitate the final conflict (144, pp.25–9).

War was now inevitable. The Queen and her allies raised another army in the North, while York and Salisbury went in pursuit, leaving Warwick in London. York's eldest son Edward went to Wales to meet the forces being raised by Wiltshire and the King's half-brother, Jasper Tudor. Four battles in the three months between 30 December 1460 and 29 March 1461 saw rapid changes of fortune. In the first, at Wakefield, York was defeated and killed, and Salisbury was captured and executed. The Queen's army marched south, defeated Warwick at St Albans, recovering the person of Henry VI, but failed to secure London, which refused to open its gates. Meanwhile, however, Edward had defeated the Lancastrians in the West, and marched to London, joining up with Warwick's remaining forces. London welcomed him, and a small group of lords, among whom only Warwick and Norfolk were of any great consequence, proclaimed him king and installed him in Westminster Abbey. He consolidated his claim by victory in another bitter battle at Towton in Yorkshire three weeks later, and although Henry, Margaret and their son escaped, effective authority in the realm remained with the victors, and in June Edward returned to London for his coronation (144, pp.30–41).

The Lancastrian threat did not disappear immediately, but became less serious, and the battles in the next few years are best regarded as mopping-up operations by Edward and his allies. There were Scottish and French raids, ostensibly in support of Lancaster, but they did not really threaten the new King's position. More serious was the survival of Lancastrian garrisons in Wales and in the North. Most of the Welsh castles fell by 1462, although Harlech remained a centre of resistance and did not finally fall till 1468. The area towards the Scottish border did not remain a centre of Lancastrian support for so long, although in the early years of Edward's reign it saw fairly constant fighting, with several of the Northumbrian castles changing hands on various occasions before they finally passed into Edward's control. It was 1464 before the new King really secured authority in the North, when John Neville defeated the last major Lancastrian army at Hexham, and the castles were subsequently surrendered, in one case after a siege. There was still sufficient sympathy for Henry VI for him to remain at large for a further year, but his capture in Lancashire in 1465 removed a further danger to Edward's throne (144, pp.48–9, 60–1, 120).

A more serious problem for Edward than residual military activity was the attitude of the nobility, only a few of whom had favoured him before Towton. Initially, those who came over to his side were few, and early in 1462 there was a major scare when the earl of Oxford, his son Aubrey and the former Treasurer of Henry's household, Sir Thomas Tuddenham, were convicted of treason and executed. Edward, however, was temperamentally inclined to a policy of conciliation, even of men closely related to the House of Lancaster – it is noteworthy that the most savage series of executions in the 1460s, after Hexham, was conducted by John Neville in Edward's absence. The new King's most notable effort to bury old scores was his treatment of the young duke of Somerset, Henry Beaufort (the son of his father's old rival), whose 1461 attainder was nullified two years later. This attempt to secure his adherence to the new regime failed; he defected within a year, and was ultimately executed after Hexham. Edward, however, was prepared to restore Oxford's heir, even after the 1462 plot, and the heir to the earldom of Devon also recovered a considerable part of his family's forfeited estates, though not the comital title. In neither of these cases did Edward's generosity guarantee loyalty, although other old Lancastrians did become pillars of his regime. It is true that Lord Audley had already abandoned Lancaster for York in 1460, but Richard, Lord Rivers, who fought against Edward at Towton, was pardoned in July 1461, and remained loyal to Edward, becoming his father-in-law in 1464. The real power in the realm, however, was exercised by a fairly narrow group, comprising essentially the Nevilles and a number of new men whom Edward promoted to the peerage in his early years, such as Herbert and Hastings. He seems to have employed them consciously to dominate particular parts of the country, building up their power on the basis of grants of forfeited Lancastrian estates, Herbert in Wales and Hastings in the Midlands. This gave them a material interest in the survival of the new dynasty, and it is noteworthy that the forfeitures on which their gains were based do not seem to have aroused the same general apprehensions as those of the Coventry Parliament of 1459 (144, pp.58–67, 74–80, 89).

As will be shown in Chapter 24, it was only when divisions emerged within this Yorkist establishment that Edward's position was seriously threatened. The relative stability of the new dynasty, for all the difficulties that one might expect after a usurpation, may help to throw light on the crucial problem of why the last years of Henry VI's reign were so unstable. McFarlane lays the blame squarely on Henry's shoulders: 'The war was fought because the nobility was unable to rescue the kingdom from the consequences of Henry VI's inanity by any other means.' (136) Storey, however, sees the problem as one which arose from local disorders which the government was powerless to control, and the magnates were seen as the cause of the trouble rather than as potential rescuers of the realm. For him, the weakness of the government lay less in the King's personality than in the structure of society, and the system of patronage which bound together men into connections and factions, with the resulting abuse of illegal maintenance of criminals. Henry's failure lay in his reliance on a particular baronial clique, which dominated his Council, and which involved him in its own factious interests (147, p.27).

Although Storey stresses these evils of 'bastard feudalism', one must remember that social organization on a basis of retaining was not new in the 1450s, not even in Henry's earlier years, nor was it to change after 1461. Local feuds still survived and were sometimes a serious threat to order, but they did not inevitably merge in a power struggle at the centre of government. Where Storey and McFarlane differ least is in their judgement that Henry was politically incapable, and this is the most convincing explanation of the troubles. At the same time, McFarlane's view needs modification. Henry himself was not the prime target of the Yorkist–Neville alliance. Until the autumn of 1460, York put forward no claim to the throne, and even when he did so his supporters had qualms about getting rid of the King. At Ludford Bridge a year earlier, Henry's presence with his army had encouraged the defection of members of York's army. Hostility was directed primarily against the court magnates; a chronicler who wrote only some twenty years later, and who was fundamentally sympathetic to the Lancastrians, blamed 'myscheves people that were aboute the Kynge' and their failure in France, saying that 'that made the peple to gruge ayens hym, and alle bycause of his fals lordes, and nevere of hym' (18, pp.11–12). Along with the lords, one must associate the Queen. The marriage alliance which had brought her to England had involved the surrender of lands in France, and her choice of friends, Suffolk in the 1440s and Somerset after 1450, made matters worse, for both of them had incurred widespread unpopularity for their failures in France. After 1455, Margaret herself was the effective leader of Henry's party, pursuing a more partisan policy than her husband, whose political interventions, when he was able to make them, tended to be on the side of moderation, as before the Battle of St Albans in 1455 and in the attempted reconciliation of 1458. It has been suggested that her methods of government in the late 1450s were coming close to a household tyranny comparable to that of Richard II's last years, and even if one does not view her actions as drastically as that, there is no doubt that her policies

208

exacerbated feuds rather than settled them. The substantial support that she had among the great magnates was from a particular group of them, who had benefited from the total exclusion of the others from power. The popular favour which York obtained, and which indeed he consciously courted, derived from his very exclusion from a court circle which was regarded as tyrannical and corrupt (53, pp.453–4). His son fell heir to this popularity, and may indeed have owed his victory partly to it, when London refused entry to the Queen but admitted him in 1461. Henry's friends, and perhaps most of all his wife, were the ultimate cause of his fall rather than he himself, because he was unable to control them and be King of the nation as a whole.

---

1. The view that Henry had again become mad was challenged by Lander (130, pp.82–3) but Wolffe, without specifically considering the points made by Lander, presents a well-argued case for a further relapse, although not a total one (156, pp.294–300). Griffiths (see note 1, Ch.21) is also inclined to accept that Henry was suffering from continued mental debility.

CHAPTER 24

Edward IV

The reign of Edward IV has been thoroughly studied in recent years, most notably in the life of the King by Ross (144) and in various papers by Lander (130). The King's poor reputation among earlier historians has been considerably rehabilitated as a result of this work, although some controversy remains about his personality and capacity as a ruler. The reign falls into two parts, divided by Henry VI's brief recovery of the throne in the winter of 1470–17, the so-called 'Readeption'. Two main periods can be discerned also in the earlier phase, the first, which was covered in Chapter 23, seeing the consolidation of Yorkist control and the eclipse of Lancaster, and the second the growth of internal feuds among the Yorkists, culminating in Warwick's revolts against the King. One factor in this change was a decline in Warwick's political influence, which had been dominant in both foreign and domestic politics in Edward's early years. May 1464 marked a critical dividing line; the military elimination of the last major Lancastrian army at Hexham (far more important than Henry VI's capture a year later) reduced the pressure on the Yorkists to preserve a united front for the sake of survival, and Edward's secret marriage to Elizabeth Woodville created new domestic political factions, which in the long term affected the country's overseas relations.

One of the Yorkists' early problems was to secure international recognition for the usurpation, and one of Edward's assets here was that as a bachelor king he was one of the most eligible matches in Europe. The proposed brides suggested for him in various negotiations included the daughters of the dukes of Bourbon and of Savoy (respectively a niece of the duke of Burgundy and the sister-in-law of the French King), the widow of James II of Scotland and the sister and heiress of the King of Castile (144, pp.84–5, 91). The political struggles within France, notably between the Crown and the duchy of Burgundy, were reflected in these schemes, and indeed were to play an important part in English diplomacy throughout Edward's reign. Louis XI, who succeeded Charles VII in France shortly after Edward's accession, and whose reign was to last for virtually the same length as the English King's, was the subtlest politician of his age, whose intrigues extended throughout Europe and had a major effect on English politics, particularly in the critical years 1470–71. Before his accession, Louis, in opposition to his father, had supported the Yorkists, but it was uncertain whether he would continue to do so. The international situation was highly fluid, and in the search for allies most parties were prepared to adopt a very flexible policy.

Although Edward's marriage removed his person as a factor in international negotiations, it did not immediately affect England's position in relation to the European powers. Indeed, had Warwick not committed himself so strongly to a policy of good relations with France, it need not have influenced this at all. It was the rise of the Woodvilles, and Warwick's resentment at it, which led to the alignment of internal factions in England with different foreign allies. Indeed the position of the Woodvilles played a critical part in English politics for the next two decades, both provoking Warwick's opposition to Edward in the 1460s and determining the factions which were involved in the power struggle after his death, which culminated in Richard III's usurpation. Their fall in 1483 was not to be permanent, however, for they were to come to terms with the Tudors and the eldest daughter of Edward and Elizabeth was to marry Henry VII. The suggestion that the Woodville marriage, the first occasion since 1066 when an English king had married one of his subjects, was a calculated move by Edward to shake off Warwick's tutelage is unconvincing; it is simpler to accept it at face value as a love match made without regard to its political consequences. Indeed, Edward's concealment of it during the summer of 1464 suggests that he himself appreciated some of the problems which it would raise, and that he was trying to postpone a possible clash with his followers. To contemporaries, Elizabeth was not a suitable queen for various reasons. Her rank was comparatively modest – although her mother was the daughter of a Burgundian count and the widow of Henry V's brother, the duke of Bedford, her father had risen from the lesser landed class through service to the Crown – she herself was a widow with two sons by her first marriage, and her first husband had been a Lancastrian. She had numerous relatives, a father, five brothers and seven unmarried sisters, as well as her sons, and these all were to make material gains as the result of her sudden elevation. The resulting antagonism to her family was hardly surprising.

Several chronicles suggest that Warwick had actually been negotiating a marriage for Edward in France during the summer of 1464, but this has now been shown to be an error. The King's failure to consult him on so major a matter, however, could only be construed as a snub. Initially, however, he accepted the situation, escorting Elizabeth into the chapel of Reading Abbey on Michaelmas day, when she was publicly introduced to the royal court. Edward was still willing to employ the earl on various embassies, particularly to the French court, and Warwick seems to have convinced Louis that his friendship was still worth cultivating, because of the influence which he possessed. The tensions between the King and the earl did not yet bring about a breach between them, and Warwick was still in sufficient favour in 1466 to be godfather to the King's eldest child, the Princess Elizabeth. (8, p.117; 144, pp.92, 115 n).

By this time the Woodvilles were also making material gains, but some of these have perhaps been exaggerated. A number of Elizabeth's relations held posts in her household, although as this was fairly small – it contained fewer members than had Margaret of Anjou's – the extent of her patronage in this area may have been fairly limited. The posts which they held were all ones already established, and they received no more than the usual salaries. Her father made gains both in office and in status; he was appointed Treasurer in March 1466 and was made an earl in May of the same year. Most important, however, was a spectacular series of marriages. One of the Queen's brothers married the elderly dowager duchess of Norfolk, and several of her sisters found husbands among the higher nobility, one to the young duke of Buckingham (grandson of the duke killed in

1460), and others to the heirs of the earls of Arundel, Essex and Kent, and of Edward IV's trusted servant Lord Herbert. Young Herbert was created Lord Dunster, thereby offending Warwick, who had wished for the lordship himself in 1461. Even more provocative was the Queen's purchase of a marriage for a son by her first husband. The girl concerned was the King's niece, Anne Holland, heiress of the duke of Exeter; she had previously been betrothed to the son of Warwick's brother John, now, through the forfeiture of the Percies, earl of Northumberland. Warwick had a further grievance; he had two daughters approaching marriageable age, and these Woodville marriages had virtually monopolized all the eligible partners for them, apart from the King's two brothers, the dukes of Clarence and Gloucester. Edward, however, set his face against this posibility (144, pp.92–4). Individual Woodvilles marrying well might have been just tolerated, but the cumulative effect of all the weddings, and their implications for Warwick's own interests, could have aggrieved a less patient man than the earl.

In a situation where Warwick had reasonable cause for resentment, his disagreement with the King over foreign policy was more serious. The best chronicle of the period, the *Croyland Continuation*, states explicitly that foreign policy rather than Woodville advancement caused the breach. There is no need to seek a single motive for the earl's actions at this time, but it is noteworthy that while he continued to serve the King during the period of the Woodville marriages, his discontent became more determined at the time when Edward was assiduously pursuing Burgundian friendship. *Warkworth's Chronicle*, with some justification, sees the moment when the split became irreconcileable as the dismissal of Warwick's brother George from the Chancellorship (14, p.551; 18, pp.3–4). When this occurred, Warwick was engaged in negotiations in France and a Burgundian party was in London for a tournament between the Bastard of Burgundy and the Queen's brother Anthony. The welcome given to the Burgundians contrasted with a chilly reception accorded to a French embassy which arrived in England shortly afterwards in Warwick's company. Clearly Edward was more inclined to favour a Burgundian alliance, and in 1468 his sister Margaret married the new duke, Charles, who had succeeded his father in the previous year. It is a measure of Edward's greater security on the throne that he embarked on so definitely an anti-French policy, compared with the bargaining of his earlier years. He concluded an alliance with Brittany as well as an agreement with Burgundy. His motives were probably military rather than mercantile; certainly the commercial clauses of the Burgundian treaty were unpopular with English merchants in that they annulled earlier prohibitions on Burgundian imports into England (144, pp.109–12).

Warwick's opposition to Edward's foreign policy led him to retire to his estates in dudgeon, and rumours began to circulate on the Continent that he might come to terms with the Lancastrians. There is, however, no reason to believe that he as yet wished to do this. His grievances were directed at the court, but his ambitions were to regain control over policy and dominate the King rather than to restore Henry. Edward made some effort to conciliate him, conferring grants on him and offering him a share in the work of the Council (144, pp.115–16, 437–8).

The events of 1469–71, which were years of serious political upheaval, throw light on the political aims of both the King and the earl. Details of these struggles are by no means clear, but the broad line of events needs little elaboration. In 1469 Warwick, assisted by Edward's brother Clarence, now his son-in-law, stirred up – or at least exploited – a rising in the north of England, the origins of which are rather obscure, to turn on the court faction, several of whom, including the Queen's father and her brother John, and William Herbert, were put to death. Edward was temporarily in the custody of his opponents, but Warwick could not rule without him and a reconciliation was patched up in the autumn. Early in 1470 fresh troubles broke out in Lincolnshire, Warwick and Clarence were again involved, and when Edward defeated the rebels they had to flee to France. There Louis XI negotiated a settlement between Warwick and Margaret of Anjou, the earl returned to England with an army in the autumn and restored Henry VI to the throne. With the collapse of Edward's cause, he fled to Burgundy, but returned in the spring of 1471, defeated all his enemies, winning two major victories at Barnet, where Warwick was killed, and Tewkesbury, which saw the death of Henry VI's son Edward. Henry himself was put to death shortly afterwards, and with virtually all the old Lancastrian supporters and the Nevilles destroyed, Edward returned to his throne with new and increased authority. (144, pp.126–77).

Why was the political situation so unstable? How important was foreign intervention? What were Warwick's aims? Why was Edward ultimately victorious? These are the critical problems of the period. Discontent was not confined to the higher nobility, and Warwick certainly was able to turn popular unrest to good account. Clarence probably wished a more prominent political role than his brother would allow, and was easily tempted into an alliance with the earl, whose daughter Isabel, whom he married at Calais in 1469, was a major heiress. Although the leader of the northern rising, who called himself Robin of Redesadle, was probably a member of the Conyers family, who were Neville retainers, it is not certain that Warwick actually prompted the revolt. Certainly his brother John Neville attempted to suppress it in its early stages. There was probably enough popular discontent, particularly over taxation, to provoke a genuine rising. Warwick and Clarence concentrated their attack on a clique at court, whom they denounced in a manifesto which they issued on returning to England from Calais. (14, p.542; 18, pp.6, 46–8). Edward acted indecisively, being perhaps too confident that he had popular support, an error which he repeated in the autumn of 1470, and which perhaps contributed to the changes of fortune which he suffered. Many men were perhaps more loyal to Edward than to his friends, and were not sorry to see some of them losing their lives. With only limited numbers of people actively involved on either side, a small shift of power could be decisive. Many stood aloof from the struggle, being more concerned with their own survival than with supporting a party in it; this is perhaps most evident in the Readeption period, when a number of Edward's former adherents, including the duke of Norfolk and the Bourchiers (the archbishop of Canterbury, the earl of Essex and his son Lord Cromwell), made their peace sufficiently with Lancaster to be summoned to the Parliament of November 1470. Others, such as the duke of Suffolk, seem always to have been more concerned with pursuing their private interests than with participation in national politics and were content to go with the tide. Most indicative of all, John Neville, earl of Northumberland, did not always join with his brother Warwick, but remained an independent actor on the political stage. The creation of his son as duke of Bedford, on his betrothal to the King's eldest daughter in early 1470, probably helped to ensure his loyalty for a time, but Edward's restoration of the earldom of Northumberland to the Percy heir to strengthen his support in the North was to outweigh this. Neville's grants of lands elsewhere and the title of Marquess Montagu did not seem adequate compensation for what he lost, and his defection to his brother during the invasion in the autumn of 1470 was a critical factor in Edward's overthrow (144, pp.136–7, 152–5; 148). His rival Percy also showed an ability to trim his sails to changes in the political wind; he survived as earl during the Readeption, and assisted Edward by his benevolent neutrality in 1471.

With so many men waiting on events, those who had definite policies could derive advantages from pursuing them vigorously. Most particularly, it gave scope for Louis XI, after Warwick and Clarence fled into exile, to negotiate a settlement between them and Margaret of Anjou, by no means an easy task in view of their former enmity. Louis's main aim was to reverse England's alignment with Burgundy, and Warwick was prepared to do this for him. This, however, prompted Charles of Burgundy, whose welcome to his exiled brother-in-law Edward had originally been markedly cool, to supply him with forces to invade England. The importance of foreign intervention in English affairs, therefore, was crucial from late 1470 onwards, though it had been unimportant earlier.

Warwick's alliance with Lancaster was a desperate attempt to recover his position in England, and it was his last resort; initially he had hoped to regain it in other ways. However, possession of the King in late 1469 did not yield the same advantages as the custody of Henry VI had done in 1460, for Edward was not prepared to be a puppet ruler. By the spring of 1470 Warwick was probably planning to replace Edward by Clarence, and even after Louis XI had turned him into an agent of Lancaster, he was still determined to secure effective authority for himself. This probably explains his actions during Edward's return in 1471. Although Margaret of Anjou was expected in England with reinforcements, he attempted to defeat Edward himself without awaiting her arrival. Indeed he may have regarded this more as a threat than as a potential advantage, and as his troops were more numerous than Edward's he may have hoped to obtain her favour from handing her enemy Edward over to her, dead or alive. Had he delayed, there was some likelihood that the old Lancastrians would secure greater influence and that he himself might be isolated.

One factor which contributed to Edward's victory was undoubtedly such divisions within the Neville–Lancaster alliance, for these enabled him to destroy his enemies one by one. Suspicions that Marquess Montagu was planning a second change of sides are probably unfounded; his failure to attack Edward on his march south, before the latter secured substantial reinforcements and when, as even his official account of the campaign suggests, he had little popular support (2, pp.3–7), was probably because he was keeping a watchful eye on his old rival Percy. Montagu did subsequently join his brother and fall with him at Barnet. A more critical switch of allegiance was that of Clarence, always an odd man out in the Lancastrian camp. Edward, with the help of friends who had remained in England, seems to have sounded him out during his time in exile, and when he landed Clarence followed events closely. A series of his letters from this time has survived, and they show him remaining notably non-committal. It is not clear whether the shifty duke was merely concealing his intentions from Warwick, who was expecting him to bring reinforcements, or if he was keeping his own options open to ensure that his brother had a fair prospect of success before he defected to him. By the time that he joined Edward, the latter's forces had increased considerably, and Clarence's move tilted the balance further in Edward's direction. Even so, Warwick still had the larger army, and it may well have been Edward's greater capacity as a soldier which was decisive. He also benefited from good fortune; in misty conditions at Barnet the similarity between the liveries of his followers and those of the earl of Oxford led Warwick's men to fire on the latter in error, thereby creating panic in the Lancastrian army. At Tewkesbury, too, the fortune of battle went Edward's way, not least in that the Lancastrian heir, Prince Edward, was killed. Henry VI was the sole surviving focus for his party's loyalty, and he was put to death on Edward's return to London. A revolt in the North collapsed on the news of Tewkesbury, and another in Kent, led by a bastard of the Neville family, Thomas Fauconberg, caused damage in London but came too late to be politically important. The rebels were repelled from the city, and Edward's march into Kent subsequently was essentially a mopping-up action. One or two other pockets of resistance had to be crushed, but the King's hold on the realm was now secure (144, pp.181–3).

This remained true for the rest of the reign, during which there were only a few ripples on a quiet domestic political scene. Warwick's surviving brother, the archbishop of York, was arrested in 1472, probably for intrigues with the exiled earl of Oxford, who had escaped abroad in 1471. In the autumn of 1473 Oxford himself, after an unsuccessful attempt to land in Essex, seized St Michael's Mount in Cornwall, clearly hoping to raise support against the King, but this came to nothing. Louis XI may have been behind this, and more seriously, Clarence too may have been involved. The latter was in fact the most troublesome figure of English politics in the 1470s. Contemporary sources attest to his good looks and eloquence, which may have given him some appeal, but he combined these with a remarkable lack of political judgement. Indeed, one of the few well-judged moves of his entire career was his change of allegiance in the spring of 1471, which made it virtually incumbent on Edward to pardon his earlier offences; indeed he was even reappointed to the lieutenancy of Ireland and obtained grants of a number of forfeited lands in the autumn of 1471. Clarence, however, was jealous of the greater gains made by his younger brother Richard of Gloucester, whose loyal support, politically and militarily, to Edward since 1469 had attracted considerable rewards. More especially, Richard was granted substantial portions of the Neville inheritance in Yorkshire and Westmorland, and became the pillar of Edward's regime in the North. He handled relations with Northumberland tactfully, and indeed was to derive considerable advantage from this in 1483 (144, pp.186–7, 199–201).

The quarrel between Clarence and Gloucester was exacerbated by Richard's intention to marry Warwick's younger daughter Anne, a widow since Prince Edward's death at Tewkesbury. Clarence tried to frustrate the marriage plans in an attempt to secure the whole Warwick inheritance as the husband of Anne's older sister. Edward remained conciliatory, making various concessions, and Gloucester, too, showed moderation in not asserting his own claims harder. Before the dukes could secure the lands there were various legal hurdles to be surmounted, but two acts in Parliament in 1474 respectively debarred Warwick's widow, from whom the Warwick title and many of the estates derived, from a right in her own inheritance, and excluded the heirs of John Neville from succeeding to the entailed paternal lands of the family. Although the whole transaction showed an unscrupulous disregard of landed rights, it was politically advantageous to Edward, and the elimination of the Nevilles as a political force in 1471 meant that there was no rival who might have hoped to gain the lands whose grievances left a dangerous legacy of discontent. Richard's share of the lands in the North gave him standing in his own right in a part of the country where he proved a capable deputy to the King, who formally created him Lieutenant of the North during the Scottish War in 1482, although as early as 1474 he had reached an agreement with Northumberland, which gave unofficial recognition to his power there (144, pp.187–91, 199–203). It is clear, however, that relations between Gloucester and Northumberland were a matter of some delicacy. The settlement of the Warwick inheritance also gave Clarence an opportunity to make peace with the King, and Edward could reasonably have hoped that George, who owed him all the obligations of a prodigal brother returning home, would be content with his fatted calf.

Clarence, however, remained disgruntled. Jealousy of Richard may have persisted, although his later offences were more directed against the King than against his younger brother. On the death of his duchess, probably from the after-effects of childbirth, his sister Margaret of Burgundy proposed her stepdaughter Mary, now heiress to a vast inheritance after the death in battle of Duke Charles early in 1477, as a new wife for him, but Edward refused to tolerate this, proposing his brother-in-law Earl Rivers as an alternative husband for Mary, though it is hard to know if he thought that this suggestion would be acceptable. Shortly after this Clarence engaged in an act of violence which could be construed as encroachment on the King's judicial powers, abducting a former servant of his wife, terrorizing a jury into condemning her on a charge of poisoning her mistress and having her hanged. About the same time a member of the duke's household, Thomas Burdett, was one of a group of men accused of necromancy, including attempts, over some years, to forecast the dates of death of the King and the prince of Wales. Although Clarence was not directly inculpated, his reaction to the execution of those involved, breaking into a meeting of the Council and having the declarations of innocence of the offenders read out, was exceedingly tactless. His choice of spokesman, a Franciscan friar who had declared Henry VI's title to the throne in 1470, was equally ill-judged (144, pp.240–1, 251). It is hardly surprising that Edward's patience at last gave way, and that Clarence was arrested and had a bill of attainder brought against him in the Parliament of 1478. This contained a long list of charges, but in the last resort the details of these are of only limited importance, because Clarence was condemned more for political incorrigibility than for any particular crime. Even though one of the charges, that he had preserved an exemplification of an agreement made during the Readeption period that he would be heir to the throne if Henry's line failed, may have been forged (130, pp.253–7, 265–6), the duke's general conduct over a decade had been so persistently unreliable that his long survival is more surprising that his ultimate downfall. Possibly the Queen's family, which had suffered at Clarence's hands in 1469, may also have urged Edward to execute his brother. Certainly the Speaker of the Commons, who asked that the sentence be carried out when Edward seemed to be dragging his feet on the matter, was associated with the Woodvilles (144, pp.241–5; 193, pp.284–9).

Clarence's execution left Edward's power unchallenged. Political tensions, however, persisted and were controlled only by his overriding authority. These are reflected in the bitterness of the crisis which followed his death, notably in the hostility to the Queen's family on the part of two men on whom Edward relied heavily, his brother Richard and his close personal friend Lord Hastings. Edward may have hoped to balance the influence of these factions by granting different powers to each, but in the event he left the rival contenders for power to fight it out when his own authority was removed.

Although Edward succeeded in dominating the domestic scene, his European policies turned out less successfully. Louis XI's support for Lancaster in 1470 made Edward hostile to him, and both the Burgundians and the Bretons tried to draw him into war against the French King. In 1472 Edward concluded an alliance with Brittany, became involved in negotiations with Burgundy and appealed to Parliament for a grant of supply. His arguments for this rested more on the need to defend the realm than on any reassertion of the English claim to lands in France, but it is not certain how far the King took this line because he hoped that it would have more effect on his subjects. Breton irresolution delayed any campaign, though not Edward's continued levying of money. Only when the Burgundians signed a formal alliance in 1474 did Edward take steps to raise an army to invade France and to come to terms with the Hanseatic League and the Scots, both possible allies for Louis (130, pp.228–30; 144, pp.207–14). The French King took the threat seriously, taking precautions to defend his kingdom and to neutralize Charles of Burgundy. The latter, in the event, proved an unrealiable ally for Edward, getting involved in a struggle for power in the Rhineland and failing to produce an army to join with the English. The alliance had probably always been one of convenience rather than of conviction; Edward may already have considered a possible accommodation with Louis before he even crossed to France, and after some futile marching around northern France, he entered on negotiations for a settlement, which was reached in the Treaty of Picquigny. By this, Edward withdrew from France, a truce for seven years was agreed and Louis promised to pay a substantial pension to the English King. Freedom of trade was agreed between the two countries, and plans were put forward for a marriage alliance (144, pp.226–34). Even more striking is the fact that English territorial claims in France were not mentioned.

Edward lost some face with his subjects by the treaty, but in fact it let him escape without disaster, indeed with profit, from a campaign in which his principal ally had let him down. There was resentment at the taxes which had been levied, but with his French pension Edward was able to remit part of these. However, as Louis's pensioner, Edward's freedom in diplomacy was severely curtailed for the rest of his reign. This became evident after Charles of Burgundy's death in 1477, when, as we have seen, his widow attempted to marry her stepdaughter Mary to Clarence. Desire to preserve his pension may have been one factor in Edward's opposition to this, though he probably also wanted to curb his brother's ambitions. His proposal that Mary marry Earl Rivers was turned down, hardly surprisingly; instead she married Maximilian of Austria, the son of the Emperor Frederick III, a match that was to affect the political geography of Europe for over three centuries in that it gave the Habsburgs a territorial interest in the Low Countries. In the complex diplomacy which ensued, Edward was always concerned with preserving his pension; indeed when he came to an agreement with Maximilian in 1480, the latter promised to take over the role of paymaster. Louis retaliated by stirring up the Scots against England and by exploring the possibility of a direct settlement with Maximilian. This was achieved in the Treaty of Arras of 1482, from which England was excluded. Thereafter Louis withheld payment of the pension, as he no longer had to buy Edward off (144, pp.236–7, 284, 292). The English King had been outmanoeuvred, and was virtually excluded from European affairs. Some contemporaries even thought that this humiliation hastened his death, though this is unlikely (3, pp.58–9). The most important effect of these years for the development of England was not a temporary relegation to the fringes of the European power struggle but the implicit abandonment of territorial claims in France at the time of the Treaty of Picquigny. Since 1066 Continental interests had played a vital part in the concerns of English kings, and since 1337 the related issues of homage for French lands and the will-o'-the-wisp claim to the French throne had been a constant and insoluble source of hostility. The war had indeed been one of the dominant factors in the development of English society and government throughout this period. Although Edward could only regard his invasion of France and his subsequent diplomatic outmanoeuvring as a defeat, this very failure may in the long run have been more beneficial to his kingdom than any domestic successes. Apart from one futile attempt by Henry VIII to reassert old claims in France (Ch.27), England's future involvement in Europe was not to take the form of territorial aggrandizement. When after a period of concentration on insular affairs England again sought to expand overseas, it was not to be in Europe, but across the oceans of the world.

This leaves a final problem, how successful a king was Edward? The general assessment of him by recent historians, as a man who consolidated royal power by restoring firm government and re-establishing the finances of the realm, has much to commend it, particularly if one considers the years after 1471. Ross, however, makes certain valid reservations about his ability. His policies were not always far-sighted, nor were his judgements always sound. In his marriage he was impulsive, and his favours to the Woodvilles gave needless offence to the men who had done most to put him on the throne. In the years 1469–71 he was twice caught unprepared, and his final recovery of the throne owed as much to his enemies' errors as to his own ability. He was inconsistent in his dealings with his enemies, treating them sometimes with surprising generosity and sometimes with unexpected harshness. Neither approach was necessarily successful; generosity could be interpreted as weakness and harshness could provoke revenge. Even in the areas of government where he has been praised most, there were limits to his achievement. He did not succeed in eliminating local feuds, attempts to deal with the abuse of retaining remained largely nominal and the problems of curbing malefactors were probably as great in 1483 as in 1461 (Ch.14; 144, pp.411–13, 419–20). Perhaps his greatest success was in the financial field, (Chs. 29 and 30) and he was the first English King to die solvent for more than two centuries. It is worth remembering that his son-in-law Henry VII, perhaps the shrewdest king in money matters in the whole history of England, was to build on the foundations which Edward had laid. He failed, too, to hand on a peaceful succession to his heir, and his dynasty collapsed within two and a half years of his premature death. In this he compares unfavourably with Henry V, who also died young, and whose heir was even younger than Edward's. Edward's successes depended essentially on his personal authority rather than on any institutional basis, and although his ability was considerable, he falls short of being a great king.

CHAPTER 25

The establishment of the Tudors

The relative peacefulness of Edward IV's later years gives a false impression of the security of his dynasty. His son lost the throne within three months of his death, his male heirs were probably both dead before the end of the year, and within two and a half years a new dynasty, the Tudors, secured the Crown. This did not create dynastic stability; not only did the Tudors' early years see attempts to overthrow them but both Henry VII and Henry VIII showed a morbid fear of possible rivals. Although the dynasty survived for over a century, and in consequence acquired ultimately a certain air of inevitability, this is essentially a retrospective view, and there were times in its early years when its tenure looked shaky. It is hard too, viewing events through the perspective of the Tudors' achievements, to remember how unlikely a candidate Henry, earl of Richmond, was for the English throne. It is a major historical problem how this obscure man of twenty-eight, who had been an exile since he was fourteen, obtained and held the mastery of England. Edward IV's sporadic attempts to gain possession of his person (110, p.18), show that he was seen as a possible threat to Yorkist power, but this does not diminish the odds against him when he made his first attempt to invade England in the autumn of 1483.

Edward IV's premature death was the ultimate cause of Henry's success. The circumstances of Richard of Gloucester's usurpation undermined the stability of the realm and opened the door to rivals, one of whom, Henry of Buckingham, was to fall before the end of 1483. Although Richard was popular in some parts of the kingdom, notably in the North, he also seems to have aroused considerable antagonism from which Henry, as the surviving challenger to him, derived benefit. It is hard to say quite how extensive this hostility was, because several of the writers who have most affected the historical interpretation of the reign were mainly concerned with glorifying the new Tudor dynasty. The prejudices of Polydore Vergil and Thomas More, both of whom wrote well after the events, sketched a picture of Richard III as a villain, and Shakepeare's melodramatic portrait represents the culmination of a tradition. Although this image has provoked a counter-view of Richard as the victim of a propaganda campaign, the King's defenders have tended to overstate their case, starting from the assumption that all criticism of the King was unjust. Even early sources, however, from before Richard's usurpation, show signs of hostility to him – there are hints of his complicity in the death of Henry VI (18, p.21) and of his willingness to use violence against his enemies. What certainly cannot be proved, whether or not it is true, is the belief inherent in the narrative of the usurpation that Richard was planning to seize the throne from the start.

Although there had been rumours a year or two earlier that Edward IV's health was poor, the best contemporary accounts suggest that his death was unexpected (3, pp.58–9; 14, pp.563–4; 158). It came after a short illness and created a political vacuum, with the most important persons in the realm being dispersed around the country. The new King, Edward V, was at Ludlow with his maternal uncle, Earl Rivers, and his paternal uncle, Richard of Gloucester, was in the North. In London there was rivalry between the Woodville faction, headed by the Queen-mother and her elder son by her first marriage, the marquess of Dorset, and Edward IV's Chamberlain, Lord Hastings. The next three months were to see a swing of the political pendulum, with the Woodvilles holding some advantage at the start, but with Gloucester steadily establishing his control and eventually usurping the throne. Perhaps the most important factor in this was the activity of some of the magnates and of men who had been old advisers of Edward IV, but who had no great love for the Woodvilles. They were prepared to acquiesce, although perhaps with some reservations, in the actions of the Queen's party while she possessed real power, but were quite happy to desert her when Gloucester asserted himself by force. It may have been their influence which secured a restriction in the size of the escort which accompanied the new King from Ludlow to London, as Hastings demanded, but they also appear to have accepted the Woodville-inspired decision to proceed to an early coronation, although this ran counter to Edward IV's will, in which he had named Gloucester as Protector (158). The Woodville group also had a firm grip of the administration, and dominated the lists of commissioners appointed at the end of April to collect a tax on aliens levied in Edward IV's last Parliament.

The first open use of force came at the end of April, when Gloucester, travelling south from York, met Rivers and the duke of Buckingham at Northampton. The meeting was clearly prearranged, and the evidence suggests that the weeks immediately after Edward's death had seen a good deal of correspondence between the interested parties. Buckingham's adherence to Gloucester was probably prompted by his resentment at having been married as a minor to one of the Queen's sisters, and was to give Richard a powerful ally with extensive territorial resources. Rivers certainly did not suspect Richard, and walked into a trap. After an apparently friendly first meeting, the dukes arrested Rivers and went to Stony Stratford where they seized various other Woodville supporters and took possession of the King's person. Richard alleged that the Woodvilles were plotting against him, and when he arrived in London tried to stir up popular sentiment against them (3, pp.76–7, 82–3). Once in London, he was recognized as Protector and assumed control of affairs. The Queen fled into sanctuary with her second son. How we interpret Gloucester's motives depends on whether he genuinely believed there was a Woodville plot. If Richard planned the usurpation from the start, these accusations may have been fabricated, but he may equally have been concerned with securing his own position and obtaining the office of Protector for which the late King had designed him. The actions of the Queen and Dorset in London could have given him a motive to act firmly, while Rivers's lack of caution could be explained by his failure to perceive that Richard felt his position threatened.

Possession of the young King gave Richard the political initiative, but only partial control of the government. There were some changes in the great offices of State; Archbishop Rotheram of York, who may have been pro-Woodville, had to surrender the Great Seal to Bishop Russell of Lincoln, but there is no proof that Russell, the Keeper of the Privy Seal, was a partisan of Gloucester. It is more likely that he was a career administrator, and the same can be said of Sir John Wood, who filled the vacant post of Treasurer, which had not been filled since the death of the earl of Essex a few days before that of Edward IV. He had previously been Under-Treasurer and had been Speaker in the Parliament two or three months earlier. The Council cannot, however, have given whole-hearted support to Gloucester, because his attempt to have Rivers and his fellow prisoners condemned for treason was unsuccessful (3, pp.84–5). Men who disliked the Woodvilles did not necessarily wish to pursue them to death.

During May, the most conspicuous development was the grant of lands and offices to Buckingham, who progressed from relative obscurity to become the second most important man in the kingdom. Other grants were made to former servants of Edward IV, who had rallied to the Protector, as well as to members of Richard's own affinity. Only the Woodvilles and their immediate circle suffered serious losses at this time. It is not clear whether Richard had a clear policy at this time, for his actions were compatible either with an intention to usurp or with preserving his position as Protector. His crucial problem was the relationship between the young King and his mother's family. A coronation would, *ipso facto*, terminate the protectorate, and Edward might then turn to the Woodvilles, whom he knew better, a potentially dangerous situation for Richard, particularly after the events at Stony Stratford. Richard may have hoped to defer the coronation indefinitely, for writs summoning Parliament were issued well before a date was fixed for the coronation (158). It may have been some of Edward IV's old followers in the Council who urged that the coronation should proceed, possibly against Gloucester's wishes. By the time that a date was fixed for the ceremony, relations between him and the Queen had reached a complete impasse; she was in sanctuary with the duke of York, Edward V's younger brother, and was a possible focus of opposition to the Protector. If Edward were to be crowned in the absence of his brother, the divisions in the realm would be emphasized with cruel clarity.

There is a sharp controversy over how the impasse was broken, affecting not only the interpretation of events but also the facts. It is known that on 10 June Richard appealed to the city of York for help against the Queen, alleging a plot against him, but there is no evidence that this existed. It is also certain that on 16 June the duke of York was handed over from sanctuary to Gloucester, although his mother remained there. About the same time, Richard accused three prominent men of treason, Lord Hastings, who was executed, and Archbishop Rotheram of York and Bishop Morton of Ely, who were imprisoned. The date of this is disputed, but on balance the evidence suggests that it took place on 13 June rather than a week later.[1] It seems clear that by 10 June Richard was expecting a showdown with the Queen, for which he would need reinforcements. Probably he had by this time decided to seize the throne, even if this had not been his earlier intention; such an action could have been prompted either by ambition or by the wish to protect himself against a possible Woodville resurgence following the coronation. If the three victims of the coup had supported an early date for Edward being crowned in discussions in the Council, this might explain why Richard wished them out of the way. It would have been unlikely for them to give willing support to a usurpation after having so recently urged the coronation of another.

The fate of Hastings raises various problems. He was executed for treason without a proper trial, but was then given honourable burial at Windsor beside his friend and master Edward IV. All the evidence suggests that the charge against him caught him totally off his guard, so it is unlikely that he was actually involved in a conspiracy, but if he were innocent, why was he executed? There are two possible explanations, either that Richard knew that he would never desert Edward's heirs, and that he had to be removed, lest his influence turned the Council against the Protector, or that he was the victim of a private conspiracy. There is a tentative hint of this in More's *History of Richard III*, a source which, though late and unreliable, is sometimes correct on obscure details. More suggests that Richard's councillor, William Catesby, may not have sounded out Hastings's views on the personal assumption of power by the protector, as he was supposed to do, because he coveted some of his offices, and that he then gave Richard an unfavourable report of Hastings's attitude (38, pp.46, 214–16).

A further problem from this period is why the Queen surrendered her second son to Richard. The most likely explanation is duress, because although the death of Hastings, whom she disliked, might not have worried her, the arrests of Rotheram and Morton, and earlier of her brother Rivers, cannot have left her confident of the Protector's goodwill. Certainly there was a display of force outside the sanctuary. Elizabeth may also have hoped that Edward's coronation during the following week would be a guarantee of the duke of York's safety. With both his nephews in his hands, Richard was able to delay the proposed Parliament, perhaps after having already obtained the Council's assent (158). Thereafter pulpit propaganda, suggesting that the princes (and possibly also Edward IV) were illegitimate, and some vigorous public relations activity by Buckingham among the magnates and the citizens of London, prepared the way for Richard to take possession of the throne.

At the beginning of Richard's reign, he continued to exercise patronage in the same way as he had done while Protector. Many of his brother's old servants continued to hold office and they shared new grants with members of Richard's own affinity. Some of the men who had supported Richard received greater rewards. John, Lord Howard, obtained the duchy of Norfolk, to which he was heir by blood, but from which he had been excluded in Edward IV's later years; that king's younger son, who had been married to the Mowbray heiress Anne when both parties were small children, had retained a claim on the lands after Anne's death in 1481. Howard was to remain loyal to Richard and fell with him at Bosworth. By contrast, an even greater beneficiary, Buckingham, rebelled before the year was out. Why did he do so? His gains had been immense; in addition to the grants of authority which had been given in Wales, while Gloucester was still Protector, he was given the office of Constable shortly after Richard became king, and in influence he was second only to the King. There is also evidence that Richard acknowledged the justice of his claim to that part of the Bohun inheritance which had passed to the Crown with the accession of the Lancastrians,[2] so he had no justifiable territorial grievance. There was little more that Buckingham could reasonably expect short of the kingdom, which may indeed have been his aim. If the Yorkists were eliminated, Buckingham, as heir of Thomas of Woodstock [B.1], could put forward a claim, and his activity on Richard's behalf during the usurpation may not have been entirely disinterested. More particularly, he may have been responsible for the allegations of Edward IV's illegitimacy, because Richard, who was actually living in his mother's house at the time, would hardly have been likely to use this argument.

There is another problem about Buckingham's revolt; he was in touch with Henry Tudor, whom he could not regard in any other light than that of a possible rival. Here the important fact is that the rebellion may have been under way before he joined it – indeed it is simpler not to describe it as his rising at all. More suggested that Bishop Morton, of whom the duke had custody, encouraged him to rebel, but the other late writer, Polydore Vergil, who stresses the part played by Lady Margaret Beaufort, may be nearer the mark. Her participation is confirmed by the proceedings against her in the 1484 Parliament, when her lands were forfeited, though she was spared the attainder which the other rebels suffered. As Buckingham's mother had been a Beaufort, he might have been willing to join with her, and although Lady Margaret put forward her son, Henry Tudor, as the claimant for the throne, the duke might still have hoped to turn the political trouble to his own advantage. Lady Margaret's prominence could also explain why Elizabeth Woodville, who from sanctuary was involved in the complex network of intrigue, and who brought the Woodville connection, headed by Dorset, into the conspiracy, was willing to join in a plot with her old enemy Buckingham.

Many of the participants in the rebellion were men who had been old supporters of Edward IV, and with rumours, probably well founded, that the late King's two sons were dead, there was some spontaneous popular discontent which could be exploited against Richard. How the princes died is not surely known, a fact which remained politically important until Henry VII's reign. It has also given rise to wild speculation, particularly by those who start from the premise that Richard could not have been responsible. In fact it is impossible to see where else the ultimate responsibility for their deaths could lie; their survival after the usurpation would have left a focus for discontent against the new King, who had therefore the strongest possible motive for actually ordering their deaths. The only plausible alternative to him, Buckingham, is not as strong a candidate for the part of murderer (127, pp.411–18). The princes were probably dead by the autumn of 1483, because otherwise Richard could have scotched the prevailing rumours by producing them in public.

Despite his obscurity, Henry Tudor had advantages over Buckingham as a figure-head for the revolt. The plan to marry him to Edward IV's eldest daughter, which seems to have been considered from the start of the conspiracy, could confirm Woodville support, he could appeal to old Lancastrian sympathizers, such as Edward Courtenay, heir to the dormant earldom of Devon, and he had the possibility of securing support from the duke of Brittany, who was looking for an English ally against the threat of French encroachment, although Louis XI's death made this less urgent for him. Buckingham had little beyond his own resources, and the Woodvilles were hostile to him for his part in Richard's usurpation. Buckingham's weakness is shown by the break-up of his army without a battle, and his subsequent capture and execution. Although Henry failed to keep his fleet together, he avoided being persuaded ashore into a trap, and escaped safely back to Brittany, where various fugitives, headed by Dorset, soon joined him. In return for his pledge to marry Elizabeth of York, they did homage to him as if he were already king (13, pp.195–6; 110, pp.19–27).

Richard's easy victory might suggest that his position was already strong, and it should have been further consolidated early in 1484 when Parliament confirmed his title and attainted the rebels. In fact the King's actions demonstrate how lacking in confidence he was. The participation of many of Edward IV's old servants in the rising led him to turn increasingly to his own followers from the North, whom he rewarded with forfeited lands in the areas most seriously affected by the rebellion. The unpopularity of these men was to reflect on the King himself, and as Richard's throne was threatened again from the middle of 1484 by the possibility of invasion and by discontent at home, he found himself relying on a narrow circle of men. Richard's failure to broaden the basis of support for his regime was a major contributory factor to his defeat at Bosworth.

Various measures taken by the King demonstrate how lacking in confidence he was; he tried to secure the title of his son as heir by oath of the lords spiritual and temporal, a fruitless measure as the boy died soon afterwards, and attempted to come to terms with Elizabeth Woodville, presumably to try to prevent a Tudor – Woodville marriage alliance. His nervousness about Henry Tudor's new prominence as a challenger for the throne is shown by his diplomatic actions towards Brittany. As the duke was ill, the dominant figure in the duchy was his unpopular treasurer, Pierre Landois, who appears to have hoped that English support would strengthen his position against his enemies. He agreed in June 1484 to surrender Henry, but the latter was forewarned and escaped to France. The French did not give immediate support for a new invasion attempt, but Henry was a useful bargaining counter for them, to discourage Richard from supporting Breton attempts to remain free of Valois control. Henry continued to receive a trickle of support from defectors: James Blount, Captain of Hammes Castle near Calais, deserted to him in company with the Lancastrian earl of Oxford, who had been a prisoner there for ten years (110, pp.29–34). In England too, men were looking to him, though most were more cautious than William Colyngbourne, executed for treason in the summer of 1484, who was charged with sending Tudor a message urging him to invade England as well as with writing the famous lampoon on Richard and his councillors:

> The Cat, the Rat, and Lovell our dog,
> Rule all England under a hog (127, p.301).[3]

When Richard's son died in April 1484, the succession problem again became open. After considering the possibility of designating Clarence's son, the earl of Warwick, as his heir (though this would have made nonsense of this line being passed over in Richard's favour in 1483), Richard chose the son of his sister Elizabeth, John de la Pole, earl of Lincoln. He was granted lands and offices, becoming Lieutenant of Ireland and President of the newly established Council of the North, succeeding to Richard's own dominance in that region (148). There is evidence, however, that by this time Richard's popular reputation was low. When his queen died in the spring of 1485, rumours arose which Richard had to deny publicly only fifteen days after her death, that he was intending to marry his niece Elizabeth. These probably had little foundation – the prospects of obtaining a dispensation for this were negligible and such a match would have been tantamount to denying the illegitimacy allegations made in 1483 – but they do reflect popular and perhaps widespread doubts about the succession. The only indication that Richard's hold on the realm was thought to be secure was an attempt by Dorset, on his mother's persuasion, to desert Tudor. The date of this episode is uncertain, but if it were late, it may have been one factor which prompted Henry to attempt a further invasion, on the assumption that time could only strengthen Richard's position (26, pp.173–4; 110, pp.35, 38).

Nevertheless, he was still little more than an adventurer embarked on a huge gamble when he landed in Wales in August 1485. Although he encountered no opposition on his rapid march through that country and into the Midlands, he also attracted little support, and when he met Richard at Bosworth, the battle was closely contested. It swung Henry's way when the Stanley family, with a substantial force, came over to him. Northumberland too, who had been one of Richard's major allies in 1483, stood apart from the conflict and surrendered to Tudor without striking a blow. Both these magnates had probably been in touch with Henry, but delayed their desertion until they were reasonably confident of the invader's victory. Lack of positive popular support and these desertions among the higher nobility were the reason for Richard's defeat, and it is hard to resist the conclusion that they feared his rule so much that they were prepared to support a virtually unknown alternative. The most powerful magnate who stood by the King, Norfolk, died alongside him (110, pp.46–9).

It was one thing to overthrow Richard, but quite another to secure the Tudor dynasty. Henry's main advantage was the relative paucity of rival claimants, though some of these remained and were later involved in conspiracies against him. He also had to face two pretenders to Yorkist blood. But Henry was concerned with the realities of power rather than with legal niceties; his coronation preceded the meeting of his first Parliament, which he told that he was king by just hereditary title (whatever that vague phrase meant) and by the judgement of God, as shown by his victory in the field. His marriage to Elizabeth of York, early in 1486, was probably less intended to strengthen his legal claim than to preclude the possibility that she might marry someone else who could then put forward a claim on her account. However, the birth of two sons of the marriage, Arthur in 1486 and Henry in 1491, did strengthen the dynasty. A possible Yorkist rival was the earl of Warwick, the last Plantagenet of the male line, whom Northumberland may have favoured in 1485. He was put in custody in the Tower, where he remained until his execution in 1499 for alleged conspiracy with the pretender Perkin Warbeck. There was also Richard's heir designate, Lincoln, who had fought for him at Bosworth, but who quickly came to terms with Henry and was present at his coronation. He did not, however, abandon his own ambitions, and he and his brothers remained a factor in later dynastic manoeuvres (110, pp.51, 59, 62, 92).

The aims of the first revolt against Henry in early 1486, led by Viscount Lovell and the brothers Humphrey and Thomas Stafford, are not clear, but it soon collapsed. Lovell escaped to Flanders, where Margaret of Burgundy remained at the centre of anti-Tudor plots for a number of years. More serious was Lincoln's flight there a year later, for it suggests that he had rejected Henry's early clemency. He, Lovell, and 2,000 German mercenaries then went to Ireland, where they joined the first of the pretenders, Lambert Simnel, the son of an Oxford tradesman, who claimed to be the earl of Warwick and who was proclaimed king as Edward VI. Although Polydore Vergil suggests that the priest Richard Simons, who coached Simnel in this part, was acting on his own initiative (19, pp.12–13), this is unlikely, and the participation of Lincoln in the plot, though he was presumably well aware that the real Warwick was Henry's prisoner, is comprehensible only on the assumption that he hoped to use Simnel to overthrow Tudor before laying claim to the throne himself. Some of the de la Pole estates were at Ewelme, not far from Oxford, so he may have known something about the plot from the start. Irish hostility to English rule probably explains why the earl of Kildare gave countenance to the pretender (Ch.10) and why the Irish reinforced the invasion army which landed in Lancashire early in June 1487. It was defeated in a hard battle at Stoke, where many of the leaders, including Lincoln, were killed. The pardon granted to Simnel, who was given a menial post in the royal household, suggests that he was regarded as the cat's-paw of others. Clemency was also extended to Kildare, in the hope that he would remain loyal in future, but this policy failed, and he may have given some support to another pretender later. (110, pp.75–82).

Simnel's imposture had little support outside England, apart from the mercenaries supported by Margaret of Burgundy. The second pretender, Perkin Warbeck, by contrast, was able to obtain external support which made him a more serious threat to Henry. The origins of the plot are obscure; originally he may have been set up as another pseudo-Warwick, but later he claimed to be Edward IV's second son, the duke of York. His own personal ineffectiveness, seen in the failure of everything he touched, suggests that others were behind the imposture, and he was certainly valuable to those who wished to create problems for Henry, including Charles VIII of France, James IV of Scotland, Margaret of Burgundy and the Habsburgs, Maximilian of Austria and his son the Archduke Philip, ruler of the Low Countries in the right of his late mother Mary of Burgundy. Warbeck even secured support in England from Henry's step-uncle, Sir William Stanley, who was executed for treason in 1495. There is no reason to think that anyone believed the imposture, except possibly James IV, who gave a kinswoman of his own to Warbeck in marriage, and certainly when Henry came to terms with his supporters they gladly dropped the pretender. The Treaty of Étaples of 1492 with France, by which Henry abandoned support for Brittany (and a claim of his own to the French Crown) provided for an indemnity payment to him along with the arrears of Edward IV's pension under the Treaty of Picquigny. Maximilian's support for Warbeck may have been prompted by this settlement with France, but he gave little practical support. The Scots King was probably concerned with trying to recover Berwick, taken by Richard of Gloucester in 1482. However, an invasion of England on Warbeck's behalf in 1496 was totally futile, and in the following summer James let Perkin go. The pretender's final gamble was to try to raise support in Cornwall, where there was still discontent after the failure of a rising against royal taxation early in 1497. At first he rallied support, but his force melted away when faced with a royal army, and Warbeck fell into Henry's hands. Like Simnel he was treated leniently, but he abused the King's generosity, first by attempting to escape and then by plotting with the earl of Warwick. In 1499 he was hanged (110, pp.85–92, 282).

Although the pretenders created trouble, potential rivals of genuine royal blood were possibly a more serious threat. After Lincoln's death, the de la Pole claimant was his brother Edmund, who succeeded to the Suffolk title, though with the reduced rank of earl, after his father's death in 1492. The King drove a hard bargain with him over the restoration of the family lands, so his dislike of Henry is understandable (148). His career was marked by some violence, and in 1501 he fled, with his brother Richard, to Maximilian's court, where he began to plot in his own interest. Another brother, William, was imprisoned at this time, and remained so for the rest of his life, and other conspirators, including Richard III's former servant Sir James Tyrell, whom Henry had restored to favour, were executed (110, p.93). It was not until 1506 that Edmund was surrendered to Henry, when his host, the Archduke Philip accidentally fell into English hands. Edmund remained in custody till 1513, when Richard, who had avoided being handed over, secured French recognition as King of England, and Henry VIII, more brutal than his father, decided to eliminate the older brother for good. This foreshadowed the fate of many other descendants of the Yorkists, especially in Henry VIII's paranoiac later years, when possession of a possible claim to the throne was virtually tantamount to a suspended death sentence.

The last great victim of dynasticism before the Reformation was Edward, duke of Buckingham, in 1521. Even under Henry VII, who had annulled his father's attainder, he was regarded as a possible heir to the throne, and in 1519 the Venetian ambassador thought that if Henry VIII had no heir, the duke might succeed him. Not only was Buckingham's own territorial power extensive, but he was also brother-in-law to the earl of Northumberland, who had a significant following in the North. His dislike of Wolsey and opposition to his foreign policy may have been exaggerated as a factor in his fall, for had he not acted and spoken foolishly, stressing his royal descent, the cardinal could have done little about it. He also had treated some of his servants badly, and their wish to pay off scores made them willing to provide evidence of his incautious remarks. Though the evidence was little more than hearsay and the statements were probably distorted, they were enough to secure his condemnation and execution for treason (97, pp.36–44; 146, p.165).

The Tudor succession never looked particularly secure, and it must be remembered that there were never more than a few lives between the dynasty and extinction. This is crucial to understanding the great crisis of Henry VIII's divorce and his desperate search for a male heir. The obstetric history of his first wife, Catherine of Aragon, with several miscarriages, stillbirths or perinatal deaths, and the survival of only one child, Mary, left the succession in the 1520s even more fragile than when Henry himself became king in 1509 (146, p.201). England had never had a queen regnant, and after his daughter, Henry's next heirs were his sisters, the elder of whom could bring in an alien Scottish ruler to succeed. Henry's lust for Anne Boleyn was undoubtedly genuine, and the circumstances of the King's marriage enabled her to gamble for higher stakes than she could have done had the succession been secure, but one must remember that other people besides the King could see the threats to political stability which were looming on the horizon if the succession issue were not solved. In this, perhaps as much as in fear of the King, one can see an explanation for the support which Henry obtained in the crisis of the 1530s. The Tudors' earlier assiduous elimination of possible dynastic rivals had created its own new problem.

---

1. The case for a later date was argued by A. Hanham (121; 122; 123) and the principal defender of the earlier one is B. P. Wolffe (155; 157). C. T. Wood (158) accepted the redating and made various important contributions to the discussion, several of which are valuable whether or not one accepts the revised view on the timing of events. I should now wish to modify my own views (149) on why an error arose in one key source (26) in the light of Dr Wolffe's arguments.
2. Mary and Eleanor, the co-heiresses of Humphrey, the last Bohun earl of Hereford (d.1374), had married respectively Henry of Lancaster, later Henry IV, and Buckingham's ancestor, Thomas, duke of Gloucester.
3. The 'cat' was William Catesby and the 'rat' Richard Ratcliff. Viscount Lovell had a dog in his crest (188, p.13b) and Richard III's own armorial device was the white boar.

CHAPTER 26

The recovery of royal power

Political stability depended on the maintenance of royal authority over the noble class, and there were two ways in which this could be secured. Either the King had to exercise it, as Henry V had done, through magnate goodwill, or he had to possess sufficient power to overrule them. Henry VI's failure in the mid fifteenth century was clearly the result of his inability to stand above and dominate noble factions. The first half of Edward IV's reign saw no diminution in the rivalries of great men; indeed the King's patronage of the Woodvilles exacerbated them. After 1471, however, there was some decline in magnate disorder, and under Richard III political unrest was directed more against the King's actions than caused by his inability to control his subjects. In this one can see a recovery of royal power preceding the advent of the Tudors, although the relative ease with which Richard was overthrown underlines its limitations. Under Henry VII the authority of the Crown was to be greatly enhanced.

Recent writing has played down the importance traditionally assigned to 1485 as a turning-point in English history, and it has been shown that many of the methods of government employed in the early Tudor period had been foreshadowed under Edward IV. Indeed it is fair to say that Henry VII's approach to government was strongly traditional, and that parallels to it, notably in his reliance on professional administrators, can be traced in the fourteenth century. It was the reign of Henry VI, when magnate influence was excessive, which in fact deviated from customary practice. The search of historians for a 'New Monarchy' or a 'more modern' form of kingship, whether of the Yorkists or the Tudors, is in that sense the pursuit of a myth. In political terms, however, there is some justification in regarding Henry VII's accession as the start of a new epoch, because the dynastic change brought with it in the long run a more securely based royal authority than had previously existed. However far Edward IV dominated the nobility in his later years, he was far more lavish in the grants which he made to them than Henry VII was ever to be. Admittedly his creations of peers were far more numerous before 1469 than after 1471, and it may be argued that it was necessary for him to reward his followers with dignities and lands in order to establish the Yorkist regime, but one must remember that even in his early years Henry VII was markedly sparing in creating new peers. Both Edward IV and Henry VII used appointment to the Order of the Garter as a reward for their closest servants, and it may reflect the former's greater dependence on the nobility that a higher proportion of his appointments were made from the noble than the knightly class (110, p.140; 144, pp.331–3). Henry also relied far less on particular great men to act as his agents in particular parts of his realm – no one in his reign possessed the power which Lord Herbert had had in South Wales before 1469 nor the authority in the north of England which made Richard of Gloucester his brother's most powerful subject in the 1470s. This may have been partly due to chance; Henry benefitted from the death of the earl of Northumberland in the Yorkshire rising against royal taxation in 1489, because it removed from the scene the head of the greatest surviving northern family and left a boy of twelve as his heir, although even before then there are signs that Percy influence was declining. Other great families which were fortuitously weakened included the Staffords and the Courtenays – Edward, duke of Buckingham, was a minor in the wardship of the King's mother, and the earl of Devon owed his restoration to Henry, with whom he had returned from exile and by whom he had been knighted fifteen days before Bosworth (97, p.35; 112, pp.63, 137).

These factors contributed to the greater independence of the nobility which Henry VII possessed compared with Edward IV. Another was that he had no close relations who could challenge his position. For three-quarters of his reign, Edward had had his brother Clarence hovering in the wings, successively as his heir general, his heir male and a disgruntled prince of the blood. Also, although Gloucester remained faithful to Edward during his lifetime, his proximity to the throne gave him a special ability to attract political support, particularly when in 1483 there was strong hostility to the Woodville group which was threatening to dominate the realm under the young Edward V. By contrast, Henry's one close relative among the nobility, his paternal uncle Jasper Tudor, earl of Pembroke, had no royal aspirations, because it was from his Beaufort mother than the King's claim derived. Indeed Jasper was to be one of his nephew's strongest allies, with a vested interest in his survival, as their fortunes were closely bound together. It is true that there were still possible claimants to the throne of Yorkist descent, who posed problems for both Henry and his son (Ch.25) but none of them secured sufficiently widespread support among the nobility to threaten the Tudor dynasty seriously, at least after the death of the earl of Lincoln at Stoke in 1487. This remained true even after the death of Prince Arthur in 1502 left the male line of the Tudors surviving only in one person, the future Henry VIII. Those nobles who did become involved in rebellion against Henry VII, namely Viscount Lovell, Lord Fitzwalter and Lord Audley, were also markedly less powerful and important than men such as Warwick or Montagu, who had risen against Edward.

Henry looked widely in his choice of councillors, and there is no truth in the belief that he neglected the peerage when selecting them. About two-thirds of the peers are known to have attended the Council on some occasion, and some of them held major offices. Between 1486 and 1501 Lord Dinham was Treasurer, and his successor, the earl of Surrey, remained in office until 1522. The King also employed various churchmen in governmental posts, notably Archbishop Morton, Chancellor from 1486 until his death in 1500, and Bishop Fox, successively King's Secretary and Keeper of the Privy Seal, holding the latter post from 1487 to 1516 (110, pp.102–9). The length of tenure enjoyed by such men is in itself a reflection of the stability of the regime. Besides these there was a group of influential men, from knightly or gentry families, who attended the Council regularly without holding major offices. These included some who had been with Henry in exile from 1483, Reginald Bray and Thomas Lovell, who seem to have specialized in financial matters, Giles Daubeney, primarily though not exclusively a military leader and perhaps for this reason the only one of the group whom Henry created a peer, Richard Guildford and John Riseley. Under them professional administrators like John Heron did much to keep the machinery of government working, and lawyers, such as Richard Empson and Edmund Dudley, both men without powerful relatives, were assiduous agents of the King's policies (110, pp.110–13, 316–17). Henry employed talent where he could find it, looking more widely than a narrow circle of great families.

It has also been argued that Henry made a deliberate attempt to stress the dignity of the Crown and the royal prerogative, a concept which was never clearly defined, and indeed was useful for that very reason. His expenditure on ceremonial display, including his creation of the Yeomen of the Guard, was surprisingly lavish for so notoriously parsimonious a ruler. Certainly one should not underrate the importance of this in his propaganda, especially as it was to be further developed by his successors, but one should guard against thinking that this was particularly novel. Not only, as Elton points out, can one see the precedent of Richard II's later years in which great attention was given to maintaining the formal dignity of the King, but one can see a similar position under Edward IV. One of the characteristic points noted about the English court by a Bohemian traveller in 1465 was the reverence paid to the King and Queen, when even the great magnates had to kneel to them (25, pp.45–7; 51, pp.43, 46).

Perhaps the ultimate test of a king's authority may be found in the way in which he treats his defeated enemies, and here again one can see some differences between Henry VII and his Yorkist predecessors. In the second half of the fifteenth century, defeated rebels were often attainted by Act of Parliament. Naturally such Acts were most common during periods of civil war or after a rebellion, and the large number of attainders during Richard III's reign, totalling 100, was entirely due to the rising in the autumn of 1483. Richard's short and disturbed reign cannot well be compared with any other, but those of Edward IV and Henry VII, which were similar in length, just over twenty-two years and a little under twenty-four, afford scope for some comparison. The total figures of attainders, 140 under Edward and 138 under Henry, are also close, but here the similarity ends. The bulk of those in the earlier reign, 113, took place near its beginning, and affected men who had fought against Edward at Towton. Moreover, the King showed a willingness to pardon his enemies and reverse the attainders against them. Such reversals might involve merely a personal pardon, or they could include a partial, or even total, restoration of estates. This could raise problems, because forfeited estates might have been granted away to the King's supporters, who were then unwilling to surrender their gains, as for example John Neville's resentment at the restoration of Henry Percy as earl of Northumberland in 1470 (Ch.24). On the other hand, the prospect of restoration allowed former rebels to work their way back into favour, and Edward was prepared to accept this. Indeed, after his return in 1471, when his authority was at its greatest, there were substantially more reversals than new attainders. Most cases where attainders were not reversed were those of men or families which had proved intransigent despite Edward's attempts at clemency, such as the earls of Oxford or Devon (130, pp.132–41).

Although, as with Simnel and Warbeck, Henry might pardon his enemies, his clemency was generally more likely to benefit those who counted for little politically. The records show attainders being enacted in every Parliament of his reign but one, and the greatest number of fifty-one occurred in the last one, in 1504. It is, however, misleading to say that Henry's severity to his enemies increased in his later years, because in 1504 there had been no Parliament for seven years, and those attainted included participants in the Cornish revolt of 1497 and in the earl of Suffolk's conspiracy of 1501. Earlier in the reign Parliaments had been more frequent [D], and the smaller number of attainders reflects the shorter gaps between them. The annual average number of men attainted does not seem to have increased markedly in the later years of the reign. Where Henry contrasts more sharply with Edward is in his much tougher attitude towards reversals of the attainders which were inflicted in his time (33, vi, 544–6; 130, pp.129–30, 143, 307). Those who were pardoned included a number of those Yorkist supporters who had fought at Bosworth, but who were willing to make their peace with Henry. In such circumstances a man's restoration to favour could be related to the service which he could offer in return. A conspicuous instance of this was the Howard heir, Thomas, earl of Surrey. His father, the duke of Norfolk, had fallen with Richard at Bosworth, and he himself was attainted and imprisoned in the Tower, where he remained until 1489. On taking an oath of allegiance, he was released, and the attainder was partially reversed. He did not yet recover his father's ducal title, and he secured only a limited proportion of the lands. Service to the King in quelling the northern insurgents who had killed the earl of Northumberland was rewarded by the recovery of further lands later in the year, and ultimately, through continued loyalty and work for the Crown, he recovered his hereditary lands, although he had to negotiate with the new holders of those which the King had previously granted away. Not until 1514, in the next reign, however, was the title of duke of Norfolk restored to Surrey, after long years of service in war and government to Henry VII and Henry VIII. This included the treasurership from 1501 till 1522, and in 1513 the command of the victorious English army at Flodden (110, p.108). Surrey's case illustrates clearly one of the ways in which Henry VII controlled the magnate class; forgiveness for past offences could be forthcoming, if a man was willing to support the new dynasty faithfully, and he could have the opportunity to better himself, with rewards which were never so great that he might not hope for more. One may contrast this with Buckingham's meteoric rise under Richard III – his gains were so great that he could well have felt that he had exhausted the King's generosity. Henry VII was particularly judicious in the way in which he balanced the carrot and the stick; even when employing the former, he never forgot to keep the latter in reserve. The nobility were more likely to secure a reversal of attainder than were lesser men; the great majority of the attainders which had not been reversed at the end of the reign were those of knights, esquires and yeomen (130, p.307).

The reason for this may well have been that the King possessed another effective sanction against the wealthier men of the realm in the use of financial penalties. Not only could money payments secure the reversal of attainders, but the King also manipulated the system of bonds and recognizances for good behaviour. The mulcting of offenders was not a new alternative to physical punishment, and there was little doubt that a well-lined purse, emptied at the right moment, could save a man from a worse fate: a London chronicler, writing of Edward IV's suppression of the Kent rising of 1471, stated: 'Such as were Rych were hangid by the purs, and the othir that were nedy were hangid by the nekkis', and another writer said of the same events that Edward 'hade out of Kent myche goods and lytelle luff' (18, p.22; 40, p.221). Henry VII was not only able to secure wealth from his attainders through confiscation of property (110, p.207 n.3) but also used the threat of money sanctions to discourage men from opposing him in future. He developed the system of recognizances on an unusual scale, although his measures were not complete innovations. During the magnate feuds of the mid fifteenth century, men had frequently been compelled to enter into recognizances to keep the peace with each other, or to appear in court at a particular time, and Edward IV employed the same system to guarantee the allegiance of men whose attainder was being reversed, such as Henry Percy in 1470. Indeed, even in Henry VII's early years recognizances were employed in the same manner, but from about 1502 there was a marked increase in the number of those who were bound in this way to keep their allegiance to the King and his heirs (130, pp.276–80). Two factors may have contributed particularly to this intensification of royal pressure on the magnates – the activities of Edmund de la Pole, which showed that a Yorkist claim was still a real possibility, and the death of the King's elder son, Arthur, leaving as sole male heir the eleven-year-old Henry, still younger than Edward V had been in 1483. With a third son, Edmund, having died in 1500 aged sixteen months, the dynasty suddenly looked much more vulnerable.

The most striking facts about these recognizances were the sums involved and the number of people affected. In many cases the sums in which men were bound over were enormous and could put their estates largely or entirely in the King's power. It has been estimated that about three-quarters of the noble families in England were at some time in the reign either under attainder or bound to the King by recognizances of this kind (130, p.292). These included some of the greatest families in the kingdom. An early example of such pressures being applied to a prominent magnate can be found in Henry's dealings with his wife's stepbrother, the marquess of Dorset. The King may never have trusted him fully after his attempt to come to terms with Richard III and return from exile, and it may be symptomatic of this distrust that he was left in France as a hostage for Henry's debts during the invasion of 1485. Although Henry reversed the attainder passed against him by Richard's Parliament of 1484, for his rebellion in the previous autumn, he insisted that he first renounce various of the territorial gains which he had made in Edward IV's reign. Dorset appeared secure under the new dynasty, but in 1492, for no particular known reason, he had to grant his lands by indenture to trustees, to be held to the King's use, except for two small manors. If he avoided committing various offences during his lifetime, the indenture was to become void and his heir was to inherit in the normal manner. He also had to grant the wardship and marriage of his heir to the King, and give recognizances for this both in his own name and in those of various sureties. In fact Henry seems to have held the power in reserve, not enforcing the agreement fully and terminating it before Dorset's death. His main concern seems to have been to have a sanction to discourage the marquess from possible disloyalty. Dorset's case shows that Henry employed the system of recognizances from early in the reign, but the most drastic financial penalties which he imposed date from near its end in the prosecution of Lord Burgavenny for unlawful retaining (Ch.14). For this offence he had incurred a massive fine, far exceeding his capacity to pay, and a settlement was reached whereby he would pay the King £5,000 in instalments over ten years, a penalty which, though still severe, was not beyond him (130, pp.287–9).

The King did not always enforce such bonds, and the amount which came to him in cash was much smaller than the sums stated in them, which the magnates were theoretically liable to pay. This must be remembered when one is trying to explain why Henry employed this system in his dealings with the nobility (110, p.216). It seems likely that control of them mattered more to Henry than the incidental financial gains, although these were also welcome to him. Although Polydore Vergil stressed the King's avarice, he also held that he wished to keep his people obedient through fear (19, pp.126–9, 146–7). This is borne out by the statement of one of the principal agents of Henry's government, Edmund Dudley. After his arrest at the beginning of the next reign, he presented a petition that, for the discharging of his conscience, steps be taken to make restitution to those who had been wronged. In this he listed those, from a wide spectrum of society, who had in his opinion been unjustly treated under the previous King. Most strikingly, in the preamble, Dudley alleged that Henry's wish had been 'to have many persons in his danger at his pleasure'. As Dudley, under sentence of death, seems to have been more concerned with the salvation of his soul than with receiving a pardon, there is no reason to doubt the accuracy of his allegations, many of which can also be substantiated from other evidence. The substance of many of the charges was that large sums had been extorted for trivial matters or on suspicion alone, and this illustrates the arbitrary, but none the less effective, power of Henry's government.

While it is doubtful how far Henry strengthened his financial position by these measures, there is no doubt that he did so in other ways. Although the level of wool exports was lower throughout the reign than it had been 50 or 100 years before, and continued to drop during this period – average wool exports in the King's last five years were 25–30 per cent lower than those in the first five – this was more than compensated for by the substantial increase in cloth exports, which rose by over 65 per cent between the same two quinquennial periods (66, pp.68–70, 109–113) [A2][1]. The benefits which the Crown derived from this in revenue are clear, although the increase in customs receipts from an average of £33,000 in the first decade of the reign to one of £40,000 for the remainder of it is more impressive as a percentage than as an actual quantity of cash. Another branch of revenue which Henry attempted to improve was extraordinary taxation, where efforts were made, though with limited success, to break away from the traditional, and largely fossilized direct imposition, the tenth and fifteenth.

Further gains were made in the exploitation of the revenues from the Crown lands, though the precise scale of these cannot be measured (110, pp. 195–212; Chs 29–30).

In the long run, however, what is most important for royal power is less the amount of money available to the King in absolute terms than its sufficiency to meet his needs. Henry's major achievement was that his revenue exceeded his expenditure, and seems to have done so from quite early in the reign. Henry himself was prepared to keep control of his financial position, checking the Treasurer's account books personally. His avoidance of war, however, was the main reason for the favourable balance which was established in the royal revenues, and why he was able to end the reign in credit. The overall surplus which he obtained was invested in plate and jewels rather than being kept in cash, and the amount of specie which Henry handed on to his son should not be exaggerated (51, p.56; 110, pp.217–18). Nevertheless, his father's measures did allow Henry VIII to begin his reign on a secure financial footing.

Whether all these actions, the curbing of the magnates and the strengthening of royal government, particularly in financial matters, left the kingdom fundamentally stable remains questionable. Henry VIII's actions on his accession give the impression of a king who wished to conciliate his subjects by easing the pressures on them. The principal victims of this were Empson and Dudley, who were arrested, charged with treason, found guilty and sent to the scaffold, without a shred of evidence against them. Their real offence was that they had been agents of extortion, a charge of which many men were prepared to accuse them, but they could show that they had acted in accordance with the King's instructions. If the new King was to secure the popularity which he was evidently seeking by making scapegoats of them – and this appears to have been his intention – he could do so only by perpetrating a manifest injustice on two loyal servants of the Crown, the first, but by no means the last, to suffer in this way during his reign. Henry also sought popularity by easing the system of recognizances, although, significantly, he still reserved the right to recover debts owed to the Crown. During the first five years of the new reign a substantial number of recognizances was cancelled. The response to these actions was favourable; Thomas More, who had incurred the old King's wrath by opposing his fiscal demands, wrote enthusiastically of the new reign, and Lord Mountjoy, who had himself been bound to Henry VII by numerous recognizances, was no less lavish in his praise in a letter to his old master Erasmus (130, pp.284, 297–9; 146, p.28).

The change of domestic policy on Henry VIII's accession was one of methods rather than of aims. The new King seems at this stage to have preferred to rule by public favour rather than by coercion, although the tyrannical streak in his character was evident from the start, as was shown both by his treatment of Empson and Dudley and by his execution of Edmund de la Pole in 1513. Nevertheless, he succeeded in winning popularity, and was able to present himself as the natural head of a magnate class which still saw its most important function as military. His enthusiasm for tilting and his commissioning of an English translation of Tito Livio's *Life of Henry V* both show his acceptance of the traditional chivalric role of the monarch (146, pp.42–3), and his pursuit of glory in a campaign in France suggests that his ambition was to model himself on his namesake and predecessor whose reputation still stood high, indeed uniquely so, after the turmoils of almost a century. This desire to idealize war was in sharp contrast to the hard-headed pragmatism of his father, who had avoided it, and although Henry VIII was ultimately to pursue policies which further strengthened the authority of the Crown, it must be remembered that in his early years his actions could have gone far to weakening it in pursuit of unrealistic ambitions. Indeed, had he not entered into an inheritance of royal control over the nobility and of sound royal finances, which his father had achieved, he would have not had the same freedom for foreign adventuring.

---

1. These figures can be only approximate, because of gaps in the series of enrolled customs accounts, but the general development is clear. A comparison of sexennial periods rather than quinquennial ones shows a slight difference in percentages, but the general trend is the same. P. Ramsey, 'Overseas trade in the reign of Henry VII: the evidence of the customs accounts', *EcHR*, 2nd ser., **6** (1953–54).

CHAPTER 27

The new European diplomacy

The second half of the fifteenth century saw a number of important changes in the western European state system, and the political units which emerged from them were to remain the principal forces in diplomacy until Italy and Germany were unified in the nineteenth century. The marriage of Ferdinand of Aragon and Isabella of Castile in 1469 laid the foundations for a Spanish state which, despite the existence of separatist forces, was to inherit the political traditions of each of its parts and become a major force in Continental politics as neither of the old kingdoms had ever been. The Valois monarchy in France rounded off its territories by successively eliminating the greatest of its semi-independent feudatories; the English kings, with lands in Normandy and Gascony, were driven out in the middle of the century, the Burgundian duchy became a prey to the rivalry of the French King and the German Emperor after the defeat and death of Charles the Bold in 1477, with some of its lands reverting to the French, and finally in the 1490s the duchy of Brittany was absorbed by the marriage of the last duke's heiress, Anne, to Charles VIII, and after his death, to Louis XII. The Habsburg share of the Burgundian inheritance, in the Low Countries, gave the imperial family a new focus of political interest in northern Europe which it had not hitherto possessed. The increasing power of the rulers of Spain and France particularly affected the English King. Although the early Tudor rulers were more powerful in domestic matters than their immediate predecessors, their kingdom was relatively weaker in both wealth and population than the new super-states which had emerged on the Continent (154, pp.12–13), and their relations with their neighbours were no longer as vital a factor in European diplomacy as they had been earlier. Whereas in 1378 the political alignments of the Anglo-French War had played a vital part in determining the lines of obedience in the Great Schism, a century later England was more liable to be tossed about in the diplomatic crosscurrents which flowed from the enmities of more powerful countries. English interests played a relatively small part in deciding the alignments of the powers.

If one reason for this, as has been suggested, was the relative weakness of England compared with its neighbours, another was a change in the main focus of European political rivalry. In the 1490s the uneasy power balance which had been established between the major Italian states collapsed, and the competing claims of outside powers made the peninsula the cockpit of European politics. Both France and Aragon had claims in the kingdom of Naples, a state technically under papal suzerainty. France also had an interest in Milan, an old imperial fief. In the ensuing struggles, the Empire, France and Spain all played a part along with the surviving Italian powers. It was not until the reign of Henry VIII that the English were drawn into the volatile diplomatic manoeuvres which arose from the problems of Italy, and it is likely that this was due to his own driving ambition for glory; his father's diplomacy, by contrast, was concerned essentially with maintaining his hold on the English throne.

Above all, English foreign policy was dominated by the country's relations with France. One element in the traditional rivalry of the kingdoms had been effectively removed when the English King ceased to hold lands for which he was the French King's vassal, but there was not yet in England a total willingness to cut these losses. As long as the French King had problems with other great vassals, it was tempting to ally with them in the hope of recovering at least part of what had been lost. From the late fourteenth century, successive English rulers had found allies in Burgundy and Brittany, and the elimination of these duchies as independent forces in the fifteenth, together with the French reconquest of Normandy, left the Valois King in control of the southern shore of the Channel. It is noteworthy that Henry VII's establishment of a naval base at Portsmouth to strengthen the English south coast defences followed Charles VIII's absorption of Brittany (154, p.63).

Defence of his position was the key to Henry VII's foreign policy, the fundamental aim which remained consistent beneath the changes in alliances and apparent shifts of policy which were forced on him by the manoeuvrings of other powers. This is apparent from his early actions as king. It is hardly surprising, in view of the support which he had had from France during his invasion, that he immediately proclaimed a year's truce with that country, and subsequently extended it, although there was no fundamental goodwill between the two kingdoms. By July 1486 he agreed a commercial treaty with Brittany, in 1487 he renewed Edward IV's treaty with Maximilian of Habsburg and early in 1488 began negotiations for the marriage of his son Arthur with Catherine, a daughter of Ferdinand of Aragon and Isabella of Castile. A year later this was agreed by the Treaty of Medina del Campo (110, pp.279–80).

Clearly the European powers expected Henry to survive in England and were accepting the new dynasty. On the other hand, old enmities still persisted, notably with France, and the expansionist policy pursued by the regency government of Anne of Beaujeu, sister of the young Charles VIII, posed Henry with his first major diplomatic problem. Her plan, to marry her brother to the heiress of the ageing Francis II of Brittany and to bring the duchy into the royal demesne, was not popular there, and the duke sought an alternative match for his daughter in Maximilian of Habsburg, who had been left a widower by the death of Mary of Burgundy in 1482. Duke Francis intrigued with the regent's enemies in France, thereby provoking retaliation in the form of an invasion in 1488. The support which the Bretons obtained from Maximilian, Aragon and England was limited, and their own leadership was divided, with the result that they were overwhelmed at the Battle of St Aubin-du-Cormier in July. In August the duke had to agree to a humiliating peace, which provided that he should not again call for foreign help, and that his daughters should not marry without the consent of the French King. He died within three weeks, and the French secured the wardship of the heiress Anne (144, p.291; 154, pp.33–4).

How was Henry VII to respond to these events? He did not wish a direct clash with France, and indeed tried to mediate between the two parties, but Brittany was a valuable ally from whose friendship England had frequently benefited. It also possessed harbours which might become strategic bases for a future French attack on England. There is evidence, too, of popular support for a Breton war (8, pp.253, 255), although this evaporated when the cost in taxation provoked the Yorkshire revolt in which the earl of Northumberland was murdered. Despite the terms of surrender of 1488, the Bretons were prepared to negotiate a treaty with Henry in the following year. He agreed to send a limited contingent of troops to Brittany, at the Bretons' expense, as did the Spanish rulers, but he was unable to prevent a French victory. In December 1491 the Duchess Anne, previously married to Maximilian by proxy, threw over the match and married the French King. This left Henry in a further dilemma. To withdraw tamely from the scene would not only leave the impression that he could be discounted as a serious political force but might also encourage his enemies to challenge his own position in England. On the other hand, to take military action on his own would incur the risk of defeat, with possibly even worse consequences. In fact, he extricated himself from the situation with a measure of success. He showed that he was not pusillanimous by reasserting the old English claim to the French throne, taking an army to Calais in 1492 and laying siege to Boulogne, but he did not press his claims too far. The French King, ambitious to invade Italy in pursuit of military success, was willing to buy him off as his father had done with Edward IV, and a peace settlement was rapidly reached at Étaples. By this Henry secured two major gains, a promise by the French King not to assist rebels against him – this was fulfilled by Warbeck's banishment from France – and the payment of a substantial indemnity for the costs of his intervention in Brittany together with the arrears of payments due under the Treaty of Picquigny. This may have given him some compensation for the failure of his attempt to prevent the French absorption of Brittany (110, p.282; 154, pp.35–6, 40).

A common hostility to French ambitions in the Breton succession struggle was one factor which involved Henry in negotiations with the Spanish rulers, culminating in the marriage agreement between Prince Arthur and Catherine of Aragon. This was a considerable diplomatic success for Henry, in that it involved recognition of his own title, and closed Spain to Yorkist claimants and pretenders. On the other hand, since the wedding was not to take place until the children attained more marriageable years, and since such political marriage agreements were easily broken, it might be dangerous to overrate the importance of the treaty. Certainly Spain gave only a little support in Brittany.

Although Maximilian's initial response to the Anglo-French settlement at Étaples was hostile, he soon found that it was desirable to come to terms with Henry again. After 1494, the success of the French campaigns in Italy, which threatened traditional imperial claims in Lombardy, weighed more heavily in this than the economic sanctions which Henry had imposed on his lands in the Netherlands; these had merely provoked a counter-embargo on Burgundian trade with England. Agreement was reached in 1496 on the treaty which came to be known as the *Intercursus Magnus*, which provided for the restoration of trade and the abandonment of support for rebels. In the same year, the agreement with Spain for the marriage of Catherine and Arthur was renewed, and it was eventually solemnized by proxy in 1499. Spanish hostility to French actions in Italy was a strong incentive to consolidating the English alliance, as well as to establishing closer ties with the Habsburgs, and by the time that Catherine arrived in England in 1501 to be married to Arthur in person, there existed a strong dynastic and political coalition directed against France (110, pp.233, 383; 154, pp.42–5). Spain was at the centre of this; in 1496 Catherine's older sister Joanna had married Maximilian's son, the Archduke Philip, to whom his father had made over the government of The Netherlands, which was his inheritance from his mother Mary of Burgundy. In fact, a series of unexpected deaths made the ties between the Spanish kingdoms and the Habsburgs closer than had originally been planned, and probably closer than the Spanish rulers at any rate wished. Between 1497 and 1500 there died successively Ferdinand and Isabella's only son, whose posthumous child was stillborn, their oldest daughter, the wife of the King of Portugal, and then her son. Joanna thus became heir to the Spanish lands, and her son Charles, born in 1500, had the even more dazzling prospect of uniting to these the old Burgundian lands and those of the Habsburgs. These close dynastic and political ties between Spain and the Low Countries, already economically linked by the growing Spanish wool trade, explain why friendship with England was valuable to both of them. The Channel sea route was their main artery of communications, and its southern seaboard was in the hands of a hostile France. Habsburg dominance in Spain, however, was not accomplished without problems, and the complexities of Henry VII's diplomacy in his last years were largely caused by the tensions, and sometimes open ruptures, in the Spanish–Habsburg alliance.

In the first years of the sixteenth century, relations between the English and Spanish courts were friendly, as is evident from the way in which, after Arthur's sudden death in 1502, both parties were prepared to agree that his young widow should marry his brother Henry, although some time elapsed before the necessary dispensation for their consanguinity was forthcoming from the Pope, and longer yet before the marriage took place. Quite simply an unmarried prince, even one who had been pledged, was a more valuable diplomatic counter than a married one. It was the Spanish who were more enthusiastic to hasten the remarriage, principally because of their increasing rivalry with France over Italian affairs. Louis XII had secured possession of Milan in 1500, but had been driven out of Naples in 1502–3, after agreeing to partition the kingdom with the Spanish in 1501. The French King had retaliated by coming to terms with the Habsburgs, and although the alliance was both unlikely and short-lived, it left England as the only available ally for Ferdinand and Isabella.

Just after this Franco-Habsburg agreement, Isabella's death introduced a new complication into the political scene, as the Castilian nobility saw an opportunity to recover some of the authority which they had lost under her rule by playing off Joanna and Philip against Ferdinand. For Henry VII this meant that he could no longer look to both Spain and the Habsburgs for support against France. He pursued a twofold approach to the situation, trying to maintain peaceful relations with a willing France – Louis XII proposed that Prince Henry should marry a French princess rather than Catherine – and aligning himself with the Habsburgs rather than with Ferdinand. As Henry VII himself had been a widower since Elizabeth of York's death in 1503, he also negotiated for a marriage with Maximilian's daughter, the widowed duchess of Savoy, although this came to nothing. More importantly, he supported Philip's attempts to gain control of Castile for his wife, lending his money in 1505 to prepare an expedition. When, shortly after, Philip was driven into Weymouth harbour by a storm which severely damaged his fleet, Henry exploited the situation to strengthen the alliance. He recognized Philip's claim to the title of King of Castile, and promised him support. In return for this Philip surrendered Edmund de la Pole and made substantial trading concessions to England in the Netherlands, although these were later dropped by Henry, a fact which shows that, as on other occasions, the English King regarded trading interests as something subordinate to politics (110, p.290; 154, pp.51–6, 69–71). Henry came out of the political crisis with some success: despite a settlement between Ferdinand and the French, the latter did not break with Henry, and the subsequent uneasy agreement between Ferdinand and Philip meant that the English King was not committed to any active policy on the Continent which might cost money or endanger his own position. The main victims of the agreement were Edmund de la Pole and the unfortunate widow Catherine, left in England without certainty of remarriage.

Hardly had this crisis been settled when in 1506 the situation was again upset, by Philip's death and Joanna's subsequent deranged melancholy, which was to persist until she died in 1555 and prevented her from taking any active part in political affairs. Ferdinand resumed control in Castile as regent for his grandson Charles, while in the Low Countries the same role fell to Maximilian. English diplomacy over the next three years was somewhat tortuous, and although the facts are not in doubt, historians have disagreed about Henry's motives. Elton suggests that he had abandoned his old restraint in order to make England's influence felt on the Continent, while Wernham considers that he was desperately trying to patch up a system of alliances to secure his own position in the face of a series of crises which he could not reasonably have foreseen (51, pp.39–41; 154, pp.57–61). In general, Wernham's interpretation is the more convincing – there is no evidence that Henry's political restraint deserted him elsewhere, and even at the start of Henry VIII's reign his father's old councillors were generally inclined to a policy of peace abroad. It is, however, possible that the King's concern for security was not altogether justified, and that he did not fully appreciate how Italian affairs were the main preoccupation of the other European powers. The League of Cambrai of 1508, which drew together Ferdinand, Louis, Maximilian and the Pope against Venice, did not leave Henry isolated; indeed all three lay powers seem to have been concerned with remaining on friendly terms with him. Henry's main fear, a possible French expansion into the Low Countries, was for the moment removed by the good relations between France and Maximilian. An even clearer indication of Henry's place in the European political scene was the Emperor's agreement that his grandson, the Archduke Charles, should marry Henry's daughter Mary by proxy. In view of Charles's expected inheritance, this plan suggests that Henry was regarded not only as undisputed King of England, but also as a figure of European importance.

When Henry died in 1509, the orientation of English foreign policy was changed. Where the father had been cautious, responding to circumstances and committing himself to military action only as a final resort, the son was ambitious for glory and from the start of his reign showed himself determined to secure it. Like many of the aristocracy over whom he ruled, he saw war as the natural function of the ruling class and France as the ancient enemy. If viewed retrospectively, Henry VIII's search for martial glory may appear a fantasy, but his subjects would not have thought so. All his actions after his accession made his aims clear, a calculated insult to a French envoy, his marriage to Catherine, postponed while his father had explored other matrimonial prospects for him, followed by an enquiry to her father Ferdinand if he would be willing to join an invasion of France, and the dispatch of Archbishop Bainbridge of York as an envoy to Rome to negotiate a peace between the Pope and Venice, which could leave the French isolated. In fact Henry moved too rapidly for both his possible allies and his own advisers. Ferdinand cautioned him to wait for a more propitious moment, and his older councillors, mainly men who had served his father, seem to have prevailed over the more bellicose younger courtiers, with the result that the existing truce with France was renewed in March 1510, probably contrary to the King's wishes and certainly to the considerable embarrassment of Bainbridge in Rome (146, pp.41–6; 154, pp.80–3; 206, pp.23, 32).

As so often at this period, however, Italian politics lay at the heart of European diplomacy, and it was this which gave Henry his opportunity for war. Pope Julius II had been at the heart of the coalition against Venice, but after the defeat of the republic came to regard French domination of northern Italy as a more serious threat. A crisis over Ferrara, where the duke was under French protection, provided a pretext for papal intervention and a renewal of war. Louis XII sent troops to support his North Italian allies and, more seriously, gave support to a group of rebel cardinals who in May 1511 attempted to summon a general council of the Church. The French King was therefore guilty of schism, a fact which may have influenced Henry VIII's ecclesiastical councillors, who had previously resisted his war policy but who were also loyal to the Pope, to support the King's more militant line. Henry joined the alliance against France, despite Louis's attempts to preserve his neutrality by continuing payment of the pension due under the Treaty of Étaples. Queen Catherine, too, played an influential part in drawing together her father and her husband (146, pp.46–7; 154, pp.80–3; 206, pp.33–4).

The first serious campaign on which the English embarked in 1512 was in fact in alliance with Ferdinand, who soon made it clear that he was not prepared to do anything for Henry, but hoped to use an English contingent to assist him in his seizure of Navarre. Lack of agreement on the object of the campaign led to squabbling between the English commanders and the Spanish King, and shortages of food and other supplies soon reduced the English force to a mutinous rabble, which returned home with nothing accomplished. Failure did not, however, deter Henry from military adventuring, although it was not until the following year that he launched a further attack in alliance with Maximilian. After long indecision, the Emperor entered a league with England, Spain and the Pope in April 1513, although Ferdinand defaulted on the alliance by concluding a treaty with France almost simultaneously. Before this, an attempt to harry Brittany by sea failed, and the English Admiral, Lord Edward Howard, lost his life, but Henry still crossed to France at the end of June and joined Maximilian. The subsequent campaign had limited success, capturing Thérouanne and Tournai, and defeating a French cavalry force at the so-called Battle of the Spurs in August. This might have provided a foundation for a further campaign in the following year, on which Henry could have embarked with even greater assurance, as the defeat of the Scots and the death of James IV at Flodden in September made it certain that England would be safe from diversionary attacks in the North for some time. Plans were made for a combined Anglo-imperial invasion of France and for the marriage of Henry's sister to the Archduke Charles, as had been proposed some years earlier (146, pp.50–3, 56–60; 154, pp.85–6).

Henry's allies, however, who had been keeping open alternative political options, found these preferable, and were quite prepared to pull out of the alliance almost as soon as it was signed. Julius II's death, even before the 1513 campaign, and the succession of the Medici Pope Leo X opened up prospects for a reconciliation between the Papacy and France. Ferdinand was won away from Henry by bribery and Maximilian also soon defected. Henry attempted to go on alone, but his sole effort was a raid near Cherbourg, and before long he too came to terms with France. One factor behind this may have been financial; he had used up both the reserves which he had inherited from his father and the proceeds of the taxation which he himself had levied. Papal pressures, aided by support for peace from two of Henry's most influential councillors, Richard Fox and Thomas Wolsey, led to the conclusion of an Anglo-French treaty in August 1514. Henry's French pension under the 1492 treaty was to be restored, and his sister Mary married the French King, not the Emperor's grandson (146, pp.77–82; 154, pp.87–8).

With this settlement, the first phase of Henry VIII's reign was over. The most important consequence of it lay not in the bitter lessons that war was costly and allies unreliable, not even that it was possible for the English to outwit their allies in duplicity and emerge relatively unscathed at the end, but in the incidental emergence of a new and dominating force in English politics, Thomas Wolsey. He had been the King's Almoner since 1509, when he also became dean of Lincoln, but it was his ability as the organizer of the army which invaded France in 1513 which first brought him to the forefront of Henry's government. There he soon became equally prominent in diplomatic negotiations, being probably, along with the veteran Bishop Fox, the most vigorous English advocate of a peace with France. Increasingly he became indispensable to Henry, who rewarded him well. These years, 1513–14, saw him appointed bishop of Tournai, then of Lincoln, and finally archbishop of York, before he even attained a secular post. This he added to his other positions when he became Chancellor in 1515. Holding high office in Church and State, he was to dominate English government for the next decade and a half.

CHAPTER 28

The age of Wolsey

Wolsey's emergence in public affairs during and after the French War of 1513 was due, above all, to the influence which he possessed with the King. His eventual fall, which one may date to his surrender of the Great Seal in 1529, came when other men could secure royal favour better than he. In order to play the part which he desired in the affairs of the nation and of Christendom as a whole, it was necessary for him to retain the goodwill of an unpredictable master, whose whims might lead to drastic changes in policy. Scarisbrick's summary of Henry's character demonstrates the reasons both for Wolsey's rise and fall and for the erratic nature of English foreign policy during the second and third decades of the sixteenth century: 'a taxing man to serve – now glad to release all into his minister's hands, now irrupting suddenly and decisively into affairs both big and small, now in enthusiastic partnership with his servant, now, equally unpredictably, lapsing into lazy indifference to public business' (146, p.301). Henry lacked the detailed concern for administration which had been the hallmark of his father's rule, and it was Wolsey's willingness to deal with such routine business which first commended him to the King. George Cavendish, Wolsey's gentleman usher and biographer, whose professed intention was to counter the slanders and untruths which he alleged had been spread about his master, suggested that he had advanced himself in the King's favour by urging Henry to pursue his own pleasures and leave the affairs of the realm in other hands, contrary to the advice of the King's other councillors. Henry was nothing loath to heed this advice, perhaps because he was still young and irresponsible and his closest associates were his boon companions of the tiltyard and the hunting-field. In these circumstances, and probably with the support of some of Henry's clerical councillors who distrusted the magnates, Wolsey obtained formal power as Chancellor in December 1515. He was already archbishop of York and a cardinal, and in 1518, when the Pope created him legate *a latere*, he secured power over the entire English Church, not only his own province of York (37, pp.4, 12–13; 146, pp.66, 101).

The emergence of a dominant clerical minister is surprising if viewed in the perspective of the early years of the reign, which saw an apparent reversal of Henry VII's attitude to the aristocracy. Whereas the old King had been markedly sparing about creating new peers, the young one was prepared to re-create various titles which had lapsed. In 1510 the duke of Buckingham's younger brother was made earl of Wiltshire, and in 1513 the King's close friend Charles Brandon, a mere esquire in 1509 but by then a knight, was granted the title of Viscount Lisle, along with the wardship and marriage of the child heiress. Brandon rose even higher within a year, being created duke of Suffolk with the grant of the greater part of the forfeited lands of the de la Poles. At the same time, the title of duke of Norfolk was restored to Thomas Howard, earl of Surrey, Charles Somerset, an illegitimate Beaufort who held the title of Lord Herbert in the right of his wife, was made earl of Worcester, and the earl of Derby's younger son became Lord Mounteagle (188, pp.551–2).

Brandon's rapid promotion was the more startling as he was not from the higher aristocracy. His father, Sir William, had been killed at Bosworth, where he had been Henry Tudor's standard-bearer. The Venetian ambassador suggested that he was promoted so that he could marry the Emperor's daughter Margaret, but this seems hardly likely – Maximilian could have found a more suitable match for her elsewhere – and Polydore Vergil's suggestion that his intended bride was Henry's sister Mary is probably nearer the mark (9, pp.157–8, 161, 184; 19, pp.222–3). Certainly the only parallel case of such speedy advancement in this period was that of George Neville, the son of the earl of Northumberland, to be duke of Bedford in 1470, in anticipation of his marriage to Edward IV's daughter (Ch.24). There are still some difficulties with this explanation of Brandon's rise; he not only had to detach himself from any obligations to the Lisle heiress (which would have applied also in the case of a Continental marriage) but Mary was also a piece on the chessboard of matrimonial diplomacy. Within a year of Brandon's promotion, she was married to the ageing Louis XII of France (Ch.27), but when Louis died within three months, she did marry Suffolk. It has been suggested that this led to the duke's temporary disgrace, although the Venetian ambassadors, Badoer and Giustinian, suggest that Henry remained friendly, although there was disapproval of the marriage elsewhere. The same source, however, suggests a year later that Suffolk was less in favour – unfortunately it gives no reason – although he recovered this by the spring of 1517. The instability of Brandon's position may reflect the King's unpredictability, as indeed may also the matrimonial plans for Mary. His temporary fall from favour may have consolidated Wolsey's rise to dominance under the King, as Brandon, through his closeness to Henry and his service in war, might well have appeared as a potential rival to the cardinal in his earlier years. By 1517 Wolsey and Suffolk seem to have been friendly; the papal nuncio said that the latter's recovery was due to the person who had formerly degraded him. According to Cavendish, Wolsey later claimed that he had saved Suffolk from execution, but this may have been exaggeration. Suffolk and the other magnates, however, were not the kind of men to immerse themselves in routine administration, and it was there that Wolsey excelled. There seems, too, to have been less magnate pressure to obtain paid offices than in the fifteenth century, possibly because the recovery of population was tilting the economic balance between land and labour back in their favour. The political and social pressures of this period and the magnate factions of the early years of the reign require further exploration, but examination of them would probably show that the apparent magnate recovery after 1509 faded out because of the needs of administration (9; 37, p.90; 142, pp.14, 108–9).

Wolsey undoubtedly sought the central place on the stage. Superficially this took the form of conspicuous display in his household and way of life, a not unusual manifestation of success by a self-made man who not only worshipped his creator but wished others to do so as well. But what were his basic aims?

Pollard suggested that loyalty to the Papacy was fundamental to his foreign policy, which he altered to remain in harmony with papal wishes. (51, p.92; 142, p.122). It has also been thought that his own ultimate ambition was to be pope, but this is unlikely; he was shrewd enough to realize that his real power came from his dominance at the English court, not from influence which he could exercise at the Curia, and it has been shown that when his name was put forward as a candidate during a papal vacancy the driving force was Henry rather than himself. The most convincing view of Wolsey's policy is Scarisbrick's, that he shared the desire of his humanist contemporaries such as More and Erasmus to establish peace in Christendom and that his diplomacy was directed to this end. It is worth remembering that during Wolsey's embassy to France in 1527, he was called 'le Cardynall pacyfike'. Certainly if one assumes that this was his fundamental aim, the details of his policies appear more consistent. Even though he sometimes failed to keep England out of war, and employed military action to curb the belligerence of others, he does not appear to have been the first to urge war on others. When England appeared bellicose, this may well have been due to Henry, whose desire for military glory could not always be controlled (20, p.24; 37, p.50; 146, pp.72–7). The pursuit of peace in Europe, however, involved England in Continental affairs more than was really necessary in its own interests, as these were not affected by the Habsburg–Valois rivalry which focused essentially on Italy. The Continental rulers could determine whether there was to be peace or war, and although England might threaten to throw its weight against a breaker of the peace, this was not a sufficient deterrent. England could have stayed out of the wars without serious harm to its own concerns, but both Henry and Wolsey wished to be prominent in European affairs.

The peace with France in 1514 had been made with Louis XII. His death, and the succession of his cousin Francis I at the beginning of 1515, brought France under an ambitious young ruler, who was soon to renew French activity in Italy, securing control of Milan after his victory at Marignano in September 1515. Henry negotiated with Ferdinand of Aragon, Maximilian and the Swiss, who were prepared to supply an army in return for money, but this counter-attack against the French position in Italy soon staggered to a halt with quarrels between the allies. In England, Henry was more enthusiastic than his councillors for an invasion of France, and Wolsey even seems to have had recourse to writing secretly to Richard Pace, the English envoy to the Emperor and the Swiss, urging him to get them to put pressure on Henry to abandon his plans. His principal aim seems to have been to avoid expense, a wise judgement, as the Continental powers regarded England primarily as their financial backer, and were prepared to deceive her if the money were not forthcoming. Maximilian did so in 1517, when, having already received English money, he accepted a French offer of cash to come to terms and join a treaty with them and the Archduke Charles, whose Spanish interest had already brought him to an arrangement with Francis (146, pp.88–96).

Henry, like most of his subjects, instinctively preferred a Habsburg alliance to one with France. His comment on Francis in 1515 was that he was indeed a worthy sovereign, but nevertheless a Frenchman and not to be trusted. Later

Wolsey, too, spoke of French perfidy, despite his willingness to negotiate, and a brother of the marquess of Dorset is said to have boasted that if he had a drop of French blood in his body, he would cut himself open to get rid of it. It may have been because of this distrust that Wolsey's most important attempt to reach a peaceful settlement of disputed issues with France was linked to a wider attempt at a collective peace in Europe. This he envisaged early in 1518, and his manipulation of a papal proposal for a crusade, which nobody really wanted except the Pope. into a scheme to resolve more immediate European problems, was his most far-reaching effort of statesmanship. The Treaty of London, which brought prestige to both Wolsey and Henry because it was concluded under their auspices, bound the great powers, and over twenty lesser ones, to act collectively against anyone guilty of breaking the peace. However much Wolsey may have gratified his master and himself in this, there is no reason to believe that the proposals contained in the treaty were not sincerely intended. In the event the settlement proved shortlived, breaking down in the wrangles of the imperial election which followed Maximilian's death in 1519. Francis I tried to challenge the claim of the Archduke Charles, and Henry VIII put his own name forward, though it is hard to judge how serious his candidature was. In fact Charles succeeded his grandfather with little difficulty, adding the imperial lands in Germany to those which he already possessed as archduke of Burgundy and King of Aragon, and as ruler in Castile on account of his mother's madness. This Habsburg conglomeration threatened to encircle France, and Francis I had genuine fears at its power, as well as being piqued by his failure in the election (146, pp.103–6, 138–9; 154, pp.93–5). Charles, too, had good reasons for hostility to the French, who still held Milan and Genoa, thereby controlling one of the main routes from his Spanish dominions to those in Germany. Because the English Channel was thereby left as the major artery of communications between his lands, England had a potential role in European diplomacy, and the two greater powers were prepared to cultivate its goodwill.

Wolsey tried to remain neutral, proposing that Henry should meet both the new Emperor and the French King, although the idea that all three monarchs should forgather was beyond the bounds of practical politics. He succeeded, however, in arranging a series of summit meetings for Henry in 1520, with Charles in England at the end of May, with Francis in June on the borders of the French kingdom and the English lands in France, at the so-called Field of Cloth of Gold, and with Charles again at Calais in July. Although the Anglo-French goodwill expressed at the Field of Cloth of Gold was all that was fulsome and insincere, the vigour of Wolsey's efforts to preserve the ideals of the Treaty of London cannot be seriously doubted. The most notable evidence for this is his refusal to listen to imperial blandishments to join an alliance against France. To say that Wolsey pursued a pro-French policy is only partially true, in so far as he avoided traditional hostility; it is fairer to say that his aim was to use English resources to deter either of the Continental rivals from attacking each other. Even when the French undoubtedly provoked Charles, Wolsey struggled to maintain his position as arbitrator, even perhaps misleading Henry as to his true aims, when he engaged in negotiations with the Emperor's ambassadors in 1521. The latter wished for English military intervention against France, but Wolsey tried to reassure the French that his own aims were still peaceful. The probable sincerity of his intentions is shown by the fact that when an Anglo-imperial treaty was agreed, promising military support in return for the Emperor pledging himself to marry Henry's daughter Mary when she became twelve, Wolsey succeeded in delaying the date when the English troops would actually be involved (146, pp.108–13, 119–25; 154, pp.101–2). Even when the Continental armies were already at war, Wolsey continued to struggle for peace; it was not until the middle of 1522 that England formally declared war on France, and even then Wolsey repeatedly tried to postpone the date of active English participation in the fighting. Wolsey was not alone in desiring peace; Sir Thomas More also expressed a wish for it at this time. There was a sudden intensification in English military activity in the autumn of 1523, when the French King had to face the treason of Charles, duke of Bourbon, who sought help from France's external enemies, but this English bellicosity may have been due to Henry rather than Wolsey, whose attempts to work for peace were swept off course by Bourbon's recourse to arms. In fact, the duke's revolt collapsed just when it was decided to send an army to support him (146, pp.131–3, 171–82).

War was costly, and under financial pressure Parliament met in April 1523. There was vigorous resistance to the King's demands, and an attempt by Wolsey to browbeat the Commons had no success. A smaller grant was made than requested, and the Commons tried, albeit unsuccessfully, to have its payment spread over two years. More strikingly, the Commons were prepared to criticize the whole policy of intervention on the Continent. This kind of criticism was different from the attitude of Parliament a century earlier, when war as such was regarded as honourable, and resistance was directed only at financial burdens. One can perhaps see in this a realization that English dynastic claims in France were essentially a thing of the past, and that involvement in Europe was not necessarily advantageous. There was no longer talk of the King's ancient rights in France, but a feeling that war was unprofitable. Even when the tax was granted, difficulties in collecting it meant that the King's financial position was weak. Wolsey may have resented the actions of Parliament – their tendency to be anti-clerical made him hostile to parliaments as such – but he may not have been altogether unhappy at the resulting necessity of a peace policy. Even while the war was in progress he had shown his attitude by insulting the imperial ambassador and by beginning secret negotiations with France. By March 1525 these had come near to a settlement (146, p.187; 154, pp.104–6; 193, pp.327–30).

As events turned out, the timing of this was disastrous. In February 1525, Francis I's army was destroyed at Pavia, and he himself was captured. At a stroke, Charles V became the dominant figure in Europe. When the news reached England, Henry hoped to exploit the situation to advance his claims in France, and tried to raise a substantial army and to levy the money to pay for it, the so-called Amicable Grant. It is impossible to say how great his ambitions were, but his plans were soon shown to be an unrealizable fantasy. Charles V made it clear that he now wanted peace rather than a further war with France, and that he had no intention of winning a kingdom for his wavering English ally. He made the unacceptable demand that Mary and her dowry should be sent immediately to Spain, and when this was refused, he broke the engagement. At the same time, the attempt to levy the Amicable Grant had provoked widespread riots – in Kent, men declared that the French wars had ruined the nation, and in East Anglia the troubles amounted virtually to a popular uprising (Ch.4). Henry was able to wriggle out of the odium for the taxation by casting the blame on Wolsey, but the latter had at least some recompense in knowing that some peace settlement with France might be possible. Within three months of the news of Pavia prompting Henry to a scheme for dismembering France, negotiations were again in progress, and before long a treaty was signed (146, pp.187–9; 154, pp.108–9).

For the rest of Wolsey's years of dominance, England and France were aligned against the Emperor, with English policy being determined by events on the Continent. The formation of the League of Cognac against the Emperor in 1526 was brought about partly through English diplomacy, and Wolsey's desire to support the Pope, from whom he derived his legatine powers and who could dispense him to hold benefices in plurality. Although England itself did not join the League, remaining on the fringes and offering financial support, Wolsey tried to act as a mediator, declaring to Henry that he would obtain glory from the conclusion of a peace (46, pp.193–4). A new Anglo-French treaty was signed in 1527, with the evident intention of putting pressure on Charles to come to terms, but when Wolsey went to meet Francis later in the year, it was under the cloud of yet another crisis in Italy.

Ever since Pavia, the Emperor's army had been on the prowl in Italy, largely unpaid. Imperial opposition to Clement VII probably lay behind the sack of the papal palace by Charles's allies, the Colonna, in 1526, and threats to Rome itself seem to have been made at the same time. In May 1527 the imperial forces under Charles of Bourbon captured and sacked Rome. The Pope, besieged in the Castel S. Angelo, was at the Emperor's mercy, and after a month surrendered to the imperial army. Wolsey's response to this was to try to apply diplomatic pressure for the Pope's release, and a scheme was also voiced for a regency of the Church by the cardinals as long as the Pope was a prisoner. Wolsey attempted secretly to get the Pope to authorize him to act as his vicar for the duration of this captivity. This scheme was probably designed also to meet the rising problem of English domestic politics, the King's desire for the annulment of his marriage to Catherine of Aragon, as well as to give the Papacy a diplomatic role independent of the Emperor. However, Clement was allowed to escape to Orvieto in December 1527, and Wolsey's hopes of exercising a regency over the Church were ended. The fortunes of war in Italy wavered between 1527 and 1529, but eventually the French were again defeated, the Pope made a treaty with the Emperor, and the French followed his example (154, pp.117–20). England was disregarded, as the Continental powers settled their own differences. Effectively, this meant the collapse of the policy of intervention which had been pursued since the start of the reign. This, together with a shift in the main focus of English political activity to domestic issues, marked the beginning of a partial withdrawal of England from the centre of European diplomacy.

The history of Henry VIII's earlier years has generally been written in terms of Wolsey's foreign policy, and domestic issues have, comparatively speaking, been neglected; indeed there is scope for a study of magnate political manoeuvrings between 1509 and 1529. In many ways domestic politics were quiescent, and Cavendish's statement that 'in my Iugement I neuer sawe thys realme in better order quyotnes & obedyence than it was in the tyme of his auctoryte & Rule ne Iustice better mynestred with indifferencye' (37, p.4) sums up the view that Wolsey's dominance established peace and stability at home. Certainly the occasional disorders which occurred appear to have been single episodes rather than the result of continuing political pressure, such as one saw in the mid fifteenth century. This is true of the outbreak of anti-clericalism over the issue of benefit of clergy in 1515, when Wolsey had to submit to the King, the anti-foreign riots on May Day 1517 and the disorders, already mentioned, in 1525 over the levy of the Amicable Grant. There is little doubt that Wolsey's influence was as pronounced in domestic affairs as in foreign diplomacy, and although the King might occasionally act against his wishes in matters of detail, his authority was never really seriously challenged between his submission on behalf of the clergy in 1515 and his fall over the issue of Henry's divorce. The appointment of Henry Standish, who had been the King's chief spokesman on benefit of clergy, as a bishop may have riled Wolsey, and there was some disagreement between the cardinal and the King over the choice of commissioners in 1522 to conduct a military and fiscal survey. In this, Wolsey ultimately seems to have had his way (42, pp.43–52; 146, p.98).

Since the King rarely attended formal meetings of the Council, Wolsey presided there, and it reflects his dominance in foreign affairs and matters of defence that little time was spent in discussing them. Domestic issues considered included such matters as illegal retaining and the problems of vagrancy in London (170). The existence of this latter problem may well explain why Wolsey took considerable interest in the question of land enclosures, and made some effort to reverse them (Ch.5). The Council's most important function, and the reason for its continued activity during the Wolsey era, was in the judicial field, where he did much to develop its equity jurisdiction, increasing the range of matters within its competence, and giving it additional powers of enforcement (Ch.33). Wolsey was willing to open the court to poor men's suits, but had eventually, under pressure of excessive demands, which reflect the popularity of his measures, to refer minor matters back to the common law courts. His judicial measures provoked hostility in two quarters; the common lawyers opposed encroachments on their traditional spheres, and the magnates resented the use of conciliar courts to enforce Wolsey's political dominance, as in 1516 when the earl of Northumberland was committed to the Fleet prison 'for diverse Contempts', or in 1518, when Sir Robert Sheffield, who had been the Speaker of the anti-clerical Parliament of 1512–14, was sent to the Tower, after public humiliation before the Council (51, pp.82–3; 170).

Men were jealous of Wolsey's dominance, but as long as he could retain the King's favour, his enemies could do little against him. Indeed, despite murmurings at him, he had some support in the Council, as in 1519 when a number of the King's boon companions were expelled from court and replaced by middle-aged gentlemen, although the favourites' banishment was not permanent. The

cardinal's position was strengthened too when the King had doubts about magnate loyalty; in 1520 or early 1521 he became suspicious of some of the higher
aristocracy and wrote to Wolsey, telling him to keep a watch on the dukes of
Suffolk and Buckingham, and the earls of Northumberland, Derby and Wiltshire
(146, pp.161, 164). The inclusion in the list of Suffolk, the King's close friend
and brother-in-law, is surprising, although it is known that he had been out of
favour two or three years before; more striking is the fact that three of the five
men named were closely connected, Buckingham, his brother Wiltshire and his
brother-in-law Northumberland. The King's letter was a prelude to Buckingham's
fall; in the spring of 1521 he was brought to trial on a charge of treason, found
guilty on dubious evidence and executed (Ch.25). The fact that the original letter
had emanated from the King suggests that it was probably he rather than Wolsey
who was the driving force behind the prosecution.

Not until the late 1520s can one see a group emerging at court which was able
to challenge the cardinal, and the key to its appearance may be found in Henry's
passion for Anne Boleyn. She had been around the court for some time, and her
family had been prominent since at least 1515, her father serving in diplomacy
and her sister Mary having been Henry's mistress. There was no love between
Wolsey and the Boleyns; Sir Thomas had been disappointed of office and his
promotion to the peerage may have been delayed, although he still became Lord
Boleyn in 1523 and Viscount Rochford two years later, and Anne had lost a suitor
in the person of Northumberland's son Lord Percy, through Wolsey's actions
(142, p.222; 146, p.200). The duke of Norfolk, whose sister was Anne's mother,
was closely associated with the Boleyns. Yet the cardinal could hardly find an
obvious ally in Queen Catherine, who disliked his willingness to negotiate with
France, so when the validity of the King's marriage was questioned, he was in a
dilemma, politically as well as legally. Polydore Vergil's suggestion that it was
Wolsey who suggested to Henry that he should get rid of Catherine with a view
to marrying a French wife is not impossible, but is equally not proven, and Cavendish's statement that Henry denied Wolsey's initiative in the campaign against
the Queen is perhaps preferable (19, pp.324–7; 37, pp.82–3). More probably
Henry himself was the driving force, and it is impossible for the historian to say
what relative importance should be attached to the political problem of the
succession and the personal question of the King's desire for Anne, as both
undoubtedly were real factors. Certainly, as Catherine became older, and it was
clear that there would be no male heir, the issue of who might succeed Henry
became increasingly important. Possible marriages for the Queen's one surviving
child, Princess Mary, played a part in the diplomacy of the years up to 1525, and
Charles's repudiation of her after Pavia was not merely a snub to Henry but an
incentive to him to seek other solutions. The creation of his illegitimate son
Henry, the child of his early mistress Elizabeth Blount, as duke of Richmond in
1525 may have been intended to prepare the way for his legitimation (154, p.111),
but this scheme seems to have been dropped. The choice of title, held by the
Tudors before 1485, had a significance which contemporaries would hardly have
missed.

Access to the King was the key to winning political influence. Through Anne, the cardinal's enemies had this. She herself seems to have calculated her chances of becoming queen rather than Henry's mistress, and exploited the succession difficulty to fulfill her ambition. Henry had sufficient knowledge of theology to see the possibilities of having his marriage to Catherine annulled, although canonist opinion on the law applicable to his situation was generally contrary to his claims (146, Ch.7). But while he might have been able to secure his annulment from a complaisant pope in a time of political calm, the diplomatic implications of his demands were such that the Pope, with whom the final decision rested, could not comply. By the time that Henry formally sought release from his marriage, Clement VII was at the mercy of Charles V, who was not only Catherine's nephew – that need not have counted in an age when family ties were so ruthlessly exploited for political ends at one moment and disregarded at the next – but was also politically hostile to Henry, who had been willing to turn against him and ally with France.

Henry seems to have had no desire to break with Rome, though he was prepared to exploit the unstable situation in the Church after Luther's revolt by threatening this in the hope of bending the Pope to his wishes. The length of the negotiations with Rome, some three years, does however suggest that this far from patient king was still willing to recognize papal authority. He wished for two things, a dispensation to marry Anne, on the grounds of the affinity resulting from Mary Boleyn having been his mistress, and more fundamental, a declaration that the marriage to Catherine was void. The Pope was prepared to grant the first conditionally on the second being permissible, but on the latter he delayed, appointing a commission to examine the case without the right of giving a definite sentence. Further diplomatic pressure secured ambiguous grants from the Pope, who was torn between fear of Charles, a need for Henry's support and his own sense of justice. How far this was vacillation, how far obstinacy, or even the hope of keeping Henry compliant, is hard to judge. When eventually Cardinal Campeggio was sent as legate, his first approach was to try to bypass the critical question by persuading Catherine to enter religion, which, according to some theologians, could be regarded as tantamount to death to the world and would leave Henry free to remarry. Catherine refused to accept this suggestion, and the integrity of her attitude, and her claim to be Henry's true wife, both then and when the legatine court opened its proceedings in 1529, left Campeggio's worldly wisdom looking both shabby and ineffective. Wolsey belaboured Rome with demands for the case to be heard in England, warning Clement that refusal could mean the end of papal authority there, while Henry tried to nullify popular support for Catherine by proclaiming hypocritically and untruthfully that he was the victim of his conscience, and that if the union was contrary to God's law, he must put aside one whom he would choose above all other women. Catherine's friends however, were more influential at Rome, and were ultimately able to halt the proceedings of the legatine court, in which Campeggio had been using every possible device to postpone a decision (146, pp.270–87, 297–300).

Although there is no reason to believe that Wolsey dragged his feet in efforts to further Henry's cause, he was to be the scapegoat for the final failure of the attempts to persuade Rome to grant a dissolution. Even in the earlier part of the proceedings there were signs of acute tension between the King and his minister, although the differences were patched up, but when the suspension of the legatine court, which Henry hoped would resolve the divorce question in England, coincided with the collapse of Wolsey's foreign policy in the summer of 1529, it was the beginning of the end for the cardinal. Wolsey's immersion in political affairs, while the King was in daily contact with his enemies, headed by the dukes of Norfolk and Suffolk and by the Boleyns, denied him the opportunity to use any personal appeal to the King, and when he came to court in September, he was unable to prevail with his master and had to surrender the Great Seal. Even at this stage Henry seems to have hesitated, sending him a ring in token of his favour, and granting him a pardon when he was found guilty on a charge of *praemunire*, that is, of having recourse to, a court outside the realm. Even during the last year of Wolsey's life, Henry on occasion sent him messages of encouragement, which may have led him to hope for rehabilitation, and if Cavendish is correct, his enemies still feared that he might be recalled, Ultimately, however, he was suspected of secret intrigues with Rome, and on 4 November 1530 he was arrested. What fate the King intended for him is not known, but his death from sickness at Leicester three and a half weeks later on his journey south from York ended his career peacefully (37, p.150; 146, pp.308–16).

By this time the Reformation Parliament was in session, the body which, in conjunction with the King, brought about some of the most drastic changes in English history. The break with Rome ended one reason for involvement on the Continent and helped to turn English political concern to domestic matters. The Dissolution of the Monasteries brought about the most extensive tenurial revolution in England since 1066. The details of these events lie beyond the scope of this volume, which ends with the emergence of Henry himself as the leading actor on the political stage. Sir Thomas More, who succeeded Wolsey as Chancellor, accepted office reluctantly, and only after the King had promised that the divorce would be handled solely by those who were prepared in conscience to further it. As this was the most critical political problem of the day, it was clear that More would not inherit Wolsey's mantle as the King's factotum. More's own words to Thomas Cromwell show that he had no illusions about his position; 'if a Lion knewe his owne strength, harde were it for any man to rule him' (20, p.57). As Chancellor, More was not even second in the realm to the King; the men who counted politically were the group which had brought Wolsey down – Norfolk, Suffolk and Anne Boleyn's father, created earl of Wiltshire in December 1529. All of these, however, were subordinate to the King, whose role in determining policy became increasingly prominent. The proverb, 'the wrath of the king is death', appears to have been well known at this time; Cavendish reports Wolsey as having used it to explain why he yielded on the *praemunire* charge, and later the duke of Norfolk cautioned More in the same words (20, p.71; 37, p.137). In many ways this saying provides an epitome of the second half of Henry's reign.

PART FOUR

The structure of government

CHAPTER 29

The royal revenues: taxation and loans

In any consideration of political developments during the later Middle Ages, one factor which constantly recurs is the need of the Crown to obtain money from its subjects. Indeed, many of the problems which the kings of the period had to face arose from men's reluctance to pay all the taxes which were demanded. These demands were particularly marked in periods of foreign warfare but were not confined to them; even in times of peace a monarch might have to appeal for financial assistance, although not necessarily on the same scale. Popular criticism might suggest that the King was extravagant, but this was not always justified. Taxation had important implications for constitutional developments, because Parliament showed a willingness to criticize some of the policies which necessitated its being levied, and also on occasions asserted claims to supervise the way in which the revenues were employed.

What were the resources possessed by the Crown?. These took many forms; there were payments derived from the royal demesne lands and from rights which the kings exercised by virtue of their feudal lordship over the realm, but these were small in comparison with what was derived from taxation, both direct and indirect. The latter, comprising various dues which were levied on exports and imports, had developed gradually since the last quarter of the thirteenth century, and by the middle of the fourteenth had become effectively fixed in form. The main factor in the development of the customs system had been the financial demands of Edward III during the early stage of the Hundred Years War, when the parliamentary grant of the 'subsidy' on wool, in addition to earlier customs payments, had become the largest single element in the royal revenues. In essence it was a tax to meet war costs, but the renewal of the wool subsidy by the Commons in 1362, 1365, 1368 and 1369, during the years of peace after the Treaty of Brétigny, marked its development into a permanent levy, which would contribute to the King's coffers in peace as well as in war. From this time, the wool tax was to be renewed virtually automatically, apart from one or two occasions in the 1380s when Parliament insisted deliberately on brief interruptions, as a means of asserting that the King could not claim the tax as a right, but that it derived from a parliamentary grant. In practice, however, there was no serious attempt to suggest that the King could do without this revenue, which was now effectively regarded as a part of the ordinary resources of the Crown. The principal way in which Parliament employed its recognized right to control the tax was by varying the level of duty according to circumstances; in 1362 it was levied at 20s. per sack, half the previous rate, but in 1365 it was restored to the 40s. level. After the renewal of the war, a differential tax was introduce, with denizens paying 43s. 4d. and aliens 53s. 4d. (167, pp.20–1; 173, pp.466–9).

The history of other forms of indirect taxation, tonnage, an import duty on wine, and poundage, an import duty on other commodities and an export duty on goods other than wool, woolfells and hides, closely resembles that of the wool tax. Originally the King had secured grants by direct negotiations with the merchant community, but by the 1380s Parliament had taken control of them, often making the grants at the same time as those of the wool subsidy. In general, Parliament was willing to comply with the kings' wishes and to grant them taxes, provided that the necessity for them was shown, even when it had originally raised objections. There was a striking instance of this in 1378; initially Parliament had asked to be excused from making any grant of taxation, but once the needs of the government had been explained, it not only extended the term of the current grant, but also raised the rate (167, pp.23, 33).

Behind this development of permanent indirect taxation was the fact that other royal revenues were insufficient to meet the King's needs. A series of documents from the years 1362–64 shows the existence of this general deficit at a time when there was no additional financial burden caused by the French War. The fact that Parliament was prepared to make grants to meet this deficit shows a growing awareness of the needs of public finance. It was recognized that the King could not rely solely on his personal resources to maintain the policies which he was pursuing, and that it was necessary for the nation also to contribute. The recognition was in many ways tentative, but it had important long-term implications, because it reflected a growing sense of national identity and of a right on the part of the political nation to share in the conduct of public affairs. Both the Crown and Parliament were prepared to see that there were advantages to be gained from co-operation; the King was willing to present a case to Parliament, usually through the Chancellor, justifying his need for financial assistance rather than assuming it as an automatic right, and presumably hoped that parliamentary approval of grants might make his subjects more willing to pay the sums demanded, while Parliament may have felt that by making grants of this kind it could at least have some say in fixing the rate, whereas if the King were left on his own there was a danger that he might try to raise money by completely arbitrary means. The attempts by Parliament to control the expenditure of the taxes levied also presuppose some idea that the policies which were being financed were in some way national and not merely personal to the monarch (Ch.31; 173, pp.471–88, 503, 508).

Such imposition of limitations on the King occurred more in the context of direct taxation than in connection with customs payments. The reason for this is almost certainly that revenues from wool were increasingly regarded as routine. This was particularly true in the fifteenth century, when there was a growing tendency to grant the King the customs for life rather than for a limited period of years. The first instance of this, to Richard II in 1398, may have been extorted by a tyrannical king from a submissive Parliament, and the second, to Henry V in 1415, could have been a euphoric emotional response to the victory at Agincourt, but from the middle of the fifteenth century life grants became increasingly common. One was made to Henry VI in 1453, by the strongly pro-court Parliament which met between the King's judicial perambulations in the West Country and the Midlands and his first attack of insanity (Ch.23), at a time when his political position was strong. Edward IV received the same grant earlier in his reign, in his second Parliament in 1465, after he had consolidated his position by effectively crushing the Lancastrians throughout the realm. The first King to obtain a life grant in his first Parliament was Richard III in 1484, and thereafter life grants from the start were invariable until 1625 (167, p.23 and n.15). This strengthened the financial position of the Crown, because as it received customs payments virtually automatically, Parliament had less scope to challenge the ways in which the money received was employed.

This was not true of direct taxation, which was levied only intermittently, essentially when the needs of war demanded it. It is noteworthy that there were no requests for it during the years of peace in the 1360s, and the same was true of the early years of Henry VI's minority, when, although there was fighting in France, it seems to have been assumed that war costs should be met from the English-held lands there (167, p.24). By the late fourteenth century, the standard form of direct lay taxation, what was called the 'fifteenth and tenth', had already become fossilized. As the name of the tax suggests, the sum demanded had originally been a proportion of an individual's wealth, in fact of his movable property, at a rate of a fifteenth from most rural areas and a tenth from boroughs and ancient demesne lands. This was a pattern of taxation which had been normal in the early fourteenth century (with different proportions of tax on different occasions), but in 1334 the assessment was made not on individuals but on communities, probably in an attempt to evade corruption on the part of the assessors. Two years later, the taxers were ordered to collect the same quotas from each county, and each community within it, as had been assessed in 1334, and from this time the term 'fifteenth and tenth' came to denote a fixed sum, of some £37,500 to £38,000, which could be levied, either as such or possibly in multiples or fractions of it. It was to survive as a form of taxation, although not the only one, until the seventeenth century. The weakness of this form of taxation, by which each county and community had its fixed quota, was that it could take no account of changes in how wealth was distributed throughout the country, a problem which became increasingly acute after the Black Death and the resultant economic disruption. In the fifteenth century some attempts were made to deal with the inequities which arose from the uneven incidence of the tax, by granting it subject to a deduction, which could be used to reduce the quotas on impoverished communities. In 1433, the deduction allowed on each complete fifteenth and tenth was £4,000 and in 1445 this was raised to £6,000 (167, pp.30–1).

The tax fell most severely on the ordinary inhabitants of the realm, perhaps because there were many taxed areas where there was no lord. The feudal classes admittedly had their own obligations of service to the King, and of the payment of various dues to him. However, the development of the system of uses (Ch.12) had provided them with a means of tax avoidance, and although in theory the Crown had possible means of compensation by insisting on its right to demand payment for a licence to alienate land, in practice it was not feasible for the King to control alienations nor to enforce rights of wardship (57, pp.207, 213–15). It is worth stressing that a number of the attempts which were made to modify the fiscal system, particularly in the fifteenth century, seem to have been particularly directed at the feudal landed class, so as to ensure that it would contribute to meeting the King's needs.

The administrative problems of conducting a reassessment probably lay behind the long survival of the fifteenth and tenth as the normal method of direct taxation, even although contemporaries appreciated that it had its weaknesses. The number of experiments which were made to find other ways of raising money from the people, despite their lack of success, are proof that doubts about the traditional tax could not be allayed; indeed in 1380 Parliament affirmed explicitly that fifteenths and tenths were very grievous to the Commons in many ways (167, p.29). It is worth looking in detail at the possible approaches which were tried and the circumstances in which they took place, because they reveal both the pressures which rendered direct taxation necessary and the areas of national wealth which were seen as a potential profitable source of supply. The history of the late medieval fiscal system, indeed, may be said to comprise the attempts of the Crown to strengthen its financial hold on the country.

It is noteworthy that the first period of fiscal experimentation came in the 1370s, when the renewal of the French War made it essential for the King to raise extra funds. It was in the same decade that the economic consequences of the Black Death, in both its primary and its later visitations, were becoming apparent in terms of magnate incomes (Ch.2) and probably also in declining prosperity in some regions or individual communities, which, however fairly they had been assessed in 1334, were now relatively overtaxed. The first attempt to find a new basis for taxation was the parish levy of 1371. As the King required £50,000 for the war, and on the assumption that there were 45,000 parishes in the country, Parliament stated that each should contribute an average sum of 22s. 3d., although it also stipulated that the commissioners making the assessment should vary the figure according to the wealth of the individual parish. It was soon realized that the assumed number of parishes was excessively high, and a Great Council was called to revise the average assessment. The notional average laid down in the revision, of 116s., gives a figure of just over 8,600 parishes. Again it was provided that the parishioners of wealthier parishes should assist those in less prosperous ones (167, pp.27-8). The lack of information which the government originally possessed and the problems of correcting the initial error perhaps explain why it was continually prepared to revert to the fifteenth and tenth, for which assessments were available.

It must have been felt that the parish levy was unsuccessful, for a new experiment was tried later in the decade with the three poll-taxes. The first of these, in 1377, was levied at a flat rate, but in 1379 a graduated system of payment was laid down. In the final poll-tax there was again a flat rate, but, as with the parish levy, it was stated that the strong ought to aid the weak (167, p.29). The difficulty with this stipulation was that there was no way of enforcing it, and it is likely that the weak were the worst sufferers. While there was something to be said in favour of a shift from the taxation of communities to that of individuals, the system adopted did not find a way of levying the heavier taxes on those best able to pay them, and the consequent outbreak of the Peasants' Revolt ruled out the possibility of continuing with this particular experiment.

It was not until the beginning of the fifteenth century that there were again attempts to vary the form of direct taxation. Although in Henry IV's reign there was technically a truce with France, the King still had to face the costs of defending his position in Gascony, of suppressing magnate revolts and of dealing with the threat of the Welsh under Glyn Dŵr. Henry IV's statement on his accession that he would avoid the oppressions inflicted on his people by Richard II made him more dependent on the goodwill of Parliament. The most important point to note is that Parliament did not abandon the fifteenth and tenth, but granted further taxes to supplement it. In 1404 it conceded two fifteenths and tenths, payable in three instalments, the first of one and the others of a half each, renewed the payment of customs and also voted a tax of 20s. on every £20 of income from land valued at over 500 marks a year. It also nominated two war treasurers to receive the money. In 1410 Parliament did not try to innovate, merely granting one and a half fifteenths and tenths, but in 1411 it again conceded a tax on land. The rate, 6s. 8d. for every £20 worth of land, was at a lower rate, but would affect far more people. To judge by the amount of cash actually received, the tax was fairly successful (33, iii, 546–7, 635, 649; 197, p.101).

Despite the French War under Henry V, this reign saw no attempted innovations in taxation, although the traditional payments were levied at higher rates (202, pp.95–6). The King's military successes probably explain how he was able to do this. The first of several fiscal experiments of Henry VI's reign came in 1428, when, along with a renewal of the customs, a grant was made of 6s. 8d. on every knight's fee, and a tax was imposed on the parishes of the realm at varying rates, depending on their wealth and whether they were in the country or in boroughs. The non-renewal of this tax suggests that it had little success, and an attempt in 1431 to impose a land tax, of 20s. per knight's fee or the equivalent in cases of lands held other than by feudal tenure, also came to nothing, being annulled in the next Parliament. More important were the attempts to introduce a form of graduated income tax on lands and other revenues; in 1435 the rate was fixed at 6d. in the pound on income from £5 to £100, at 8d. in the pound on further income between £100 and £400, and 2s. in the pound on any income above £400. The same principle was followed again in 1449, although the detailed tax bands and rates were altered to make the levy even more comprehensive; the lower level of the 6d. rate was reduced to £1 for freehold land and £2 for customary tenures, and its upper limit, for both, was lowered to £20. Between £20 and £200 the rate was raised to 1s., after which point it was 2s. A distinction must, however, be drawn between the tax levels and the actual amount of money which was brought into the royal coffers, for it is clear that 1435 was markedly more productive, perhaps because hostility to Henry VI's ministers encouraged evasion at the late date (33, iv, 318, 367–70, 409–10, 486, v, 172–4; 197, pp.208, 234).

The main aim of these various new taxes was to enable the King to draw more easily on the resources of the community, and as they were granted by Parliament it is clear that the politically dominant classes were prepared to go at least some way to recognizing their responsibilities for keeping the King adequately supplied. The fact that the increases in taxation were directly related to the wealth of the parties concerned does not reflect an altruistic attempt to make the system socially more just, but merely displays a realization that only the wealthy had the resources which could be made available to the Crown. The only aspect of fiscal policy which does show an attempt to secure a more equitable incidence of burdens lay in the modification of the fifteenth and tenth, mentioned earlier, which provided allowances for impoverished communities, and this was an adjustment between communities rather than classes.

The existence of these various experiments in the first half of the fifteenth century shows an awareness of the inadequacy of the fifteenth and tenth. Why, therefore, were there so few attempts to levy an income tax in the second half? One answer, almost certainly, must be found in the administrative simplicity of the older system, because each community would know the quota which it owed, whereas a tax on income involved a reassessment on each occasion, and probably greater opportunities for evasion. The poor yield of the 1449 income tax, compared with that of 1435, highlights this problem; the situation is perhaps parallel to that of the poll-taxes under Richard II, where the third levy saw massive evasion (Ch.3) [A.4]. Another reason may have been simply that there was a decline in the Crown's need for additional revenue after the end of the fighting in France, which undoubtedly was the greatest single drain on royal resources before 1453. It is worth stressing that the occasions on which there were experiments in taxation were all connected with the involvement of England in a possible Continental campaign. In 1472 Edward IV secured a grant from the Commons of a tax of 2s. in the pound on the issues and profits of lands, rents, fees, annuities and offices, to raise a force of 13,000 archers, which the King was planning to lead abroad. The grant stipulated that if the army were not raised by Michaelmas 1474, the tax was to be annulled, and this in fact was the case. Under Henry VII there were two experiments in raising revenue by direct taxation; in 1489 the pattern of 1472 was followed, but the actual levy fell short of the sum required, and in 1497 a compromise was devised between the schemes of 1472 and 1489, which did not provide a fixed and foreseeable yield, and the traditional fifteenth and tenth, which gave a sum that would be known in advance. The grant provided for a subsidy equivalent to two fifteenths and tenths, but commissioners were appointed to assess the contributions of individuals within each country, although the payments for each shire were to be on a fixed quota (110, pp.198–200).

Under Henry VIII too, proposed fiscal changes were prompted by the needs of war finance. In 1513, when he required to raise £160,000 to pay for his Continental adventures, an attempt was made to draw all adults into the net. Those aged over fifteen, who did not receive wages, were to pay 4d., and wages and yearly rents were taxed at 6d. in the pound. Aliens in the realm were also to pay, but at a double rate. It was clearly expected that the administration of the tax, involving the first comprehensive assessment of wealth throughout the country since 1334, would require much effort, because the annexed list of commissioners for the levy extends to eight pages in the folio volume of the statutes. The assessments cannot have been completely successful, for in 1522 there were further investigations for the levy of a loan, which gave the government an even clearer idea of the real distribution of national wealth. This probably assisted in the assessment of a tax in 1523, when Parliament granted 1s. in the pound for two years on lands and on personal goods worth over £20, with a reduced rate of 6d. on personal goods between £2 and £20. As in 1513, aliens were to pay double (36, iii, 105–6, 112–19, 231). By this time, then, new forms of direct taxation were clearly proving more fruitful than the traditional fifteenth and tenth, but it was to be a considerable time before the latter finally disappeared. The newer forms of taxation were intended to be more flexible, but they in turn became fossilized, and the 'subsidy' of later Tudor and Stuart times became a fiscal expression for a certain sum of money, which could be levied in multiples, just as its medieval predecessor had been.

The mention of the loan of 1522 serves as a reminder that there was also a tradition that the Crown could meet its short-term needs by borrowing. Loans to the King fell into two distinct categories, those which were more or less obligatory and those which were made voluntarily in the hope of gain. Certainly some loans to the Crown were made without interest, when the King had argued a need for them on the grounds of his resources being inadequate to meet his requirements. In 1382, however, there is record of a group of merchants contrasting these with loans made at interest, so there clearly were occasions when the King had to pay for his borrowings (171; 183).[1] There were forms of putting pressure on potential but reluctant lenders to make them agree to giving a loan, notably the threat that they might be summoned to appear before the King's Council. Similar sanctions might be applied to a person who agreed to the demand for a loan, but then failed to produce the cash. Such measures, however, did not invariably produce money for the King; even during the last authoritarian years of Richard II, the commissioners appointed to levy loans do not seem to have obtained payment from more than about one person in three of those whom they approached (108; 171).

At times loans virtually shaded into taxes, because the Crown might fail to repay the money which it had compelled its subjects to lend. This took place under Richard II, and was equally the case with Henry VII and Henry VIII. One way in which the King might evade reimbursement of a loan was to make the repayment not in cash but by a tally of assignment, perhaps on the customs or on the security of a future tax, but there was no guarantee that such a tally would be honoured. A comparable practice to this was to pay royal debts by tally; this practice was particularly rife during Henry VI's minority, when various magnates were in effect compelled to underwrite the Crown's finances at their own cost through not being paid their salaries and expenses for offices. Not all kings, however, defaulted on payment – Henry VII repaid over £10,000 of loans incurred in the first year of his reign, though one wonders how far his aim in this was to secure goodwill towards his usurpation (51, p.78; 108; 171; 197, pp.xxxiii, 189–90).

On some occasions the King explicitly demanded a gift from his subjects, possibly on the grounds that it would be regarded as a substitute for personal service.

As with obligatory loans, the King's needs were stated, and the demand was made particularly on the wealthier members of the community. It is interesting that Edward IV raised money in this way to finance his expedition to France in 1475, rather than trying to raise a direct tax as he had proposed in 1472. Such payments, euphemistically called 'benevolences', seem to have been regarded as tyrannical devices – they were criticized by Richard III in an attempt to secure popular favour – but this did not prevent the Tudors from demanding them too. The selection of lenders and donors, however, seems to have been done with care, and the sums demanded were related to their known circumstances (53, pp.477, 499; 171). Arbitrary though the method was of raising money, it is possible that it was not only more effective from the King's point of view than the traditional fifteenth and tenth, but also fairer in its incidence in that the payers were chosen according to their ability to contribute.

---

1. There has been considerable debate among historians concerning the question of how far kings had to pay interest. The most recent article, by Harriss (171), largely supersedes the views of McFarlane (183), although the latter writer showed clearly that there were some occasions on which interest was paid.

CHAPTER 30

The royal revenues: Crown lands and financial administration

The greater part of the King's resources in the later Middle Ages came from the various taxes and quasi-taxes, such as forced loans and benevolences, which were discussed in Chapter 29. There was one further substantial source of royal revenues, the estates which the Crown owned and exploited directly. Traditionally, it has been thought that the demands which were sometimes made in the later Middle Ages that the King should 'live of his own' implied that the yield from these lands should normally suffice for his needs and that he should not demand more from his subjects, but recent work has made it almost certain that contemporaries did not take so limited a view of the King's 'own', but also included in it normal customs revenue and even some taxation. What was particularly attacked was the practice of purveyance for the royal household, whereby the King might arbitrarily take his subjects' goods for his own use (202, pp.48–50).

Until 1399, however, the royal lands did not make a major contribution to the national revenue. Their primary function was to support the King's family; it was from them that cadet branches of it were endowed, and it seems to have been acceptable that a king's half-brothers on his mother's side, such as the Hollands under Richard II, could be treated in the same way as full members of the royal house. The Crown estates were similarly employed under the Lancastrians, although the infertility of Henry IV's younger sons meant that there was no permanent drain on them. Indeed Henry VI's Tudor half-brothers were among the major beneficiaries of such grants. Secondarily, the Crown lands provided scope for patronage outside the royal house, subject to the limitations of land being available; estates which had escheated through failure of heirs were particularly employed for this, as when Michael de la Pole secured the Suffolk inheritance and title of the Ufford family. Only when these functions of family support and patronage had been fulfilled did the estates make a contribution to the current expenses of government (202, pp.58–65).

In the late fourteenth century too, there was a further difficulty in employing the Crown estates to bolster the King's finances. Like all landowners, the King was faced with the problem that the pressures of labour shortage and land surplus were reducing the yields from real property. This could also affect the employment of grants as a form of patronage, as can be seen in a claim made by Michael de la Pole in 1386. He swore that, having been granted lands to a particular value, he had been advised by the King to take them at an old rather than a new valuation, although this would be less advantageous to him financially; he would, however, avoid a charge that as Chancellor he might have tried to influence the assessments in his favour, because, with a fall in land values, a newer valuation would have shown that more lands would have been required to make up the total of his grant (202, p.69).

In view of the diminishing returns available from land, it is at first sight somewhat surprising that it was in the early fifteenth century that demands were first heard that the King should live of his own, in the sense of financing his court and government from his landed resources. The reason for this was probably that the Lancastrian usurpation represented a revolution in the Crown's territorial holdings, because Henry IV united the duchy of Lancaster lands with those of the Crown, although they still continued under separate administration. The duchy lands were substantial; three surviving figures from the last quarter of the fourteenth century show an average annual value of over £13,700 and five sets of figures from Henry IV's reign an average of over £14,600. In the light of the general decline in landed revenues at this time, this suggests that the estates were well managed as well as extensive. Henry himself may have given a hostage to fortune when he claimed, in his first Parliament in October 1399, that when the realm did not have the burden of war expenses he should be able to live without oppressing his people from the issues of the kingdom and from the royal patrimony (33, iii, 419). This affirmation was clearly directed at Richard II's arbitrary taxation, and the reference to war expenses as a reason for exceptional levies may have been intended to emphasize the fact that Richard's extortions had taken place in time of peace. However politically motivated the claim was, it did focus greater attention on the Crown lands as a source of revenue, and in 1404 Parliament petitioned the King to resume such lands as had been granted away by the Crown since the fortieth year of Edward III (202, p.82). Such demands for resumption and various attempts to comply with them were to recur regularly throughout the century.

Clearly Henry IV had doubts about such a policy. He replied that he lacked the information to carry out a resumption, but announced his intention of appointing a committee to put the petition into execution. Once Parliament was dissolved, however, it became clear that he had little enthusiasm for carrying matters any further. In 1406, when Parliament was able to put pressure on Henry concerning membership of his Council (Ch.32), the new councillors were instructed to discover the true value of the royal manors and lordships which had been leased out, and then to relet them at their true value. Existing holders were to have the first right to lease them at the new rate, but if they were not prepared to do so, the lands were to be taken away after reasonable warning (202, pp.84–5 and n.27). It is not certain what effect these instructions had, but there does seem to have been a decline in the number of royal grants which diminished the revenue after 1406.

Henry V's reign saw a lull in the demands that the Crown exploit its demesne resources more fully, apart from a resumption of annuities in his first Parliament. Some purchases of lands suggest that the King was prepared to build up his resources, and it may have been possible for him to do this because he could employ conquered territories in France as his main source of patronage. During Henry VI's minority too, the royal patrimony was preserved from any lasting diminution, because it was held that until the King came of age no permanent alienation of it should be allowed. In consequence the main concern shown by the Council for the Crown lands was for the better employment of the income from them, and attempts were made to ensure that the entire resources of the duchies of Cornwall and Lancaster should be paid into the Exchequer (202, pp.86–8, 96).

By contrast, Henry's coming of age was followed by very substantial alienations, as he seems to have seen his main role as that of a giver of grants. The greater part of these, between 1437 and 1450, went to members of the royal household or men otherwise connected with it. Over half the beneficiaries in this period fell into this class, and they were also the men who received the larger grants. Some of these were very favourable to the recipients; Lord Cromwell held the manor of Castle Rising in Norfolk for ten years, paying £20 per annum to the King, but a valuation of the lands shows that even after he had met the costs due on them he received over £70, leaving him with a very handsome margin of profit. Such gains by the courtiers were an important, though not the only factor in the reaction against them in 1450 (Ch.22). The introduction into Parliament of further Acts of resumption shows that contemporaries regarded the exploitation of royal favour by such men as a major abuse. The first Act, of 1450, contained a considerable number of exemptions, with the result that only about one-third of the lands granted to household men fell under it, but another in 1451 was markedly tougher, and was largely able to undo the excessive grants of 1437–50. Indeed the Crown not only recovered alienated lands, but it also increased the revenue from its estates by allowing competitive leasing, although the existing holder of a lease was to be given the opportunity to match any other offer made. (202, pp.101–9, 127–35). These resumptions marked a turning-point in the granting of lavish rewards to large numbers of royal servants to the impoverishment of the King; neither the Yorkists nor the Tudors showed such prodigal generosity.

The policy of resuming lands, as well as forfeiting those of attainted Lancastrians, continued after Edward's accession. It is hardly surprising that his first Act, directed largely against grants made by the Lancastrians, contained few exemptions, whereas his later Acts, of 1465, 1467 and 1473, has substantially more, as he wished to maintain gifts which he had made himself. The last of these three Acts was the toughest, probably because after 1471 there was no need to make concessions to the Nevilles. One cannot measure how much the King himself gained from these acts, because some of the resumed lands were sold, others were taken into the King's hands and others again were granted to Yorkist supporters, although on a less lavish scale than Henry's donations. Edward had strong political motives for such grants, which probably justified financial concessions: the establishment of his supporters in various parts of England gave him a group of allies with a vested interest in resisting any Lancastrian counter-attacks (202, pp.156–8).

Richard III made no resumptions of Crown lands, probably because the forfeiture of those who had rebelled in the autumn of 1483 gave him a reservoir of lands which he could redistribute to his supporters to bind them more closely to him. There is, however, no evidence that he dispersed the Crown estates from his brother's reign, and indeed, as will be shown later, he appears to have been concerned with securing better returns from these. Henry VII did begin his reign with an Act of resumption, and it is worth stressing that, unlike Edward IV's of 1461, this contained a very large number of exemptions, most of which confirmed grants made by his Yorkist predecessors (202, p.198). This suggests that as far as the estates of both the Crown and the landed class were concerned, 1485 may have seen less upheaval than 1461.

As important in the long run as the resumption of lands were the attempts made in the second half of the fifteenth century to exploit them more effectively. The Lancastrian period had seen no major administrative innovations, but Edward IV's accession was soon followed by various changes in the management structure of the royal estates. The aim of these appears to have been to bring the Crown lands under a similar organization to that followed on the earldom of March estates. In 1462 special surveyors for eight groups of contiguous counties were appointed, all men of considerable administrative experience. Although they were assigned to collect the payment of farms due to the Exchequer, they had to pay the money not into that body but to the Treasurer of the Household. Gaps in the records make it hard to judge the effectiveness of the system, though the fact that a new team of receivers was appointed in 1472 suggests that the King had confidence in it (202, pp.159–61). For the next three-quarters of a century, the household, where royal control was tighter, rather than the Exchequer was to be the controlling body in the financial system, although until the sixteenth century the latter still remained the sole court of record in accounting matters (apart from the separately administered lands of the duchy of Lancaster). The auditors of the chamber had to deliver their accounts to the Exchequer, although the latter no longer had the power to audit them itself. Office in the Exchequer could still, however, be an important step in a man's career and might be held by men of influence; a number of the under-treasurers of the Exchequer under Edward IV were also members of the Council, and one, John Say, had also served as Speaker of the Commons (182; 202, pp.168, 176–7).

Contemporaries reckoned that Edward IV died a wealthy man, but it is hard to say what the main reason for this was. Certainly more efficient management of the Crown lands may have contributed, but one must not forget that he had other resources at his disposal, such as the pension paid by Louis XI under the Treaty of Picquigny. (Such payments from France were to remain an element, albeit a precarious one, in the English revenue well into the Tudor period.) The absence of war costs cut his expenditure, and there is also some evidence for attempted retrenchment in the household; an ordinance of 1478 tried to reduce the permitted number of officials there and trim the allowances paid to them. The extant household accounts for the last years of the reign suggest that something was achieved by this measure, and that its costs were lower than they had been under Henry VI or were to be under Henry VII, for all the latter's reputation for parsimony. These economies seem to have been effected without giving up the propaganda benefits of conspicuous display at court.

Despite this, it is likely that Richard III was not entirely satisfied with the efficiency of the financial administration. The appointment in 1483 of the Under-Treasurer, Sir John Wood, a career administrator, to be Treasurer (182) may hint at this, and in the following year a special auditor, John Stanford, was given the task of supervising the accounts of all officers and ministers, although there is no evidence that he ever had the opportunity to do much in this post. It was possibly at the same time that a scheme was put forward to improve the organization of both the Exchequer and other parts of the financial structure. The proposals included more rapid measures against Crown debtors, and a restriction on grants of respite from payment from officials. The Exchequer auditors were to compile an annual book of the revenues, and the Treasurer was to make a yearly declaration of the money received by his office. Various lands were to account separately, and their revenues were to be checked by special auditors, who were also to make an annual declaration of accounts, so that the King should know what his revenues were, what was paid and what was owing. It also reflects a significant social change of the period that it was recommended that posts as king's stewards should be given to men learned in the law.

The advent of the Tudors created some temporary administrative confusion, and the Exchequer seems to have tried to recover its old central role in the control of the finances from the chamber. However, before long Henry VII reverted to the practice of his Yorkist predecessors in relying on the chamber. By the early 1490s a substantial proportion of the Crown's land revenues were again being paid in there, and by 1493 it was also obtaining independent powers of audit. The difference between the proportion of chamber revenues deriving from land in the two earliest surviving account books of the reign, 17.6 per cent in 1487–89 and 40.7 per cent in 1492–95, illustrates clearly its recovery of control. The King became personally involved in accounting matters, as can be seen from his participation in the procedures of auditing – he initialled the accounts of his Household Treasurer, John Heron (202, pp.199–210) – and by his choice of the men to be responsible to him in revenue matters. At the start of the reign the key figures were Sir Thomas Lovell, then Treasurer of the Household and Chancellor of the Exchequer, and Sir Reginald Bray, Chancellor of the duchy of Lancaster and Under-Treasurer of England. Both of these remained trusted royal servants until they died, Bray in 1503 and Lovell well into Henry VIII's reign. By 1492 Lovell had handed over some of his responsibilities to his assistant John Heron, who was to remain at the centre of chamber financial administration until 1521, becoming increasingly important after Bray's death. Indeed it may well have been his personal influence that maintained the importance of the chamber in finance, for it seems to have declined in importance after his retirement (110, pp.110–11, 126; 191, pp.14–15, 67, 132, 419).

Of all the King's servants, Bray was perhaps the one closest to him, and he effectively supervised all matters pertaining to Crown lands and their revenues, despite the fact that he had neither appointment by patent nor statutory authority to do this. Within the duchy of Lancaster, where his work is better documented, there is evidence of persistent and successful efforts to recover arrears of debt and to improve the administration of duchy manors. More efficient collection seems to have been more characteristic of his work than attempts to increase the level of leases. Bray's importance rested above all on the fact that he was the King's man, and this in turn reflects the monarch's central role in government.

Henry VII's inclinations involved him in detailed administrative work, and he left a personal stamp on the working of government; his personal control probably contributed to the accumulated financial reserve which he left at the end of the reign. Henry VIII left his officials rather more in charge, and developments in government resulted more from their actions. One cannot really say that the system became more bureaucratic, because this would imply that the offices of State were able to operate effectively more or less irrespective of who was running them, whereas what one sees is a proliferation of different offices, which tended to rise and fall in influence depending on who was at their head. Henry VIII established a more personal private treasury for his own use, and the jewel house was also developed as a treasury within the chamber system. This was the office from which Thomas Cromwell was to rise to influence. But although the institutions showed considerable flexibility, it is important to remember that they were controlled by professional administrators; Sir Edward Belknap held the post of 'surveyor of the King's prerogative', collecting money penalties for violations of the King's prerogative rights, and later took control of the general surveyors of land revenues, and Brian Tuke moved from being Henry VIII's secretary to be treasurer of the chamber (191, pp.76, 91–7, 195–204, 214, 239–40).

The most important institutional development was that of the general surveyors, who controlled and audited the revenues of the Crown lands. Until 1503, Bray was chief auditor; after his death Sir Robert Southwell virtually took over the duties. He had, however, no patent of appointment and the office existed only at the King's pleasure. The auditors were essentially a group of members of the Council who had been given a particular task to perform, and for this reason they, like other councillors, depended on the King. On Henry VII's death there was a reaction against the auditors, but clearly they were seen to be doing a necessary job, because before long they were given statutory standing. A series of Acts regulated their work and extended their administrative jurisdiction (191, pp.184–9, 248–50; 201, pp.76–7). They were freed from attempts made by the Exchequer to make them render their accounts there, although the older body was allowed to retain the right of settling certain legal matters. The surveyors never perhaps possesed quite as great powers formally as they had been able to exercise informally under Henry VII, although in 1515 they did regain the power of imposing financial penalties on defaulters. Nor at this time did they retain control over such large sums as they had had under Henry VII, as gifts of lands made by the new King led to a decline in actual revenues. One may suspect that although the King remained uninterested in the surveyors' activities, Wolsey was prepared to reinforce their legal and administrative powers in the hope of strengthening the royal finances (191, p.252; 201, pp.79–84). Certainly by the end of the 1520s, the office of the general surveyors had become the most important of the three financial departments of the government, with an annual net revenue exceeding £40,000, slightly greater than that of the Exchequer and over three times that of the duchy of Lancaster. The division of the sources of revenue between the two major departments seems to have been somewhat haphazard, though in general the Exchequer drew its funds from customs, the farms of shires and boroughs and legal profits, while the general surveyors derived theirs from

Crown lands, wardships, woods and mines and from vacant bishoprics and abbeys (191, pp.277–8). The whole situation was ill organized, and it is hardly surprising that the 1530s were to see further changes in the pattern of administration, which were able to develop further the kind of administrative structures concerned with particular areas of revenue, which had been emerging in the previous thirty years. These were to depress for a time, still further, the old primacy of the Exchequer.

The administration of the King's resources between the reigns of Edward IV and Henry VIII saw various changes which pushed the traditional Exchequer administration into the background, and it was not really to recover until Mary's reign. The changes were largely connected with a reassertion of royal power after its collapse in the mid fifteenth century. Until that time, the Exchequer had been able to perform a useful function, and it was after all its officials who had been able to furnish estimates of government income and expenditure in earlier years, particularly at times when the King was seeking a grant of parliamentary taxation.[1] Although such 'budget' statements were essentially exercises in public relations, it still reflects the Exchequer's operational efficiency that it could produce them when required – after all, its primary function was not to do this to audit the enrolled accounts of the sheriffs. Exchequer efficiency seems to have declined in the mid century; accounts fell into arrears, and so many assignments were made on the shire revenues that men were reluctant to undertake the office of sheriff in case they might end up out of pocket, through having less revenue to collect than commitments to meet (191, pp.41–3). The various administrative experiments after 1461, while going some way to restoring the royal resources both by improving returns and by controlling expenditure, tended to bypass the Exchequer, although it never entirely lost its power, a fact no doubt which gave scope for it to regain its influence later. No general statements of income and expenditure survive from the later period, although one suspects that Henry VII's officials had at least some idea of what this would be; probably the less frequent attempts at securing parliamentary taxation explain why these were not made.

The financial fortunes of the kings in this period were determined more by variations in their expenditure than in their income, and above all by whether or not they were involved in foreign wars. The kings who were financially successful, Edward IV and Henry VII, both avoided these, and it is noteworthy that it was when Henry VIII began to pursue a more active foreign policy than his father that pressure on the royal finances re-emerged, and with it the reappearance of experiments in methods of raising funds. Wolsey's attempts to tap the nation's resources for his master in the 1520s were the most determined effort hitherto made to make the tax system more effective. That this was necessary when the administration of the ordinary royal revenue from customs and lands had already been improved is a measure of how great the demands were that military activity put on the national resources, and how far fiscal history must be understood in terms of the nation's external relations.

1. See (30, pp.211–14) for a summary of the figures for 1411, 1421 and 1433. See also an analysis of a series of estimates from the 1360s (173, pp.473–96) and those for 1433 (181).

CHAPTER 31

Parliament[1]

In the chapter on the revenues which the Crown derived from taxation, frequent references were made to grants from Parliament (Ch.29). The making of such grants was one of the main functions performed by Parliament in the later Middle Ages, and indeed was an increasingly important role which it played. In the first ten years of Edward III's reign, there were grants of supply in only about a quarter of the Parliaments which met, but between 1350 and 1450 there were grants in about 80 per cent of them (167, p.16). There can be no doubt about the reasons for this dramatic increase in the fiscal activity of Parliament, which was due firstly to the needs of the wars in France and secondly to the pressures which the Crown had to face, along with other landowners, in the years of agricultural recession which followed the population decline of the late fourteenth century. One must not, however, see the role of Parliament being limited to financial matters; it was also coming to play a prominent part in the formulation of law, and the idea developed that statutes which it approved were superior to the common law and were binding in the King's courts. Most important of all, it was developing as a forum of political discussion, where great matters of State were considered and where the conduct of the King's ministers might be called in question.

In much writing on English constitutional development, stress has been laid on the growth of representative government, and the main theme in the history of Parliament has been the emergence of the House of Commons as the dominant element within it. Although this is undoubtedly an important facet of the making of modern Britain, the historian should not allow this particular aspect of constitutional growth to get out of perspective when he is considering the conditions of the later Middle Ages. The part which Parliament played in political affairs did not depend on it being a representative institution, although it is true that from the latter part of the fourteenth century onwards elected members began to play an increasingly active part in its deliberations. But when in 1365 Chief Justice Thorpe referred to Parliament representing the body of all the realm, he was not necessarily thinking of the elected element within it.

Although there were many aspects of Parliament which were still only partially formed by 1370, it already possessed certain characteristics which foreshadowed later developments. Most notably, one sees the existence of two broad divisions among those attending it, those summoned as individuals and the representatives of the remainder of the community. County representation had already developed a consistent form; two members were sent from each of thirty-seven shires, the palatinates of Durham and Chester being excluded. There were, however, fluctuations in the numbers of boroughs which sent men to Parliament; in the first half of the fourteenth century there had been a decline in the figures of burgess representatives, but from around 1350 these began to rise again, and they continued to do so throughout the fifteenth and sixteenth centuries. It is impossible to give precise numbers of the boroughs represented, for there is no reliable list of men who attended most Parliaments, but it seems likely that between the late fourteenth century and the Reformation the total membership of the Commons rose from about 250 to just under 300, the increase being caused purely by the enfranchisement of a number of new boroughs, as the figures for shire members remained unaltered. Although this increase in membership was substantial, it was relatively slight compared with the much greater growth of numbers in the late Tudor period. The initiative in summoning representatives, of course, lay with the King, although it is noteworthy that boroughs now were more willing to send Members to Parliament, regarding this as a privilege rather than a burden.

Another pointer to the future was the development in the late fourteenth century of the office of Speaker in the Lower House. Originally his function was to represent the Commons in joint discussions with the Lords and the King, a task which may well have been performed originally by different men on particular occasions within an individual Parliament. Some time in the last quarter of the century, however, a new practice emerged, by which one individual performed this task for the duration of a whole Parliament. The likely date for this was 1376, in the Good Parliament, when the post of Speaker was held by Sir Peter de la Mare. Certainly the record of this Parliament, which was particularly well documented, suggests that his continuous spokesmanship for the Commons throughout the parliamentary session was regarded as unusual by contemporaries. After this time, however, a Speaker was regularly elected for a whole Parliament, and acquired the further task of presiding over the Commons. This whole development undoubtedly strengthened the corporate identity of the Lower House (167, pp.68–71).

The most marked difference between late medieval and modern Parliaments lay in their centre of gravity. To a modern man, the term 'Member of Parliament' denotes a member of the House of Commons, and the Upper House is seen as having only a subsidiary role to play. However, Parliament took its origin from those men who formed the nucleus of the later House of Lords, when the King summoned them individually to strengthen, or, to use the technical term, 'afforce' his Council. The inclusion of representatives of the various communities within the realm as a necessary part of Parliament was a later development. The fact that the title 'Clerk of Parliament' is still borne by the principal clerk of the Lords reflects the time when the Upper House was politically dominant. Even when Parliament was already coming to be established as an institution, the King still sometimes summoned afforced councils to advise him, consisting of men who would have been in the Upper House of a Parliament, and the uncertainty of comtemporaries as to what precisely constituted Parliament illustrates the fluidity of its place in national life. Records of 1372 and 1373 actually designate a Great Council of 1371, which had met to conclude business which had been incomplete at the end of the previous Parliament, as a Parliament in its own right (190). Great Councils continued to meet in the fifteenth century, perhaps even more frequently than Parliament, although the suggestion of Plucknett (187) that they were much more common appears to be erroneous as he gives a much smaller number of Parliaments than that recorded in the *Handbook of British Chronology* (50).

Parliament met irregularly, and the details of its meetings [D] show that although there were times when these were frequent, at other times there were considerable gaps between them. These were also considerable variations in the duration of parliamentary sessions, and it is significant that those before 1450 which lasted longest were the ones with which the Crown had greatest difficulties. The initiative in relations between the King and Parliament rested with the King; he summoned it and decided when it was to be dissolved, and it is clear that unless he had a very special need for it, he could, and usually did, avoid calling one. It is also very striking that from the end of the Lancastrian period there was a very marked decrease in the frequency of Parliaments. An examination of the meetings shows that between 1370 and 1530 there were 92 Parliaments, 72 of which before 1461. The reigns of both Richard II and Edward IV lasted for 22 years; in the former there were 25 meetings (including that in which Henry IV secured the throne), whereas in the latter there were 6. It is true that the later Parliaments tended to have more than one session, and that these tended to be rather longer than at an earlier date, but there were still greater gaps between meetings. The longest intervals between the close of one Parliament and the assembly of the next were all in the Tudor period – $7\frac{1}{4}$ years between those of 1515 and 1523, $6\frac{3}{4}$ years between those of 1497 and 1504, $6\frac{1}{4}$ between that of 1523 and the Reformation Parliament of 1529 and $5\frac{3}{4}$ between those of 1504 and 1510. The longest gap under the Yorkists was just under 5 years, between the meetings of 1478 and 1483, and under the Lancastrians $3\frac{2}{3}$ years between 1456 and 1459.

The variations in the number of Parliaments between different periods are best explained by looking at the functions which they performed. The kings called Parliaments because they needed them, rather than because they wanted them, and the principal reason for this need was money. It was established usage by the mid fourteenth century that parliamentary consent was required for direct general taxation, and by the 1390s the Commons were the formal grantors of it. An episode in 1400 makes it clear that the acquiescence of the Commons was essential. In that year a Great Council, which did not include representatives of the Commons, granted an aid from the lords spiritual and temporal rather than calling a Parliament, which would be necessary if the 'common people' were to be taxed. The Commons also became responsible for the amount of taxation which was to be levied – at the time of the 1380 poll-tax they settled the figure of three groats per head, as opposed to the Lords' suggestion of four or five groats. In 1407, it was agreed that the Lords should merely assent to what the Commons had granted, and by the middle of the fifteenth century all that the Lords could do with taxation was to decrease the amount of a grant; they could not increase it (167, pp.39–40; 168, p.317; 190).

Parliament tended to grant direct taxation only intermittently, whereas it normally renewed automatically indirect taxes, such as the subsidy on wool and tonnage and poundage (Ch.29). Twice under Richard II, Parliament left a gap between grants of the wool subsidy, to emphasize that the King received it as a favour and not as a right, but for the greater part of our period the payment of customs dues was continuous. In 1398 Richard II secured a life grant of the custom on wool, and, as we have seen in an earlier chapter, his fifteenth-century successors from Henry V onwards, were able to secure similar grants, a precedent which was followed until the accession of Charles I in 1625 (167, pp.19–23; Ch.29). Such grants undoubtedly gave the Crown a greater element of financial security, although not to the extent that it was able to dispense with Parliament entirely, because customs revenues and the returns from the royal estates would not meet any extraordinary expenditure such as that for financing wars. In the Tudor period Parliament became increasingly willing to comply with the King's wishes in fiscal matters, even granting retrospective approval to other forms of tax, such as benevolences and forced loans, which had been taken between meetings and therefore without prior parliamentary agreement (168, pp.318–19).

In addition to the Crown's strengthened financial position from an automatic entitlement to customs revenues, the ending of the Anglo-French War probably contributed to the decline in the frequency of Parliaments, because the costs of this were the greatest single factor contributing to the difficulties which the earlier kings had had in keeping their expenditure within their income. More frugal management of the royal resources under the Yorkists and Tudors, and the possibility of obtaining money other than by taxation, such as one sees in the payments of pensions by various French kings to Edward IV and Henry VII, also made it less necessary for the Crown to appeal to its subjects for grants, and therefore to summon Parliament (Ch.30).

Parliamentary concern with the royal finances was not limited to granting or refusing taxes, or even to fixing the rate at which they were to be paid. The Commons also tried to ensure that the money granted would be spent only on acceptable purposes. As early as 1371 they petitioned that the taxes granted for the war should be spent on that and on nothing else, and later in the decade one sees the appointment of special treasurers to handle the revenue from a tax or the concession to Parliament of a right to audit the accounts of it. This assertion of a right to check expenditure did not survive long into the fifteenth century, and such claims by the Commons, which reflected a distrust of the Crown and determination to ensure that taxation revenues would not be spent purely at a monarch's whim, were largely confined to the reigns of Richard II and Henry IV. The tradition of imposing curbs of this nature was probably broken by popular willingness to support the successes of Henry V and by the greater participation of the magnates in government during Henry VI's minority, as this itself could guard against the possibility of arbitrary action by a monarch. It is perhaps noteworthy that the one later appointment of special treasurers came in 1450, at a time when Henry VI's government was particulary unpopular (168, p.320).

Finance apart, Parliament's main field of activity was the presentation of petitions to the King. These fell into two categories which were dealt with by different procedures, 'singular' petitions, concerned with the interests of an individual, who need not even be a Member of either House of Parliament, or 'common' petitions, which touched the interests of the people as a whole. By

1400, singular petitions themselves fell into two different classes; those which were submitted direct to the King, and those which were directed to the Commons in Parliament, so that they could submit them to the King; by Henry V's time many of those which had been presented directly to the King were referred back to the Commons for their support. Behind the whole procedure of petitioning lay the idea that the King was the ultimate source of justice for his subjects, but what is striking here is the apparent wish of the King to associate the Commons with his decisions and with the redress of individual grievances. Common petitions often lie at the basis of statutes, and it was through them that the Lower House began to participate in legislation, although it took some time to develop a regular procedure by which bills could be approved as laws. Petitions were sent from the Commons to the Lords, and then to the King, and both the Lords and the King could amend or reject them. The Commons were able to co-ordinate individual petitions which were submitted to them; in 1423 a common petition concerning disorders in Herefordshire stated that the Commons had received several petitions from individual persons on this subject. Already the procedure had developed beyond what had occurred in 1410 when there had been cases of contradiction between different petitions which the lower house had made to the King. Besides the procedure of passing petitions upwards, there was also a downward traffic in bills from the Lords to the Commons, so that the lower house could assent to them. The first known instance of this was in the reign of Henry V, and the practice became more common from the 1430s. By the reign of Henry VII, the participation of the Commons in legislation was recognized as essential; in 1489 the judges ruled that an Act of Parliament without their consent was invalid (167, pp.46, 61–5).

It is not always easy to judge how far Parliament generally concerned itself with great matters of public affairs. Of course one can isolate individual crises in which it was prominent; one thinks of the Commons' attack on the court in 1376, its resistance to royal tax demands in 1406, the impeachment of Suffolk in 1450 and the attack on Wolsey's foreign policy in 1523 (Chs 16, 19, 22, 28); but there were many Parliaments which were far less outspoken. Possibly the very attention which the chroniclers gave to the 1376 Parliament may have been prompted by the unusual degree of initiative which it took in attacks on the court and its high level of political consciousness. However, parallels to its procedures on other occasions suggest that its method of working was not abnormal. The fact that the legislation of later medieval Parliaments covered topics which were of interest to people other than the King – one thinks of matters such as wage-rates or clothing regulations – suggests that they were prepared to concern themselves with political matters on their own initiative. The efforts made by great men to influence elections to the Commons are an even more significant pointer to the importance of Parliament; these would hardly have been worth while if Parliament in general, including the Commons, was not regarded as playing a significant part in public affairs. The most famous instance of this was Richard II's enquiry to the sheriffs in 1387 if it would be possible to prevent the election of knights of the shire who were not agreeable to the King, and his subsequent instruction that the knights chosen should be neutral in the current disputes. In the mid fifteenth century, too, the evidence of the Paston Letters shows how the great lords attempted to influence the elections of shire knights in East Anglia; irrespective of whether they were successful or not in these endeavours, they clearly regarded it as valuable to secure the choice of members of their affinity (150, p.112, 184).

In these elections one sees how men who themselves received individual writs of summons to the Upper House were also interested in who might sit in the Lower. The division of Parliament into two houses was partly, although not entirely, connected with the growth of the idea of a peerage. As was shown earlier (Ch.12), the idea of a parliamentary peerage was not finally established in the 1380s – Sir Thomas Camoys, who was elected as knight of the shire for Surrey in 1383, was also summoned individually in his own right. By the fifteenth century, however, the idea of differentiating socially those individuals who were personally summoned from the representatives of the rest of the community seems to have been generally agreed. A major development in the history of the parliamentary peerage came when Henry VI created Ralph Boteler as Lord Sudeley in 1441 with succession to heirs male but not to heirs general. This was to become the norm, and increasingly the peerage consisted of lords whose title had been created by writ, whereas previously the right of summons had been granted to those holding particular large estates. By the reign of Henry VIII one sees the abandonment of the older principle, closely connected with the idea of the peerage as a group of men who hold particular lands, that the husband of the heiress of a lord was entitled to a summons in the right of his wife.

The only persons who sat in the Upper House whose position was still ambiguous were some of the King's more influential councillors. In the 1461 Parliament, from which a fragmentary record has survived in a late transcript, one can see that matters might be referred by the Lords to a small group which included men who were not of their own number, Peter Ardern, a judge, and the dean of St Severin at Bordeaux. On the other hand, the sederunt lists preserved in the same document name only men who were spiritual or temporal lords. The same is true of those present on an earlier occasion in 1449, from which again a record survives (185). In many cases, of course, the great officers of State were either bishops or hereditary lords, who were as such entitled to individual writs of summons, but it is clear that some men of lesser rank might be in attendance and act with the lords on behalf of the Upper House as a whole. At the same time, the most assiduous attenders among the lords were those who were members of the Council, to the extent indeed that the Upper House was frequently little more than an afforced session of it. Of those who were entitled to attend, the most frequent absentees were the abbots of the great monasteries, who were the least involved in politics of those summoned individually. The result of this was that the Dissolution of the Monasteries under Henry VIII had less effect on the normal composition of the Upper House than on its formal membership (196).

It is likely, therefore, that the Crown's interests were well represented in the Upper House, where the great officers of State were present. It also had its men in the Commons; a number of Speakers of the late fourteenth and early fifteenth centuries, Bussy, Savage and Tiptoft, for example, were close advisers of Richard II and Henry IV, and at a later date there are numerous cases of household officials or men in lesser government posts being elected to the Commons. Many sat for borough seats, including a number of collectors of customs, although holders of more important offices, such as the treasurership of the household, were more likely to have shire seats. There is a conspicuous change, however, in the early Tudor period – under Henry VII some of the King's most important councillors, including Sir Reginald Bray and Sir Thomas Lovell, were elected to the Commons. It is uncertain whether the reason for this was that the King wished his councillors to influence the Commons on his behalf – and it is perhaps not just coincidence that most of Henry's Parliaments were unusually co-operative with the King's wishes – or merely that he was reluctant to create peers, but the effect was the same, to limit the Upper House to the hereditary peerage and the spiritual lords and to bring about the presence of royal officials in the Commons, thereby enhancing the dignity of the Lower House. This was perhaps the most important permanent contribution made in this period to the subsequent development of Parliament as an institution (168, pp.7, 11; 194, pp.55, 57, 134).

The social history of the Lower House at this time was marked by the increasing influence of the landed class and of lawyers in the borough seats. Although a substantial number of the burgess members had active trading interests, many of the smaller boroughs were represented by members of the country gentry. Only one of the twelve Cornish borough representatives in 1422 was a merchant. Later in the century, and at the other end of the country, one sees that many borough representatives were non-residents, and that the smaller the borough the greater was the likelihood that this would be the case. The non-resident element was more marked in the smaller boroughs, such as Scarborough, Appleby and Carlisle, than in the larger centres of York, Hull and Newcastle. An appreciable number of these incomers seem to have been royal servants, and one gains the impression that the King's patronage in the North was of greater importance in securing election to Parliament than that of the greatest magnate families in the area, the Nevilles and the Percies, in the late Lancastrian and early Yorkist periods. This seems to have been the time when gentry penetration of the borough seats was most systematic, although the practice can be traced back to the first half of the century, and indeed in isolated cases as early as the reign of Edward II (189; 194, pp.49–50, 125, 127).

What is not always clear is how the gentry secured the seats; in some cases the boroughs may themselves have taken the initiative in the election, a relatively simple matter when, as was frequently the case, the franchise pertained to a limited group such as the borough council, and chose outsiders in the hope that they could provide favours in return. On the other hand, the evidence of some Norfolk elections recorded in the Paston Letters suggests that men who had sought the favour of a great lord in a shire election and been disappointed there might often obtain a borough seat; in such cases there is at least some implication that the lord may have succeeded in influencing the borough electors (184).

The fact that a borough seat was regarded as second best to a shire one reflects the higher social standing of the latter, and it was the shire members who were regarded as the leaders of the Commons. There is some evidence that the shire knights provided the representatives of the Lower House when it sent delegations to the Lords to confer, or 'intercommune', on particular matters. Even more conspicuous is the fact that the Speaker was invariably chosen from their ranks, although he might hold a borough seat on other occasions. John Say, Speaker in 1449, 1463–65 and 1467–68, was MP for Cambridgeshire on the first occasion and for Hertfordshire on the other two, but had sat for Cambridge in 1447 and was to be MP for Tavistock in 1472. Many of the shire knights, however, possessed a legal training as well as being landowners, and this became increasingly common in the fifteenth century. Earlier there had been considerable hostility to lawyers; in 1372 there had been a statute against them being elected as knights of the shire, although it never seems to have been observed. The increasing extent to which the Commons were involved in legislation through forwarding petitions to the King gave lawyers an important part to play and probably explains why the attempt to exclude them, prompted perhaps by the fear that they might turn their position too much to their own advantage, was allowed to lapse. Legal training indeed created a new class, which was neither landed gentry nor burgess; Sir Thomas More, Speaker in the 1523 Parliament, and the son of a judge, is its most distinguished representative. The existence of such men, and the tenure of parliamentary seats by royal officials, helped to blur the distinction between knights and burgesses as much as the infiltration of gentry into borough seats. The assimilation of the groups was still a gradual one; although in 1433 the Chancellor referred to knights, esquires and merchants as comprising one of the estates of the realm, there is some evidence that some division between shire knights and borough representatives persisted in the sixteenth century. In 1475 a justice could still speak as though the shire knights only possessed legislative powers, and in 1523 there was considerable tension between the two groups over the extent of the grant to be made to the King. The burgesses even appear to have met separately and declared that the knights, in offering more, were enemies to the realm (167, pp.15, 51; 193, pp.329, 336, 341; 194, pp.55–6).

The late Middle Ages also saw persistent efforts to clarify the system of electing members of the Commons, and the electoral laws of the period survived until the nineteenth-century reforms. Legislation touched on the procedures of election and the qualifications of both electors and those elected. This presupposes that there was some prospect of elections being contested, and certainly some contests occurred, although these were probably in a minority of seats. The impression given in the Paston Letters is that the election itself was often a formality and that the really crucial manoeuvres in the choice of a shire knight took place before the meeting of the county court. In some cases the great men of the shire might agree to share the seats between their protégés, but efforts were undoubtedly made to ensure that the nominees would be acceptable to the members of the gentry class, although if they were not the lord might still persist in his choice.

The key figure in the conduct of elections was the sheriff, and legislation tried to provide a middle way between arbitrary action on his part and a totally open election. In 1362 there were complaints that the sheriff's deputies in Lancashire had returned themselves (189), and a statute of 1406, approved by a Parliament which had pertinaciously resisted royal demands, provided that the return of shire knights should be made by an indenture under the seals of the participants. A further statute of 1410 provided penalties for a sheriff who broke this law, but it is likely that this system soon became formalized, as surviving indentures suggest that before many years the names of fictitious witnesses were employed. The sequence of legislation, however, makes clear the feeling which existed that sheriffs were likely to commit sharp practice during elections. At the same time, there was also fear of disorder during elections in the county court and that the traditional county landed class might lose its control. In 1353, 1355 and 1371, demands were made that knights of the shire should be knights by rank, and in the Good Parliament of 1376 there was a petition that representatives should be elected from the better men of the shires. The economic problems of the landed class at this time (Ch.2) may have led them to fear that they were threatened with subversion, and prompted them to use the law to defend their position. The response to the petition, that the knights should be elected by common consent of the whole county, was non-committal, avoiding the question of who should sit and dealing with the actual business of the election in the most general terms. The writs for the next Parliament did not expressly require such a form of election, although there was a clause to that effect in those for the Parliament which met in the autumn of 1377. By the middle of the fifteenth century it was clearly recognized that knights alone could not bear the whole responsibility for shire representattion, when the statute merely provided that a man could not be elected who was of yeoman rank or less, thereby confirming, what was already the practice, that gentry could be elected. The title 'knight' of the shire was already an anachronism, which reflected earlier practices (33, ii, 355; 36, ii, 162, 340–2; 189; 194, pp.5–8).

Besides limiting representatives by rank, attempts were also made to enforce a residence qualification. In 1413 it was enacted that earlier statutes concerning the election of knights of the shire should be observed at all points, and also that the knights should not be elected unless they were resident in the counties for which they were elected on the day when the writ of summons to the Parliament was issued. A similar provision was made for borough representatives (36, ii, 170). It is not clear how successful this measure was as far as shire members were concerned, although it cannot have been fully implemented, judging by the disgust of one of John Paston's correspondents in 1455 at the prospect of having a Suffolk knight elected for Norfolk (184). As far as the boroughs were concerned, as we have seen, the attempt to enforce residence failed completely.

The most famous electoral statute of the period is that of 1429, which limited the county franchise to those with freehold land worth 40s. a year, and authorized the sheriff to examine the qualifications of the electors. Behind this there seems to have been fear of disorder, for the preamble to the Act alleged that there was a danger of riots and divisions between the greater and lesser men of the shires, if a remedy were not provided for the excessive number of people with small means who claimed an equal voice with the most valiant knights and esquires who participated in the elections (36, ii, 243–4). However, although the county franchise was limited in this way, there was no comparable qualification laid down concerning borough electors. It may well have been felt unnecessary, because the normal practice seems to have been that the governing bodies of towns, which were themselves becoming increasingly oligarchic, chose the Members of Parliament. Bristol, which had the status of a county, followed the 40s. freehold rule from 1432, but this was not the case in other cities of similar legal standing. There was to be no general definition of the urban franchise until 1832.

It is clear that Parliament was representative, above all, of the landed class, both through its control of the shire seats, with their greater prestige, and by its infiltration into the boroughs. Changes in electoral law were aimed at preserving its authority against both the Crown and its inferiors. As far as the latter were concerned, there is no reason to believe that the threat was serious, but there is a real historical problem in trying to estimate how much influence Parliament could exercise against the King. Historians have long ago, and justifiably, abandoned the idea of Stubbs that the Lancastrian period, particularly Henry IV's reign, saw a great constitutional experiment, by which the King ruled in partnership with Parliament, to which he owed his title, and that in this there was a premature flowering of a democratic system of government, which was to fall to a 'New Monarchy' later in the century. One cannot build such an argument on the volume of criticism levelled at Henry IV and his government, for such criticism antedates the Lancastrian usurpation; during Edward III's last years and the first half of Richard II's reign criticism of the Crown was no less vocal than under Henry IV. What must be remembered is that Parliament had the opportunity to criticize, because the kings needed money, and that it could make demands as the price for granting taxation. It is noteworthy that the kings were better able to avoid parliamentary criticism in the latter half of the fifteenth century, at precisely the time when their financial problems were less overwhelming. There is no reason to believe, however, that Parliament became fundamentally more docile, and its criticism was by no means muted when the King's financial problems gave it an opportunity to insist on being heard. This is clearly shown by the bitter hostility to Wolsey's foreign policy shown by the Parliament of 1523 (193, pp.327–30). Parliament might also oppose royal policies even when there was no financial question involved, although in such matters it was less likely to prevail against the King. One sees this in the way in which Henry VI refused to accept the impeachment of Suffolk in 1450 and in the existence of opposition in 1485 to the attainders in Henry VII's first Parliament, which did not prevent the King having his way.

But although Parliament could oppose the King, in the last analysis it depended on him, as he alone could summon or dissolve it. It lacked any autonomous existence, so it cannot be held to have possessed anything which can reasonably be described as sovereignty. At the time of the various usurpations during the period, assemblies which contemporaries regarded as Parliaments, irrespective of whether or not they were summoned in strictly legal form, expressed their support for the victor, but one cannot argue from this that the kings consequently relied on any form of parliamentary title; the usurpations were acts of political force, which were later acclaimed by Parliament, but Parliament did not possess any form of authority to legalize them. The search for a 'Lancastrian constitutional experiment' was based on anachronistic premisses concerning the nature of Parliament and the powers which it possessed. The late medieval Parliament could be a forum for political manoeuvres, it could attempt to limit the monarchy in particular matters, but if it was faced with a determined king there was little it could do, so long as the King curbed his expenses and kept clear of expensive foreign entanglements. It was in association with the King, not on its own initiative, that Henry VIII's Reformation Parliament achieved a new prominence in national affairs, because the King used it as his agent to carry out a revolution, but it was not until the seventeenth century that it achieved any significant measure of corporate autonomy.

Nevertheless, one must not underestimate the extent of parliamentary development betwen 1370 and 1530, because this period saw various changes which foreshadowed its later power. Conspicuous among these were the extent to which it gained control over legislation, with the Commons playing an increasingly important part, and the consolidation of its powers over taxation. At the same time too, one sees the beginnings of special privileges for Members of Parliament and their servants. Most notable of these was that of freedom from arrest, although in times of political crisis this was not always secured. Because Parliament had a strong corporate identity, it was able to play a greater part as the forum of debate within the nation, and the implications of this included both the increased activity of the great men of the realm to secure the election of their supporters to the Lower house and the development of efforts by the King to manage Parliament through the presence of his officials there. Parliament could not be controlled by the King completely; he had to learn the arts of persuading it to comply with his wishes rather than relying on a simple command to have his will done. In return, Parliament was willing to recognize that the initiative in government lay with the King, and while it could be outspokenly critical on practical matters which affected it, notably where they touched the pockets of the King's subjects, it did not wish to upset the traditional social order.

1. While this book was in the final stages of revision, an important new book was published on the medieval Parliament, R. G. Davies and J. H. Denton, eds, *The English Parliament in the Middle Ages*, Manchester, 1981. The chapters in this by A. L. Brown and A. R. Myers are of particular value to the student of parliamentary developments between 1370 and 1530. It has been possible to make some adjustment to the text to incorporate material from this, but it was not feasible to give specific page references.

CHAPTER 32

The King's Council

As we saw Chapter 31, Parliament had already by the late Middle Ages developed the characteristics of an independent institution. By contrast, the Council was a much more fluid body; indeed the very title was used in a flexible manner to denote different groups of men. These ranged from the Great Council, which might be the same as the lords who attended Parliament, to a small 'continual council' comprising essentially a small group of officials. As we have seen, Parliament had developed out of afforced sessions of the Great Council, but the growth of Parliament did not mean the demise of the earlier body; Great Councils were still called at a time when Parliament was recognized as the most solemn way in which the King could consult his subjects. The process of summoning a Great Council seems to have been less cumbersome than that for calling a Parliament, and the King had a freer choice of whom he might bid to attend. In the early fifteenth century, members of the Great Council might even grant a tax on themselves, although not on the whole nation (190). Under Henry VII, Great Councils also appear to have authorized the levying of taxation in anticipation of later parliamentary approval, although the fact that Parliament later ratified these grants suggests that the action of the Great Council was regarded as no more than an emergency action at a time when there might be a threat of war or rebellion. It is by no means clear how many Great Councils met during the later medieval period, nor even indeed what precisely constituted one; a meeting at Durham in 1403, which was described as a Council, had a distinctly northern bias, consisting of lords and knights from the region who had been called to discuss the custody of the castles there after the defeat of the Percies, whereas neither Henry IV himself nor any of his regular councillors was present. In essence, the Council comprised the available men whom the King had summoned to give counsel concerning his affairs or those of the State, and any attempt at a more precise definition is liable to exclude meetings to which contemporaries applied the description (110, p.144; 180; 187).

Besides the Great Council, and gatherings of great men such as that at Durham in 1403, which were only occasional assemblies, one can also identify a much smaller 'continual Council' of the King's close advisers, on whom he would rely both for political counsel and for the daily conduct of administration. This, too, lacked any regular clear-cut membership, although there were times in the fourteenth and fifteenth centuries when some attempts were made to define this. It cannot, however, be regarded merely as an accidental gathering of the King's officials, but must be seen as something possessing a measure of organization; one of the noteworthy developments of the late fourteenth century was the establishment of the post of Clerk of the Council to record its business. This gave it a rather more clearly defined character, and although one cannot talk of a Council with a precisely fixed membership, it is reasonable to assume that it was recognized as a corporate body which performed certain acknowledged tasks in government. Its history in the fifteenth century bears out the perceptive reminder by Williams that institutions are human beings in action, and the result of ambitions, rivalries and decisions rather than of evolutionary logic (200).

The problems of writing a history of the late medieval Council result from the patchy survival of its records. Unlike Parliament, chancery or the courts of law, the Council did not have its Acts enrolled, for it was not a court of record. If it made a decision which led subsequently to the issue of letters under the Great Seal, the letter of warranty authorizing this may survive in the chancery records, or the chancery roll may be endorsed with the note that the letters were issued by conciliar authority. Some Council documents have survived in the records of the privy seal office, but this series has not been well preserved. Surviving petitions to the Council may bear endorsements that a decision was taken on them on a particular day. Endorsements may also list the names of those attending, and are a valuable guide to membership of the Council, but as some of these lists end with 'etc.' one cannot regard them as a complete indication of those present. More particularly, one suspects that the names omitted might have been those of men of socially lower rank, who were nevertheless important in the work of administration. There were some periods when the Council clerks made a special record of its business, although the emphasis on the items selected for recording varied from time to time. For example, the 'Book of the Council', kept by Richard Caudray from 1421, shows a marked interest in the judicial matters heard by the Council until the death of Henry V, after when state documents relating to the arrangements for the minority government or to finance bulk more largely. This cannot be explained by assuming that the changed circumstances of the minority alone affected the range of the Council's work, because other material surviving in files shows that Caudray did not include all the business of the Council in the book. The keeping of such a book was itself intermittent, a sign that the recording of business was not considered absolutely essential, and in the 1470s Sir John Fortescue argued for the keeping of a Council register, although his concern seems to have been more with ensuring regularity in procedures rather than with recording business done (30, pp.148–9; 163, pp.2–4, 21–2, 35–7).

However, despite all that can be said about the lack of formal arrangements for the Council and its business, there are definite signs of an increase in systematic organization in the last quarter of the fourteenth century. This is seen most clearly in the emergence of the post of Clerk of the Council. There is no evidence that any such office existed before 1377, but the arrangements for the Council which served at the start of Richard II's minority included the provision of a clerk to be regularly at its disposal. At the same time, a system of regular salaries for councillors was devised, evidence that they were formally appointed to serve and did not attend casually. The abnormal conditions created by a minority may have contributed to these developments, but the advantages of having a permanent clerk seem to have been appreciated, for when Richard II resumed control of the government from the Appellants in 1389, a new clerk, John Prophete, was appointed. He seems to have been a king's man, and certainly received a number of rewards from Richard shortly after. When the King had asserted on his resumption of power that he would call whom he wished to his Council, he may have included also the appointment of a new clerk. In 1392, Prophete for the first time appears with the designation of 'Clerk of the Council'. It reflects the lack of clear differentiation between the Great Council and the continual Council that in the two earliest surviving uses of the title he is variously entitled 'clericus magni concilii' and 'clericus concilii'. As clerk, Prophete received a regular fee and also a position in the privy seal office, although, for no known reason, he ceased to hold official posts from 1395 until the Lancastrian usurpation. His time as clerk saw the start of a new period of Council record-keeping, and a journal which he kept in 1392–93 provides a fuller record of Council activity than survives for the years either preceding or succeeding it (160, pp.121, 130; 163, pp.6–10, 13–15).

Prophete's journal illuminates both the composition and the activity of Richard's Council. It reflects the fact that the term 'council' was still a flexible one, because it records both the meeting of a Great Council in February 1392 and the day-to-day gatherings of a much smaller body. Clearly membership of the Council was determined by the King's wishes and needs at any particular moment. The Great Council, which met for at least five days, and was attended by forty-three men at least once, dealt with major political issues such as negotiations with France, customs regulations, and the possible modification of the statutes of Provisors and Praemunire. The King was personally present, and may have raised the possibility of recalling Archbishop Neville and Robert de Vere, both of whom had been in exile since the crisis of 1387–88. By contrast, the thirty-four other meetings recorded between January and May of the same year had a different range of business and a much smaller attendance. The matters dealt with on these occasions were less political, but comprised technical questions of administration, such as the scrutiny of royal grants, the authorization of payments due and settling the terms of official appointments. The King was not present, and out of the twenty-four men who attended only seven were there regularly, contributing between them three-quarters of the total attendance. The average number of councillors present was between six and seven. The regular attenders were the Chancellor and the Treasurer (Archbishop Arundel of Canterbury and Bishop Waltham of Salisbury), three other bishops, all with legal and diplomatic backgrounds, and two knights, both of whom had had long experience in military, diplomatic and administrative affairs. The nucleus of the continual Council, therefore, was a small group of professional administrators, and did not include any member of the lay magnate class. Although this period is a relatively short one, the membership was typical of the Council for much of the later Middle Ages. In the last years of Richard II's reign its central core consisted of the three great officers, the Chancellor, the Treasurer and the Keeper of the Privy Seal, along with three knights, an esquire and two clerks, and although in the period immediately after Henry IV's usurpation the numbers attending increased, by 1400 the figure had again fallen, and until 1406 the most prominent members were of the familiar kind, the great officers – it was very rare when at least two of the three were not present – and a group of knights and esquires who had been retained by the King (164; 180).

The greatest crisis in the Council under Henry IV came in 1406, when, under pressure from Parliament, the knights and esquires were dropped from the Council and a stronger magnate element was introduced. At the end of the Parliament twelve councillors took an oath to observe thirty-one principles which were laid down for their guidance. They included a number of barons or earls, as well as a group of prelates, but it seems likely that in practice there was little drastic change in the active membership. Not only did the three great officers head the list of councillors, but they remained markedly the most assiduous attenders (164; 180). It is not quite clear that what lay behind the pressure for these changes, but probably the reasons were political rather than constitutional. There is no real evidence of an attempt to restrict the power of the Council, and the exclusion of the knights and esquires may have been prompted by the fear that they would be more inclined to favour the King's interests rather than those of the prince of Wales, who was now the most prominent figure opposed to Henry IV's policies. Unfortunately, the documentation of the Council's activity is much sparser after 1406 than before, so it is impossible to say if there was any significant change in the range of its work.

Records are also scarce for the early years of Henry V, and there is only a slight improvement in documentation for the middle years of the reign. Enough survives, however, to show that a small group of councillors, among whom the great officers or their deputies were still prominent, carried on the routine business of government. Circumstances were different from Henry IV's time, as the King spent a considerable part of his reign campaigning in France, where he was accompanied by the majority of the magnates. Even when Henry was in England, however, the nobility played only a small part in the Council, and the official and clerical members of it were the most active. Apart from the absence of a group of household knights and gentry, the Council was very similar in composition and, probably, in functions to what it had been in the two previous reigns (164).

The minority following Henry V's death created a totally new, and abnormal, situation. Hitherto the choice of councillors had been the King's concern, subject only to occasional constraints as in 1406. Now, instead of a single ruler, there were noble factions struggling for influence, and the man who might have been most effective in preserving royal authority, the King's senior uncle, the duke of Bedford, was left with the responsibility of defending his nephew's claims in France. The leading figure in England was Humphrey of Gloucester, but his aspirations to authority were resisted by many of the other magnates, and an attempt was made to ensure that the government of the realm would be in the hands of the Council rather than of the duke (Ch.21). Despite this, the magnates played a relatively slight part in conciliar activity except at times of political crisis, and although theoretically the lay element was more numerous, in practice the clerical minority, comprising the three great officers and five bishops, three of whom had previously been major office-holders, made up the majority of those who attended. Among the laity the most active members were two barons and two knights who later became peers, all of whom had held administrative posts previously, either in the household or as Treasurer of the realm. Those who had not yet held the latter post were to do so in future. The prominence of this administrator group is reflected in the fact that they were granted regular salaries in 1424. There was a decline in the attendance of the earls after the first two or three years, apart from times when the quarrels between Gloucester and Beaufort reached a critical point, both in the 1420s and in the last years of the minority, and when such crises passed, it was the administrators who remained active (164). Magnate interest in conciliar activity in times of crisis illustrates how the Council was at the centre of political struggles as well as of the administration, but the intermittent nature of their interest in its proceedings makes it clear that they had little concern for administrative routine.

In the early period of the King's majority, the number of active councillors was fairly high, and the most assiduous attenders were the great officers. They were followed closely by Suffolk, whose influence derived from his position in the household rather than from tenure of a traditional office of State. The 1440s saw an increased prominence of such court figures in government, probably because Henry tended to be influenced by his close associates, rather than seeking counsel from the magnate class as a whole. In consequence, the distinction between the court and the Council tended to be blurred. When in 1443, Lord Sudeley, the Chamberlain of the Household, replaced Lord Cromwell as Treasurer he continued to hold his court post. The Council seems to have been a rather looser group than formerly, although there are still signs of an active core of officials, many of them churchmen. The crisis of 1449–50 saw a collapse of the court group rather than of the Council as such, and a small group of ministers remained active in the early 1450s. As far as the Council was concerned, the real change in character came not with the fall and death of Suffolk but with Henry's insanity, when the aristocratic element in the Council attained new prominence and substantial numbers of magnates began to attend meetings. Indeed at a time when Parliament was sitting any small continual Council may have effectively ceased to exist, and the Council, to which references are made, may have consisted of the magnate group as a whole. This, of course, was possible because there was no clear idea of what precisely the Council was. Later a smaller council was established, including a number of great men, but containing also a nucleus of professional administrators, some of whom survived into the Yorkist period. The rather thin surviving evidence suggests that the late 1450s saw the clerical members still showing the greatest assiduity in attendance, evidence of the need for professional administrators even in times of political upheaval (160, p.199; 164; 199).

Under the Yorkists, there seems to have been an extension of the title 'councillor' to men involved in a wide range of government activities, notably in diplomacy, these including both magnates and officials. As the records of the Council's actions are largely missing, it is impossible to judge which of these councillors were regular attenders and did most of the work. There are some pointers, however, to the persistence of a professional tradition in government, even though the Council included a number of men whose power rested on their territorial holdings rather than on their tenure of office. The proportion of officials who were designated as councillors rose in the second part of Edward IV's reign, when the King's position was stronger. A substantial number of these were later to serve Henry VII, so it is clear that their concern was with administration rather than politics and that they did not depend particularly on the Yorkist dynasty. Routine matters were left in the hands of administrators, and even when the King was outside London, a Council remained in the capital, and sent letters to Edward and *his* Council in the provinces (130, pp.188–9, 205–6, 218–19). The fact that such a division was not completely unprecedented may explain why Richard of Gloucester aroused no suspicions in June 1483 when he had one half of the Council remaining at Westminster to discuss the arrangements for Edward V's coronation and summoned the other half to the Tower, where he staged the arrests of Rotheram and Morton and the execution of Hastings. Chronicle sources for the whole usurpation period, indeed, show that the Council was the centre of both political and executive activity, although no documentary records survive to give additional information on it (3, pp.70–5, 80–5; 14, pp.564–6).

Henry VII's Council had a strongly professional character, and the length of tenure of the great offices by individuals suggests that he relied greatly on their expertise in government. The career of one of the greatest of these, John Morton, Chancellor from March 1486 and archbishop of Canterbury from December of the same year until his death in 1500, illustrates this. Morton had first entered royal service under Henry VI, remaining loyal to Lancaster until the débâcle of Tewkesbury. He than made this peace with Edward IV, who recognized his talents and took him into his own service. His career again seemed in ruins when Gloucester arrested him in 1483, but he escaped to the Continent after the autumn rebellion of that year, and on his return to England became the Tudor King's most influential councillor. The vicissitudes of his career reflect his involvement in politics, but his restoration to office under successive dynasties shows that talent could be more important than past connections when a king was choosing his administrators. A similar willingness to bury the political past is shown by the fact that both Henry's two treasurers, Lord Dinham and the earl of Surrey, had been favoured by Richard III (110, pp.105–8).

A number of Edward IV's closer advisers, such as Herbert and Hastings, had their origins in the lesser landed class, but were promoted to the peerage. Henry VII's most important advisers, outside the holders of the major offices, were also drawn from the ranks of the knights and gentry, but did not normally receive such promotion. The Yorkist and early Tudor lay councillors, therefore, were similar in origin to the men who had been prominent in the Councils of Richard II and Henry IV, even if their rewards were different. The extent of the Council's influence varied with the amount of concern which the King himself displayed in government, and in the period between Henry VII's death and the rise of Wolsey the Council seems to have secured rather more power than it had exercised before 1509, with a magnate Treasurer and an episcopal Keeper of the Privy Seal, along with a number of knights, being the new King's principal advisers. Most ecclesiastical councillors at this period were drawn from the episcopate, but apart from those churchmen who held one of the great offices they do not appear to have been particularly prominent in government; there were no longer lesser clerks who played an active part in the Council because of their importance in the royal administration, which was becoming increasingly laicized. This did not change with the rise of Wolsey, although he himself became dominant in the Council, being normally left to preside over it, although on great occasions the King might be present. The largest recorded attendance at an individual meeting during the Wolsey years was fifty-four, but the figure could fall as low as eleven. Some attempt may have been made to differentiate between different kinds of councillors; in 1535 Sir Robert Wingfield stated that he had been sworn of the Council above twenty years, and of the Privy Council above fourteen years. The term 'Privy Council', does not seem to have been given any precise meaning until the 1530s, but there is a pointer to the future in the implication that some attempt was made to distinguish an inner circle of councillors from the rest of the King's advisers, and that contemporaries recognized the distinction (110, pp.110–12; 160, p.450; 170; 174; 200).

The history of the Council's variable membership clearly demonstrates its character. The amount of power which it could exercise depended on the King, and this is why the reign of Henry VI, where ineffective rule followed a protracted minority, saw a tendency for it to fall into magnate hands. Even then, however, the administrators who attended most assiduously were probably responsible for ensuring that Council decision on routine governmental questions were carried out. The Council's duties were as flexible as its membership, and it is hard for the historian to say what took most of its time and concern. This is partly due to the patchy survival of its records, which tend to reflect decisions rather than discussion; decisions on administrative matters involved the issue of letters which were recorded, whereas the consideration of political questions might leave little trace. Chronicle records of such debates, as in 1483, are rare. The judicial activities of the Council, however, are relatively well documented. They were not separated from its other business, and could involve men without any specialist knowledge of law. As late as 1526, in an attempt to formalize the structure of the Council, the Eltham ordinances proposed that there should be a smaller group of twenty members within it, drawn from the principal officers of State and of the household, and laid down that they could commune on any matter of the King's business as well as hearing poor men's complaints on matters of justice. This last matter was an important part of conciliar activity, representing the exercise of an equity jurisdiction distinct from the courts of common law. Further proposals were put forward shortly afterwards for differentiating the Council's judicial and administrative functions, with a number of lesser councillors and lawyers dealing with the former (Ch.33; 160, pp.446–7; 170). These various reform proposals in the 1520s came to nothing, but their importance to the historian is to show that, even before Wolsey's fall, men were concerned about the Council's place in government and perhaps also about the volume of conciliar judicial business, and that it was felt that there was a need for a greater formalization of its structure to make it more effective.

Throughout the late Middle Ages, then, the Council remained normally only loosely organized. As the King's Council it had an important role in government, and it is hardly surprising that its character varied with the effectiveness of each individual king. Generally speaking, however, it was not a place where the magnates were much involved except when royal authority was in abeyance, as in a minority. Despite its lack of clear organization and its fluidity of membership, it was still involved in many aspects of routine administration as well as giving advice to the monarch. The nucleus of the Council, as far as the conduct of such business was concerned, comprised the professional administrators, who might well survive even major political upheavals. These were both clerical and lay, although during the period the clerical element became less important. As professionals, such men followed customary administrative practices, and are best regarded as bureaucrats rather than as politicians.

CHAPTER 33

Lawyers, law and justice

In the chapters dealing with financial administration we saw that the English kings in the late Middle Ages became increasingly inclined to employ lawyers in administrative posts. This emergence of the legal profession was a significant social development, because it reflected the appearance of a class of laymen whose interests were professional rather than military, and opened up a new way by which an able man could rise in the social scale. The fortunes of two fifteenth-century families, who are well known to historians from the survival of their correspondence, the Pastons and the Stonors, can both be traced to ancestors who were judges. In the case of Justice Paston indeed there were suspicions that his near ancestors had not even been free, so it appears that a man could rise far if he were successful in the law. The majority of the bench in the mid fifteenth century seems to have been recruited from the upper gentry or the lesser nobility; the judges were chosen from an élite group of pleaders, the serjeants-at-law, and it is noteworthy that of a group of nine men who were admitted to this grade in 1495, only two were really well born. Promotion to serjeant gave a man rank equivalent to a knight. The higher lawyers, comprising serjeants and judges, were a select body, usually not more than about 20 in number, and indeed the number of men practising in the courts at Westminster, including attorneys and various clerks, probably did not exceed 400; of these about 150 were of sufficient standing in 1523 to be rated for the levy of the subsidy. Besides these practitioners there were perhaps 200 or 300 students of law in training, not all of whom would pursue the course to the end (175, p.61; 176, ii, 486; 177).

Before the fourteenth century, important judicial posts had often been filled by churchmen, but the King's Bench was already laicized by 1341. It was just at this time too that the lawyers, for the first time, began to take over administrative posts hitherto held by the clergy; the first lay Chancellor, Sir Robert Bourchier in 1340, was a lawyer (55, p.168), and although it was not long before the Great Seal returned to clerical hands, to remain there for the greater part of the next two centuries, the occasional lay holders of it included lawyers as well as some magnates. Most significant were two appointments in the 1370s, when there was a reaction against Edward III's clerical ministers. In 1371 the Chief Justice of the Common Pleas, Sir Robert Thorp, was appointed, and on his death in the following year he was succeeded by his opposite number from the King's Bench, Sir John Knyvet [C]. At the end of our period there was another appointment of notable importance, when Sir Thomas More succeeded Wolsey; he was not only the first Chancellor who had studied in the Inns of Court, but he was the first of a line of lawyer chancellors to bring this training to the post. The latter half of the fifteenth century saw the lawyers also capturing a number of other posts; they provided 7 out of 10 Chancellors of the duchy of Lancaster between 1471 and 1529, and all 22 Speakers of the House of Commons between 1484 and 1559. They were active in the Council of Edward IV and even active in that of Henry VII. Under Henry VIII their role may have been slightly less prominent in central administration, but they were to play a leading part in the new organizations set up after the Reformation (177).

The increasing complexity and technicality of the law necessitated a professional expertise among its practitioners. The most striking idiosyncrasy of the common law was the continued use of French in its formal business, despite a statute of 1362 which had ordered that pleas should be heard in English and enrolled in Latin. Law French, however, possessed greater technical precision in its terminology, which obviously commended it to lawyers. The survival also reflects legal conservatism, because it was only in the common law courts that French was employed; the records of the equitable jurisdiction of the Chancellor were kept in English from the start and the highest court of the land, Parliament, also began keeping its records in English at this time. Another indication of the need for professionalism can be seen in the multiplication of civil remedies, and of the number of writs required to put them into effect. In the first half of the thirteenth century there had been about 60 writs, around 1320 the figure had risen to about 890, but when the first printed register of writs appeared in 1531, there were no fewer than 2,500. It is not surprising that one also sees treatises on writs being produced for the guidance of lawyers (176, ii, 477–81, 522).

It seems to have been in the early fifteenth century that the system of legal education developed, which, with some modifications, was to be the basis of training for practice in the courts down to the present time. The student began by attending an inn of chancery, where he acquired a basic knowledge of writs and legal practice. Thence he would proceed to one of the four great Inns of Court, where he would attend readings given by more advanced students, participate in 'mootings', discussions of points of law, and listen to actual cases in court. The senior members of the Inn, the benchers, would decide when he was sufficiently expert to be called to the bar, and this would entitle him to practise in any court except the Common Pleas, where the monopoly of pleading was in the hands of the serjeants-at-law. Their promotion was by royal authority on the command of the Chancellor, and its importance was marked by an expensive ceremony. It is clear that the rewards attached to the rank were high, as were the prospects of further promotion to judge. Not all men, of course, attained such high ranks, but a professional lawyer who did not become a serjeant could still have an active practice. Also, members of the land-owning class might well wish to equip themselves with some knowledge of the law to assist in running their estates, or they might obtain administrative positions in the service of the Crown or of a powerful magnate on the strength of their legal studies (4, ii, 128–30; 175, pp.63–75). Law and land-owning went well together, and successful lawyers could hope to acquire estates for themselves, while still continuing to practise. Here they were more fortunate than merchants, who, after buying land, would have to abandon trade if they wished to be regarded as gentlemen.

Legal training was protracted for a man who was aiming for the highest positions, and it probably reflects the growing professionalism of the law that many of those involved in it in the fifteenth century seem to have taken little interest in politics. The last occasion in the Middle Ages when the bench suffered severely for pronouncing on a political question as a matter of law was in the Merciless Parliament of 1388, when Chief Justice Tresilian was executed and his fellow judges were banished to Ireland for expressing views on the King's prerogative rights which were contrary to the liking of the victorious magnates. By contrast, the fortunes of the judges during the struggles of Lancaster and York suggest that the vast majority of them were either indifferent to the dynastic struggle or at least unwilling to allow themselves the luxury of partisanship. In 1460, when the duke of York claimed the throne in Parliament, the judges and serjeants, when asked to express a view on the legality of his title refused to do so. Of the 28 men who were justices of the Common Pleas between the reigns of Henry VI and Richard III, only 6 had ever served as MPs, and only 3 had reputations of being partisans of either faction. Further evidence for the non-political character of the judiciary is the fact that new kings, even after seizing the throne by force, regularly reappointed existing judges to office. One must not generalize from the example of the judge best known to historians, Sir John Fortescue, Chief Justice of the King's Bench, who went into exile with Margaret of Anjou, serving as her Chancellor there, and did not come to terms with the Yorkists until after the final extinction of Lancastrian hopes at Tewkesbury. Fortescue's fate was exceptional in that he lost his position because of political activity; the only other case of a judge being dismissed at this time, Chief Justice Markham, removed by Edward IV for directing a jury to give a verdict of concealment of treason rather than of treason itself, must be seen as royal interference with the bench and not as direct political involvement. The very fact that Markham's fate was regarded as a scandal is itself testimony to a general belief that the judiciary was above politics (175, pp.91–3; 176, ii, 560–8).[1]

If one compares Fortescue's career with that of his greatest contemporary, Thomas Littleton, one sees how a lawyer could remain unaffected by political turmoil. The latter first appears as a rising lawyer in the 1440s, becoming a serjeant-at-law in 1453 and a king's serjeant two years later. Edward IV reappointed him as such in 1461, appointed him a justice of the Common Pleas in 1466 and created him a knight of the Bath in 1475. Both Fortescue and Littleton made noteworthy contributions to the literature of English government and law, but there is little doubt that the former's fame among historians is greater. The reason for this is presumably that his interest in the constitution and government is more congenial to them than the technical details of land-holding, covered by Littleton in his *Tenures*, a work described by Holdsworth as one of the five pre-eminent books in the history of English law, along with those of Glanvill, Bracton, Coke and Blackstone (176, ii, 572–3).[2] Another reason for the relative attention paid to the two writers may be that Fortescue's most famous works, the *Governance of England* and the *De Laudibus Legum Anglie* were written respectively in English and Latin, languages with which educated men at a later date were familiar, whereas the *Tenures* was in highly technical law French, so few apart from lawyers would be likely to consult it in its original form.

Among lawyers, however, it soon came to be regarded as a classic, and it is a comment on its importance that it was the first work on English law to be printed; the earliest edition appeared in 1481 or 1482, over twenty editions by the end of Henry VIII's reign and more than seventy by 1628, the year when Coke's famous commentary on it was published. It was also translated into English early in the sixteenth century, and thereby became available to a far wider audience; indeed in the seventeenth century there is reference to Norfolk men, who were said to keep Littleton's *Tenures* 'at the plough's tail'.[3] Through the excellence of the work lawyers came to regard it as far more than a textbook and virtually as a codification of the law. Paradoxically, however, there were ways in which the *Tenures* was virtually out of date by the time it appeared, for Littleton wrote of land-holding purely within the terms of the common law, which failed to take proper cognizance of the development of the use, leaving it to the Chancellor's equitable jurisdiction to deal with the resulting problems. His academic lack of interest in uses, which he mentioned only in connection with a technical point of conveyancing, did not, however, prevent him from employing them; in his will he provided for the disposition of lands held by his feoffees (4. ii, 30, 178; 176. ii, 574, 593).

The late fifteenth and early sixteenth centuries saw the printing of other legal works besides Littleton's. The most famous of these were the year books, records of cases pleaded in the courts. These had been compiled from the thirteenth century onwards, presumably by lawyers to meet their professional needs, and the process of reporting the cases had developed over the years in parallel with the growth of the legal profession. As the Inns of Court grew in importance, they may have played a part in making the year books, which became less students' notebooks and more something which was given a quasi-authoritative standing. As such legal literature proliferated, it became necessary for lawyers to have recourse to abridgements, of which the most important was Fitzherbert's *Graunde Abridgement* of 1514–16 (4. ii, 31, 162; 176. ii, 538, 542). Such works provided the material for training lawyers, who were already playing a major part in government as the King's servants, and who were later to provide an opposition to authoritarian monarchy. The precedents contained in the year books were to be set up as a rival authority to the absolute will of later kings.

During this period, the busiest court in the country was the Common Pleas, which heard far more cases than the King's Bench. Debt cases provided the greater part of its business; a sample from the plea rolls of Edward IV's reign shows that these amounted to over 70 per cent of its total work. In 1483 the jurisdictional sphere of the King's Bench was defined as pleas touching the King, writs of error, and actions of debt, detinue and account when the defendant was in the custody of the marshal. It was this last area of jurisdiction which gave the King's Bench scope to extend its civil jurisdiction at the expense of the Common Pleas through the device known as the bill of Middlesex, which alleged (usually fictitiously) that the defendant was in the marshal's custody. Despite the fiction, the bill was allowed, and by the seventeenth century it was the King's Bench which attracted the greater part of civil litigation. The greater expeditiousness of the King's Bench, and hence lower costs for litigants, may explain why they were prepared to acquiesce in the fiction. The King's Bench was also able to hear civil suits if some element of force had been involved, in, for example, a disputed title to land. The preference for the Common Pleas in the earlier period was probably due to the fact that it had been a fixed court when the King's Bench was still peripatetic, moving around with the King and his Council. In fact, by 1400, the King's Bench had also become virtually static, holding nearly all its sessions at Westminster (4, ii, 57; 162, p.2; 175, pp.16, 25–7; 176, i, 207, 210, 219).

These courts did not, of course, have a monopoly even of royal justice. Itinerant justices might visit the shires to hold the assizes, and from the early fourteenth century it had been provided that they were to be discreet men who were knowledgeable in law. The power of local magnates might raise problems for those who administered law, and in 1384 the Commons petitioned that no man of law should be a justice of assize 'en son propre pais', because there had been justices who had fees and robes from lords, and were of their affinities. In the same petition, the Commons asked that the chief justices should be excluded from sitting as assize judges, because they had the responsibility of correcting errors from lower courts. The King accepted the first half of the petition but not the second. The willingness of litigants to attend the assizes, which heard civil suits before a jury, speaks favourably for their effectiveness. Criminal proceedings were also conducted outside the central courts, usually by commissioners of gaol delivery or of oyer and terminer. The former might be granted to justices, with or without lay assistance, who were directed to try prisoners in particular gaols; the scope of the latter was wider, for the commissioners might have to enquire into and deal with all offences within their area, or possibly into certain specified crimes. A statute of 1394 ordered that commissions to deliver gaols should contain at least two lawyers; in this, as in the appointment of men to sit on assizes, one sees the importance that was attached to legal professionalism (33, iii, 200; 176, i, 274; 178, pp.33, 143–5). An active king who was trying to enforce order could appoint important men to these commissions; for example Edward IV named a substantial number of his councillors to sit on them, and in a major case, such as the proceedings for treason against Burdett and Stacy in 1477, the commission of oyer and terminer contained some of the greatest men in the realm as well as a number of the judges. When treason was accompanied by open revolt, the King had an alternative method of proceeding, by trying the rebels under the law of arms in the Constable's court. Edward was prepared to employ common law procedures on other occasions, and one contemporary writer states that he perambulated the country with the judges to try to enforce order (14, p.559; 144, pp.240, 399; 179).

For most Englishmen of the period, their contacts with the law, either as litigants in civil suits or as defendants in criminal proceedings, were more likely to be in one of the local courts than in the central ones at Westminster. Locally, the most important judicial body was the Commission of the Peace. Essentially this was a non-professional body; its members were drawn from the local landed class and were in practice the leading men in county society. A statute of 1414 provided that they should reside in their counties, and another of 1439 stipulated that they should have land worth £20 per annum. Some of these might in fact be legally trained; as we have seen, members of the landed class might have spent some time in an inn of chancery or of court, and an analysis of the personnel of various commissions shows that professional lawyers also played an active part in their proceedings. The commission had begun to emerge to importance early in Edward III's reign, when it acquired the right to receive presentments of crimes and to punish offenders. After the Black Death, it was made responsible for implementing the Ordinance, and then the Statute, of Labourers, and later it acquired other powers. In 1363 it was laid down that sessions were to be held four times a year, and about the same time the change in nomenclature from keepers of the peace to justices of the peace reflected their enhanced power. They made a substantial gain in authority in 1461 in Edward IV's first Parliament, when it was enacted that they were to take indictments of offences and the sheriffs were forbidden to arrest persons without process from the sessions. This Act marks a significant decline in the power of the sheriff, who had been the key figure in local judicial administration at an earlier date. By the Tudor period the Commission of the Peace had increased in size, and contained most of the more influential landed men in the shire; these were the natural agents on whom the King would rely in local matters (36, ii. 390–1; 176, i. 288–9; 178, p.146).

How effective was the system of justice provided by these courts? As far as maintaining law and order was concerned, there is little doubt that they left a great deal to be desired. It has been said that 'when the criminal law dealt with the poor it was callous but inefficient, when it dealt with the better off merely inefficient'. Even if a defendant could not plead a technical flaw in an indictment, the first way of trying to avoid a judgment, there were various methods of blocking proceedings. In a non-capital case, a defendant who denied a charge might offer to pay a fine to avoid the trouble and expense of disproving it, and this would often be acceptable. A person who admitted his guilt might obtain a pardon, even for a felony. If a civil suit came to trial, there might be attempts to influence a jury by violence or bribery, or a defendant's lord might 'maintain' him, threatening the court. The evidence of the Paston Letters shows widespread disorder in mid-fifteenth-century East Anglia, but it is worth remembering that this not only occurred when royal political power was at its nadir for over a century, but also that the region was particularly prey to magnate rivalries. The letters of the Stonors in Oxfordshire reflect less disorder in local society, although it is not entirely absent, and there is insufficient evidence to say which part of the country was more typical. There were other weaknesses in the legal system too, particularly in the existence of areas of litigation with which the common law was not well equipped to deal, most notably in matters concerning real property, because the courts were not prepared to treat enfeoffments to uses (Ch.12) as anything other than simple conveyances of land (162, pp.25, 52–5; 175, pp.218–22).

These weaknesses in the common law were responsible for one of the major developments in English law in the fifteenth century, the emergence of new courts to deal with particular problems. The main new jurisdictions were that of the Chancellor in matters of equity and that of the Council, and behind the growth of both of these was the idea that the King had a responsibility to do justice to his subjects even when the law did not provide a remedy for them. The two developments were originally closely connected, for the Chancellor initially exercised his equity jurisdiction in the Council – a petition to the Chancellor around 1390 is endorsed as having been heard by the Council. Gradually, however, the Chancellor's court was differentiated from the Council and came to exercise more specialized functions. The most marked increase in the number of petitions to the Chancellor came between 1420 and 1450, and at the same time their character changed. In 1420 almost three-quarters of the Chancellor's business concerned matters for which the common law normally provided a remedy, but one unavailable in a particular case for a special reason, the poverty of the claimant or the maintenance of his opponent by too powerful a person. By 1450, almost all the cases related to questions for which there was no common law remedy, 90 per cent of these being concerned with enfeoffments to uses. The strength of equity was that the Chancellor was less bound by technicalities than was the increasingly constipated common law; a flaw in the form of a common law writ could invalidate a suit, but petitions to the Chancellor did not have a set form and could be treated on the merit of their contents. When, in a case recorded in a year book, counsel argued that a plaintiff had no remedy, because a man who had made an enfeoffment without a deed was simple and had only himself to blame, the Chancellor replied that he would have a remedy in chancery, 'because God protects the simple'. The stress laid on chancery here, of course, makes it clear that counsel's claim would have been valid in the common law courts. The substance of most chancery cases in the late fifteenth century was topics such as uses, contracts and matters of account (159; 160, p.251; 176, i. 406, ii. 551).

Cases which were heard before the Council came to a body which was as yet fluid in composition, and those who heard litigation were no different from those who advised the King on political matters. Again, much of the business was civil in character, although the petitions presented to the Council might disguise the fact that a suit was basically concerned with a question of title, in so far as they allege that the other party had been guilty of violence or of perversion of legal process against the plaintiff. The judgment given, however, could be concerned as much with the question of title as with the disorder or any corrupt practices. Not more than 10 per cent of the litigation before Henry VII's Council was essentially concerned with criminal matters, and official prosecutions were exceptional. There may have been some decline in conciliar judicial activity after Henry VII's death, but it revived under Wolsey. Again, the weighting of cases is overwhelmingly towards the civil side; only 9 cases of official criminal prosecutions can be identified from his chancellorship, compared with over 800 suits between contending parties. It is hardly surprising that the Council tried to steer criminal proceedings to the common law courts, which possessed the right to impose severer sentences; when the Council investigated and tried felonies, it did not have the power of imposing capital sentences and had to punish them as misdemeanours, with fines or imprisonment (169).

This does not mean that the government paid no attention to disorder. The Act of 1487, which for long was erroneously thought to have set up the court of the Star Chamber, in fact created a tribunal distinct from the Council (although its members were also councillors), with special responsibility for dealing with various offences concerning breaches of public order and maladministration of the common law. It gave summary powers to the principal officers of State and certain councillors to take proceedings in these cases and to punish offenders in accordance with statute. Little survives in the way of records from this body, so it is impossible to judge its effectiveness (110, pp.154–6). The tribunal may be regarded as an offshoot from the Council, but one which was still completely distinct.

The Council itself remained a unitary body until the reforms of the 1530s, without formal differentiation of its various functions. There does, however, seem to have been some informal attempt to organize its legal business separately. As early as 1494 a reference in a letter stated that the Council was so busy on the King's affairs that the Chancellor had not kept the star chamber for over a week. At this stage the 'star chamber' was merely a place of meeting, not the court it later became. In 1517 Wolsey tried to reserve two days a week for the Council to hear cases, and in the Eltham ordinances of 1526, there was a suggestion that a reduced group within the Council should hear judicial matters, although it is not certain if this was to be their exclusive task (169, pp.14, 37–47). The structure and scope of conciliar jurisdiction were still very fluid and required clarification. This was attained in the middle years of the sixteenth century; the 'court of the Star Chamber' was formally separated from the Council in 1536 and thereby acquired a new standing, and in the years which followed, a more formal organization was also given to the 'court of requests', which heard the pleas of poor men, a task which had also been performed by members of the Council from Henry VII's time. It is not clear, however, what differences there were in jurisdictional function between these various offshoots of the Council in the early Tudor period (51, pp.412–15; 110, pp.152–3).

It is hard to judge how far chancery and the Council were threatening to supersede the existing common law courts. The number of cases heard by the latter appears to have declined from the 1430s until the middle of the sixteenth century, precisely the same period as that in which there was a spectacular growth of proceedings in chancery. The common lawyers certainly complained at the activities of chancery and the conciliar courts. At the same time, however, the central courts of common law were gaining ground at the expense of both local lay courts and, even before the Reformation, the ecclesiastical courts (4, ii. 51, 65–79; 162, p.25; Ch.36, below). In retrospect it may well seem that 1529 was the year which saw a crucial event in the recovery of the common law courts, when Sir Thomas More, himself a brilliantly successful barrister of Lincoln's Inn and the son of a justice of the King's Bench, became Chancellor. Many of his successors in the office had similar legal backgrounds and it was not likely that they would be as ready as their clerical predecessors to ride roughshod over common law custom. As chancery, like other branches of government became more secular, the common law was in a better position not only to recover its influence, but to go on from strength to strength. By the early seventeenth century common lawyers like Coke were self-confident and formidable enough to put themselves in the van of opposition to what they saw as the misuse of the royal prerogative in general as well as of the prerogative courts in particular. By such opposition to arbitrary royal power, the common lawyers must rank high among the architects of the later British State.

---

1. Two sources from the early sixteenth century which mention the case (38, p.70; 40, p.207), refer to the episode as a scandal. The latest study of the relevant case, M. A. Hicks, 'The case of Sir Thomas Cook, 1468', *EHR*, **93** (1978), concentrates on whether or not Cook was guilty and says little about Markham's position.
2. The historians' neglect of Littleton may be seen in the absence of any reference to him in the index of either (52) or (53), although both these works contain several references to Fortescue.
3. I am indebted to Professor G. S. Holmes for this reference.

PART FIVE

The Church and education

Entries in *italics* are intended to provide cross-references to the Framework of events – Social and economic, and the Framework of events – Political.

1351	First Statute of Provisors (sanctions against papal provisions to benefices).
1353	First Statute of Praemunire (restriction on access to Curia in judicial matters). Agreement on precedence between the archbishops of Canterbury and York.
1365	Second Statute of Praemunire.
Early 1370s	Wyclif's philosophical teachings begin to provoke controversy in Oxford.
1371	Foundation of London Charterhouse (only second foundation of Carthusian house in England since thirteenth century and on a larger scale than earlier establishments).
1372–73	Papal demands for financial support from England.
1375	Concordat between England and Papacy.
1377	*Accession of Richard II.* Commons petition for the expulsion of aliens, including monks. First prosecution of Wyclif; various of his propositions condemned by the Pope.
1378–1417	Great Schism of the Papacy.
1378	Major crisis over breach of sanctuary at Westminster.
1381	*Great Revolt.* Condemnation by University of Oxford of Wyclif's teaching on Eucharist. Foundation of Coventry Charterhouse.
1382	Collapse of Wyclifite influence at Oxford. Prosecution of William Swinderby for heresy by Bishop Buckingham of Lincoln. Foundation of Winchester College by Bishop Wykeham.
1388	Urban VI seeks financial aid from England.
1389	Inquest into the government and endowment of guilds and fraternities.
1389–90	Second Statute of Provisors.
1391	Boniface IX claims to annual Statute of Provisors.
1393	Third Statute of Praemunire.
1395	Lollard manifesto calling for ecclesiastical disendowment.
1396	*Twenty-eight year truce with France. Richard II's second marriage.* Crusade of Nicopolis.
1398	Concordat between England and the Papacy.
1399	*Accession of Henry IV.*
1401	Statute *De Heretico Comburendo.* Execution of William Sawtry for heresy.
1409	Council of Pisa fails to end the Great Schism.
1410	Parliament sympathetic to proposals for Church disendowment. Execution of John Badby for heresy.
1411	Commission at Oxford produces list of errors in Wyclif's writings.
1413	*Accession of Henry V.* Trial of Sir John Oldcastle for heresy.
1414	Oldcastle rebellion. Suppression of alien priories and foundation of Sheen Charterhouse.
1414–18	Council of Constance. Ending of Great Schism.
1415	Foundation of Bridgettine House at Twickenham (moved to Syon, 1431).
1417	Capture and execution of Oldcastle.
1418	Concordat between England and the Papacy.
1422	*Accession of Henry VI*
1423–28	Papal attempt to secure repeal of the Statute of Provisors.

1428	Arrest of considerable number of Lollards in Kent.
1428–31	Bishop Alnwick's heresy proceedings in the Waveney valley, Norfolk.
1430	Completion of William Lyndwood's *Provinciale*.
1431	Anti-clerical revolt at Abingdon.
1431–49	Council of Basel (election of anti-pope, 1439).
1440	Foundation of Eton College.
1449–75	Intermittent tithe disputes in London.
1450	Cade's rising. Some anti-clerical overtones, including murder of Bishop Ayscough of Salisbury.
1461	*Accession of Edward IV.*
1462–64	Heresy proceedings in the Chilterns.
1462	Convocation of York agrees to accept that all the provincial constitutions of Canterbury should normally be accepted in the northern province also.
1477	Caxton established first English printing press at Westminster.
1481	John Anwykyll appointed master at Magdalen College School, Oxford.
1482	Foundation of Observant Franciscan house at Greenwich.
1483	*Accession and deposition of Edward V. Accession of Richard III.*
1485	*Accession of Henry VII.*
1489	Statute limiting benefit of clergy.
1491	Statute limiting benefit of clergy.
1494	*Outbreak of Italian wars.*
1496	Suppression of nunnery of St Radegund's, Cambridge; endowments employed for the foundation of Jesus College.
1509	*Accession of Henry VIII.*
c. 1510	Foundation of St Paul's School by Dean Colet.
1511	Heresy trials in Kent and Chilterns.
1511–12	Heresy trials in Coventry.
1512	Statute limiting benefit of clergy.
1514–15	Richard Hunne's case.
1521	Burning of Lutheran books in London.
1521–22	Heresy trials in the Chilterns.
1524	William Tyndale flees to Germany.
1525	First edition of Tyndale's *New Testament* in English published at Cologne (second edition, 1526, Worms).
1529	Sir Thomas More's *Dialogue Concerning Heresies* published. Meeting of the Reformation Parliament.

CHAPTER 34

The organization and structure of the secular Church

The English Church in the late Middle Ages was, first and foremost, a part of Western Christendom, owing obedience to the Papacy. Relations with the popes, at Avignon and then in Rome, were not always easy, and some of the problems of this will be considered in Chapter 35. The Church also had a more immediate master in the King, and this too raised problems; many of these were not new and were to be resolved only with the Reformation. Before these topics are considered, however, there is the question of what exactly the *ecclesia anglicana* was. In a general sense of course, it represented the *congregatio fidelium*, and as, since Edward I's expulsion of the Jews, there were no other religions to the country, this was equivalent to the people as a whole. In a more specialized sense, however, it consisted of the clergy, although this group too was not clearly defined; a man in minor orders might proceed no further and have little clerical status apart from some legal protection from the lay courts. The men who really mattered within the Church were those who had received at least the order of the subdiaconate, the level at which compulsory celibacy became the rule. It is these clergy with whom we shall be concerned in this chapter.

Theoretically the English Church comprised two provinces, under the archbishops of Canterbury and York. The former contained fourteen dioceses in England and four in Wales, the latter only three. No new dioceses were established in the country between 1133 and the reign of Henry VIII, when a number of former abbeys were transformed into cathedrals. Until the fourteenth century there had been rivalry, often bitter, between the two archbishoprics, but in 1353 an agreement was reached between Islip of Canterbury and Thoresby of York. Both of these men were royal servants by training and former Keepers of the Privy Seal, and may perhaps have been personal friends. If so, their willingness to bury old feuds may be the more understandable. The precedence of Canterbury was confirmed, but each archbishop was given the right to carry his primatial cross within the other's province. If both archbishops were present, their cross-bearers were to have no priority if the way was wide; only if it were narrow would the Canterbury bearer take precedence. While this agreement was concerned with essentially formal matters, it represented a real admission of the greater dignity of Canterbury. In practical terms this was recognized more fully in 1462 when the Convocation of York agreed that all the provincial constitutions of Canterbury which were not repugnant to York should be accepted in the North also. In 1530 Bishop Tunstall of Durham was to remind Wolsey that it was customary for York to wait and see what decisions were made by Canterbury and then decide whether or not to assent to them. The initiative rested with Canterbury, and it was only when a particular archbishop of York was more dominant than his southern colleague – Wolsey is the most conspicuous example – that his fellow primate was not the leading churchman in the realm.

The jurisdiction exercised by archbishops and bishops was primarily limited by the geographical bounds of their dioceses, but there were a number of anomalous situations where a bishop might have powers over certain churches in other dioceses, which were called 'peculiars'. A number of parish churches in the city of London came directly under the archbishop of Canterbury, who also had jurisdiction over some parishes in the diocese of Chichester. The bishop of Exeter also had powers over some Chichester parishes. Peculiar jurisdictions could even cross the boundaries of provinces; the priory of St Oswald at Gloucester came under the authority of the archbishop of York, and remained so until 1545. Such privileges did not, however, always work in favour of archbishops; the archdeaconry of Richmond was exempt from the authority of York (239, pp.3–4, 52 n.1, 60, 75). These apparent oddities probably reflect earlier patterns of Church government which had become fossilized; certainly the Canterbury peculiars, which were to survive till the nineteenth century, appear to comprise churches which had been granted to the see as early as Anglo-Saxon times.

In practical terms the existence of the peculiars probably did little to upset the day-to-day running of the Church. It does, however, highlight one of its characteristics, a concern with law, which predominated over any pastoral role. The language of the episcopal chancery tended to depict the bishop less as a shepherd of souls and more as a judge who corrected offenders. This was emphasized all the more by the position of the bishop's various deputies, his vicar-general, who exercised episcopal jurisdiction during his master's absence, and his official, who could hold courts on his behalf at all times. In fact there was an increasing tendency for these two posts to be amalgamated in the same person. These diocesan administrators were drawn from the upper class of the clergy, and might well aspire to ending their own days as bishops. They were the kind of men who were active in Convocation, and might well have served intermittently in royal government also. There was only one aspect of the bishop's work which these men could not perform, those spiritual duties which required episcopal orders, such as the conduct of confirmations or ordinations. For these tasks, recourse was had to a suffragan; many of these were friars who held sees *in partibus infidelium* or in parts of Ireland to which they could not obtain access. They were only occasionally important in themselves, and there are no cases where one was promoted to a territorial bishopric in his own right. They might even exercise their functions in more than one diocese, a clear indication that their place in the ecclesiastical order was as channels of spiritual grace rather than as rulers of other churchmen (205, p.24; 239, pp.40–1, 47–51).

It would not be an exaggeration to describe the clergy as two nations, those who ruled and those who obeyed, with little opportunity to move into the higher class. The Church certainly still offered a career to men of talent irrespective of origin, and the differentiation between the two nations must be sought in the merits of those in each; William of Wykeham in the fourteenth century and Thomas Wolsey in the early sixteenth both rose to high positions from humble backgrounds. These represent the peak of achievement, but there was substantial rewards for those who did not go quite so far, such as cathedral canonries, combined perhaps with a wealthy parochial benefice, which a successful man might serve by deputy while drawing the bulk of the emoluments. The division between the two nations came increasingly in our period to be drawn on the basis of education, which meant, essentially, training at a university. This is demonstrated most clearly by comparing some fourteenth-century bishops with those of the early Tudor period. When in 1389 Richard II reasserted his own authority at the expense of the Appellants, the key administrative positions of Chancellor and Treasurer were given to two bishops, Wykeham of Winchester and Brantingham of Exeter respectively. Neither of these were graduates, both having made their early careers in the royal administration and worked their way up from one office to another. If one wishes to trace their early lives, the best record is found in Tout's *Chapters in Administrative History* (198, iii, 235–9, 261). Brantingham had worked in the wardrobe, a department which was a particularly plentiful source of bishops in Edward III's reign, Wykeham was a clerk of the king's works and a surveyor of royal manors before he first achieved a major office of State as Keeper of the Privy Seal. Such office was generally an important step towards the episcopate.

Men with administrative experience did not, of course, disappear from the ranks of the bishops, but such administrators, by early Tudor times, had usually also had a university training. For information in their early careers the best source is Emden's *Biographical Register of the University of Oxford* or, in a few cases, the corresponding volume for Cambridge. The names of all the best known of the early Tudor bishops, Morton, Warham, Wolsey and Fox, may be found there (48). It is also worth stressing that after the completion of their studies, they did not begin in the lower reaches of the Civil Service and work their way up; when they obtained government office, the post was often a responsible one. The most conspicuous example of this was Wolsey; he made his early career in the Church rather than in administration, and his first appointment from the Crown was as chaplain to Henry VII. Under Henry VIII he was appointed royal almoner, and employed his talents to advance the King's secular concerns before he was appointed to any office of State. The first such office which he held was the chancellorship, when he was already archbishop of York and a cardinal. Possibly the growing secularization of the administration, which was noted above (Ch.30), was giving fewer opportunities to able clerks to make a career there. The decline in the number of canons of York who were described as *clerici regis* in the fifteenth century may reflect the same development, particularly as there too graduates secured a virtual monopoly of the chapter after 1435 (210). A study of the origins of the minor administrators in the early Tudor period, if this could be made, might show how far promotion was still possible for churchmen who chose a career in royal administration. It would appear, however, that it was only some of the major government posts which still fell to clerics, and that the lesser positions were increasingly filled by laymen. Possibly service to a bishop was a better avenue to ecclesiastical promotion than service to the King – certainly a number of future bishops had experience of this sort, and it is noteworthy that the active parish clergy did not provide recruits to the episcopate.

Because practical ability was the principal criterion for ecclesiastical advancement, it is hardly surprising that there were no great spiritual leaders among the bishops. Only one appointed during this period has been canonized, John Fisher of Rochester, and his sanctity was displayed primarily in his resistance to Henry VIII in the 1530s. In general, however, they were competent men and were able to do the tasks expected of them, and their failure was at the higher level of religious inspiration rather than in routine management of the Church's affairs. Men of ability were drawn from all social levels; we have already noted men from humble origins, and others, such as Chichele, Kemp and Morton came from the lesser landed class. The higher nobility, too, provided a number of bishops; the family of the earls of Devon, the Courtenays, produced three, including an arch-bishop of Canterbury, between 1370 and 1500, and the royal family itself two, both of whom eventually became cardinals, Henry Beaufort and Thomas Bour-chier, respectively a grandson and a great-grandson of Edward III. Such aristocratic prelates became increasingly prominent in the second half of the fourteenth century, and there seem to have been about twenty of them between 1350 and 1480 (232, p.23; 239, p.38). Their influence in major posts is shown by the fact that three of them, Courtenay, Arundel and Bourchier, held the see of Canterbury for about sixty-two years between 1381 and 1486. It is not quite clear why this occurred, nor indeed why aristocratic bishops tended to disappear after the advent of the Tudors. Between 1485 and 1529, only one man of noble rank received promotion to the episcopate, James Stanley, who became bishop of Ely in 1506; in addition, two bishops of noble family in 1485, Edmund Audley of Rochester and Peter Courtenay of Exeter, were translated to more important sees under Henry VII. This change in the social background of the episcopate may perhaps be explained by the attitude of the nobility. At a time when profits from land were decreasing, it could have been tempting for them to push their younger sons into the Church, exploiting their rights of patronage to give them a good start, in order to preserve undivided inheritances for the firstborn. As yields from land recovered, the incentive for this may have been less, and alternative possibilities, such as law, may have provided other forms of career for younger sons. Another possible explanation is that the Tudors were less willing to see major benefices being conferred on scions of the aristocracy than their predecessors had been, and recommended to the Pope for promotion men from lower in the social scale. The attainment of high ecclesiastical office by such cadets of the aristocracy was not, however, due merely to family influence, and there is no doubt about the ability of men such as William Courtenay or Beaufort. Courtenay was popular with his subjects in London, who in 1378 and 1379 wrote to Urban VI deprecating the proposal to make him a cardinal, because this would deprive the citizens of his personal influence. Where aristocratic prelates did have an advantage was that their promotion to high office came young – Courtenay received his first bishopric at twenty-five and Beaufort his at twenty-three. Similarly in the fifteenth century, Thomas Bourchier was also consecrated under the canonical age of thirty (48, i, 230–2; 232, p.23).

The limited number of bishoprics meant that the top prizes in the Church were few, but cathedral canonries were a good second best. Their value varied; at

Hereford and Lichfield even the richest were rarely assessed for taxation at more than £20 per annum, whereas over two-thirds of those at York exceeded this figure. In the 1291 assessment, the average annual value of the thirty-six prebends of York was £48, £8 more than that of the second wealthiest chapter in the country, Lincoln. The York prebends included the richest in England, Masham, valued at £166 13s. 4d., and various cathedral and diocesan offices were worth even more; the deanery of York was worth over £370, the treasurership £233 and the archdeaconry of Richmond £200. A comparison of the 1291 assessment with the *Valor Ecclesiasticus* of 1535 suggests that the values of cathedral benefices fell during the later Middle Ages, but they were still vastly greater than the emoluments of the ordinary parish priest.

Many of the more valuable canonries were held by absentees, usually men who were involved in episcopal or royal service. Among the holders of Masham in the fifteenth century were three future bishops, George Neville, John Shirwood and John Blythe, and the same was true of the second wealthiest of the York prebends, Wetwang, which numbered among its holders Lawrence Booth (though only for some six months before his promotion to Durham), John Arundel and Robert Stillington. Resident canons were only a small minority of the chapter; indeed only two who 'protested their residence' in fact moved on to higher positions, and they may well not have done so until they felt that their prospects of further promotion were small. In the 1370s the residentiaries numbered seven or eight, but this figure was never exceeded for the rest of the Middle Ages. It dropped to four early in the fifteenth century, and though there were short spells when it rose to six or even seven, before 1500 it fell again to three or even less (210).

The social backgrounds of the residentiary canons were as diverse as those of the men who became bishops. There were a few from the nobility and the knightly class, but a substantial number derived from obscure backgrounds and presumably owed their achievement to ability rather than to social connections. This is borne out by the high proportion of graduates among them – only one non-graduate can be found among those who took up residence at York after 1435. This had not been true of the late fourteenth century, when important royal clerks held a number of the canonries, but they disappear from the scene early in the fifteenth, perhaps because more government administrators were being drawn from the laity. Graduates also dominated another wealthy chapter, Lincoln. Of the 15 canons who undertook residence there between 1495 and 1520, the majority held higher degrees, and only 2 were non-graduates. The same is true of the non-residents at Lincoln, of whom there were 125 in the same period. At least 105 of these are known to have been graduates, nearly three-quarters of them with higher degrees. Only 7 were certainly not graduates; the origins of the other 13 are unknown. The canons of collegiate churches, as well as of cathedrals, were also largely drawn from the ranks of university-trained men, although their educational standards may have been slightly lower. In the Newarke College at Leicester, there were 20 graduates among the 32 clerks who held prebends between 1495 and 1520, but only about a third of these held degrees higher than MA (205, pp.157–63; 210).

The wealth of such men was often enhanced by their holding benefices in plurality. Before he became bishop of Winchester, William of Wykeham was the richest churchman in England outside the episcopate, holding the archdeaconry of Lincoln and ten prebends in various churches. In the early Tudor period another high royal servant, Christopher Urswick, was very similar. The bulk of his preferment came in the latter half of Henry VII's reign, and he continued to hold numerous benefices until his death in 1522. At that time, he held canonries in London, Salisbury, York and Southwell, archdeaconries in Wiltshire, Surrey and Oxford, and was chancellor of Exeter. Besides this he was rector of Hackney, of Felpham (Sussex) and Ashbury (Berkshire), and had a pension of £22 from the rectory of Gedney (Norfolk), which he had held between 1504 and 1519 (48, iii, 1935–36; 232, p.36).

By holding more than one parish church, Urswick was contravening the rule of canon law, although he presumably had secured dispensation for doing so.[1] If only one of a man's benefices involved cure of souls, no such legal problem arose, because canonries in cathedrals could lawfully be held in plurality. Indeed, as we have seen at York and Lincoln, absenteeism was normal, and the canon's duties in choir would be performed by a vicars-choral. These were a poorer group of men than the canons, and had probably worked their way up from being cathedral choristers or poor clerks. Promotion from the ranks of the vicars-choral was hard to find, and there are cases of a man remaining one for a quarter of a century. In a majority of cases, however, they were able to combine their choral duties with the tenure of one of the chantries in the cathedral, a position which could help to supplement their income (205, pp.164–5).

Chantry priests were the least fortunate members of the late medieval clergy. Vicars-choral, and some vicars who served parish churches on behalf of absentee rectors, might at least hope for some security of tenure, even if their emoluments were exiguous, but not all chantry priests could even hope for this, since, to an increasing degree in the fifteenth century, chantries were endowed only for a term of years and not in perpetuity. There was a statutory wage laid down for chaplains, of 7 marks (£4. 13s. 4d.) per annum, but in London at any rate the normal level of salary seems to have been nearer 10 marks in the fifteenth century, and sometimes more in the early sixteenth. In York, however, and elsewhere outside the capital, only a minority of chantry foundations were endowed above the statutory minimum (212, p.22; 240, p.209; 242, p.191).

Such impoverishment, and the existence of this clerical proletariat, probably affected the general religious life of the nation less than the inadequate standard of the men who served the 8,500 to 9,000 parish benefices, although one must not automatically assume that a lower level of education made the parish vicars and curates poorer pastors than their graduate absentee rectors might have been. Two studies of the parish clergy in pre-Reformation England, based on the records of different dioceses, give a very similar picture, so it is likely that the conditions described in them were fairly general (205; 212). It is clear that there were few cases of highly educated university men being actively engaged in the cure of souls, although some patrons did try to secure graduates for parish benefices. This was particularly striking in London, where the mayor and corporation tried to lay down regulations for the appointment of incumbents to two churches in their patronage, St Peter Cornhill (1445) and St Margaret Pattens (1478); in the former case it was stipulated that the person nominated should be a graduate in theology, in the latter, a poorer benefice, a master of arts or a theology graduate. The corporation also laid down that the person appointed should reside. An examination of those appointed suggests that at St Peter's the standard was attained immediately, and in the latter from the start of the sixteenth century.[2] London may have been exceptional in the number of graduates, particularly with degrees in the higher faculties, who held parish benefices, but even there one can see signs of an increase in the number of graduate incumbents during the fifteenth century. Possibly other city patrons followed the example of the corporation (240, pp.7, 10–11).

Outside London there was a similar increase in the number of graduates appointed to parishes. Between 1421 and 1431 only $3\frac{1}{2}$ per cent of those presented to benefices in the diocese of Lincoln were MAs, but by the years 1495–1520 the figure was $11\frac{1}{2}$ per cent. In both cases the figures can take no account of men who had proceeded no further than BA, or who had attended university without taking a degree, as they cannot be differentiated by the title of *magister*. How many fell into this category is hard to judge, but it is hardly surprising that men did not complete their courses; a BA required four years of study, an MA seven and a degree in a higher faculty fourteen, and study cost money for fees as well as for the necessities of life. The authorities, however, were concerned with raising educational standards, possibly under the pressure of lay criticism of their existing level. It is hard to say how great the educational shortcomings of the clergy were. An examination conducted by Bishop Stokesley of London in 1530 resulted in 22 out of the 56 men examined (39 per cent) being banned from practising as curates within the dioceses, and 6 more being allowed to remain only on condition of undertaking further study (205, pp.45–6; 212, pp.73–4, 79, 81). As 4 of these 28 were MAs one is left with doubts as to whether the educational attainments of even graduates were sufficient. Lay attacks on clerical ignorance must also be related to rising educational standards among the laity. While the clergy had a monopoly of learning, it was easier for them to overawe their parishioners, but the kind of literate layman who began to emerge in the late Middle Ages could judge for himself how well trained his parish priest was. If a layman was devout and concerned about the well-being of the Church, his natural reaction would be to demand a higher standard of clerical education than had previously been acceptable. The level of literacy in London may explain the pressure to secure graduates for the parish churches there.

The emoluments of the parochial clergy could hardly appeal to able and ambitious men, compared with those obtainable elsewhere in the Church. The wealthier benefices were often held by absentees, whose duties were performed by deputies receiving fixed salaries. A rector [F] with a right to the parish tithes might draw considerable revenues from it, although these, depending as they did on the parishioners' prosperity, could fall in times of economic recession. On balance, a graduate had a better opportunity of obtaining a rich living, but even he might have to be content with a fairly meagre one. Most benefices were meagre; it has been estimated that in the late Middle Ages three-quarters of the parish livings in the country were worth less than £15 per annum and half less than £10. Assistant clergy, such as chaplains, were even worse off: 100 out of 166 (60 per cent) of the chaplains in the archdeaconry of Stafford in 1525 received only £4. A beneficed clerk, with possession of tithes, might appear to be well endowed, but his income could easily be eroded by various obligations, such as that of maintaining the fabric of the chancel in his church. Where priests were on a fixed stipend, their standard of living could be affected by external factors, such as the increasing extent of clerical taxation from 1450, which became more severe under the Tudors, and, in the 1520s, a general rise in the cost of living. The willingness of men to turn up to funerals where small doles were paid to priests who attended suggests that many of them felt the need of such supplementary benefit. A recorded case from 1525, when eighty priests came, and were apparently given doles, even although money had been left for only thirty, suggests that even small sums were sought after. The tendency of the clergy to insist on their financial rights, and the dues payable to them by the laity, may have been prompted, at least in part, by genuine need. Demands for mortuary payments were particularly resented, and the notorious case of Richard Hunne in London (Ch.38) was not unique. Such demands may have come particularly from the poorer clergy who could not compensate for the poverty of an individual benefice in the manner of a graduate pluralist. It is noteworthy that the proportion of graduate non-residents in the diocese of Lincoln ($35\frac{1}{2}$ per cent) was markedly greater than the proportion of university-trained incumbents who were appointed (205, pp.97, 138, 149; 212, pp.23–4, 36, 146, 155–6, 173–4).

The absence of a rector did not, of course, mean that a church was totally unprovided with services. Absolute absenteeism is rare, although there are cases when a church had not even a curate, such as St Mary Staining in London in 1440. More normal was the dependence on a deputy, who may have been conscientious in his task, and perhaps competent at it, but who was almost always less well educated than the rector. Some visitation records certainly show that a benefice was not necessarily neglected when it was served by a deputy. Where all was going well, there were no complaints which left a trace in the records, and only when parishioners complained that services were being neglected does evidence survive which suggests to the historian that the system provoked discontent (212, pp.65–7; 240, p.6). The very fact that the parishioners were prepared to voice their complaints may have put some pressure on the resident priest, whether he was the rector or a deputy, to fulfill at least his basic pastoral obligations, and although one can see lay protests as evidence of anti-clericalism, there is a danger of exaggerating its scale (Ch.38).

In general, the structure of the English Church in the late Middle Ages was well equipped to meet the demands made of it. It provided for the training and selection of able men to fill its high offices, and the smooth way in which it generally ran suggests that the hierarchy was well able to fulfill its tasks. Its weakness lay in the wide gap which existed between the higher and the lower clergy, with many of the latter living on or below the level of poverty, which might in turn compel them to make undue demands on the laity. It is true that there was some tension between clergy and laity, and criticism by the latter of low clerical standards, but much of the latter may have been due to the increasing level of literacy and learning in lay society and greater expectations of the same among churchmen rather than to any decline in the ability of the clergy themselves.

---

1. The papal registers, which could throw light on whether or not he had obtained dispensations to hold more than one benefice, are not in print after 1492.
2. The names of the incumbents in G. Hennessy's *Novum Repertorium Parochiale Londiniense* (1898) have been checked against A. B. Emden's *Registers* of Oxford and Cambridge graduates (47; 48; 49). Three of the rectors of St Peter's came from each university between 1445 and the Reformation; there were three Oxford graduates at St Margaret's after 1506. St Peter's was a much wealthier parish; a tax assessment of 1428 rated it at £20 per annum and St Margaret's at only 5 marks (£3 6s. 8d.). In Henry VIII's time the respective valuations of the two parishes were £39 5s. 8d. and £10.

CHAPTER 35

Church and State. I – England and the Papacy

The phrase 'Church–State relations' possesses two distinct, although not totally different, connotations. Firstly, it can be applied to the political and administrative bonds which linked the universal Church, and its central government, to the churches in the individual nations of Christendom. When disputes arose between popes and secular rulers, the clergy's sympathies might well lie with the latter rather than with the former. Secondly, it refers to the relationship between the secular and spiritual powers within individual countries. The common factor in these was the clergy in particular countries, who had to face the problems of serving two masters, whose aims might be very different but who might both be determined to assert their authority over their subjects. These topics will provide the substance of the next two chapters.

In the late Middle Ages the balance of power between central and national authority in the Church was never clearly defined, although attempts were made in concordats between the Papacy and individual countries to draw working lines of demarcation. The theoretical claims of the popes had been developed since the Gregorian reform movement of the late eleventh century, and their practical authority had increased between then and the thirteenth century, particularly in the legal sphere and in the area of ecclesiastical appointments. The papal Curia became a final court of appeal in matters of canon law, and could also provide dispensations from it, it was recognized as having the right to pronounce on disputed Church appointments, and, because administration was costly, it also developed the right to levy taxation. In such matters as appeals, appointments and taxation it was hardly surprising that the Papacy came into conflict with the lay power. Kings could reasonably expect a say in naming the holders of major church offices, for such dignitaries held lands by feudal tenure, and had similar obligations of loyalty to the Crown as lay feudal tenants. The most bitter conflicts between England and the Papacy were probably the crisis over Archbishop Becket in Henry II's reign and the Canterbury election dispute under John, which led first to an interdict on the kingdom and later to the King's excommunication.

Many of these disputed matters were not formally resolved, but in practice one can see that a working system developed, as pope and king alike recognized the desirability of a measure of compromise. Agreement was tacit rather than explicit, and there were still intermittent crises, but these should not obscure the fact that on many practical matters there was often substantial co-operation. The Pope might theoretically claim supremacy over all Christians, but could still appreciate that little was to be gained by alienating the secular ruler, while a king could realize that with papal goodwill he could enhance his authority over an important section of his subjects. Indeed, the fact that some English late medieval anti-papalism emanated from Parliament suggests that the laity, as well as the clergy, might see dangers in too close an *entente* between the King and the Pope.

Both masters of the English Church were concerned with maintaining their authority over it, but their mutual relations were affected at any particular moment by external considerations. For this reason, the most satisfactory historical divisions in Anglo-papal relations are those determined by political factors, especially those affecting the Pope. Immediately before the start of our period and in its early years, when the Papacy was still at Avignon, fears that a French pope might be hostile to England soured relations with it. The outbreak of the Great Schism in 1378, and the consequent rivalries of contending claimants to the Papacy, shifted the balance of power firmly in favour of the secular rulers, who could play off rival contenders against each other and seek favours as the price of loyalty. Even after unity was restored to the Papacy, through the action of general councils of the Church, the claims which these made to authority over the Pope set some curbs on its recovery of authority, and the political needs of the fifteenth-century popes meant that they were always concerned with retaining the goodwill of at least some of the major princes of Christendom. Such goodwill became increasingly important after the outbreak of the Italian wars in 1494, which were to stress the political role of the Papacy at the expense of its ecclesiastical responsibilities (243).

Between the late fourteenth century and the start of the English Reformation, there were only two periods of really acute tension between the Crown and the Papacy, and in both of these the critical issue was one of ecclesiastical appointments. Both periods must be seen against a background of a number of 'anti-papal' statutes enacted in the middle of the century, those of Provisors (1351) and of Praemunire (1353, 1365). These were concerned respectively with the filling of benefices by papal provision, the procedure by which normal patrons or electors lost their right of appointment, which passed to the Pope, and the hearing of legal cases in courts outside the realm. The letter of the law of 1351 stated that men receiving provisions should be imprisoned, and that if the normal patron, or the electors in the case of benefices where the appointment was made by election (such as the monks in a monastery or the canons of a cathedral), were afraid to proceed because of the Pope's action, the right of patronage would pass to the King. The first Statute of Praemunire forbade cases to be taken to courts outside the realm in matters of which the King's courts should have cognizance, and in the second statute the papal court was particularly mentioned. The rules appear rigorous, but their implementation was less so; they tended to be held in reserve to prevent royal rights from being overridden, but they were often quietly ignored by the King if the Pope was prepared to provide royal protégés at the expense of men appointed to benefices by traditional canonical means (55, p.28; 219, p.192). This was most obvious in appointments to bishoprics, where the Church's two masters showed a notable tendency to co-operate, and the influence exercised by each of them depended on the immediate circumstances operating at any particular moment.

The Papacy made two major attempts to have the offending statutes annulled, the first during the Schism, in the early 1390s, and the second after its end, in the

1420s. In view of papal weakness *vis-à-vis* the secular power, the former attempt seems at first sight surprising, but it becomes more comprehensible in the light of tensions which developed into an open quarrel over a period of years. In 1388, Urban VI, in need of money, tried to obtain financial aid from the English clergy; in September of the same year this provoked a sharp reaction from Parliament, which forbade men to seek favours at the court of Rome. This is probably a good indication of popular attitudes, because at this date the King was temporarily powerless after the Appellants' victory in the previous winter, but the Appellants themselves were coming under attack from the Commons. Urban retaliated by attempting to reserve benefices and by appointing his own men to them, even to bishoprics. The Pope's death and the succession of Boniface IX in 1389 did not prevent the crisis from intensifying, even although the new Pope annulled the reservations. Parliament, which was markedly more anti-papal than the Crown, reiterated old legislation against papal encroachments, prohibiting provisions and imposing severe penalties on those who sought them, or who even supported those seeking them. Distrust of royal authority was shown by an attempt to ensure that the great officers of State would not apply the statute leniently. The Commons went too far for the King, who had by this time recovered his influence, and he refused to accept their demand that the papal collector should be expelled within forty days and that his successor should not be accepted unless he were English. However, the King's Council was prepared to protest to Rome about the abuses which had resulted from the Pope's fiscal demands. The door to negotiation remained open, and it was perhaps rather surprising that in February 1391 the Pope annulled the statutes of Provisors as contrary to the liberties of the Church (150, pp.134–6; 233, pp.305–19).

Surprisingly, however, this had little result. Over the next two years negotiations continued and, even more significantly, there was no marked reduction in the number of English clerks who had recourse to the Curia, while some men who had obtained papal provisions before the date of the statute were allowed to retain their benefices. Rumours, however, were circulated that the Pope was preparing further reprisals against clerks who had been promoted through royal action, notably that he might translate to foreign sees those bishops who were the King's close councillors. Whether or not these rumours were true, they united the English clergy and laity against the Pope; Parliament retaliated by approving a new Statute of Praemunire (1393), which forbade papal citations, sentences of excommunication and bulls of provision from entering England. Boniface had to accept the check to his authority – he dared not drive Richard into the anti-pope's camp at a time when English foreign policy was moving towards peace with France, which supported the Avignon claimant – and before long negotiations were resumed. The statutes were not enforced vigorously, and Parliament was prepared to let the King negotiate for modifications to them. Ultimately these exchanges led to a concordat in 1398, which was largely concerned with how benefices should be filled. Boniface agreed to confirm candidates for bishoprics if the King notified him in time of the man whom he wished to have appointed. The Pope was conceded the right to appoint his own candidate to every third vacancy in major cathedral dignities, though it was stipulated that no foreigner, other than a cardinal, should benefit from such provisions, An arrangement even more favourable to Rome was made for lesser benefices, that for the next two years the Pope should have the first right of collation and the ordinary patron the second. This agreement. however, seems to have lapsed after Richard's fall, and in Henry IV's second Parliament in 1401, the Statute of Provisors was extended. About 1409–10 too, Henry IV may have hinted to the Pope that he did not want any relaxation of the statutes dealing with provisions (36, ii, 121; 215, p.75; 233, pp.326–34, 349).

The second major crisis in Anglo-papal relations came after the end of the Schism. It is hardly surprising that Martin V, who was concerned with rebuilding papal authority, was interested in the crucial issue of ecclesiastical appointments. His position in the 1420s was clearly stronger than Boniface's thirty years before: not only was his own title unchallenged but England was facing the problems of France and of Henry VI's factious minority. Indeed Martin began to reassert his position, by promoting candidates other than those chosen by the King, even before Henry V's death, but there is no evidence of any deep ill-will between England and Rome at the outset of the new reign. The lack of firm royal control played an important part in the deterioration of relations between England and Rome in the ensuing years, as various individual churchmen tried to advance their own interests at the Curia without ensuring that the minority government approved of their actions. The bitterness of the later struggle also owed something to personal tensions between the Pope and Archbishop Chichele; the latter complained that Martin was infringing the traditional privileges of his see and refused to implement a provision of the Pope's nephew to the archdeaconry of his cathedral. At first, from 1423, Martin seems to have tried to secure the repeal of the Statute of Provisors by negotiation, but a series of difficulties over episcopal appointments complicated the issue by creating ill-will in England. He provided the ambitious Bishop Fleming of Lincoln to the see of York, probably as a reward for his work on the Pope's behalf at the Council of Siena, but this was not allowed to stand and Fleming had to be translated back to Lincoln. The English Council and the episcopate were divided, and the political problems of Bedford, anxious to secure papal support for the English position in France (Ch.21), were a further complicating factor. Bedford's willingness to compromise with Martin for this reason led him to make concessions to the Pope on appointments (207).

In 1426 Martin began to increase his pressure to have the statutes of Provisors abolished, and a new crisis occurred when he suspended Archbishop Chichele's legatine powers in 1427. This action, however, merely stiffened English resistance. Admittedly, Chichele and his fellow archbishop, John Kemp, presented Martin's case against the statute in Parliament in 1428, but this had no effect – they probably had not expected that it would. The Pope abandoned his measures against the statute and even restored Chichele's legatine authority. Clearly he felt that his attempt to have the acts revoked was futile, because he made no further effort to renew it. His successor, Eugenius IV, was too deeply involved in his struggle with the Council of Basel to be concerned with England, and later popes appear to have acquiesced in the situation which they inherited. The Curia did not entirely forget about the legislation – a question was raised about the Statute of Praemunire in 1506 – but no action was taken (207; 219, p.220). Presumably the popes of this period felt that they stood to gain more co-operation with the English Crown than by asserting a theoretical authority over the Church. Not least, they had a financial interest in maintaining good relations. Acquiescence in the candidates approved by the King could be recompensed by the speedy payment of dues liable for the bulls of provision.

These tensions over appointments existed quite independently of the political complications resulting from the division in the Western Church between 1378 and 1417, although there is no doubt that the secular power was better able to take a tough line in any controversy when the Pope was under threat from a rival. The allegiance of individual countries to particular popes was determined essentially by political motives, and it is noteworthy how closely the lines of demarcation between the Roman and Avignonese obediences during the Schism corresponded to the political alignments of the Anglo-French War. French support for the dissident cardinals and their pope, Clement VII, led England to adhere to Urban VI, and although the rebels sent a mission to plead their case, its arguments fell on deaf ears. The leader of the embassy, the dean of St Emilion at Bordeaux, and hence a subject of the English Crown, was imprisoned for twenty months and was not released until he had abjured the Schism. There was considerable English enthusiasm for Urban; even Wyclif spoke favourably of him for a time, saying that he was a true pope, whereas Clement VII was a disciple of Lucifer. Urban showed his appreciation of English support by offering a cardinalate to Bishop Courtenay of London. In fact the bishop did not accept it, possibly because he did not wish to leave his see where he was evidently popular, but another Englishman, the Benedictine Adam Easton, was then granted the red hat (233, pp.56–67).

There is little doubt that throughout Christendom the Schism was regarded as a scandal, but the difficulty lay in finding an acceptable way of ending it. As long as the secular powers could not agree on a method of solution, the temptation was always present to try to end it by force, and the rival popes were always willing to bless the political and military activities of their supporters. A papal legate played an important part in the negotiations between England and the Emperor Wenceslas which culminated in Richard II's marriage to Anne of Bohemia, and papal support was forthcoming for English military adventures on the Continent. The futile campaign in Flanders under Bishop Despenser of Norwich in 1383 was given the status of a crusade, and was partially financed by the alms of the faithful. Later in the decade, the Pope also blessed John of Gaunt's campaigns in Spain, but the Flemish disaster seems to have discouraged the English from supporting the expedition with voluntary contributions (55, p.431; 233, pp.140–1, 149–50, 235).

Another reflection of papal desires to remain on good terms with the secular power can be seen in the ease with which politically unacceptable prelates could be removed from positions of power. In 1388 Urban VI complied with the wishes of the Appellants to translate Archbishop Neville of York and Bishop Rushook of Chichester, both of them supporters of the King. Neville was nominated to St Andrews, then owing obedience to the schismatic Pope at Avignon, and Rushook to the Irish see of Kilmore. Various of the wealthier sees were filled by partisans of the magnates, with York being given to Bishop Arundel of Ely, brother of the Appellant earl, Nine years later, during Richard's revenge, Boniface IX meted out to Arundel, whom he had only recently promoted to Canterbury, the same fate as had been inflicted on Neville, and this time it was the King's adherents who received episcopal promotion (233, pp.303–4, 340–5).

The close connection between the Schism and international politics is clearly shown by the way in which Anglo-French diplomacy in the 1390s was often as concerned with solving the problems of the Church as with ending hostilities between the two kingdoms. At the practical level it was possible for English and French to share in the campaign against the Turks which ended in disaster at Nicopolis in 1396, and it is possible that if Richard II had not been deposed, Anglo-French pressure might have brought about an earlier Church council than that of Pisa. Certainly the University of Oxford seems to have moved much closer to that of Paris in its attitude to applying compulsion to the rival popes to make them stand down, and it is unlikely that this would have been possible without the easing of Anglo-French hostilities.

Popular concern over the Schism was reflected in a request by the Commons to Henry IV in 1401 to use his influence to unite the Church, though without any indication of how he should do it and with a stipulation that it should involve no great cost. In 1402, when the Chancellor reported optimistically, and prematurely, that unity was in sight, this proviso on cost was renewed. This interest in ecclesiastical affairs was later reflected by a willingness to participate in the general councils of the Church, although the total contribution of Englishmen to conciliar activity was, with one or two exceptions, fairly limited. Support for a council remained closely linked to residual distrust of the French, even after 1407 when the news of Gregory XII's election seems to have provoked the feeling that drastic measures would be required to end a Schism which was being perpetuated by the action of the cardinals in electing a successor to Innocent VII. The desire to restore unity in the Church was also linked with a wish for reform, this being nowhere more marked than in the activity of Bishop Hallum of Salisbury, who led the English delegation at the councils of Pisa and Constance, at the latter of which he played an important role. At Basel the English were less prominent, perhaps because the Council's decision to abandon the system of voting by nations led to them being instructed to absent themselves from its proceedings. Their withdrawal may have been prompted by fear that the French might be able to exploit their greater numbers to obtain ecclesiastical support for their position in the war. The failure of the Council of Basel cleared the way for a further recovery of the papal position, although it was never to be as strong as it had been before 1378. The ghost of conciliar claims to supreme power in the Church could still be raised to haunt the Papacy in times of crisis as late as the early sixteenth century (215, pp.59, 70–8; 216, p.136; 243, Ch.1).

Most later fifteenth-century popes accepted the limitations on their authority, although as far as England was concerned they did so tacitly rather than by such formal agreements, as those of 1375, 1398 and 1418. None of these concordats had provided for a comprehensive settlement of the problem in Anglo-papal relations; the nearest approach to this was the agreement of 1398, discussed earlier in this chapter. The 1375 settlement was concerned essentially with immediate matters; the English allowed the Pope to raise a subsidy of about £9,000 from the clergy, and in return Gregory XI made various concessions to English clerks who had obtained benefices contrary to attempted papal collations. Various legal suits between royal and papal nominees were settled in favour of the former, the majority of whom, significantly, were clerks in the royal administration. Arrangements were also made for cases due to be heard in the papal courts to be heard at Bruges if war made it difficult for the litigants to go to Avignon. Also, although no formal statement was made on the subject, it was probably not mere coincidence that several papal provisions to bishoprics and translations of bishops in 1375 were of men whose advancement was acceptable to the Crown (124, pp.46–9).

The concordat at the end of the Council of Constance in 1418 did not touch on fundamental matters, such as appointments to benefices and the related issue of annate payments, but was concerned with the control of indulgences, limitations on the appropriation of parish churches to religious houses and control of dispensations to hold benefices in plurality. It was also stated that the cardinals should be appointed from various nations of Christendom, and that Englishmen should obtain a share of posts at the Curia. This concordat was much narrower in scope than those agreed with the other nations of Christendom, probably because it was felt unnecessary to lay down more precise rules than those which were already being tacitly followed. In practice, both the College of Cardinals and the Curia became increasingly dominated by Italians during the next century.

The three issues which were fundamental to relations between England and Rome between the Schism and the Reformation were all familiar – appointments to benefices, taxation and jurisdiction. As we have seen, the first gave trouble for a time, but eventually ceased to be contentious. Taxation, too, had given rise to troubles in the past, although by conceding a share to the King the thirteenth-century popes had usually been able to secure some money in taxes from the clergy. In the late fourteenth century, the financial demands of Gregory XI gave rise to severe criticism, not least from Wyclif, and in 1388 the Commons petitioned that anyone who sought to levy a tax for Urban VI without royal assent should be regarded as a traitor. Later papal attempts to levy such taxes were unsuccessful (53, pp.205–6; 124, pp.12–14, 167; 219, pp.134–5).

Direct taxation of the clergy was not, however, the only way in which the Pope obtained money from England. There were also the ancient payment called Peter's pence, *census* paid by monasteries which were exempt from episcopal control, procurations to the papal collector and, most important of all, payments of services and annates on benefices filled by papal provision. The extent of these last provoked some criticism; complaints were made in Parliament in 1404 about excessive sums being demanded, and it was enacted that those who paid more than the amounts customarily due should forfeit their goods to the King. The complaints about annates and services seem to have declined in the fifteenth century, although the amount of money leaving the country may actually have increased during the period. In addition to the yields of these specific taxes, the

Papacy also secured some money from voluntary payments by the faithful, either in the form of fees paid by those seeking dispensations or as offerings for indulgences [F]. Although these were normally granted to benefit ecclesiastical institutions in England, the papal collector might take his share, as indeed might the King, either directly or through imposing a tax on the export of money. The Pope in fact received far less from the English clergy than did the King; it has been estimated that the ratio of the Crown's gains to the Pope's was in the region of $2\frac{1}{2} : 1$ (36, ii. 148–9, 223; 237).

In legal matters, the statutes of Praemunire provided a barrier which could be applied to excessive papal interference. However, those acts referred only to matters within the cognizance of the royal courts, and there were other aspects of ecclesiastical jurisdiction where the rights of the Papacy were never challenged. A glance at the *Calendars of Papal Registers* shows the range of the papal power to dispense from the normal provisions of canon law and the favours which popes could still grant. Litigants at the Curia were served by proctors [F], some of whom spent considerable time there. The letter-book of one proctor, William Swan, is most informative on the tasks which they performed and the life which they led. He went first to Rome in 1404 or 1405, and followed the perambulations of the papal court in the ensuing years, remaining loyal to Gregory XII after the Council of Pisa. After a spell in England, probably from 1411 to 1415, he rejoined the Curia at Constance and remained with it, apart from a brief visit to England in 1418–19, until about 1429. In his later years he became involved in official missions, and served as Archbishop Chichele's proctor, but much of his work was concerned with private litigation. Later in the century the office of king's proctor at the Curia anticipated the post of resident ambassador there. Early in the sixteenth century a number of Italian prelates were given English bishoprics as non-residents, to reward them for their assistance in maintaining diplomatic representation in Rome (216, pp.60–9, 81; 219, p.222; 243, p.102).

Special envoys might also be sent to deal with legal questions. In the middle of the fifteenth century a dispute broke out in London over the payments due in tithes from the citizens to their parish clergy, and the civic authorities sent orators to Rome to defend a citizen who had been condemned in the diocesan court for non-payment, clearly regarding this as a test case. They were able to secure the suspension of the sentence, although the question at issue was referred back to England with instructions to reach a compromise (244). There was never any question of the Curia's right to hear the case, as it undoubtedly fell within the competence of clerical jurisdiction. Among the important matters which came within the province of the higher Church courts were, of course, matrimonial issues, many of which might involve the papal power of dispensation. It was just such an issue, involving the highest in the land, which provided the spark to ignite the controversy between England and Rome under Henry VIII.

This crucial dispute must also, however, be seen in a political context. From the outbreak of the Italian wars in 1494, the political concerns of the Papacy involved it deeply in the struggles of the great European powers. Initially, this had not seriously affected Anglo-papal relations, presumably because Henry VII had, as far as possible, avoided Continental entanglements and remained on good terms with the Pope. He had good cause to be friendly, because the Pope had given him valuable support, granting a dispensation for his marriage to Elizabeth of York and threatening anathema against those who disturbed his succession (219, p.220). Under Henry VIII, Wolsey, too, was generally concerned with maintaining friendly relations with Rome (Ch.28). The growing English involvement in Europe did not, therefore, raise any real problems which might upset the status quo in matters of ecclesiastical administration. Indeed, since Henry's religious sentiments were conservative, the outbreak of the Lutheran crisis in Germany might well, in normal times, have drawn England and Rome closer. But circumstances in the 1520s were not normal; Henry was concerned about the succession and had developed a passion for Anne Boleyn. He was bent on obtaining an annulment of his marriage to Catherine of Aragon, but just at the time that he opened his suit at the papal court, Pope Clement VII fell into the hands of the imperial forces, and ceased to be a free agent. He procrastinated in the hope of avoiding trouble, but Henry's patience became exhausted and as a means of browbeating Rome he determined to employ his effective power over the Church in England.

CHAPTER 36

Church and State. II – *Ecclesia Anglicana*

The term *Ecclesia Anglicana* was frequently used in the late Middle Ages to describe the English Church. It did not imply, of course, that the Church within England was in any way separated from the rest of Christendom, and the problems discussed in the last chapter clearly show the closeness of the ties between England and the Papacy; indeed disputes over the relative powers which the King and the Pope could exercise reflect the basic assumption that the English Church was, in different ways, subject to them both, However, there were ways in which the 'chirch of the royaume of England' had its own independent traditions, and even if its canon law, represented by the statutes of successive archbishops, was only supplementary to the law of the universal Church, when the latter was uncertain, it still was at times distinctive from the law of the Church in other parts of Christendom (12, pp.119–20; 27, p.70b). The Church also had to face the implications of royal authority; in financial matters, kings' demands for taxes imposed considerable burdens, and the relations of the Church courts to the secular power, especially where churchmen possessed any privileges, gave rise to problems. At the same time, it must be recognized that the secular and spiritual powers were by no means always mutually hostile, but that they could support each other in enforcing the law over their subjects.

The theoretical position of the English Church is indicated in the work of one of its most distinguished writers of the period, the canonist William Lyndwood, whose *Provinciale*, completed in 1430, provides a full picture of the operation of canon law in England. This comprises a collection of the constitutions of the province of Canterbury, accompanied by a lengthy gloss, and much of what these contain would have been applicable in the northern province also. Lyndwood was well qualified to write such a work, because he was a distinguished clerical administrator, and as he also served the Crown, he could speak with authority on matters of Church and State. He was Archbishop Chichele's chancellor from 1414 to 1417, and later his official, and served as prelocutor in the Convocation of Canterbury on five occasions between 1419 and 1426. He had been a king's clerk as early as 1402, was regularly involved in overseas embassies and presumably was still closely involved with secular government, for in 1432 he was appointed Keeper of the Privy Seal, retaining the post till 1443. The range of his experience makes him a good witness for historians (47, pp.380–1).

Some of his most interesting statements refer to relations between the secular and spiritual powers within England; a most significant inclusion in the work is Edward I's writ *circumspecte agatis*, which appears in the section describing which courts were appropriate for dealing with particular matters. In fact the gloss says little of importance, but it is striking that a churchman and a canonist was willing to accept a royal command as authoritative in limiting the jurisdictional competence of the Church courts. Churchmen clearly recognized a substantial measure of lay authority over themselves, because Lyndwood also discusses when the secular power could act against individual clerks, If a churchman committed an offence which was a matter of public law, such as robbery or sedition, and there was a danger that he would take refuge in flight, the lay judge was entitled to detain him, if his clerical judge could not be found, although he was to be surrendered to his ordinary [F] for punishment. If, however, the offence was a private one, only the aggrieved party, or a close relative, could make the arrest without incurring the pains of excommunication. Such permission to take custody of an offending clerk seems to have been particularly forthcoming in cases of sexual offences. In other circumstances, a layman could not arrest a clerk without a mandate from an ecclesiastical judge. Even although such actions were permitted, Lyndwood made it clear that laymen should not have the power to pass judgments on clerks, nor the power to interfere in matters arising out of their status as spiritual men (27, pp.92b, 96a–97b, 129b).

The Church authorities claimed assistance from the lay power in enforcing their jurisdictional rights, notably by means of writs of signification. By these, bishops could notify the Chancellor of the names and offences of persons who had not submitted after excommunication, and ask that they be arrested. This sanction could be employed only as a last resort, against those who were declared contumacious in failing to come to court when cited or for not obeying its decisions; it could not be applied immediately after excommunication. Such contumacy could arise out of a wide range of original offences, drawn from both the broad divisions of ecclesiastical jurisdictions, 'ex officio', namely prosecutions by the Church authorities for some moral or spiritual offence, and 'instance', pleas brought by one party against another. The writ was employed against a wide range of people, from a broad cross-section of society, including clerks, although the majority of offenders were lay (27, pp.264b–265a, 351a–352a; 221, pp.43–6, 50–2, 62–5).

The use of signification to bring an offender to heel seems to have declined in the later Middle Ages, if the figures compiled from surviving dated writs correspond, even approximately, to the numbers actually issued at particular times. In the first quarter of our period (1370–1409), there were 3,982 recorded cases, an average of just under 100 a year, from 1410 to 1449 the figure dropped to 1,175, averaging below 30. The middle years of the century saw little change, but from about 1470 there was a further pronounced drop, which lowered the figures for 1450–89 to 828, averaging just over 20, and those for 1490–1529 to 436, averaging just under 11. The very high figures for the late fourteenth century, much greater than in the years immediately preceding, although lower than those for the late thirteenth century, were probably increased markedly by the employment of the writ against clergy who failed to pay taxes to the King. The Church formally granted a tax in 1371, although in the previous year the King had tried to levy one without consent. In these circumstances, it is noteworthy that the higher clergy, who possessed jurisdictional power, were generally willing to cooperate with the lay authorities against recalcitrant fellow churchmen. Not less than 1,500 clerics were excommunicated and signified for arrest in the next thirty-five years, until the middle of Henry IV's reign, as a result of their persistent resistance to the subsidy levies. Thereafter the sanction was used more rarely for this offence, although Henry VIII was to employ it again, albeit less widely, in the early 1530s. Even apart from this particular type of case, there was still a decline in the number of writs over the period as a whole, so it is possible that the ecclesiastical authorities may have become more chary of seeking lay support to reinforce their own power in the late fifteenth and early sixteenth centuries. Although signification survived the Reformation, it virtually died out during the sixteenth century (221, pp.56–8, 68, 156–7).

The fact that the majority of those signified as excommunicated were laymen is a reminder that canon law did not concern only the clergy. It was recognized that the Church possessed full jurisdictional rights in certain matters, and its exercise of them is shown in the surviving records of its courts. The enforcement of morality, particularly sexual, was one of the major ways in which Church law impinged on the laity, but as the teachings of the Church were the foundations of social morality generally, there was little reason to expect anything but co-operation in this field between it and the lay power. Certainly the ex officio proceedings in the Church courts were dominated by sexual offences; a sample year (1474) examined in the records of the Canterbury diocesan courts showed that over two-thirds of the cases heard fell into this category, and approximately half the cases in the London Church courts between 1496 and 1500 were of the same type (240, p.261; 249, p.79).

Other offences, which were less concerned with fundamental morality and more with Church law, such as failure to attend church or unlawful trading on Sunday, were heard in a lower ecclesiastical court, such as that of the archdeacon; more serious offences, such as heresy, were reserved to the bishop or the archbishop, and are normally recorded in the episcopal registers. Even in matters such as these, there was little serious tension between clergy and laity. In 1392 Bishop Braybrook of London issued a warning against working on Sundays and feast days, and in 1413 Archbishop Arundel commanded the barbers of London to close their shops on Sunday. The sanction laid down by Arundel should be noted, for the penalty was financial rather than spiritual, and it was stated that this was thought more likely to have effect than the threat of excommunication. The involvement of the laity in enforcing the Church's rules was shown by the fact that the fine was not payable to the Church, but was to be divided between the city authorities and the wardens of the barbers' company. Even more indicative of the laity's co-operation with the Church in such matters is their willingness to issue decrees on it themselves; the wardens of the London grocers did so in 1429 and the city common council in 1444 (240, pp.256–7). Such co-operation, however, while preventing the appearance of jurisdictional disputes, did not necessarily enforce Sunday observance; prosecutions in the Church courts and the recurrence of measures commanding it both point to considerable disregard of this particular law.

Another area of public conduct where clergy and laity shared a common attitude was in the suppression of usury. This was prosecuted both in the Church courts and by the secular authorities, and could also be the subject of an instance suit. In London there were civic proclamations against the offence, although there is little evidence that they had any marked degree of success. The Canterbury act-books contain only a small number of such cases, but it is not clear if this reflects a lower incidence of the offence in a predominantly rural area, or merely a lack of concern with it (240, pp.252–3; 249, p.87).

In these matters, therefore, there was reasonable co-operation between the secular and the ecclesiastical authorities. Even more remarkable is the fact that the Church courts compensated for weaknesses in the secular administration of justice. The great bulk of instance proceedings in the Canterbury courts are described as perjury, but closer examination suggests most of these cases originated as petty debts, and that the broken oath (which gave rise to the perjury charge) was a pledge to pay money to a creditor (249, pp.84, 89–91). Similar figures can also be recorded in other dioceses. Under the early Tudors there seems to have been a decline in such suits, possibly because a new remedy, the action called *assumpsit*, was being increasingly employed in the common law courts. The rise in the number of these cases recorded in the King's Bench plea rolls in the second decade of the sixteenth century occurred at precisely the same time as the decline in the figures of perjury cases in the Church courts. The growth of secular jurisdiction on obligations had nothing to do with the Henrician Reformation, but antedated it by a number of years.

Canon law, of course, was concerned not only with spiritual offences but also, more generally, with offences committed by churchmen, and the claims of the lay power to punish criminous clerks had been a major issue of controversy in the twelfth century. Later, the privilege of benefit of clergy, which allowed the convicted clerk to be handed over to his bishop instead of undergoing the full penalties of the law, was gradually clarified. Although there is no doubt that the practice was open to abuse, it may be fair to say that in the case of some lesser felonies, justice may not have been entirely ill served by the mitigation of some of the rigours of harsh law; clerks were not subjected to capital penalties, although they might be sentenced to imprisonment for life with forfeiture of both lands and chattels. The privilege did not extend to all crimes; high treason was excluded, and petty crimes or misdemeanours were 'non-clergyable', as were offences heard in manorial courts. Nor were clerks normally exempt from civil suits, apart from being protected against imprisonment for debt. The extent of this exemption was defined in the middle of Edward III's reign, and was further clarified by statute under Henry IV (211, pp.58–9).

Restrictions on benefit of clergy were also concerned with defining who were entitled to it. As early as 1300 it was no longer possible to equate an ability to read with membership of the clerical order, although the use of a reading test to determine a man's 'clergy' survived for much longer. With the spread of literacy in the later Middle Ages, however, the use of reading ability as the criterion for determining the punishment to be inflicted for a crime became increasingly unacceptable. Although nothing seems to have come of a petition against it in 1455, this was a pointer to later developments. The secular power was able to take the initiative in restricting the privilege; already under Edward IV the secular courts were determining the validity of claims to be clerks, and under the early Tudors there were various statutory restrictions of the right, applying both to persons and to offences. The most important of these, in 1489, removed the full privilege from those who had not been once admitted to a benefice. Such men, if convicted, were to be branded on the thumb, and were not to be allowed to plead with their clergy a second time. The restriction did not apply to those genuinely of clerical status, but any churchman who was brought to trial a second time, after having previously pleaded his clergy, was required within a set time to produce his letters of ordination (36, ii. 538; 211, pp.100–1, 118).

Some of the other restrictive Acts show clearly how far the privilege had come to be extended. One of 1491 declared that soldiers who had deserted the King's army in a way which would be adjudged felonious were not to benefit from it, and another of 1512 made the same provision for those committing a murder or felony in a church, chapel or hallowed place, or highway robbery, or robbery or murder in a man's house, 'suche as ben within holy orders only excepte' (36, ii. 549, iii. 49). This last clause is particularly revealing. These statutes still protected offenders who were genuinely churchmen, but no longer gave a way of escape to those who had merely been tonsured or received minor orders, or who were assumed to be clerks because they were literate.

Although legal penalties might be mitigated, there were other deterrents to priestly misconduct. In London, priests found guilty of sexual offences were exposed to public ridicule, being led through the city with minstrels, and having their misconduct proclaimed at the street corners. It was probably in the late fourteenth century that a priest who was three times taken with a woman was compelled to forswear the city permanently. There is no evidence that the ecclesiastical authorities took any exception to these measures in the case of genuine offenders, although in the Convocation of 1439 allegations were made of churchmen being falsely indicted of various offences (21, iii. 282; 240, p.274). As far as the enforcement of public morality on layman and cleric alike was concerned, the Church seems to have accepted secular assistance within certain reasonable limits.

These limits involved recognition that certain ecclesiastical liberties had to be maintained, and that Church courts should not be subject to intimidation. Equally, it was recognized that the Church should support the lay power – excommunication could be imposed on those who disturbed the King's peace or withheld his rights. Difficulties could arise where clerical claims were challenged, and a notable instance of this could be found in the privilege of sanctuary, which was increasingly eroded in the century before the Reformation. There were two different kinds of sanctuary, the normal privilege of every parish church and churchyard to afford protection for forty days, during which time an offender might abjure the realm, and the more extensive rights enjoyed by various places which could afford permanent protection to fugitives. The former privilege was purely ecclesiastical, and in 1463 Archbishop Bourchier declared that lay officers who had been exceeding their powers in making arrests in consecrated places would *ipso facto* incur greater excommunication. The latter originally had no essentially ecclesiastical character; some of the liberties had been purely secular franchises which had enjoyed freedom from royal justice. The power of lay lords to hold these rights had, however, been gradually eroded, and although some survived, as in the Welsh Marches, the most important of the remaining liberties were held by churchmen. These sanctuaries were unpopular, not only because they gave protection to criminals but also because they afforded a refuge to debtors, and complaints against them embraced both these groups. In times of political unrest, there was also the danger that sanctuary men might emerge and commit further depredations, and the two great liberties of Westminster and St Martin le Grand in London were particularly liable to cause trouble (12, pp.108–9, 21, iii. 257; 238, pp.182–6).

As early as 1377 an Act was passed to give creditors rights over the goods of debtors who had made collusory gifts of their assets to friends, so as to avoid paying what they owed. As this Act specifically mentioned Westminster and St Martin's, it is likely that the pressure for it came from the Londoners, who were to play an active part in trying to restrict sanctuary privileges during the fifteenth century. Economic motives could explain London's initiative in this, because not only did sanctuaries provide an easy escape for debtors, but also craftsmen within them were able to produce work without guild supervision, work which might be inferior in quality to, but also cheaper than, that which would have been required outside. At least one dean of St Martin's recognized that the citizens had a valid grievance and took steps against offenders in this matter, to try to alleviate civic hostility, but although the action secured him personal goodwill, the privilege was allowed to remain (238, pp.186–8, 193).

There were also a number of occasions when trouble arose out of breaches of sanctuary, notably at Westminster. Particularly notorious was one in 1378, when two escaped prisoners were pursued there by the Constable of the Tower of London, and one of them was murdered on the altar steps, Not surprisingly, the Church authorities reacted strongly, and Bishop Courtenay of London excommunicated those involved. John of Gaunt, though out of England when the outrage occurred, unwisely allowed himself to be drawn into the ensuing controversy by supporting the Constable, bringing Wyclif into Parliament to argue against the abbey's privileges, though without result. Not all churchmen were so willing to uphold ecclesiastical liberties against the State; in 1388, when Richard II's Chief Justice, Robert Tresilian, was removed from sanctuary, he claimed its privileges when on trial before the Merciless Parliament, only to have the Chancellor, Bishop Arundel, give the decision against him. Arundel, as the brother of one of the Appellants, may have been prejudiced politically, but Bishop Wykeham of Winchester may also have acquiesced, and even Courtenay does not appear to have protested (55, pp.403–4; 204, pp.346–7). During much of the fifteenth century sanctuaries were generally left inviolate, and in the struggles of Lancaster and York provided a haven for political fugitives; Edward IV's queen took refuge at Westminster in both 1470 and 1483. The thought that they might themselves need protection in future may have been one reason why kings were by no means enthusiastic in trying to curb sanctuaries.

It was not until the Tudor period that the lay power was able to restrict them, and the most effective limitations were those resulting from judicial interpretation of the law. The judges insisted that sanctuaries should have a proper legal basis, namely an origin in a royal grant and recognition of their status in a general eyre. Failure to possess this last qualification was the basis for the removal of the rebel Humphrey Stafford from sanctuary at Culham in 1486 and his subsequent execution. In the same period, various men accused of treason were removed from sanctuary on the ground that the charters of the liberties did not specifically mention treason as an offence for which they could provide protection. It is perhaps noteworthy that a lawyer, Thomas More, in his *History of Richard III*, put words into the mouth of the duke of Buckingham attacking the two sanctuaries in the neighbourhood of London, Westminster and St Martin's respectively: 'What a rabble of theues, murtherers and malicious heyghnous Traitours, and that in twoo places specyallye. The tone of the elbowe of the Citie, the tother in the verye bowelles.' (38, p.30) Almost certainly More was thinking of the debates over sanctuary at the time when he was writing rather than recording something said a generation before. In reducing these privileges, the lay power secured some co-operation from the Papacy, which issued a number of bulls to meet royal demands, by depriving sanctuary men of their privileges if they committed a second offence. There was some clerical resistance to the encroachments on sanctuary, perhaps in part because the attacks on it were connected with those on the benefit of clergy. In the 1512 Parliament, clerical opposition to the reduction of the latter led also to the abandonment of an attempt to restrict sanctuary (238, pp.197–200).

Action could not be taken against such privileges without royal approval, and Henry VIII played a conspicuous part in curbing sanctuary. His views on the subject were expressed as early as 1519, when he attacked the legalistic way in which the sanctuary holders defended their claims. He declared that those who had initially granted the privilege had not intended it to serve for murder, or for crimes committed by men who had come out of sanctuary and hoped to return there, and affirmed that he hoped to reduce it where it had been encroached on by abuse (238, pp.201–7). In the Reformation Parliament the restriction was largely achieved, but this lies beyond the scope of this volume, as does the increasingly vestigial survival of some sanctuary rights as late as the eighteenth century.

A final area of tension between the Church and the secular power was taxation. The problems of papal demands were discussed in Chapter 35, but the clergy also owed various payments to the King. Those originating in the feudal ties between the King and the higher clergy, namely the fines paid for the restoration of the temporalities [F] of a monastery or a bishopric to a newly appointed abbot or bishop, seem generally to have been accepted without question. These were worth on average some £3,500 per annum to the Crown (237). More controversial was the direct taxation of the clergy in the clerical subsidy; this corresponded to the lay payment of the fifteenth, although the assessment, at a tenth, was higher. It was paid by beneficed priests, and was granted by Convocation on behalf of the lower clergy, who had generally ceased to attend Parliament by the middle of the fourteenth century, although there are occasional references to the election of proctors to represent them there at later dates. Indeed the absence of churchmen from Parliament, which was the King's source of extraordinary taxation, may explain some of the friction which arose in the late fourteenth century; because when Parliament made a grant to the King it sometimes stipulated that this should be conditional upon the clergy doing likewise. Arguments may have been put forward in the 1371 Parliament that the secular power was entitled to use the Church's property in cases of necessity, and this may have been the first occasion when Wyclif was involved in politics as a royalist spokesman (124, p.168; 226, p.60). It was not, of course, a new issue; it had been one of the questions at stake in the 1290s between Boniface VIII and Edward I, and even then the Pope had to concede that under certain circumstances the King might tax the clergy. Possibly, however, in the economic conditions of the late fourteenth century the controversy developed a new sharpness, with royal demands becoming more clamant at a time when the clergy were less well able to pay.

The most vigorous spokesman for the clergy in this matter was William Courtenay, both as bishop of London and later as archbishop of Canterbury. His aristocratic background may have given him more self-assurance in resisting the King than might have been found in a man of humbler origins, and the fact that he was relatively little involved in government meant that he had little opportunity to see the genuineness of the King's needs. (Apart from a brief period in the autumn of 1381, when he was Chancellor, he never held one of the great offices of State.) He resisted parliamentary attempts to put pressure on Convocation in the 1370s, and in 1384 he demanded that the Commons delete from their grant a condition that the clergy should match it. His actions incurred some hostility from the Lords as well as from the Lower House, but he secured some support from the King, who clearly hoped that separate bargaining with Convocation might be to his advantage. Courtenay was no more willing to yield to royal pressure than to Parliament's; in 1385 he persuaded Convocation not to make the grant which the King demanded. In 1386, however, despite questioning whether the King needed the funds he sought, Convocation did make the requested grant. These years saw the establishment of a regular pattern of clerical taxation; it was accepted that it was Convocation, not Parliament, which should make the grant, and that the clergy should have considerable freedom in administering the details of the tax. Poor benefices might be exempted from the requirement to pay, and a timetable could be set for making the payments. On the other hand, the higher clergy were prepared to seek secular aid to ensure that demands would be met, as can be seen from the widespread use of writs of signification against recalcitrant taxpayers, mentioned earlier in this chapter.

Under Henry IV, when Parliament was particularly resistant to royal fiscal demands (Ch.19), there were further disputes over clerical taxation. The parliamentary knights suggested that the clergy did not bear a fair share of national burdens, and attempts were made, possibly under Lollard influence, to confiscate their temporalities. In 1404 demands were made that non-beneficed clergy, such as stipendiary chaplains, should also contribute to the tax, and in 1406 provision was made for this. In fact, the King seems to have had considerable success in obtaining clerical taxes, and to have had fewer conditions imposed by Convocation than by Parliament concerning his expenditure. Relations between Parliament and the clergy seem to have eased after 1414, possibly because the laity were alarmed by the Lollard revolt under Oldcastle. Convocation made substantial grants to Henry V, although in the early years of his son no taxes were forthcoming until 1425. Then, and in 1426, the payment was small, half a tenth on each occasion, but in 1428 strong pressure was brought to bear on Convocation, which consented to a whole tenth. In the 1430s there was again resistance; a grant in 1435 was agreed only by a majority, and in 1438 demands for a tax were met by an absolute refusal (21, i. cxxiv–cxxvi).

By the latter half of the century, however, Convocation seems normally to have met royal demands, although it attached to each grant lists of those to be exempted from paying. As the names on these varied from one occasion to the next, the clergy clearly continued to exercise control over the detailed administration of the taxes. Such payments were of considerable value to the King, the more so as they were made at a time when parliamentary grants were in decline. Between 1471 and 1483 the contribution of the clergy to the King's revenues, totalling £77,100, was almost 83 per cent of the sum raised by taxes on the laity, despite the far larger number of contributors to parliamentary levies. Under the early Tudors clerical subsidies continued to be a significant part of the revenues, being worth on average some £9,000 per annum. The extent of these payments makes clear the effectiveness of secular control over clerical wealth, although the vast increases in taxation after the break with Rome suggest that before the 1530s there were still some limits to the demands which a king could enforce (12, pp.xxx, 93–8, 111–12, 137–42; 144, p.385; 237).

In general, however, relations between the spiritual and the secular powers remained fairly amicable in this period. Friction undoubtedly existed, but there were no protracted struggles between the kings and their clerical subjects. Compromise was generally possible, and this is hardly surprising, because kings and prelates alike could see the advantages to be gained from it. Furthermore the kings, as we have seen (Ch.35), had a large say in the choice of the higher clergy, and none of those appointed showed any desire to emulate Becket in standing for ecclesiastical liberties against the King. It was not until Henry VIII decided to break with Rome that any vital issue of principle arose on which there was widespread disagreement between the clergy and the lay power.

CHAPTER 37

The regular clergy

The orders of regular clergy, monks and friars alike, played a relatively unimportant part in the life of the late medieval Church. They were no longer the dynamic force which they had been in the period up to the thirteenth century, when successive orders, with varying ideals, had set the pace in the life of the whole Western Church. The twelfth century had seen the zenith of the black monks and the Cistercians in both membership and influence, and the thirteenth the greatest impression made by the friars. The decline in influence is shown by looking at the appointment of regulars to the see of Canterbury; between 1066 and 1189 all but one of the archbishops were regulars, mainly Benedictines, but thereafter there was only one monk, Simon Langham (1366–68), one Augustinian canon, Henry Dean (1501–3) and two friars, Robert Kilwardby (1273–78) and John Pecham (1279–92). Increasing royal influence over the appointment of the higher clergy was probably the main explanation of this change, as old royal servants often secured the highest ecclesiastical posts, and regulars did not serve in the royal administration. They were not entirely excluded from the episcopate, but it is noteworthy that of those who became bishops, many held either Welsh sees or one of the less well-endowed English ones. The part played by the regulars was no longer supported by administrative authority, and their power depended more on how they could affect individuals; the friars provided a number of confessors to the early Lancastrian kings, and were also active in public preaching (217, pp.709–10; 218, i, 321, ii, 145, 370, iii, 492).

The result of this declining part in Church government was that the regulars became more inward-looking, and their history is increasingly an account of how their rules were observed rather than one of how they affected ecclesiastical ideals. This was not new in 1370; traditional monasticism, which sought to withdraw from the world, lost force under the impact of mendicant teaching in the thirteenth century, but the new orders failed to sustain their original momentum, and consequently made a decreasing impression on Church life. This was particularly true of the Franciscans, whose initial appeal had been based on their life of poverty and sanctity, but who had, almost at once, to compromise with their founder's aims, facing various crises in their attempts to reconcile idealism and practicality. By the fourteenth century all the regular clergy were part of the clerical establishment rather than constructive critics, openly or tacitly, of its abuses. Organizational problems bulked large, particularly in the monasteries, which had to face the problems of the agricultural recession, when their lands were giving declining returns. All monastic houses were affected by this, and others had to face difficult local circumstances, notably those northern monasteries which were vulnerable to Scottish raids. Under economic pressure, the monks were more poorly placed than the laity, as they had fewer ways of compensating for the loss in landed income; they could not seek office under the Crown, nor, in view of the limitations imposed by Edward I's Statute of Mortmain, was it easy for them to acquire extra lands to provide additional income. This may have led them to try enforcing traditional labour services with particular vigour, with the result that in the revolt of 1381 there were conspicuous outbreaks of discontent on monastic lands, as at St Albans and Bury St Edmunds. The only specifically monastic way of trying to raise extra money was by the sale of corrodies, or allowance of a share in the common funds of the house, in return for the down payment of a lump sum. A man could buy one for himself, possibly with a remainder to his wife, and it was a gamble for the monastery whether or not the transaction would show a profit (239, pp.174–5). But even if the house gained financially, the residence of corrodians within the monastic premises could only lead to the introduction of secular attitudes there.

However, if the economic fortunes of the monasteries were closely tied to those of the nation, this could mean that an improvment in the latter could benefit them. It is perhaps significant that in the early Tudor period, when economic activity seems to have increased, and when, possibly, the renewal of population pressure on land was tipping the balance of power back in favour of the landowner against the tenant, there was increased activity in monastic building. Among the large houses one can see this at Canterbury, Gloucester, Evesham and Westminster, to name but a few, and it was not only such large abbeys which were able to afford renovations (218, iii. 22, 24).

Certainly many monks of this period were concerned with practical matters, such as maintaining buildings and lands, and it is striking that the men who made the most marked impression as abbots were those whose talents lay in this field. This was not new; after all one of the best-documented abbots of the twelfth century, Samson of Bury St Edmunds, was a practical man rather than a spiritual inspiration. But whereas the twelfth century also produced men such as Ailred of Rievaulx, whose charismatic qualities could inspire men to the higher reaches of religious life and fulfil the ultimate aim of monasticism to bring souls closer to God, in the fifteenth century there was a striking lack of men whose distinction lay in their spiritual qualities. At best they were devout and punctilious in their observance, but seem to have lacked the capacity to lead others to the loftier heights of contemplation. A few examples illustrate this. The dominant English Benedictine of the late fourteenth century was Thomas de la Mare, abbot of St Albans for forty-seven years, a man who was active in the reform of other monastic houses as well as his own, and an enthusiastic builder. His private life was ascetic, he was punctilious in observing the offices and he won the affection of his monks, but we do not know if he had the final quality of holiness. Certainly one hears nothing of the spiritual qualities of the house over which he ruled. John Wessington, prior of the cathedral monastery of Durham from 1416 to 1446, possessed similar characteristics; he too was concerned with the religious observances of his house – there seems to have been an improved attendance at cathedral services under his rule – and was also a builder, both at the cathedral and at the prior's lodgings. The evidence of his expenses, however, suggests that he was less ascetic than de la Mare in both clothing and diet, and his literary interests, as a historian of his house and as a compiler of legal tracts defending its rights, reflect a man who was an administrator rather than a spiritual father. There were other men of this type, John Whethamstede at St Albans (1420–41, 1452–65) who was an energetic ruler of his monks and a writer admired by his contemporaries, despite what seems to moderns a pretentious literary style. His retirement from office may have been prompted by a reluctance to enforce discipline, but his later recall suggests that his monks respected him. At a later date, and from the Cistercians, Marmaduke Huby of Fountains (1494–1526) was regarded as the natural leader of the order in England and was an effective head of his own house. Not only was he responsible for considerable building there, but in his time the number of monks rose from twenty-two to fifty-two. Again, however, nothing is known of his spiritual qualities (209, pp.101, 104, 110, 379; 218, ii. 41–7, 193–7, iii. 35–7).

Besides contending with the economic difficulties of the time, these abbots were also faced by the damage done to their orders' morale by the Great Schism and the tendency of the national churches to loosen ties with Rome during the conciliar period. Those orders, with a closely knit structure binding daughter houses to senior ones, such as the Cluniacs and the Cistercians, were particularly hard hit, as the superior houses fell within the Avignon obedience. The friars, whose headquarters were based in Rome, were less affected, because England could remain loyal to the existing heads of the orders. Some problems of the Schism, indeed, had been foreshadowed even before 1378, because of the Anglo-French War. There were a number of English houses which depended on monasteries in enemy territory, and which might number aliens among their number. In 1377 the Commons petitioned for the expulsion of aliens, including monks, and this was done, apart from those who were conventual priors. Under the combined pressures of war and schism, the lands of a number of these 'alien priories' passed into lay hands, notably through Henry V's statute of 1414 which sanctioned their suppression, although ultimately most of them were restored to religious purposes. Some were given to Henry V's new foundations at Sheen and Syon, and others passed into the hands of various colleges of secular churchmen later in the century (218, ii. 163–4).

As far as constitutional problems were concerned, the Papacy took steps to safeguard the government of the orders, where the mother houses lay within the Avignonese obedience. A chapter of the Cluniacs was set up in England, and in general worked well. Indeed, even after the end of the Schism, Cluny never recovered its earlier control over the English houses. Initially a similar course was taken with the Cistercians, but the old ties with Cîteaux were resumed after the Council of Pisa in 1409. During the fifteenth century, there were some occasions when war interfered with communications with the mother houses of the order, so English and Welsh abbots were exempted from the requirement to attend the general chapter, and the contributions due from the English houses were sent to support representatives of the order at the Curia rather than to Cîteaux (218, ii, 167–9). For much of the time, however, it was possible to keep in touch with the centre of the order, and the letters of the English abbots to Cîteaux in the late fifteenth and early sixteenth centuries show that the international character of the order was still preserved, despite some pressures from the secular power. In 1497, for example, a royal agent was reported as having been investigating how much money the order had sent overseas in recent years.

When one turns from the government of the monasteries to examine the standards of observance within them, the balance of the evidence undoubtedly points to considerable decline. In some cases this took the form of a slackening of traditional discipline, such as the appointment of monks to the honorific title of papal chaplain, which could exempt the recipient from regular obedience (a practice particularly common during the Schism), or the granting of permission to religious to hold a benefice, either with or without cure of souls. The granting of money payments to monks, in lieu of the issue of clothes, and the development of private chambers in the monasteries, also reflect a decline in traditional communal life. But besides such abandonment of earlier levels of austerity, some records of episcopal visitations also show worse failings; both in the fifteenth century and in the early sixteenth cases of serious moral lapses were reported. In some cases the vow of chastity was disregarded, even by heads of houses, in others there were accusations of drunkenness, gambling or brawling. However, this was not universal; elsewhere visitations by bishops or by superiors within the order reported that all was well with a house, or at least that the matters requiring correction were slight. (218, ii. 171–3, 211–12, 241–4; iii. 65).

Visitation records are difficult evidence to handle, not least because they do not cover all houses comprehensively. Also, if factiousness existed between individuals within a house there was the danger that accusations made to a visitor might be exaggerated, while on the other hand, there was the possibility that the monks might either be in a conspiracy of silence against an outsider or be afraid to make any accusations for fear of later reprisals. It is, however, worth noting that a number of guilty persons had difficulties in finding the required number of compurgators to testify to their innocence, so there is at least reasonable cause to accept at face value statements of *omnia bene* ('all well') when these were made. A more serious problem revealed by the records was that the authorities found it difficult to take firm disciplinary action when this was required. Men who had been found guilty of various offences by Abbot Redman of Shap, visitor of the English province of the Premonstratensians from 1459 to 1505, were subsequently appointed to offices of responsibility in their houses. Bishops might fail to remove heads of houses who had lapsed; an abbot of Dorchester, who in 1441 was accused of keeping five married women as mistresses, escaped immediate judgment, and when another abbot was appointed to the house, the old offender was allowed private quarters and a comfortable pension (218, ii. 213, iii. 46; 239, p.180).

One has only tentative indications of how widespread moral decline was, but perhaps one of the best samples of evidence is found in Redman's visitations. He was clearly a man of ability, who became an abbot young and was made visitor of the order in England only a year later. His good reputation probably explains why he was allowed to hold a bishopric concurrently with his abbey – in fact he held three in turn – technically an irregularity for a regular. He was active in visiting the twenty-nine houses of the order, where he found varying conditions. A third were consistently satisfactory, and only about a quarter were persistently low in standard. The remainder varied from time to time between reasonably satisfactory and moderately poor (218, iii. 39–42). What the general situation was in the other orders is hard to say, in part because of the patchiness of surviving records, but it would not be surprising if the majority of houses of the older orders showed a comparable range of observance.

One way of assessing how far the regular clergy were meeting the standards expected of them is to consider contemporary opinions of them, but it is necessary not to rely overmuch on the writings of men such as Chaucer, whose *Prologue* is sometimes cited by historians as though he were a dispassionate reporter for posterity on the Church of his day rather than a literary artist with a strong satirical bent. No doubt there were monks, friars and prioresses who correspond to his characters – had there not been, the satire would have lacked bite – but one is not entitled to assume that they were typical, any more than a bumbling vicar in a twentieth-century farce can be taken as an accurate picture of a modern churchman. Despite critical expressions in literature, there is evidence that the orders retained a fair measure of popular respect. When in 1495 the Benedictines moved the site of their triennial chapter from Northampton to Coventry, they were given a civic welcome there (218, iii. 10). In London, some two-fifths of the wills in a sample examined from the fifteenth and early sixteenth centuries contained bequests to one or more of the orders, most notably to the friars, even although the latters' idealization of poverty was hardly likely to appeal to the city merchant class (242). On the other hand, the very limited scale of opposition to the dissolutions of the 1530s shows that there were only a few men who were prepared to support the orders at great cost to themselves. Recruitment of regulars was quite well sustained, and although the mid-fourteenth-century epidemics took a heavy toll (perhaps about half the regulars in England, compared with a fall of about a third in the population as a whole), losses seem to have been made up at least partially in the fifteenth century. A writer of 1489 speaks of the mendicant orders as flourishing, and we have already noted how the community at Fountains increased under Huby's rule. Even although the number of regulars was lower than it had been at its peak, it is clear that the monastic life could not have lost its appeal entirely.

Indeed, certain sections of regular observance flourished in the late Middle Ages as never before. When Wolsey issued a book of reforming statutes, which would have tightened up standards of observance, this provoked opposition, evidence of how much standards had become relaxed. It was acknowledged that an attempt to apply the rules rigorously could lead to widespread apostasy, and that few could follow the rule of the Carthusians, the Bridgettines or the Franciscan Observants. In 1370 there were only three Carthusian houses in England, by 1420 there were nine, and although the number of monks in the order cannot have been high, probably never more than 175 at any one time, their spiritual vigour was considerable. There were sufficient men who were drawn to the Carthusian ideals of austerity and seclusion to sustain the expansion of the order, and benefactors showed a willingness to endow it, particularly from the resources of the dissolved alien priories. Many of these were from the highest levels of society; Richard II and his queen founded the Coventry Charterhouse, his half-nephew Thomas Holland Mount Grace, and Henry V Sheen (218, iii. 159; 236; 239, p.182).

Recruits were also drawn from men with a court or administrative background. A former baron of the Exchequer, Adam Horsley, entered the Beauvale Charterhouse in the fourteenth century, and in the fifteenth Henry VI's former chaplain and hagiographer, John Blacman, a man of academic background, joined the order, although he may never have become fully professed in it (222). Many early-sixteenth-century Carthusians were also from distinguished backgrounds; John Houghton, the last prior of the London house, began his career in law, before becoming first a secular priest and then a monk, and Sebastian Newdigate had been a page at court and a gentleman of the privy chamber to Henry VIII. Both these men were among the Carthusians who suffered atrocious pains for their resistance to Henry VIII's demands in the 1530s. Newdigate came from a devout background, with two brothers who were knights of Malta and two sisters who were nuns in strictly observant houses. It perhaps emphasizes the reputation of the Carthusians that when he decided to become a monk, that was the order to which he was drawn. Even men who did not join them could come under their influence, sharing their devotions and living in the precinct of their house; around the turn of the sixteenth century the young Thomas More did so, and even although he eventually chose an active rather than a contemplative life, his admiration for them remained to the end. The increasing number of benefactions to the order is yet another manifestation of popular esteem for it (218, iii. 224–36; 242).

Contemplation was the hallmark of the Carthusian tradition, and the English houses of the late Middle Ages were active in the transmission of devotional literature. They were in touch with the most active religious movement on the Continent, the *Devotio Moderna* of the Low Countries, and played the main part in bringing into England, and in translating into English, the greatest spiritual classic produced by it, the *Imitation of Christ*. Another Continental writer whose works were translated by the Carthusians was the Flemish mystic Ruysbroeck, and an English version of the pseudo-Bonaventuran *Meditationes Vitae Christi* was produced by Nicholas Love of the Mount Grace Charterhouse about 1410. The monks were also concerned with the native tradition of mysticism; a substantial number of the surviving MSS of the English mystics, notably Richard Rolle and Walter Hilton, have a Carthusian provenance, and many of their works reached the Continent through the same order. Furthermore, although the fifteenth century did not produce the same level of spiritual writing as the fourteenth-century mystics had done, the Carthusian Richard Methley, who was acquainted with some of their writings, came perhaps closer to them in spirit than any other man of his age (218, ii. 224–6; 222; 236).

Henry V, who founded the Sheen Charterhouse, also established another monastery which retained a high level of fervour and austerity, the house of the Bridgettines, an order of Swedish origin for men and women, which was founded at Twickenham in 1415 and moved to Syon, just across the Thames from Sheen, in 1431. The first English recruits to the order made their profession in 1420, by which time it was securely established. The devotional life of the house was sustained by the resources of an exceptionally good library, and its members retained a reputation for strict observance. The nunnery had a strong aristocratic character, usually coming near its full complement of sixty, while the men who provided the chaplains and spiritual directors were often drawn from an academic background, combining learning with personal austerity. The most distinguished member of the house in the century and a quarter of its life was Richard Reynolds, who joined it about 1515. Formerly a Fellow of Corpus Christi College, Cambridge, he was learned in Latin, Greek and Hebrew, and was one of the leading theologians in England. In the crisis of the 1530s he was closely associated with More and Fisher, and stood firmly with Queen Catherine. Like them and the Carthusians, he was to be executed (218, ii. 177–81, iii. 212–18).

The third group of rigorous regulars mentioned in the reply to Wolsey's reform decrees was the Franciscan Observants. They emerged as an independent group on the Continent by the early fifteenth century, but did not reach England until a house was established at Greenwich in 1482. The early development of the order was slow, but increased in momentum under Henry VII, in whose reign some further foundations were made and some older houses were transferred to the new order. Ultimately they had seven houses, of which the two most notable were the original one at Greenwich and one at Richmond, which was closely in touch with the Carthusians at Sheen and the Bridgettines at Syon. They, like the Carthusians, were common recipients of benefactions from the laity in London. The order had close ties with Rome, and theologically was strongly conservative, more so than the other orders of friars, some members of which in the 1520s were tending to favour the new doctrines which were coming into England from the Continent. In view of this, it is hardly surprising that they too suffered for strong opposition to the King in the 1530s (218, iii. 11–13, 206–11; 242).

Although the Dissolution of the Monasteries in England was essentially part of the ecclesiastical revolution of the 1530s, there were some precedents for it. The suppression of the alien priories during the Schism, culminating in Henry V's statute of 1414, was of relatively minor importance, but in the late fifteenth and early sixteenth centuries a number of other houses disappeared, largely through the agency of prelates who transferred their revenues to support colleges at Oxford and Cambridge. In some cases there can have been little real disturbance of existing regulars; there were only two nuns at St Radegund's in Cambridge when it was suppressed in 1496 for the foundation of Jesus College, and the situation was very similar in 1524 when no less a person than Bishop Fisher of Rochester, Henry VIII's future opponent and victim, obtained two decaying nunneries for the benefit of St John's College, Cambridge. As the number of regulars in the country was probably lower than the number of places which existing houses could support, such actions might well be regarded as a rationalizing of ecclesiastical resources, which were no longer being employed for the purposes for which they were originally given. Indeed, when one remembers how many regular houses there were in the country and the costs of sustaining them, the casualties were perhaps surprisingly few. There was, however, one group of dissolved houses, those suppressed by Wolsey in his search for endowments for his college at Oxford, whose fate was less predictable, because their condition was less parlous than those which had fallen previously. St Frideswide's Oxford still had a fair-sized community, and even in those where the numbers were small there is little reason to believe that their observance was lax (218, iii. 157, 161–2).

Contemporaries, however, do not seem to have been alarmed by such actions, and even during the early sessions of the Reformation Parliament monastic life apparently pursued the even tenor of its way, unconscious of any impending storm. This can be seen in the letters of Robert Joseph, a monk of Evesham, dating from 1528 to 1531. He was a scholarly man, interested in the new humanist learning, and an admirer of Erasmus, though he did not share the latter's critical attitude to traditional religion. Theologically he was prepared to follow Scotus, although he wrote in a more classical style. He does not appear to have been much concerned with public affairs, nor to have felt that there was any urgent need to reform his house. His correspondents likewise were touched by the new scholarship, and may have hoped to absorb it into the traditions of monastic learning, which saw no conflict between the love of letters and the pursuit of holiness. What may appear to us as complacency more accurately reflects a genuine sense of stability on the verge of the great crises of the 1530s, the enforcement of the royal supremacy and the subsequent destruction of the monasteries which marked the end of an epoch in the religious history of England (218, iii. 100–7).

CHAPTER 38

Laity, clergy and religion

In studying ecclesiastical history, it is dangerous to concentrate exclusively on the clergy and forget that the Church, as the *congregatio fidelium*, includes lay as well as clerical members. In the Middle Ages, the laity played an active part in the life of the Church, by sharing in its administration at the local level and by supporting its observances, both financially and by personal involvement. The historian should also examine the relations between the clergy and the laity in the parishes, to see how far one can accept the idea that there was widespread hostility to churchmen. It is almost commonplace to talk of this: Keen refers to 'the strong anti-clerical tenor of popular feeling' and Elton, referring to a slightly later period, says that 'men were tired of being ruled or badgered by priests' and suggests that London in particular was strongly anti-clerical (51, p.104; 53, p.224). Certainly one can see some manifestations of this hostility; politically it could take the form of anti-papal statutes in Parliament, or of demands that the clergy should pay a higher sum in taxes to the King (Chs 35, 36); in literature there was criticism by major writers such as Chaucer and Langland, and sometimes scurrilous depiction of churchmen by lesser writers. But this does not give the whole picture, and it is necessary to remember than in late medieval England one can also see positive signs of loyalty to the Church and all for what it stood, as well as evidence of friendliness to individual churchmen. And although this period saw the appearance of Lollard heresy, this drew only limited support, and must be viewed strictly in perspective (Ch.40).

The laity's principal obligations to the Church were in the parish. It was there too, in many cases, that they undertook further commitments beyond the minimum laid down in canon law. Potentially too, the parish was the main focus for discontent with the Church, because many of the troubles which occurred resulted from the actions of particular priests, which provoked a hostile reaction from their parishioners, rather than from demands made by the ecclesiastical authorities on the whole body of the laity. A layman's basic obligations to the Church were relatively slight; in strictly religious matters, he had to attend service on Sundays and feast days, make his confession and receive the Eucharist at least once a year, and on the material side there was the requirement to pay tithes and other dues such as mortuaries. The parishioners also had a collective responsibility for maintaining the fabric of their church; from the late thirteenth century the normal practice was that while the rector was responsible for the upkeep of the chancel, the parishioners had to bear the cost of repairing the nave (240, pp.24, 26).

How willingly did the parishioners meet these demands? There is a basic problem of evidence, for the records of the Church courts, which show the breach of obligations rather than their observance, have survived better than parish accounts, which can show how the system worked when the laity met their recognized responsibilities. Enough of the latter, however, have been preserved from the late fifteenth century onwards to provide a corrective to court proceedings, which are concerned with only a small proportion of the total population. One of the most complete sets of churchwardens' accounts, from Ashburton in Devonshire, which is continuous from 1482 to 1580, gives some indication of how the parish financed itself; the sale of ale made a substantial contribution, but the wardens also received gifts from individuals and rents from various properties. On some occasions they made considerable payments for repair work – in 1500–1 the steeple was roughcast, new bell-ropes were made and there were repairs to the organ. One additional way employed to raise funds was the holding of a play, and this was found elsewhere in the country also – in 1527 the London court of aldermen agreed to the petition of the rector of All Hallows on the Wall that the parish should have a licence to hold a play, and that no other parish should have one at the same time, as the church was in 'grete Ruyne and dekeye'. The accounts show that the play yielded a profit of £5. 8s. 9½d., although this was markedly less than a collection which was made for repairs shortly afterwards. This amounted to £10. 0s. 8d., the subscription list being headed by 'the wyffs', who gave £2. 12s. 0d. (240, p.237). In these cases the parish was operating as a social unit to meet the needs of its church, and there was no disagreement over disbursements of money for ecclesiastical needs. It is likely that such co-operation was fairly general; any traveller around England who visits its parish churches can see that a substantial amount of rebuilding took place in the late Middle Ages, and even where the buildings no longer survive, the writings of the early antiquaries, such as John Stow's great *Survey of London*, testify to the work that was done and the gifts which were made. However much tension existed between churchmen and laymen, it is certain that the latter were still prepared to make substantial gifts to their parish churches.

Such extensions to and beautification of churches were voluntary acts, which went beyond the obligations of routine maintenance. The best measure of popular religious sentiment is the existence of activities which went beyond the requirements of canon law, of which the most marked are the activities of the various religious guilds. Some guilds were primarily concerned with economic matters, but even they took part in various spiritual observances, which show how the influence of the Church permeated all aspects of social life. This is seen in an ordinance of the London Merchant Tailors in 1371, which provided that when a workman miscut or spoiled cloth which had been entrusted to him, two-thirds of the fine should be paid to the chamber of the guildhall and one-third to the guild's fraternity of St John the Baptist, with the money going to the priests and the poor. The religious guilds associated with such companies were, however, sufficiently independent of them to include outside persons in their membership (240, pp.126–9).

Far more important were the guilds which existed in many parish churches. These are quite well documented, because in 1389 Parliament laid down that the masters and wardens of guilds and fraternities should make a return to chancery of their foundation, form of government, feasts and meetings, and give a list of the property which they held (247, p.36). Some 500 returns survive, from a wide variety of places, although it is certain, from other more isolated surviving references, that these were by no means complete. Either some guilds failed to make returns, or these have been lost. The calendar of these returns (247, pp.138–238) provides a good guide to what the guilds did. About a third of them had social as well as religious functions, more particularly in providing a form of insurance for members who had accidentally fallen into poverty. The most common rate of benefit was 7d. per week, if the guild could afford it, but clearly this might be varied in accordance with the availability of resources. In the guild of St Mary, in St Botulph's Church, Cambridge, where the basic relief rate was 7d., it was stipulated that if the guild had to maintain two poor, the weekly sum would have to be cut to 4d. Such provisions, however, were found in only a minority of guilds (247, p.41), and the common aim in all of them was to support services in their churches, more particularly services for the souls of deceased members, and to maintain lights there. The form of this varied according to the resources which each guild possessed, and could range from the support of a light annually on Corpus Christi day, provided by the society of Corpus Christi in St Nicholas' Church, Great Yarmouth, to the wide range of benefits offered by the guild of St Stephen in St Sepulchre without Newgate, London; this maintained a permanent chaplain to sing for the guild before the image of the patron saint, provided five candles at the mass of a deceased guild brother, as well as trentals of masses by the Franciscan, Carmelite and Austin Friars, and brought home the body of a brother who died within 20 miles, as well as offering insurance benefits at 14d. per week to those in accidental poverty. Another aim of a fraternity might be to provide for the singing of particular prayers and antiphons; that of the Salutation of the BVM and St Thomas the Martyr in St Magnus, London (a union of two earlier brotherhoods) rebuilt a chapel on London Bridge, and supported a chaplain to sing the anthem *Salve Regina* and the antiphon of St Thomas. The guild of the Purification in the church of the BVM, Beverley, supported a procession of the guild brothers and sisters, which was virtually a religious pageant. One member was dressed as a queen, to represent the Virgin, and two others played the parts of Joseph and Simeon. It was only a small step from this to the production of religious plays as was done by various craft guilds, such as those of York.

Some guilds may have depended for funds on the continuing subscriptions of their members, but others might also hold endowments of land. That of the BVM and St Giles, in St Giles, Cripplegate, took payments of ½d. per week from members, but it also held sufficient landed property for them to have to pay £40 for licence to hold it in mortmain. Endowment, clearly, could provide a guarantee of permanence, whereas those fraternities which depended for income on members' payments were more likely to prove ephemeral. Certainly one finds many references in the fifteenth century to guilds which were not mentioned in the 1389 returns, and it may well be that many of them were founded by a group of pious men and survived only as long as the founders did. Guilds could proliferate even within a single church; in 1524 a draper, John Maidenhead, left four torches to each of the five brotherhoods in St Michael Cornhill, London. It is worth noting that such a multiplication of brotherhoods could persist to this date, so shortly before the English Reformation, because it suggests that earlier traditions of devotion were still active (240, pp.88, 93–4).

The support of chaplains to celebrate for the souls of former guild members and for the welfare of those still living makes it clear that the fraternities can be regarded as a kind of collective chantry, supported in some cases by men who could not afford to endow one on their own account. Behind such foundations was the fundamental outlook of those who established them, the belief that life on earth was but a passing phase of existence, that man's true destiny was eternity and that the sacraments which were necessary for salvation could be administered by the clergy alone. The tendency to view the celebration of masses in a mechanical light – the more that were said, the greater the benefit for the person for whom they were said – clearly encouraged guild practices and the endowment of chantries, either in perpetuity or for a term of years. Even although theologians might debate the question of predestination, prayers for the dead were acceptable, because no one knew who were saved and who were reprobate. When the great Bristol merchant William Canynges, a devout man, who himself took orders after his wife's death, drew up ordinances for a chantry in St Mary Redcliffe in 1467, the preamble stressed the mediating effect of prayer, particularly long prayer. Many late medieval wills, from different walks of society, contain affirmations of personal devotion to Christ and the saints, and lay down precise services to be said, or affirm their loyalty to the doctrines taught by the Church (235, pp.11–13; 240, pp.64–7; 245, pp.14–18).

Such provision for the hereafter varied according to the resources of the individual, and might take the form either of endowing services or of giving charitable gifts, in return for which the beneficiaries were expected to pray for the soul of the donor. It is anachronistic for the historian to distinguish between purely pious endowments and charitable gifts; both, paradoxically, were a form of selfishness on the part of the giver. The nobility might found splendid chapels, staffed by several chaplains and endowed in perpetuity, but men of more modest means could make a similar endowment on a smaller scale, or, if they could not afford to establish a perpetual chantry, they could leave a cash sum to support a priest for a term of years. One finds this among both the gentry and the merchant class. In London and York, indeed, temporary foundations were markedly more numerous than perpetual ones. One reason for the popularity of this type of foundation was that it was relatively inexpensive; in fifteenth-century London the normal annual salary of a chantry chaplain was 10 marks (£6. 13s. 4d.), but in York it was only £5 and elsewhere it might be even lower. Those whose resources were yet smaller could still endow votive lights in a church (235, p.39; 240, pp.209, 214–18; 245, p.31).

Many of those who endowed such foundations laid down precise regulations concerning the prayers to be said and the names of those to be commemorated. This would suggest that the laity, in a wide range of classes, had sufficient knowledge of the liturgy to lay down such rules or were on sufficient terms of friendliness with the clergy to seek their guidance. It is reasonable to assume that such persons were regular in their religious observance, and other evidence suggests that this was not untypical. A foreign observer, writing about 1500, commented on the regularity of attendance at mass by the English and their liberal giving of alms, and mentioned also that those who could read followed the office of the Virgin as it was being said. The possession of various religious and particularly liturgical books by laymen is shown by reference in wills, and it is worth stressing that some 45 per cent of Caxton's publications and 40 per cent of those of his successor Wynkyn de Worde were religious in character. While some of these may have been intended to supply a clerical market, it is likely that the laity also were among the purchasers (35, p.23; 235, pp.27–8; 240, pp.23–4; 245, p.15).

Yet a further sign of religious zeal was the popularity of pilgrimages. No doubt, for many pilgrims there were other motives for travel besides the purely spiritual, but in view of the discomforts which they would have to endure it is likely that religious devotion provided the main spur to their action. There is no reason to believe that Chaucer was being ironical when he described his Canterbury pilgrims, a motley crowd of predominantly worldly minded people, assembling with devout hearts, and such characters could no doubt be matched in the world of fact. Some pilgrims were indefatigable travellers, one of the most notable being the emotional Margery Kempe of Lynn in the first half of the fifteenth century, who journeyed to Italy and the Holy Land, to Compostella and to shrines in the Baltic. Margery, who aspired to, although she probably did not attain, the deeper levels of religious contemplation, was certainly driven by a spiritual quest, and while other pilgrims may have been less devout than she, and indeed found her weepings and outbursts annoying, there is every likelihood that they too set store by the religious purpose of their journeys.

Within England, Canterbury was a favourite destination, but other major shrines were to be found at Durham, Walsingham, Glastonbury and Bury St Edmunds, and there were also various lesser centres with a more local appeal. Overseas there were three major places of pilgrimage, the Holy Land, Rome and Compostella. Even the most humble might find their way to Rome – a serf from the lands of Croyland Abbey died on the journey there – and the appeal of Compostella was such that even during the Schism, when it lay within the Avignonese obedience, the government could not enforce a veto on travel there. In the two months of May and June 1395 licences were issued for 11 ships to take up to 970 pilgrims there. It is not of course known whether the number who actually made the journey came anywhere near this figure, but it is clear that there was a considerable market for ships to make the voyage, and that pilgrimages were not confined to the few. Nor is there any evidence that enthusiasm for them declined in the years immediately before the Reformation, as criticism of the practice remained one of the most common traits of Lollard teaching (209, p.28; 240, pp.52, 56; 241, p.246).

In the light of these active manifestations of popular religious activity, what judgement should be made on the belief that anti-clericalism was rife? A certain hostility to the ordained clergy is not of course incompatible with religious enthusiasm, and may indeed exist when men feel that the clergy are not providing the example which they should, but in the late Middle Ages many manifestations of spiritual zeal involved positive support for the clergy. Where one can see elements of anti-clericalism most clearly is in areas where the interests of the clergy and the laity came directly into conflict. Even there one should guard against dangers of exaggeration; it was possible for some *modus vivendi* to be reached on legal matters, although there were areas where jurisdictional tensions persisted (Ch.36). The financial demands of the Church too were an obvious point of tension, but hostility to them was sometimes surprisingly muted. The Church's right to tithes seem to have been accepted, and criticisms were directed at their misuse rather than at them *per se*. Bequests to parish churches in wills to recompense for dues withheld and proceedings in the Church courts for the recovery of unpaid tithes show that men were reluctant to pay, but this does not necessarily mean more than the unwillingness of a man to hand over his money to someone else. Protracted disputes were relatively rare, although one such occurred in London in the third quarter of the fifteenth century; then the civic authorities defended a citizen who had refused to pay certain dues, even sending spokesmen to Rome to plead the case at the Curia. At the same time, however, direct negotiations on the issue continued with the city parish clergy, a fact which suggests that the city authorities were concerned with reaching an amicable agreement rather than with inflicting a defeat on the Church. It was clearly recognized that certain payments had to be made; what was at issue was their extent (244; 249, p.86).

More contentious, and more productive of ill-feeling, were the demands of the Church for mortuary payments; certainly this provided the background to the famous early-sixteenth-century case of Richard Hunne, who refused to hand over the bearing sheet of his infant son, who died in 1511. His rector sued successfully for this in the following year, but Hunne retaliated in turn, bringing a *praemunire* suit against the rector and various of his associates, including the bishop's summoner, and a slander action against the parish chaplain who had declared that he was excommunicate, and had thereby damaged him in his business dealings. Subsequently he was arrested on a heresy charge, and died, probably murdered by one of the bishop's officers, in the Lollards' Tower in London. Although it is unlikely that the bishop himself was involved in a plot against Hunne, he became somewhat hysterical during the resulting furore, and alleged that the Londoners were so favourable to heresy that a city inquest would condemn his chancellor, one of the other suspects, 'were he as innocent as Abel', a charge which was indignantly denied by the court of aldermen (241, pp.163–70). Certainly the episode made a strong popular impression and provoked a hostile reaction against the clergy which persisted after the immediate trouble had died down; more than a decade later More discussed the case at length in his *Dialogue of Heresies*, so it was clearly something which had remained vividly in people's minds and may well have helped to set the tone of popular feeling against the Church authorities at the time of the Reformation Parliament. Nevertheless, there are certain aspects of the case which make it dangerous to deduce from it that the country was ripe for a popular religious revolution; not only does its very notoriety suggest that it was regarded as something out of the ordinary but also Hunne's claim in his slander action that his business dealings had been affected by the allegation that he was excommunicate is hardly compatible with any suggestion that the people had little regard for the Church. To balance the idea that there was seething discontent, one should note that in the late 1520s one still finds bequests in London wills to churches to recompense them for unpaid dues and to endow services, with the clergy being named among the overseers of such wills.

The clearest evidence of anti-clericalism can be found in malicious attacks on churchmen, and in surviving court proceedings where they took action to redress these. In 1514 a London priest facing a paternity allegation brought a slander suit in the consistory court, and there are also recorded cases of priests appealing to the Chancellor's equity jurisdiction against allegedly malicious charges, with a suggestion being made that an inquest had been packed to bring in a hostile verdict. There were also cases of physical assault on priests, and one man who made such an attack said he did so in order that other 'knave priests' should take warning (240, pp.270–2). What is not known is whether such assailants merely represent a hooligan element in society or if such hostility was widespread, nor, in cases where churchmen alleged malicious attacks, if they may not have been guilty of misconduct but hoped to escape by exploiting their clerical privileges. Even the defenders of the clergy admitted that they were not all faultless, although their most distinguished advocate, Sir Thomas More, also claimed that their general moral standards were as high as or higher than those of churchmen elsewhere. He continued: 'If a lewde preste do a lewde dede than we say, lo se what sample the clergye gyveth us, as though that preste were the clergye. But than forgete we to loke what good men be therin, and what good counsayle they gyve us, and what example they shew us.' More's comment is not merely a reproof to the muckrakers, who (as in all ages) were inclined to stress failure at the expense of success, but should also remind us that there were churchmen whose good example was appreciated.

In judging relations between the clergy and the laity, one must strike a fair balance between favourable and hostile elements. There was undoubtedly some anti-clericalism, which may indeed have been growing in strength in the last decade before the meeting of the Reformation Parliament, possibly as rumours of the new teachings in Germany began to filter into the country and undermined the standing of the priesthood. Equally, however, it is impossible to say that the Church had lost its grip on popular sentiment; even although much religious observance may have been essentially conventional, many men and women were prepared to do far more than give mere lip-service to the Church's demands. It required the external force of the King's proceedings to bring about an effective revolution in the Church, and a good deal more than that revolution to alienate decisively the affections of the bulk of the laity from the old religious ways.

CHAPTER 39

Education and learning

Traditionally, learning was associated with the Church, as is clearly shown by the fact that the term 'clerk', denoting someone who had been ordained, came to be applied more or less indiscriminately to any literate person. But, as we have seen, by the late Middle Ages such an identification of literacy with the clerical order was becoming increasingly outmoded. The law had emerged as a literate profession for laymen, and men questioned the right of those who could read to share the privileges of the clerical order (Chs 33, 36). Nevertheless, there were ways in which the Church was still closely involved in learning, not least in its connection with the system of education which was provided. This was certainly true at the start of our period, and although one can see some erosion of its position during the fifteenth and sixteenth centuries, churchmen still played the dominant part in schooling up to and beyond the Reformation. During this period, however, one sees the appearance of a class of schoolmasters who had not proceeded beyond minor orders, perhaps because they had chosen a married rather than a celibate life, and a growing measure of educational patronage by the laity.

Institutions fell into two broad divisions, reading and song schools, which provided a basic elementary education, and grammar schools, which concentrated on the study of Latin. Beyond these, there was the higher scholarship of the universities and the Inns of Court, which provided training for men who were normally preparing for careers in the Church or the law, but who might have been sent there to study without any specific career in mind. There is a danger, however, in applying too rigid categories, and undoubtedly there were overlaps between the different levels of the education system. Since some grammar schools expected their pupils to have some knowledge of the basic grammar text, that of Donatus, before entry, a requirement found in the Winchester College statutes of 1400 and the Eton statutes of 1447, it is clear that some song schools must have taught the subject at least at a rudimentary level. On the other hand, one also finds some grammar schools providing elementary instruction; the 1525 statutes of Manchester Grammar School laid down that the scholars should take it in turn to teach the alphabet to the infants who sat at one end of the schoolroom. There may also have been some overlap between grammar schooling and the universities, because some Oxford colleges made provision for instruction to be given in plainsong and grammar before boys embarked on the study of logic and the rest of the arts course. As far as can be seen, however, they were generally taught outside the colleges by professional schoolmasters (229, pp.69–70, 185–6).

The fact that one staple of primary education was song reflects ecclesiastical influence, because it was in the Church that this had practical application. It explains the role of the monasteries in education, because with the elaboration of polyphonic composition boys' voices would be required for the proper performance of services; it is noteworthy that some of the greatest composers of the day served as monastic choirmasters, such as Tallis, who was organist and master of the choristers at Waltham for some years before the Dissolution. However, the number of boys in these monastic schools was often small, seldom more than a dozen and often fewer. In most schools, song was probably limited to plainsong, which could lay the foundations of saying the daily office for those who ultimately proceeded to take orders. The study of Latin grammar, the basis of secondary education, was equally related to the needs of the Church (218, iii. 17–19; 228, p.8).

For these reasons, it is hardly surprising that churchmen played an important part as patrons of education, although pious lay people might also endow schools as a form of chantry, with stipulations that the master should celebrate mass for their souls. The earliest of the great foundations was that of William of Wykeham, whose college at Winchester, set up in 1382, provided places for seventy scholars. Its scale was much greater than anything which had preceded it; even more important was the radically different emphasis placed on education, which was seen as the college's principal aim, instead of it being merely an adjunct to the saying of the offices. It provided a model for later founders, although few could match the lavishness of the endowment; only Henry VI's college at Eton, which was closely modelled on it, and Wolsey's at Ipswich, which survived his fall only on a reduced scale, were in any way comparable. The foundation of Eton, however, may have provided an incentive to various court prelates to establish further, though smaller, schools; certainly there was a sudden flurry of new establishments in the years immediately before the outbreak of the wars of Lancaster and York. Bishop Alnwick of Lincoln, in whose diocese Eton lay, was to found a grammar school in the town of the same name, presumably his place of origin, and John Chedworth, a later holder of the same see, set up one at Cirencester. Thomas Beckington, the King's secretary, laid down new statutes for the schooling of the choristers in his cathedral at Wells, which not only provided for the teaching of grammar, plainsong and polyphony, but also showed marked moderation in matters of discipline – pupils were to be warned first for offences, and flogging was to be employed only if this failed. A further founder influenced by Eton was its second provost, William Waynflete, who established two grammar schools, one at his birthplace in Lincolnshire and the other in connection with the college of St Mary Magdalen which he founded in the University of Oxford (228, pp.80–1; 229, pp.187, 197–200).

Many foundations, however, were markedly smaller, such as that set up in 1384 by Lady Katherine Berkeley at Wotton-under-Edge in Gloucestershire. As at Winchester, its near contemporary, the main purpose was educational, although as it was stipulated that masses be said, it was necessary for the master to be a priest. This endowment had one important characteristic which differed from customary practice: it was directed to maintaining the teacher rather than meeting the expenses of pupils, who would then support the teacher by fees. Such an association of school and chantry remained normal until the early sixteenth century, when one begins to find prayers for the founder being recited in class rather than offered in the mass, and it then became possible to appoint a lay master rather than a priest. Forms of endowment continued to vary; sometimes provision was made for free education for all, at other times it was laid down that while it was to be free for those who could not afford it otherwise, fees were to be charged for those who could pay (228, pp.192–3; 229, pp.188–9, 196).

The greatest problem in assessing how many schools were available in the late Middle Ages is the absence of direct evidence. The existence of many can be deduced only from isolated references in a wide range of sources, and it is often impossible to deduce how long a particular establishment survived, or if, when two references survive from dates half a century apart, a school's existence was uninterrupted. Certainly there were times when masters were hard to find; in the mid fifteenth century complaints were made that some schools which had previously existed were now empty because of the shortage of masters, and petitions were presented for the endowment of houses to teach grammar. Even when schools did not go into abeyance, it was possible that there may have been times when the qualifications of the masters declined; it seems clear that after the Black Death there was a fall in the number of arts graduates who became teachers, possibly because men with degrees had better prospects of advancement if they obtained a benefice. Even in major centres, such as York, where a graduate master had probably been the norm, one sees the appearance of masters who had not taken degrees. The universities appear to have accepted the situation, even establishing an alternative degree, that of master of grammar. At Cambridge there seems to have been a definite course leading to the degree, at Oxford men who had already taught grammar appear to have supplicated for a formal licence to do so, their capacity being assessed by some token exercise. This qualification disappeared again about the middle of the sixteenth century, presumably as the number of arts graduates willing to teach increased. It is likely, however, that for the greater part of our period most schoolmasters had not attained degrees in arts, and that the qualification of master of grammar was sought only by men who wished posts for which some stipulation was laid down concerning graduate status (227, p.6; 229, pp.151–4, 221; 231, pp.186–7).

It has also been argued that the declining level of qualifications brought in its train a fall in grammar standards. One of the best known early-fifteenth-century grammar masters was John Leland; he wrote various works on syntax and was admired by his contemporaries, one of whom described him as 'flos gramaticorum'. However, his grammatical tracts, which are extant, show an approach markedly less critical than that of earlier writers, and provide a simplified manual of instruction. Perhaps the modern critic's description of this as 'debasement' is unduly harsh; if Leland was attempting to produce a basic grammar for school pupils rather than a treatise for grammarians, simplification was a practical necessity. Some teachers preserved considerable academic interests; John Seward, a master in London during the reigns of Henry IV and Henry V, wrote a number of small treatises, particularly on Latin prosody, although his views on this were untouched by the new ideals of Renaissance humanism. His writings hint at the existence of a group of schoolmasters who engaged in disputes on literary matters (231, pp.169–70, 181–4; 246, p.11).

The award of such qualifications as master of grammar by the universities, which were clerical bodies, reflects the Church's supervisory role in educational matters. Another manifestation of this was its attempts to control the number of existing schools. In late medieval York, the chancellor of the cathedral and the chapter claimed a right to license grammar masters, and there were regular attempts in London to limit the number of schools to three. In neither case were these attempts particularly successful; there is evidence of various schools existing in York without authorization, and in London the authorities seem to have bowed to the inevitable. The existence of Seward and his circle shows that other schools already existed in the early fifteenth century, and later in it a number of new establishments were actually licensed. The culmination of such educational expansion came in the sixteenth century when John Colet, dean of St Paul's and the son of a former mayor of the city, refounded the cathedral school there as a free grammar school (227, pp.8–9; 229, pp.212–14). This foundation was to be particularly important in propagating the new humanist learning, and will be considered again later in this chapter.

New schools were established elsewhere too, although as their foundation depended on the whims of individual benefactors, these were distributed somewhat fortuitously throughout the country. What Colet was to do at St Paul's had already been foreshadowed elsewhere, because a number of ancient cathedral schools became free grammar foundations during this period. But the absence of records often makes it impossible to say whether or not schools existed; we have no mention of them in places such as Newcastle or Southampton, yet there is no reason to believe that they were likely to be without one when comparable towns, such as Bristol and Coventry, possessed schools which are mentioned fairly frequently in surviving sources. Such references, however, suggest that in those towns the schools possessed a greater measure of popular favour. As far as can be judged, the fifteenth and early sixteenth centuries saw some increase in the number of endowed free grammar schools in the larger towns, although it was not until after the Reformation that the existence of these became the norm.

Records are even more patchy concerning song and reading schools, but surviving evidence suggests that these were often taught by the parish clergy, who might also provide some grammar instruction. Again, numbers seem to have grown; recent work has suggested that in the diocese of York reading schools in the parishes increased from about 15 at the end of the fourteenth century to almost 60 in 1500 and 96 in 1548. In the south-western counties too, a substantial number of village schools appear to have been set up in the early Tudor period (227, p.15; 228, p.6; 229, p.220). One may even infer the existence of otherwise unknown schools from the evident spread of literacy in the late Middle Ages. Proceedings in various heresy prosecutions, particularly a well-documented one at Coventry in 1512, show that an ability to read existed even in the artisan class, and Thrupp's examination of educational standards in London shows that 40 per cent of male witnesses who appeared before the consistory court during Edward IV's reign were literate. It is likely that this term implied the knowledge of at least a little Latin, and it is reasonable to assume that others again could read English. Since company regulations might stipulate that apprentices should show some ability to read and write, there must have been places where they could acquire such skills (104, pp.156–8; 241, pp.113–14). Writing indeed was becoming increasingly a social and economic necessity, and it is no accident that this period sees the first survival of collections of family correspondence, such as those of the Pastons, the Stonors and the Celys. Although some correspondents might require an amanuensis, the idea of communicating by letter was well established in the course of the fifteenth century.

It is not always certain how such literacy was attained. It is quite possible that not all education was given formally in schools, nor that it was all controlled by the Church. In London there are one or two allusions to schools held by scriveners, and in York the same group of men even protested against priests who taught writing. Their role may have extended beyond simple instruction in penmanship, because they may also have taught some simple conveyancing. Some schools certainly provided instruction in business skills; in the late fifteenth century accounts as well as writing were included in the curriculum of elementary schools at Acaster Selby and Rotherham. One suspects, however, that most merchants picked up the essentials of writing and accounting in the course of their work – certainly the records of the Cely family suggest that they were without any formal training. It is true that some men may have tried to cash in on the requirements of business; a number of treatises survive on letter-writing and conveyancing, and in 1432 Oxford University issued regulations for teachers who instructed people in Latin composition, speaking French, drafting charters and pleading in the English manner (104, p.159; 227, pp.24–5). One may, however, doubt if a training in writing Latin and French contributed much to business skills at a time when the vernacular was coming increasingly into use, and instruction in modes of pleading was probably taken over by the developing Inns of Court (Ch.33).

At the highest level of education, the universities, the period saw various organizational developments, although for much of the time little intellectual vigour. Much is obscure about the history of the universities, even on such basic questions as the numbers attending them. There seems to have been a decline in the student population at Oxford between the late fourteenth century and 1438, to about 1,000, but numbers increased again by the beginning of the sixteenth century. Cambridge was smaller, but its reputation and numbers grew during the fifteenth century, perhaps in part because Oxford had incurred suspicion as the source of Wycliffite heresy. The increase in the number of graduate parish clergy (Ch.34) may reflect this recovery in the student population. The most important development in both universities was the foundation of colleges, although these contained only a minority of students, most of whom lived in various private halls or in lodgings. It was not until the end of the sixteenth century that the colleges became dominant within the universities. In the late Middle Ages they were normally graduate establishments for students who had completed their arts course and were studying in one of the higher faculties such as theology or law. This was still true of such fifteenth-century foundations at Oxford as Lincoln and All Souls, although in the late fourteenth century a new kind of college had been founded when William of Wykeham established New College, which provided a large number of places for undergraduates. This precedent was followed in two mid-fifteenth-century colleges, King's at Cambridge and Magdalen at Oxford. Henry VI, in his foundation of King's, was consciously imitating Wykeham, in the same way, as we have seen, in which he followed Wykeham's college at Winchester in his foundation of Eton. William Waynflete, the founder of Magdalen, was clearly influenced by the King, who had appointed him headmaster of Eton and secured his appointment to the great see of Winchester, so it is hardly surprising that his college, too, owed much to the model of New College.

A striking feature of the statutes in many of the fifteenth-century colleges was the express stipulation that strong measures should be taken against any Fellow who was found guilty of heresy (241, pp.212–14). The background to this was the fear of Lollardy, which had taken its origins from the intellectual life of late-fourteenth-century Oxford (Ch.40). This had been a period of some speculative vigour, but the fifteenth century saw a retreat into orthodoxy and fears that theological enquiry was potentially too dangerous for men to indulge in it freely. Not until the new influences of Renaissance humanism began to affect the curriculum did the universities again make a significant contribution to intellectual innovation.

Such ideas developed slowly; the study of fifteenth-century humanism in England is essentially a record of patrons who collected books and occasionally employed visiting Italian scholars. The most notable of these was Humphrey, duke of Gloucester, whose fame as a collector has been perpetuated by the large gifts of books which he presented to Oxford. A scrutiny of the titles, however, suggests that he was primarily a bibliophile and less a pure humanist, for many of the books in his donation were texts of medieval authors. William Grey, bishop of Ely, another book collector and benefactor of Balliol College, also included classical texts in his donation, but the majority were traditional theology. He was, however, undoubtedly interested in the new learning, having spent some ten years in Italy, partly in study and partly as Henry VI's proctor at the Curia. After his return to England, he supported the young scholar John Free's journey to Italy, but although the latter's classical talents won respect even from Italian humanists, he died young and was able to contribute only his books, acquired after his death by other Englishmen in Italy, to the later development of humanism in his own country. In the early Yorkist period, the two men whose patronage was most influential in England were John Tiptoft, earl of Worcester, and Archbishop George Neville of York, both of whom were noted book collectors, and the latter of whom gave support to the development of Greek studies (246, pp.42, 45, 61–2, 66, 92, 107, 115, 144).

In Italy, an important influence in spreading the new learning was that of various professional educators, and it was around 1480 that men with humanist interests began to appear as schoolmasters in England for the first time. Here the key man was John Anwykyll, who was appointed master of the grammar school attached to Magdalen College, Oxford, in 1481, and whose *Compendium Totius Grammaticae* was printed in Oxford in 1483. The contents of this showed a marked break with older grammar texts, drawing on the work of Italian scholars such as Niccolo Perotti and Lorenzo Valla, and giving citations from various classical authors. Anwykyll's deputy and successor at Magdalen College School, John Stanbridge, also produced various works of grammar, which, through the new medium of the printed book, achieved wide circulation; although he was perhaps rather more traditional in outlook than Anwykyll, he too cited a substantial number of usages from ancient rather than medieval writers. This school was to play a seminal role in the development of English humanism, and a variety of men who were active in its growth in the early sixteenth century could trace its influence on their early careers (225, p.50; 229, pp.107–8).

By the 1480s too, England was a country to which occasional visiting Italian humanists came in search of patrons, although not always with success. Pietro Carmeliano arrived there in 1481, and seems to have eked out a living either by teaching or working for printers until the accession of Henry VII, who extended to him the favour which he had attempted to secure from the last Yorkists. He was associated with English scholars and wrote two poems in praise of Anwykyll. Henry VII may well have welcomed cultivated Italians to his court in the hope that their writings could serve to justify his dubious title to the other princes of Europe, and when Polydore Vergil arrived in England in 1502, as deputy to the papal collector, he was well received by the King, who encouraged him to work on the history of the country. By this time England was being more drawn into the main stream of European cultural development, and new patrons were able to attract scholars of the first rank. Most notable of these was Erasmus, whose pupil in Paris, William Blount, Lord Mountjoy, brought him to England, where he spent some time in Cambridge as well as making friends in London, most notably with the two finest English scholars of the day, Sir Thomas More and John Colet. Of these two, More was the writer of greater distinction, but in the long run Colet's influence may have been the greater, through his foundation of the new school at St Paul's, which was intended to provide for teaching the laity a humanist piety of the kind which was the Erasmian ideal. It is noteworthy that William Lily, incidentally a married man, whom Colet chose to be headmaster of his new school, combined scholarship and piety in his outlook (225, pp.6, 48–9; 246, pp.171–2).

There are other indications, too, of how far the new learning was becoming established in England by the early sixteenth century. Significantly, by 1520 the old medieval grammars, which had appeared from some of the earliest English presses, were going out of print – clearly there was no longer a demand for them – and were being supplanted by new humanist works, such as Erasmus's *De Duplici Copia Verborum*, which was to become the standard manual of literary style in English schools. It is a further measure of English participation in Renaissance culture that the second decade of the sixteenth century saw an increase in the number of humanist books which appeared from presses in the country, although it must be admitted that these did not include any of the major scholarly critical texts, which still appeared on the Continent (225, pp.31, 65–6; 229, p.112).

At the higher educational level, the foundation of Corpus Christi College, Oxford in 1515–16 marked a new departure. Bishop Richard Fox of Winchester was a long-standing royal servant, and was closely associated with the circle of scholars around Erasmus, More and Colet. In his new college, he provided for a public lecturer in Greek and for readers in Latin and theology, thereby drawing together, in true Erasmian fashion, the strands of new learning and of piety. Significantly, in theology, stress was to be laid on the patristic writers, Greek as well as Latin, rather than on medieval writings. Nor was he the only founder with a sympathy for the new learning; another such was Wolsey, who encouraged humanists to come to Oxford in the following decade, and whose own Cardinal College, later Christ Church, was intended to encourage the new learning (225, p.83). It is likely that Robert Joseph, the humanist Evesham monk, whose letters we noted earlier (Ch.37), had laid the foundations of his scholarly interests in Oxford as a result of such educational benefactions.

Undoubtedly such places played an important part in forming the educational standards of only a relatively small intellectual group, but these values were passed on in the next generation to a wider group at court and among the aristocracy, as well as influencing teachers in the best of the grammar schools. How extensive their influence was over the country as a whole is less certain, because for most men education was purely functional and concerned with the basic skills of literacy and numeracy. For them, the spread of local schools was far more important. Nevertheless, it was the combination of such ideals with a developing literacy at the lower level which created the cultural milieu which fostered the spread of Reformation teachings both through criticisms of the traditional Church order and by creating a society capable of reading religious literature in its own language. The same cultural development also laid the foundations for the literary flowering of the Elizabethan age.

CHAPTER 40

Wyclif and Lollardy

Lollardy [F] was a complex phenomenon, and in examining its origins one has to look at various factors to explain why it arose, and why England, which had hitherto been singularly free of heresy, proved a suitable ground for it. The movement, moreover, was unusual in character, originating in the speculations of a theologian but ending far away from the subtle distinctions of the schools. It was hardly surprising that theologians should incur suspicion of heresy – it was almost an occupational risk for them that their intellectual speculation might overstep the bounds of accepted orthodoxy – but it was less normal for them to persist in it. Usually they would submit to the Church's teaching, withdrawing or modifying such of their views as had been criticized. Where Wyclif was unusual was that he not only persisted in affirming views which had been condemned but even proceeded beyond them to others even more repugnant to orthodox opinion. Even more surprising was the development of a popular movement after Wyclif's condemnation; professors are not naturally revolutionary leaders. To understand why this occurred, it will be necessary later to examine how his ideas affected the milieu of contemporary popular religion and led to the growth of dissent.

The background to Wyclif's own unorthodoxy must be sought first in the intellectual life of fourteenth-century Oxford. Since the middle of the century, it had been falling out of the main stream of European thought, possibly because of the death of a number of its younger scholars in the Black Death, but more probably because the Anglo-French War had broken the ties it had had with the greatest centre of European theological thought, the University of Paris. As the number of English students there declined, Oxford in turn became more parochial in outlook. Links were not broken entirely – one finds occasional references to Parisian thought in texts originating in Oxford – but they were less close than they had been. Whereas in the thirteenth century, theological innovations were attacked almost simultaneously on both sides of the Channel, by Wyclif's time the two universities were developing more independent traditions. These did, however, have a common background in the philosophical works of the English Franciscan William of Ockham (d.1347), whose writings had stressed the impossibility of establishing a purely rational foundation for faith, and had emphasized the absolute freedom of God's will in relation to creation. Such teachings led to greater stress being laid on revealed truth and on faith. It also led to greater concern with what God would do with the individual, whether or not he would be saved, and how the process of salvation worked. Irrespective of whether later scholars accepted or rejected Ockham's metaphysics, they were deeply concerned with the issues which arose from them.

In the years immediately before the outbreak of the Wyclif crisis, there were various academic controversies in Oxford, both in the faculty of arts and among the theologians. In 1368 Archbishop Langham censured the writings of the Durham monk Uthred of Boldon and banned his views from the schools, although he does not appear to have been required to make any formal recantation. However, his house withdrew him from the university, although it did not disgrace him. His thought was eclectic, including some views tending to Pelagianism [F], which were probably of Ockhamist origin, but also an affirmation that it was impossible for things to be annihilated, an opinion closely associated with the realist metaphysics being taught at the same time by Wyclif in the faculty of arts (218, ii. 49–51; 234, pp.103, 109–10). Until the 1370s, however, Wyclif himself was not a controversial figure; his troubles began only when he moved from the faculty of arts to that of theology. His first major controversy, with the Carmelite friar John Kenningham, which was concerned with the issue of the eternity of being, was in the early 1370s, when Wyclif was incepting in theology and was concerned with applying some of his metaphysical views to theological matters. This remained true of the later controversies which Wyclif provoked, notably his views on the Bible and on the Eucharist. His fundamentalist view of the Bible rested not only on a belief that it was the yardstick by which matters of faith should be measured, but also in the idea that it was eternally present in God. His concern for the Bible was clearly shown by him producing a *Postilla* or commentary on the whole of it, probably in the early 1370s, something which none of his contemporaries did. Later he was to affirm that it should be translated into the vernacular, and the translation which emanated from his followers was to be a crucial text for the popular movement which grew up. His refusal to accept that matter could be annihilated lay at the basis of his insistence that the material bread and wine in the Eucharist remained after consecration, although he did not (as did some later Lollards) deny the spiritual presence of Christ in the host, which he saw as being transmuted sacramentally but not physically. Although his Eucharistic views were his most striking deviation from contemporary orthodoxy, one should stress that he was slow to formulate his final ideas on this topic; despite his earlier metaphysical opinions, he tried for a long time to remain within the limits of orthodoxy on the doctrine of transubstantiation, ultimately departing from it only reluctantly. A lack of clarity in his views suggests a man who was reluctant to break with official teaching, despite the direction in which his own earlier thought was tending (220, ii. 503–5, 550–6; 231, pp.267–8, 283; 234, p.195).

Another aspect of Wyclif's career, however, probably also affected his thinking. As well as being a scholastic philosopher and theologian, he was also engaged in the political world. From the early 1370s he served the Crown in diplomacy and as a controversial writer. His presentation to the benefice of Lutterworth in 1374 was presumably a reward for earlier service, and in the same year he was a member of an embassy sent to negotiate with the Pope at Bruges on various matters connected with royal and papal rights over the clergy. He might have expected further promotion but did not attain it, and it is possible, although one cannot prove it, that his later cantankerousness may have been partly caused by disappointment at this. In the early 1370s he may have been associated with the

Black Prince, but he seems to have entered John of Gaunt's service by the time of the Good Parliament in 1376. When Wyclif was summoned before the bishops in 1377 to answer for his contumacy in attacking the episcopate, it was Gaunt who defended him, both by retaining the services of various doctors of divinity and by trying to overawe the Convocation at which Wyclif was cited to appear. Although the proceedings were stayed, this did not narrow the rift between the Oxford theologian and his ecclesiastical superiors. Wyclif's debt to the secular power may explain some of his views on rightful lordship, which were yet another point of divergence between him and the Church's teaching. By affirming that dominion could be rightly possessed only by those in a state of grace, who were unknowable because of God's absolute freedom to save or reject men irrespective of their lives, Wyclif might have been expected to deny all forms of authority, but in fact he denied this only to the visible Church, while asserting that royal power came from God; it had therefore to be obeyed in all matters, including ecclesiastical ones (220, ii. 518–19, 543–4; 226, pp.55–7, 63, 74–6). This respect which Wyclif afforded to the laity reflects more the views of a royal servant than those of a philosopher following through the logic of his argument to its final conclusion.

Not surprisingly, Wyclif's radicalism attracted both support and criticism, as different groups of men employed his arguments to back up their own. His attitude to possession made him allies among the friars, who did not finally break with him until 1380–81, probably on account of his Eucharistic views. By this time, of course, Wyclif had already come under attack; a number of propositions from his *De civili dominio* were condemned by Gregory XI in 1377 (220, ii, 560; 234, pp.190–1). The English authorities, however, were slow to move, particularly those at Oxford, who were not prepared to abandon one of the university's leading scholars. Instead they declared publicly that although Wyclif's conclusions sounded bad to the ear, they were still true. The university's efforts to preserve its independence from outside interference were a major factor in giving Wyclif and his academic followers some respite from prosecution. In 1378 Wyclif was again summoned to appear before the bishops, but all they did was to enjoin him to abstain from arguing disputed opinions. The outbreak of the Great Schism protected him from further papal pressure, and also hardened his views on the Papacy as such; in the next year or two his writings on the subject became increasingly strident in tone. More important, the development of his thought on the Eucharist gave his opponents within the university an opportunity to counterattack. In the winter of 1380–81, a commission appointed by the chancellor of the university found by a narrow majority that he was guilty of maintaining erroneous doctrines. It was at this point that Wyclif made the crucial decision not to submit, and after an unsuccessful attempt to appeal to the lay power, he left Oxford for Lutterworth. He remained there unmolested and continued writing in increasingly extreme terms, until he died of a stroke at the end of 1384, aged about fifty-five. The absence of action against him by the authorities, however, suggests that his influence was thought to be slight (226, pp.81–2, 97–9, 116–18).

The movement which developed from the 1380s onwards certainly derived some of its beliefs from Wyclif's teaching, and members of it undoubtedly looked to him as a major influence. Some groups of later heretics may also, however, have come under the influence of a Continental dissident group, the Brethren of the Free Spirit, some of whose views are occasionally echoed in Lollard trials (214). How these reached England can only be conjectured, but trading links with the Low Countries may have provided a channel of communication. There were three main groups among the early Lollards, only one of which was closely connected with Wyclif, namely the academics at Oxford who were attracted by his teaching. Some of these were men of distinction and high reputation, such as Nicholas Hereford and Philip Repingdon, and as long as they adhered to Wyclif's views, they attracted the attention of the authorities. Secondly, some of his teachings appealed to members of the knightly class, who extended patronage to Wycliffite clerks. Such members of the lower clergy, by no means all of them graduates, and their lay followers, comprised the third group. Occasionally one sees connections between the groups; one knight, Sir William Neville, spoke well of Nicholas Hereford, and another, Sir Thomas Latimer, who is known to have presented a Lollard priest to a benefice in his gift, may well have supported him in preaching heresy to his congregation (135, pp.194–9). A surviving Wycliffite commentary on the Apocalypse, the colophon of which states that it was written in prison in 1389, contains too many references to have been produced from memory, and was the work of a heretical scholar whose gaoler may perhaps have been well disposed to his views. The later geographical distribution of Lollards tends to reflect the activity of individual preachers, and in some cases at any rate their areas of teaching correspond to places where they might have sympathetic lay patrons.

It is hardly surprising that Wyclif had academic followers. The atmosphere of the schools was conducive to the growth of scholarly discipleship, and a distinguished theologian, such as he was, would naturally attract admirers. Also, the university's dislike of episcopal interference in its affairs gave the academic Lollards some protection even among men who did not share their views – indeed twice in thirty years an archbishop of Canterbury had to overcome opposition from men who were in no way unorthodox, but who were prepared to defend the university's privileges. The first such occasion was in 1382 when Courtenay secured the condemnation of various Wycliffite propositions by a synod at Blackfriars in London, and tried to impose this on Oxford. The most vigorous supporters of the measure were mainly regulars, whereas Wyclif's followers were mostly seculars, and Courtenay's proceedings occurred at a time when tension was rising between the two groups of clergy. Richard Rigg, the chancellor of the university and a secular, although no heretic, was prepared to support his fellow seculars, and chose two of Wyclif's more noted followers, Hereford and Repingdon (the latter in fact an Augustinian canon), to preach the university sermon on the major feasts of the Ascension and Corpus Christi. It was on the latter day that the Blackfriars decrees were due to be promulgated in Oxford. The resistance, however, was futile; Rigg himself was cited before the archbishop and compelled to submit, while Courtenay strengthened his position by securing the support of the royal Council. Immediate Lollard resistance in Oxford soon collapsed, with a number of Wyclif's major supporters submitting, notably

Repingdon, who rose in the hierarchy to end his career ultimately as bishop of Lincoln. Hereford was slower to surrender, not coming to terms with the authorities until about 1391 (220, ii. 564–9). Not all the submissions seem to have been sincere, but Courtenay's measures did purge the university of open heresy.

Wyclif's influence did not entirely disappear, particularly from the philosophical teaching of the university. Free speculation was not entirely curbed, and an interest in Wyclif's logic persisted until about the turn of the century. Men who were by no means prepared to follow him into heresy were impressed by his philosophy; even the man who wrote the fullest academic confutation of Wyclif, Thomas Netter of Walden, was among their number. A substantial number of manuscripts of his philosophical work were copied after his condemnation, although significantly, his name is not included in them; presumably it was erased to guard the owner of the work from suspicion of heresy. Even as late as 1403, his *Postilla* on the New Testament was being copied in Oxford. Men could still discriminate between the different issues on which Wyclif had put forward controversial views; Richard Ullerston, who wrote one treatise against the Lollard attack on endowments, produced another in defence of translating the Scriptures into English (215; 234, pp.223–5, 243).

Such survivals of Wycliffite teaching form the background to a certain resurgence of its activity in Oxford in the first decade of the fifteenth century, notably at St Edmund Hall. In 1406, its principal, William Taylor, in a sermon at St Paul's Cross, supported the right of lay lords to deprive the religious of their temporal possessions. About the same time another Oxford Lollard, Peter Payne, secured possession of the university seal and attached it to a eulogy of Wyclif which he sent to the Prague reformers. He himself had to flee therein 1413, and played an active part in the Hussite movement. These years also saw renewed archiepiscopal pressure on the university, with Arundel being markedly clumsier and less effective than Courtenay. The university, ever conscious of its rights, was slow to appoint a commission to investigate Wyclif's writings, not doing so until 1409. It was not until 1411 that this produced a list of 267 errors taken from them, to be sent to the Canterbury Convocation, whence they were forwarded to the Pope and condemned in 1413. Later in the year Arundel tried to conduct a visitation of the university, but this only provoked a further disorder, during which one of the proctors defied an interdict imposed by the archbishop on the university church (220, ii, 571–3). These proceedings ended with the triumph of official orthodoxy, closed the door to further debates on the legitimacy of translating the Scriptures and marked the beginning of a period in which the university was firmly committed to the maintenance of approved teaching. Lollardy, too, reached a turning-point, being bereft of its academic leadership. Its theology, which had been developed in the subtle learning of scholastic disputation, became static, and, as the movement became predominantly lay, simplified. A few academic heretics survived beyond the crisis of Oldcastle's rebellion, but were gradually hunted down, the last, Richard Wyche, being put to death as late as 1440. It is, however, fair to say that intellectual Lollardy received its death-blow from Arundel.

The second group of Wyclif's followers, the Lollard knights, has recently been shown to have comprised a number of influential men, who supported unorthodoxy and patronized Lollard preachers (135). One of them indeed, Sir John Clanvow, wrote a religious treatise contrasting the ways to heaven and to hell; although this contained little that was specifically unorthodox, its omission of customary pious practices showed where the author's views lay. At one point too he was prepared to identify himself with the despised sect of Lollards. It is never quite clear what attracted these men to dissent, but it is worth remembering that there was a genuine concern for spiritual matters among the laity at this time, and in such circumstances individual ideas could easily slip into heresy. Lay piety, after all, could also be completely orthodox, as can be seen from the *Livre de Seyntz Medicines*, written in 1354 by Henry, duke of Lancaster, a noted soldier in the early part of the Hundred Years War. The search for salvation in popular religious practices reflects a concern of the age, and it is not always easy to draw the boundary between orthodoxy and heresy. There is a strand of puritanism in some aristocratic religious beliefs, which could occur independently of unorthodoxy. One sees this, for example, in the Arundel family; the archbishop's father and brother both asked that their funerals be conducted without pomp, a point worth bearing in mind when one considers the terms of the archbishop's own will, which in its description of himself as an unworthy sinner and of his body as a foetid and putrid cadaver is curiously close to the phraseology employed in the wills of men with Lollard connections. It may have been such family tradition, rather than her late husband's friendship with Lollard sympathizers, which prompted Arundel's niece, Joan Beauchamp to make a similar will. When such common ground existed between heresy and orthodoxy, it is perhaps less surprising that one noted Lollard knight, Sir William Neville, was brother of the archbishop of York (118, p.106; 135, pp.166, 201–6, 214–19; 232, pp.231–3).

How the Lollard knights were subjected to Wyclif's teaching is not known, and is by no means easy to explain. It is only a plausible inference that their court connections, particularly with the Black Prince, may have brought them under his influence at a time when he was a royal servant. Possibly some of Wyclif's views on dominion and on the clerical ownership of goods appealed also to their cupidity; it is worth noting that a number of them were able to invest in the lands of alien priories, which had been taken into the King's hands because of the war. They were not alone in this, of course, but they may have been happy to rationalize their encroachments on Church property by reference to the heresiarch. Clerical wealth undoubtedly attracted the lesser landed class in an age of agricultural recession; although Parliament took no notice of a Lollard manifesto posted in London in 1395, in 1410 it was willing to listen to proposals for ecclesiastical disendowment. Sympathy for Lollardy was also shown by those knights who in the Coventry Parliament of 1404 kept their heads covered in the presence of the host, a gesture which showed open defiance of the Church's teaching on transubstantiation (135, pp.189–92, 221; 226, pp.147, 155). It seems clear that various factors contributed to this unorthodoxy, but to estimate the relative importance of radical religious sentiment, anti-clericalism and economic motives of varying degrees of cynicism is impossible.

The knights' most important contribution to the movement was their patronage of preachers, and they may also have provided havens for the copying and transmission of Lollard texts. Study of manuscripts of these, such as the heretical sermon cycle, suggests that the copying was done with considerable care and was thoroughly checked thereafter. The existence of a substantial number of extant texts of the cycle, containing few serious variations, suggests competent organization behind the production and that it took place within a fairly short time span. Many of the manuscripts are too large for easy concealment, so it is likely that those responsible for them felt that they were well protected. Much the same can be said of other Wycliffite writings, including the vernacular Bible and the theological commonplace books, the *Floretum* or *Rosarium Theologiae*, which draw heavily on Wyclif's writings. These were in Latin, but one vernacular version of the *Rosarium* also survives, and may well have been a link in the transmission of Wyclif's ideas to a wider audience than that of the schools. There are later pointers to the Lollard knights being connected with men who preserved heretical texts. In 1407, two Czech scholars transcribed, for dispatch to Prague, a copy of Wyclif's *De Dominio* at Braybrooke in Northamptonshire. The rector there, Robert Hook, was a notorious Lollard who had been presented to the benefice by Sir Thomas Latimer, one of the knights named as a heretic by two of the major chroniclers of the time. Three years later Richard Wyche wrote a letter to Hus on the same day as Sir John Oldcastle, the last important Lollard knight, wrote to one of the Hus's lay supporters, almost certainly for dispatch by the same messenger (135, pp.195–6; 226, p.162).

It is noteworthy that there were close personal ties between many of the men whom the chroniclers identify as Lollard sympathizers, these being the more striking because they were of widely scattered geographical origins. They appear together as witnesses to documents, as feoffees and as executors of wills. They also shared a close connection with the court of Richard II, and many of them had earlier served the Black Prince. Indeed the involvement of some of them in diplomacy may well have helped to forge the links between the heretical movements in England and Bohemia at the time of the King's first marriage. During the crisis of the Appellants in 1387–88, they seem to have avoided trouble, but several of them were prominent among Richard's advisers after his resumption of power. This was shown clearly by their regular attendance at the Council – Sir Richard Sturry indeed attended for 159 consecutive days in 1392–93, and other suspects who were active included Clanvow, Neville and Sir Lewis Clifford (135, pp.160–1; 150, pp.141–2). Their court connections probably helped to protect them, and those to whom they extended their support, against the Church authorities. However orthodox the King was personally, he might well trust a Lollard chamber knight more willingly than an archbishop such as Arundel who was the brother of one of his most intransigent enemies and who had been forced on him as Chancellor by the Appellants. This personal favour from the King can be the only explanation of the knights' immunity at this period, because their heresy was sufficiently notorious for more than one chronicler to mention it.

At the popular level, Lollardy appears to have been disseminated by members of the lower clergy, and to a lesser extent by sympathetic laymen. One chronicle account of the Lollards conducting their own ordinations and celebrating a modified form of the Eucharist is borne out by an entry in a Salisbury bishop's register (214). However, judging by the number of chaplains who participated in Oldcastle's rebellion in 1414, the main leadership of the popular movement came from lesser clergy who had been properly ordained. Notable among these in the 1380s was William Swinderby, the puritanical hermit of Leicester, who may have been influenced by Wyclif's teachings, although he was certainly not an extremist on the question of transubstantiation. Prosecuted by Bishop Buckingham of Lincoln in 1382, he betook himself to the West Country, where in 1391 he was brought to trial again by Bishop Trefnant of Hereford; he was, however, protected against punishment by going to court with a safe-conduct provided by some gentry of the diocese. This looks very like an example of how heretics were assisted by the patronage of the landed class, for a number of Lollard knights had either inherited or acquired by marriage lands in that part of the country. It may well have been Swinderby's teaching too which recruited the young John Oldcastle to the sect (226, pp.103–5, 121–36).

The Church authorities were sufficiently alarmed in Richard II's later years to seek the death penalty for heresy. The reaction of Parliament at that time is not known, and it was not until 1401 that it agreed to the statute *De Heretico Comburendo*. Even then, there were only two cases of heretics being put to death in Henry IV's reign, the Norfolk priest William Sawtry in 1401 and the Evesham tailor John Badby in 1410 (226, pp.150–5). One suspects that their fates, compared with the immunity of others, may have been due to the fact that they lacked influential patrons. Nevertheless, although there are still some signs of knightly sympathy for heresy in Henry IV's reign, notably in the parliamentary proposals for Church disendowment, it is likely that there was a decline in the number of prominent men who were attracted to Lollardy, as the threat of repression increased the desirability of remaining on the orthodox side of the fence. The most important man who remained attached to Lollardy was Sir John Oldcastle, and it was his prosecution in the autumn of 1413 which was to spark off a crisis in the movement and set its tone for the remainder of its history.

CHAPTER 41

Heresy, persecution and reform

One of the most striking features about the history of early Lollardy is the absence of systematic persecution, which, as was suggested in Chapter 40, was probably due to the patronage which it had from various influential men. Only after Henry V's accession, with the prosecution of Sir John Oldcastle, was a direct attack launched on an upper-class Lollard. When and how Oldcastle first became associated with heresy is not known though, as we have seen, Swinderby was a possible influence, but by the first years of the fifteenth century he was connected with some of the earlier Lollard knights; in 1404 he was named as an executor of Sir Lewis Clifford's will, of which Sir John Cheyne was the overseer. He may also have had contacts with the Clanvow family, whose lands in Herefordshire were not far from his own. He became involved in public affairs like other men of his class, serving in the Scottish campaign of 1400 and, as might be expected from the location of his lands, fighting against the Welsh rebels in the following years. Such service was rewarded in 1406 by an annuity of 100 marks. In 1409 he took part in a tournament at Lille, and in 1411–12 was again serving in the King's forces, being apparently closely associated with the prince of Wales. He was parliamentary knight for his shire in 1404, and in 1409, after marrying the heiress of Lord Cobham, he was summoned to the upper house in his own name in the right of his wife. Altogether, until his heresy came to light, he seems to have been generally well respected by his contemporaries. The first sign of his religious proclivities attracting unfavourable attention came in 1410, when Archbishop Arundel cited a chaplain who may have been associated with him on a heresy charge, although he himself was still left untouched, as the earlier Lollard knights had been. He was, however, probably now strongly suspected, and with good reason, as he may well by then have been regarded as the leading figure among the Lollards. Certainly in the same year he wrote to a lay supporter of Hus, and in 1411 to King Wenceslas of Bohemia, congratulating the Hussites on their recent successes (135, pp.207, 212; 226, pp.160–2).

Arundel's defeat of university Lollardy under Henry IV may have given him confidence to move against its lay sympathizers, but it also reflects Henry V's strongly orthodox sentiments that the archbishop felt able to attack Oldcastle, despite his earlier associations with the King. Before 1413, he may have felt that he had insufficient proof to take action, but during the meeting of Convocation in March of that year two events brought the issue to a head; a chaplain suspected of heresy admitted having celebrated mass in Oldcastle's presence, evidence incidentally for the religious practices of the Lollards, who may have been prepared to follow customary observances while holding unorthodox views on their significance, and some heretical tracts belonging to Oldcastle were discovered in an illuminator's shop. Significantly, Arundel consulted the King before acting; Oldcastle, confronted with the evidence in Henry's presence, prevaricated on the question of the tracts, and a fuller indictment was then laid against him. The King tried to persuade his former associate to return to the fold of the Church, but when it came to the moment of decision the latter was not prepared to yield. After a futile attempt to deny the archbishop's summons and barricade himself into his castle, he was brought to trial in the autumn of 1413. When questioned on his beliefs, his first replies were imprecise on crucial matters, such as the nature of transubstantiation and the necessity of confession, and Arundel pressed him further. He refused to conform to orthodoxy, denounced the hierarchy as the body of Antichrist and was ultimately condemned (226, pp.163–5).

During a forty-day stay of execution, granted apparently at the King's wishes in the hope that Oldcastle might be reconciled with the Church, the Lollard leader escaped from custody in the Tower. Instead of lying low, which would have been his best hope of survival, he attempted to raise a revolt in January 1414. This desperate, indeed hopeless, act ended in disaster and did serious damage to the Lollards as a whole; the association of heresy with treason probably discouraged other members of the landed class from giving it protection and certainly encouraged the lay power to throw its weight behind the Church authorities in hunting down offenders.

The numbers participating in the rising were small, a few hundred at most, but the revolt clearly created panic, which is reflected both in some chronicles, such as Walsingham's, and in the language of the indictments brought against the rebels. Both sources talk about 20,000 men being involved. What is more significant than the numbers is the fact that the response to Oldcastle's call came from widely separate places; he was clearly regarded as a leader to be obeyed and had channels of communication to his followers. Although some men who are known to have been Lollards both before and after 1414 did not take part in the rising, those who did came from places as far apart as Worcester in the West, Colchester in the East and Derby in the North. There was fairly strong support from the Midlands and Bristol, with other substantial contingents coming from the Chilterns and North Oxfordshire. Oldcastle's own estates in Herefordshire and Kent do not appear to have sent him support; possibly the authorities were on the alert to prevent this. Most of the rebels were artisans, with chaplains as the leaders; it is noteworthy how many of the groups delated in the investigations of 1414 were controlled by members of the lesser clergy. Only a few members of the landed class were involved, and apart from Oldcastle himself, none were of real importance. Possibly his stepson-in-law, Thomas Broke, was suspected of participation, for he was kept in custody for a time. He and his father may have sympathized with Lollardy, judging by the language of their wills, but it is clear that no open offence could be proved against them. Surviving sympathizers, none of them men of any standing, were able to afford shelter to Oldcastle while he was on the run, until he was eventually taken and put to death late in 1417 (135, p.216; 226, pp.169–79; 241, pp.9–15).

There was to be no one in future who could command the loyalty of the sect as Oldcastle had done; after the failure of the rising the movement became fragmented, although tenuous communications were maintained between different groups, in the early years principally through the agency of Lollard priests and thereafter by the activity of itinerant evangelists who were probably laymen. Certainly by the early sixteenth century, there is ample evidence of secret contacts between various groups; Joan Washingby, who was put to death at Coventry in 1512, had previously abjured heresy at Maidstone and had also stayed in London at the home of another Lollard. Thomas Man, executed for relapse in 1518 in London, after having abjured in the Chilterns in 1511, was certainly a layman, and is known to have travelled also to Newbury and Colchester (241).

Such cases illustrate clearly the strong local character of Lollardy after 1414. It was never again to gain a foothold in the universities, such as it had possessed in its early days, nor was it to secure the patronage of influential men whose territorial power could guard it against persecution. Instead it found refuge in small communities, many of which were the same as those which had sent recruits to Oldcastle during the rising – the localities where it took root were determined primarily by the men who had given it support in the early days. For example, Bristol and the Chilterns both remained important centres of heresy from the early fifteenth century to the time of the Reformation, and although there are records of recurrent persecutions throughout the period, it seems to have persisted, perhaps even gaining strength after 1500 in the latter area. The Tenterden area of South Kent was also a major Lollard centre from the 1420s to the sixteenth century, although it does not appear to have been established there before that date. Its origin can probably be attributed to the activity of a chaplain called William White, who had to flee to East Anglia in 1428 and was eventually executed at Norwich. His preaching in Kent, however, had laid firm foundations for heresy, which survived there despite repeated attempts at suppression by the authorities throughout the fifteenth and early sixteenth centuries (241, Chs 2, 3, 7).

It is hard to judge the extent of fifteenth-century Lollardy. The records on which the historian must rely are those of proceedings in trials, so our knowledge of the sect rests almost exclusively on the opinions of its opponents. Heretical communities which evaded detection by their contemporaries are equally likely to remain hidden from modern writers, and the distribution of those which are known reflects primarily the assiduity of local bishops in investigating them. Probably no major groups were able to remain totally concealed, but some small ones may possibly have survived undetected. The numbers of known Lollards, however, remained small. Probably fewer than 100 suffered the ultimate penalty of burning in over a century between the passing of the statute *De Heretico Comburendo* and the beginning of the Reformation, and the number of those known to have abjured during the same period does not approach the 1,000 mark. Even if the Lollards were adept in self-concealment, and their survival in particular areas suggests that they probably were, these figures make it clear that they represented only a tiny minority of the population as a whole.

The impression which they made, however, on the authorities of both Church and State, was sufficient to create considerable concern, even sometimes panic. The grossly exaggerated suggestions in both chronicles and official documents that Oldcastle had 20,000 followers in 1414 and the concern shown by such later writers as the prior and convent of Christ Church Canterbury in 1428, who refer to the 'high malice of these mischievous heretics and Lollards' (29, p.568), make it clear that heresy had caused genuine alarm, whether or not such fear was really justified. One does not find such signs of apprehension in the middle and later years of the fifteenth century, but they recurred early in the sixteenth; in his convocation sermon of 1512, John Colet, dean of St Paul's declared, 'We are also nowe a dayes greued of heretykes, men mad with marueylous folysshenes.' Ironically, Colet himself was, shortly after, to fall under suspicion of heresy from his bishop, the theologically conservative Richard Fitzjames, because of the stress which he laid on the literal sense of Scripture, unencumbered by scholastic commentary, and his willingness to approach texts with the critical tools of Renaissance humanism. Nothing came of this, and Archbishop Warham of Canterbury upheld the dean's orthodoxy, but the bishop's action in prosecuting one of the most important dignitaries in his diocese is a very clear indication of his apprehensiveness. This may have been prompted by a number of heresy proceedings in London during his episcopate, of which the most notorious was that against Richard Hunne (208, p.98; 241, pp.160–71, 251–2). In the course of the furore which followed Hunne's death, Fitzjames made certain hysterical statements about support for heresy in London, which make it clear that he thought that Lollardy was more deeply rooted than might appear from normal enquiries. There is, however, no reason to believe that all his fears were justified, although they should not be totally discounted.

The great majority of fifteenth-century Lollards whose background can be identified were drawn from the artisan class, and there is a conspicuous absence of men with landed wealth, such as had provided support for the sect in its early years. In one of the best-documented groups, that in the Waveney valley, which was prosecuted and suppressed by Bishop Alnwick of Norwich between 1428 and 1431, a wide range of occupations were represented, including tailors, glovers and skinners. A substantial number of weavers were involved in Oldcastle's rising, and others played an active part later (226, pp.173–8; 241, pp.64, 68, 72, 125, 152). Furthermore, some of the major centres of Lollard activity, notably that in South Kent, were important areas of textile manufacturing, so it is probable that some heretics whose occupations have not been recorded may also have been involved in it. Possibly too, the trading connections between such textile centres provided one of the channels of communication between different Lollard groups; certainly they could provide a pretext for contacts without arousing clerical suspicion.

Although craftsmen were more likely to support Lollardy than were members of the bourgeoisie, the latter class also provided occasional sympathizers. A series of proceedings in Coventry in the winter of 1511–12 named as one, a man who can be identified with a former mayor of the town, Richard Cook, who on his death in 1507 had included two English bibles among the bequests which are noted in his will, although there is no evidence that he was licensed to own any such. His choice of two parish churches as the legatees to receive them may well have been prompted by a desire to avoid inculpating any other members of the sect, although the existence of the books may have prompted the authorities to start investigations. Other leading citizens of town, associated with Cook personally and in business, also seem to have been sympathetic to Lollardy. In London, too, the octogenarian Joan Boughton, executed in 1494, was mother-in-law to Sir John Young, a former mayor of the city, and Fitzjames's proceedings against Hunne, a merchant tailor, show that the wealthier citizens were not exempt from suspicion (224). The attitude of the authorities may have been unduly alarmist, but not totally unfounded; Cook as a mercer and Hunne as a merchant tailor were both connected with the textile trade, and one certainly knows that during the early period of the Reformation there were London merchants such as Humphrey Monmouth, perhaps significantly a man involved in the cloth trade, who played an important part in supporting Lutheran ideas and in giving patronage to the reformers. It is possible that a background of mercantile Lollardy may have played a part in forming his religious outlook (208, p.106).

Although the movement was largely a lay one, a few churchmen are known to have supported heresy, most of these being chaplains but one or two beneficed priests. One of the latter, John Whithorn, rector of Letcombe Basset in North Berkshire, was executed in 1508, after relapsing into heresy which he had abjured nine years before. His influence probably played a large part in strengthening a Lollard group near his parish. Even more striking was the association of James Preston, vicar of St Michael's Coventry for almost twenty years before his death in 1507, with Richard Cook, who witnessed his will, and others connected with the Lollard circle in the town. Preston was a highly educated man, an Oxford doctor of theology, who founded four fellowships at Magdalen, and had a considerable collection of books, particularly ones relating to the Bible (224; 241, pp.80–6). It is impossible to say if he was genuinely sympathetic to Lollardy, though the language of his will has parallels to that in those of some members of the Lollard group. His friendship with them may have been based on a shared evangelical piety and on his willingness to see the border line between orthodoxy and heresy as indistinct, with the Lollards representing a radical form of popular piety rather than dissent and revolution.

This would hardly be surprising, for English heretics in the last century before the Reformation showed few signs of the millenarianism which occurred in a number of contemporary groups on the Continent. There were a few such cases, most notably in a group at Newbury in the 1490s, but it was not common. There is little reason to think that Lollardy was a movement of social revolt, clad in religious guise – indeed one Lollard tract, the *Lantern of Light*, which probably dates from the early fifteenth century, seems to accept the traditional threefold division of medieval society among those who fought, those who prayed and those who toiled, when it is describing the elect, who are the Church. Those occasions on which the Lollards were involved in risings, in 1414 and possibly 1431, were infrequent and uncharacteristic of the sect as a whole (241, pp.61, 147–8, 241). Nor is it possible to prove that economic distress had the effect of turning men to heresy; a far more likely factor in this was the activity of individual teachers and the response which they evoked from their hearers.

This influence of particular evangelists may help to explain the recorded variation in belief which occur between the different Lollard groups, although another factor which may contribute to this variety is the procedure by which heretical beliefs were elicited. The investigating clergy interrogated suspects on a series of articles of belief, and although an attempt was made to standardize these in the 1420s, different sets of articles have been preserved in formularies of a later date (241, pp.225, 229). As many Lollards were simple men, their answers may have been given a precision in the records which never existed in their own minds. There was, however, no single clearly defined Lollard creed, although certain attitudes remained common throughout the movement, and the Lollards themselves apparently regarded their beliefs as something which they shared with their fellows and taught to others. Devotion to his beliefs was clearly shown by a certain John Morden, who on his death-bed was more concerned to teach them to his son-in-law Richard Ashford than he was to return to the fold of the Church. The two most characteristic attitudes which lay at the basis of Lollard beliefs were not always compatible, a scriptural fundamentalism and a common-sense rationalism. If one takes the two most commonly held Lollard views, hostility to the veneration of images was clearly rooted in the prohibition of this in the Decalogue, while denial of transubstantiation in the Eucharist, an inheritance from the later writings of Wyclif, no doubt secured popular accept-ance among those unconcerned with the subtleties of substance and accidents [F] because an absence of change in the elements conformed with what they could see. The third most commonly recorded Lollard belief, opposition to pilgrimages, probably originated in the fact that many of these were made to particular images. Perhaps the clearest evidence for genuine Lollard communities, as distinct from individuals who had incurred suspicion because of loose talk about the Church, was the possession of texts of the vernacular Scriptures, normally small manu-scripts of individual books of the Bible. Bishop Longland's persecutions in the Chilterns in the early 1520s showed that the group there possessed almost all the New Testament, and the Coventry group broken up in 1511–12 had a complete Old Testament as well as a substantial part of the New. The best-informed observer of mid-fifteenth-century Lollardy, Bishop Pecock of Chichester, whose prolix attempts to meet the Lollards on their own ground and defeat them by argument merely led to his own downfall on suspicion of heresy in 1457, noted that there were various groups among them, as indeed one might expect in any radical sect. Among the negative views of the Lollards, strong antipapalism was the most pronounced, and was probably inherited from both Wyclif and the older political opposition to the exercise of papal authority in England. Certainly the description of the Pope as Antichrist, found on various occasions, goes beyond the nationalism of the statutes of Provisors and Praemunire, support for which was still compatible with doctrinal orthodoxy. The assertion that preaching was more important than singing in services may have been a legacy from the men-dicant tradition, and there was also a continuation of the puritanical thread of thought, seen in the earlier Lollard wills, when some men attacked the ringing of bells or the playing of organs in church (241, pp.91, 215–16, 239–50).

Some of these views might not in themselves overstep the boundaries of orthodoxy, and it is likely that by the early sixteenth century considerable numbers sympathized with at least part of Lollard beliefs. Such attitudes could have helped to prepare the ground for the break with Rome in the 1530s, when royal interests drove a wedge between England and the Papacy, and gave the new Lutheran teachings, which were infiltrating into the country from the Continent, greater opportunity to take root. Until about 1530, however, the Lollard strain seems to have been stronger than the Lutheran in English heresy. What is certain is that the channels of communication between different Lollard groups provided a ready-made means for the spread of Lutheran material in England; one such group which had existed in London before the outbreak of the crisis in Germany, and which had contacts with others in Essex and Buckinghamshire, played an important part in the distribution of Lutheran books in the late 1520s. It is significant that when Bishop Tunstall of London embarked on an extensive purge of heretics in 1527, the main centres of his activity were in areas where there is record of Lollardy at an earlier date (208, pp.47–53).

The future leaders of the English Reformation did not, however, come from Lollard communities. Two streams contributed to the intellectual formation of these men, the development of Erasmian humanism and the spread of Lutheran theology from Wittenberg. Erasmianism did not necessarily lead to dissent, and it is noteworthy that none of Erasmus's personal associates in England was prominent among the reformers; indeed his closest friend there, Sir Thomas More, was a pillar of orthodoxy. However, a number of men who were active in a Lutheran cell at Cambridge in the 1520s were influenced by the Dutch scholar's work on the New Testament. By the start of this decade, some of Luther's writings had also begun to penetrate into England; the ledger of an Oxford bookseller records sales of some of these during 1520 (although a much greater number of Erasmian works were sold by him), in the following winter a number of Luther's books were burned at Cambridge, and in May 1521 Wolsey himself presided at a formal burning of Lutheran works in London. Such measures, however, did not check the flow of imported literature, and in Cambridge particularly some of the younger men met regularly but informally at the White Horse Inn to exchange ideas on the religious innovations which were being developed on the Continent. The most important figure in these meetings was Robert Barnes, perhaps significantly an Augustinian friar, as was Luther himself. By the mid 1520s he was involved in importing English New Testaments from Germany, these translations being the work of William Tyndale, who had fled there in 1524. It is not certain how closely he had been connected with the group at the White Horse during a brief spell in Cambridge, and it is likely that the main influence on him, which prompted his translation, came from the writings of Erasmus (208, pp.101–3; 225, pp.88–90; 248, pp.5, 9–11, 23). Tyndale was not a natural revolutionary; he had first sought patronage for his work from Bishop Tunstall of London, and only when this was not forthcoming did he secure it from the cloth merchant Humphrey Monmouth, whose trading connections with the Continent meant that he was in touch with Lutheran ideas, and who may also have had some contacts with old Lollard groups in London. Further evidence of the way in which the new reformers drew on earlier English dissent may be found in the printing of old Lollard tracts, although there is little sign of this being done before about 1530 (203).

It is impossible to judge how far reformed doctrines had penetrated into England during the 1520s, but ecclesiastical reactions suggest that their spread was considerable. Two main approaches were taken to meet the threat; suspected dissidents might be hunted down, or their views might be confuted by argument. Bishop Tunstall began a persecution in 1527, which his successor Stokesley contined after 1530. Tunstall also employed argument, commissioning Sir Thomas More to study and reply to heretical literature. The latter's *Dialogue of Heresies*, published in 1529, dealt with the doctrines and practices of the Church which were being criticized by the reformers. In essence, More based his case on the inerrancy of the Church, upholding its position as the interpreter of Scripture and the preserver of tradition. Where he was most clearly influenced by his English background was in his reluctance to allow the laity access to vernacular Scriptures, something which his friend Erasmus had considered an ideal for which to strive. The identification of the English Bible with Lollardy, however, obviously conditioned More's outlook. This controversy between Tyndale and More continued into the 1530s, one in which two high-principled men, with the same fundamental aim of furthering religion, could find no agreement on method (208, p.50; 248, pp.38, 102–5).

Tyndale was the most distinguished Protestant controversialist in the late 1520s, but there were other writers who were also active. Simon Fish was a very different kind of man from Tyndale, although he had helped in distributing his New Testament translation. His approach to controversy was through the violent anti-clerical invective of his *Supplication of Beggars*, which claimed that the Church absorbed wealth that should be employed to relieve the needy, and also gathered together all possible slanders against the clergy. Exaggerated though these were, the authorities regarded them sufficiently seriously for More to take up his pen to counter them in the *Supplication of Souls* (1529). Though Fish's tone is that of tavern scurrilities, he had in fact been originally trained in law, and one reason for the violence of his views may have been his opposition to the exercise of ecclesiastical jurisdiction at the expense of the lay courts. Background, however, is an inadequate explanation of his attitude; although there were other legal writers such as Christopher St German, who supported reform ideas, their most vigorous opponent, More, came from similar circles (208, pp.143–6).

The events of the 1520s provide an overture to the English Reformation. They saw the emergence of new movements of thought, sometimes independent of, sometimes merging with, older religious ideas, which, however, still displayed considerable durability. They saw the appearance of articulate criticism of the existing Church order, which could not be stifled by the ecclesiastical establishment. When, therefore, Henry VIII called Parliament in 1529, he was able to harness this to support his actions against Rome, and the subsequent development of the English Church was affected by a complex blend of religion and politics, idealism and greed.

Epilogue. England in 1529

When one compares England immediately before the Reformation crisis and in Edward III's later years, the most striking difference which one sees is that it was no longer a Continental power. Apart from a small enclave at Calais, which was to remain in English hands for a further generation, the lands over which Henry VIII ruled were entirely insular. The loss of the old French lands in the second quarter of the fifteenth century had been followed by years of domestic unrest, which had made it impossible to mount any campaign to recover them, and it seems clear that by the time of the Tudors the kings were prepared to accept the loss as irreversible. The most important implication of this transformation into a purely island power for the first time since the eleventh century was that English rulers now could choose whether or not to become involved in Continental affairs, whereas previously a refusal to defend their ancient rights could have led to a serious loss of face with their subjects; a king was expected to defend lands to which he had a title irrespective of the cost, even if his people had little interest in supporting him and were reluctant to give him financial assistance. Henry VII was able to avoid European entanglements in a way that would have been impossible a century earlier, and although Henry VIII and Wolsey did try to play the game of international power politics, they did so more from choice than from necessity.

Not only had England's position in Europe changed, but the political geography of the Continent also showed drastic alterations from that of the fourteenth century. The French monarchy had increased in power, with the closer incorporation of Brittany under the Crown as well as with the conquest of the English lands in the South-west, the old Spanish kingdoms of Aragon and Castile had been united and subsequently became linked, under the Emperor Charles V, with the Habsburg agglomeration which included the Empire and the former Burgundian lands in the Low Countries. The dominant force in European international politics was now the rivalry of Valois and Habsburg, whereas in the late fourteenth century it had been that of Valois and Plantagenet, as can be seen from the way in which the alignments of the Great Schism paralleled those of the Hundred Years War. The main centre of European conflict was now Italy rather than France, with the result that England was relegated to a more peripheral role among the actors on the international stage. By the late sixteenth century, England was to find a new role, as it became involved in overseas expansion, but this still lay in the future. The one earlier move in this direction, the Bristol voyages associated with the Cabots in Henry VII's reign, had been allowed to peter out under Henry VIII, and exploration of the world beyond Europe had been left to other nations.

Less dramatic than the change in England's relations with its Continental neighbours, but still important for the later development of Britain, were the attitudes of the English to the other countries within the British Isles. By the time of Henry VIII, Wales, already legally united to England in the late thirteenth century, was being drawn more closely to it. In the fifteenth century Welsh families such as the Tudors and the Herberts had entered the English aristocracy, the former even securing the throne following a lucky marriage and the elimination in war of rival claimants. The final abolition of Welsh law and the establishment of counties in the Principality on the English pattern in the 1530s was the logical outcome of earlier developments. Although Welsh national identity was not completely submerged, the country was in future to be more closely linked to England than were Ireland or Scotland. English rule in Ireland had always been more theoretical than effective, and there were fewer links between the Irish aristocracy and England than existed among their Welsh counterparts. The indigenous Irish remained virtually free from government control, and even the Anglo-Irish noble families were more tempted to align themselves with the native ones than with the English. The failure to resolve the tensions between Gaelic Ireland and those parts of the island under English rule was to lie at the root of many of its later troubles.

The third of England's insular neighbours, Scotland, had survived through the late Middle Ages as an independent kingdom, and often a hostile one. The sixteenth century saw a number of occasions of open hostility; the battles of Flodden (1513) and Pinkie (1547) are sufficient examples of this. Nevertheless, the background to the latter, an attempt to enforce a marriage between the young Edward VI and the even younger Scots Queen Mary, and the earlier marriage between Margaret Tudor and James IV, shows that there were times when it was acceptable to try to unite the two royal houses. One cannot say that there was a conscious willingness to accept the idea of uniting the two countries by marriage; Scottish resistance to the 'rough wooing' of 1547 testifies to this, even although there were now men in Scotland who were prepared to adopt a pro-English rather than a pro-French stance in international affairs. The Anglo-Scottish Union of 1603 resulted from the accidental infertility of the senior Tudor line through Henry VIII rather than from any conscious scheming; indeed it is possible that one reason for that monarch's concern at his failure to have a male heir may have been the fear of a disputed succession in which the Scots would have a claim.

In internal affairs, the monarchy was more powerful and more stable in 1529 than it had been in 1370, particularly in relation to the great nobility. This may have been due partly to chance; one factor in magnate power in the late fourteenth century was the number of cadet branches of the royal house, members of which might challenge the power of the King. Henry VIII's problem was quite the opposite: the absence of a possible male successor. The history of the Tudor period, however, shows that the kings regarded potential challengers with acute suspicion; intermittently drastic action was taken against men whose descent might give them a possible claim to the throne, and although this became more marked in Henry VIII's paranoiac later years, he had already in 1521 been prepared to execute one of the greatest lords of the realm, the duke of Buckingham, who was descended from Edward III, on a dubious charge of treason. Even earlier, Henry VII had taken steps to curb magnate power by taking recognizances for good behaviour from them. Even more important, however, in ensuring royal power was the fear which the King could inspire personally; this was probably the most important reason for his not being faced with the large-scale magnate revolt to which fourteenth- and fifteenth-century kings had been vulnerable.

A marked difference in government between the late fourteenth and early sixteenth centuries was the frequency with which Parliament was summoned, there being a pronounced decline. Nevertheless, the late Middle Ages was an important period in Parliament's development, seeing that it was playing an increased role in legislation as well as asserting claims in fiscal matters. It became more conscious of its rights, was able to secure various privileges, and showed a willingness to criticize royal policies. This compelled the Crown to improve its techniques of managing it, and it is not fortuitous that the most influential minister of the 1530s, Thomas Cromwell, was adept at this. Also, although fewer Parliaments were called, meetings tended to last longer from the late fifteenth century onwards than they had in the fourteenth. The practice of proroguing a Parliament, and then recalling it for a further session, instead of calling a new one, became increasingly common and may have helped to create a greater sense of national identity by strengthening ties between men from different parts of the realm. The greater infrequency of meetings from the late fifteenth century can be explained by the absence of Continental wars, which had earlier put such a heavy demand on royal resources and necessitated parliamentary grants. At the same time too, new methods were developed to improve the King's other revenues, so it became less necessary for him to have recourse to his subjects for extra funds.

The administration of these and the development of new departments was somewhat haphazard, and in the 1530s there was to be considerable reorganization in government. Within the administration, one very marked development was the decline of clerical influence, something which has perhaps been veiled by the importance of one churchman, Wolsey. The Civil Service, however, was increasingly staffed by laymen, and the more important offices were often held by lawyers. Such professional administrators were far more the pillars of Tudor society than were the higher nobility, particularly those from the older families, who played a markedly less important part in political affairs under Henry VIII than they had done in the fifteenth century. This may have been partly due to fear of the uncertain fortunes of court life, and partly to an improvement in their economic conditions; as the economy expanded with a rise in population, they probably possessed better opportunities for exploiting their own estates and perhaps had less need to seek royal patronage and grants of offices.

The late Middle Ages had seen important changes in the English economy, more particularly in agricultural society where serfdom had virtually disappeared in the years of labour shortage and declining population, leaving the rural worker free in law. The development of a rent-paying yeoman class was also a consequence of population change. The same conditions had also contributed to the beginnings of land enclosure, and although initially this had been possible without major social disruption, by the early Tudor period this was no longer the case. As the population began to recover, the balance between land and labour was shifting again in favour of the lords, who were able to put pressure on their tenants. When land was not available for occupation, there was a growth of pauperism and vagrancy, problems which became increasingly a concern of government in the sixteenth century. Certainly some of the social discontents of the period were focused specifically on the enclosed lands, although one must not allow these to get out of perspective; their extent was still small compared with the later enclosures of the seventeenth and eighteenth centuries.

A further important economic development in the period was the growth of cloth manufacturing, and the replacement of wool by cloth as the country's principal export commodity. This was the most important departure from a purely agricultural economy in England before the Industrial Revolution, and contributed to some shifts in the distribution of the national wealth, which became increasingly concentrated in the South and East. Certainly some of the most prosperous areas in early-sixteenth-century England, in East Anglia, Kent and the West Country, were those in which textiles were manufactured. London, too, was generally prosperous, having major trading connections with the Continent, but this was not new, although it is probably true that it had succeeded better than some of the other towns in resisting the economic problems of the period. There was little change yet in the trading connections of England from what they had been in the fourteenth century; it was only after their expansion into lands beyond Europe that the pattern was altered significantly.

A final area of English society which was effectively changed in the late Middle Ages was the Church, which fell increasingly under royal influence. It was, of course, not new for the Crown to secure the appointment of its own nominees to high ecclesiastical office, but it seems likely that from the time of the Great Schism onwards, the Papacy was never able to recover more than a nominal power in such matters. This background perhaps explains why there was a lack of effective resistance in the 1530s when the King, supported by Parliament, took steps to encroach further on traditional ecclesiastical rights, such as appeals to Rome and the payments of annates and services. Only one bishop, Fisher, was prepared to resist the King to the end, and paid for it with his life. The statutory royal supremacy, the basis of the Church of England, which was established in the 1530s, meant little more in practice than the existing authority which the popes of the previous century had had to concede tacitly to the secular power. Another factor which may have contributed to the Church's vulnerability was the laicization of government, because many of the secular administrators may have hoped to make personal gains at the expense of the Church. However, the principal factor leading to ecclesiastical change was the Lutheran Reformation in Germany; this served as á catalyst to release new religious ideas in a way that traditional English Lollardy had not, and although Henry VIII's own theological conservatism affected the doctrinal outlook of the new national Church, it is doubtful whether the break with Rome could have occurred had it not been for the interaction of politics and religion in Europe from the 1520s onward. How the English Reformation developed, with its cross-currents of theology, politics and economics, lies beyond the scope of this book, but there is little doubt that the ground had been prepared for them by changes in the government of the Church in the previous century and a half.

COMPENDIUM OF INFORMATION

Compendium of information

A. ECONOMIC AND SOCIAL TABLES

Table A.1: Prices and wages in Southern England, 1370–1529

Indexes (1451–75 = 100) of (1) price of composite unit of consumables, comprising basic elements of food, drink, fuel and textiles; (2) equivalent of wage-rate of building craftsman, expressed in the above composite physical unit

	(1)	(2)		(1)	(2)		(1)	(2)		(1)	(2)
1370	184	45	1410	130	—	1450	102	98	1490	106	94
1371	164	51	1411	106	—	1451	109	92	1491	112	89
1372	132	63	1412	103	97	1452	97	103	1492	103	97
1373	131	63	1413	108	93	1453	97	103	1493	117	85
1374	125	66	1414	108	93	1454	105	95	1494	96	104
1375	125	66	1415	115	87	1455	94	106	1495	89	112
1376	146	57	1416	124	81	1456	101	99	1496	94	106
1377	112	74	1417	129	78	1457	93	108	1497	101	99
1378	95	87	1418	114	88	1458	99	101	1498	96	104
1379	94	88	1419	95	105	1459	95	105	1499	99	101
1380	106	78	1420	102	98	1460	97	103	1500	94	106
1381	119	70	1421	93	108	1461	117	85	1501	107	93
1382	111	75	1422	97	103	1462	115	87	1502	122	82
1383	108	77	1423	108	93	1463	88	114	1503	114	88
1384	116	72	1424	103	97	1464	86	116	1504	107	93
1385	112	74	1425	109	92	1465	108	93	1505	103	97
1386	104	80	1426	103	97	1466	109	92	1506	106	94
1387	100	83	1427	96	104	1467	108	93	1507	98	102
1388	102	81	1428	99	101	1468	106	94	1508	100	100
1389	100	83	1429	127	79	1469	107	93	1509	92	109
1390	106	78	1430	138	72	1470	102	98	1510	103	97
1391	133	62	1431	115	87	1471	103	97	1511	97	103
1392	104	80	1432	102	98	1472	104	96	1512	101	99
1393	100	83	1433	112	89	1473	97	103	1513	120	83
1394	101	82	1434	109	92	1474	95	105	1514	118	85
1395	93	89	1435	105	95	1475	90	111	1515	107	93
1396	99	84	1436	95	105	1476	85	118	1516	110	90
1397	116	72	1437	93	108	1477	81	123	1517	111	90
1398	121	69	1438	128	78	1478	89	112	1518	116	86
1399	113	73	1439	154	65	1479	97	103	1519	129	78
1400	104	80	1440	140	71	1480	103	97	1520	137	73
1401	130	64	1441	93	108	1481	115	87	1521	167	60
1402	127	65	1442	85	118	1482	145	69	1522	160	63
1403	119	—	1443	97	103	1483	162	62	1523	136	74
1404	99	—	1444	102	98	1484	128	78	1524	133	75
1405	99	—	1445	87	115	1485	99	101	1525	129	78
1406	100	—	1446	95	105	1486	86	116	1526	133	75
1407	99	—	1447	100	100	1487	103	97	1527	147	68
1408	107	—	1448	102	98	1488	110	90	1528	179	56
1409	120	—	1449	106	94	1489	109	92	1529	159	63

Source: From (65) pp. 311–12.

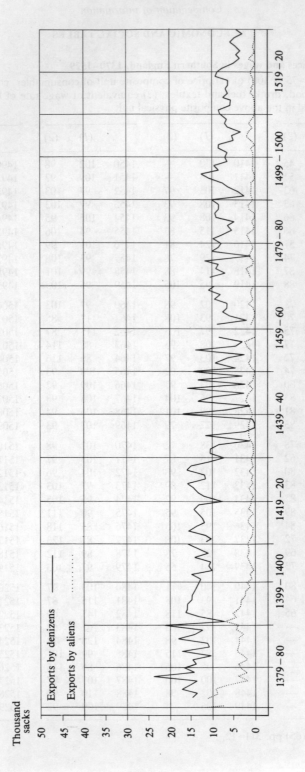

Table A.2: Exports of raw wool

Thousand sacks

Exports by denizens ——
Exports by aliens ·········

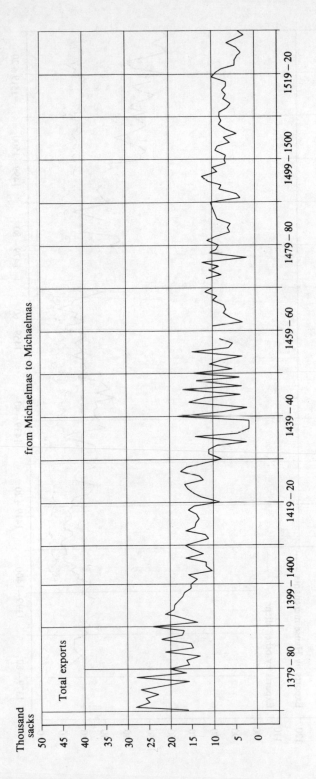

Thousand sacks

from Michaelmas to Michaelmas

Total exports

Table A.2: Cont'd

Source: From (66) pp. 122–3.

Thousand
cloths

Exports by denizens ——
Exports by Hanse merchants ----
Exports by other aliens ....

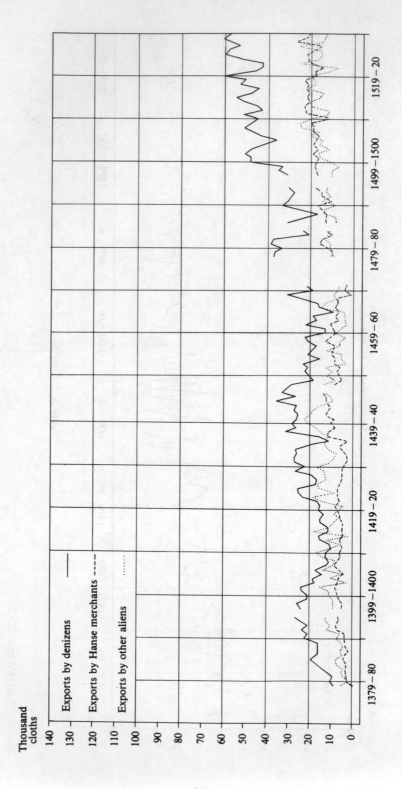

Table A.3: Exports of cloth

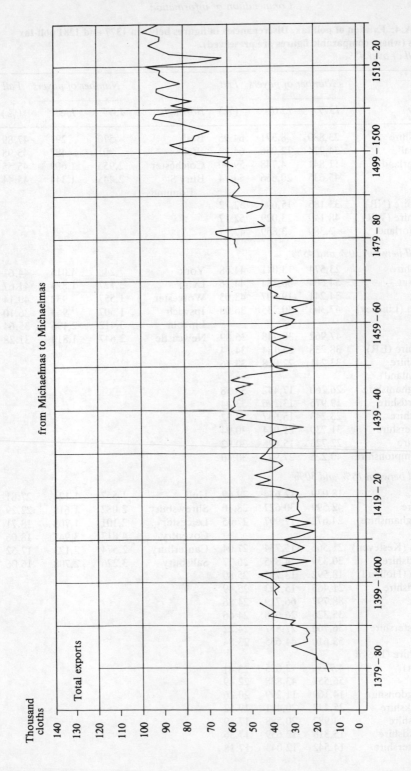

Source: From (66) pp. 138–9.

Table A.3: Cont'd

Table A.4: Evasion of poll tax. Discrepancies in figures between 1377 and 1381 poll-tax returns (where comparable figures are preserved).

(a) Fall of over 45%

County	Number of payers 1377	1381	Fall (%)	Borough	Number of payers 1377	1381	Fall (%)
Lancashire	23,880	8,371	64.95	Bath	570	297	47.89
Cornwall	34,274	12,056	64.82	Wells	901	487	45.95
Cumberland	11,841	4,748	59.90	Colchester	2,955	1,609	45.55
Devon	45,635	20,656	54.74	Bury St Edmunds	2,445	1,344	45.44
Yorkshire (NR)	33,185	15,690	52.72				
Yorkshire (WR)	48,149	23,029	52.17				
Westmorland	7,389	3,859	47.77				

(b) Fall between 30% and 45%

County	Number of payers 1377	1381	Fall (%)	Borough	Number of payers 1377	1381	Fall (%)
Shropshire	23,574	13,041	44.68	York	7,248	4,015	44.61
Somerset	54,604	30,384	44.36	Lynn	3,127	1,824	41.67
Dorset	34,241	19,507	43.03	Worcester	1,557	932	40.14
Lincoln (Lindsey)	47,303	30,235	36.08	Ipswich	1,507	963	36.10
				Lincoln	3,412	2,196	35.64
Essex	47,962	30,748	35.89	Newcastle	2,647	1,819	31.28
Yorkshire (ER)	38,238	25,184	34.14				
Hampshire (mainland)	33,241	22,018	33.76				
Nottinghamshire	26,260	17,442	33.58				
Hertfordshire	19,975	13,296	33.44				
Derbyshire	23,243	15,637	32.72				
Leicestershire	31,730	21,914	30.94				
Berkshire	22,723	15,696	30.92				
Northamptonshire	40,225	27,997	30.40				

(c) Fall between 15% and 30%

County	Number of payers 1377	1381	Fall (%)	Borough	Number of payers 1377	1381	Fall (%)
Surrey	18,039	12,684	29.69	Hull	1,557	1,124	27.81
Wiltshire	42,599	30,627	28.10	Shrewsbury	2,082	1,618	22.29
Buckinghamshire	24,672	17,997	27.05	Leicester	2,101	1,708	18.71
				Coventry	4,817	3,947	18.06
Lincoln (Kesteven)	21,566	15,734	27.04	Canterbury	2,574	2,123	17.52
Bedfordshire	20,339	14,895	26.77	Salisbury	3,226	2,708	16.06
Lincoln (Holland)	18,592	13,795	25.80				
Staffordshire	21,465	15,993	25.49				
Norfolk	88,797	66,719	24.86				
Sussex	35,326	26,616	24.66				
Gloucestershire	36,760	27,857	24.22				
Suffolk	58,610	44,635	23.84				
Hampshire (Isle of Wight)	4,733	3,625	23.41				
Kent	56,557	43,838	22.49				
Huntingdonshire	14,169	11,299	20.26				
Warwickshire	25,447	20,481	19.52				
Oxfordshire	24,982	20,588	17.59				
Herefordshire	15,318	12,659	17.36				
Worcestershire	14,542	12,043	17.18				

Table A.4: Cont'd

(d) *Fall of below 15%*

County	Number of payers 1377	1381	Fall (%)	Borough	Number of payers 1377	1381	Fall (%)
Middlesex	11,243	9,937	11.62	Oxford	2,357	2,005	14.93
Cambridgeshire	27,350	24,324	11.06	London	23,314	20,397	12.51
Rutland	5,994	5,593	6.69	Nottingham	1,447	1,266	12.51
				Bristol	6,345	5,662	10.76
				Chichester	869	787	9.44
				Exeter	1,560	1,420	8.97
				Southampton	1,152	1,051	8.77
				Cambridge	1,902	1,739	8.57
				Norwich	3,952	3,833	3.01
				Northampton	1,477	1,518	(2.78)

Source: From (11) pp. 55–7.

B. GENEALOGICAL TABLES

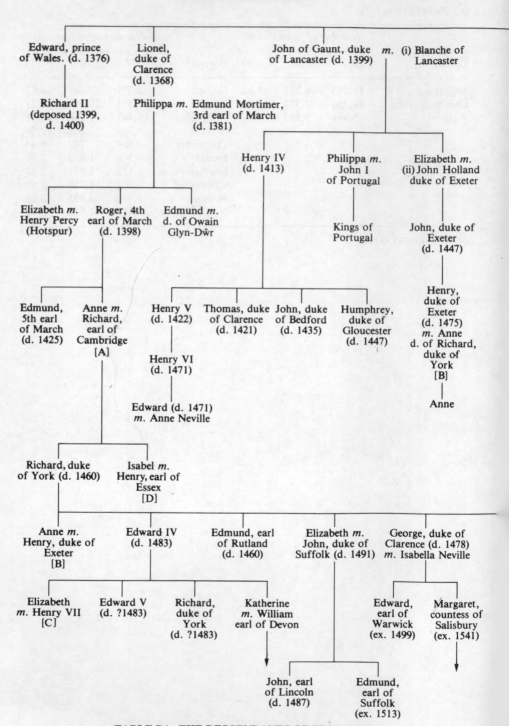

TABLE B1: THE DESCENDANTS OF EDWARD III

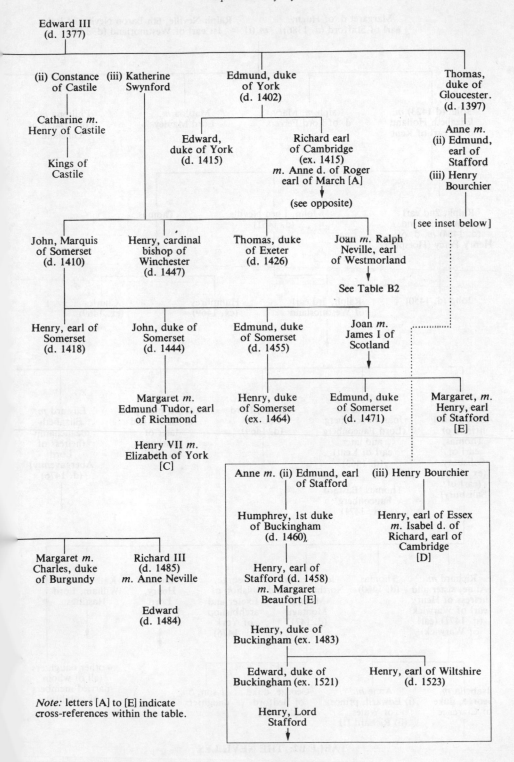

Edward III
(d. 1377)

(ii) Constance
of Castile

Catharine *m.*
Henry of Castile

Kings of
Castile

(iii) Katherine
Swynford

Edmund, duke
of York
(d. 1402)

Edward,
duke of York
(d. 1415)

Richard earl
of Cambridge
(ex. 1415)
m. Anne d. of Roger
earl of March [A]

(see opposite)

Thomas,
duke of
Gloucester.
(d. 1397)

Anne *m.*
(ii) Edmund,
earl of
Stafford

(iii) Henry
Bourchier

[see inset below]

John, Marquis
of Somerset
(d. 1410)

Henry, cardinal
bishop of
Winchester
(d. 1447)

Thomas, duke
of Exeter
(d. 1426)

Joan *m.* Ralph
Neville, earl
of Westmorland

See Table B2

Henry, earl of
Somerset
(d. 1418)

John, duke of
Somerset
(d. 1444)

Edmund, duke
of Somerset
(d. 1455)

Joan *m.*
James I of
Scotland

Margaret *m.*
Edmund Tudor, earl
of Richmond

Henry, duke
of Somerset
(ex. 1464)

Edmund, duke
of Somerset
(d. 1471)

Margaret, *m.*
Henry, earl
of Stafford
[E]

Henry VII *m.*
Elizabeth of York
[C]

Margaret *m.*
Charles, duke
of Burgundy

Richard III
(d. 1485)
m. Anne Neville

Edward
(d. 1484)

Anne *m.* (ii) Edmund, earl
of Stafford

(iii) Henry Bourchier

Humphrey, 1st duke
of Buckingham
(d. 1460),

Henry, earl of Essex
m. Isabel d. of
Richard, earl of
Cambridge
[D]

Henry, earl of
Stafford (d. 1458)
m. Margaret
Beaufort [E]

Henry, duke of
Buckingham (ex. 1483)

Edward, duke of
Buckingham (ex. 1521)

Henry, earl of Wiltshire
(d. 1523)

Henry, Lord
Stafford

Note: letters [A] to [E] indicate
cross-references within the table.

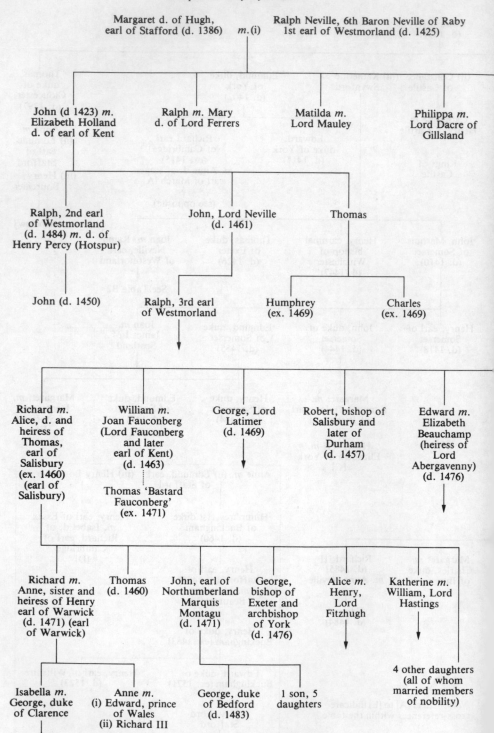

TABLE B2: THE NEVILLES

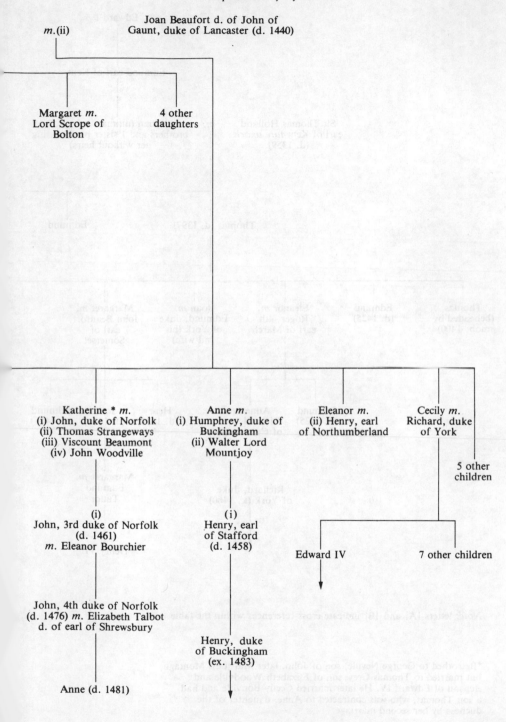

Joan Beaufort d. of John of
Gaunt, duke of Lancaster (d. 1440)

m.(ii)

Margaret *m.*
Lord Scrope of
Bolton

4 other
daughters

Katherine * *m.*
(i) John, duke of Norfolk
(ii) Thomas Strangeways
(iii) Viscount Beaumont
(iv) John Woodville

Anne *m.*
(i) Humphrey, duke of
Buckingham
(ii) Walter Lord
Mountjoy

Eleanor *m.*
(ii) Henry, earl
of Northumberland

Cecily *m.*
Richard, duke
of York

5 other
children

(i)
John, 3rd duke of Norfolk
(d. 1461)
m. Eleanor Bourchier

(i)
Henry, earl
of Stafford
(d. 1458)

Edward IV

7 other children

John, 4th duke of Norfolk
(d. 1476) *m.* Elizabeth Talbot
d. of earl of Shrewsbury

Henry, duke
of Buckingham
(ex. 1483)

Anne (d. 1481)

*Still living in 1483.

389

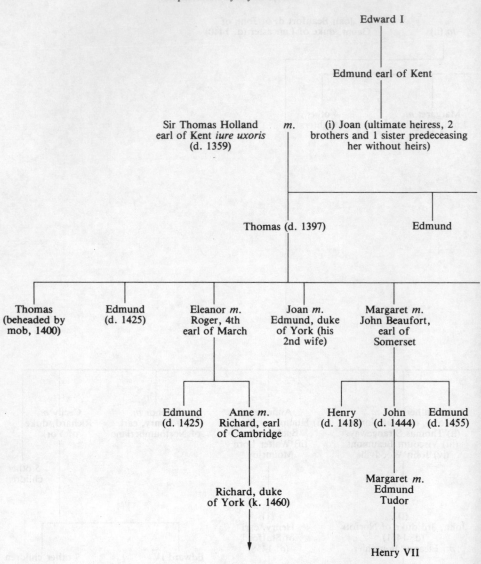

Edward I

Edmund earl of Kent

Sir Thomas Holland   *m.*   (i) Joan (ultimate heiress, 2
earl of Kent *iure uxoris*   brothers and 1 sister predeceasing
(d. 1359)   her without heirs)

Thomas (d. 1397)   Edmund

Thomas   Edmund   Eleanor *m.*   Joan *m.*   Margaret *m.*
(beheaded by   (d. 1425)   Roger, 4th   Edmund, duke   John Beaufort,
mob, 1400)   earl of March   of York (his   earl of
                                               2nd wife)   Somerset

                 Edmund   Anne *m.*   Henry   John   Edmund
                 (d. 1425)   Richard, earl   (d. 1418) (d. 1444) (d. 1455)
                             of Cambridge

                             Richard, duke   Margaret *m.*
                             of York (k. 1460)   Edmund
                                                           Tudor

                                                           Henry VII

Note: letters [A] and [B] indicate cross-references within the table.

*Betrothed to George Neville, son of John, later Marquess Montagu,
but married to Thomas Grey, son of Elizabeth Woodville and
stepson of Edward IV. He later married Cecily Bonville and had
a son Thomas, who was contracted to Anne, daughter of the
duchess by her second marriage.

TABLE B3: THE HOLLANDS

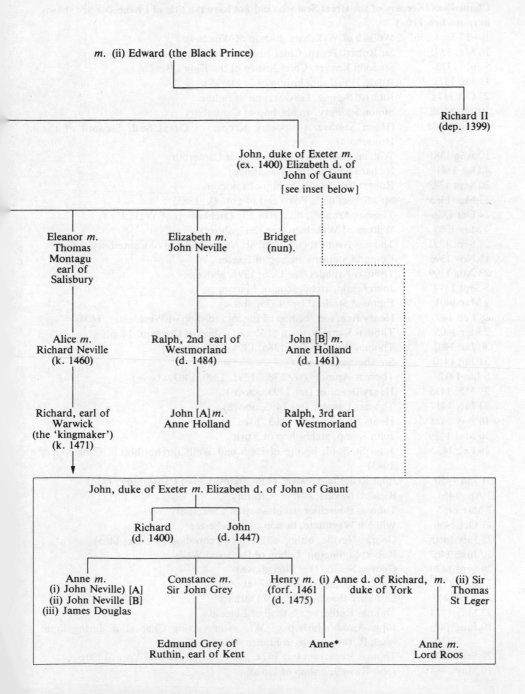

m. (ii) Edward (the Black Prince)

Richard II
(dep. 1399)

John, duke of Exeter *m.*
(ex. 1400) Elizabeth d. of
John of Gaunt
[see inset below]

Eleanor *m.*
Thomas
Montagu
earl of
Salisbury

Elizabeth *m.*
John Neville

Bridget
(nun).

Alice *m.*
Richard Neville
(k. 1460)

Ralph, 2nd earl of
Westmorland
(d. 1484)

John [B] *m.*
Anne Holland
(d. 1461)

Richard, earl of
Warwick
(the 'kingmaker')
(k. 1471)

John [A] *m.*
Anne Holland

Ralph, 3rd earl
of Westmorland

John, duke of Exeter *m.* Elizabeth d. of John of Gaunt

Richard
(d. 1400)

John
(d. 1447)

Anne *m.*
(i) John Neville) [A]
(ii) John Neville [B]
(iii) James Douglas

Constance *m.*
Sir John Grey

Henry *m.* (i) Anne d. of Richard,
(forf. 1461   duke of York
(d. 1475)

m. (ii) Sir
Thomas
St Leger

Edmund Grey of
Ruthin, earl of Kent

Anne*

Anne *m.*
Lord Roos

391

C. MAJOR OFFICE-HOLDERS

Titles shown are those held at time of appointment to office – those obtained during tenure of office are given in round brackets.

Chancellors (Keepers of the Great Seal who did not have the title of Chancellor are shown in round brackets.)

10–17 Sept 1367	William of Wykeham, bishop of Winchester
26 Mar 1371	Sir Robert Thorp, Chief Justice of the Common Pleas
5 July 1372	Sir John Knyvet, Chief Justice of the King's Bench
11 Jan 1377	Adam Houghton, bishop of St David's
29 Oct 1378	Richard Scrope, Lord Scrope of Bolton
30 Jan 1380	Simon Sudbury, archbishop of Canterbury
16 June 1381	(Hugh Segrave, temporary Keeper of Great Seal, Steward of the Household)
10 Aug 1381	William Courtenay, archbishop of Canterbury
4 Dec 1381	Richard Scrope (*see* 1378, above)
20 Sept 1382	Robert Braybrook, bishop of London
13 Mar 1383	Sir Michael de la Pole (earl of Suffolk, 1385)
24 Oct 1386	Thomas Arundel, bishop of Ely (archbishop of York, 1388)
4 May 1389	William of Wykeham (*see* 1367, above)
27 Sept 1391	Thomas Arundel (*see* 1386, above, archbishop of Canterbury, 1396)
15 Nov 1396	Edmund Stafford, bishop of Exeter
23 Aug 1399	Thomas Arundel (*see* 1386, 1391, above)
5 Sept 1399	John Scarle, archdeacon of Lincoln
9 Mar 1401	Edmund Stafford (*see* 1396, above)
28 Feb 1403	Henry Beaufort, bishop of Lincoln (bishop of Winchester, 1404)
2 Mar 1405	Thomas Langley, dean of York (bishop of Durham, 1406)
30 Jan 1407	Thomas Arundel (*see* 1386, 1391, 1399, above)
31 Jan 1410	Sir Thomas Beaufort
5 Jan 1412	Thomas Arundel (*see* 1386, 1391, 1399, 1407, above)
21 Mar 1413	Henry Beaufort (*see* 1403, above)
23 July 1417	Thomas Langley (*see* 1405, above)
16 July 1424	Henry Beaufort (*see* 1403, 1413, above)
16 Mar 1426	John Kemp, archbishop of York
26 Feb 1432	John Stafford, bishop of Bath and Wells (archbishop of Canterbury, 1443)
31 Jan 1450	John Kemp (*see* above, 1426, archbishop of Canterbury, 1452)
2 Apr 1454	Richard Neville, earl of Salisbury
7 Mar 1455	Thomas Bourchier, archbishop of Canterbury
11 Oct 1456	William Waynflete, bishop of Winchester
25 July 1460	George Neville, bishop of Exeter (archbishop of York, 1465)
20 June 1467	Robert Stillington, bishop of Bath and Wells
29 Sept 1470	George Neville (*see* 1460 above)
? Apr 1471	Robert Stillington (*see* 1467, above)
27 July 1473	Laurence Booth, bishop of Durham
27 May 1474	Thomas Rotheram, bishop of Lincoln
10 June 1475	John Alcock, bishop of Worcester (acting Chancellor during time when Rotheram was in France with the King)
29 Sept 1475	Thomas Rotheram (*see* 1474, above, archbishop of York, 1480)
10 May 1483	John Russell, bishop of Lincoln

18 Sept 1485	Thomas Rotheram (*see* 1474, 1475, above)
7 Oct 1485	John Alcock (*see* 1475, above, bishop of Ely, 1486)
6 Mar 1487	John Morton, archbishop of Canterbury
13 Oct 1500	(Henry Dean, archbishop of Canterbury, Keeper of the Great Seal)
11 Aug 1502	(William Warham, bishop of London, Keeper of the Great Seal, archbishop of Canterbury, 1503)
21 Jan 1504	William Warham, archbishop of Canterbury
24 Dec 1515	Thomas Wolsey, archbishop of York
26 Oct 1529	Sir Thomas More

Keepers of the Privy Seal

28 Oct 1367	Peter Lacy, canon of Lichfield and Dublin
26 Mar 1371	Nicholas Carew
26 June 1377	John Fordham, dean of Wells
13 Dec 1381	William Dighton, canon of St Paul's
9 Aug 1382	Walter Skirlaw, dean of St Martin's-le-Grand (bishop of Coventry and Lichfield, 1385, bishop of Bath and Wells, 1386)
24 Oct 1386	John Waltham, archdeacon of Richmond (bishop of Salisbury, 1388)
4 May 1389	Edmund Stafford, dean of York (bishop of Exeter, 1395)
16 Feb 1396	Guy Mone (bishop of St David's, 1397)
14 Nov 1397	Richard Clifford, dean of York (bishop of Worcester, 1401)
3 Nov 1401	Thomas Langley, dean of York
2 Mar 1405	Nicholas Bubwith, archdeacon of Dorset (bishop of London, 1406)
4 Oct 1406	John Prophete, dean of York
3 June 1415	John Wakering, archdeacon of Canterbury (bishop of Norwich, 1415)
11 Sept 1416	Henry Ware, canon of London (bishop of Chichester, 1418)
3 Oct 1418	John Kemp, archdeacon of Durham (bishop of Rochester, 1419)
25 Feb 1421	John Stafford, dean of St Martin's-le-Grand
19 Dec 1422	William Alnwick, archdeacon of Salisbury (bishop of Norwich, 1426)
25 Feb 1432	William Lyndwood, archdeacon of Oxford (bishop of St David's, 1442)
18 July 1433	Thomas Beckington, archdeacon of Buckingham (bishop of Bath and Wells, 1443)
11 Feb 1444	Adam Moleyns, dean of Salisbury (bishop of Chichester, 1445)
20 Jan 1450	Thomas Kent (temporary)
31 Jan 1450	Andrew Holes, archdeacon of York
5 April 1452	Thomas Kent (temporary)
12 May 1452	Thomas Lisieux, dean of St Paul's
24 Sept 1456	Laurence Booth, dean of St Paul's (bishop of Durham, 1457)
28 July 1460	Robert Stillington, archdeacon of Wells (bishop of Bath and Wells, 1465)
24 June 1467	Thomas Rotheram, canon of Lincoln (bishop of Rochester, 1468)
24 Oct 1470	John Hales, bishop of Coventry and Lichfield
? April 1471	Thomas Rotheram (*see above*, 1467, bishop of Lincoln, 1472)
28 May 1474	John Russell, archdeacon of Berkshire (bishop of Rochester, 1476, bishop of Lincoln, 1480)
10 May 1483	John Gunthorp, dean of Wells
8 Sept 1485	Peter Courtenay, bishop of Exeter (bishop of Winchester, 1487)
24 Feb 1487	Richard Fox, bishop of Exeter (bishop of Bath and Wells, 1492, bishop of Durham, 1494, bishop of Winchester, 1501)

18 May 1516	Thomas Ruthall, bishop of Durham
14 Feb 1523	Sir Henry Marny (Lord Marny, 1523)
25 May 1523	Cuthbert Tunstall, bishop of London

Treasurers

27 June 1369	Thomas Brantingham (bishop of Exeter, 1370)
27 Mar 1371	Richard Scrope, Lord Scrope of Bolton
26 Sept 1375	Sir Robert Ashton
14 Jan 1377	Henry Wakefield, bishop of Worcester
19 July 1377	Thomas Brantingham (*see* 1369, *above*)
1 Feb 1381	Sir Robert Hales, prior of the Hospital of St John of Jerusalem in England
10 Aug 1381	Sir Hugh Segrave
17 Jan 1386	John Fordham, bishop of Durham
24 Oct 1386	John Gilbert, bishop of Hereford
4 May 1389	Thomas Brantingham (*see* 1369, 1377, *above*)
20 Aug 1389	John Gilbert (*see* 1386, *above*, bishop of St David's, 1389)
2 May 1391	John Waltham, bishop of Salisbury
20 Sept 1395	Roger Walden (archbishop of Canterbury, 1397)
22 Jan 1398	Guy Mone, bishop of St David's
17 Sept 1398	William Scrope, earl of Wiltshire
3 Sept 1399	John Norbury, esquire
31 May 1401	Laurence Allerthorp, canon of London
27 Feb 1402	Henry Bowet, bishop of Bath and Wells
25 Oct 1402	Guy Mone (*see* 1398, *above*)
9 Sept 1403	William Roos, Lord Roos
5–9 Dec 1404	Thomas Neville, Lord Furnival
15 Apr 1407	Nicholas Bubwith, bishop of London (bishop of Salisbury, 1407, bishop of Bath and Wells, 1407)
14 July 1408	Sir John Tiptoft
6 Jan 1410	Henry Scrope, Lord Scrope of Masham
23 Dec 1411	Sir John Pelham
21 Mar 1413	Thomas FitzAlan, earl of Arundel
10 Jan 1416	Sir Hugh Mortimer
17 Apr 1416	Sir Roger Leche
6 Dec 1416	Henry FitzHugh, Lord Fitzhugh
26 Feb 1421	William Kinwolmarsh, dean of St Martin's-le-Grand
18 Dec 1422	John Stafford, dean of Wells (bishop of Bath and Wells, 1424)
16 Mar 1426	Walter Hungerford, Lord Hungerford
26 Feb 1432	John Scrope, Lord Scrope of Masham
11 Aug 1433	Ralph Cromwell, Lord Cromwell
7 July 1443	Ralph Boteler, Lord Sudley
18 Dec 1446	Marmaduke Lumley, bishop of Carlisle
16 Sept 1449	James Fiennes, Lord Saye and Sele
22 June 1450	John Beauchamp, Lord Beauchamp of Powick
15 Apr 1452	John Tiptoft, earl of Worcester
15 Mar 1455	James Butler, earl of Ormond and Wiltshire
29 May 1455	Henry Bourchier, Viscount Bourchier
5 Oct 1456	John Talbot, earl of Shrewsbury

30 Oct 1458	James Butler, earl of Ormond and Wiltshire (*see* 1455, *above*)
28 July 1460	Henry Bourchier, Viscount Bourchier (*see* 1455, *above*, earl of Essex, 1461)
14 Apr 1462	John Tiptoft, earl of Worcester (*see* 1452, *above*)
24 June 1463	Edmund Grey, Lord Grey of Ruthin
24 Nov 1464	Walter Blount (Lord Mountjoy, 1465)
4 Mar 1466	Richard Woodville, Lord Rivers (earl Rivers, 1466)
16 Aug 1469	Sir John Langstrother, prior of the Hospital of St John of Jerusalem in England
25 Oct 1469	William Grey, bishop of Ely
10 July 1470	John Tiptoft, earl of Worcester (*see* 1452, 1462, *above*)
20 Oct 1470	Sir John Langstrother (*see* 1469, *above*)
22 Apr 1471	Henry Bourchier, earl of Essex (*see* 1455, 1460, *above*)
17 May 1483	Sir John Wood
6 Dec 1484	John Tuchet, Lord Audley
14 July 1486	John Dinham, Lord Dinham
16 June 1501	Thomas Howard, earl of Surrey (duke of Norfolk, 1514)
4 Dec 1522	Thomas Howard, earl of Surrey (succeeds his father as duke of Norfolk, 1524)

Archbishops of Canterbury

Provided	Release of temporalities		Death translation
11 Oct 1368	15 Jan 1369	William Whittlesey, bishop of Worcester	5 or 6 June 1374
4 May 1375	5 June 1375	Simon Sudbury, bishop of London	14 June 1381
9 Sept 1381	23 Oct 1381	William Courtenay, bishop of London	31 July 1396
25 Sept 1396	11 Jan 1397	Thomas Arundel, archbishop of York	Tr to St Andrews 1397
8 Nov 1397	21 Jan 1398	Roger Walden	(deprived, 1399)
—	21 Oct 1399	Thomas Arundel (restored)	19 Feb 1414
27 Apr 1414	30 May 1414	Henry Chichele, bishop of St David's	12 Apr 1443
13 May 1443	25 June 1443	John Stafford, bishop of Bath and Wells	25 May 1452
21 July 1452	6 Sept 1452	John Kemp, archbishop of York	22 Mar 1454
21 June 1454	22 Aug 1454	Thomas Bourchier, bishop of Ely	30 Mar 1486
6 Oct 1486	6 Dec 1486	John Morton, bishop of Ely	15 Sept 1500
26 May 1501	2 Aug 1501	Henry Dean, bishop of Salisbury	15 Feb 1503
29 Nov 1503	24 Jan 1504	William Warham, bishop of London	22 Aug 1532

Archbishops of York

Provided	Release of temporalities		Death/translation
17 Oct 1352	8 Feb 1353	John Thoresby, bishop of Worcester	D. 6 Nov 1373
3 Apr 1374	6 June 1374	Alexander Neville,	Tr. to St Andrews 30 Apr 1388
3 Apr 1388	14 Sept 1388	Thomas Arundel, bishop of Ely	Tr. to Canterbury 25 Sept. 1396
5 Oct 1396	6 Mar 1397	Robert Waldby, bishop of Chichester	D. 6 Jan 1398
15 Mar 1398	23 June 1398	Richard Scrope, bishop of Coventry and Lichfield	D. 8 June 1405
14 May 1406	Not released	Robert Hallum	Tr. to Salisbury, 23 Oct 1407
7 Oct 1407	1 Dec 1407	Henry Bowet, bishop of Bath and Wells	D. 20 Oct 1423
14 Feb 1424	Not released	Richard Fleming, bishop of Lincoln	Resigned 20 July 1425
20 July 1425	22 Apr 1426	John Kemp, bishop of London	Tr. to Canterbury 21 July 1452
21 July 1452	6 Sept 1452	William Booth, bishop of Coventry and Lichfield	D. 12 Sept 1464
15 Mar 1465	17 June 1465	George Neville, bishop of Exeter	D. 8 June 1476
31 July 1476	8 Oct 1476	Laurence Booth, bishop of Durham	D. 19 May 1480
7 July 1480	9 Sept 1480	Thomas Rotheram, bishop of Lincoln	D. 29 May 1500
18 Jan 1501	29 Apr 1501	Thomas Savage, bishop of London	D. 2–3 Sept 1507
22 Sept 1508	12 Dec 1508	Christopher Bainbridge, bishop of Durham	D. 14 July 1514
15 Sept 1514	Not recorded	Thomas Wolsey, bishop of Lincoln	D. 29 Nov 1530

There were also two archbishops who were elected, but who failed to secure provision and had their elections quashed, Thomas Langley in 1405 and Philip Morgan in 1423.

D. MEETINGS OF PARLIAMENT

These took place at Westminster, unless noted to the contrary.

Summoned	Assembled	Terminated	Notes
8 Jan 1371	24 Feb 1371	29 Mar 1371	
No details	8 June 1371	17 June 1371	Winchester. (A Great Council comprising some prelates and magnates, with one knight per shire and one burgess per borough, from those returned to January Parliament.)
1 Sept 1372	3 Nov 1372	24 Nov 1372	Initially summoned for 13 Oct, but prorogued to later date
4 Oct 1373	21 Nov 1373	10 Dec 1373	
28 Dec 1375	28 Apr 1376	10 July 1376	'The Good Parliament'. Initially summoned for 12 Feb, but prorogued to later date
1 Dec 1376	27 Jan 1377	2 Mar 1377	
4 Aug 1377	13 Oct 1377	28 Nov x 6 Dec 1377	
3 Sept 1378	20 Oct 1378	16 Nov 1378	Gloucester
16 Feb 1379	24 Apr 1379	27 May 1379	
20 Oct 1379	16 Jan 1380	3 Mar 1380	
26 Aug 1380	5 Nov 1380	6 Dec 1380	Northampton
16 July 1381	3 Nov 1381	25 Feb 1382	Initially summoned for 16 Sept, but prorogued till later date. Further prorogation from 13 Dec 1381 to 24 Jan 1382
24 Mar 1382	7 May 1382	22 May 1382	
9 Aug 1382	6 Oct 1382	24 Oct 1382	
7 Jan 1383	23 Feb 1383	10 Mar 1383	
20 Aug 1383	26 Oct 1383	26 Nov 1383	
3 Mar 1384	29 Apr 1384	27 May 1384	Salisbury
28 Sept 1384	12 Nov 1384	14 Dec 1384	
3 Sept 1385	20 Oct 1385	6 Dec 1385	
8 Aug 1386	1 Oct 1386	28 Nov 1386	
17 Dec 1387	3 Feb 1388	4 June 1388	'The Merciless Parliament'. Amended writs concerning election of knights of the shire, 1 Jan 1388. Prorogued 20 Mar to 13 Apr 1388

Summoned	Assembled	Terminated	Notes
28 July 1388	9 Sept 1388	17 Oct 1388	Cambridge
6 Dec 1389	17 Jan 1390	2 Mar 1390	
12 Sept 1390	12 Nov 1390	3 Dec 1390	
7 Sept 1391	3 Nov 1391	2 Dec 1391	
23 Nov 1392	20 Jan 1393	10 Feb 1393	Winchester
13 Nov 1393	27 Jan 1394	6 Mar 1394	
20 Nov 1394	27 Jan 1395	15 Feb 1395	
30 Nov 1396	22 Jan 1397	12 Feb 1397	
18 July 1397	17 Sept 1397	31 Jan 1398	Prorogued from 29 Sept 1397 to 27 Jan 1398 at Shrewsbury
19 Aug 1399	30 Sept 1399	30 Sept 1399	Writs of summons were regarded as invalidated by the deposition of Richard II on 29 Sept.
30 Sept 1399	6 Oct 1399	19 Nov 1399	
9 Sept 1400	20 Jan 1401	10 Mar 1401	Initially summoned for 27 Oct 1400 at York, but prorogued to later date at Westminster.
19 June 1402	30 Sept 1402	25 Nov 1402	Initially summoned for 15 Sept, but prorogued to later date
20 Oct 1403	14 Jan 1404	20 Mar 1404	Initially summoned for 3 Dec 1403 at Coventry but prorogued to later date at Westminster
25 Aug 1404	6 Oct 1404	13 Nov 1404	Coventry
21 Dec 1405	1 Mar 1406	22 Dec 1406	Initially summoned for 15 Feb 1406 at Coventry, prorogued first to Gloucester and then to Westminster. Mid-session prorogations 3 Apr to 25 Apr and 19 June to 13 Oct
26 Aug 1407	20 Oct 1407	2 Dec 1407	Gloucester
26 Oct 1409	27 Jan 1410	9 May 1410	Initially summoned to Bristol and resummoned to Westminster. Mid-session prorogation, 15 Mar to 6 Apr 1410
21 Sept 1411	3 Nov 1411	19 Dec 1411	
1 Dec 1412	3 Feb 1413	20 Mar 1413	Ended by death of Henry IV and proceedings nullified
22 Mar 1413	14 May 1413	9 June 1413	

Summoned	Assembled	Terminated	Notes
1 Dec 1413	30 Apr 1414	29 May 1414	Leicester. Initially summoned for 29 Jan 1414, but prorogued to later date
26 Sept 1414	19 Nov 1414	No details	
12 Aug 1415	4 Nov 1415	12 Nov 1415	Initially summoned for 21 Oct, but prorogued to a later date.
21 Jan 1416	16 Mar 1416	No details	Prorogued from 8 Apr to 4 May
3 Sept 1416	19 Oct 1416	18 Nov 1416	
5 Oct 1417	16 Nov 1417	17 Dec 1417	
24 Aug 1419	16 Oct 1419	13 Nov 1419	
21 Oct 1420	2 Dec 1420	No details	
26 Feb 1421	2 May 1421	No details	
20 Oct 1421	1 Dec 1421	No details	
29 Sept 1422	9 Nov 1422	18 Dec 1422	
1 Sept 1423	20 Oct 1423	28 Feb 1424	Prorogued from 17 Dec 1423 to 14 Jan 1424
24 Feb 1425	30 Apr 1425	14 July 1425	Prorogued from 25 to 31 May
7 Jan 1426	18 Feb 1426	1 June 1426	Leicester. Prorogued from 20 Mar to 29 Apr
15 July 1427	13 Oct 1427	25 Mar 1428	Prorogued from 8 Dec 1427 to 27 Jan 1428
12 July 1429	22 Sept 1429	23 Feb 1430	Initially summoned for 13 Oct, but date advanced. Prorogued from 20 Dec 1429 to 16 Jan 1430
27 Nov 1430	12 Jan 1431	20 Mar 1431	
25 Feb 1432	12 May 1432	17 July 1432	
24 May 1433	8 July 1433	After 18 Dec 1433	Prorogued from 13 Aug to 13 Oct
5 July 1435	10 Oct 1435	23 Dec 1435	
29 Oct 1436	21 Jan 1437	27 Mar 1437	Initially summoned to Cambridge, but resummoned to Westminster
26 Sept 1439	12 Nov 1439	15–24 Feb 1440	Earlier summons to Oxford. Prorogued from 21 Dec 1439 to 14 Jan 1440, reassembling at Reading
3 Dec 1441	25 Jan 1442	27 Mar 1442	

Summoned	Assembled	Terminated	Notes
13 Jan 1445	25 Feb 1445	9 Apr 1446	Prorogued from 15 Mar. to 29 Apr 1445, 5 June to 20 Oct. 1445, 15 Dec 1455 to 24 Jan 1446
14 Dec 1446	10 Feb 1447	3 Mar 1447	Initially summoned to Cambridge, but resummoned to Bury St Edmunds
2 Jan 1449	12 Feb 1449	16 July 1449	Prorogued from 4 Apr to 7 May and from 30 May to 16 June, with final session at Winchester
23 Sept 1449	6 Nov 1449	5–8 June 1450	Adjourned to London 6 Nov, returned to Westminster 4 Dec 1449. Prorogued from 17 Dec 1449 to 22 Jan 1450, and from 30 Mar to 29 Apr 1450, reassembling at Leicester
5 Sept 1450	6 Nov 1450	24–31 May 1451	Prorogued from 18 Dec 1450 to 20 Jan 1451 and from 29 Mar to 5 May 1451
20 Jan 1453	6 Mar 1453	16–21 Apr 1454	Reading. Prorogued from 28 Mar to 25 Apr 1453, reassembling at Westminster, from 2 July to 12 Nov 1453, reassembling at Reading, and from 12 Nov 1453 to 14 Feb 1454, reassembling at Westminster
26 May 1455	9 July 1455	12 Mar 1456	Prorogued from 31 July to 12 Nov 1455 and from 13 Dec 1455 to 14 Jan 1456
9 Oct 1459	20 Nov 1459	20 Dec 1459	Coventry
30 July 1460	7 Oct 1460	No details	Prorogued probably from 1 Dec 1460 to 28 Jan 1461. May have continued to sit till accession of Edward IV, 4 Mar 1461
23 May 1461	4 Nov 1461	6 May 1462	Initially summoned for 6 July, but prorogued to later date. Prorogation from 21 Dec 1461 to 6 May 1462
22 Dec 1462	29 Apr 1463	28 Mar 1465	Initially summoned for 5 Feb at York, prorogued, first to Leicester and then to Westminster. Five mid-session prorogations continuing from 17 June 1463 to 21 Jan 1465 (one of these proposed a meeting at York)

Summoned	Assembled	Terminated	Notes
28 Feb 1467	3 June 1467	7 June 1468	Three mid-session prorogations, continuing from 1 July 1467 to 12 May 1468 (one of these proposed a meeting at Reading)
15 Oct 1470	26 Nov 1470	No details	Probably prorogued over Christmas. May have sat until the restoration of Edward IV in Apr 1471
19 Aug 1472	6 Oct 1472	14 Mar 1475	Prorogued from 30 Nov 1472 to 8 Feb 1473, from 8 Apr to 6 Oct 1473, from 13 Dec 1473 to 20 Jan 1474, from 1 Feb to 9 May 1474, from 28 May to 6 June 1474, from 18 July 14⁄4 to 23 Jan 1475
20 Nov 1477	16 Jan 1478	26 Feb 1478	
15 Nov 1482	20 Jan 1483	18 Feb 1483	
9 Dec 1483	23 Jan 1484	20 Feb 1484	
15 Sept 1485	7 Nov 1485	*c.* 4 Mar 1486	Prorogued from 10 Dec 1485 to 23 Jan 1486.
No details	9 Nov 1487	*c.* 18 Dec 1487	
No details	13 Jan 1489	27 Feb 1490	Prorogued from 23 Feb to 14 Oct 1489, and from 4 Dec 1489 to 25 Jan 1490
12 Aug 1491	17 Oct 1491	5 Mar 1492	Prorogued from 4 Nov 1491 to 26 Jan 1492
15 Sept 1495	14 Oct 1495	21–22 Dec 1495	
20 Nov 1496	16 Jan 1497	13 Mar 1497	
No details	25 Jan 1504	*c.* 1 Apr 1504	
17 Oct 1509	21 Jan 1510	23 Feb 1510	
28 Nov 1511	4 Feb 1512	4 Mar 1514	Prorogued from 30 Mar to 4 Nov 1512, from 20 Dec 1512 to 23 Jan 1514
23 Nov 1514	5 Feb 1515	22 Dec 1515	Prorogued from 5 Apr to 12 Nov 1515
No details	15 Apr 1523	13 Aug 1523	First session at Blackfriars, London. Prorogued from 21 May to 10 June, 29–31 July 1523

Summoned	Assembled	Terminated	Notes
9 Aug 1529	3 Nov 1529	14 Apr 1536	Summoned to Blackfriars, London and prorogued to Westminster for 4 Nov when first session opened. Eight sessions of the Parliament were held before it was dissolved.

Details of Parliaments have been taken from 50, pp. 525–35. Some dates of termination of Parliaments are approximate.

E. SELECTED STATUTES

These statutes have been selected to illustrate points which have been discussed in the text, whether or not they fall within the precise period 1370–1529.

Date	Designation of statute	Subject matter	Statutes of the Realm
1350–51	25 Edward III, St. 2.	Statute of Labourers	I. 311–13
	25 Edward III, St. 4.	First Statute of Provisors	I. 316–18
1353	27 Edward III, St. 1, c. 1.	First Statute of Praemunire	I. 329
1360–61	34 Edward III, c. 1.	JPs. empowered to determine felonies and trespasses	I. 364–5
1362	36 Edward III, St. 1, c. 15.	Pleadings to be heard in English	I. 375–6
1363	37 Edward III, cc. 8–15	Restriction on clothing to be worn by persons of different classes	I. 380–2
1363–64	38 Edward III, St. 1.	Second Statute of Praemunire	I. 385–7
1377	1 Richard II, c. 7.	Restriction of maintenance and liveries	II. 3
1389–90	13 Richard II, St. 2, cc. 2–3	Second Statute of Provisors	II. 69–74
	13 Richard II, St. 3.	Restriction of maintenance and liveries	II. 74–5
1392–3	16 Richard II, c. 4.	Restraint on liveries	II. 84
	16 Richard II, c. 5.	Third Statute of Praemunire	II. 84–6
1399	1 Henry IV, c. 7.	Restriction on grants of liveries	II. 113
1400–1	2 Henry IV, c. 3.	Extension of statute of Provisors	II. 121
	2 Henry IV, c. 12.	Restriction of rights of Welshmen	II. 124
	2 Henry IV, c. 14.	*De Heretico Comburendo*	II. 125–8
	2 Henry IV, c. 21	Confirmation and amendment of 1 Henry IV, c. 7, *above*	II. 129–30
1402	4 Henry IV, cc. 26–34	Restriction of rights of Welshmen	II. 140–1
1405–6	7 Henry IV, c. 2.	Entail of inheritance of the Crown	II. 151
	7 Henry IV, c. 14.	Confirmation and amendment of 1 Henry IV, c. 7, *above*	II. 155–6
	7 Henry IV, c. 15.	Knights of the shire to be returned by indenture	II. 156

Date	Designation of statute	Subject matter	Statutes of the Realm
1409–10	11 Henry IV, c. 1.	Penalties imposed on sheriffs and knights for non-fulfilment of 7 Henry IV, c. 15 *above*	II. 162
1411	13 Henry IV, c. 3	Rehearsal and confirmation of 1 Henry IV, c. 7, and 7 Henry IV, c. 14, *above*	II. 167
1413	1 Henry V, c. 1.	Knights of the shire and electors to reside in shire	II. 170
	1 Henry V, c. 5.	Status of defendants to be recorded in personal actions	II. 171
1414	2 Henry V, c. 7	Procedures for lay power in suppressing Lollardy	II. 181–4
1429	8 Henry VI, c. 4.	Extension of statutes concerning livery and maintenance	II. 240–1
	8 Henry VI, c. 7	Shire electors to be resident 40s. freeholders	II. 243–4
1444–45	23 Henry VI, c. 12	Fixing of wage-rates for servants	II. 337–9
	23 Henry VI, c. 14	Provisions for elections of knights of the shire and burgesses. Yeomen and below debarred from election	II. 340–2
1461	1 Edward IV, c. 2	Indictments in criminal matters to be heard by JPs	II. 389–91
1463	3 Edward IV, c. 5	Restrictions on apparel according to rank	II. 399–402
1468	8 Edward IV, c. 2	Confirmation of laws on liveries	II. 426–9
1472	12 Edward IV, c. 4	Prince of Wales may give liveries despite former statutes	II. 436–7
1482–83	22 Edward IV, c. 1	Restrictions on apparel	II. 468–9
1487	3 Henry VII, c. 1	Council empowered to proceed in cases of abuse of maintenance	II. 509–10
	3 Henry VII, c. 15	Act against retaining of the King's tenants	II. 522–3
1488–89	4 Henry VII, c. 13	Restriction of benefit of clergy for persons not in orders	II. 538
	4 Henry VII, c. 16	Act against amalgamating farms in the Isle of Wight	II. 540

Date	Designation of statute	Subject matter	Statutes of the Realm
	4 Henry VII, c. 19	Act to prevent waste of houses and conversion of tilled land to pasture	II. 542
1491	7 Henry VII, c. 1.	Deserters from army not to be entitled to benefit of clergy	II. 549–50
1495	11 Henry VII, c. 2	Act against vagabonds and beggars	II. 569
1503–4	19 Henry VII, c. 14	Act against illegal retainers	II. 658–60
1509–10	1 Henry VIII, c. 14	Act against wearing costly apparel	III. 8
1512	4 Henry VIII, c. 2	Restriction of benefit of clergy for murder to those in holy orders	III. 49
1514–15	6 Henry VIII, c. 1	Act concerning apparel	III. 121–3
	6 Henry VIII, c. 5	Act against decay of towns and conversion of land from tillage to pasture	III. 127
	6 Henry VIII, c. 24	King's general surveyors	III. 145–52
1515	7 Henry VIII, c. 1	Act against decay of towns and conversion of lands from tillage to pasture	III. 176
	7 Henry VIII, c. 7	Act concerning apparel	III. 179–82
1523	14 & 15 Henry VIII, c. 15	King's general surveyors	III. 219–30
	14 & 15 Henry VIII, c. 20	Attainder of duke of Buckingham	III. 246–58
1529	21 Henry VIII, c. 2	Limitations on sanctuary rights	III. 284
	21 Henry VIII, c. 6	Restriction on taking mortuary payments	III. 288
1531–32	23 Henry VIII, c. 20	Restraint of annates and services	III. 385–8
1532–33	24 Henry VIII, c. 12	Restraint of appeals to Rome	III. 427–9
1535–36	27 Henry VIII, c. 26	Laws and justice to be administered in Wales as England	III. 563–9

F. GLOSSARY OF ECCLESIASTICAL TERMS

Accidents:	the visible and variable elements which could differentiate individual examples of the same species (*see also* Substance).
Annates:	a payment of the first year's revenues made by a cleric to the Papacy on his appointment to a non-elective benefice (a benefice other than a bishopric or an abbacy) reserved to the Holy See. The term was also used loosely to include services (*see below*).
Chantry:	the endowment, either in perpetuity or for a term of years, of a priest to celebrate mass for the soul of the founder.
Collation:	the act by which a bishop presented and instituted a clerk to a benefice in the bishop's jurisdiction.
Indulgence:	originally the remission of a temporal penalty incurred as a canonical penance for a sin. By the late Middle Ages, it had come to mean the commutation of a deed of penance for a payment of money.
Lollard:	a term of doubtful origin applied as an abusive designation to English heretics who were influenced by the teachings of Wyclif. Usually taken to mean a mumbler (of prayers).
Mortmain:	the grant of land into the 'dead hand' of a corporate body, which, on account of its perpetual existence, could not be liable for the payment of succession dues. This applied to churches, monasteries and colleges at universities.
Ordinary:	one who has of right immediate jurisdiction in ecclesiastical cases; e.g. an archbishop in a province and a bishop or his deputy in a diocese.
In partibus infidelium:	literally, in lands under the infidel. This was the term given to suffragan bishops (*see below*), who were given titles of sees in lands no longer under Christian rule.
Pelagianism:	doctrine of fifth-century heretic that man might attain to salvation through his own free will without the aid of grace.
Prebend:	a benefice in a cathedral or collegiate church.
Proctors:	legal representatives of individuals or corporate bodies.
Provision:	a papal appointment to a benefice normally in the patronage of someone else.
Rector:	the individual or corporate body entitled to the tithes of a parish. In the late Middle Ages, this was often not the parish priest, who received only a fixed stipend, but a corporate body such as a monastery or a college at a university.
Services:	payments made to the Papacy by bishops and abbots on their appointment, if their benefices were assessed at more than 100 florins per annum.
Spiritualities:	the resources of a church derived from its ecclesiastical rights, such as tithes, offerings, and lands held in return for spiritual services such as prayers. The opposite of temporalities (*see below*).
Substance:	the essential being in something which underlies its appearance and gives it its real nature. This contrasts with accidents (*see above*).
Suffragans:	bishops who were ordained so that they could conduct such services as required the possession of episcopal orders; these included ordinations and confirmations. They did not, however, possess

jurisdictional powers such as those enjoyed by a diocesan bishop. They were given titles of sees either *in partibus infidelium* or in parts of Ireland which they might not be expected to visit.

Temporalities: the resources of a church (especially a bishopric or a monastery) which it held in return for secular services such as the fulfilment of feudal obligations as a tenant-in-chief.

Tithes: payments due by the laity to their parish church, comprising a tenth of their produce.

Transubstantiation: the doctrine that in the Eucharist the substance of the elements was transmuted from bread and wine, which were annihilated, into the body and blood of Christ, although the accidents of the elements remained unaltered (*see also above*, Accidents, Substance).

G. MAPS

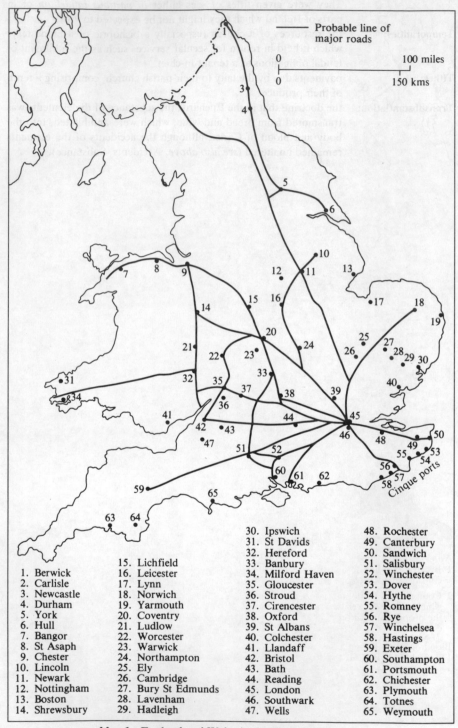

Probable line of
major roads

| 0 | | 100 miles |
| 0 | | 150 kms |

30. Ipswich
31. St Davids
32. Hereford
33. Banbury
34. Milford Haven
35. Gloucester
36. Stroud
37. Cirencester
38. Oxford
39. St Albans
40. Colchester
41. Llandaff
42. Bristol
43. Bath
44. Reading
45. London
46. Southwark
47. Wells

48. Rochester
49. Canterbury
50. Sandwich
51. Salisbury
52. Winchester
53. Dover
54. Hythe
55. Romney
56. Rye
57. Winchelsea
58. Hastings
59. Exeter
60. Southampton
61. Portsmouth
62. Chichester
63. Plymouth
64. Totnes
65. Weymouth

15. Lichfield
16. Leicester
17. Lynn
18. Norwich
19. Yarmouth
20. Coventry
21. Ludlow
22. Worcester
23. Warwick
24. Northampton
25. Ely
26. Cambridge
27. Bury St Edmunds
28. Lavenham
29. Hadleigh

1. Berwick
2. Carlisle
3. Newcastle
4. Durham
5. York
6. Hull
7. Bangor
8. St Asaph
9. Chester
10. Lincoln
11. Newark
12. Nottingham
13. Boston
14. Shrewsbury

Map 1   England and Wales in the Later Middle Ages

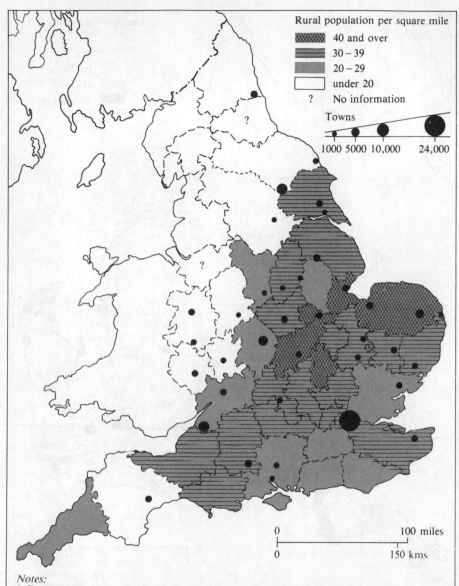

Rural population per square mile

- 40 and over
- 30 – 39
- 20 – 29
- under 20
- ? No information

Towns

1000 5000 10,000 24,000

0   100 miles

0   150 kms

Notes:

1 Because population density is averaged on a county basis, this map does not show the considerable variations which could exist within the limits of a shire.

2 Comparisons of population density, as shown on the map, involve the assumption, which cannot be verified, that there were no significant variations between shires in the proportion of non-taxpayers (those under 14 years of age, mendicants, and tax evaders).

Based on J. C. Russell, *British medieval population* (Alberquerque, 1948), 132–3, 142–3 (P.R.O. Exchequer Lay Subsidies E. 179).

Map 2   **The Population of England, 1377**

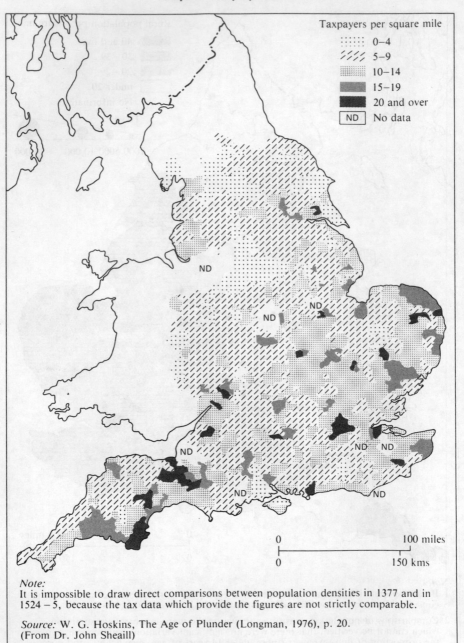

Taxpayers per square mile

:::::: 0–4
////// 5–9
▒▒▒▒ 10–14
▓▓▓▓ 15–19
████ 20 and over
| ND | No data

0 _____ 100 miles
0 _____ 150 kms

Note:
It is impossible to draw direct comparisons between population densities in 1377 and in 1524–5, because the tax data which provide the figures are not strictly comparable.

Source: W. G. Hoskins, The Age of Plunder (Longman, 1976), p. 20.
(From Dr. John Sheaill)

Map 3   The Population of England, 1524–5

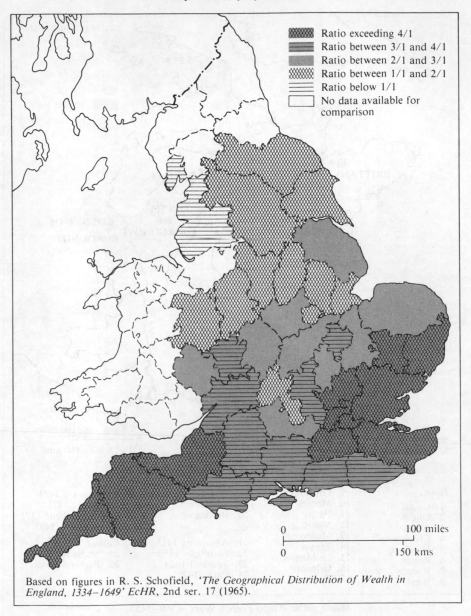

Legend:
- Ratio exceeding 4/1
- Ratio between 3/1 and 4/1
- Ratio between 2/1 and 3/1
- Ratio between 1/1 and 2/1
- Ratio below 1/1
- No data available for comparison

0   100 miles

0   150 kms

Based on figures in R. S. Schofield, *'The Geographical Distribution of Wealth in England, 1334–1649' EcHR*, 2nd ser. 17 (1965).

Map 4   Changes in the distribution of lay taxable wealth, 1334–1515

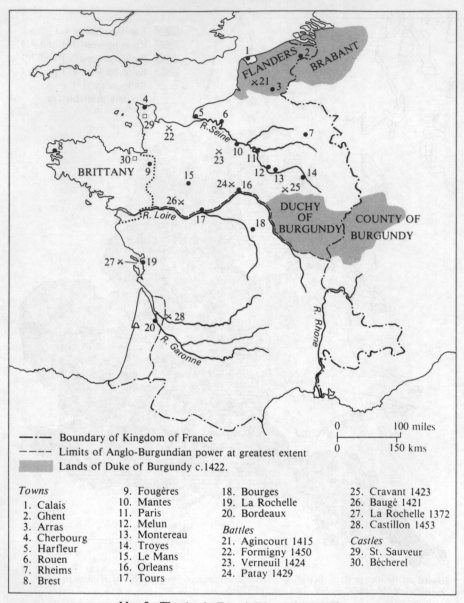

Boundary of Kingdom of France
Limits of Anglo-Burgundian power at greatest extent
Lands of Duke of Burgundy c.1422.

Towns			
1. Calais	9. Fougères	18. Bourges	25. Cravant 1423
2. Ghent	10. Mantes	19. La Rochelle	26. Baugé 1421
3. Arras	11. Paris	20. Bordeaux	27. La Rochelle 1372
4. Cherbourg	12. Melun		28. Castillon 1453
5. Harfleur	13. Montereau	*Battles*	
6. Rouen	14. Troyes	21. Agincourt 1415	*Castles*
7. Rheims	15. Le Mans	22. Formigny 1450	29. St. Sauveur
8. Brest	16. Orleans	23. Verneuil 1424	30. Bécherel
	17. Tours	24. Patay 1429	

Map 5   The Anglo-French Wars, 1369–1453

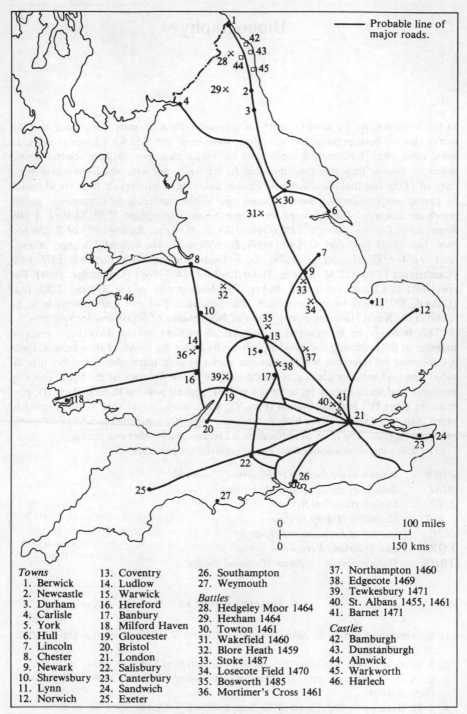

Probable line of major roads.

Map 6 The Wars of Lancaster and York

Towns
1. Berwick
2. Newcastle
3. Durham
4. Carlisle
5. York
6. Hull
7. Lincoln
8. Chester
9. Newark
10. Shrewsbury
11. Lynn
12. Norwich
13. Coventry
14. Ludlow
15. Warwick
16. Hereford
17. Banbury
18. Milford Haven
19. Gloucester
20. Bristol
21. London
22. Salisbury
23. Canterbury
24. Sandwich
25. Exeter
26. Southampton
27. Weymouth

Battles
28. Hedgeley Moor 1464
29. Hexham 1464
30. Towton 1461
31. Wakefield 1460
32. Blore Heath 1459
33. Stoke 1487
34. Losecote Field 1470
35. Bosworth 1485
36. Mortimer's Cross 1461
37. Northampton 1460
38. Edgecote 1469
39. Tewkesbury 1471
40. St. Albans 1455, 1461
41. Barnet 1471

Castles
42. Bamburgh
43. Dunstanburgh
44. Alnwick
45. Warkworth
46. Harlech

Bibliography

In this bibliography, the need to select has imposed certain arbitrary restrictions, and the works chosen, both primary and secondary, have been included for various reasons. In some cases, their fundamental importance has meant that they virtually selected themselves, in others, they owe their inclusion to the frequency with which they have been cited or to the fact that they illuminate current historical controversies. Readers who wish to pursue subjects further should consult one of the numerous bibliographical guides which are available. The following are among the more important: E. B. Graves, *A bibliography of English history to 1485* (Oxford, 1975), C. Read, *Bibliography of British history, 1485–1603* (2nd edn, Oxford, 1959), B. Wilkinson, *The high Middle Ages in England, 1154–1377* (Cambridge, 1978), D. J. Guth, *Late-medieval England, 1377–1485* (Cambridge, 1976) and M. Levine, *Tudor England, 1485–1603* (Cambridge, 1968). For specialists in Church history, D. Baker, *The bibliography of the Reform, 1450–1648* (Oxford, 1975) may be recommended. The best record of new publications is to be found in the Royal Historical Society, *Annual bibliography of British and Irish history*.

This bibliography is arranged as follows; all primary sources have been grouped together at the beginning and listed alphabetically under the names of their editors; these are followed by reference books and some useful general textbooks; thereafter it is divided into four sections which correspond roughly to the structure of the book, covering economic and social history (as in Parts I and II), general political history (Part III), government (Part IV) and the Church (Part V). Some books could have been assigned to more than one division of the bibliography, and have been included in whichever seems more appropriate. The place of publication is London unless otherwise stated.

The following abbreviations have been employed for periodicals:

BIHR: *Bulletin of the Institute of Historical Research*
BJRL: *Bulletin of the John Rylands Library*
EHR: *English Historical Review*
EcHR: *Economic History Review*
JEH: *Journal of Ecclesiastical History*
LQR: *Law Quarterly Review*
TRHS: *Transactions of the Royal Historical Society*

1. PRIMARY SOURCES

1. S. Armitage-Smith, ed., *John of Gaunt's Register, 1372–76*, Camden Third Series, 20, 21, 1911.
2. J. Bruce, ed., *The Arrival of Edward IV*, Camden First Series, 1, 1838.
3. C. A. J. Armstrong, ed., D. Mancini, *The usurpation of Richard III*, 2nd edn, Oxford, 1969.
4. J. H. Baker, ed., *The reports of Sir John Spelman*, Selden Society, 94, 1978.
5. C. G. Bayne, ed., *Select cases in the Council of Henry VII*, Selden Society, 75, 1956.

6. *Calendar of Inquisitions post mortem, Henry VII*, HMSO, 1898–1955.
7. *Calendar of Patent Rolls*, HMSO, 1914 and after.
8. *Calendar of State Papers, Milan, 1385–1618*, HMSO, 1912.
9. *Calendar of State Papers, Venetian, 1509–19*, HMSO, 1867.
10. S. B. Chrimes, ed., J. Fortescue, *De laudibus legum Anglie*, Cambridge, 1942.
11. R. B. Dobson, ed., *The Peasants' Revolt of 1381*, 1970.
12. F. R. H. DuBoulay, ed., *The register of Thomas Bourgchier*, Canterbury and York Society, Oxford, 1957.
13. H. Ellis, ed., *Three books of Polydore Vergil's English History*, Camden First Series, 29, 1844.
14. W. Fulman, ed., *Rerum Anglicarum scriptorum veterum*, I, Oxford, 1684.
15. F. J. Furnivall, ed., *The Babees book*, Early English Text Society Original Series, 32, 1868.
16. J. Gairdner, ed., *The historical collections of a citizen of London in the fifteenth century*, Camden Second Series, 17, 1876.
17. J. Gairdner, ed., *The Paston letters*, 6 vols, 1904.
18. J. O. Halliwell, ed., *Warkworth's chronicle*, Camden First Series, 10, 1839.
19. D. Hay, ed., *The Anglica Historia of Polydore Vergil*, Camden Third Series, 74, 1950.
20. E. V. Hitchcock, ed., W. Roper, *The lyfe of Sir Thomas Moore, knighte*, Early English Text Society Original Series, 197, 1935.
21. E. F. Jacob, ed., *The register of Henry Chichele*, 4 vols, Oxford, 1938–47.
22. C. L. Kingsford, ed., *Chronicles of London*, Oxford, 1905.
23. C. L. Kingsford, ed., *The first English life of Henry V*, Oxford, 1911.
24. C. L. Kingsford, ed., *Stonor letters and papers*, Camden Third Series, 29, 30, 1919.
25. M. Letts, ed., *The travels of Leo of Rozmital, 1465–67*, Hakluyt Society Second Series, 108, Cambridge, 1957.
26. L. Lyell, ed., *Acts of court of the Mercers' Company, 1453–1527*, Cambridge, 1936.
27. W. Lyndwood, *Provinciale*, Oxford, 1679.
28. T. More, *Dialogue of heresies*, 1529.
29. A. R. Myers, ed., *English historical documents*, IV, 1969.
30. C. Plummer, ed., J. Fortescue, *The governance of England*, 1885.
31. B. H. Putnam, ed., *Proceedings before the justices of the peace, Edward III – Richard III*, Ames Foundation, 1938.
32. H. T. Riley, ed., T. Walsingham, *Historia Anglicana*, Rolls Series, 1863–64.
33. *Rotuli Parliamentorum*, Record Commission, 1767–83.
34. R. R. Sharpe, ed., *Calendar of letter-books of the city of London, H, K. L*, 1899–1912.
35. C. A. Sneyd, ed., *Italian relation of England*, Camden First Series, 37, 1847.
36. *Statutes of the realm*, I – III, Record Commission, 1816.
37. R. S. Sylvester, ed., G. Cavendish, *The life and death of Cardinal Wolsey*, Early English Text Society Original Series 243, 1959.
38. R. S. Sylvester, ed., T. More, *History of Richard III*, New Haven, Conn. and London, 1963.
39. F. Taylor and J. S. Roskell, eds, *Gesta Henrici Quinti*, Oxford 1975.
40. A. H. Thomas and I. D. Thornley, eds, *The Great Chronicle of London*, 1938.
41. *Valor Ecclesiasticus*, Record Commission, 1810.
42. R. Virgoe, 'Some ancient indictments in the King's Bench referring to Kent, 1450–52', in *Documents illustrative of medieval Kentish Society*, Kent Archaeological Society Record Series 17, Ashford, 1964.

43. G. Warner, ed., *The libelle of Englyshe polycye*, Oxford, 1926.
44. C. H. Williams, ed., *English historical documents*, V, 1967.
45. J. A. Williamson, ed., *The Cabot voyages and Bristol discovery under Henry VII*, Hakluyt Society Second Series, 120, Cambridge, 1962.

2. REFERENCE WORKS

46. G. E. Cokayne (ed. V. Gibbs and others), *The complete peerage*, 1910–59.
47. A. B. Emden, *Biographical register of the university of Cambridge to 1500*, Cambridge, 1963.
48. A. B. Emden, *Biographical register of the university of Oxford to 1500*, 3 vols, Oxford, 1957–59.
49. A. B. Emden, *Biographical register of the university of Oxford, 1501–1540*, Oxford, 1974.
50. *Handbook of British chronology*, 1961.

3. GENERAL TEXTBOOKS

51. G. R. Elton, *England under the Tudors*, 2nd edn, 1974.
52. E. F. Jacob, *The fifteenth century*, Oxford, 1961.
53. M. H. Keen, *England in the later Middle Ages*, 1973.
54. J. R. Lander, *Government and community, England, 1450–1509*, 1980.
55. M. McKisack, *The fourteenth century*, Oxford, 1959.

4. ECONOMIC AND SOCIAL

56. J. N. Bartlett, 'The expansion and decline of York in the later Middle Ages', *EcHR*, 2nd ser., **12** (1959–60).
57. J. M. W. Bean, *The decline of English feudalism, 1215–1540*, Manchester, 1968.
58. M. Beresford, *The lost villages of England*, rev. edn, 1965.
59. I. Blanchard, 'Population change, enclosure and the early Tudor economy', *EcHR*, 2nd ser., **23** (1970)
60. A. R. Bridbury, 'The Black Death', *EcHR*, 2nd ser., **26** (1973).
61. A. R. Bridbury, *Economic Growth*, 1962.
62. A. R. Bridbury, 'Sixteenth century farming', *EcHR*, 2nd ser, **27** (1974)
63. D. Burwash, *English merchant shipping, 1460–1540*, repr. Newton Abbot, 1969.
64. E. M. Carus-Wilson, *Medieval merchant venturers*, 1954.
65. E. M. Carus-Wilson, ed., *Essays in economic history*, II, 1962.
66. E. M. Carus-Wilson and O. Coleman, *England's export trade 1275–1547*, Oxford, 1963.
67. J. Cornwall, 'The early Tudor gentry', *EcHR*, 2nd ser., **17** (1964–65).
68. C. S. L. Davies, 'The Pilgrimage of Grace reconsidered', *Past and Present*, **41** (1968).
69. A. G. Dickens, 'Secular and religious motivation in the Pilgrimage of Grace', *Studies in Church History*, **4** (1967).
70. R. B. Dobson, 'Admissions to the freedom of the city of York in the later Middle Ages', *EcHR*, 2nd ser., **26** (1973).

71. R. B. Dobson, 'Urban decline in late medieval England', *TRHS*, 5th ser. **27** (1977).
72. W. H. Dunham, *Lord Hastings' indentured retainers, 1461–1483*, New Haven, Conn., 1955.
73. A. Fletcher, *Tudor rebellions*, 1972.
74. H. L. Gray, 'Incomes from land in England in 1436', *EHR*, **49** (1934).
75. J. Hatcher, *Plague, population and the English economy, 1348–1530*, 1977.
76. J. Hatcher, *Rural economy and society in the duchy of Cornwall 1300–1500*, Cambridge, 1970.
77. J. W. F. Hill, *Medieval Lincoln*, Cambridge, 1948.
78. R. H. Hilton, *Bond men made free*, 1973.
79. R. H. Hilton, *The decline of serfdom in medieval England*, 1969.
80. R. H. Hilton, *The economic development of some Leicestershire estates in the 14th and 15th centuries*, Oxford, 1947.
81. R. H. Hilton, *The English peasantry in the later Middle Ages*, Oxford, 1975.
82. W. G. Hoskins, *The age of plunder*, 1976.
83. W. G. Hoskins, *The Midland peasant*, 1957.
84. T. H. Lloyd, *The English wool trade in the Middle Ages*, Cambridge, 1977.
85. K. B. McFarlane, 'Bastard feudalism', *BIHR*, **20** (1943–45).
86. K. B. McFarlane, 'England and the Hundred Years War', *Past and Present*, **22** (1962).
87. K. B. McFarlane, 'The investment of Sir John Fastolf's profits of war', *TRHS*, 5th ser., **7** (1957).
88. K. B. McFarlane, *The nobility of later medieval England*, Oxford, 1973.
89. D. A. L. Morgan, 'The King's affinity in the polity of Yorkist England', *TRHS*, 5th ser. **23** (1973).
90. C. Platt, *The English medieval town*, 1976.
91. M. M. Postan, 'The costs of the Hundred Years War', *Past and Present*, **27** (1964).
92. M. M. Postan, *The medieval economy and society*, 1972.
93. M. M. Postan, 'Some social consequences of the Hundred Years War', *EcHR*, 1st ser., **12** (1942).
94. E. Power and M. M. Postan, *English trade in the fifteenth century*, repr. 1951.
95. T. B. Pugh and C. D. Ross, 'The English baronage and the income tax of 1436', *BIHR*, **26** (1953).
96. P. Ramsey, 'Overseas trade in the reign of Henry VII: the evidence of the Customs Accounts', *EcHR*, 2nd ser., **6** (1953–54).
97. C. Rawcliffe, *The Staffords, earls of Stafford and dukes of Buckingham*, Cambridge, 1978.
98. A Réville, *Le soulèvement des travailleurs d'Angleterre en 1381*, Paris, 1898.
99. J. C. Russell, *British medieval population*, Albuquerque, 1948.
100. G. V. Scammell, 'Shipowning in England, c. 1450–1550', *TRHS*, 5th ser., **12** (1962).
101. R. S. Schofield, 'The geographical distribution of wealth in England, 1334–1649', *EcHR*, 2nd ser., **18** (1965).
102. J. F. D. Shrewsbury, *The history of bubonic plague in England*, Cambridge, 1970.
103. J. Thirsk, ed., *The agrarian history of England and Wales*, IV, Cambridge, 1967.
104. S. L. Thrupp, *The merchant class of medieval London*, Chicago, 1948.

5. POLITICAL EVENTS

105. C. T. Allmand, 'The Anglo-French negotiations, 1439', *BIHR*, **40** (1967).

106. S. Armitage-Smith, *John of Gaunt*, repr. 1964.
107. C. A. J. Armstrong, 'Politics and the Battle of St Albans', *BIHR*, **33** (1960).
108. C. M. Barron, 'The tyranny of Richard II', *BIHR*, **41** (1968).
109. R. Bird, *The turbulent London of Richard II*, 1949.
110. S. B. Chrimes, *Henry VII*, 1972.
111. S. B. Chrimes, 'Richard II's questions to the judges', *LQR*, **62** (1956).
112. S. B. Chrimes, C. D. Ross and R. A. Griffiths, *Fifteenth century England, 1399–1509*, Manchester, 1972.
113. D. Clementi, 'Richard II's ninth question to the judges', *EHR*, **86** (1971).
114. R. R. Davies, 'Colonial Wales', *Past and Present*, **65** (1974).
115. J. G. Dickinson, *The Congress of Arras*, Oxford, 1955.
116. G. Donaldson, *Scotland: James V to James VII*, Edinburgh, 1965.
117. F. R. H. DuBoulay and C. M. Barron, eds, *The reign of Richard II*, 1971.
118. A. E. Goodman, *The loyal conspiracy*, 1971.
119. R. A. Griffiths, 'Duke Richard of York's intentions in 1450 and the origins of the Wars of the Roses', *Journal of Medieval History*, **1** (1975).
120. R. A. Griffiths, 'Local rivalries and national politics: the Percies, the Nevilles and the Duke of Exeter, 1452–55', *Speculum*, **43** (1968).
121. A. Hanham, 'Hastings Redivivus', *EHR*, **90** (1975).
122. A. Hanham, *Richard III and his early historians, 1483–1535*, Oxford, 1975.
123. A. Hanham, 'Richard III, Lord Hastings and the historians', *EHR*, **87** (1972).
124. G. A. Holmes, *The Good Parliament*, Oxford, 1975.
125. R. H. Jones, *The royal policy of Richard II*, Oxford, 1968.
126. M. H. Keen and M. J. Daniel, 'English diplomacy and the sack of Fougères in 1449', *History*, **59** (1974).
127. P. M. Kendall, *Richard III*, 1955.
128. C. L. Kingsford, *Prejudice and promise in fifteenth century England*. repr. 1962.
129. J. L. Kirby, *Henry IV of England*, 1970.
130. J. R. Lander, *Crown and Nobility, 1450–1509*, 1976.
131. J. E. Lloyd, *Owen Glendower*, Oxford, 1931.
132. L. R. Loomis, 'Nationality at the Council of Constance', *American Historical Review*, **44** (1938–39).
133. J. Lydon, *Ireland in the later Middle Ages*, Dublin, 1973.
134. M. MacCurtain, *Tudor and Stuart Ireland*, Dublin, 1972.
135. K. B. McFarlane, *Lancastrian kings and Lollard knights*, Oxford, 1972.
136. K. B. McFarlane, 'The Wars of the Roses', *Proceedings of the British Academy*, **50** (1964).
137. K. Nicholls, *Gaelic and Gaelicised Ireland in the Middle Ages*, Dublin, 1972.
138. R. G. Nicholson, *Scotland: the later Middle Ages*, Edinburgh, 1974.
139. A. J. Otway-Ruthven, *A History of medieval Ireland*, 1968.
140. J. J. N. Palmer, *England, France and Christendom, 1377–99*, 1972.
141. E. Perroy, *The Hundred Years War*, 1951.
142. A. F. Pollard, *Wolsey*, 1929.
143. G. Roberts, 'Wales and England: antipathy and sympathy', *Welsh Historical Review*, **1** (1960–63).
144. C. D. Ross, *Edward IV*, 1974.
145. P. E. Russell, *The English intervention in Spain and Portugal in the time of Edward III and Richard II*, Oxford, 1955.
146. J. J. Scarisbrick, *Henry VIII*, paperback edn, 1976.
147. R. L. Storey, *The end of the House of Lancaster*, 1966.

148. J. A. F. Thomson, 'John de la Pole, Duke of Suffolk', *Speculum*, **54** (1979).
149. J. A. F. Thomson, 'Richard III and Lord Hastings: a problematical case reviewed', *BIHR*, **48** (1975).
150. J. A. Tuck, *Richard II and the English nobility*, 1973.
151. M. G. A. Vale, *English Gascony 1399–1453*, Oxford, 1970.
152. R. Vaughan, *John the Fearless*, 1966.
153. R. Vaughan, *Philip the Good*, 1970.
154. R. B. Wernham, *Before the Armada: the growth of English foreign policy 1485–1588*, 1966.
155. B. P. Wolffe, 'Hastings reinterred', *EHR*, **91** (1976).
156. B. P. Wolffe *Henry VI*, 1981.
157. B. P. Wolffe, 'When and why did Hastings lose his head?', *EHR*, **89** (1974).
158. C. T. Wood, 'The deposition of Edward V', *Traditio*, **31** (1975).

6. GOVERNMENT, LAW AND THE CONSTITUTION

159. M. E. Avery, 'History of the equitable jurisdiction of Chancery before 1460', *BIHR*, **42** (1969).
160. J. F. Baldwin, *The King's Council in England during the Middle Ages*, repr. Oxford, 1969.
161. J. G. Bellamy, *The law of treason in England in the later Middle Ages*, Cambridge, 1970.
162. M. Blatcher, *The Court of the King's Bench, 1450–1550*, 1978.
163. A. L. Brown, *The early history of the clerkship of the Council*, Glasgow, 1969.
164. A. L. Brown, 'The King's councillors in fifteenth century England', *TRHS*, 5th ser., **19** (1969).
165. S. B. Chrimes, *English constitutional ideas in the XV century*, Cambridge, 1936.
166. R. R. Davies, 'The twilight of Welsh law, 1284–1536', *History*, **51** (1966).
167. (J.) G. Edwards, *The second century of the English Parliament*, Oxford, 1979.
168. E. B. Fryde and E. Miller, *Historical studies of the English Parliament*, II, Cambridge, 1970.
169. J. A. Guy, *The Cardinal's Court*, Hassocks, 1977.
170. J. A. Guy, 'Wolsey, the Council and the Council Courts', *EHR*, **91** (1976).
171. G. L. Harriss, 'Aids, loans and benevolences', *Historical Journal*, **6** (1963).
172. G. L. Harriss, 'Cardinal Beaufort – patriot or usurer?', *TRHS* 5th ser., **20** (1970).
173. G. L. Harriss, *King, Parliament and public finance in medieval England to 1369*, Oxford, 1975.
174. G. L. Harriss, 'Medieval government and statecraft', *Past and Present*, **25** (1963).
175. M. Hastings, *The Court of Common Pleas*, Ithaca, NY, 1947.
176. W. Holdsworth, *History of English law*, 1903–72.
177. E. W. Ives, 'The common lawyers in pre-Reformation England', *TRHS*, 5th ser., **18** (1968).
178. H. M. Jewell, *English local administration in the Middle Ages*, Newton Abbot, 1972.
179. M. H. Keen, 'Treason trials under the law of arms', *TRHS*, 5th ser., **12** (1962).
180. J. L. Kirby, 'Councils and councillors of Henry IV', *TRHS*, 5th ser., **14** (1964).
181. J. L. Kirby, 'The issues of the Lancastrian Exchequer and Lord Cromwell's estimates of 1433', *BIHR*, **24** (1951).
182. J. L. Kirby, 'The rise of the under-treasurer of the Exchequer', *EHR*, **72** (1957).

184. K. B. McFarlane, 'Parliament and bastard feudalism', *TRHS*, 4th ser. **26** (1944).
185. A. R. Myers, 'A parliamentary debate of the mid-fifteenth century', *BJRL*, **22** (1938).
186. R. A. Newhall, 'The war finances of Henry V and the Duke of Bedford', *EHR*, **36** (1921).
187. T. F. T. Plucknett, 'The place of the Council in the fifteenth century', *TRHS*, 4th ser., **1** (1918).
188. J. E. Powell and K. Wallis, *The House of Lords in the Middle Ages*, 1968.
189. H. G. Richardson, 'John of Gaunt and the parliamentary representation of Lancashire', *BJRL*, **22** (1938).
190. H. G. Richardson and G. O. Sayles, 'Parliaments and great councils in medieval England', *LQR*, **77** (1961).
191. W. C. Richardson, *Tudor chamber administration 1485–1547*, Baton Rouge, 1952.
192. A. Rogers, 'Henry IV, the Commons and taxation', *Mediaeval Studies*, **31** (1969).
193. J. S. Roskell, *The Commons and their Speakers in English Parliaments, 1376–1523*, Manchester, 1965.
194. J. S. Roskell, *The Commons in the Parliament of 1422*, Manchester, 1954.
195. J. S. Roskell, 'The office and dignity of Protector of England, with special reference to its origins', *EHR*, **68** (1953).
196. J. S. Roskell, 'The problem of the attendance of the lords in medieval Parliaments' *BIHR*, **29** (1956).
197. A. Steel, *The receipt of the Exchequer, 1377–1485*, Cambridge, 1954.
198. T. F. Tout, *Chapters in the administrative history of medieval England*, Manchester, 1920–33.
199. R. Virgoe, 'The composition of the King's Council, 1437–1461', *BIHR*, **43** (1970).
200. P. Williams, 'The Tudor State', *Past and Present*, **25** (1963).
201. B. P. Wolffe, *The Crown Lands 1461–1536*, 1970.
202. B. P. Wolffe, *The royal demesne in English History*, 1971.

7. THE CHURCH AND CULTURE

203. M. E. Aston, 'Lollardy and the Reformation: survival or revival?', *History*, **49** (1964).
204. M. E. Aston, *Thomas Arundel*, Oxford, 1967.
205. M. Bowker, *The secular clergy in the diocese of Lincoln 1495–1520*, Cambridge, 1968.
206. D. S. Chambers, *Cardinal Bainbridge in the Court of Rome*, Oxford, 1965.
207. R. G. Davies, 'Martin V and the English Episcopate, with special reference to his campaign for the repeal of the Statute of Provisors', *EHR*, **92** (1977).
208. A. G. Dickens, *The English Reformation*, rev. edn, 1967.
209. R. B. Dobson, *Durham Priory 1400–1450*, Cambridge, 1973.
210. R. B. Dobson, 'The residentiary canons of York in the fifteenth century', *JEH*, **30** (1979).
211. L. C. Gabel, *Benefit of clergy in England in the later Middle Ages*, repr. New York, 1969.
212. P. Heath, *The English parish clergy on the eve of the Reformation*, 1969.
213. A. Hudson, 'The debate on Bible translation, Oxford 1401', *EHR*, **90** (1975).
214. A. Hudson, 'A Lollard mass', *Journal of Theological Studies*, NS, **23** (1972).
215. E. F. Jacob, *Essays in the conciliar epoch*, 2nd edn, Manchester, 1952.

216. E. F. Jacob, *Essays in later medieval history*, Manchester, 1968.
217. M. D. Knowles, *The monastic order in England*, Cambridge, 1940.
218. M. D. Knowles, *The religious orders in England*, 3 vols, Cambridge, 1948–59.
219. C. H. Lawrence, ed., *The English Church and the Papacy*, 1965.
220. G. Leff, *Heresy in the later Middle Ages*, Manchester, 1967.
221. F. D. Logan, *Excommunication and the secular arm in medieval England*, Toronto, 1968.
222. R. W. Lovatt, 'The *Imitation of Christ* in late medieval England', *TRHS*, 5th ser., **18** (1968).
223. W. E. Lunt, *Financial relations of the Papacy with England 1327–1534*, Cambridge, Mass., 1962.
224. I. Luxton, 'The Lichfield Court Book: a postscript', *BIHR*, **44** (1971).
225. J. K. McConica, *English humanists and Reformation politics*, Oxford, 1965.
226. K. B. McFarlane, *John Wycliffe and the beginnings of English Nonconformity*, 1952.
227. J. H. Moran, *Education and learning in the city of York 1300–1560*, York, 1979.
228. N. Orme, *Education in the west of England*, Exeter, 1976.
229. N. Orme, *English schools in the Middle Ages*, 1973.
230. G. R. Owst, *Literature and pulpit in medieval England*, repr. Cambridge, 1961.
231. *Oxford studies presented to Daniel Callus*, Oxford Historical Society, NS., **16**, 1964.
232. W. A. Pantin, *The English Church in the fourteenth century*, Cambridge, 1955.
233. E. Perroy, *L'Angleterre et le grand schisme d'occident*, Paris, 1933.
234. J. A. Robson, *Wyclif and the Oxford schools*, Cambridge, 1961.
235. J. T. Rosenthal, *The purchase of paradise*, 1972.
236. M. G. Sargent, 'The transmission by the English Carthusians of some late medieval spiritual writings', *JEH*, **27** (1976).
237. J. J. Scarisbrick, 'Clerical taxation in England, 1485 to 1547', *JEH*, **11** (1960).
238. R. W. Seton-Watson, ed., *Tudor studies presented . . . to A. F. Pollard*, London, 1924.
239. A. H. Thompson, *The English clergy and their organization in the later Middle Ages*, Oxford, 1947.
240. J. A. F. Thomson, 'Clergy and laity in London, 1376–1531', unpublished Oxford D.Phil, thesis, 1960.
241. J. A. F. Thomson, *The later Lollards 1414–1520*, rev. edn, Oxford, 1968.
242. J. A. F. Thomson, 'Piety and charity in late medieval London', *JEH*, **16** (1965).
243. J. A. F. Thomson, *Popes and princes 1417–1517*, 1980.
244. J. A. F. Thomson, 'Tithe disputes in later medieval London', *EHR*, **78** (1963).
245. M. G. A. Vale, *Piety, charity and literacy among the Yorkshire gentry 1370–1480*, York, 1976.
246. R. Weiss, *Humanism in England during the fifteenth century*, 2nd edn, Oxford, 1957.
247. H. F. Westlake, *The parish gilds of mediaeval England*, 1919.
248. C. H. Williams, *William Tyndale*, 1969.
249. B. L. Woodcock, *Medieval ecclesiastical courts in the diocese of Canterbury*, 1952.

Index

Individuals are normally given the title they held at death, although in the text they are designated by the title they held at the time of the events being discussed. The following abbreviations are employed: a, archbishop; abb. abbot; bp. bishop; card. cardinal; css. countess; d. duke; dss. duchess; e. earl; k. king; m. marquess; q. queen.